Ventilation and Indoor Air Quality

Ventilation and Indoor Air Quality

Editors

Ashok Kumar
Alejandro Moreno-Rangel
M. Amirul I. Khan
Michał Piasecki

MDPI • Basel • Beijing • Wuhan • Barcelona • Belgrade • Manchester • Tokyo • Cluj • Tianjin

Editors

Ashok Kumar
The University of Toledo
USA

Alejandro Moreno-Rangel
University of Strathclyde
UK

M. Amirul I. Khan
University of Leeds
UK

Michał Piasecki
Building Research Institute
Poland

Editorial Office
MDPI
St. Alban-Anlage 66
4052 Basel, Switzerland

This is a reprint of articles from the Topic published online in the open access journals *Atmosphere* (ISSN 2073-4433), *Environments* (ISSN 2076-3298), *Buildings* (ISSN 2075-5309), and *International Journal of Environmental Research and Public Health* (ISSN 1660-4601) (available at: https://www.mdpi.com/topics/Ventilation_Indoor_Air).

For citation purposes, cite each article independently as indicated on the article page online and as indicated below:

LastName, A.A.; LastName, B.B.; LastName, C.C. Article Title. *Journal Name* **Year**, *Volume Number*, Page Range.

ISBN 978-3-0365-5981-0 (Hbk)
ISBN 978-3-0365-5982-7 (PDF)

Contents

About the Editors

Ashok Kumar

Dr. Ashok Kumar (Distinguished University Professor Emeritus). Ashok's research work has focused on finding innovative solutions to fundamental and applied problems in air quality modelling, risk assessment and environmental data analysis. His recent projects include mobile source modelling, pollution prevention, and indoor radon detection in Ohio. He has received 44 grants from industry and regulatory agencies. He is the author or co-author of more than 450 peer-reviewed papers, book chapters, conference papers and reports. He has edited three conference proceedings and three books, and has additionally co-authored five books. He was the guest editor of 11 journal issues by different publishers. The work of his group on model evaluation, indoor radon, indoor air quality in public buses, biodiesel, and modelling techniques has received extensive citations in the literature. He has served as a reviewer for several journals, publications, and corporations. He received Layman A. Ripperton Award for distinguished achievement as an educator in the field of air pollution control in June 2003 from the Air and Waste Management Association (A&WMA), and is now an honorary member of A&WMA.

Alejandro Moreno-Rangel

Dr. Alejandro Moreno-Rangel (Lecturer in Building Performance Evaluation and Net Zero Design). Alejandro has extensive experience in sustainable architecture, particularly in Passivhaus buildings and their connections to health and human behaviors. Through this work, Alejandro explores the architectural design, energy efficiency methods, passive techniques and their impact on the indoor environment—indoor air quality (IAQ) and thermal comfort. He particularly focuses on these aspects of homes and their relation to the urban environment with the aim of creating healthy homes. Architecture has responded well to climate change, mitigating the effects of the built environment and achieving net zero carbon emissions. However, its impact on human health is often left aside. Alejandro's approach to architectural design seeks to improve the quality of life and health for all citizens, delivering net zero interventions that take a "whole house" approach, improving IAQ and comfort. Alejandro's research uses design research methods to explore the interactions of building occupants' behavior and net zero buildings to deliver healthier indoor environments, considering the impact of bio-psychological-social aspects of health, climate change, and energy efficiency method interactions. Alejandro's research interests also extend to the use of low-cost sensors as research tools, in retrofitting and in maintaining a net zero policy.

M. Amirul I. Khan

Dr. M. Amirul I. Khan (Lecturer in Environmental Fluid Mechanics) has extensive experience in innovative computational approaches for applications of wall-bounded turbulent flow modelling to indoor built environments and outdoor environments. He has expertise in mathematical modelling, numerical optimization methods and high-performance computing. His expertise in turbulent flow modelling allowed him to lead and co-lead several inter-disciplinary research projects, including a CONFAP-Newton Fund award, EU-GeoTech, EPSRC HECOIRA, UKRI GCRF COVID-19 grant. He is currently co-leading the computational group of Leeds Institute for Fluid Dynamics (LIFD), which is a university-wide hub to facilitate world-leading research and education in fluid dynamics. He has developed computational fluid dynamics (CFD)-based optimization approaches to design healthcare environments and developed the novel massively parallel lattice Boltzmann (LBM)-based method for real-time building environment simulation, which was recognized with the Best Paper Award.

He has also developed a novel sensor data assimilation-based indoor air quality (IAQ) forecasting technique. He has over 50+ peer-reviewed journal and conference papers across top journals in fluid mechanics and computational methods, including leading journals for the built environment.

Michał Piasecki

PhD, D.Sc. eng. Michał Piasecki is a senior researcher at the Building Research Institute (ITB). In 2009, he obtained a doctoral degree in civil engineering (sustainable assessement). From 2010 to 2021 he joined the Department of Thermal Physics, Acoustics and Environment at ITB as an assistant professor. From 2016 to 2019, he served as head of deparment. In 2021, he obtained a doctor of science degree (habilitation) in Civil Engineering from the Lodz University of Technology (indoor comfort). Currently, he is employed as the Institute's professor. Piasecki specializes in issues of sustainable construction concerning buildings and products related to VOC emissions, the assessment of indoor environment comfort and quality (IEQ), indoor air quality (IAQ), carbon footprint (CF) and economic assessment (LCC), as well as determinations of the thermal and moisture properties of buildings and thermal comfort (PMV/PPD). He is the Chairman of the KT 307 Committee at Polis Standards PKN for Sustainable Construction, a member and expert of numerous scientific organizations in Poland and Europe and a thematic editor and a reviewer in several scientific journals. His achievements include over 130 peer-reviewed publications, including 22 in the Web of Science database with citation h-index = 13. Recent achievements include the creation of a model for assessing the indoor environment of buildings. In 2019, he completed a research internship at the Lviv University of Technology. In the last dozen or so years, he help to lead and participate in several scientific and research projects, including European Commission research projects in the prestigious FP7, Erasmus+, Norway Grants and Horizion programs (energy performance, IAQ, IEQ, sustainable building).

Preface to "Ventilation and Indoor Air Quality"

Indoor air quality (IAQ) issues have been important since the 1980s for protecting the health and well-being of the general public. This book focuses on the application of ventilation and IAQ in real-life situations, and provides state-of-the-art analysis and reviews to researchers, consultants, graduate students, and faculty members.

Ashok Kumar, Alejandro Moreno-Rangel, M. Amirul I. Khan, and Michał Piasecki
Editors

atmosphere

Editorial

Ventilation and Indoor Air Quality

Ashok Kumar [1,*], Alejandro Moreno-Rangel [2,3], M. Amirul I. Khan [4] and Michał Piasecki [5]

1 Department of Civil and Environmental Engineering, The University of Toledo, Toledo, OH 43606, USA
2 Department of Architecture, University of Strathclyde, 75 Montrose Street, Glasgow G1 1XJ, UK
3 Lancaster Institute for the Contemporary Arts, Lancaster University, Bailirg LA1 4YW, UK
4 School of Civil Engineering, University of Leeds, Woodhouse Lane, Leeds LS2 9JT, UK
5 Department of Thermal Physic, Acoustic and Environment, Building Research Institute, Filtrowa 1, 00-611 Warsaw, Poland
* Correspondence: akumar@utoledo.edu; Tel.: +1-419-934-0878

Keywords: indoor air quality; ventilation; regulations; homes; modeling; field studies; technology

Citation: Kumar, A.; Moreno-Rangel, A.; Khan, M.A.I.; Piasecki, M. Ventilation and Indoor Air Quality. *Atmosphere* **2022**, *13*, 1730. https://doi.org/10.3390/atmos13101730

Received: 21 September 2022
Accepted: 17 October 2022
Published: 21 October 2022

Indoor air quality (IAQ) issues became important in the 1980s to protect the public's health and well-being. Since then, people have become aware of the fact that buildings not only provide them with a sense of security but can also significantly affect their health and well-being.

A significant number of scientific organizations and universities undertake research in the field of IAQ to this day, and the number of discoveries in this field is increasing. Ventilation and IAQ standards have been developed over the years by professional associations for engineering design and standard organizations such as CEN (European Committee for Standardization), ASHRAE (American Society of Heating, Refrigerating and Air-Conditioning Engineers) or ISO (International Organization for Standardization). Since the COVID-19 crisis, the interest in IAQ and ventilation has grown exponentially—even though ventilation is not enough to eliminate the risk of airborne virus exposure. Ventilation is a critical part of a larger strategy to improve IAQ issues in modern buildings, including schools, restaurants, public transport vehicles, and spaces. Poor indoor air quality has been linked to sick building syndrome, reduced productivity of office workers, and impaired learning over the last several decades. Ventilation enables the removal of air pollutants and can help in controlling indoor humidity as well as contaminant levels.

In connection with the growing need to determine the level of indoor air pollution, new research centers performing tests and investigating new methods have been created with research scopes including an increasing number of harmful substances and test methods. This Special Issue, titled "Ventilation and Indoor Air Quality", aims to provide readers with a comprehensive summary of the case studies based on the current work being carried out to solve ventilation and IAQ problems. It presents 19 papers related to regulations, homes, modelling, field studies, and technology related to IAQ. The papers are published in *Atmosphere*, *Environments*, *Buildings*, and *IJERPH*. The focus of the papers ranges from data collection to modelling.

Government agencies and professional associations develop indoor air quality standards and guidelines to protect public health. This Special Issue has two technical papers on the efforts of the government and health organizations. The paper by Hu and Cheng [1] discusses the efforts of the Taiwanese government in regulating IAQ since 2011. Eventually, the Taiwanese government implemented the self-managed IAQ certification in 2021. The authors conducted a questionnaire survey before the Taiwanese government officially implemented the certification. They found that the proposed IAQ certification complies with international standards and has continuous monitoring and information disclosure methods. In another paper, Wakefield and Glantz [2] examined efforts by health organizations seeking comprehensive smoke-free ordinances over Louisiana casinos and bars.

They found that ongoing local campaigns, social justice themes, and cultural messaging with coalitions in cities can secure smoke-free laws covering casinos and bars and that local ordinance campaigns are a viable method for advancing smoke-free protections over those venues in states where the state legislatures are resistant to action.

People naturally love their places of residence and would like them to be safe for families and guests. Four papers have been published in this issue to study IAQ problems in homes and apartments. Research by Moreno-Rangel et al. [3] focuses on indoor air quality in Latin America's Passivhaus homes. They concluded that Passivhaus dwellings could provide better and healthier indoor air quality in Latin America. A similar theme was examined in the homes of those employees working from home during the COVID-19 pandemic by Roh et al. [4]. In this research, the authors suggested that working from home might have a detrimental health impact due to poor IAQ and providing interventions to remote employees. The IAQ issues caused by unregulated chemical substances in Korean residential environments, i.e., in homes, are explored by Kim et al. [5]. Authors suggest that it is essential to reduce the emissions of α-pinene and limonene through the processing of wood, extending its drying period, and determining the most appropriate time of use. The performance of a five-story apartment building equipped with modern passive stack ventilation in Nordic conditions was examined by Kravchenko et al. [6]. The results show a significant effect of poor maintenance and the possibility of opening windows to control the CO_2 concentration.

IAQ modelling is a cost-effective alternative to experimental studies, although it may be associated with greater uncertainties in the obtained results. This issue has six modelling papers dealing with different aspects of indoor air quality. Zhao et al. [7] showed that errors in predicting household formaldehyde concentrations using a time-varying model were substantially less than those using a traditional constant emission rate model, despite requiring less unique building information. Rasmussen and Cornelius [8] developed a theoretical model for balancing an acceptable radon concentration in indoor air. Matheis et al. [9] presented a computational modelling study of the transmission of SARS-CoV-2 in the main types of public transport vehicles and stations to comparatively assess the relative theoretical risk of infection of travelers. Yu et al. [10] investigated the mediating effects between solid fuel use and self-rated health by using structural equation modelling (SEM). Air flow distribution and contamination control in an operating room have been examined by Wang et al. [11] using computational fluid dynamics (CFD) and field measurements. Under normal operating conditions, the contaminant concentration slightly increased while performing surgery, with an average value of 420 ppm. Abdullah and Alibaba [12] proposed a performance-based window design model for optimized natural ventilated offices.

Experimental work gives an insight into the physical processes involved in originating IAQ problems as well as solving them. Four provided papers discuss the new type of experimental work. Oda et al. [13] examined the different approaches undertaken in Japan to prevent COVID-19 against pollen and house dust antigens in patients with allergic rhinitis. The study found that 47.5% of the pollinosis patients reported improvement in nasal symptoms after the three seasons of pollen dispersion in the COVID-19 era based on the clinical records of the patients. Guo et al. [14] measured air quality inside three different brands of new vehicles. A higher concentration and different volatile organic compounds (VOCs) released from the indoor materials were observed during sunny conditions. Wallenius et al. [15] examined the data collected from 2010 to 2019 on VOC and formaldehyde in Finnish offices, schools, kindergartens, and health care offices. They found that the concentrations of individual VOCs and formaldehyde in these work environments were generally very low and posed no health risks which is due to the reduction in the use of formaldehyde resins in indoor products. The characteristics of airflow to prevent the dissemination of contaminants such as viruses were studied by Kim et al. [16] using a mobile slipstream measuring device in a motorcar.

This Special Issue contains three papers related to indoor quality technologies and applicable techniques. The paper by Alexei et al. [17] tested the effectiveness of a novel window windcatcher device (WWC) for improving natural ventilation in buildings. The proposed window windcatcher has been shown to improve both thermal comfort and indoor air quality. Another interesting paper by Siebler et al. [18] evaluated indoor airborne virus transmissions using two methods (a generalized experimental set up and a trace gas method) for several ventilation measures. Readers will enjoy a review of indoor air quality cleansing technologies by Mata et al. [19]. The paper discusses physicochemical as well as biological technologies. Meta et al. [19] concludes that the optimum solution may involve the use of a combination of technologies to solve IAQ problems.

Overall, this Special Issue provides new information to the readers and introduce new research areas for solving IAQ problems. It is hoped that readers of this Special Issue will be inspired and their minds stimulated to conduct further research on IAQ issues.

Funding: This research received no external funding.

Acknowledgments: The authors would like to thank their institutions for providing facilities for this work.

Conflicts of Interest: The authors declare no conflict of interest.

References

1. Hu, C.-P.; Cheng, J.-H. Indoor Air Quality Certification and Consumers' Willingness: Taiwan's Experience and Survey. *Atmosphere* **2021**, *12*, 1320. [CrossRef]
2. Wakefield, T.D.; Glantz, S.A. Securing Smokefree Laws Covering Casinos and Bars in Louisiana via Messaging, Continuous Campaigning and Health Coalitions. *Int. J. Environ. Res. Public Health* **2022**, *19*, 3936. [CrossRef] [PubMed]
3. Moreno-Rangel, A.; Musau, F.; Sharpe, T.; McGill, G. Indoor Air Quality Assessment of LatinAmerica's First Passivhaus Home. *Atmosphere* **2021**, *12*, 1477. [CrossRef]
4. Roh, T.; Moreno-Rangel, A.; Baek, J.; Obeng, A.; Hasan, N.T.; Carrillo, G. Indoor Air Quality and Health Outcomes in Employees Working from Home during the COVID-19 Pandemic: A Pilot Study. *Atmosphere* **2021**, *12*, 1665. [CrossRef]
5. Kim, H.; Kim, T.; Lee, S. A Study on the Measurement of Unregulated Pollutants in Korean Residential Environments. *Buildings* **2022**, *12*, 243. [CrossRef]
6. Kravchenko, I.; Kosonen, R.; Jokisalo, J.; Kilpeläinen, S. Performance of Modern Passive Stack Ventilation in a Retrofitted Nordic Apartment Building. *Buildings* **2022**, *12*, 96. [CrossRef]
7. Zhao, H.; Walker, I.S.; Sohn, M.D.; Less, B. A Time-Varying Model for Predicting Formaldehyde Emission Rates in Homes. *Int. J. Environ. Res. Public Health* **2022**, *19*, 6603. [CrossRef] [PubMed]
8. Rasmussen, T.V.; Cornelius, T. Model to Balance an Acceptable Radon Level Indoors. *Buildings* **2022**, *12*, 447. [CrossRef]
9. Matheis, C.; Norrefeldt, V.; Will, H.; Herrmann, T.; Noethlichs, B.; Eckhardt, M.; Stiebritz, A.; Jansson, M.; Schön, M. Modeling the Airborne Transmission of SARS-CoV-2 in Public Transport. *Atmosphere* **2022**, *13*, 389. [CrossRef]
10. Yu, Q.; Cheng, Y.; Li, W.; Zuo, G. Mediating Factors Explaining the Associations between Solid Fuel Use and Self-Rated Health among Chinese Adults 65 Years and Older: A Structural Equation Modeling Approach. *Int. J. Environ. Res. Public Health* **2022**, *19*, 6904. [CrossRef] [PubMed]
11. Wang, F.; Permana, I.; Rakshit, D.; Prasetyo, B.Y. Investigation of Airflow Distribution and Contamination Control with Different Schemes in an Operating Room. *Atmosphere* **2021**, *12*, 1639. [CrossRef]
12. Abdullah, H.K.; Alibaba, H.Z. A Performance-Based Window Design and Evaluation Model for Naturally Ventilated Offices. *Buildings* **2022**, *12*, 1141. [CrossRef]
13. Oda, T.; Maeda, F.; Takeno, S.; Tsuru, Y.; Ishikawa, C.; Ishino, T.; Takemoto, K.; Hamamoto, T.; Ueda, T.; Kawasumi, T.; et al. Impact of Preventive Measures on Subjective Symptoms and Antigen Sensitization against Japanese Cedar, Cypress Pollen and House Dust Mites in Patients with Allergic Rhinitis: A Retrospective Analysis in the COVID-19 Era. *Atmosphere* **2022**, *13*, 1000. [CrossRef]
14. Guo, R.; Zhu, X.; Zhu, Z.; Sun, J.; Li, Y.; Hu, W.; Tang, S. Evaluation of Typical Volatile Organic Compounds Levels in New Vehicles under Static and Driving Conditions. *Int. J. Environ. Res. Public Health* **2022**, *19*, 7048. [CrossRef] [PubMed]
15. Wallenius, K.; Hovi, H.; Remes, J.; Mahiout, S.; Liukkonen, T. Volatile Organic Compounds in Finnish Office Environments in 2010–2019 and Their Relevance to Adverse Health Effects. *Int. J. Environ. Res. Public Health* **2022**, *19*, 4411. [CrossRef] [PubMed]
16. Kim, M.; Lee, Y.; Park, D. Analysis of the Airflow Generated by Human Activity Using a Mobile Slipstream Measuring Device. *Environments* **2021**, *8*, 97. [CrossRef]

17. Fawwaz Alrebei, O.; Obeidat, L.M.; Ma'bdeh, S.N.; Kaouri, K.; Al-Radaideh, T.; Amhamed, A.I. Window-Windcatcher for Enhanced Thermal Comfort, Natural Ventilation and Reduced COVID-19 Transmission. *Buildings* **2022**, *12*, 791. [CrossRef]
18. Siebler, L.; Calandri, M.; Rathje, T.; Stergiaropoulos, K. Experimental Methods of Investigating Airborne Indoor Virus-Transmissions Adapted to Several Ventilation Measures. *Int. J. Environ. Res. Public Health* **2022**, *19*, 11300. [CrossRef] [PubMed]
19. Mata, T.M.; Martins, A.A.; Calheiros, C.S.C.; Villanueva, F.; Alonso-Cuevilla, N.P.; Gabriel, M.F.; Silva, G.V. Indoor Air Quality: A Review of Cleaning Technologies. *Environments* **2022**, *9*, 118. [CrossRef]

atmosphere

MDPI

Article

Indoor Air Quality Certification and Consumers' Willingness: Taiwan's Experience and Survey

Chih-Pei Hu [1,]* and Jen-Hsiung Cheng [2]

1 Department of Public Administration, Chung Hua University, Hsinchu 30012, Taiwan
2 Taiwan Indoor Environment Quality Management Association, New Taipei City 23555, Taiwan; ieqm.tw@msa.hinet.net
* Correspondence: billhu0711@gmail.com

Abstract: People spend about 80–90% of their time in indoor environments, and poor indoor air quality (IAQ) can seriously endanger people's health, work quality, and efficiency. The Taiwan Government began regulating IAQ in 2011 and implemented the self-managed IAQ certification in 2021. Before the Taiwan Government officially implemented the certification, we conducted a questionnaire survey from 26 to 27 September 2020. Moreover, this survey selected Banqiao and Wuri High-Speed Rail Plaza as the survey sites and completed 337 valid questionnaires. According to the hierarchical regression results, this research found the following: firstly, IAQ certification complies with international standards and has continuous monitoring and information disclosure methods, both of which are key factors affecting people's willingness to consume; secondly, the respondents, who are female, familiar with the regulations, and living in the northern Taiwan area, have more willingness to consume in the certificated places.

Keywords: indoor air quality; IAQ citification; consumers' willingness; Taiwan's experience

Citation: Hu, C.-P.; Cheng, J.-H. Indoor Air Quality Certification and Consumers' Willingness: Taiwan's Experience and Survey. *Atmosphere* **2021**, *12*, 1320. https://doi.org/10.3390/atmos12101320

Academic Editors: Ashok Kumar, M Amirul I Khan, Alejandro Moreno Rangel and Michał Piasecki

Received: 8 September 2021
Accepted: 8 October 2021
Published: 9 October 2021

1. Introduction

According to the Environmental Protection Administration of the R.O.C. (TW EPA), each person spends about 80–90% of the time in an indoor environment (including homes, offices, or other buildings) [1]. Therefore, when the indoor air quality (IAQ) is poor, it can seriously endanger people's health, work quality, and efficiency. In particular, if indoor ventilation is insufficient in a closed building for a long time, pollutants are likely to accumulate and deteriorate the IAQ. Sometimes, people within closed buildings experience acute uncomfortable symptoms caused by unknown reasons that often disappear after leaving. This is known as the so-called "sick-building syndrome" condition (sick-building syndrome—SBS). If people stay in such buildings over long periods of time, in which the IAQ is poor or the indoor air is polluted, this will easily lead to abnormal human symptoms such as neurotoxic symptoms (including eye, nose, and throat irritation), a pungent or unpleasant smell, and induced asthma attacks. Indeed, the IAQ impacts human health, especially during the COVID-19 outbreak, in which people have significantly increased their indoor time. To prevent the spread of COVID-19, many people may not open doors and windows to allow in the fresh air, resulting in poor ventilation and deterioration of IAQ.

1.1. Indoor Air Quality

1.1.1. Definition and Its Effects

The IAQ is particularly important since people stay indoors for a long time. Steinemann et al. [2] pointed out that IAQ definitions can vary depending on the perspectives of the user, as well as the indoor air of the space and the source of indoor air pollution. In fact, indoor air quality is affected by outdoor sources and building design, especially regarding ventilation and physical parameters (relative humidity and temperature) [3]. The

World Health Organization (WHO) [4] defined healthy IAQ as "no harmful concentrations of pollutants are found in the air, and at least 80% of users are not dissatisfied with air quality." The US Environmental Protection Agency [5] also defined IAQ as the air quality inside and around buildings and structures, especially because it is related to the health and comfort of the occupants of the building. Understanding and controlling common indoor pollutants can help reduce risks related to indoor health problems.

In 1988, the WHO held the first meeting on the IAQ and health and generated a vast amount of reliable information on the impact of degraded IAQ on workers' health and productivity. Past research on IAQ usually focused on ventilation, health hazards, and creating a comfortable environment. In general, the scientific literature shows that good or improved indoor air quality increases productivity in the workplace and reduces absenteeism, which provides substantial financial benefits, which usually greatly exceeds the associated costs [6]. In other words, improving IAQ can not only protect the health and well-being of building occupants but also generate considerable financial returns on investment.

1.1.2. Organizations and Improvements

The IAQ is not only related to health outcomes, indoor air pollutant exposure, and occupants' satisfaction with the environment but also to overall human well-being, cognitive performance, and learning [7]. Therefore, organizations and governments, within their technical documents and position papers, have always emphasized the determinants of IAQ on human health and the potential existence of harmful pollutants released from indoor sources [8].

The first study on comfort and IAQ conditions was in the 19th century, which measured fresh air. With the energy crisis in the second half of the 19th century, research on IAQ increased rapidly [9]. Many organizations and governments are currently working to improve information about indoor air quality, setting priorities and goals, and providing various legal research, monitors, setting standards, and environmental protection for indoor air quality. Table 1 highlights IAQ-related work in some countries and organizations.

Table 1. Countries and organizations working on IAQ.

Country	Organization	Country	Organization
Worldwide	WHO	China	AQSIQ, SEPA
Worldwide	ISO	Malaysia	DOSH
Worldwide	International Society of Indoor Air Quality and Climate	Japan	MHLW
Worldwide	AIVC	Korea	KEITI
USA	ASHRAE, OSHA, US EPA	Taiwan (R.O.C.)	TW EPA
UK	HSC	Germany	MAK
EU	REHVA The Joint Research Center CEN, the European Committee for Standardization	Canada	Health Canada

According to research, poor IAQ has an important impact on human health, performance, and productivity and should be regarded as a public health issue. Therefore, indoor environmental conditions improved through enhanced ventilation strategies should be opportunities for people's health, performance, and productivity [10]. Hawkins et al. [6] argued that improvements in the IAQ have also been found to reduce employee absenteeism, reduce reported work stress, and increase job satisfaction. Some specific IAQ improvements related to these benefits include increased ventilation; reduced emissions of chemicals and other pollutants; improved air filtration, temperature and humidity control; and reduced moisture and mold in buildings. In other words, building design, construction, renovation, and ongoing maintenance can enable the identification and resolution of potential and actual IAQ issues.

1.2. Taiwan's Experience

1.2.1. Legislation and Regulated Places

Since 1998, the TW EPA has conducted surveys and research on the indoor and IAQ of relevant occupational sites. Accordingly, the Taiwan Government passed the "Indoor Air Quality Management Promotion Plan" drafted by the TW EPA in 2005 and then announced the "Recommended Indoor Air Quality Values" at the end of 2005 to provide users with a reference for management [11]. After years of research and policy formulation, the Taiwan Government passed the "Indoor Air Quality Act" on 8 November in 2011 and became the second country (after South Korea) to compulsorily incorporate indoor air quality management into legislation and extended air quality management from outdoor to indoor. Today, Taiwan's Indoor Air Quality Act has been formally implemented for 10 years and has a total of 10 relevant regulations, orders, and directions (see Table 2). The Indoor Air Quality Information Network. Available online: https://iaq.epa.gov.tw/indoorair/introduction_importance.aspx (accessed on 1 September 2021).

Table 2. IAQ regulations in Taiwan.

Rank	Title	Announced Date
Act	Indoor Air Quality Act	23 November 2011
Order	Indoor Air Quality Act Enforcement Rules	23 November 2012
Order	Indoor Air Quality Standards	23 November 2012
Order	The Regulations of Establish Specialized Personnel for Indoor Air Quality Maintenance and Management	11 August 2016
Order	The Regulations of the Indoor Air Quality Inspection and Determination in Specific places	23 November 2012 9 August 2021 (amended)
Order	The Regulations of the Violate Indoor Air Quality Act Penalty Limits and Guidelines	23 November 2012
Order	The First Batch of Specific Places Comply with the Indoor Air Quality Act	23 January 2014
Order	The Second Batch of Specific Places Comply with the Indoor Air Quality Act	11 January 2017
Direction	Operation Directions for Self-Management Marks of Indoor Air Quality by Environmental Protection Administration of the Executive Yuan	2 July 2021
Other	Indoor Air Quality Maintenance and Management Plan Document	June 2016 (amended)

In 2014, the TW EPA made an announcement: "The First Batch of Specific Places Comply with the Indoor Air Quality Act"; therefore, the objects of this study are people gathering, entering, and exiting specific public and private places or the risk of indoor air pollutants and the special needs of these places. The First Batch of Specific Places includes colleges, libraries, medical institutions, social welfare institutions, government offices, railway transportation stations, civil aviation stations, mass rapid transit systems, transportation stations, exhibition rooms, conference halls, shopping malls, and another ten types.

Moreover, "The Second Batch of Specific Places Comply with the Indoor Air Quality Act" was also announced in 2017. Under this order, owners, managers, and users of specific places were also required to complete management plans, inspections, and records every year. This announcement included an additional six types of places, including museums and art galleries, financial institutions, performance halls, cinemas, KTVs, and sports centers, with a total of 940 places under regulation.

To date, there has been no clear time schedule for the third batch of specific places that could be announced. In addition, small public places, such as kindergartens, gyms, and long-term care centers, that were selected in this research may be included in the next regulation. In other words, Taiwan's implementation of the IAQ management continuously expands the policy coverage within 10 years.

1.2.2. Standards, Inspections, and Certifications

The concentration of indoor air pollutants is closely related to the activities of indoor personnel and the use of equipment. According to the IAQ standards announced by the Taiwan Government, controlled pollutants include carbon dioxide (CO_2), carbon monoxide (CO), formaldehyde (HCHO), total volatile organic compounds (TVOC), bacteria (bacteria), fungi (fungi) (the indoor and outdoor concentration ratio is less than or equal to 1.3, which is no longer limited), 10 microns suspended particles (PM_{10}), 2.5 microns suspended particles ($PM_{2.5}$), and ozone (O_3). At the same time, the standard clearly stipulates the relevant pollutant audit and prohibition penalty standards (see Table 3).

Table 3. Standard values of indoor air pollutants in Taiwan.

Item	Standard Values		Unit
CO_2	8 h	1000	ppm
CO	8 h	9	ppm
HCHO	1 h	0.08	ppm
TVOC	1 h	0.56	ppm
Bacteria	Highest value	1500	CFU/m^3
Fungi	Highest value	1000	CFU/m^3
PM_{10}	24 h	75	$\mu g/m^3$
$PM_{2.5}$	24 h	35	$\mu g/m^3$
O_3	8 h	0.06	ppm

At the same time, IAQ inspection and determination are divided into two categories:

1. Regular inspection: specific places that are under-regulated should conduct indoor air pollutant concentration measurements within a prescribed period and regularly announce the inspection and measurement results.
2. Continuous monitoring: government-designated specific places must set up automatic monitoring facilities. The owner, manager, or user who approved the automatic monitoring facilities should continue to measure indoor air pollutant concentrations and display the latest measured values in real time.

In 2021, the Taiwan Government's management of IAQ made another leap forward. To advocate self-maintenance of the IAQ in public and private places, the Taiwan Government announced the self-management certification of IAQ. If the IAQ of public and private spaces is deemed to meet the standard of the certification mark after review, then those sites will be awarded a certification. The self-management certification is applicable to 19 categories—colleges and universities, libraries, museums and art galleries, medical institutions, social welfare institutions, government offices, railway stations, airports, mass rapid transit system stations, financial institutions, performance halls, exhibition rooms, cinemas, KTV, shopping malls, gyms, kindergartens, post-natal care institutions, and baby care centers. Specific places, regardless of whether or not they have been previously regulated, are divided into two levels (see Figure 1):

1. Excellent: the certification is valid for three years, within self-inspections every six months and regular inspections completed once every three years.
2. Good: the certification is valid for two years, with self-inspections before regular inspection and regular inspection completed once every two years.

Once a private or public place has applied for the mark, the certification is placed on the service counter or at an obvious location at the entrance for public identification. According to current regulations, different types of places have designated certified IAQ standards (see Table 4). Only the selected three categories of places—related to this research—are shown here.

In the past, IAQ research focused on instrument measurement and controlling air pollutants; however, recent public awareness of IAQ also gained traction. Firstly, IAQ surveys in Taiwan are generally based on presenting technical monitoring data—the subjects are mostly medical institutions. At the same time, the surveys can be roughly divided into three types: measurement quality and comparative analysis [12,13], measurement as the main part and supplemented by some subjective questionnaire surveys [14], and pure public IAQ perception surveys [15,16]. Secondly, IAQ surveys around the world have also shown different characteristics in recent years: combining instrumental measurements and subjective questionnaires [17–21] and IAQ perception surveys for specific spaces [22,23]. It is worth mentioning that some research has emphasized public IAQ perception surveys and conducted comparative analyses [24].

Figure 1. IAQ certification mark in Taiwan.

Table 4. Selected cases of the IAQ certification standard in Taiwan.

Place	Indoor Air Pollutant Items	Monitoring Period	Excellent Level Standard (Unit)	Good Level Standard (Unit)
Gym/kindergarten	CO_2	8 h	800 (ppm)	1000 (ppm)
	HCHO	1 h	0.03 (ppm)	0.08 (m)
	Bacteria	Highest value	800 (CFU/m^3)	1500 (CFU/m^3)
	PM_{10}	24 h	50 (μg/m^3)	75 (μg/m^3)
Long-term care center * (social welfare institutions)	CO_2	8 h	800 (ppm)	1000 (ppm)
	CO	8 h	2 (ppm)	9 (ppm)
	HCHO	1 h	0.03 (ppm)	0.08 (ppm)
	Bacteria	Highest value	800 (CFU/m^3)	1500 (CFU/m^3)
	PM_{10}	24 h	50 (μg/m^3)	75 (μg/m^3)

* Long-term care centers refer to use social welfare institution standards.

According to the above analysis, the differences between this research and others are: First, this is a first-hand survey and pilot study before the Taiwan Government officially implemented the self-management IAQ certification; second, the questionnaire contains not only traditional basic information, symptoms, and cognition of IAQ but also the opinions and evaluations of the IAQ certification system; finally, this research extended the subject—of IAQ's survey—to the consumer behavior field and conducted a regional comparative analysis. Therefore, this is a subject that has rarely appeared in related research yet is an innovative and practical topic.

Related studies have pointed out that having excellent IAQ can promote human health and increase productivity; however, there is little discussion regarding whether these environmental conditions can cause people to go or even have the willingness to consume. Accordingly, this research aims to use empirical investigations to understand whether government-certified IAQ places can promote people's willingness to consume and related relevant influencing factors.

As mentioned above, this research mainly aims to understand the public's views on the self-management certification system promoted by the Taiwan Government and whether it will affect their willingness to consume. This research proposes the hypothesis that the public's cognition of IAQ certification and displaying certification information are both key factors that affect people's willingness to consume.

2. Materials and Methods

2.1. Research Design and Methods

The IAQ standards and specifications are discussed in many related studies, but the impact on consumption willingness is seldom discussed. To understand the relationship between IAQ certification and consumption willingness, this research specifically designed a questionnaire using the public's cognition of IAQ certification and certification information as an independent variable and the consumption willingness of certified locations as a dependent variable. Therefore, this research proposes the following hypotheses:

Hypothesis 1 (H1). *The cognition of IAQ certification will affect their willingness to consume.*

Hypothesis 2 (H2). *The display method of IAQ certification information will affect their willingness to consume.*

Hypothesis 3 (H3). *Both the cognition of IAQ certification and the way of displaying information will strengthen their willingness to consume.*

To ensure survey respondents have a certain degree of regional representativeness, this research specifically selected areas with dense populations, high economic development, and urbanization in Taiwan. Therefore, the high-speed rail station plaza, with a large crowd and an important transportation hub, was selected as the survey site. For the feasibility and convenience of the investigation, this research cooperated with the Taiwan Indoor Environment Quality Management Association—TIEQMA is one of the few non-governmental professional organizations in Taiwan that focuses on IAQ-related issues. It also gathers experts in various fields such as environmental protection, air conditioning, construction, and improving technology to promote the indoor air quality industry to formulate unified standards, technical guidance, education and training, and assistance in the promotion of related laws and regulations. Official Website: https://www.tieqm.com/, accessed on 1 September 2021 (TIEQMA)'s annual activities to conduct two-day investigations at Banqiao and Wuri High-speed Railway Station Plaza.

The survey is combined with TIEQMA's annual public welfare activities. The association regularly promotes IAQ-related information and improvement methods every year. At the same time, on the two days of the survey, the association mobilized many volunteers, university professors, and students to randomly invite people concerned about IAQ issues to fill out the questionnaire. Each respondent is fully informed of the purpose of the questionnaire and how the relevant information will be used.

Therefore, the survey subjects of this research can be divided into two groups: one is the people living cycle around the Banqiao High-Speed Station (north area of Taiwan), and the other is around the Wuri High-Speed Station (middle area of Taiwan). For the questionnaire (see Appendix A), we consulted and communicated with the TIEQMA several times during the design process, and so it has a certain degree of expert validity. The questionnaire was also pre-tested before being formally conducted and was revised according to the results.

The questionnaire used in this research can be divided into five parts: (1) basic information of the respondents, including four variables, i.e., gender, age, marriage, and education; (2) practical experience and knowledge of the IAQ scale section, in which there are also six questions; (3) certification cognition scale section, including four questions (Cronbach's Alpha = 0.760); (4) certification displays scale section—there are only three questions that require responses (Cronbach's Alpha = 0.872); and (5) willingness to consume at certified places scale section, in which there are four questions that require answering by respondents (Cronbach's Alpha = 0.772).

2.2. Data and Survey Sites Selection

The survey was conducted between 09:00 and 17:00 from 26 September (Banqiao) to 27 (Wuri) in 2020—at that time, the COVID-19 pandemic in Taiwan had not broken out seriously, and the main pandemic prevention measures in place during this period were mask wearing and maintaining social distancing—and as mentioned above, it mainly included two types of respondents. In addition, Banqiao Station, which is close to the north area of Taiwan including Taipei City and New Taipei City, both have a population of approximately 6.9 million (30% of Taiwanese residents); Taipei City is Taiwan's economic and financial center, and many domestic and foreign corporate headquarters and financial institutions; New Taipei City is the most populous city in Taiwan and is dominated by manufacturing and construction industries; the Wuri Station near to the middle area of Taiwan includes three counties, with a population of approximately 4.7 million (25% of Taiwanese residents), and it is the second-largest metropolitan area in Taiwan, mainly in manufacturing areas and agricultural and fishing villages. Therefore, northern Taiwan is the most densely populated area with the best economic development, while the middle area of Taiwan is an emerging metropolis. According to statistics from the Taiwanese Government in 2020, the monthly consumption expenditure of residents of northern Taiwan is about USD 1100, while that of central Taiwan is close to USD 850.

High-speed rail is currently one of Taiwan's most important modes of transportation, connecting many important cities and driving regional population growth and economic development. The main reasons why Banqiao and Wuri Station were selected as the survey bases in this research are: First, Banqiao Station is a three-rail joint construction (high-speed rail, railway, and MRT), connecting the largest metropolitan area in northern Taiwan; second, Wuri Station is a transportation hub in the adjacent area, with expressways and railways connecting Taiwan's second-largest central metropolitan area; finally, both sites are crowded and traffic-heavy and are important transportation locations for Taiwan's important population clusters and high urbanization areas.

This research is limited by funding, so convenience sampling is mainly adopted, and the results cannot be inferred to other groups. There were 337 copies of valid questionnaires, including 189 copies from Banqiao and 148 copies from Wuri.

3. Results

3.1. Descriptive Analysis of the Results

This survey applied the hierarchical regression analysis, using the certification cognition and display as the independent variable, the willingness to consume at certified places as the dependent variable, and testing whether there were significant differences among the three scales (background information, experience, and knowledge of the respondents as the control variable).

3.1.1. Features of Samples

According to the basic information of the 337 respondents, the main components were as follows: 56.1% of respondents live around the north of Taiwan, 68.8% of the sample were females, 22.3% respondents were aged 41–50 and 51–60 years old, 57.3% of the respondents are married, and 42.4% hold a college or university education degree. Furthermore, the Banqiao and Wuri samples collected in this research have the following characteristics (see Table 5):

Firstly, most of the respondents at Banqiao Station are female, older, with higher education, and have relatively no air allergy symptoms.

Secondly, the samples at Wuri Station are also mostly female, younger, have college degrees, and more are acknowledgeable of relevant laws and regulations.

These results are not completely consistent with the real demographic characteristics of Taiwan. The main reason for this bias is that the survey was conducted on weekends, and the convenience sampling design was adopted.

Table 5. Comparison of Banqiao and Wuri sample features.

Survey Site		Banqiao (N = 189)		Wuri (N = 148)	
Items		Frequency	Percentage	Frequency	Percentage
Gender	Female	133	70.4%	99	66.9%
	Male	56	29.6%	49	33.1%
Age	Under 20	7	3.7%	14	9.5%
	21–30	21	11.1%	36	24.3%
	31–40	37	19.6%	20	13.5%
	41–50	41	21.7%	34	23.0%
	51–60	41	21.7%	34	23.0%
	Above 61	42	22.2%	10	6.8%
Marriage	Married	120	63.5%	73	49.3%
	Unmarried	69	36.5%	75	50.7%
Education	Junior high school	17	9.0%	10	6.8%
	High school	29	15.3%	27	18.2%
	College	19	10.1%	13	8.8%
	University	71	37.6%	72	48.6%
	Master or PhD	53	28.0%	26	17.6%
Air allergy	Yes	82	43.4%	74	50.0%
	No	104	55.0%	74	50.0%
	Missing	3	1.6%	0	0%
Know the law	Yes	83	43.9%	85	57.4%
	No	100	52.9%	52	35.1%
	Missing	6	3.2%	11	7.4%

In addition, on the practical experience and knowledge scale, this research designed questions related to understanding the real situation of the respondents. Firstly, 52.8% of the respondents have no symptoms of air allergy, and 49.9% of the respondents are aware of the government-enacted IAQ management laws. Secondly, the respondents are familiar with some indoor air quality pollutants and focus on specific items (see Table 6).

Table 6. The cognition of indoor air pollutants.

Item	N	Percentage	Item	N	Percentage
$PM_{2.5}$	230	68.9%	TVOC	149	44.6%
CO_2	213	63.8%	Bacteria	129	38.6%
HCHO	213	63.8%	O_3	127	38.0%
PM_{10}	183	54.8%	Fungi	75	22.5%
CO	177	53.0%	None	22	6.7%

Thirdly, most respondents are aware that the government has regulated some specific places; however, 24.9% of them express that they are unaware of any places (see Table 7).

Table 7. Top five responses of regulated specific places.

Places	N	Percentage
Medical institutions	186	55.7%
Mass rapid transit system stations	155	46.4%
Libraries	153	45.8%
Government offices	139	41.6%
Railway stations/airports	132	39.5%

3.1.2. Description of Scales

This research designed three scales to inquire about respondents' views and attitudes towards the IAQ certification, contents, and their willingness to consume in the certified places. These scales used a five-point Likert scale (5 = strongly agree), and the mean and standard deviation (of the descriptive statistics) were used to analyze the results (see Table 8).

Table 8. The IAQ Certification cognition, displays, and the consumer's willingness.

Scale	Items	N	Mean	Standard Deviation
Certification cognition	Certification classification	335	4.4687	0.72472
	Comply with international standards *	334	4.4461	0.69431
Certification display	Monitoring equipment and bulletin board	327	4.3670	0.68723
	Replace paper poster	327	4.2813	0.76366
Consumer's willingness	Willing to pay a higher price	327	4.1468	0.87388
	Case1: Gym	327	4.3700	0.75986
	Case2: Kindergarten	327	4.5443	0.64377
	Case3: Long-term Care Center	326	4.5583	0.62362

* Since the respondents of the questionnaire in this study are public, not professionals, they are not familiar with various highly professional standards. Therefore, in the questionnaire design, the IAQ international standard description used in this research is used as an example of the IAQ standard in the WELL healthy building certification.

According to Table 8, the following findings can be summarized.

First, most of the respondents are willing to express their opinions, and their degree of agreement is very high (all means are above 4), especially some questions in the certification cognition and consumer's willingness scales.

Second, some responses in the scale are relatively consistent, e.g., the certified kindergartens (S.D. = 0.64377) and long-term care centers (S.D. = 0.62362) are willing to consume; some are relatively more divergent and appear in all three scales, such as the willingness to pay a higher price (S.D. = 0.87388), the certified gym (S.D. = 0.75986), replace the paper poster (S.D. = 0.76366), and certification classification (S.D. = 0.72472).

Overall, the responses in the survey are positive and affirmative—also expressed in the IAQ adopting certification, classification, and international standards items. In addition, if there are specific places that have been certified, their willingness to consume is also highly aggressive. Relatively speaking, regarding the certification display scale, respondents' opinions are minorly divergent.

3.2. *Hierarchical Regression Analysis of Certification and Consume*

For this section, this research used the respondents' seven-basic information as the control variable: gender (1 = man; 0 = female), age (1 = 15–39; 0 = above 40), marriage (1 = yes; 0 = no), education (1 = collage; 0 = high school), air allergy (1 = yes; 2 = no), know the law (1 = yes; 2 = no), and area (1 = Banqiao; 2 = Wuri). In addition, the certification cognition and display were used as the independent variable, the willingness to consume at certified places as the dependent variable, and the hierarchical regression analysis was employed to test for any significant differences in the scales.

3.2.1. Cognition Effect the Consumer's Willingness

In the certification cognition scale, this research designed two concepts: classification and compliance with the international standards. Therefore, we used these as the independent variable and tested whether there were significant differences in the consumer's willingness scales by regression analysis. According to the results in Table 9, the cognition of certification does affect the willingness to consume (all models $p < 0.001$); classification and compliance with international standards also show a low moderately positive correlation with consumer willingness and have certain predictions (all models Adj R^2 between 0.264 and 0.365). From the analysis results of the control variables, females are more willing to pay more for certified places, and people in northern Taiwan are also willing to send their children to certified kindergartens. This result may be because females may pay more attention to environmental cleanliness; since northern Taiwan is a densely populated area with strict living conditions, people pay more attention to environmental quality.

Table 9. Certification cognition regression.

Independent Variables	Model 1 Pay High Price		Model 2 Gym		Model 3 Kindergarten		Model 4 Long-Term Care Center	
	B	(S.E.)	B	(S.E.)	B	(S.E.)	B	(S.E.)
Certification cognition								
Classification	0.291 **	(0.105)	0.305 ***	(0.078)	0.264 ***	(0.067)	0.418 ***	(0.067)
Comply with the international standards	0.368 ***	(0.098)	0.352 ***	(0.071)	0.345 ***	(0.062)	0.175 **	(0.062)
Control Variables								
Gender	−0.232 *	(0.101)	0.063	(0.075)	−0.006	(0.065)	0.059	(0.064)
Age	0.060	(0.114)	−0.014	(0.085)	0.011	(0.073)	0.010	(0.073)
Marriage	−0.221	(0.113)	−0.081	(0.084)	0.016	(0.072)	−0.042	(0.072)
Education	0.043	(0.111)	−0.149	(0.082)	−0.022	(0.070)	−0.062	(0.070)
Air allergy	−0.064	(0.096)	−0.069	(0.071)	−0.065	(0.061)	−0.060	(0.061)
Know the law	−0.088	(0.096)	−0.038	(0.071)	−0.018	(0.061)	−0.083	(0.061)
Area	0.030	(0.096)	−0.069	(0.071)	−0.135 *	(0.061)	−0.066	(0.061)
Constant	1.024 **	(0.358)	2.017 ***	(0.264)	1.867 ***	(0.226)	1.825 ***	(0.225)
Statistics	N = 265 F(9255) = 10.310 $p < 0.001$ $R^2 = 0.267$ Adj $R^2 = 0.244$		N = 265 F(9255) = 15.559 $p < 0.001$ $R^2 = 0.354$ Adj $R^2 = 0.332$		N = 265 F(9255) = 17.743 $p < 0.001$ $R^2 = 0.385$ Adj $R^2 = 0.363$		N = 265 F(9255) = 17.858 $p < 0.001$ $R^2 = 0.387$ Adj $R^2 = 0.365$	

Note: *** $p < 0.001$; ** $p < 0.01$; * $p < 0.05$.

3.2.2. Monitors and Bulletin Enforce the Attitude

In the certification display scale, this research also designed two concepts: monitors and information disclosure forms. Again, we used these to test the effects on consumers' willingness. According to the results in Table 10, the certification has a strong effect on the willingness to consume (all models $p < 0.001$); the monitors and bulletin have a moderately positive correlation with consumer willingness and have a prediction of around 40% (all models Adj R^2 between 0.381 and 0.396). Furthermore, we find that respondents who are familiar with the regulations pay a higher price in certified spaces, especially in the long-term care center. These people are aware of the relevant laws and regulations, and they also know that the certified places have better IAQ.

3.2.3. International Standards and Information Disclosure as the Key Factors

Finally, we combine the certification cognition and display scale and investigate the consumer's willingness results. From the previous analysis, a synergy result can be observed (see Table 11):

1. International standards and monitors still have a significant effect on consumer's willingness, in particular, the continuous monitors and bulletin is a key factor.
2. Further improvement in the degree of prediction, with an effect of close to 45% (all models Adj R^2 between 0.384 and 0.454).
3. Some features of the respondents still have a significant influence on different models, e.g., gender in high price, living area in kindergarten, and know the law in the long-term care center.

Table 10. Certification display regression.

Independent Variables	Model 1 Pay High Price		Model 2 Gym		Model 3 Kindergarten		Model 4 Long-Term Care Center	
	B	(S.E.)	B	(S.E.)	B	(S.E.)	B	(S.E.)
Certification display								
Monitors and bulletin	0.667 ***	(0.087)	0.617 ***	(0.070)	0.475 ***	(0.061)	0.488 ***	(0.061)
Replace paper poster	0.157 *	(0.077)	0.022	(0.062)	0.095	(0.054)	0.092	(0.054)
Control Variables								
Gender	−0.176	(0.092)	0.102	(0.075)	0.020	(0.065)	0.075	(0.064)
Age	−0.028	(0.104)	−0.073	(0.084)	−0.048	(0.073)	−0.024	(0.072)
Marriage	−0.115	(0.104)	−0.019	(0.084)	0.065	(0.073)	0.008	(0.072)
Education	0.122	(0.101)	−0.081	(0.082)	0.007	(0.071)	−0.020	(0.070)
Air allergy	−0.066	(0.087)	−0.079	(0.070)	−0.070	(0.061)	−0.051	(0.060)
Know the law	−0.193 *	(0.087)	−0.121	(0.071)	−0.111	(0.061)	−0.166 **	(0.060)
Area	0.076	(0.088)	−0.059	(0.071)	−0.107	(0.061)	−0.048	(0.061)
Constant	1.114 *	(0.437)	2.038 ***	(0.354)	2.415 ***	(0.306)	2.032 ***	(0.210)
Statistics	N = 266 F(9256) = 18.478 $p < 0.001$ $R^2 = 0.394$ Adj $R^2 = 0.372$		N = 266 F(9256) = 18.036 $p < 0.001$ $R^2 = 0.388$ Adj $R^2 = 0.367$		N = 266 F(9256) = 17.488 $p < 0.001$ $R^2 = 0.381$ Adj $R^2 = 0.359$		N = 266 F(9256) = 18.641 $p < 0.001$ $R^2 = 0.396$ Adj $R^2 = 0.375$	

Note: *** $p < 0.001$; ** $p < 0.01$; * $p < 0.05$.

Table 11. Certification cognition and display regression.

Independent Variables	Model 1 Pay High Price		Model 2 Gym		Model 3 Kindergarten		Model 4 Long-Term Care Center	
	B	(S.E.)	B	(S.E.)	B	(S.E.)	B	(S.E.)
Certification cognition								
Classification	0.036	(0.100)	0.143	(0.077)	0.110	(0.066)	0.277 ***	(0.066)
Comply with the international standards	0.197 *	0(.091)	0.229 **	(0.070)	0.261 ***	(0.060)	0.086	(0.060)
Certification display								
Monitors and bulletin	0.563 ***	(0.090)	0.422 ***	(0.073)	0.332 ***	(0.063)	0.334 ***	(0.062)
Replace paper poster	0.118 **	(0.079)	−0.017	(0.061)	0.067	(0.052)	0.032	(0.052)
Control Variables								
Gender	−0.183 *	(0.092)	0.090	(0.070)	0.018	(0.060)	0.085	(0.060)
Age	−0.011	(0.103)	−0.061	(0.079)	−0.028	(0.068)	−0.030	(0.068)
Marriage	−0.119	(0.103)	−0.028	(0.079)	0.064	(0.068)	0.010	(0.067)
Education	0.131	(0.101)	−0.083	(0.077)	0.030	(0.067)	−0.010	(0.066)
Air allergy	−0.050	(0.086)	−0.055	(0.066)	−0.055	(0.057)	−0.050	(0.056)
Know the law	−0.155	(0.087)	−0.072	(0.067)	−0.049	(0.058)	−0.117 *	(0.057)
Area	0.074	(0.087)	−0.049	(0.067)	−0.116 *	(0.057)	−0.044	(0.057)
Constant	0.513	(0.476)	1.293 ***	(0.364)	1.601 ***	(0.314)	1.618 ***	(0.311)
Statistics	N = 265 F(11,253) = 15.990 $p < 0.001$ $R^2 = 0.410$ Adj $R^2 = 0.384$		N = 265 F(11,253) = 18.613 $p < 0.001$ $R^2 = 0.447$ Adj $R^2 = 0.423$		N = 265 F(11,253) = 20.288 $p < 0.001$ $R^2 = 0.469$ Adj $R^2 = 0.446$		N = 265 F(11,253) = 20.944 $p < 0.001$ $R^2 = 0.477$ Adj $R^2 = 0.454$	

Note: *** $p < 0.001$; ** $p < 0.01$; * $p < 0.05$.

4. Discussion

The IAQ is a topic of increasing interest in green and energy-renovated buildings [25] and provides a compelling opportunity for the building industry; human health has recently emerged as a priority, as reflected in the Green Building Certification Program [7]. The purpose of this research was to understand whether the IAQ certification can influence people's willingness to consume. From the above results, it is shown that there is a significant correlation between them.

Mothersbaugh et al. [26] stressed that the factors that affect consumer behavior could be summarized into two types: external and internal influences. The IAQ cognition and display discussed in this research can be regarded as the internal influence factors of consumer perception, attitudes, and self-concepts.

Indeed, the empirical survey results confirm that IAQ-certified places have certain standards and continuous public disclosure of information, which is enough to change the willingness of the people to consume. In addition, the survey results also show additional influencing factors, such as gender, knowledge of the regulations, and living area, etc. These additional factors are mostly related to personal perceptions and objective conditions in Taiwan.

5. Conclusions

The WHO continuously emphasizes IAQ determinants on human health and the potential existence of harmful pollutants released from indoor sources [8]. The Taiwan Government, in 2011, enacted the "Indoor Air Quality Act" and continues to maintain the air pollution standards and related operating directions. Moreover, The TW EPA began promoting IAQ certification in 2021 and adopted a self-management approach to encourage various places to apply for the certification.

The survey conducted by this research found that certified places can indeed increase people's willingness to consume, and the certification can comply with international standards, as well as continuously monitor and disclose information—both of which are important factors. These findings also partially verify the three hypotheses proposed in this research. Concurrently, the results of this study are only applicable within the scope of the investigation and represent some regional findings; however, they retain a certain reference value. Similarly, these findings are partly different from previous past IAQ-related findings because other surveys mainly focused on exploring the possible symptoms of people in indoor spaces and their perception of the IAQ. This research links the public's perception of the IAQ with potential consumer behaviors, so these findings can indeed serve as a reference for business places, corporations, and the government.

According to the results of this research, compared with the current IAQ certification promoted by the Taiwan Government, there are two shortcomings that need to be further improved: firstly, the certified pollutant testing project excludes $PM_{2.5}$, which is currently an important source of air pollution and is also a common international air pollutant setting standard; secondly, in the process of applying the certification, the continuous testing requirement was canceled—only a simple mark shows the IAQ status. The biggest problem with this approach is that it is difficult to know whether the IAQ of places has changed over time and if the public has immediate access to IAQ information.

With today's modern lifestyle, people spend a greater amount of time indoors and often visit various indoor places. The Taiwan Government has promoted IAQ for ten years. Although there are still some shortcomings that need to be improved, the Taiwan Government still intends to move forward. Accordingly, the effectiveness of the currently implemented IAQ self-management certification in Taiwan remains to be further verified by more research.

Author Contributions: Conceptualization, methodology, and formal analysis, C.-P.H.; investigation and resources, J.-H.C.; data curation and writing—original draft preparation, C.-P.H.; writing—review and editing, C.-P.H. and J.-H.C. All authors have read and agreed to the published version of the manuscript.

Funding: This research received no external funding.

Institutional Review Board Statement: Not applicable.

Informed Consent Statement: Not applicable.

Conflicts of Interest: The authors declare no conflict of interest.

Appendix A. The IAQ Certification and Consumers' Willingness Questionnaire

Survey Site □Banqiao □Wuri

1. Basic Information

1.1 Gender □male □female

1.2 Age □ < 20 years old □ 21–30 years old □ 31–40 years old □ 41–50 years old □ 51–60 years old □ 61 years old and above.

1.3 Marriage □ Married □ Unmarried

1.4 Education □Junior High school □High school □College □University □Master or PhD

2. The Practical Experience and Knowledge of IAQ Scale Section

2.1 Do you have symptoms of air allergy? □Yes □No

2.2 Have you ever heard of air quality-related issues?

□News media □Newspapers and magazines □Television

□Government propaganda □Related websites □Tell from family and friends □Education and training □None

2.3 Do you know that the government has enacted the "Indoor Air Quality Act"? □Yes □No

2.4 Do you know those indoor air pollutants?

□Carbon monoxide (CO) □Carbon dioxide (CO2) □Ozone (O3) □Formaldehyde

□Total volatile organic compounds (TVOC) □Bacteria □Fungi □Suspended particulates (PM_{10})

□Fine suspended particles ($PM_{2.5}$) □None

2.5 Do you have the following symptoms of physical discomfort indoors?

□Dizziness □Dry eyes (itch) □Stuffy nose □Runny nose □Sneezing □Cough □Dry throat □Body neck, shoulder, back pain or stiffness □Dry skin □Chest tightness □Tiredness □Drowsiness □Lack of concentration □Tight nerves □None

2.6 Do you know that the government currently regulates the indoor air quality of the following public places?

□College □Library □Medical institution □Annuity institution □Social welfare institution □Government office □Railway station and air station □MRT station □Exhibition room □Shopping mall □Financial institution □Museum/art gallery □Performance hall □Movie theater □KTV □Sports center □None

3. The Certification Cognition Scale Section

3.1 Do you agree that all public places should be marked with a healthy indoor air quality label, and a grading system should be adopted to show different levels of indoor air quality? (1 to 5, 5 = strongly agree)

3.2 In your opinion, should the healthy indoor air quality labels used in various public places in the future be divided into several levels?

□1 level (passed) □2 levels (normal/excellent) □3 levels good/excellent/excellent)

3.3 Do you think that to mark the indoor air quality mark in public places, the design must be combined with relevant international air quality certification standards? (such as WELL healthy building certification standards) (from 1 to 5, 5 = strongly agree)

3.4 In the future, if the indoor air quality mark is to be displayed in public places, which authority do you expect to review and issue?

□A fair third party with professional testing equipment □Indoor Environmental Quality Association □Local Environmental Protection Bureau □Central Environmental Protection Agency □All of the above

4. The Certification Displays Scale Section

4.1 Do you think that to obtain the certification of the healthy indoor air quality mark in public places, air quality monitors and display boards are installed at the entrance and exit. These are necessary conditions for applying for the certification? (from 1 to 5, 5 = strongly agree)

4.2 Do you agree to replace the original government-regulated test result poster with a healthy air quality label in the future? (from 1 to 5, 5 = strongly agree)

4.3 What other types of public places do you think should be given priority to obtain relevant indoor air quality testing or certification in the future?

□Kindergarten □Elementary, Junior High, and High School □Children's Recreation Center □Gym □Long-term care Center □Office Building □Post Office □Restaurant □Hotel

5. The Willingness to Consume at Certified Places Scale Section

5.1 Are you willing to pay a higher fee to go to public places certified by the healthy indoor air quality mark? (from 1 to 5, 5 = strongly agree)

5.2 If there is a gym that has obtained the "Healthy Indoor Air Quality Mark" certification, would you be more willing to consume? (from 1 to 5, 5 = strongly agree)

5.3 If there is a kindergarten certified with the "Healthy Indoor Air Quality Mark", would you be more willing to send your children to school? (from 1 to 5, 5 = strongly agree)

5.4 If there is a long-term care center certified by the "Healthy Indoor Air Quality Mark", would you be more willing to be included as a nursing facility? (from 1 to 5, 5 = strongly agree)

References

1. The Indoor Air Quality Information Network. Available online: https://iaq.epa.gov.tw/indoorair/introduction_importance.aspx (accessed on 1 September 2021).
2. Steinemann, A.; Wargocki, P.; Rismanchi, B. Ten questions concerning green buildings and indoor air quality. *Build. Environ.* **2017**, *112*, 351–358. [CrossRef]
3. Kozielska, B.; Mainka, A.; Zak, M.; Kaleta, D.; Mucha, W. Indoor air quality in residential buildings in Upper Silesia. *Poland Build. Environ.* **2020**, *177*, 106914. [CrossRef]
4. WHO. *The Right to Healthy Indoor Air. Report on WHO Meeting: Bilthoven, Netherlands, 15–17 May 2000*; WHO: Copenhagen, Denmark, 2000.
5. Introduction to Indoor Air Quality. Available online: https://www.epa.gov/indoor-air-quality-iaq/introduction-indoor-air-quality (accessed on 1 September 2021).
6. Hawkins, V.R.; Marcham, C.L.; Springston, J.P.; Miller, J.; Braybrooke, G.; Maunder, C.; Feng, L.; Kollmeyer, B. *The Value of IAQ: A Review of the Scientific Evidence Supporting the Benefits of Investing in Better Indoor Air Quality*; AIHA®Ergonomics Committee: Falls Church, VA, USA, 2020.
7. Licina, D.; Langer, S. Indoor air quality investigation before and after relocation to WELL-certified office buildings. *Build. Environ.* **2021**, *204*, 108182. [CrossRef]
8. Settimo, G.; Manigrasso, M.; Avino, P. Indoor Air Quality: A Focus on the European Legislation and State-of-the-Art Research in Italy. *Atmosphere* **2020**, *11*, 370. [CrossRef]
9. Umaroğulları, F.; Seitablaiev, M.O. Regulations Regarding Indoor Air Quality. In Proceedings of the 14th International Conference "Standardization, Protypes and Quality: A Means of Balkan Countries' Collaboration", Tirana, Albania, 21 September 2018.
10. Palacios, J.; Steele, K.; Tan, Z.; Zheng, S. Human health and productivity outcomes of office workers associated with indoor air quality: A systematic review. *MIT Cent. Real Estate Res.* **2021**. [CrossRef]
11. Tsai, W.-T. Overview of Green Building Material (GBM) Policies and Guidelines with Relevance to Indoor Air Quality Management in Taiwan. *Environments* **2018**, *5*, 4. [CrossRef]
12. Yang, W.-T.; Chiang, C.-M.; Ho, M.-C.; Chen, J.-L.; Lo, S.-C. Indoor Air Quality and Its Determinants in Taiwan Child Care Centers. *J. Archit.* **2011**, *75*, 61–80.
13. Lee, M.J.; Shih, W.-C. Discussion on Indoor Air Quality in Different Space Plan in Dental Clinics. *J. Archit.* **2019**, *110*, 33–48.
14. Huang, Y.-T.; Chen, Y.-K. Methods for the Diagnosis of Indoor Environment Quality on Health Affection, Evaluation in the Research Building Type of Taiwan. *J. Archit.* **2010**, *73*, 143–159.
15. Hu, C.-P.; Lin, H.-K.; Cheng, J.-H. The Study of the Cognition and Evaluation of the Indoor Air Quality Management in the Department Stores-Take the Shin Kong Mitsukoshi Xinyi Place as an Example. *J. Prop. Manag.* **2019**, *10*, 13–23.

16. Hu, C.-P.; Cheng, J.-H. The Study of the Cognition and Management Strategies of the Indoor Air Quality in the Living Places. *J. Prop. Manag.* **2020**, *11*, 1–13.
17. Goldin, L.J.; Ansher, L.; Berlin, A.; Cheng, J.; Kanopkin, D.; Khazan, A.; Kisivuli, M.; Lortie, M.; Peterson, E.B.; Laura Pohl, L.; et al. Indoor Air Quality Survey of Nail Salons in Boston. *J. Immigr. Minority Health* **2014**, *16*, 508–514. [CrossRef] [PubMed]
18. Shang, Y.; Li, B.; Baldwin, A.N.; Ding, Y.; Yu, W.; Cheng, L. Investigation of Indoor Air Quality in Shopping Malls during Summer in Western China using Subjective Survey and Field Measurement. *Build. Environ.* **2016**, *108*, 1–11. [CrossRef]
19. Langer, S.; Ramalho, O.; Le Ponner, E.; Derbez, M.; Kirchner, S.; Mandin, C. Perceived Indoor Air Quality and Its Relationship to Air Pollutants in French dwellings. *Indoor Air* **2017**, *27*, 1168–1176. [CrossRef] [PubMed]
20. Wu, Y.; Lu, Y.; Chou, D. Indoor Air Quality Investigation of a University Library Based on Field Measurement and Questionnaire Survey. *Int. J. Low-Carbon Technol.* **2018**, *13*, 148–160. [CrossRef]
21. Wong-Parodi, G.; Dias, M.B.; Taylor, M. Effect of Using an Indoor Air Quality Sensor on Perceptions of and Behaviors toward Air Pollution (Pittsburgh Empowerment Library Study): Online Survey and Interviews. *JMIR Mhealth Uhealth.* **2018**, *6*, e8273. [CrossRef] [PubMed]
22. Huizenga, S.C.; Zagreus, L.A.; Arens, E. Air Quality and Thermal Comfort in Office Buildings: Results of a Large Indoor Environmental Quality Survey. *Proc. Healthy Build.* **2006**, *3*, 393–397.
23. Saleem, M.; Kausar, M.A.; Khatoon, F.; Anwar, S.; Shahid SM, A.; Ginawi, T.; Hossain, A.; Al Anizy, A.A.S.A.; Alswaidan, M.A.A.; Aseeri, A.S.; et al. Association between Human Health and Indoor Air Pollution in Saudi Arabia: Indoor Environmental Quality Survey. *J. Pharm. Res. Int.* **2020**, *32*, 57–66. [CrossRef]
24. Yap, H.S.; Roberts, A.C.; Luo, C.; Tan, Z.; Lee, E.H.; Thach, T.Q.; Kwok, K.W.; Car, J.; Soh, C.K.; Christopoulos, G. The Importance of Air Quality for Underground Spaces: An International Survey of Public Attitudes. *Indoor Air* **2021**. [CrossRef] [PubMed]
25. Yang, S.; Pernot, I.G.; Jorin, C.H.; Niculita-Hirzel, H.; Perret, V.; Licina, D. Energy, indoor air quality, occupant behavior, self-reported symptoms and satisfaction in energy-efficient dwellings in Switzerland. *Build. Environ.* **2020**, *171*, 106618. [CrossRef]
26. Mothersbaugh, D.L.; Hawkins, D.I.; Kleiser, S.B. *Consumer Behavior: Building Marketing Strategy*, 14th ed.; McGraw Hill: New York, NY, USA, 2020.

International Journal of
Environmental Research and Public Health

MDPI

Article

Securing Smokefree Laws Covering Casinos and Bars in Louisiana via Messaging, Continuous Campaigning and Health Coalitions

Tanner D. Wakefield and Stanton A. Glantz *

Center for Tobacco Control Research and Education, University of California, San Francisco, CA 94143-1390, USA; tanner.wakefield@ucsf.edu
* Correspondence: stanton.glantz@sonic.net; Tel.: +1-415-564-4801

Abstract: In this paper, we examine efforts by health organizations seeking comprehensive smokefree ordinances over Louisiana casinos and bars between 2010 and 2020 to determine best practices for increasing coverage. Bars and casinos remain less protected from secondhand smoke compared to other workplaces in the United States. Casino behavior is compared to the Policy Dystopia Model (PDM), a tobacco industry strategy framework. We performed a historical case study using snowball searches for news on the Access World News Database and the internet. We performed web searches using the names of key actors, organizations, and locations and interviewed nine participants. Starting in 2010, the Louisiana Campaign for Tobacco-Free Living ran ordinance campaigns supplemented by an ongoing statewide smokefree media initiative. Utilizing consistent strategies, including promoting performers as cultural emblems deserving protection, health organizations coalesced in New Orleans during 2014 and Baton Rouge in 2016 and 2017 to pursue ordinances. The coalitions secured ordinances in Louisiana's population and tourism centers despite business resistance. Organizations obtained 30 smokefree laws across Louisiana by 2021. Casinos used PDM strategies to resist ordinances, indicating the framework may predict strategies by non-tobacco entities resisting tobacco control. Louisiana shows that ongoing local campaigns, social justice themes and cultural messaging with coalitions in cities can secure smokefree laws covering casinos and bars and that local ordinance campaigns are a viable method for advancing smokefree protections over those venues in states where the state legislatures are resistant to action.

Keywords: smokefree; industry; regulation; advocacy; tobacco control

Citation: Wakefield, T.D.; Glantz, S.A. Securing Smokefree Laws Covering Casinos and Bars in Louisiana via Messaging, Continuous Campaigning and Health Coalitions. *Int. J. Environ. Res. Public Health* **2022**, *19*, 3936. https://doi.org/10.3390/ijerph19073936

Academic Editors: Ashok Kumar, M Amirul I Khan, Alejandro Moreno Rangel and Michał Piasecki

Received: 15 February 2022
Accepted: 23 March 2022
Published: 25 March 2022

1. Introduction

As of January 2022, casinos remain less protected by smokefree laws than other workplaces despite implementation of temporary policies in response to the COVID-19 pandemic. Of 36 U.S. states having smoking restrictions as of October 2021, 20 have prohibited smoking in casinos and 30 in bars [1]. COVID-19 led to commercial casinos in New Jersey [2], Pennsylvania [3] and Michigan [4] and over 160 sovereign tribal casinos implementing temporary smokefree indoor air policies, starting debates on making them permanent. In November 2021, the Navajo Nation made all its casinos permanently smokefree as part of a larger clean indoor air law [5].

The years-long battle for smokefree laws in Louisiana helped lay the foundation for local ordinances there covering bars and casinos. The 2006 Louisiana Smoke-Free Air Act, passed with support from advocates who had sought to replace ineffective statewide smokefree laws since 2001, exempted bars and casinos [6]. The Coalition for a Tobacco-Free Louisiana (CTFLA), consisting of national and state health organizations, accepted the exemptions to avoid political resistance. Significantly, the law repealed state preemption of stronger local ordinances enacted with tobacco industry support. Since the 2006 law did not cover all workplaces and political inertia at the state level prevented comprehensive statewide smokefree legislation, health organizations pursued local smokefree ordinances starting in 2011 to extend smokefree policy coverage to bars and casinos. Louisiana's nonprofit tobacco control program, Louisiana Campaign for Tobacco-Free Living (TFL), working with national, state and local organizations (including as a member of CTFLA), secured 30 local laws between 2011 and 2021 [7] despite resistance from the bar and gaming industries. The local smokefree ordinance battles in Louisiana provide insight into overcoming political opposition and securing smokefree laws for workplaces not yet protected by state laws.

To understand the success of campaigns pursuing comprehensive local smokefree ordinances covering bars and casinos in Louisiana, we analyzed the efforts of advocates and health organizations to pass local laws between 2011 and 2021. We found that health organizations overcame industry opposition to smokefree bars and casino interests with innovative campaigns expanding upon established smokefree organizing tactics [8–12] (extended and consistent media campaigns and news media engagement on secondhand smoke, messaging focusing on health and workplace protection, multilevel alliances, local organizing and countering industry claims) by integrating jazz musicians in messaging and campaign events to highlight how smokefree laws would protect employees as well as promote local culture.

This paper also tests the applicability of the Policy Dystopia Model [13] (PDM) for predicting non-tobacco industry behavior against smoking restriction laws. The PDM is a framework that was developed to understand tobacco industry discursive and instrumental strategies against taxes and advertising restriction legislation. Discursive strategies outlined by the PDM focus on predicting secondary adverse social and economic outcomes of tobacco control legislation while instrumental strategies include coalition building, litigation, information management and policy interference to support tobacco industry positions. While the model was created by analyzing tobacco industry behavior against tax increases and advertising restrictions, it has been used to interpret tobacco industry opposition to smokefree laws in countries outside the United States [11,14]. The tobacco industry mobilized opposition nationally against smokefree policies in bars and casinos since the 1990s by arguing smokefree laws harmed those businesses in order to develop alliances with trade associations [15,16]. We compared casino industry behavior directed against smokefree ordinances in New Orleans and Baton Rouge to categories of arguments and strategies outlined by the PDM to determine if a non-tobacco industry would use tactics established by the model when opposing tobacco control policies. Louisiana's experience shows that the PDM can be used to understand and anticipate gaming industry tactics against smokefree policies.

2. Materials and Methods

We performed a case study to understand health organization tactics and activities around passing local smokefree laws in Louisiana that combined information from the documentary record with key informant interviews. Snowball searches [17] were conducted for news on the Access World News Database, Google, and websites for the *Times-Picayune*/nola.com (New Orleans) and *The Advocate* (Baton Rouge) between 2000 and 2020. Search terms included "smoking," "smoking restrictions," and "ordinance," followed by searches of key actors, organizations and locations. Key actors were those involved as campaign officials, operatives or representatives from business, government or advocacy organizations supporting or opposing smokefree ordinances. Key organizations were industry associations, businesses and health organizations that were involved in smokefree advocacy or policy campaigns as supporters or opponents, while locations were places where smokefree legislation was debated. News stories were read and cited if they added context or information on campaign activities, attitudes, messaging or strategies to local smokefree ordinance battles.

Interviews were conducted with employees from 3 national and 4 state health organization representatives. Participants were approached if they served as health organization staff involved in local ordinance efforts, media messaging or were campaign officials in the New Orleans or Baton Rouge smokefree law campaigns in Louisiana. Interviews were performed under a protocol approved by the UCSF Committee on Human Research. We did not track who declined interviews, nor did we approach opponents of smokefree legislation for interviews since the focus of our research was on health organization strategies. Interview questions were unstructured and questions were developed organically based on information collected during research and prior interviews. Interviews were transcribed. TW and SAG have interacted with some of the interviewees at public health meetings. Two interviewees (Cynthia Hallett and Jennifer Cofer) serve on the external advisory committee for the UCSF Center for Tobacco Control Research and Education.

Our paper particularly analyzes smokefree battles in New Orleans and Baton Rouge. Both cities warranted focus because they are the largest population and tourism centers within Louisiana, they manifested the most intense efforts by casino entities to defeat smokefree coalitions and smokefree legislation, and represented the largest deployments of health organizations' planning, coalition building and resources. New Orleans and Baton Rouge were two of three jurisdictions among the 30 towns and cities that prohibited smoking in bars and casinos in Louisiana that had operating casinos at the time the law was being debated.

We analyzed gaming industry behavior from smokefree ordinance campaigns in New Orleans and Baton Rouge to determine similarities and differences with tobacco industry tactics outlined by the PDM. We compared data to the PDM's discursive and instrumental categories and subcategories. Arguments and activities that matched the PDM were placed in the corresponding category.

There are two reference lists for this paper. The references enclosed in square brackets and preceded with "S" refer to original source materials and appear in the Supplement File.

3. Results

3.1. Laying the Groundwork with a Focused Media Campaign

TFL launched a paid advertising and social media campaign "Let's Be Totally Clear" in 2010 to advocate for employees and musicians' rights to smokefree air [18]. The campaign directed viewers to TFL's website with advocacy resources [19]. Rebranded as "Healthier Air For All" in 2012 according to one interviewee [20], the campaign generated capacity for ordinances.

3.2. Local Campaigns Build Support

TFL initially won comprehensive ordinances in localities without significant gaming industry presence, beginning in Alexandria in 2011 [21] after it responded favorably to TFL's media campaign and grassroots education efforts according to one interviewee [22]. TFL organized smokefree events, provided promotional packages to bars and bingo halls and advertised on billboards and social media. One interviewee stated that TFL conducted air quality studies finding hazardous secondhand smoke (SHS) levels in local bars, prepared packets for lawmakers and recruited and trained speakers for hearings [22]. A law was passed, and TFL ran local ads to assist with its implementation [23].

Five additional municipalities adopted ordinances between 2012 and 2014 (Table 1), providing experience to pursue laws in New Orleans, Baton Rouge and elsewhere. While most locations that adopted comprehensive smokefree legislation covering bars and casinos did not host casinos such as New Orleans or Baton Rouge, the laws generated momentum and normalization for prohibiting smoking in places that had casinos.

Table 1. Localities in Louisiana with 100% Smokefree Laws including Casinos [7,24,25].

Year	Number of Cities that Adopted Smokefree Law Covering Casinos	Number of Cities with Casinos	City
2012	2	0	Alexandria
			Woodworth
2014	4	0	Cheneyville
			Monroe
			Ouachita Parish
			West Monroe
2015	3	1	Hammond
			New Orleans *
			Abbeville
2016	1	0	Bogalusa
2017	5	1	Glenmora
			Lafayette Parish
			Town of Lecompte
			Baton Rouge/East Baton Rouge Parish *
			Colfax
2018	2	0	Roseland
			Village of McNary
2019	12	0	Fenton
			Boyce
			Cullen
			Ruston
			Pineville
			Ponchatoula
			Haynesville
			Natchez
			Reeves
			Oak Grove
			Athens
			Angie
2020	1	1	Shreveport *

* Casino operating when ordinance was being considered.

TFL conducted research and ran its media campaign in New Orleans to generate support for an ordinance. It produced five studies on SHS and air quality, the economy and health relevant to New Orleans between 2011 and 2014 [26,27] using "Healthier Air for All and an affiliated statewide smokefree concert series held there in May 2014 [28].

3.3. *Smokefree NOLA*

In August 2014, CTFLA members formed Smokefree NOLA (the acronym for New Orleans) (Table 2). Four interviewees recalled that the coalition formed after New Orleans councilmember LaToya Cantrell told health organizations she was introducing a comprehensive ordinance [29,30]. Smokefree NOLA (SFNOLA) shared TFL's statewide media campaign's themes and branding [23,31].

Table 2. Composition of the Smokefree NOLA and Smoke-Free East Baton Rouge Coalitions [27,29,30,32].

	Smokefree NOLA	Smoke-Free East Baton Rouge
National Health Voluntaries	American Cancer Society Cancer Action Network	American Cancer Society Cancer Action Network
	American Heart Association	Red Team
	American Lung Association	American Lung Association
	Americans for Nonsmokers' Rights	Americans for Nonsmokers' Rights Foundation
	Campaign for Tobacco-Free Kids	Campaign for Tobacco-Free Kids
	March of Dimes	March of Dimes
Louisiana Organizations	Tobacco-Free Living/Louisiana Public Health Institute	Tobacco-Free Living/Louisiana Public Health Institute
	Louisiana Comprehensive Cancer Control Partnership	Musicians for a Smoke-Free Louisiana
	Oschner Health Systems	National Association of Social Workers Louisiana Chapter
	Louisiana Cultural Economy Foundation	Louisiana Budget Project
	LSU Tobacco Control Initiative	–
	Smoking Cessation Trust	–
Local Organizations	Communities of Color Network	SEIU Local 21 LA
	Fresh Campus Campaign	–

SFNOLA branding celebrated New Orleans's culture and musical heritage while linking with Healthier Air For All [23,29,31,33] (Figure 1). One interviewee stated SFNOLA recruited musician spokespersons through the Louisiana Cultural Economy Foundation [34], which helped performers obtain economic assistance and healthcare [35]. TFL had partnered with the foundation since 2011 to hold smokefree music events [34]. Musicians wrote letters and attended hearings and campaign events [36].

Figure 1. Smokefree NOLA Campaign Logo used the fleur-de-lis, a symbol of New Orleans' French origins, and a trumpet, reflecting the city's jazz legacy.

SFNOLA held "Smoke-Free Week 2.0" in November 2014 to promote smoking restrictions [37] during the American Public Health Association's (APHA) annual meeting (around 12,000 attendees [38]) in New Orleans [39]. The ordinance was introduced on the last day of Smoke-Free Week [37,40].

SFNOLA leveraged APHA's meeting to press for legislation [29,30], with four interviewees recalling the coalition persuading APHA to declare it would not meet again in New Orleans unless the city adopted an ordinance meeting APHA's smokefree meetings policy [41]. The American Heart Association, which held a large meeting (17,000 attendees [42]) in New Orleans every few years also threatened to avoid the city until a law was enacted [43].

SFNOLA organized promotions to engage the public. During Smoke-Free Week 2.0 it held a traditional New Orleans second line parade [44] that rallied for the ordinance at APHA's meeting [45]. According to two interviewees, the coalition hosted smokefree events at LGBT and African-American bars, industry nights for service employees and placed announcements in churches [30]. It held a townhall [30,46], prayer breakfast and rally in January [46] and other events promoted on TFL's Healthier Air for All website [36].

SFNOLA obtained USD 2.8 million in earned media by February 2015 [47] and funded advertising using partner contributions.

3.4. Business Opposition

Gaming, bar and restaurant entities formed the Freedom to Choose Coalition to oppose the ordinance. One founder, Harrah's [48], operated Louisiana's only land-based casino. Other participants were the Louisiana Amusement and Music Operators Association, Louisiana Video Gaming Association, Louisiana Casino Association [49], French Quarter Business League, Louisiana Restaurant Association (LRA) and Louisiana Association of Wholesalers (LAW) [49]. LRA helped the tobacco industry resist statewide smokefree legislation in the 1980s and 1990s [6]. Altria and other tobacco companies sponsored LAW in 2015 [50] and its executive director worked for Philip Morris as a coordinator during the 1990s [51,52]. LAW's director also had Altria (Philip Morris) as his lobbying firm's client [53].

New Orleans' vapers fought to exclude e-cigarettes from the ordinance [6], including speaking at the subcommittee hearing. According to two interviewees, local e-cigarette retailers formed the Louisiana Association of Electronic Cigarette Retailers (LAECR) to oppose the ordinance [30]. An out-of-state retailer [54] and the national Consumer Advocates for Smoke Free Alternatives Association [55] supplemented LAECR with action alerts encouraging e-cigarette advocates to attend town halls and contact lawmakers.

3.5. Hearings

The New Orleans City Council considered the ordinance at a subcommittee hearing on 7 January [56] and a full hearing on 22 January [57].

The subcommittee started with a panel of health experts, a musician and a nightclub owner who testified on SHS's dangers [56], countered economic harm claims and argued workers lacked choice regarding working in smoke. TFL provided councilmembers with briefs containing studies on air quality, SHS exposure, health effects, and the economic impact of smokefree laws [26,56].

At the hearings, health professionals, health organization representatives and residents supported the ordinance after being prepared by SFNOLA according to two interviewees [30]. They highlighted policy benefits, refuted economic harm claims [56,57], and argued smokefree laws protected employees and performers and their cultural contributions. They argued ventilation and smoking areas could not protect people from SHS and that e-cigarettes were underregulated and contained harmful components in aerosols.

Freedom to Choose argued the ordinance would harm businesses and employees, reduce tourism, lower tax revenue, drive customers to neighboring casinos and limit choice [56,57].

Harrah's contracted with the state for its gaming license [58] and had a city lease [59]. The state contract prevented employment below 2455, while the lease required enhanced severance packages for employees terminated below 2550 [59]. Harrah's claimed resulting revenue losses justified reducing employment required by its contract [56], a number it wanted lowered since 2007 [60].

Vaping proponents tried excluding e-cigarettes from the ordinance, arguing e-cigarettes are healthier than cigarettes and aid cessation [56]. They questioned research [56] and referenced statements from public health officials supporting legal access to e-cigarettes or their harm reduction potential including FDA Center for Tobacco Products Director Mitch Zeller and UK Royal College of Physicians Tobacco Advisory Group Chair John Britton [56]. LAECR referenced a World Health Organization letter advocating against prohibiting e-cigarettes [56]. (We could not locate any such letter.) LAECR accused the Council of succumbing to threats of losing conferences [57].

The Council unanimously adopted the ordinance on 22 January 2015 [57], effective 22 April [61].

3.6. Health Organizations Support Implementation despite Industry Resistance

SFNOLA members assisted with implementation. According to two interviewees, Americans for Nonsmokers' Rights (ANR), a national organization, organized a meeting between the New Orleans Health Department and southern health officials to learn implementation strategies [29]. Four interviewees recalled that ANR helped fund the department's implementation website and toolkits [29,30,36]. SFNOLA provided promotional materials to casinos and bars, advertised and sent education teams to local events.

Harrah's resisted the ordinance, announcing in March 2015 that it sought exemptions to its contract because of expected revenue declines [62]. It offered to create smoking sections [63] and offered cessation services and smoking education to employees and customers to be exempted [63]. Harrah's claimed the law threatened its lease payments and USD 3.6 million annually to New Orleans [63]. Harrah's claimed it could renegotiate its lease if the city refused, which city officials rejected [62].

Harrah's and 54 other bars, restaurants and strip clubs filed a class action lawsuit against the ordinance, claiming procedural errors and that the legislation was vague [64]. The court dismissed the case [65].

Harrah's partnered with a state senator to introduce legislation allowing renegotiation of its state contract [60,66], including reducing Harrah's employment requirement [67]. The Senate Judiciary Committee delayed consideration after a member found New Orleans officials were unaware of the attempted employment reduction [67]. New Orleans' officials opposed the bill; the Committee rejected it [60].

The State Legislature's Joint Budget Committee twice refused to renew the Louisiana Gaming Control Board's contract with New Orleans for hosting Harrah's, slowing USD 3.6 million [68], as threatened by Harrah's [63]. Altria and Harrah's shared lobbyists supported Harrah's request with the committee [68], but the contract was renewed without change.

Health organizations did not join this debate.

Harrah's complied with New Orleans' ordinance upon effect in April 2015 [69], but blamed it for revenue declines in May, June and August 2015 compared to the prior year; Harrah's' profits increased in July and September [70].

Health organizations contested Harrah's economic assertions. TFL released a study in July 2015 finding Harrah's was experiencing a 10-year revenue decline because of unrelated factors [71]. Harrah's failed to resist the law, eventually building outdoor smoking courtyards for gaming [72].

A June 2015 air quality study found that hazardous indoor air quality improved to safe levels [73].

3.7. Forming Another Coalition for Baton Rouge in 2016

Louisiana's state capitol, Baton Rouge, and its parish, East Baton Rouge, have a consolidated government [74]. Health organizations, many involved in CTFLA and SFNOLA, formed the Smoke-Free East Baton Rouge Coalition (SFEBR; Table 2) to pursue an ordinance.

A community meeting launched the campaign in January 2016 [75]. A SFEBR representative spoke to the local Rotary about protecting employees from SHS [76] and SFEBR hosted smokefree events, including a happy hour, karaoke night and music performance [77]. The American Association of Retired Persons Louisiana Chapter, Miss Louisiana, Baton Rouge musicians [78] and local hospitals and medical groups endorsed the coalition [79,80].

SFEBR spent approximately USD 300,000 on advertising in its first six months for radio, billboards, social media and television [81]. The coalition disseminated SHS facts, articles on smokefree policies, casino employee testimonials and action alerts via social media [77,82].

3.8. Opposition

Gaming industry resistance started in March 2016. L'Auberge Casino owner, Pinnacle Entertainment, claimed the law would reduce income and tax revenue, referencing fallen profits after smoking bans [83,84]. In April, as hearings neared, Baton Rouge's three casinos claimed they expected the ordinance to inflict economic harm, reduce tax revenues, disadvantage them with smoking venues and potentially reduce their purchases from local vendors [85]. They argued that SHS was not problematic in employee surveys and the ordinance would harm workers by lowering business and tips [85].

3.9. Hearings

East Baton Rouge's Metro-Parish Council considered the ordinance in April 2016 [86]. Health organization representatives, doctors, nurses, entertainers, faith leaders and casino employees asserted the ordinance protected personal rights and health and did not harm businesses, particularly casinos.

Gaming officials and workers testified that smokefree laws harmed casino and tax revenue and reduced purchases from local vendors [86]. They argued that working in SHS was a choice and asserted that ventilation made the ordinance unnecessary, a common tobacco industry argument [16,86]; ventilation cannot prevent harmful SHS exposure [87]. L'Auberge employees and officials claimed workers desiring smokefree areas were accommodated [86]. The Council voted six to six, defeating the ordinance [86].

3.10. Pursuing Ordinances throughout Louisiana

Municipalities, many with TFL's assistance, won ordinances in seven Louisiana communities between 2015 and 2017 (Table 1) to build capacity [6].

3.11. The Second Baton Rouge Campaign in 2017

SFEBR announced in May 2017 that it would pursue another ordinance [88]. and in June, 7 out of 12 East Baton Rouge Metro-Councilmembers co-sponsored legislation [89].

The coalition disseminated information, secured endorsements and held events to support the ordinance. It released a poll showing local women supported a law by 79% and college educated women supported the law by 69% [90]. SFEBR organized a smokefree bar night, happy hours, music performances, a comedy night and a dance night, and circulated flyers, informational videos, tobacco health statistics, news, blog posts and lawmakers' contact information [77,82]. It also partnered with Miss Black Louisiana U.S. Ambassador LeighAnna Kingvalsky for promotional efforts [77,91], Three ordinance sponsors participated in a local radio show [92–94]. SFEBR secured letters in the Baton Rouge *Advocate* [91,95] and released an air quality study on local casinos and bars finding unhealthy air conditions [96].

3.12. Hearings

The Baton Rouge Metro-Parish Council considered the second ordinance in June [97] and August 2017 [98].

Coalition members, health representatives, city employees, performers, bar industry members and locals supported the ordinance [97,98]. They highlighted SHS's harms and costs, asserted the right to smokefree workplaces, discussed local bars and casinos' poor air quality and how smokefree policies improved public health. Proponents countered claims that restrictions harm income and that ventilation systems "solve" SHS. They reported 20 states and various localities prohibited smoking in casinos.

Opponents argued smokefree laws cost jobs, profits, employee income and tax revenue. They asserted customers and employees chose to frequent casinos [97,98] while claiming workers wanting smokefree environments were accommodated, that most employees did not work in smoking areas, and that ventilation protected people.

Baton Rouge lawmakers approved the ordinance with an effective date of 1 June 2018 [98].

SFEBR supported implementation by promoting the law and SHS's harmfulness on social media, sponsoring events [77,99], producing implementation toolkits [100] and educating Baton Rouge police about the ordinance [101]. An air quality survey conducted a month after implementation found a 98.8% improvement in air quality in places that previously allowed smoking [102].

4. Discussion

Louisiana illustrates how health organizations can shift to local campaigns to secure ordinances covering bars and casinos when state progress is blocked. Local governments are more responsive to constituents where the tobacco industry [103] and other sectors [104] have less influence on policymaking. After state smoking restrictions stagnated following 2006, Louisiana health organizations pursued local comprehensive ordinances covering casinos and bars, enabled by the 2006 repeal of preemption. Louisiana organizations sustained their partnerships after 2006, allowing deployment of an existing coalition network that facilitated cooperation [105] to pass comprehensive local ordinances over business resistance. Starting in 2011, TFL secured ordinances using policy campaigns supported by its "Let's Be Totally Clear/Healthier Air for All" media initiative. Efforts to pass local smokefree ordinances in Louisiana serve as a model for passing comprehensive protections in states that currently lack statewide smokefree protections for bars and casinos because of political resistance at the state legislature, as long as they are not preempted by state law.

4.1. A Theoretical Framework: The Policy Dystopia Model

The PDM [13] identifies two forms of resistance, discursive and instrumental. Discursive arguments seek to cast regulation as economically harmful to the economy or society, as criminalizing or crime generating, are unbeneficial to public health, regressive, ineffective, beneficial to undeserving interests and a form of government overreach as well as harmful to business interests and employees. Instrumental tactics include funneling information to the public that benefits the industry's image and position, hides its role in information sharing, weakens public health organizations' claims and standing and portrays the regulation as ineffective. Other instrumental strategies include recruiting or manufacturing allies, breaking public health alliances, suing and directly interfering in the policy process.

Louisiana indicates the gaming industry, which has opposed smoking restrictions in partnership with the tobacco industry [16], deployed PDM tactics (Table 3). In New Orleans and Baton Rouge, they claimed the ordinances would inflict economic and tax harm while denying their effectiveness. Harrah's formed a coalition, participated in a class action lawsuit and interfered in legislative and contractual processes in attempts to block the New Orleans ordinance. None of the casinos in New Orleans or Baton Rouge used PDM strategies such as discursive arguments that smokefree policies benefited undeserving groups or inadvertently harmed public health, nor did they engage in illicit trade. Gaming industry strategies indicate that, similar to the tobacco industry, they seek external institutional lanes to failing policy venues where they have more influence. Louisiana shows that the PDM can be used to understand industry opposition to smokefree laws inside and outside the Unites States [11,14], not just opposition to advertising restrictions and taxes, which were used to develop the PDM.

4.2. Health Coalition Effectiveness in Countering Industry Political Influence

TFL's ongoing "Healthier Air for All" media campaign on the effects of SHS [106] and social justice themes [107] facilitated ordinance campaigns across Louisiana. TFL supplemented these general messages with SHS-impacted musicians and other performers to equate smokefree environments to preserving local culture, while also messaging the need for workplace protections. Focusing on policy solutions through those impacted by a policy change reoriented the media narrative from victim responsibility to a public issue [108]. Cobranded local campaigns tied smoking restrictions to a statewide movement, using norm changes to enable victories.

In Louisiana, as in other successful campaigns inside [8,9] and outside [10,11] the United States, joining with health organizations at higher political levels provided resources and expertise to combat well-financed and coordinated industry resistance. Louisiana's framing around musicians and performers, workers and customers in an adult rights and cultural context, as opposed to youth as was conducted in Duluth Minnesota [8], facilitated the passage of stronger ordinances than in Duluth, where focusing on youth led to weak restrictions allowing smoking sections in restaurants, exemptions for some restaurants and smoking in bars.

SFNOLA and SFEBR's aggressive media engagement via events and outreach as well as advertisements countered casino industry claims of economic harm and highlighted the need to protect workers. This experience is consistent with Mexico City, where a coalition of international and state organizations obtained and defended a smokefree law [10]. The Mexico City campaign, similar to the Louisiana campaigns, had dedicated legislative champions and promoted the protective and beneficial qualities of smokefree laws. Comparing local campaigns in Louisiana, El Paso [9] and Mexico City [10] to Duluth [8] indicates that consistent media outreach, messaging around worker and public protection, collaborating with strong legislative champions, countering opponents' economic arguments and relying on support from larger health organizations are essential to campaigns seeking comprehensive legislation.

4.3. Limitations

This paper relies on interviews and testimony from people involved with government and health organizations. Our findings from interviews may be influenced by personal bias, as not all health organization participants were interviewed, or by recall bias since years have passed from the events covered. Interviews were conducted between 2014 and 2017, so subjects could have forgotten or recalled details incorrectly. We were unable to obtain detailed funding information for local campaigns in Louisiana, preventing analysis of the financial asymmetry between smokefree proponents and opponents. We relied on news coverage and hearings to analyze bar and gaming industry behavior, because in the past, representatives from these groups consistently declined to be interviewed. We may have missed clandestine tobacco industry involvement.

Table 3. Comparison of the Policy Dystopia Model and use of its Tobacco Industry Discursive and Instrumental Strategies by the Gaming Industry in Major Louisiana Policy Battles [6,13].

	Themes	New Orleans	Baton Rouge
Discursive	Unanticipated Costs to Economy and Society	- Harms casino revenue - Harms tax revenue - Harms tourism - Reduces funding for law enforcement	- Harms casino revenue - Harms tax revenue - Harms local vendors dependent on casinos - Business choice
	Unintended Benefits to Undeserving Groups	Not used	Not used
	Unintended Costs to Public Health	Not used	Not used
	Denial of Intended Public Health Benefits	Not used	- Ventilation systems already clean air - Majority of establishments are nonsmoking - Casino employees are accommodated - Customers can attend casinos that permit no smoking if they desire - Not a workplace that all members of the public must frequent (grocery stores for example) - Secondhand smoke studies are unreliable and lack quality
	Expected Industry Costs *	- Casino employees will lose income and work hours - Casino employees will lose jobs	- Casino employees will lose income - Casino employees will lose jobs
Instrumental	Coalition Management	- Harrah's helped form the Freedom to Choose Coalition.	Not used
	Information Management	- Repeatedly blamed smokefree ordinance for revenue declines	Not used
	Direct Involvement and Influence in Policy	- Threats by Harrah's to renegotiate contract with New Orleans and the State - Legislation to renegotiate Harrah's contract and reduce employment - Louisiana gaming board delays casino contract approval	Not used
	Litigation	Harrah's and its allies filed a lawsuit to repeal New Orleans' smokefree law	Not used
	Illicit Trade	Not used	Not used

* The Policy Dystopia Model was built using the tobacco industry's behavior for its marketing and tax policy efforts, and this category was specifically labeled for the tobacco industry. We modified the label to refer to the casino industry.

5. Conclusions

Louisiana health organizations secured 30 local smokefree laws covering casinos and bars, including in New Orleans and Baton Rouge, between 2011 and 2021. Louisiana's experience indicates that effective established strategies for enacting smokefree laws (a sustained media campaign, local organizing, polling and countering industry claims) can be combined with an emphasis on worker protections and local culture to mount successful campaigns to enact smokefree laws.

Author Contributions: Conceptualization, T.D.W. and S.A.G.; methodology, T.D.W. and S.A.G.; software: NA; validation: NA; formal Analysis, T.D.W. and S.A.G.; investigation, T.D.W.; resources: S.A.G.; data curation, T.D.W.; writing—original draft preparation, T.D.W.; writing—review and editing, T.D.W. and S.A.G.; visualization: NA; supervision, S.A.G.; project administration, S.A.G.; funding acquisition, S.A.G. All authors have read and agreed to the published version of the manuscript.

Funding: This work was supported by a National Cancer Institute grant R01CA061021, the National Institute on Drug Abuse Cancer grant R01DA043950 and the William Cahan Professorship to Glantz from the Flight Attendant Medical Research Institute. The funding agencies played no role in the conduct of the research or preparation of the manuscript.

Institutional Review Board Statement: Interviews were conducted under protocol 10-01262, approved by the UCSF Committee on Human Research.

Informed Consent Statement: All interviewees granted informed consent.

Data Availability Statement: Interviews have been deposited in the UCSF Tobacco Control Archive, maintained by Archives and Special Collections at the UCSF Library. All other materials are publicly available at the cited sources.

Conflicts of Interest: The authors declare no potential conflicts of interest with respect to the research, authorship and/or publication of this article. Glantz serves as a consultant to the World Health Organization on other projects.

References

1. No Author. Summary of 100% Smokefree State Laws and Population Protected by 100% U.S. Smokefree Laws. Berkeley: American Nonsmokers' Rights Foundation; 2021 updated 1 October 2021. Available online: https://no-smoke.org/wp-content/uploads/pdf/SummaryUSPopList.pdf (accessed on 3 January 2022).
2. Johnson, B. Smoking Ban in Atlantic City Casinos due to COVID Ends Sunday. Murphy Wants Permanent ban. 2021. Available online: https://www.nj.com/coronavirus/2021/06/smoking-ban-in-atlantic-city-casinos-due-to-covid-ends-sunday-murphy-wants-permanent-ban.html (accessed on 10 January 2022).
3. Felton, J. Gamblers Light Up in Pennsylvania Casinos with Lifting of Smoking Ban. 2021. Available online: https://triblive.com/local/regional/gamblers-can-again-light-up-in-pennsylvania-casinos-as-smoking-ban-lifts/ (accessed on 10 January 2022).
4. Eggert, D. Michigan: No Smoking, 15% Capacity when Detroit Casinos open. 2020. Available online: https://www.fox47news.com/news/local-news/michigan-no-smoking-15-capacity-when-detroit-casinos-open (accessed on 10 January 2022).
5. Native News Online Staff. Navajo Nation Bans Indoor Smoking. 2021. Available online: https://nativenewsonline.net/currents/navajo-nation-bans-indoor-smoking-in-public-places (accessed on 11 November 2021).
6. Wakefield, T.; Glantz, S. *Blowing Smoke out of the Bayou: The Battle for Tobacco Control in Louisiana*; UCSF, Center for Tobacco Control Research and Education: San Francisco, CA, USA, 2020; Available online: https://escholarship.org/uc/item/1cc903g7#main (accessed on 10 January 2021).
7. No Author. Healthier Air for All: Goals and Progress. Tobacco-Free Living. 2022. Available online: https://healthierairforall.org/goals-progress (accessed on 3 January 2022).
8. Tsoukalas, T.; Glantz, S.A. The Duluth clean indoor air ordinance: Problems and success in fighting the tobacco industry at the local level in the 21st century. *Am. J. Public Health* **2003**, *93*, 1214–1221. [CrossRef]
9. Reynolds, J.H.; Hobart, R.L.; Ayala, P.; Eischen, M.H. Clean indoor air in El Paso, Texas: A case study. *Prev. Chronic Dis.* **2005**, *2*, A22.
10. Crosbie, E.; Sebrié, E.M.; Glantz, S.A. Strong advocacy led to successful implementation of smokefree Mexico City. *Tob. Control.* **2011**, *20*, 64–72. [CrossRef]
11. Bhatta, D.N.; Crosbie, E.; Bialous, S.A.; Glantz, S. Defending comprehensive tobacco control policy implementation in Nepal from tobacco industry interference (2011–2018). *Nicotine Tob. Res.* **2020**, *22*, 2203–2212. [CrossRef]
12. Magzamen, S.; Glantz, S.A. The new battleground: California's experience with smoke-free bars. *Am. J. Public Health* **2001**, *91*, 245–252.

13. Ulucanlar, S.; Fooks, G.J.; Gilmore, A.B. The policy dystopia model: An interpretive analysis of tobacco industry political activity. *PLoS Med.* **2016**, *13*, e1002125. [CrossRef]
14. Egbe, C.O.; Bialous, S.A.; Glantz, S. Role of stakeholders in Nigeria's tobacco control journey after the FCTC: Lessons for tobacco control advocacy in low-income and middle-income countries. *Tob. Control.* **2019**, *28*, 386–393. [CrossRef]
15. Dearlove, J.V.; Bialous, S.A.; Glantz, S.A. Tobacco industry manipulation of the hospitality industry to maintain smoking in public places. *Tob. Control.* **2002**, *11*, 94–104. [CrossRef]
16. Mandel, L.L.; Glantz, S.A. Hedging their bets: Tobacco and gambling industries work against smoke-free policies. *Tob. Control.* **2004**, *13*, 268–276. [CrossRef]
17. Anderson, S.J.; McCandless, P.M.; Klausner, K.; Taketa, R.; Yerger, V.B. Tobacco documents research methodology. *Tob. Control.* **2011**, *20* (Suppl. S2), ii8–ii11. [CrossRef]
18. Louisiana Cancer Research Consortium. 2010 Annual Report New Orleans: Louisiana Cancer Research Consortium. 2010. Available online: https://www.louisianacancercenter.org/annual-reports/2010 (accessed on 25 January 2017).
19. Rudov, L.; McCormick-Ricket, I.; Kingsmill, D.; Ledford, C.; Carton, T. Evaluation recommendations for nonprofit social marketing campaigns: An example from the Louisiana campaign for tobacco-free living. *Int. J. Nonprofit Volunt. Sect. Mark.* **2017**, *22*, e1507. [CrossRef]
20. Conrad, L.M. Interviewed by Wakefield, T. 23 May 2016.
21. No Author. Alexandria Council Bans Smoking in City Bars. The Associated Press. 2011 Updated October 5. Available online: https://infoweb.newsbank.com/apps/news/document-view?p=AWNB&docref=news/13A310311272F238 (accessed on 8 May 2019).
22. Gilchrist, J. Interviewed by Barry, R. 22 January 2014.
23. No Author. City and Parish Smoke-Free Ordinances. Louisiana Public Health Institute. 2015. Available online: https://web.archive.org/web/20151031011426/http://tobaccofreeliving.org/news/media-campaigns/ordinance/ (accessed on 25 January 2017).
24. No Author. Municipalities with Local 100% Smokefree Laws Currently in Effect as of 2 January 2020. Berkeley: American Nonsmokers' Rights Foundation. 2020. Available online: http://no-smoke.org/wp-content/uploads/pdf/100ordlisttabs.pdf (accessed on 25 May 2021).
25. Moore, T. Statement from the Louisiana Campaign for Tobacco-Free Living Regarding Shreveport's Smoke-free Ordinance. Louisiana Public Health Institute. 2020 updated June 18. Available online: https://web.archive.org/web/20201020084729/http://tobaccofreeliving.org/news/press-releases/statement-from-the-louisiana-campaign-for-tobacco-free-living-regarding-shreveports-smoke-free-ordinance (accessed on 21 January 2021).
26. No Author. New Orleans Data Briefs. Louisiana Campaign for Tobacco-Free Living; 2014 updated December. Available online: https://lphi.org/the-latest/the-louisiana-campaign-for-tobacco-free-living-and-well-ahead-announce-new-tobacco-data/ (accessed on 1 January 2016).
27. Cofer, J.; Rodas, C.F. Smokefree NOLA. 2016. Available online: https://lphi.org/work/tobacco-prevention-and-control/smoke-free-nola/ (accessed on 12 May 2017).
28. Conrad, L.M. Healthier Air for All Partners with WWOZ for Statewide Smoke-Free Concert Series. New Orleans: Cision PRWeb. 2014. Available online: https://healthierairforall.org/the-movement (accessed on 12 May 2017).
29. Hallett, C.; Frick, B. Interviewed by Wakefield, T. 25 July 2016.
30. Cofer, J.; Hurst, A. Interviewed by Wakefield, T. 14 April 2017.
31. No Author. City and Parish Smoke-Free Ordinances. Louisiana Public Health Institute. 2020. Available online: https://tobaccofreeliving.org/media/media-campaigns/city-and-parish-smoke-free-ordinances (accessed on 19 January 2021).
32. No Author. Smoke-free East Baton Rouge. Baton Rouge, LA: Smoke-Free East Baton Rouge. 2015. Available online: https://web.archive.org/web/20160915063552/http://www.smokefreeebr.org/ (accessed on 13 December 2016).
33. No Author. Smokefree NOLA Twitter Post. Twitter. 2014. Available online: https://twitter.com/SmokeFreeNOLA/status/540926090395799552 (accessed on 28 May 2019).
34. Richard, K. Interviewed by Wakefield, T. 11 January 2017.
35. No Author. History. New Orleans: Louisiana Cultural Economy Foundation. 2015. Available online: https://web.archive.org/web/20160210062324/http://culturaleconomy.org/about/history/ (accessed on 11 May 2017).
36. Truth Initiative. Smoke-Free New Orleans. 2015 updated 5 August 2016. Available online: https://www.youtube.com/watch?v=sdbUYeM1zM8 (accessed on 5 January 2021).
37. Rainey, R. New Orleans to kick off Smoke-Free Week 2.0 at City Hall. The Times-Picayune [Serial on the Internet]. 2014. Available online: https://web.archive.org/web/20150102192218/http://www.nola.com/politics/index.ssf/2014/11/new_orleans_to_kick_off_smoke-.html (accessed on 7 December 2016).
38. No Author. Frequently Asked Question: APHA 2020 Virtual. American Public Health Association. 2020. Available online: https://www.apha.org/events-and-meetings/annual/frequently-asked-questions (accessed on 21 December 2020).
39. No Author. Online Program: APHA 142nd Annual Meeting & Expo Online. American Public Health Association. 2014. Available online: https://apha.confex.com/apha/142am/webprogram/start.html (accessed on 16 May 2017).

40. McClendon, R. Proposal Banning Smoking Introduced-Business Coalition Prepared to Fight City Council Plan. The Times-Picayune. (New Orleans). 21 November 2014. Available online: https://infoweb.newsbank.com/apps/news/openurl?ctx_ver=z39.88-2004&rft_id=info%3Asid/infoweb.newsbank.com&svc_dat=AWNB&req_dat=0F8328B6120203A5&rft_val_format=info%3Aofi/fmt%3Akev%3Amtx%3Actx&rft_dat=document_id%3Anews%252F151BBFDC63516990 (accessed on 29 October 2020).
41. APHA. APHA Annual Meeting Opening Session: 'You Are the Heart of Public Health'. Washington: American Public Health Association. 2014. Available online: http://aphaannualmeeting.blogspot.com/2014/11/apha-annual-meeting-opening-session-you.html (accessed on 16 November 2017).
42. No Author. AHA (American Heart Association) Scientific Sessions 2014. 2014. Available online: https://healthmanagement.org/c/cardio/event/aha-american-heart-association-scientific-sessions-2014#:~{}:text=The%20American%20Heart%20Association\T1\textquoterights%20Scientific,from%20more%20than%20100%20countries (accessed on 21 December 2020).
43. No Author. The American Heart Association's Smoke-Free Meeting Policy 2015. 2020 (November 2). Available online: https://playbook.heart.org/the-american-heart-associations-smoke-free-meeting-policy/ (accessed on 2 November 2020).
44. McNulty, I. Block Parties In Motion: The New Orleans Second Line Parade. n.d. Available online: http://www.frenchquarter.com/secondline/ (accessed on 21 July 2016).
45. APHA. Closing General Session: 'We can make health everyone's business'. American Public Health Association. 2014. Available online: https://aphaannualmeeting.blogspot.com/2014/11/ (accessed on 19 November 2021).
46. No Author. SmokeFreeNOLA Facebook Page. Facebook. 2019. Available online: https://www.facebook.com/SmokeFreeNOLA/ (accessed on 29 May 2019).
47. Moore, T.; Rodas, C.F.; Smith, O.; Cofer, J. Laying the Groundwork for Smoke-Free NOLA (2015 APHA Annual Meeting & Expo (31 October–4 November 2015). 2015. Available online: https://apha.confex.com/apha/143am/videogateway.cgi/id/72810?recordingid=72810 (accessed on 16 March 2021).
48. Goins, B. When Smokers Stay Home. 2015. Available online: http://bestofswla.com/2015/09/03/when-smokers-stay-home/ (accessed on 16 May 2017).
49. McClendon, R. Smoking Ban Introduced before New Orleans City Council; Cantrell Wants Vote before March 1. The Times-Picayune [serial on the Internet]. 2014. Available online: https://web.archive.org/web/20141124064811/http://www.nola.com/politics/index.ssf/2014/11/smoking_ban_introduced_before.html (accessed on 22 July 2016).
50. No Author. Louisiana Association of Wholesalers: Membership Services. Louisiana Association of Wholesalers. 2016. Available online: https://web.archive.org/web/20160107062051/https://www.louisianawholesalers.org/Membership.cfm (accessed on 5 March 2018).
51. No Author. ProActive Communications. Field Action Team Campaign 98 National Overview Volume II. January 27 1998. Philip Morris Records; Master Settlement Agreement. Available online: https://www.industrydocumentslibrary.ucsf.edu/tobacco/docs/#id=stcf0167 (accessed on 1 December 2021).
52. Proactive Communications. Field Action Team Ally Meeting Reports. June 29 2001. Philip Morris Records; Master Settlement Agreement. Available online: https://www.industrydocumentslibrary.ucsf.edu/tobacco/docs/#id=llwy0177 (accessed on 12 November 2021).
53. No Author. Archived Tatman Group Web Page. Baton Rouge: The Tatman Group. 2020. Available online: https://web.archive.org/web/20200804194517/http://www.tatmangroup.com/our-firm (accessed on 19 January 2021).
54. Julie. New Orleans, Louisiana Call To Action: Ordinance Would Ban Vaping Wherever Smoking is Prohibited. 2015. Available online: https://casaa.org/get-involved/state-locator/louisiana/ (accessed on 28 July 2016).
55. Woessner, J. New Orleans, Louisiana Call to Action: Ordinance would Ban Vaping Wherever Smoking is Prohibited. CASAA: Consumer Advocates for Smoke-Free Alternatives Association. 2015. Available online: https://casaa.org/education/vaping/historical-timeline-of-electronic-cigarettes/ (accessed on 12 May 2018).
56. Commmunity Development Meeting Minutes, Community Development, New Orleans City Council. 7 January 2015. Available online: http://cityofno.granicus.com/MediaPlayer.php?view_id=7&clip_id=1976 (accessed on 5 August 2016).
57. Regular City Council Meeting, New Orleans City Council. 22 January 2015. Available online: http://cityofno.granicus.com/MediaPlayer.php?view_id=7&clip_id=1985# (accessed on 5 August 2016).
58. No Author. Anti-Smoking Advocates Question Link between New Orleans Ban and Casino Revenue Drop. The Times-Picayune [Serial on the Internet]. 2017. Available online: https://www.nola.com/news/business/article_da72cc1e-1941-562d-a711-f18ce160549e.html (accessed on 4 January 2020).
59. Eggler, B. Harrah's Gets Earful from Committee-Council Members Say Casino Got Deal, then Broke Promises. The Times-Picayune. (New Orleans). 19 July 2001. Available online: https://infoweb.newsbank.com/apps/news/openurl?ctx_ver=z39.88-2004&rft_id=info%3Asid/infoweb.newsbank.com&svc_dat=AWNB&req_dat=0F8328B6120203A5&rft_val_format=info%3Aofi/fmt%3Akev%3Amtx%3Actx&rft_dat=document_id%3Anews%252F0F131BD7283CB0D6 (accessed on 21 December 2020).
60. Rainey, R. Harrah's New Orleans Loses Fight to Cut Jobs under Smoking Ban. The Times-Picayune [serial on the Internet]. 2015. Available online: https://web.archive.org/web/20150716032504/http://www.nola.com/politics/index.ssf/2015/05/arrahs_new_orleans_job-cutting.html (accessed on 3 August 2016).

61. Rainey, R. French Quarter Cigar Bar's Permit Fight to Test New Orleans Smoking, Drinking Laws. The Times-Picayune [Serial on the Internet]. 2015. Available online: https://web.archive.org/web/20150226112528/http://www.nola.com/politics/index.ssf/2015/02/french_quarter_cigar_bars_perm.html (accessed on 25 May 2017).
62. Adelson, J. Harrah's Seeks Exemption from Smoking Ban, Says City could Lose Millions. The New Orleans Advocate [Serial on the Internet]. 2015. Available online: http://www.theadvocate.com/new_orleans/news/politics/article_17365f07-77e3-5ece-b69c-6e7c6675db42.html (accessed on 4 August 2016).
63. Rainey, R. Harrah's Casino in New Orleans Renews Push to Dodge City Smoking Ban. The Times-Picayune [Serial on the Internet]. 2015. Available online: https://web.archive.org/web/20170602183248/http://www.nola.com/politics/index.ssf/2015/03/harrahs_casino_in_new_orleans.html (accessed on 4 August 2016).
64. Grimm, A. Judge Denies Bar Owners' Bid to Stall New Orleans Smoking Ban. The Times-Picayune [serial on the Internet]. 2015. Available online: https://web.archive.org/web/20150420150243/http://www.nola.com/politics/index.ssf/2015/04/new_orleans_smoking_ban_lawsui.html (accessed on 3 August 2015).
65. Rainey, R. Bars' Lawsuit against New Orleans Smoking Ban Flames out. The Times-Picayune [Serial on the Internet]. 2015. Available online: https://web.archive.org/web/20150707123924/http://www.nola.com/politics/index.ssf/2015/06/bars_lawsuit_against_new_orlea.html (accessed on 2 November 2020).
66. SB236 by Senator Edwin, R. Murray, SB236. Regular Session. Louisiana State Legislature. Available online: http://www.legis.la.gov/Legis/BillInfo.aspx?s=15RS&b=SB236&sbi=y (accessed on 3 April 2021).
67. Ballard, M. Harrah's New Orleans wants to reduce staff by 400; Sen. Karen Peterson said city not told of plans. The Advocate [serial on the Internet]. 2015. Available online: http://www.theadvocate.com/baton_rouge/news/politics/legislature/article_2ff06976-2bb9-570a-97dc-5fb6c3ab2748.html (accessed on 3 August 2016).
68. Adelson, J.; Bridges, T. Several Bars, Restaurants Join in Suit to Strike down New Orleans' Smoking Ban. The New Orleans Advocate [Serial on the Internet]. 2015. Available online: http://www.theadvocate.com/new_orleans/news/politics/article_3eab1ad0-2017-532f-ba8b-713f4ae5d1ae.html (accessed on 3 August 2016).
69. Rainey, R. Hope is Not Extinguished in Fight against Smoking Ban. The Times-Picayune. (New Orleans). 23 April 2015. Available online: https://infoweb.newsbank.com/apps/news/openurl?ctx_ver=z39.88-2004&rft_id=info%3Asid/infoweb.newsbank.com&svc_dat=AWNB&req_dat=0F8328B6120203A5&rft_val_format=info%3Aofi/fmt%3Akev%3Amtx%3Actx&rft_dat=document_id%3Anews%252F154E2ABBD5831480 (accessed on 4 June 2019).
70. Buchanan, S. Harrah's Seeks Assistance as it Adjusts to City's Smoking Ban. The Louisiana Weekly [Serial on the Internet]. 2015. Available online: http://www.louisianaweekly.com/harrahs-seeks-assistance-as-it-adjusts-to-citys-smoking-ban/ (accessed on 4 August 2016).
71. No Author. TFL Reveals The Real Facts Behind Harrah's Casino Gaming Revenue. [Press Release] New Orleans: Louisiana Public Health Institute; 2015 updated July 24. Available online: https://web.archive.org/web/20160428003538/http://lphi.org/home2/section/2-158/announcement-archive/view/222/ (accessed on 4 August 2016).
72. Chaffin, S. Gambling in the Great Outdoors. 2020. Available online: https://www.casinocenter.com/gambling-in-the-great-outdoors/?utm_source=rss&utm_medium=rss&utm_campaign=gambling-in-the-great-outdoors (accessed on 22 January 2021).
73. Travers, M.J.; Vogl, L. New Orleans, Louisiana Indoor Air Quality Study. Buffalo: Roswell Park Cancer Institute, Department of Health Behavior and Air Pollution Exposure Research Laboratory. August 2015. Available online: https://www.tobaccofreekids.org/assets/content/press_office/2015/2015_08_04_nola_aqm.pdf (accessed on 29 December 2020).
74. No Author. City of Baton Rogue Parish of East Baton Rouge: Our Government. Baton Rouge: City of Baton Rouge Parish of East Baton Rouge. n.d. Available online: https://www.brla.gov/1062/Our-Government (accessed on 4 January 2019).
75. Gallo, A.; Peveto, K. Group Pushing Bar, Casino Smoking Ban in East Baton Rouge includes Doctors, Musicians, Public Officials. The Advocate [Serial on the Internet]. 2016. Available online: http://www.theadvocate.com/baton_rouge/news/article_e1a047bf-7567-530c-8a92-0225773e6338.html (accessed on 13 December 2016).
76. Riegel, S. As Effort to Ban Smoking in Baton Rouge Bars and Casinos gathers Steam, Both Sides Prepare to Face off. Greater Baton Rouge Business Report [Serial on the Internet]. 2016. Available online: https://web.archive.org/web/20160218091958/https://www.businessreport.com/business/effort-ban-smoking-baton-rouge-bars-casinos-gathers-steam-sides-prepare-face-off (accessed on 5 June 2017).
77. No Author. Facebook Page for Tobacco Free Louisiana and Smoke-Free East Baton Rouge. Facebook. 2019. Available online: https://www.facebook.com/TobaccoFreeLouisiana/ (accessed on 6 June 2019).
78. WAFB Staff. Campaign to Make EBR Smoke Free Gains Several Endorsements 2016. Available online: http://www.wafb.com/story/31192375/campaign-to-make-ebr-smoke-free-gains-several-endorsements (accessed on 5 June 2017).
79. Wester, S.; Fontenot, T.G.; McMillen, E.; Olson, R.; Stevens, T.; Slyter, M. Area Health Professionals Announce Support for Smoke-Free EBR Movement. Baton Rouge, LA. n.d. Available online: https://web.archive.org/web/20180903135838/http://www.smokefreeebr.org/docs/SFEBR-Hospitals-Letter-of-Support.pdf (accessed on 13 December 2016).
80. Burris, A. Area Medical Exectives Back Smoke-Free East Baton Rouge Campaign. Greater Baton Rouge Business Report [Serial on the Internet]. 2016. Available online: https://web.archive.org/web/20160220102824/https://www.businessreport.com/article/east-baton-rouge-parish-medical-executives-back-smoke-free-east-baton-rouge-campaign (accessed on 5 June 2017).

81. Broussard, R. Smoke-free EBR Coalition has Spent Roughly $300k in Advertising to Push for Full Smoking Ban. Greater Baton Rouge Business Report [Serial on the Internet]. 2016. Available online: https://web.archive.org/web/20160418085601/https://www.businessreport.com/article/smoke-free-ebr-coalition-spent-roughly-300k-advertising-push-full-smoking-ban (accessed on 5 June 2019).
82. No Author. Tobacco Free Louisiana SmokeFree EBR Twitter Page. Twitter. 2019. Available online: https://twitter.com/latobaccofree (accessed on 6 June 2019).
83. Broussard, R. L'Auberge Parent Company Exec Says Baton Rouge Smoking Ban could put Casino at Competitive Disadvantage. Greater Baton Rouge Business Report [Serial on the Internet]. 2016. Available online: https://web.archive.org/web/20160404120043/https://www.businessreport.com/article/lauberge-parent-company-exec-says-baton-rouge-smoking-ban-put-casino-competitive-disadvantage (accessed on 7 June 2017).
84. Griggs, T. Casino Says Smoking Ban could cost EBR, State Millions in Tax Revenue. The Advocate [Serial on the Internet]. 2016. Available online: http://www.theadvocate.com/baton_rouge/news/business/article_22ad917c-0f5d-588f-b429-16b16c4a0eb8.html (accessed on 7 June 2017).
85. Gallo, A. Casinos Say Smoking Ban would be Costly; Anti-Smoking Forces Plan Show of Force for Metro Council Vote. The Advocate [Serial on the Internet]. 2016. Available online: http://www.theadvocate.com/baton_rouge/news/article_17bc4528-c848-5647-b324-0418e1f1e9d1.html (accessed on 7 June 2017).
86. City of Baton Rouge. 13 April 2016 Metropolitan Council Hearing. Baton Rouge, LA2016 updated April 13. Available online: http://batonrougela.swagit.com/play/04132016-784/#5 (accessed on 5 July 2017).
87. American Society of Heating RaA-CEA. *ASHRAE Position Document on Environmental Tobacco Smoke*; ASHRAE: Atlanta, GA, USA, 2020.
88. Gallo, A. Effort Revived to Ban Smoking in Casinos, Bars with Baton Rouge Mayor on Board. The Advocate. (Baton Rouge). 31 May 2017. Available online: https://infoweb.newsbank.com/apps/news/openurl?ctx_ver=z39.88-2004&rft_id=info%3Asid/infoweb.newsbank.com&svc_dat=AWNB&req_dat=0F8328B6120203A5&rft_val_format=info%3Aofi/fmt%3Akev%3Amtx%3Actx&rft_dat=document_id%3Anews%252F164CBE9994924410 (accessed on 10 June 2019).
89. Gallo, A. With Baton Rouge Smoking Ban Apparently on Track, here's Who Supports It, Who'll Enforce It, What It Covers. The Advocate. (Baton Rouge). 8 June 2017. Available online: https://infoweb.newsbank.com/apps/news/openurl?ctx_ver=z39.88-2004&rft_id=info%3Asid/infoweb.newsbank.com&svc_dat=AWNB&req_dat=0F8328B6120203A5&rft_val_format=info%3Aofi/fmt%3Akev%3Amtx%3Actx&rft_dat=document_id%3Anews%252F164F052425142830 (accessed on 11 June 2019).
90. Hardy, S. Majority want East Baton Rouge bars, casinos smoke-free, according to poll by ban supporters. The Advocate. (Baton Rouge). 17 June 2017. Available online: https://infoweb.newsbank.com/apps/news/openurl?ctx_ver=z39.88-2004&rft_id=info%3Asid/infoweb.newsbank.com&svc_dat=AWNB&req_dat=0F8328B6120203A5&rft_val_format=info%3Aofi/fmt%3Akev%3Amtx%3Actx&rft_dat=document_id%3Anews%252F1651FA647669A830 (accessed on 11 June 2019).
91. Kingvalsky, L. Letters: Support ban on smoking. The Advocate. (New Orleans). 23 June 2017. Available online: https://infoweb.newsbank.com/apps/news/openurl?ctx_ver=z39.88-2004&rft_id=info%3Asid/infoweb.newsbank.com&svc_dat=AWNB&req_dat=0F8328B6120203A5&rft_val_format=info%3Aofi/fmt%3Akev%3Amtx%3Actx&rft_dat=document_id%3Anews%252F1653F469EF95F9F0 (accessed on 13 June 2019).
92. Engster, J.; Watson, M.; Chad, L. The Jim Engster Show. 2017. Available online: http://talk1073.com/2017/06/20/jim-engster-show-06-20-17-hour-one/?fbclid=IwAR3gyTqXayNt_gGNmxi8QiIDzYPZ2N3Q3_RNcXN2m3RCKBaYOMBcJxePpew (accessed on 14 June 2019).
93. Engster, J.; Collins-Lewis, D. Donna Collins-Lewis on the Alton Sterling Tension and the Smoking Ban. Baton Rouge: WRKF. 2017. Available online: https://www.wrkf.org/show/talk-louisiana/2017-07-06/donna-collins-lewis-on-the-alton-sterling-tension-and-the-smoking-ban (accessed on 12 May 2017).
94. Engster, J.; Freiberg, B.R. Barbara Reich Freiberg on Smoking Ban Considerations. Baton Rouge: WRKF. 2017 updated June 19. Available online: https://www.wrkf.org/post/barbara-reich-freiberg-smoking-ban-considerations?fbclid=IwAR3yyrU4Xy2xjDIR-5O0BdxAezAEKb-oS9ez_rp6hq6Djl_jrZDIpV-MZWM#stream/0 (accessed on 18 June 2019).
95. Wallace, M. Letters: Smoking ban helps public health. The Advocate. (Baton Rouge, LA). 4 July 2017. Available online: https://infoweb.newsbank.com/apps/news/openurl?ctx_ver=z39.88-2004&rft_id=info%3Asid/infoweb.newsbank.com&svc_dat=AWNB&req_dat=0F8328B6120203A5&rft_val_format=info%3Aofi/fmt%3Akev%3Amtx%3Actx&rft_dat=document_id%3Anews%252F16579528A0F397B8 (accessed on 13 June 2019).
96. Daily Report Staff. Smoke-free EBR unveils new study ahead of council vote. Greater Baton Rouge Business Report [serial on the Internet]. 2017. Available online: https://web.archive.org/web/20170805001436/https://www.businessreport.com/article/smoke-free-ebr-unveils-new-study-ahead-council-vote (accessed on 14 June 2019).
97. City of Baton Rouge Parish of East Baton Rouge. 28 June 2017 Metropolitan Council Hearing. 2017. Available online: https://batonrougela.swagit.com/play/06282017-776 (accessed on 12 June 2019).
98. 9 August 2017 Metropolitan Council Hearing, Baton Rouge Metropolitan Council. 9 August 2017. Available online: https://batonrougela.swagit.com/play/08092017-828 (accessed on 18 June 2019).
99. WBRZ Staff. Baton Rouge Blues Festival releases 2018 lineup. 2018. Available online: http://www.wbrz.com/news/baton-rouge-blues-festival-releases-2018-lineup/ (accessed on 18 June 2019).

100. Smoke-Free East Baton Rouge. Smoke-Free Ordinance Toolkit. Baton Rouge: City of Baton Rouge Parish of East Baton Rouge. n.d. updated n.d. Available online: https://www.brla.gov/DocumentCenter/View/4866/EBR-Smoke-Free-Ordinance-Toolkit-PDF (accessed on 18 June 2019).
101. Boone, T. Baton Rouge Smoking Ban now in Effect; here's Where You Can, Can't Light Up. The Advocate. (Baton Rouge). 31 May 2018. Available online: https://infoweb.newsbank.com/apps/news/openurl?ctx_ver=z39.88-2004&rft_id=info%3Asid/infoweb.newsbank.com&svc_dat=AWNB&req_dat=0F8328B6120203A5&rft_val_format=info%3Aofi/fmt%3Akev%3Amtx%3Actx&rft_dat=document_id%3Anews%252F16C4B393A4C25EB0 (accessed on 22 December 2020).
102. Jones, T. How Successful is Baton Rouge's Smoking Ban? Indoor Air Pollution Has Dropped Significantly, Report Says. The Advocate. (Baton Rouge). 28 November 2018. Available online: https://infoweb.newsbank.com/apps/news/openurl?ctx_ver=z39.88-2004&rft_id=info%3Asid/infoweb.newsbank.com&svc_dat=AWNB&req_dat=0F8328B6120203A5&rft_val_format=info%3Aofi/fmt%3Akev%3Amtx%3Actx&rft_dat=document_id%3Anews%252F17000C4612EA8F50 (accessed on 22 December 2020).
103. Givel, M.S.; Glantz, S.A. Tobacco lobby political influence on US state legislatures in the 1990s. *Tob. Control.* **2001**, *10*, 124–134. [CrossRef]
104. Gorovitz, E.; Mosher, J.; Pertschuk, M. Preemption or prevention?: Lessons from efforts to control firearms, alcohol, and tobacco. *J. Public Health Policy* **1998**, *19*, 36–50. [CrossRef]
105. Weishaar, H.; Collin, J.; Amos, A. Tobacco control and health advocacy in the European Union: Understanding effective coalition-building. *Nicotine Tob. Res.* **2015**, *18*, 122–129. [CrossRef]
106. Goldman, L.K.; Glantz, S.A. Evaluation of antismoking advertising campaigns. *JAMA* **1998**, *279*, 772–777. [CrossRef]
107. Berg, C.J.; Thrasher, J.F.; O'Connor, J.; Haardorfer, R.; Kegler, M.C. Reactions to smoke-free policies and messaging strategies in support and opposition: A comparison of southerners and non-southerners in the US. *Health Behav. Policy Rev.* **2015**, *2*, 408–420. [CrossRef]
108. Wallack, L.; Dorfman, L. Media advocacy: A strategy for advancing policy and promoting health. *Health Educ. Q.* **1996**, *23*, 293–317. [CrossRef]

atmosphere

MDPI

Article

Indoor Air Quality Assessment of Latin America's First Passivhaus Home

Alejandro Moreno-Rangel [1,2,*], Filbert Musau [1], Tim Sharpe [1,3] and Gráinne McGill [1,3]

1 Mackintosh Environmental Architecture Research Unit, The Glasgow School of Art, Glasgow G3 6RQ, UK; f.musau@gsa.ac.uk (F.M.); tim.sharpe@strath.ac.uk (T.S.); grainne.mcgill@strath.ac.uk (G.M.)
2 Lancaster Institute of the Contemporary Arts, Lancaster University, Lancaster LA1 4YW, UK
3 Department of Architecture, University of Strathclyde, Glasgow G1 1XJ, UK
* Correspondence: a.morenorangel@lancaster.ac.uk; Tel.: +44-(0)-152-510873

Abstract: Sustainable building design, such as the Passivhaus standard, seeks to minimise energy consumption, while improving indoor environmental comfort. Very few studies have studied the indoor air quality (IAQ) in Passivhaus homes outside of Europe. This paper presents the indoor particulate matter ($PM_{2.5}$), carbon dioxide (CO_2), and total volatile organic compounds (tVOC) measurements of the first residential Passivhaus in Latin America. It compares them to a standard home in Mexico City. Low-cost monitors were installed in the bedroom, living room, and kitchen spaces of both homes, to collect data at five-minute intervals for one year. The physical measurements from each home were also compared to the occupants' IAQ perceptions. The measurements demonstrated that the Passivhaus CO_2 and tVOC annual average levels were 143.8 ppm and 81.47 μg/m^3 lower than the standard home. The $PM_{2.5}$ in the Passivhaus was 11.13 μg/m^3 lower than the standard home and 5.75 μg/m^3 lower than outdoors. While the results presented here cannot be generalised, the results suggest that Passivhaus dwellings can provide better and healthier indoor air quality in Latin America. Further, large-scale studies should look at the indoor environmental conditions, energy performance, and dwelling design of Passivhaus dwellings in Latin America.

Keywords: Passivhaus; indoor air quality (IAQ); Latin America; particulate matter ($PM_{2.5}$); carbon dioxide (CO_2); total volatile organic compounds (tVOC)

Citation: Moreno-Rangel, A.; Musau, F.; Sharpe, T.; McGill, G. Indoor Air Quality Assessment of Latin America's First Passivhaus Home. *Atmosphere* **2021**, *12*, 1477. https://doi.org/10.3390/atmos12111477

Academic Editor: Ashok Kumar, Amirul I Khan, Alejandro Moreno Rangel and Michał Piasecki

Received: 4 October 2021
Accepted: 3 November 2021
Published: 8 November 2021

1. Introduction

Sustainable building design is in constant evolution; such a process has been emphasised due to climate change issues. Sustainable architecture aims to deliver buildings that balance their ecological impact, and even go further. The construction industry has faced significant challenges, to reduce energy demand while providing better indoor environmental quality [1]. Buildings have reduced heat losses through the building envelope and introduced active and passive techniques to reduce energy use further. However, these changes have been mainly motivated by environmental concerns, energy prices, and an increased demand for housing [2]. Other factors, such as indoor environmental comfort and health, have not been addressed adequately in the past, but have seen increased attention, particularly indoor air quality (IAQ); after the COVID-19 lockdowns [3,4]. Different organisations have developed benchmarking systems and certifications to promote and recognise energy-efficient buildings through different design and construction criteria. Some examples include BREEAM (Building Research Establishment Environmental Assessment), LEED (Leadership in Energy and Environmental Design), and the Passivhaus standard, on which this work is based.

A Passive House, or 'Passivhaus', which is the original German term, is '[...] a building, for which thermal comfort (ISO 7730) can be achieved solely by post-heating or post-cooling of the fresh air mass, which is required to achieve sufficient indoor air quality conditions—without the need for additional recirculation of air [5]'. Nevertheless, the

Passivhaus does not have specific criteria for IAQ and relies on the DIN1946 suggested airflow rates to manage ventilation and, hence, the removal of indoor air pollutants. The German standard DIN1946 establishes air flow rates between 0.5 and 1.0 ach^{-1}, suggesting that these ventilation rates should be sufficient to avoid CO_2 peaks above 1500 ppm.

The Passivhaus standard is based on five fundamental concepts: thermal insulation, thermal bridge-reduced design, airtightness, adequate ventilation strategy (usually through mechanical ventilation with heat recovery (MVHR) systems), and the use of Passivhaus windows and doors (for a detailed explanation of the Passivhaus principles see [6]). Additionally, the building must adhere to strict design criteria detailed in the Passive House Planning Package (PHPP, currently version 9) [7]. Although the Passivhaus standard was first developed for cold central European countries, its methodology has been introduced to warmer climates such as those found in Latin America.

Between 1990 and 2005, a few Passivhaus homes were built, mainly in cold climates from European countries. The interest in Passivhaus buildings has expanded outside of Europe. According to the Passivhaus Institute in Latin America (ILAPH), the uptake of the Passivhaus standard in Latin America started in 2010 with a non-residential Passivhaus pilot building in Chile. However, it was not until 2014 that the first dwelling received certification, in Mexico. Since then, other dwellings have achieved certification, but have only been subject to scientific scrutiny through virtual modelling, mainly through the PHPP; until now. These studies show evidence of the thermal comfort [8], energy [9,10], economic [11,12], and environmental [13] performance, as well as the feasibility [14,15] of Passivhaus buildings in Latin America. Their measured performance evaluation is limited to thermal comfort [16], energy [17], or limited to short ($\leq$3 months) term studies [18]. Passivhaus dwellings have attracted scientific scrutiny of their energy performance [19–21], thermal comfort [22–25], and IAQ [21,26–29] in other parts of the world.

Indoor air quality (IAQ) refers to the indoor concentration of air pollutants that can harm human wellbeing [30]. Nevertheless, what constitutes safe or adequate levels is a current debate. Some authors claim that this should be a complete absence of air contaminants [31]. In contrast, others suggest that low concentrations, which are not detrimental to public health, are acceptable [32]. In 2000, the World Health Organisation (WHO) recognised healthy air as a human right [33] and published guidelines for safe thresholds of different indoor air pollutants [34]. The Passivhaus standard does not explicitly address off-gassing from building materials or other air pollution issues in buildings. Instead, it relies on ventilation rates (30 m^3/h per person or 0.3 ach/h) to achieve acceptable levels. Hence, IAQ in Passivhaus dwellings is a topic that has captivated the interest of researchers.

Several studies [35–39] suggest that Passivhaus dwellings have the means to achieve acceptable IAQ, even when compared to other non-Passivhaus homes [40–44]. However, very few have compared the measured IAQ to the occupant's IAQ perception [29,45,46]. Other studies show conflicting results, suggesting that the IAQ in a Passivhaus may not be adequate [47–49]. Some of the Passivhaus principles, airtightness and ventilation, directly impact the IAQ in homes. For instance, the required levels of airtightness ($\leq$0.6 h-1 @50 Pa) in Passivhaus dwellings help avoid condensation and conserve energy by reducing air infiltration. However, it is unclear whether an airtight building envelope has clear IAQ benefits [39,50] or not [51]. Nevertheless, occupants' satisfaction with IAQ and indoor humidity is better than those living in non-Passivhaus dwellings [44].

A previous study [26] suggested further work on long-term studies, to understand the IAQ performance of Passivhaus worldwide, in climates different from those found in central European countries. To the authors' knowledge, this work is the first to measure and evaluate the long-term IAQ performance of a Passivhaus dwelling in Latin America. Indoor air quality parameters were measured using low-cost monitors with remote access capabilities. Additionally, the occupants' perception of IAQ was assessed and compared to the physical measurements. Finally, this paper discusses further work to support the development of the Passivhaus standard in Latin American countries. This work focuses on IAQ, as the thermal performance of this Passivhaus dwelling is discussed elsewhere [16].

2. Method

This study presents results from a monitoring campaign of a certified Passivhaus dwelling, and another built with the standard building practices in Mexico City. This campaign took place between 1 June 2016 and 31 May 2017. Locations with an Oceanic Subtropical Highland Climate (Cwb), such as Mexico City, are characterised by warm and wet summers, with dry and warmer winters [52]. Foobot was used to monitor air temperature (−40–125 °C; ±0.4 °C), relative humidity (0–100% RH; ±4% RH), particulate matter 2.5 µm ($PM_{2.5}$) (0–1300 µg/m^3; ±4 µg/m^3 or ±20%), and total volatile organic compounds (tVOC) (125–1000 µg/m^3; ±1 µg/m^3 or ±10%). As the Foobot does not have a dedicated carbon dioxide (CO_2) sensor, a Netatmo (0–5000 ppm; ±50 ppm or 5%) was used for these measurements. The accuracy of both the Foobot [53] and Netatmo [54] monitors has been tested and validated for carrying out long-term IAQ monitoring. The calibration equations used in this study are described in greater detail in a previous study from our research group [53].

We adopted a novel monitoring methodology for this research, avoiding researcher visits to the homes. Instead, the participants were asked to install the monitors and asked for the surveys online, as described in [55]. They received a pack with information on how to operate the monitors and where to place them. These monitors were used as they could be deployed remotely, with remote data collection, and were acceptable to the building owners who installed them. The Foobot monitors were installed in the living room, kitchen, and bedroom, while the Netatmos were only placed in the living room and bedroom. The sensors collected data continuously at five-minute intervals, for one year. As this was a long-term study, using these low-cost monitors for outdoor monitoring would have been difficult and added challenges for the building occupants to install a different set of sensors (i.e., outdoor air quality, doors, windows, and movement sensors).Hence, outdoor parameters were collected from the 'Hospital General de México (HGM)' station (<1 km from the homes) of Mexico City's official local atmospheric monitoring program (http://aire.cdmx.gob.mx/ (accessed on 16 August 2021), see location in Figure 1).

Occupant perceptions of IAQ were collected through a certified indoor environmental survey [56], which was adapted to an online format. Building occupants were asked to complete the surveys after the end of the monitoring phase, considering their experiences throughout the previous year. This survey examined their perception of air freshness, moisture, movement, the outdoors, and their overall satisfaction with the air quality. The survey was based on seven-option rating scales, was unipolar and bipolar, and assessed following the survey guidelines (see [56] for detailed instructions). As this was a long-term study, it was also not viable to ask the participants to keep a detailed diary of their activities, therefore, participants were asked to provide the general weekly occupancy pattern of the dwelling and window opening patterns on which the analysis is based.

Figure 1. Location of the homes in Mexico City. The red highlighted area shows the Roma Norte. The navy dot represents the location of the monitoring station. The yellow circle highlights the area of the city centre. The blue arrows the main wind direction. Source: Authors, based on Google map image.

2.1. *Indoor Air Quality Criteria*

Standard protocols for measuring the IAQ in homes are limited. Usually, such protocols are designed for general IAQ monitoring (i.e., CIBSEKS17, ASTM D6245-12, and the BS EN ISO 16000-1:2006) and are adapted for residential studies. In this study, we followed the recommendations from BS EN ISO 16000-1:2006 and used the following thresholds:

- $PM_{2.5}$: 25 μg/m^3 at 24 h mean and annual mean of 10 μg/m^3, as defined by WHO [33].
- tVOC: 300 μg/m^3 over 8 h mean, as defined by the WHO [33].
- CO_2: 1000 ppm, as defined by IDA3 (moderate IAQ based on the EN 13779:2007 [57])
- Relative humidity: 40–60%RH (ideal) and 30–70%RH (extended) as defined by CIBSE [58].

2.2. *Household Characteristics*

The dwellings are located within the Roma Norte neighbourhood in the west of Mexico City's historic centre, within less than 500 m of each other (Figure 1). The Roma Norte encompasses diverse building uses residential, restaurants, bars, clubs, shops, churches, and galleries. The borders of the neighbourhood are three principal avenues, which have dense and constant traffic, this is in combination with the winds in the city, which bring the surrounding pollution of the industrial zones to the central neighbourhoods.

Both dwellings have the same orientation, north to south, facing the predominant winds (north-west). While the homes are different in size and floor plan layout (Figure 2a,b), it was deemed adequate to compare them, as the standard home represents the most common typology [59]. Both dwellings have similar occupancy and multipurpose rooms (kitchen, living room, and dining area). Two adults and one child occupied each of the dwellings. Table 1 describes the frequency of window opening and the occupancy patterns, as depicted in the occupancy diaries. Table 2 shows a summary of the building characteristics and construction details.

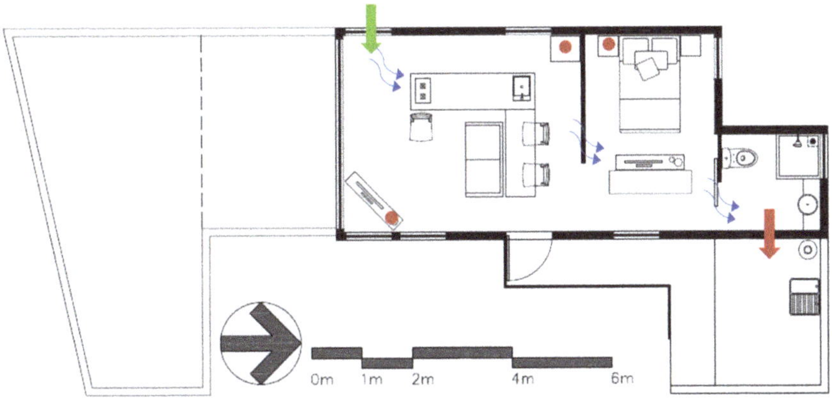

(**a**)

(**b**)

Figure 2. (**a**) Passivhaus dwelling floor plan. The red dots indicate the placement of the sensors. The blue arrows indicate the ventilation flow. The green and red arrows represent the inlet openings and extraction fan, respectively. Source: authors. (**b**) Standard dwelling floor plan. Source: Authors.

Table 1. Household characteristics. Source: Authors.

Household Characteristic	Passivhaus Dwelling	Standard Dwelling
Household occupancy Age range (years) Smoking	2 Adults, 1 child (>16). 40–50, <16 No, only outdoors	2 Adults, 1 child (>16). 40–50, 50–60, <16 No, only outdoors
	Occupancy Pattern (Daily)	
Bedroom	00:00–06:30; 22:30–24:00	00:00–06:30; 22:30–24:00
Kitchen	07:30–09:00; 14:00–16:00; 20:30–21:30	07:30–09:00; 11:00–16:00; 20:30– 21:30
Living room	09:00–09:30; 14:00–16:00; 21:30–22:30	09:00–09:30; 11:00–16:00; 21:30–22:30
	Frequency of Window Opening	
Morning	Rarely	Constantly
Afternoon	Occasionally	Regularly
Evening	Regularly	Occasionally
Night	Constantly	Rarely

Table 2. Main building characteristics of the Passivhaus and Standard Dwellings. Source: Authors.

Building Characteristic	Passivhaus Dwelling	Standard Dwelling
Airtightness (n_{50})	0.59 h^{-1}	Not tested
Floor area	42 m^2	57 m^2
Main door	PVC (Passivhaus certified)	Wood (standard)
U_g-value (window)	1.64 $W/(m^2K)$	5.78 $W/(m^2K)$
U-value (floor slab)	0.33 $W/(m^2K)$	13.66 $W/(m^2K)$
U-value (roof)	0.36 $W/(m^2K)$	13.66 $W/(m^2K)$
U-value (wall)	0.37 $W/(m^2K)$	1.18 $W/(m^2K)$
Ventilation	Mechanical extraction and cross natural ventilation. Due to the mild climate, no MVHR was needed. An extraction fan ran intermittently to provide 42 m^3/h as calculated by the PHPP calculations; no kitchen hood.	Natural (cross and stack). Calculated ventilation (89.6 m^3/h) depending on the outdoor conditions Kitchen hood fans with no extract.
Window type	Double-glazing 6 mm/ 12 mm air, 4 mm low-e-clear-claro (Passivhaus certified)	Single glazing 3 mm (Standard)
Building Standard	Passivhaus (certified)	Mexico City's Standard Building Regulation

In warmer climates, the Passivhaus ventilation strategy may differ from the one recommended in European countries. Rather than using mechanical ventilation with a heat recovery (MVHR) system, the ventilation can rely on mechanical and natural ventilation (hybrid). This Passivhaus dwelling used mechanical extraction ventilation, in the toilet, and three openings with a total of 0.05 m^2, in the living room, at the other end of the house (see green and red arrows in Figure 2a). These inlet openings were initially fitted with an F7 filter–for fine dust and PM_{1-10}. As the filters were difficult to find on the Mexican market at the time, they were removed as they could not be periodically changed. Therefore, during this study, no filters were present. Before the monitoring phase, the ventilation system was recommissioned to ensure that the air flows were as stated in the PHPP (42 m^3/h).

3. Results

3.1. *Passivhaus Ventilation*

A Passivhaus design for hybrid ventilation must ensure that the required ventilation is still met in the most unfavourable conditions, when windows are closed, and natural ventilation is restricted. Therefore, the Passivhaus still needs to provide the ventilation required by the Passivhaus calculation through mechanical means. The air flows in the house were tested and adapted accordingly to the PHPP calculation (42 m^3/h). The extraction fan claimed to have a capacity of 95 m^3/h. However, this was reduced to 74.30 m^3/h after being installed. Nonetheless, this was still higher than the 42 m^3/h required by the PHPP. The difference was compensated using a timer that regulated the fan operation at 34 min per hour and allowed manual activation/deactivation.

The CO_2 levels were used as a ventilation metric [60] (CO_2 levels are examined in detail in the next section). The CO_2 concentrations in the room were modelled using Equation (1).

$$c = (q \div nV)\left[1 - \left(e^{nt}\right)\right] + (c_0 - c_i)\left(1 \div e^{nt}\right) + c_i \quad (1)$$

Equation (1). Model for CO_2 Concentrations in Rooms with People. Source: [61].
where

c = carbon dioxide concentration in the room (m^3/m^3)
q = carbon dioxide supplied to the room (m^3/h)
V = volume of the room (m^3)
e = the constant 2.718
n = air changes per hour (1/h)
t = time (hour, h)
c_i = carbon dioxide concentration in the inlet ventilation air (m^3/m^3)
c_0 = carbon dioxide concentration in the room at start, t = 0 (m^3/m^3)

Figure 3 shows the measured CO_2 levels (continuous blue line) on 26 March 2017. The calibration model (orange short dashed line) was produced using the real occupancy and ventilation patterns (Density: two persons; activity: sleeping; time interval: 5 min; CO_2 emissions per person: 0.015 m^3/h; ventilation rates (calibration model): each hour from 0:00–0:15 at 0.001 ach, 0:15–0:30 at 0.9789 ach (74.3 m^3/h), 0:30–0:40 at 0.001 ach, and 0:45–1:00 at 0.9789 ach (74.3 m^3/h); room volume: 75.9 m^3; and outdoor CO_2: 500 ppm) assuming an outdoor level of 500 ppm, as recommended on the EN 13779:2007 [62]. Another model (blue dash-dot-dash line) evaluated the same condition but changed the extraction to a continuous rate of 42 m^3/h, as suggested by the PHPP calculations (Density: two persons; activity: sleeping; time interval: 5 min; CO_2 emissions per person: 0.015 m^3/h; ventilation rates (continuous flow): 42 m^3/h; room volume: 75.9 m^3; and ambient CO_2: 500 ppm). Finally, the last model (Density: two persons; activity: sleeping; time interval: 5 min; CO_2 emissions per person: 0.015 m^3/h; ventilation rates (continuous flow): 74.3 m^3/h; room volume: 75.9 m^3; and ambient CO_2: 500 ppm) (red long dashed line) evaluated with the total capacity of the installed fan (74.3 m^3/h). The effect can be observed in Figure 4.

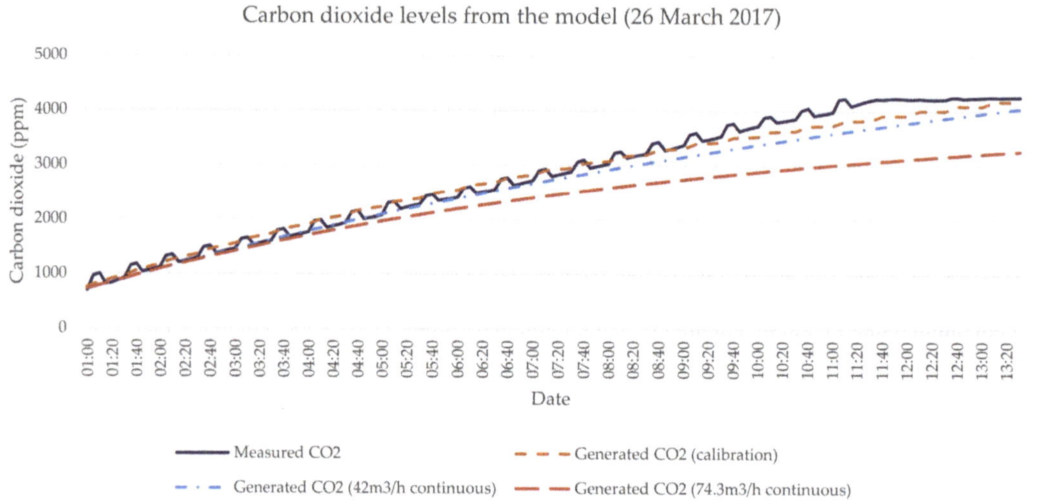

Figure 3. Measured and modelled overnight CO_2 levels. Source: Authors.

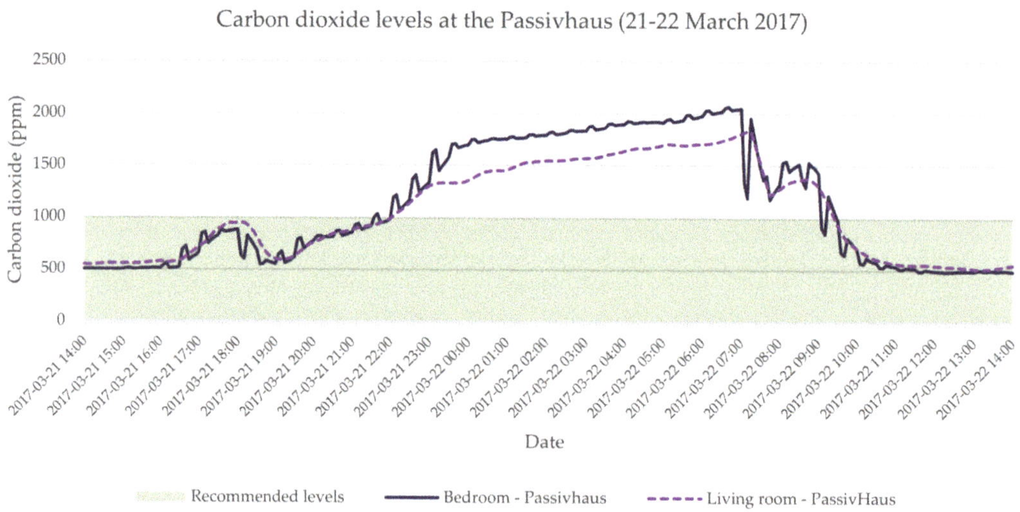

Figure 4. Monitored CO_2 levels in Mexico's Passivhaus (21–22 March 2017). Source: Authors.

3.2. Carbon Dioxide Levels

The CO_2 levels in both monitored spaces, the living room and bedroom, exceeded the recommended 1000 ppm throughout the year. The results showed that the highest levels peaks were during the colder months, when one would expect the windows to remain closed. Nonetheless, the monthly mean levels in both spaces remained below the recommended levels (Figure 5). The overall CO_2 levels in the Passivhaus were better compared to those in the standard dwelling. They remained below the recommended 1000 ppm for 85.9% of the year in the bedroom and 90.1% in the living room in the Passivhaus. In contrast, the standard dwelling bedroom CO_2 levels were above 1000 ppm for 42.9% of the time and 97.5% in the living room. The CO_2 levels of the bedroom of the standard home were of particular concern, particularly at night. A potential explanation could be the differences in the ventilation regulation in the Mexican building regulations, and the fact that windows remained closed during the night due to security concerns. Monthly CO_2 levels and a statistical analysis can be found in the Supplementary Table S1.

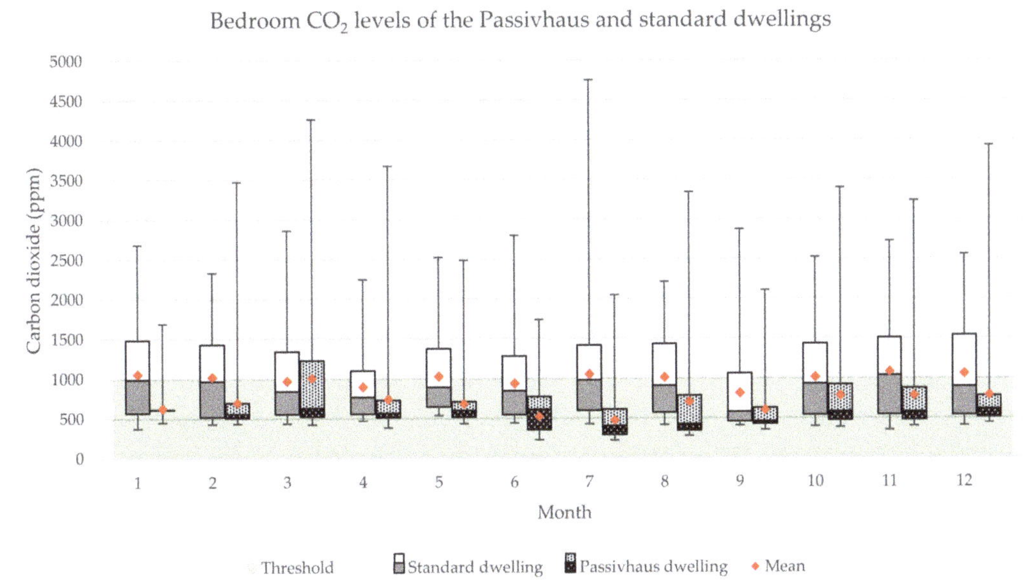

Figure 5. Bedroom annual CO_2 levels in the Passivhaus and Standard dwellings. Source: Authors.

3.3. *Particulate Matter 2.5 µm*

The recommended $PM_{2.5}$ thresholds of 10 µg/m^3 and 25 µg/m^3 were exceeded outdoors and in both dwellings (Figure 6). The measured $PM_{2.5}$ levels outdoors and in both dwellings are shown in Table 3. In comparison, previous studies found that the mean indoor $PM_{2.5}$ concentrations ranged between 28.9 µg/m^3 [63] and 35.1 µg/m^3 [64]. These levels were significantly higher than those in the Passivhaus dwelling.

The $PM_{2.5}$ levels in the Passivhaus (r_s = 0.539–0.587, ($p < 0.001$)) and the standard (r_s = 0.539–0.611, ($p < 0.001$)) dwellings were statistically similar to that outdoors, which is similar to another study where this relationship was significant at r_s = 056, ($p < 0.001$) [65] (see Section 3.3.1.). Nonetheless, further examination revealed that indoor $PM_{2.5}$ levels were also affected by indoor behaviours and ventilation strategies. For instance, cooking originated significant pollution peaks, rapidly dissipated in the standard home (Figure S1) due to higher ventilation rates, compared to the Passivhaus dwelling (Figure S2), where the pollution peaks took longer to dissipate. However, once the pollution peaks dissipated, indoor $PM_{2.5}$ levels remained lower in the Passivhaus dwelling than in the standard home. Monthly $PM_{2.5}$ levels and a statistical analysis can be found in Supplementary Table S2.

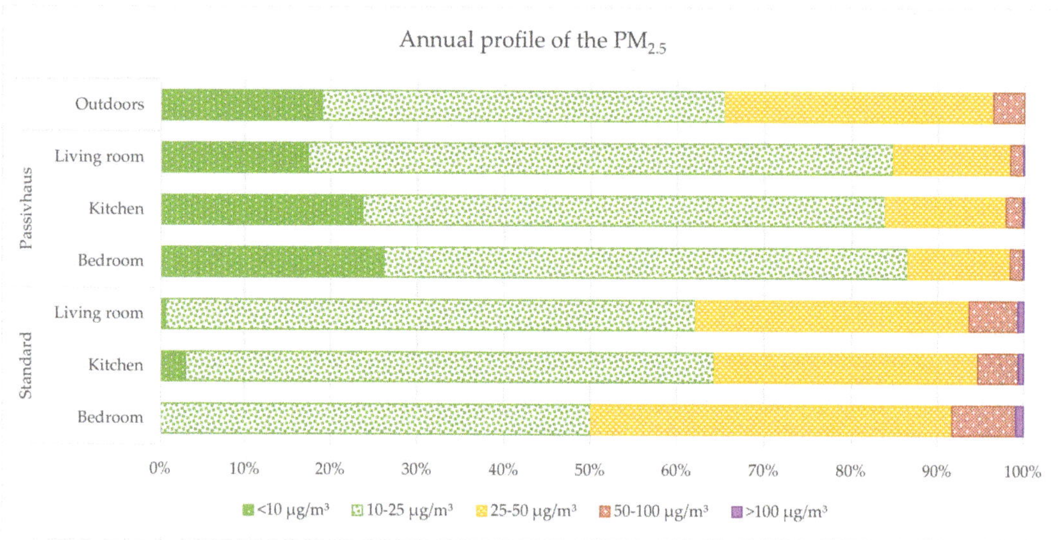

Figure 6. Annual $PM_{2.5}$ profile in the Passivhaus and standard dwellings. Source: Authors.

Table 3. Annual $PM_{2.5}$ means compared to the recommended thresholds. Source: Authors.

		Annual Mean (µg/m³)	**Standard Deviation**	**% of Time above 10 µg/m³**	**% of Time above 25 µg/m³**	**Number of Days above 25 µg/m³**
Passivhaus	Bedroom	15.8	10.9	73.8%	10.7%	40
	Living room	16.9	10.5	82.7%	12.1%	44
	Kitchen	17.2	12.0	76.3%	13.7%	50
Standard home	Bedroom	29.4	18.8	100.0%	66.0%	241
	Living room	27.8	17.1	99.4%	52.6%	173
	Kitchen	26.1	16.9	96.9%	47.4%	192
Outdoors		22.4	13.3	81.1%	35.3%	129

3.3.1. Indoor-Outdoor $PM_{2.5}$ Levels

A previous study that looked at indoor and outdoor $PM_{2.5}$ concentrations in Mexico City found that they were statically similar at $r_s = 0.56$ ($p < 0.001$), regardless of the season [64]. In this study, we found similar relationships in both dwellings. The Passivhaus indoor–outdoor correlation was significant at $r_s = 0.539$–0.587 ($p < 0.001$) and in the standard home at $r_s = 0.539$–0.611 ($p < 0.001$). Although indoor–outdoor $PM_{2.5}$ levels were significantly correlated, there were some differences between the indoor–outdoor levels measured.

$PM_{2.5}$ levels in the Passivhaus dwelling were between 5.22 µg/m^3 to 6.54 µg/m^3 below outdoor levels and those in the standard home were between 3.65 µg/m^3 and 7.04 µg/m^3 above those outdoors as shown in Table 4. Hence, the results in this study suggest that these differences could be related to building related issues or differences in the building occupants' behaviour. Outdoor $PM_{2.5}$ levels are described in Table S2.

Occupant behaviour, particularly cooking, window opening, and the use of sprays, have an important role in the $PM_{2.5}$ profiles in homes. Therefore, the impact of cooking and window opening on $PM_{2.5}$ was analysed in both homes. For instance, cooking fumes produced higher peak levels of $PM_{2.5}$ as pollution continued to accumulated (being slowly dissipated/driven outdoors). $PM_{2.5}$ levels were observed to rise in the kitchen during cooking. However, the particles travelled to the adjacent rooms, where $PM_{2.5}$ levels started rising minutes after (Figures S1 and S2).

Table 4. Monthly indoor–outdoor differences of the $PM_{2.5}$ levels. Source: Authors.

	Month	Jan	Feb	Mar	Apr	May	Jun	Jul	Aug	Sep	Oct	Nov	Dec	Annual
Standard home	Bedroom	2.42	5.4	3.2	0.4	9.7	4.6	5.8	12.9	9.7	11.9	11.2	7.1	7.0
	Kitchen	−0.92	1.2	−0.7	0.7	2.3	2.0	0.3	4.0	10.9	11.3	9.6	3.2	3.7
	Living room	1.81	1.6	5.6	−2.6	0.3	2.7	4.2	9.7	12.6	13.7	13.0	2.4	5.4
Passivhaus	Bedroom	−13.67	−9.6	−6.1	−8.8	−9.5	−7.5	−7.1	−4.0	−4.4	1.5	−1.9	−7.7	−6.5
	Kitchen	−13.49	−6.8	−4.9	−7.3	−6.2	−6.5	−5.9	−3.0	−4.4	−0.0	0.8	−4.9	−5.2
	Living room	−14.00	−7.0	−2.8	−8.8	−10.0	−5.5	−5.9	−4.0	−5.4	2.1	−0.1	−4.5	−5.5

3.4. Total Volatile Organic Compounds

As part of the study, indoor tVOC levels were measured. However, it was not possible to collect outdoor measurements, as they were not measured by the local air pollution network and the specifications of the low-cost monitors. A 7-month study found that outdoor tVOC levels in Mexico City were 1462 $\mu g/m^3$ ($\pm$763 $\mu g/m^3$) in residential neighbourhoods but could peak at up to 5364 $\mu g/m^3$ [66]. Mean indoor tVOC levels ranged between 569 $\mu g/m^3$ to 578 $\mu g/m^3$ in the Passivhaus, while in the standard home they were 587 $\mu g/m^3$ to 786 $\mu g/m^3$, as illustrated in Figure 7. Peak pollution levels were commonly observed when the occupants reported using personal cleaning products, cooking, and cleaning activities. These activities impacted the most in the early mornings, when windows usually remained closed and the ventilation rates were lower, as evidenced by the CO_2 levels. The effect of the lack of ventilation had a significant impact on the dissipating of indoor tVOC concentrations. Finally, tVOC concentrations were not directly associated with building or furnishing materials. During non-occupied periods, the levels remained relatively low (<300 $\mu g/m^3$). This could be because both dwellings are more than five years, and tVOC off-gassing is usually higher in new (<2 years) materials [67]. Monthly tVOC levels and statistical analyses can be found in Supplementary Table S3.

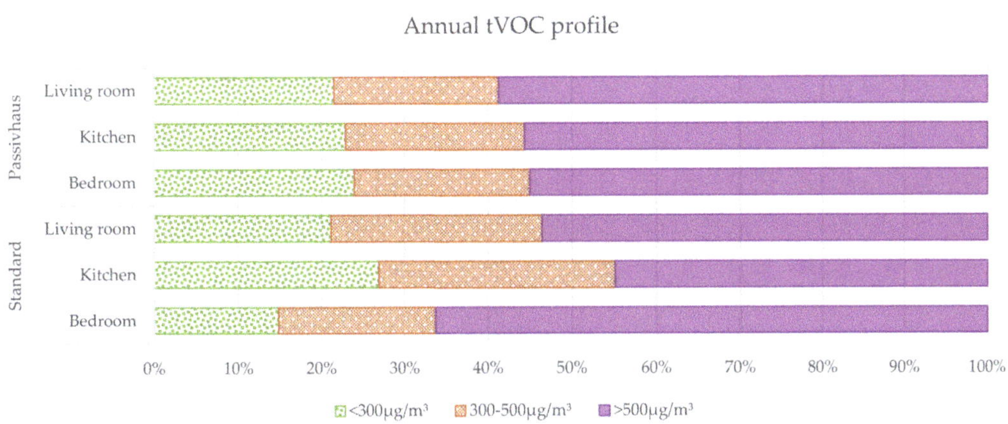

Figure 7. Annual tVOC profile in the Passivhaus and Standard dwellings. Source: Authors.

3.5. Indoor Air Quality Perception

Table 5 shows a summary of the occupants' summer IAQ perceptions. The surveys suggest that the Passivhaus fresh–stuffy scale (M = 4.67) for the summer months was rated poorly. It showed that while occupants were satisfied overall with the IAQ conditions, they did not perceive the freshness of the air as an important factor. The survey analysis suggests that occupants from the standard home had a constant dissatisfaction (M = 4.00) with the IAQ in their home, as participants perceived the air to be stale (M = 4.67), draughty (M = 5.67), and smelly (M = 5.33).

Table 5. Statistical analysis of the IAQ perceptions during summer for both homes. Source: Authors.

IAQ Perception	Home Type	Resident	Score	Mean	SD	Mean + SD	Mean - SD	Min	Max
Fresh (1)–stuffy (7) scale	Passivhaus	R1 R2 R3	4 5 5	4.7	0.6	5.2	4.1	4	5
	Standard	R1 R2 R3	3 3 3	3.0	0.0	3.0	3.0	3	3
Dry (1)–humid (7) scale	Passivhaus	R1 R2 R3	4 5 3	4.0	1.0	5.0	3.0	3	5
	Standard	R1 R2 R3	4 5 5	4.7	0.6	5.2	4.1	4	5
Still (1)–draughty (7) scale	Passivhaus	R1 R2 R3	3 4 3	3.3	0.6	3.9	2.8	3	4
	Standard	R1 R2 R3	5 6 6	4.7	0.6	6.2	5.1	5	6
Odourless (1)–smelly (7) scale	Passivhaus	R1 R2 R3	1 4 2	2.3	1.5	3.9	0.8	1	4
	Standard	R1 R2 R3	5 5 6	5.3	0.6	5.9	4.8	5	6
Satisfactory overall (1)–unsatisfactory overall (7) scale	Passivhaus	R1 R2 R3	1 1 2	1.3	0.6	1.9	0.8	1	2
	Standard	R1 R2 R3	3 5 4	7.0	1.0	5.0	3.0	3	5

The analysis of the winter IAQ perception surveys suggests that Passivhaus occupants rated the air as stale (M = 3.33). However, they stated being (M = 1.3) satisfied overall with the IAQ. Occupants of the standard home stated the air was stale (M = 4.67), draughty (M = 2.33), and smelly (M = 5.00), rating all these scales poorly. This may have led the occupants to rate very poorly the overall IAQ perception (M = 5.33), as shown in Table 6.

Passivhaus occupants reported that they did not experience condensation on windows or doors. However, they had experienced odours coming from outdoors; this may be related to the lack of filters in the inlet. Nonetheless, participants rated the odour scale on the odourless side, suggesting that the odours were not uncomfortable. Occupants of the standard home reported condensation on windows and the presence of mould in the bathroom. They also perceived smells coming from the kitchen, toilets, laundry closet, and outdoors. A possible explanation for the indoor odours could be that the windows remain closed for prolonged periods, causing the air to be stale and stuffy, as stated in the survey scale ratings.

Table 6. Statistical analysis of the IAQ perceptions during winter for both homes. Source: Authors.

IAQ Perception	Home Type	Resident	Score	Mean	SD	Mean + SD	Mean − SD	Min	Max
Fresh (1)–stuffy (7) scale	Passivhaus	R1	4	3.3	1.2	4.5	2.2	2	4
		R2	4						
		R3	2						
	Standard	R1	5	4.7	0.6	5.2	4.1	4	5
		R2	5						
		R3	4						
Dry (1)–humid (7) scale	Passivhaus	R1	3	4.0	1.0	5.0	3.0	3	5
		R2	4						
		R3	5						
	Standard	R1	3	3.3	0.6	3.9	2.8	3	4
		R2	4						
		R3	3						
Still (1)–draughty (7) scale	Passivhaus	R1	4	3.7	0.6	4.2	3.1	3	4
		R2	4						
		R3	3						
	Standard	R1	2	2.3	0.6	2.9	1.8	2	3
		R2	3						
		R3	2						
Odourless (1)–smelly (7) scale	Passivhaus	R1	1	2.7	1.5	4.2	1.1	1	4
		R2	4						
		R3	3						
	Standard	R1	5	5.0	0.0	5.0	5.0	5	5
		R2	5						
		R3	5						
Satisfactory overall (1)–unsatisfactory overall (7) scale	Passivhaus	R1	1	1.3	0.6	1.9	0.8	1	2
		R2	1						
		R3	2						
	Standard	R1	5	5.3	0.6	5.9	4.8	5	6
		R2	6						
		R3	5						

4. Discussion

This work presents long-term indoor air quality measurements conducted alongside airflow testing of the first residential Passivhaus building in Latin America. The results suggest that, in big cities in Latin America, dwellings built to the Passivhaus standard have the potential to achieve better IAQ compared to standard dwellings. This is of particular interest, as outdoor pollution in these cities usually exceeds the recommended levels of exposure [68]. Through this study, several lessons were learned that could help to develop further the Passivhaus standard in warm/temperate climates, such as the one in Mexico City.

The approach to the ventilation system may be the most important of these lessons. While the Passive House Institute would still recommend a MVHR in these climates, this study shows that hybrid ventilation may still be a viable option. However, the mechanical component of the ventilation method still needs to provide minimum airflow rates. It is recommended to use adequate filters, to ensure the best IAQ performance. It is also recommended to provide continuous, rather than intermittent, ventilation.

The levels of indoor air pollutants at the Passivhaus dwelling were lower than those in the standard home. However, pollution peaks took longer to dissipate in the Passivhaus home. This could have been related to the fact that the standard home relied on natural ventilation. Higher airflows helped to dissipate the air pollutants. Another potential explanation is related to the fact that the mechanical ventilation was not continuous (34 min on–26 min off). If a pollution event occurred during or close to when the fan was off, indoor air pollutants were not removed through ventilation. Similarly, indoor air pollutants, particularly tVOCs (Figure S3), in the standard home were higher during the night, when the windows were closed.

The $PM_{2.5}$ and tVOC decay rates were lower in the Passivhaus dwelling compared to the standard dwelling, particularly those related to fine particles after cooking. The $PM_{2.5}$ pollution decay in the Passivhaus (1.1 h^{-1}) was longer compared to the conventional home (0.24 h^{-1}) [69]. Similar to this study, a spike of $PM_{2.5}$ was measured immediately after cooking events, but levels dropped quickly and then the peak concentrations began to decay gradually. In this study, a higher stability of $PM_{2.5}$ levels across the different rooms was noted in the Passivhaus homes. This indicates the likely transport of particles from the source room to others, assisted by longer decay rates and doors opening/closing between spaces, facilitating further distribution of $PM_{2.5}$.

Filters with F7 or higher levels of filtration are designed to filter $PM_{2.5}$ and are recommended for Passivhaus. However, their use could lead to higher fan demands, noise, filter costs, maintenance, and even energy penalties. Ventilation rates and particle sedimentation primarily influence $PM_{2.5}$ decay rate, whereas tVOC may also depend on operative room temperature and relative humidity. However, proper ventilation remains the best way to control indoor pollution. In this study, it was observed that window opening behaviour was the most effective technique to control indoor pollution.

Further works should test at larger scale the indoor air quality alongside thermal comfort and energy performance in other Passivhaus dwellings in Latin America. Such a study could support the positive impact on the Sustainable Development Goals 03 (health and wellbeing), 07 (affordable and clean energy), and 09 (industry, innovation, and infrastructure) for Latin American countries.

This study suffered from some apparent limitations. First of all, this work presents the monitoring results of two homes that are different in typology. As the standard dwelling was a typical representation of the housing typologies in Mexico City, it was deemed appropriate for comparison. In addition, it was not possible to find another dwelling of a similar layout within an appropriate radius from the Passivhaus, so that the outdoor air pollution was similar between both dwellings. In addition, at the time of this research, there was no other Passivhaus dwellings in Latin America to conduct the study. Second, the use of low-cost monitors could represent a compromise in accuracy. In order to overcome this barrier, we installed three different monitors in each room, developed calibration equations, and tested the accuracy of the monitors in real-life settings, as suggested by [53,55]. Third, the long-term (one year) coverage of this study made it difficult and too onerous for the participants to keep detailed activity and occupancy diaries. Therefore, the analysis was based on a general pattern. We also considered using other low-cost sensors to monitor the door/window use, but this was not economically feasible at the time of this study. Having data on the window opening could have allowed a better data analysis, but this was not feasible in this study. Finally, difference in the monitoring technologies between the indoor and outdoor air pollution sensors could represent minimal discrepancies between the readings.

5. Conclusions

This work presented the IAQ monitoring of the first Passivhaus residential dwelling in Latin America. The measurements demonstrate that the Passivhaus CO_2 and tVOC annual average levels were 143.8 ppm and 81.47 $\mu g/m^3$ lower than the standard home. $PM_{2.5}$ levels in the Passivhaus were 11.13 $\mu g/m^3$ lower than the standard home and 5.75 $\mu g/m^3$ lower than those outdoors. While these results give insights into the trends and relative levels air pollution, some lessons were also learned for the development of the Passivhaus in Latin America. It is possible to use a hybrid ventilation strategy to provide adequate ventilation in Passivhaus dwellings. While the use of MVHR units could be dependent on outdoor weather conditions, it is still preferable to use them, particularly in cities with high outdoor pollution. The ventilation strategy, independent of the use of the MVHR unit, needs to run continuously to provide adequate airflow levels and, hence, adequate indoor air pollution removal.

While the results presented here cannot be generalised, the results suggest that Passivhaus dwellings have the potential to provide better and healthier indoor air quality in Latin America. Further large-scale studies should consider the indoor environmental conditions, energy performance, and dwelling design of Passivhaus dwellings in Latin America.

Supplementary Materials: The following are available online at https://www.mdpi.com/article/10.3390/atmos12111477/s1, Table S1. Summary of CO2 levels in both homes; Figure S1. Standard home PM2.5 profile 29–30 June 2016; Figure S2. Passivhaus home PM2.5 profile 20–21 December 2016, Table S2. Summary of PM2.5 levels in both homes; Table S3. Summary of tVOC levels in both homes; Figure S3. Hourly tVOC levels in the Passivhaus and Standard dwelling's bedrooms.

Author Contributions: Conceptualisation: T.S., F.M., G.M., A.M.-R.; Methodology: T.S., F.M., G.M., A.M.-R.; Formal analysis: A.M.-R.; Investigation: A.M.-R.; Data Curation: A.M.-R.; Writing—Original Draft: A.M.-R.; Writing—Review & Editing: T.S., F.M., G.M.; Visualisation: A.M.-R.; Supervision: T.S., F.M., G.M.; Project administration: T.S., F.M., G.M., A.M.-R.; Funding acquisition: A.M.-R. All authors have read and agreed to the published version of the manuscript.

Funding: CONACyT partially funded this research through a PhD grant. AirBoxLab (Foobot) partially funded this study, offering a discount on the monitors used in this research. The development of this article was supported by the Research England Expanding, Excellence in England (E3).

Institutional Review Board Statement: Ethical approval was sought and granted by the Glasgow School of Art Ethics Sub-committee; for further details, please refer to: https://www.gsa.ac.uk/media/497492/gsa_research_ethics_policy.pdf (accessed on 17 July 2019).

Informed Consent Statement: Informed consent was obtained from all subjects involved in the study.

Data Availability Statement: The data for this study were part of a PhD published in 2019 [55] with an embargo until March 2024. Data could be made available upon request from the corresponding author.

Acknowledgments: This work would not have been possible without the support of INHAB and the participation of the building occupants, to which we are thankful. Thanks are given to Adam Hotson, who offered useful editing and proofreading of an earlier version of this paper. The work published here was undertaken at the Mackintosh Environmental Research Unit.

Conflicts of Interest: None of the authors of this paper has a financial or personal relationship with other people or organisations that could inappropriately influence or bias the content of this article. The authors declare no conflict of interest.

References

1. Hopfe, C.J.; McLeod, R.S. *The PassivHaus Designer's Manual: A Technical Guide to Low and Zero Energy Buildings*, 1st ed.; Routledge: London, UK, 2015.
2. Sadineni, S.B.; Madala, S.; Boehm, R.F. Passive building energy savings: A review of building envelope components. *Renew. Sustain. Energy Rev.* **2011**, *15*, 3617–3631. [CrossRef]
3. Peters, T.; Halleran, A. How our homes impact our health: Using a COVID-19 informed approach to examine urban apartment housing. *Int. J. Arch. Res.* **2020**, *15*, 10–27. [CrossRef]
4. Al Khateeb, M.; Peterson, H. The impact of COVID-19 on perceptions of home and house design in Saudi Arabia. *Strat. Des. Res. J.* **2021**, *14*, 327–338. [CrossRef]
5. Passive House Institute. Passipedia. 2017. Available online: http://www.passipedia.org/ (accessed on 3 May 2021).
6. Moreno-Rangel, A. Passivhaus. *Encyclopedia* **2020**, *1*, 20–29. [CrossRef]
7. Feist, W.; Bastian, Z.; Ebel, W.; Gollwitzer, E.; Grove-Smith, J.; Kah, O.; Kaufmann, B.; Krick, B.; Pfluger, R.; Schnieders, J.; et al. *Passive House Planning Package Version 9: The Energy Balance and Design Tool for Efficent Buildings and Retrofits*, 1st ed.; Passive House Institute: Darmstadt, Germany, 2015.
8. Costanzo, V.; Carrillo Gómez, J.E.; Evola, G.; Marletta, L. Suitability of Passivhaus design for housing projects in Colombia. In *Sustainability in Energy and Buildings*; Littlewood, J., Howlett, R.J., Capozzoli, A., Jain, L.C., Eds.; Smart Innovation, Systems and Technologies; Springer: Singapore, 2020; Volume 163, pp. 97–107.

9. Valiente, E.E.; Garcia-Alvarado, R.; Celis-D'Amico, F.; Saelzer-Fuica, G. Integrated design experiences for energy-efficient housing in Chile. *Constr. Innov.* **2019**, *19*, 236–255. [CrossRef]
10. Vettorazzi, E.; Figueiredo, A.; Rebelo, F.; Vicente, R.; da Cunha, E.G. Optimization of the passive house concept for residential buildings in the South-Brazilian region. *Energy Build.* **2021**, *240*, 110871. [CrossRef]
11. Gesellschaft für Internationale Zusammenarbeit. NAMA Facility—Implementation of the New Housing NAMA Mexico. 2014. Available online: http://www.nama-facility.org/projects/mexico.html (accessed on 20 May 2009).
12. Feist, W. Technical Annex: Evaluation of Social Housing Building Types in Mexico. In *Supported NAMA for Sustainable Housing in Mexico: Mitigation Actions and Finance*; Mexico's National Housing Commission: Mexico City, Mexico, 2012.
13. Bravo-Orlandini, C.; Gómez-Soberón, J.; Valderrama-Ulloa, C.; Sanhueza-Durán, F. Energy, Economic, and Environmental Performance of a Single-Family House in Chile Built to Passivhaus Standard. *Sustainability* **2021**, *13*, 1199. [CrossRef]
14. Carrasco, J.; Kokogiannakis, G. Feasibility of PassivHaus standards and alternative passive design on climatic zones of Chile—Determination of energy requirements with dynamic simulation. *Hábitat Susten.* **2012**, *2*, 59–71.
15. Cruz, A.S.; de Carvalho, R.S.; da Cunha, E.G. Passive House Alternative Proposal for the Brazilian Bioclimatic Zone 8. *Int. J. Sustain. Dev. Plan.* **2020**, *15*, 827–833. [CrossRef]
16. Moreno-Rangel, A.; Sharpe, T.; McGill, G.; Musau, F. Thermal comfort assessment of the first residential Passivhaus in Latin America. *J. Build. Eng.* **2021**, *43*, 103081. [CrossRef]
17. Schnieders, J.; Eian, T.D.; Filippi, M.; Florez, J.; Kaufmann, B.; Pallantzas, S.; Paulsen, M.; Reyes, E.; Wassouf, M.; Yeh, S.-C. Design and realisation of the Passive House concept in different climate zones. *Energy Effic.* **2019**, *13*, 1561–1604. [CrossRef]
18. Moreno-Rangel, A.; Sharpe, T.; Musau, F.; McGill, G. Indoor Fine Particle ($PM_{2.5}$) Pollution and Occupant Perception of the Indoor Environment During Summer of the First Passivhaus Certified Dwelling in Latin America. *J. Nat. Resour. Dev.* **2018**, *8*, 78–90. [CrossRef]
19. Ridley, I.A.; Bere, J.; Clarke, A.; Schwartz, Y.; Farr, A. The side by side in use monitored performance of two passive and low carbon Welsh houses. *Energy Build.* **2014**, *82*, 13–26. [CrossRef]
20. Colclough, S.; Kinnane, O.; Hewitt, N.; Griffiths, P. Investigation of nZEB social housing built to the Passive House standard. *Energy Build.* **2018**, *179*, 344–359. [CrossRef]
21. Wang, Y.; Kuckelkorn, J.; Zhao, F.-Y.; Spliethoff, H.; Lang, W. A state of art of review on interactions between energy performance and indoor environment quality in Passive House buildings. *Renew. Sustain. Energy Rev.* **2017**, *72*, 1303–1319. [CrossRef]
22. Foster, J.; Sharpe, T.; Poston, A.; Morgan, C.; Musau, F. Scottish Passive House: Insights into Environmental Conditions in Monitored Passive Houses. *Sustainability* **2016**, *8*, 412. [CrossRef]
23. Grudzińska, M. Overheating assessment in flats with glazed balconies in warm-summer humid continental climate. *Build. Serv. Eng. Res. Technol.* **2021**, *42*, 583–602. [CrossRef]
24. Fletcher, M.; Johnston, D.; Glew, D.; Parker, J. An empirical evaluation of temporal overheating in an assisted living Passivhaus dwelling in the UK. *Build. Environ.* **2017**, *121*, 106–118. [CrossRef]
25. Finegan, E.; Kelly, G.; O'Sullivan, G. Comparative analysis of Passivhaus simulated and measured overheating frequency in a typical dwelling in Ireland. *Build. Res. Inf.* **2019**, *48*, 681–699. [CrossRef]
26. Moreno-Rangel, A.; Sharpe, T.; McGill, G.; Musau, F. Indoor Air Quality in Passivhaus Dwellings: A Literature Review. *Int. J. Environ. Res. Public Health* **2020**, *17*, 4749. [CrossRef]
27. Derbez, M.; Berthineau, B.; Cochet, V.; Lethrosne, M.; Pignon, C.; Riberon, J.; Kirchner, S. Indoor air quality and comfort in seven newly built, energy-efficient houses in France. *Build. Environ.* **2014**, *72*, 173–187. [CrossRef]
28. Feist, W.; Pfluger, R.; Hasper, W. Durability of building fabric components and ventilation systems in passive houses. *Energy Effic.* **2019**, *13*, 1543–1559. [CrossRef]
29. Wang, Z.; Xue, Q.; Ji, Y.; Yu, Z. Indoor environment quality in a low-energy residential building in winter in Harbin. *Build. Environ.* **2018**, *135*, 194–201. [CrossRef]
30. Jacobs, D.E.; Kelly, T.; Sobolewski, J. Linking Public Health, Housing, and Indoor Environmental Policy: Successes and Challenges at Local and Federal Agencies in the United States. *Environ. Heal. Perspect.* **2007**, *115*, 976–982. [CrossRef]
31. Rosseau, D.; Bowser, D.; Mattock, C. A Guide to Mechanical Equipment for Healthy Indoor Environments. 2001. Available online: https://www.cmhc-schl.gc.ca/odpub/pdf/62015.pdf (accessed on 7 November 2018).
32. American Society of Heating, Refrigerating and Air-Conditioning Engineers. *ASHRAE Standard 62.1-2007 Ventilation for Acceptable Indoor Air Quality*; American Society of Heating, Refrigerating and Air-Conditioning Engineers: Atlanta, GA, USA, 2007.
33. World Health Organization. *Air Quality Guidelines for Europe*, 2nd ed.; WHO Regional Publications: Copenhagen, Denmark, 2000.
34. World Health Organization. *WHO Guidelines for Indoor Air Quality: Selected Pollutants*, 1st ed.; World Health Organization Regional Office for Europe: Copenhagen, Denmark, 2010; Volume 9.
35. Dan, D.; Tanasa, C.; Stoian, V.; Brata, S.; Stoian, D.; Gyorgy, T.N.; Florut, S. Passive house design—An efficient solution for residential buildings in Romania. *Energy Sustain. Dev.* **2016**, *32*, 99–109. [CrossRef]
36. Fokaides, P.A.; Christoforou, E.; Ilic, M.; Papadopoulos, A. Performance of a Passive House under subtropical climatic conditions. *Energy Build.* **2016**, *133*, 14–31. [CrossRef]
37. Santin, O.G.; Grave, A.; Jiang, S.; Tweed, C.; Mohammadi, M. Monitoring the performance of a Passivhaus care home: Lessons for user-centric design. *J. Build. Eng.* **2021**, *43*, 102565. [CrossRef]

38. Kaunelienė, V.; Prasauskas, T.; Krugly, E.; Stasiulaitienė, I.; Čiužas, D.; Šeduikytė, L.; Martuzevicius, D. Indoor air quality in low energy residential buildings in Lithuania. *Build. Environ.* **2016**, *108*, 63–72. [CrossRef]
39. Less, B.; Mullen, N.; Singer, B.; Walker, I. Indoor air quality in 24 California residences designed as high-performance homes. *Sci. Technol. Built Environ.* **2015**, *21*, 14–24. [CrossRef]
40. Guillén-Lambea, S.; Soria, B.R.; Marín, J.M. Review of European ventilation strategies to meet the cooling and heating demands of nearly zero energy buildings (nZEB)/Passivhaus. Comparison with the USA. *Renew. Sustain. Energy Rev.* **2016**, *62*, 561–574. [CrossRef]
41. Langer, S.; Bekö, G.; Bloom, E.; Widheden, A.; Ekberg, L. Indoor air quality in passive and conventional new houses in Sweden. *Build. Environ.* **2015**, *93*, 92–100. [CrossRef]
42. Wallner, P.; Tappler, P.; Munoz, U.; Damberger, B.; Wanka, A.; Kundi, M.; Hutter, H.-P. Health and Wellbeing of Occupants in Highly Energy Efficient Buildings: A Field Study. *Int. J. Environ. Res. Public Health* **2017**, *14*, 314. [CrossRef]
43. Meyer, W. Impact of constructional energy-saving measures on radon levels indoors. *Indoor Air* **2019**, *29*, 680–685. [CrossRef]
44. Lim, A.-Y.; Yoon, M.; Kim, E.-H.; Kim, H.-A.; Lee, M.J.; Cheong, H.-K. Effects of mechanical ventilation on indoor air quality and occupant health status in energy-efficient homes: A longitudinal field study. *Sci. Total. Environ.* **2021**, *785*, 147324. [CrossRef]
45. Langer, S.; Ramalho, O.; Derbez, M.; Ribéron, J.; Kirchner, S.; Mandin, C. Indoor environmental quality in French dwellings and building characteristics. *Atmos. Environ.* **2016**, *128*, 82–91. [CrossRef]
46. McGill, G.; Oyedele, L.O.; Keeffe, G. Indoor air-quality investigation in code for sustainable homes and passivhaus dwellings. *World J. Sci. Technol. Sustain. Dev.* **2015**, *12*, 39–60. [CrossRef]
47. Wilson, J.; Dixon, S.L.; Jacobs, D.E.; Breysse, J.; Akoto, J.; Tohn, E.; Isaacson, M.; Evens, A.; Hernandez, Y. Watts-to-Wellbeing: Does residential energy conservation improve health? *Energy Effic.* **2013**, *7*, 151–160. [CrossRef]
48. Milner, J.; Shrubsole, C.; Das, P.; Jones, B.; Ridley, I.A.; Chalabi, Z.; Hamilton, I.; Armstrong, B.; Davies, M.; Wilkinson, P. Home energy efficiency and radon related risk of lung cancer: Modelling study. *BMJ* **2013**, *348*, f7493. [CrossRef] [PubMed]
49. McGill, G.; Sharpe, T.; Oyedele, L.; Keeffe, G.; McAllister, K. An investigation of indoor air quality in UK Passivhaus dwellings. In *Smart Energy Control Systems for Sustainable Buildings*; Smart Innovation, Systems and Technologies; 2017; Volume 67, pp. 245–268. [CrossRef]
50. Sherman, M.H.; Chan, R. *Building Airtightness: Research and Practice*; Lawrence Berkeley National Laboratory Report No. LBNL-53356; Lawrence Berkeley National Laboratory: Berkeley, CA, USA, 2004.
51. Seppänen, O.; Fisk, W.J. Association of ventilation system type with SBS symptoms in office workers. *Indoor Air* **2002**, *12*, 98–112. [CrossRef]
52. Kottek, M.; Grieser, J.; Beck, C.; Rudolf, B.; Rubel, F. World Map of the Köppen-Geiger climate classification updated. *Meteorol. Z.* **2006**, *15*, 259–263. [CrossRef]
53. Moreno-Rangel, A.; Sharpe, T.; Musau, F.; McGill, G. Field evaluation of a low-cost indoor air quality monitor to quantify exposure to pollutants in residential environments. *J. Sensors Sens. Syst.* **2018**, *7*, 373–388. [CrossRef]
54. Petersen, J.; Kristensen, J.; Elarga, H.; Andersen, R.; Midtstraum, A. Accuracy and Air Temperature Dependency of Commercial Low-Cost NDIR CO_2 Sensors: An Experimental Investigation. In Proceedings of the 4th International Conference on Building Energy & Environment, Melbourne, VIC, Australia, 5–9 February 2018; pp. 203–207.
55. Moreno-Rangel, A. Continuous IAQ Monitoring with Low-Cost Monitors: Protocol Development, Performance and Application in Residential Building. Ph.D. Thesis, The Glasgow School of Art, Glasgow, Scotland, April 2019.
56. Raw, G.J. *A Questionnaire for Studies of Sick Building Syndrome; A Report to the Royal Society of Health*; BRE Press: Watford, ND, USA, 1995.
57. European Committee for Standardization. *Indoor Environmental Input Parameters for Design and Assessment of Energy Performance of Buildings Addressing Indoor Air Quality, Thermal Environment, Lighting and Acoustics*; EN 15251:2007; European Committee for Standardization: Brussels, Belgium, 2008.
58. Chartered Institution of Building Services Engineers. *CIBSE Guide A: Environmental Design*, 7th ed.; CIBSE Publications: Norwich, UK, 2006.
59. Mendez Florian, F.; Velasco Sodi, P. *Estrategia Nacional para la Vivienda Sustentable; Componente Ambiental de la Sustentabilidad*; Fundacion IDEA: Mexico City, Mexico, 2013.
60. Wargocki, P. The Effects of Ventilation in Homes on Health. *Int. J. Vent.* **2013**, *12*, 101–118. [CrossRef]
61. Engineering ToolBox. Carbon Dioxide Concentrations in Rooms with People. 2004. Available online: https://www.engineeringtoolbox.com/pollution-concentration-rooms-d_692.html (accessed on 23 May 2018).
62. European Committee for Standardization. *Ventilation for Non-Residential Buildings—Performance Requirements for Ventilation and Room-Conditioning Systems*; EN 13779:2007; European Committee for Standardization: Brussels, Belgium, 2007.
63. Barraza-Villarreal, A.; Sunyer, J.; Cadena, L.H.; Escamilla-Nuñez, M.C.; Sienra-Monge, J.J.; Ramírez-Aguilar, M.; Cortez-Lugo, M.; Holguin, F.; Diaz-Sanchez, D.; Olin, A.C.; et al. Air Pollution, Airway Inflammation, and Lung Function in a Cohort Study of Mexico City Schoolchildren. *Environ. Health Perspect.* **2008**, *116*, 832–838. [CrossRef]
64. Holguín, F.; Téllez-Rojo, M.M.; Hernández, M.; Cortez, M.; Chow, J.C.; Watson, J.G.; Mannino, D.; Romieu, I. Air Pollution and Heart Rate Variability Among the Elderly in Mexico City. *Epidemiology* **2003**, *14*, 521–527. [CrossRef]

65. Cortez-Lugo, M.; Moreno-Macias, H.; Holguin-Molina, F.; Chow, J.C.; Watson, J.G.; Gutiérrez-Avedoy, V.; Mandujano, F.; Hernández-Ávila, M.; Romieu, I. Relationship between indoor, outdoor, and personal fine particle concentrations for individuals with COPD and predictors of indoor-outdoor ratio in Mexico City. *J. Expo. Sci. Environ. Epidemiol.* **2007**, *18*, 109–115. [CrossRef]
66. Sosa, E.R.; Bravo, A.H.; Mugica-Alvarez, V.; Sanchez, A.P.; Bueno, L.E.; Krupa, S. Levels and source apportionment of volatile organic compounds in southwestern area of Mexico City. *Environ. Pollut.* **2009**, *157*, 1038–1044. [CrossRef] [PubMed]
67. Holøs, S.B.; Yang, A.; Lind, M.; Thunshelle, K.; Schild, P.; Mysen, M. VOC emission rates in newly built and renovated buildings, and the influence of ventilation—A review and meta-analysis. *Int. J. Vent.* **2018**, *18*, 153–166. [CrossRef]
68. Bell, M.L.; Davis, D.L.; Gouveia, N.; Borja-Aburto, V.H.; Cifuentes, L.A. The avoidable health effects of air pollution in three Latin American cities: Santiago, São Paulo, and Mexico City. *Environ. Res.* **2006**, *100*, 431–440. [CrossRef] [PubMed]
69. Militello-Hourigan, R.E.; Miller, S.L. The impacts of cooking and an assessment of indoor air quality in Colorado passive and tightly constructed homes. *Build. Environ.* **2018**, *144*, 573–582. [CrossRef]

atmosphere

Article

Indoor Air Quality and Health Outcomes in Employees Working from Home during the COVID-19 Pandemic: A Pilot Study

Taehyun Roh [1], Alejandro Moreno-Rangel [2], Juha Baek [3], Alexander Obeng [4], Nishat Tasnim Hasan [1] and Genny Carrillo [4,5,*]

1 Department of Epidemiology and Biostatistics, School of Public Health, Texas A&M University, 212 Adriance Lab Road, College Station, TX 77843, USA; taehyunroh@tamu.edu (T.R.); nishat@tamu.edu (N.T.H.)
2 Lancaster Institute of Contemporary Arts, Faculty of Arts and Social Science, Lancaster University, Bailrigg, Lancaster LA1 4YW, UK; a.morenorangel@lancaster.ac.uk
3 Center for Outcomes Research, Houston Methodist, 7550 Greenbriar Drive, Houston, TX 77030, USA; jbaek@houstonmethodist.org
4 Department of Environmental and Occupational Health, School of Public Health, Texas A&M University, 212 Adriance Lab Road, College Station, TX 77843, USA; abobeng@tamu.edu
5 Program on Asthma Research and Education, Healthy South Texas, Texas A&M School of Public Health, McAllen Campus, 2102 S. McColl Road, McAllen, TX 78503, USA
* Correspondence: gcarrillo@tamu.edu

Citation: Roh, T.; Moreno-Rangel, A.; Baek, J.; Obeng, A.; Hasan, N.T.; Carrillo, G. Indoor Air Quality and Health Outcomes in Employees Working from Home during the COVID-19 Pandemic: A Pilot Study. *Atmosphere* **2021**, *12*, 1665. https://doi.org/10.3390/atmos12121665

Academic Editors: Ashok Kumar, M Amirul I Khan, Alejandro Moreno Rangel and Michał Piasecki

Received: 30 November 2021
Accepted: 9 December 2021
Published: 11 December 2021

Abstract: Indoor air quality (IAQ) has a substantial impact on public health. Since the beginning of the COVID-19 pandemic, more employees have worked remotely from home to minimize in-person contacts. This pilot study aims to measure the difference in workplace IAQ before and during the pandemic and its impact on employees' health. The levels of fine particulate matter ($PM_{2.5}$) and total volatile organic chemicals (tVOC) were measured in the employees' offices before the COVID-19 pandemic and at homes while working from home during the pandemic using Foobot air monitors. The frequencies of six sick building syndrome (SBS) symptoms were evaluated at each period of monitoring. The result showed $PM_{2.5}$ levels in households while working from home were significantly higher than in offices while working at the office for all participants ($p < 0.05$). The $PM_{2.5}$ levels in all households exceeded the health-based annual mean standard (12 $\mu g/m^3$), whereas 90% of offices were in compliance. The tVOC levels were all below the standard (500 $\mu g/m^3$). We also found a higher frequency of SBS symptoms were observed while working from home as the IAQ was worse at home. This study suggested that working from home might have a detrimental health impact due to poor IAQ and providing interventions to remote employees should be considered.

Keywords: indoor air quality; air monitor; particulate matter 2.5; COVID-19; employee health; remote work

1. Introduction

Indoor air pollution has been classified as one of the top five environmental health hazards. In the United States (US), the average person spends nearly 90% of their time indoors, where air quality is estimated two to five times worse than outdoors [1]. Indoor air quality (IAQ) is affected by outdoor factors (i.e., motor vehicle and industry), indoor activities (i.e., cooking and smoking) and building-related factors (i.e., ventilation and air conditioning systems) [2].

Outdoor chemicals, including fine particulate matter ($PM_{2.5}$), volatile organic compounds (VOCs), ozone (O_3), carbon monoxide (CO), and radon could affect IAQ. However, there are a variety of additional sources for indoor air pollution in offices and homes. In offices, most indoor pollutants are related to building materials and human activities such as carpet and other office furniture, cleaning agents, air fresheners, paints, adhesives, printers, pesticides, and biological contaminants from poor ventilation systems or water-damaged walls [3–6]. A study conducted by Serafin et al. prioritized the indoor air pollutants in office buildings and found formaldehyde, acetaldehyde, benzene, $PM_{2.5}$, and PM_{10} as priority pollutants [7]. In households, activities performed by individuals including cooking, laundry, smoking, and the use of chemicals for cleaning and hobbies increase indoor air pollution [8]. The primary indoor air pollutants include particulate matter, volatile organic compounds (VOCs), semi-volatile organic compounds (SVOCs), ozone, asbestos, tobacco smoke, nonpolar volatile organic compounds, allergens, and mold [9,10].

Modern buildings are designed to be airtight, eliminating natural ventilation as they are controlled by heating, ventilation, and air conditioning (HVAC) systems that recirculate a high percentage of the air with minimal fresh air replacement, maintaining constant IAQ across seasons [10–12]. HVAC systems have a critical role in keeping people inside buildings comfortable and healthy, and they are intended to provide an air supply to the room and have an exhaust system to remove dirty air from indoor spaces [13]. Non-residential buildings like offices usually have an mechanical ventilation for outdoor air change, with less natural ventilation or infiltration contribution, maintaining constant IAQ over seasons [14]. It is recommended to install filters (F7 grade or above) to filter fresh air to the unit to protect HVAC units and limit the ingress of outdoor particles. However, inadequate system installation and poorly maintained air ducts and filters diminish the air quality [15]. Biological particles such as bacteria, fungi, and viruses correlated with respiratory health conditions can float in the air and linger longer in poorly ventilated indoor spaces [16–18].

IAQ is a significant concern because it could adversely impact human health, comfort, well-being, and productivity [19]. Acute and chronic health effects are associated with exposure to indoor air pollutants in office environments. Sick building syndrome (SBS) is a group of acute adverse health experiences related to IAQ, including headache, eye irritation, dry cough, and itching skin for occupants of a building related to the time spent in the building [20,21]. According to a multi-country study in Europe, the most prevalence adverse health outcomes were dry eyes and headache, accounting for one-third of the office workers [22]. In the US, SBS could be responsible for an overall loss in productivity, leading to costs up to $75 billion per year [23]. Poor IAQ also increases the risk of chronic health problems including cardiovascular disease, chronic obstructive and pulmonary disease, and lung cancer [24]. Among indoor air pollutants, $PM_{2.5}$ has become a major public health hazard because it penetrates deeply into the respiratory trat, entering the circulatory system and causing oxidative stress and inflammation [25–28]. Among indoor air pollutants, $PM_{2.5}$ is a dominant indoor air pollutant causing 4000 DALYs (disability-adjusted life years) per one million population, which is 80% of the total annual burden of diseases related to indoor exposure [29].

The development of information and communication technologies have changed the work environment, increasing the adaptation of remote work in diverse occupations including managers, educators, and those working in computers, finance, and law [30,31]. In Europe, the proportion of teleworkers was less than 10% in normal times, which increased up to 31% during the COVID-19 pandemic [32]. In the US, the percentage of employees who had ever worked remotely increased from 9% in 1995 to 37% in 2015 and the average number of days working remotely per month was 2.3 [33]. The advantages of remote work include flexibility, cost and time savings on commuting, and more time with family [34,35]. In contrast, it also has negative aspects such as loss of social interaction and self-discipline and unfavorable physical conditions, leading to productivity reduction and psychological and psychological distress [36–38].

In December 2019, the COVID-19, caused by a new coronavirus, SARS-CoV-2, was first detected in Wuhan, China [39]. The World Health Organization (WHO) proclaimed the COVID-19 outbreak to be the sixth global public health emergency on 30 January 2020 [40,41]. Due to the highly contagious nature of the disease, governments decided to implement "social distancing" measures, closing businesses and enacting stay-at-home orders [42]. Some sectors of occupations such as healthcare, farm, construction, and service workers could not be carried out remotely, and therefore had higher risks of contracting COVID-19 [43]. In contrast, many employees in fields including management, education, and information technology worked remotely during 2020 and half of 2021 [31,44–46]. In the US, approximately 30% of employees changed to working from home between February and May 2020 [47]. In Canada, the percentage of remote workers increased from 13% to 39% during March 2020 [48]. In the Netherlands, 6% of workers worked from home before the pandemic, but the percentage increased to 39% during the pandemic [49]. However, the domestic spaces became offices without consideration of environmental infrastructures such as ventilation systems and subsequent indoor air quality, posing health risks to employees [50].

This study aims to evaluate the IAQ in the office before the COVID-19 pandemic and at home while working remotely from home during the pandemic and compare the health outcomes in employees between those two periods.

2. Materials and Methods

2.1. Participants and Study Design

This pilot study was conducted in McAllen, South Texas, during May–July 2019 in employees' offices before the COVID-19 pandemic and during June–September 2020 at their households while employees worked from home during the pandemic. A total of eight staff members working in the same building in an academic organization participated in the study. The study protocol was reviewed and approved by Texas A&M University's Institutional Review Boards. The methodology presented here was adapted to comply with the COVID-19 regulation from a previous study from our research group [51].

2.2. Air Quality Assessment

This study used a low-cost consumer monitor called Foobot® Air Monitor (Model# FBT0002100, AirBoxLab, San Francisco, CA, USA) to assess the IAQ in the offices and households. The performance and accuracy of the Foobot monitor were assessed and determined to be a reliable tool for measuring indoor pollution levels [52,53]. The Foobots (low-cost air monitors) were used in the offices and homes (bedroom, kitchen, and living room), where occupants stay for a longer time [54]. As suggested in previous studies, calibration equations, data quality, and data corroboration were followed by comparison [55,56]. The IAQ was measured according to the ASTM D7297-14. The Foobot monitors (air temperature (−40–125 °C), relative humidity (0–100%), $PM_{2.5}$ (0–1300 μg/m^3), and tVOC (100–1000 ppb) were installed in each office on top of a bookshelf (5–6 feet). The Foobot air monitors collected data at 5-minute intervals for two months in each office. The same procedure was done in households to avoid any accidents with children living at the house. We used hotspots in both locations to have a stable WiFi connection throughout the study periods. The data was stored automatically every five minutes in a protected online storage and were safely saved in an encrypted computer.

The outdoor temperature and $PM_{2.5}$ levels in the study area during the same periods of IAQ measurements were retrieved from the Texas Air Monitoring Information System (TAMIS), a database maintained by the Texas Commission on Environmental Quality (TCEQ). The outdoor tVOC levels were not collected because data were not available.

2.3. Health Outcomes Assessment

A brief version of the modified Office Environment Survey (OES) was implemented for all participants to assess six SBS symptoms while they were working in the office before the COVID pandemic and at home during the pandemic as well as the characteristics of residential environment and behaviors in the participants' homes [57]. The selected six SBS symptoms included in this study were: dry eyes, itchy or watery eyes, blocked or stuffy nose, dry throat, headache, and dry or irritated skin, as these were identified as more dominant and prevalent from previous studies [56–59]. The frequencies of these symptoms were assessed using a Likert scale, and scores for each symptom were assigned by the frequency of symptoms: 0 (not at all), 1 (less often), 2 (every 2–3 weeks), 3 (1–2 days each week), 4 (3–4 days each week) and 5 (every day). The surveys were conducted online via Qualtrics.

2.4. Statistical Analysis

The least-square geometric means (LSGMs) for $PM_{2.5}$ and tVOC levels were calculated from the data collected at 5-minute intervals for each monitoring period in the offices and the three locations (bedroom, kitchen, and living room) within the homes. After adjusting for temperature and relative humidity, the generalized linear model was fitted to estimate LSGMs and 95% confidence intervals (CIs) of $PM_{2.5}$ and tVOC levels and compare those levels in the offices while working at the office before the COVID-19 pandemic and at homes working from home during the pandemic in each participant and overall. The differences in levels of those pollutants among locations within the houses were assessed using Tukey's post hoc test. However, for health outcomes, statistical analyses could not be conducted for their associations with IAQ due to the small sample size. Instead, the direction of changes in IAQ and frequencies of health outcomes were manually compared between the two periods for each participant. All statistical analyses were conducted using SAS version 9.4 (SAS Institute Inc., Cary, NC, USA). A p-value less than 0.05 was considered statistically significant.

3. Results

In our study, eight female academic staff members aged 23 to 67 years old (average 36.1, standard deviation 13.1) participated. All participants lived in single-family detached houses with central air conditioning systems and electric heaters. All households had electric dryers vented outside and kitchen fans, and none of their family members smoked or worked with hazardous materials on the job. Table 1 summarizes other characteristics of the residential environment and behaviors in the participants' home. The average numbers of rooms and people living in the house were 3.3 and 3.4. Six homes had furry pets and non-carpeted floors at their homes. Seven families used electronic stoves and bathroom fans, and three households had air purifiers. Most households rarely opened windows for ventilation and only three households cleaned their floors regularly using a vacuum cleaner. Five houses used chemicals for lawn care. The averages of indoor temperature and relative humidity measured at homes during the study period were 24.6 °C (range: 23.6–26.9) and 52.8% (range: 46.3–57.5), which are within the recommended ranges of indoor temperature (23–27 °C) and relative humidity (30–60%) [60,61].

Table 1. Characteristics of residential environment and behaviors in the participants' homes.

Participants	No. of Rooms	No. of Family Members	Floor Material	Pet	Stove	Bathroom Fan	Air Purifier	Window Ventilation [1]	Vacuum Cleaning	Lawn Chemical	Temperature (°C) (SD)	Relative humidity (%) (SD)
1	5	5	Tile	Y	Electric	Y	N	1–2	N	Y	24.4 (1.9)	54.3 (3.2)
2	4	2	Hardwood	N	Electric	N	Y	1–2	N	Y	22.7 (1.5)	53.5 (3.2)
3	3	3	Tile	Y	Electric	Y	N	1–2	N	Y	24.7 (2.0)	46.3 (3.5)
4	3	5	Completely carpeted	N	Electric	Y	N	Never	Y	N	22.9 (1.4)	52.8 (3.8)
5	3	4	Hardwood	Y	Electric	Y	N	Never	N	Y	25.8 (1.2)	56.5 (6.4)
6	3	2	Tile	Y	Electric	Y	N	Never	Y	N	23.6 (0.8)	48.9 (3.3)
7	5	4	Tile	Y	Gas	Y	Y	Never	N	Y	26.9 (1.7)	57.5 (4.0)
8	0	2	Partially carpeted	Y	Electric	Y	Y	Never	Y	N	25.4 (0.7)	52.2 (1.7)

[1] Frequency per one month.

Table 2 shows the averages of $PM_{2.5}$ levels in the offices before the COVID-19 pandemic and at homes during the pandemic for each participant. The results showed that the averages of indoor $PM_{2.5}$ levels ranged from 5.6–12.2 $\mu g/m^3$ for offices and 11.2–45.7 $\mu g/m^3$ for homes in our participants. The $PM_{2.5}$ concentration levels at homes during the pandemic were significantly higher than those in the offices before the pandemic for each participant. Six homes had levels higher than the current health-based standard (12 $\mu g/m^3$) of the National Ambient Air Quality Standards (NAAQS) [62], whereas one office had $PM_{2.5}$

levels higher than this level. Only one participant had $PM_{2.5}$ levels higher than the national standard in both the office and home.

Table 2. Averages of indoor $PM_{2.5}$ levels (μg/m^3) in the offices before the COVID-19 pandemic and at homes during the pandemic (LSGMs, 95% CI).

Participants	Office	Home
1 *	8.95 (8.78–9.13)	22.5 (22.3–22.8)
2 *	4.28 (4.09–4.28)	45.7 (45.2–46.2)
3 *	8.03 (7.99–8.08)	14.8 (14.7–14.8)
4 *	7.36 (7.28–7.44)	12.2 (12.1–12.3)
5 *	9.78 (9.72–9.85)	11.2 (11.2–11.3)
6 *	7.93 (7.83–8.02)	16.8 (16.7–16.9)
7 *	12.2 (12.1–12.4)	13.3 (13.2–13.3)
8 *	5.60 (5.49–5.71)	11.5 (11.5–11.6)
Total *	8.18 (7.48–8.95)	16.3 (12.4–21.3)

* $PM_{2.5}$ level in the household was significantly higher than the office at $p < 0.05$.

Table 3 describes the mean $PM_{2.5}$ levels for different locations such as the bedroom, kitchen, and living room in each home. Bedroom $PM_{2.5}$ levels ranged from 9.95–94.51 μg/m^3 compared to 10.87–22.58 μg/m^3 for kitchens and 8.89–29.71 μg/m^3 for living rooms. In four homes (50%), the $PM_{2.5}$ levels were highest in the bedrooms compared to the kitchens and living rooms of the same home. The levels of $PM_{2.5}$ were highest in the kitchen (participants 6 and 8) and the living room (participant 5) compared to the other two locations within the same home. At homes of six participants (75%), the levels of $PM_{2.5}$ in the living room were significantly lower than in other locations.

Table 3. Averages of $PM_{2.5}$ levels (μg/m^3) at different locations in the households (LSGMs and 95% CI).

Participants	Bedroom	Kitchen	Living Room
1	80.15 (79.23–81.09) *	16.90 (16.66–17.16)	12.33 (12.23–12.44) †
2	94.51 (93.03–96.00) *	22.58 (22.21–22.96) †	29.71 (29.15–30.29)
3	17.79 (17.65–17.94) *	15.81 (15.68–15.93)	11.40 (11.33–11.47) †
4	13.04 (12.84–13.26)	13.05 (12.90–13.20)	11.37 (11.23–11.52) †
5	9.73 (9.68–9.79) †	10.87 (10.78–10.96)	12.79 (12.67–12.90) *
6	15.61 (15.37–15.85)	20.65 (20.36–20.95) *	14.30 (14.08–14.52) †
7	21.09 (20.89–21.28) *	18.39 (18.23–18.54)	10.85 (10.75–10.95) †
8	9.95 (9.78–10.13)	15.25 (15.05–15.46) *	8.89 (8.80–8.99) †

* $PM_{2.5}$ level at the location was significantly higher than other locations at $p < 0.05$. † $PM_{2.5}$ level at the location was significantly lower than other locations at $p < 0.05$.

Table 4 describes the average tVOC levels in the offices and homes for all participants. The average tVOC levels ranged from 151.65–215.08 μg/m^3 for offices and 152.87–279.86 μg/m^3 for homes. The tVOC levels were significantly higher at homes than in the offices for all participants. However, all the tVOC levels in the offices and homes were much lower than the acceptable maximum tVOC level of 500 μg/m^3 [63].

Additional analyses showed that the average tVOC levels within the house ranged from 159.4–305.2 μg/m^3 in the bedrooms, 151.1–286.1 μg/m^3 in the kitchens, and 148.9–273.8 μg/m^3 in the living rooms (Table 5). The tVOC levels at all locations within homes were much lower than the acceptable maximum level of 500 μg/m^3 [63]. In four homes (50%), the tVOC levels were highest in the bedrooms compared to the kitchens and living rooms of the same home. The tVOC levels were highest in the kitchen (participants 1, 3, and 5) and the living room (participants 2 and 7) compared to the other two locations within the same home.

Table 4. Averages of indoor tVOC levels (μg/m^3) in the offices before the COVID-19 pandemic and at homes during the pandemic (LSGMs, 95% CI).

Participants	Office	Home
1 *	166.68 (164.63–168.76)	253.48 (251.97–255.03)
2 *	172.71 (171.28–174.15)	181.27 (180.53–182.00)
3 *	168.38 (167.10–169.66)	242.89 (241.65–244.13)
4 *	173.78 (171.95–175.63)	279.86 (278.22–281.55)
5 *	215.08 (213.47–216.70)	222.05 (221.16–222.94)
6 *	164.66 (163.01–166.33)	230.00 (228.38–231.67)
7 *	151.65 (149.71–153.61)	229.11 (227.69–230.56)
8 *	168.31 (166.88–169.73)	152.87 (152.49–153.27)
Total *	175.75 (165.44–186.70)	217.49 (189.22–249.98)

* The tVOC level in the household was significantly higher than the office at $p < 0.05$.

Table 5. Averages of tVOC levels (μg/m^3) at different locations in the households (LSGMs and 95% CI).

Participants	Bedroom	Kitchen	Living Room
1	228.38 (225.02–231.78)	286.12 (280.82–291.52) *	228.40 (225.92–230.90)
2	184.97 (183.66–186.29) *	168.95 (167.70–170.20) †	178.68 (177.15–180.22) *
3	228.31 (225.34–231.32) †	264.36 (260.99–267.76) *	239.27 (236.89–241.68)
4	305.24 (300.28–310.29) *	270.70 (267.52–273.88)	273.77 (270.35–277.22)
5	226.92 (225.23–228.63) †	245.77 (243.18–248.39) *	236.35 (233.67–239.08)
6	237.75 (234.09–241.46) *	219.36 (216.24–222.54)	222.54 (222.05–229.06)
7	200.58 (198.58–202.57) †	209.91 (208.03–211.81)	223.86 (221.67–226.08) *
8	159.41 (158.17–160.68) *	151.11 (150.19–152.03)	148.89 (148.19–149.59) †

* The tVOC level at the location was significantly higher than other locations at $p < 0.05$. † The tVOC level at the location was significantly lower than other locations at $p < 0.05$.

Table 6 shows the changes in the frequency of six SBS symptoms associated with poor air quality that participants reported. Among six participants who completed the health survey at both periods, four subjects reported higher frequency of multiple symptoms while working at home than while working in the office. The $PM_{2.5}$ level while working at home during COVID-19 (greater than the standard 12 μg/m^3) was higher than at the office before the COVID-19 pandemic (less than the standard 12 μg/m^3). However, in participants 5 and 7, despite the statistically significant difference, both office and home $PM_{2.5}$ levels were lower or higher than the standard 12 μg/m^3, and the frequencies of symptoms in these participants were stable between the two different time periods.

Table 6. Frequencies of experiencing six SBS symptoms while working in the office before COVID-19 pandemic and working at home during the pandemic.

Participants	Dry Eyes		Itchy or Watery Eyes		Blocked or Stuffy Nose		Dry Throat		Headache		Dry or Irritated Skin		Number of Symptoms Changed *		
	Office	Home	Office	Home	Office	Home	Office	Home	Office	Home	Office	Home	Increased	No Change	Decreased
1	3	5	3	5	1	5	1	4	1	4	1	4	6	0	0
2	0	2	0	2	0	1	0	0	0	3	0	4	5	1	0
3	0	5	0	5	2	5	0	4	3	1	0	3	5	0	1
5	3	3	0	1	0	0	0	0	1	0	0	0	1	4	1
6	0	0	0	0	3	4	0	0	3	1	2	3	2	3	1
7	2	3	3	3	3	3	3	0	0	0	0	0	1	4	1

Each score means the frequency of symptoms: 0 (not at all), 1 (less often), 2 (every 2–3 weeks), 3 (1–2 days each week), 4 (3–4 days each week), and 5 (every day). * Change in the frequencies of the symptoms while working from home during the COVID-19 pandemic, compared to those while working in the office before the pandemic.

Table 7 displays the averages of outdoor temperatures and $PM_{2.5}$ levels in the study area before and during the COVID-19 pandemic for the same periods of office and home IAQ measurements for each participant. In all participants, outdoor air quality while working at home during the pandemic was significantly better than in the office before the pandemic. The outdoor $PM_{2.5}$ levels before the pandemic were significantly higher than the current national standard of 12 μg/m^3, whereas those during the pandemic were below the standard. The outdoor temperatures during the pandemic were lower than those before the pandemic. Study participants' homes and offices were in the same or neighboring areas, and therefore there was no difference in outdoor air conditions among the participants.

Table 7. Averages of outdoor temperature (°C) and $PM_{2.5}$ levels (μg/m^3) in the study area while working in the office before the COVID-19 pandemic and working from home during the pandemic (LSGMs and 95% CI).

Participants	Temperature (°C)		$PM_{2.5}$ Levels (μg/m^3)	
	Before COVID-19	During COVID-19	Before COVID-19	During COVID-19
1	29.9 (29.5–30.2)	29.7 (29.3–30.2)	13.9 (12.2–15.7)	8.53 (6.98–10.4) *
2	28.6 (27.9–29.3)	28.0 (27.1–28.9)	14.1 (12.5–15.9)	8.53 (6.93–10.5) *
3	30.1 (29.5–30.9)	27.9 (27.2–28.7) *	13.4 (11.7–15.4)	8.36 (6.78–10.3) *
4	30.1 (29.7–30.6)	29.7 (29.2–31.1)	13.6 (11.7–15.7)	8.49 (6.92–10.4) *
5	28.6 (27.9–29.3)	28.0 (27.2–28.8)	14.1 (12.5–15.9)	7.85 (6.54–9.43) *
6	25.1 (24.3–26.1)	25.6 (24.4–27.0)	12.1 (10.5–14.0)	7.44 (5.97–9.28) *
7	30.1 (29.7–30.5)	28.6 (28.2–29.1) *	13.4 (11.3–15.9)	10.6 (8.52–13.2) *
8	30.0 (29.2–30.9)	29.6 (29.1–30.2)	13.1 (10.1–17.1)	8.51 (6.92–10.5) *
Total	29.0 (28.8–29.3)	28.4 (28.1–28.7) *	13.2 (12.6–13.8)	8.47 (7.97–9.00) *

* The values during the COVID-19 pandemic were significantly lower than the office at $p < 0.05$.

4. Discussion

The advent of COVID-19 caused the shift of working pattern to work from home remotely for many employees. However, homes may not be a good working environment, compared to conventional office settings with better air conditioning and ventilation systems [4]. In addition, activities performed by individuals at homes may increase indoor air pollution, contributing to more negative health issues [8]. Therefore, in this pilot study, IAQ in the offices before the COVID-19 pandemic and at homes during the pandemic and employees' health status in both periods were compared to assess the impact of working from home on employees' health during the pandemic. Our study found that the IAQ in households during the pandemic was worse than that in the office before the pandemic in all participants, and participants experienced higher frequency of SBS symptoms while working from home. Specifically, home IAQ was worse than the outdoor air quality, and the $PM_{2.5}$ levels in all households while working from home were greater than the health-based standard 12 μg/m^3.

The interest in studying the impact of COVID-19 in different settings has led to higher scrutiny of the IAQ at homes during the lockdown. A recent study conducted in Northern Italy estimated the average indoor $PM_{2.5}$ levels ranged from 8.6 to 18.7 μg/m^3, which were higher than the outdoor $PM_{2.5}$ levels (7.4–15.4 μg/m^3) for a two-week study period in summer during the lockdown [4]. In a study conducted in Norway, the IAQ in home offices were evaluated for up to two weeks, and levels of CO_2 and other pollutants higher than health-based standards were detected [50]. Our findings were consistent with previous studies to investigate the IAQ at homes during the COVID-19 pandemic. However, previous studies only focused on home IAQ during the pandemic without comparing with IAQ in the office before the pandemic and the IAQ was measured for shorter time periods (2 weeks) than our study (2 months), and the health impact was not evaluated directly from the participants.

One of the strengths of our study is that evaluating IAQ in the office before the pandemic and that at home during the pandemic in the same individuals in the same season enabled us to compare personal exposure to air pollutants. In addition, their health status during those two different periods was directly assessed in each individual to investigate the negative health impact of the COVID-19 pandemic. Another strength of this study is the utilization of a low-cost Foobot air monitor, for which reliability and accuracy in collecting temporal and spatial IAQ data were validated in previous studies [51–53]. This monitor provides real-time data and was helpful to monitor multiple locations at home simultaneously, allowing longitudinal monitoring for months in each period. In addition, the user-friendly interface requiring low maintenance and power consumption allows participants to install it quickly without a researcher's visit to their homes when social distancing was in place.

There are several limitations to our study. First, due to the small sample size, we could not conduct a statistical analysis to investigate the comprehensive association between IAQ and health outcomes, adjust for characteristics of residential environments and behavioral factors, and differentiate the influences of multiple factors on health complaints. Although the changes of frequencies of health outcomes were in the same direction and degree of changes of $PM_{2.5}$, larger sample sizes should be considered to perform statistical analyses in future studies. However, the IAQ was measured at 5-minute intervals for 2 months at each location before and during the pandemic, and there were enough numbers of measurements for statistical analyses, demonstrating a significantly worse air quality at homes of all individual subjects during the pandemic, regardless of home environments. Second, the Foobot air monitor did not measure the outdoor air pollutants simultaneously because this monitor is not suitable for outdoor measurements. However, we collected the daily outdoor temperature and $PM_{2.5}$ data in our study area from TCEQ during the study periods. We found the outdoor $PM_{2.5}$ levels were significantly lower while working from home during the pandemic, which is consistent with other studies showing the reduction of ambient air pollution globally during the pandemic [64]. This indicates that the outdoor $PM_{2.5}$ levels did not confound the exacerbation of symptoms caused by home IAQ. Third, IAQ measurements were not conducted during the whole year and seasonal and temporal changes could not be addressed. In South Texas, the $PM_{2.5}$ levels were highest in summer, due to the hot and humid climate, and lowest in winter, and residents may experience more symptoms in summer and less in winter [65]. However, the seasonal difference could be excluded by assessing and comparing IAQ and health complaints in the same season. Fourth, the health outcome was assessed by self-report surveys, leading to recall biases. Finally, the effects of other behavioral factors could affect our findings. For example, some symptoms such as headache or dry eyes could be related to the increased screen time from telework [66], and other studies proposed that increased sedentary behaviors and reduced physical activity may increase the susceptibility to adverse health outcomes [46,67].

Despite these limitations, IAQ and health outcomes were measured in the office and household of the same participants, providing a unique opportunity to gather some limited but essential information, allowing the comparison of two different work environments. Especially, our findings provided us with information on whether employers need to provide a healthy place at home for a remote worker and such intervention will be possible with reasonable costs to protect and improve the health of all employees. Further large-scale studies should be conducted by addressing the limitations discussed earlier.

5. Conclusions

This pilot study assessed workplace IAQ and SBS symptoms before and during the COVID-19 pandemic in academic administrative staff members whose workplace changed from office to home due to the pandemic. Low-cost sensors were found suitable for in situ and continuous IAQ monitoring due to their simplicity, speed, and data accessibility. This study found that working from home may cause greater health issues for employees due to poor home IAQ, emphasizing the importance of the interventions to improve the home IAQ. One of the recommendations to enhance IAQ at homes can be achieved through behavioral changes such as opening windows and doors unless the outdoor air quality is harmful. Another approach is to provide remote workers with portable air purifiers with HEPA filters, particularly in locations where appropriate ventilation is difficult to attain. Lastly, integrating these strategies with smart building technologies would maximize the health and wellness of building occupants.

Author Contributions: Study design and conceptualization, G.C.; data analysis and interpretation, T.R., A.M.-R., A.O., and J.B.; writing—original draft preparation, T.R., A.O., J.B., N.T.H., and G.C.; writing–review and editing, A.M.-R., J.B., T.R., N.T.H., and G.C.; project administration and funding acquisition, G.C. All authors have read and agreed to the published version of the manuscript.

Funding: This research was funded by Research England's Expanding Excellence in England (E3) Fund, the National Institute of Environmental Health Sciences (P30 ES029067), and the State of Texas's legislative action to establish and support the Healthy South Texas Initiative. Funds were administered through Texas A&M University Health Science Center (grant number 23-183000).

Institutional Review Board Statement: The study was conducted according to the guidelines of the Declaration of Helsinki, and approved by the Institutional Review Board of Texas A&M University's Institutional Review Boards reviewed and approved the study protocol.

Informed Consent Statement: Informed consent was obtained from all subjects involved in the study.

Data Availability Statement: The data used to support the findings of this study are available from the corresponding author upon request.

Acknowledgments: The authors thank Lucy Conner for coordinating the fieldwork. AirBoxLab (Foobot) partially funded this study by offering a discount on the air monitors used in this research.

Conflicts of Interest: The authors declare no conflict of interest.

References

1. US EPA. *Introduction to Indoor Air Quality*; United States Environmental Protection Agency: Washington, DC, USA, 2021.
2. Cincinelli, A.; Martellini, T. Indoor air quality and health. *Int. J. Environ. Res.* **2017**, *14*, 1286. [CrossRef]
3. US EPA. A Guide to Indoor Air Quality. 2021. Available online: https://www.epa.gov/indoor-air-quality-iaq/inside-story-guide-indoor-air-quality (accessed on 27 July 2021).
4. Pietrogrande, M.C.; Casari, L.; Demaria, G.; Russo, M. Indoor air quality in domestic environments during periods close to Italian COVID-19 lockdown. *Int. J. Environ. Res. Public Health* **2021**, *18*, 4060. [CrossRef] [PubMed]
5. Campagnolo, D.; Saraga, D.E.; Cattaneo, A.; Spinazze, A.; Mandin, C.; Mabilia, R.; Perreca, E.; Sakellaris, I.; Canha, N.; Mihucz, V.G.; et al. VOCs and aldehydes source identification in European office buildings-The OFFICAIR study. *Build. Environ.* **2017**, *115*, 18–24. [CrossRef]
6. Spinazzè, A.; Campagnolo, D.; Cattaneo, A.; Urso, P.; Sakellaris, I.A.; Saraga, D.E.; Mandin, C.; Canha, N.; Mabilia, R.; Perreca, E.; et al. Indoor gaseous air pollutants determinants in office buildings—The OFFICAIR project. *Indoor Air* **2020**, *30*, 76–87. [CrossRef]
7. Sérafin, G.; Blondeau, P.; Mandin, C. Indoor air pollutant health prioritization in office buildings. *Indoor Air* **2021**, *31*, 646–659. [CrossRef]
8. He, C.; Morawska, L.; Taplin, L. Particle emission characteristics of office printers. *Environ. Sci. Technol.* **2007**, *41*, 6039–6045. [CrossRef]
9. Destaillats, H.; Maddalena, R.L.; Singer, B.C.; Hodgson, A.T.; McKone, T. Indoor pollutants emitted by office equipment: A review of reported data and information needs. *Atmos. Environ.* **2008**, *42*, 1371–1388. [CrossRef]
10. Weschler, C.J. Changes in indoor pollutants since the 1950s. *Atmos. Environ.* **2009**, *43*, 153–169. [CrossRef]
11. Nag, P.K. Sick Building Syndrome and Other Building-Related Illnesses. In *Office Building*; Springer: Singapore, 2019; pp. 53–103.
12. Mandin, C.; Trantallidi, M.; Cattaneo, A.; Canha, N.; Mihucz, V.G.; Szigeti, T.; Mabilia, R.; Perreca, E.; Spinazzè, A.; Fossati, S.; et al. Assessment of indoor air quality in office buildings across Europe–The OFFICAIR study. *Sci. Total Environ.* **2017**, *579*, 169–178. [CrossRef]
13. Vesitara, R.A.K.; Surahman, U. Sick building syndrome: Assessment of school building air quality. *J. Phys. Conf. Ser.* **2019**, *1375*, 012087. [CrossRef]
14. Rackes, A.; Waring, M. Do time-averaged, whole-building, effective volatile organic compound (VOC) emissions depend on the air exchange rate? A statistical analysis of trends for 46 VOC s in US offices. *Indoor Air* **2016**, *26*, 642–659. [CrossRef] [PubMed]
15. Balvers, J.; Bogers, R.; Jongeneel, R.; van Kamp, I.; Boerstra, A.; van Dijken, F. Mechanical ventilation in recently built Dutch homes: Technical shortcomings, possibilities for improvement, perceived indoor environment and health effects. *Archit. Sci. Rev.* **2012**, *55*, 151. [CrossRef]
16. D'Antonio, P. Combatting IAQ and health concerns: There are many ways to improve indoor air quality in buildings and to address COVID-19 fears. *Consult. Specif. Eng.* **2021**, *58*, 14–19.
17. Bernstein, J.A.; Alexis, N.; Bacchus, H.; Bernstein, I.L.; Fritz, P.; Horner, E.; Li, N.; Mason, S.; Nel, A.; Oullette, J.; et al. The health effects of nonindustrial indoor air pollution. *J. Allergy Clin. Immunol.* **2008**, *121*, 585–591. [CrossRef]
18. Svendsen, E.R.; Gonzales, M.; Commodore, A. The role of the indoor environment: Residential determinants of allergy, asthma and pulmonary function in children from a US-Mexico border community. *Sci. Total. Environ.* **2018**, *616*, 1513–1523. [CrossRef] [PubMed]

19. Holgate, S.; Grigg, J.; Agius, R.; Ashton, J.R.; Cullinan, P.; Exley, K.; Fishwick, D.; Fuller, G.; Gokani, N.; Griffiths, C.; et al. *Every Breath We Take: The Lifelong Impact of Air Pollution, Report of a Working Party*; Royal College of Physicians: London, UK, 2016.
20. Joshi, S.M. The sick building syndrome. *Indian J. Occup. Environ. Med.* **2008**, *12*, 61–64. [CrossRef]
21. Wolkoff, P.; Azuma, K.; Carrer, P. Health, work performance, and risk of infection in office-like environments: The role of indoor temperature, air humidity, and ventilation. *Int. J. Hyg. Environ. Health* **2021**, *233*, 113709. [CrossRef]
22. Bluyssen, P.M.; Roda, C.; Mandin, C.; Fossati, S.; Carrer, P.; De Kluizenaar, Y.; Mihucz, V.G.; de Oliveira Fernandes, E.; Bartzis, J. Self-reported health and comfort in 'modern' office buildings: First results from the European OFFICAIR study. *Indoor Air* **2016**, *26*, 298–317. [CrossRef] [PubMed]
23. Pitarma, R.; Marques, G.; Ferreira, B.R. Monitoring indoor air quality for enhanced occupational health. *J. Med. Syst.* **2017**, *41*, 1–8. [CrossRef] [PubMed]
24. Carrer, P.; Wolkoff, P. Assessment of indoor air quality problems in office-like environments: Role of occupational health services. *Int. J. Environ. Res. Public Health* **2018**, *15*, 741. [CrossRef]
25. Feng, S.; Gao, D.; Liao, F.; Zhou, F.; Wang, X. The health effects of ambient $PM_{2.5}$ and potential mechanisms. *Ecotoxicol. Environ. Saf.* **2016**, *128*, 67–74. [CrossRef]
26. Chen, H.; Burnett, R.T.; Kwong, J.C.; Villeneuve, P.J.; Goldberg, M.S.; Brook, R.D.; van Donkelaar, A.; Jerrett, M.; Martin, R.V.; Brook, J.R.; et al. Risk of incident diabetes in relation to long-term exposure to fine particulate matter in Ontario, Canada. *Environ. Health Perspect.* **2013**, *121*, 804–810. [CrossRef] [PubMed]
27. Fleischer, N.L.; Merialdi, M.; van Donkelaar, A.; Vadillo-Ortega, F.; Martin, R.V.; Betran, A.P.; Souza, J.P.; O'Neill, M.S. Outdoor air pollution, preterm birth, and low birth weight: Analysis of the world health organization global survey on maternal and perinatal health. *Environ. Health Perspect.* **2014**, *122*, 425–430. [CrossRef] [PubMed]
28. Wolkoff, P. Indoor air pollutants in office environments: Assessment of comfort, health, and performance. *Int. J. Hyg. Environ. Health* **2013**, *216*, 371–394. [CrossRef]
29. Asikainen, A.; Carrer, P.; Kephalopoulos, S.; de Oliveira Fernandes, E.; Wargocki, P.; Hänninen, O. Reducing burden of disease from residential indoor air exposures in Europe (HEALTHVENT project). *Environ. Health* **2016**, *15*, 61–72. [CrossRef]
30. Vilhelmson, B.; Thulin, E. Who and where are the flexible workers? Exploring the current diffusion of telework in Sweden. *New Technol. Work. Employ* **2016**, *31*, 77–96. [CrossRef]
31. Dingel, J.I.; Neiman, B. How many jobs can be done at home? *J. Public Econ.* **2020**, *189*, 104235. [CrossRef]
32. Boeri, T.; Caiumi, A.; Paccagnella, M. Mitigating the work-safety trade-off. *Covid Econ.* **2020**, *2*, 60–66.
33. Jones, J.M. In US, Telecommuting for Work Climbs to 37%. Gallup News. 2015. Available online: https://news.gallup.com/poll/184649/telecommuting-work-climbs.aspx (accessed on 5 December 2021).
34. Rudolph, C.W.; Baltes, B.B. Age and health jointly moderate the influence of flexible work arrangements on work engagement: Evidence from two empirical studies. *J. Occup. Health Psychol.* **2017**, *22*, 40. [CrossRef] [PubMed]
35. Conradie, W.J.; De Klerk, J.J. To flex or not to flex? Flexible work arrangements amongst software developers in an emerging economy. *SA J. Hum. Resour. Manag.* **2019**, *17*, 1–12. [CrossRef]
36. Okuyan, C.B.; Begen, M.A. Working from home during the COVID-19 pandemic, its effects on health, and recommendations: The pandemic and beyond. *Perspect. Psychiatr. Care* **2021**. Available online: https://onlinelibrary.wiley.com/doi/full/10.1111/ppc.12847 (accessed on 8 December 2021).
37. Reznik, J.; Hungerford, C.; Kornhaber, R.; Cleary, M. Home-based work and ergonomics: Physical and psychosocial considerations. *Issues Ment. Health Nurs.* **2021**. [CrossRef]
38. Wang, B.; Liu, Y.; Qian, J.; Parker, S.K. Achieving effective remote working during the COVID-19 pandemic: A work design perspective. *Appl. Psychol.* **2021**, *70*, 16–59. [CrossRef]
39. Hu, D.S.; Azhar, E.I.; Madani, T.A.; Ntoumi, F.; Kock, R.; Dar, O.; Ippolito, G.; Mchogh, T.D.; Memish, Z.; Drosten, C.; et al. The continuing 2019-nCoV epidemic threat of novel coronaviruses to global health—The latest 2019 novel coronavirus outbreak in Wuhan, China. *Int. J. Infect. Dis.* **2020**, *91*, 264–266. [CrossRef] [PubMed]
40. US CDC. Laboratory-Confirmed COVID-19- Associated Hospitalizations. 2020. Available online: https://gis.cdc.gov/grasp/COVIDNet/COVID19_3.html (accessed on 27 July 2021).
41. Thompson, R. Pandemic potential of 2019-nCoV. *Lancet Infect Dis.* **2020**, *20*, 280. [CrossRef]
42. Koren, M.; Pető, R. Business disruptions from social distancing. *PLoS ONE* **2020**, *15*, e0239113. [CrossRef] [PubMed]
43. Mongey, S.; Pilossoph, L.; Weinberg, A. Which workers bear the burden of social distancing? *J. Econ. Inequal.* **2021**, *19*, 509–526. [CrossRef]
44. U.S. Bureau of Labor Statistics. Ability to Work from Home: Evidence from Two Surveys and Implications for the Labor Market in the COVID-19 Pandemic. 2020. Available online: https://www.bls.gov/opub/mlr/2020/article/ability-to-work-from-home.htm. (accessed on 20 November 2021).
45. Barrot, J.N.; Grassi, B.; Sauvagnat, J. Sectoral effects of social distancing. *AEA Pap. Proc.* **2021**, *111*, 277–281. [CrossRef]
46. Koohsari, M.J.; Nakaya, T.; Shibata, A.; Ishii, K.; Oka, K. Working from home after the COVID-19 pandemic: Do company employees sit more and move less? *Sustainability* **2021**, *13*, 939. [CrossRef]
47. Brynjolfsson, E.; Horton, J.; Ozimek, A.; Rock, D.; Sharma, G.; Tuye, H.Y. *COVID-19 and Remote Work: An Early Look at US Data*; National Bureau of Economic Research: Cambridge, MA, USA, 2020.

48. Deng, Z.; Morissette, R.; Messacar, D. Running the Economy Remotely: Potential for Working from Home during and after COVID-19. Statistics Canada Catalogue. 2021. Available online: https://www150.statcan.gc.ca/n1/pub/45-28-0001/2020001/article/00026-eng.htm (accessed on 5 December 2021).
49. De Haas, M.; Faber, R.; Hamersma, M. How COVID-19 and the Dutch intelligent lockdown change activities, work and travel behaviour: Evidence from longitudinal data in the Netherlands. *Transp. Res. Interdiscip. Perspect.* **2020**, *6*, 100150. [CrossRef]
50. Alonso, M.J.; Jørgensen, R.B.; Mathisen, H.M. Short term measurements of indoor air quality when using the home office in Norway. *E3S Web Conf.* **2021**, *246*, 01002. [CrossRef]
51. Moreno-Rangel, A.; Baek, J.; Roh, T.; Xu, X.; Carrillo, G. Assessing impact of household intervention on indoor air quality and health of children with asthma in the US-Mexico border: A pilot study. *J. Environ. Public Health* **2020**, *2020*, 6042146. [CrossRef] [PubMed]
52. Sousan, S.; Koehler, K.; Hallett, L.; Peters, T.M. Evaluation of consumer monitors to measure particulate matter. *J. Aerosol Sci.* **2017**, *107*, 123–133. [CrossRef]
53. Moreno-Rangel, A.; Sharpe, T.; Musau, F.; McGill, G. Field evaluation of a low-cost indoor air quality monitor to quantify exposure to pollutants in residential environments. *J. Sens. Sens. Syst.* **2018**, *7*, 373–388. [CrossRef]
54. Spinazzè, A.; Borghi, F.; Rovelli, S.; Mihucz, V.G.; Bergmans, B.; Cattaneo, A.; Cavallo, D.M. Combined and Modular Approaches for Multicomponent Monitoring of Indoor air Pollutants. Available online: https://www.tandfonline.com/doi/full/10.1080/05704928.2021.1995405 (accessed on 8 December 2021).
55. Moreno-Rangel, A. *Continuous IAQ Monitoring with Low-Cost Monitors: Protocol Development, Performance and Application in Residential Buildings*; The Glasgow School of Art: Glasgow, UK, 2019.
56. Moreno-Rangel, A.; Sharpe, T.; Musau, F.; McGill, G. Indoor fine particle ($PM_{2.5}$) pollution and occupant perception of the indoor environment during summer of the first Passivhaus certified dwelling in Latin America. *J. Nat. Resour. Dev.* **2018**, *8*, 78–90. [CrossRef]
57. Whitehead, C.; Robertson, A.; Burge, S.; Kely, C.; Leinster, P. *A Questionnaire for Studies of Sick Building Syndrome: A Report to The Royal Society of Health Advisory Group on Sick Building Syndrome*; Building Research Establishment Report: Watford, UK, 1995.
58. Berglund, B.; Brunekreef, B.; Knöppe, H.; Lindvall, T.; Maroni, M.; Mølhave, L.; Skov, P. *Effects of Indoor Air Pollution on Human Health. Report No. 10. European Concerted Action: Indoor Air Quality and Its Impact on Man*; Eauropean Commission Report: Luxembourg, 1991.
59. Berglund, B.; Bluyssen, P.; Clausen, G.; Garriga-Trillo, A.; Gunnarsen, L.; Knöppel, H.; Lindvall, T.; MaclEOD, P.; Mølhave, L.; Winneke, G. *Sensory Evaluation of Indoor Air Quality. Report No. 20. European Collaborative Action: Indoor Air Quality and Its Impact on Man*; European Commission Report: Luxembourg, 1999.
60. ANSI/ASHRAE. *Standard 55-2013: Thermal Environmental Conditions for Human Occupancy*; National Standards Institute/American Society of Heating, Refrigerating, and Air-Conditioning Engineers: Atlanta, GA, USA, 2013.
61. US EPA. *Indoor Air Qqulity Tools for Schools Action Kit, EPA 402/K-07/008*; United States Environmental Protection Agency: Washington, DC, USA, 2009.
62. US EPA. NAAQS Table. 2021. Available online: https://www.epa.gov/criteria-air-pollutants/naaqs-table (accessed on 12 October 2021).
63. US GBC. LEED v4.1: Indoor Environmental Quality Performance. US Green Building Council: Washington, DC, USA, 2021. Available online: https://www.usgbc.org/credits/existing-buildings-schools-existing-buildings-retail-existing-buildings-data-centers-5 (accessed on 12 October 2021).
64. Venter, Z.S.; Aunan, K.; Chowdhury, S.; Lelieveld, J. Air pollution declines during COVID-19 lockdowns mitigate the global health burden. *Environ. Res.* **2021**, *192*, 110403. [CrossRef] [PubMed]
65. Ghahremanloo, M.; Choi, Y.; Sayeed, A.; Salman, A.K.; Pan, S.; Amani, M. Estimating daily high-resolution $PM_{2.5}$ concentrations over Texas: Machine Learning approach. *Atmos. Environ.* **2021**, *247*, 118209. [CrossRef]
66. Xiao, Y.; Becerik-Gerber, B.; Lucas, G.; Roll, S.C. Impacts of working from home during COVID-19 pandemic on physical and mental well-being of office workstation users. *J. Occup. Environ. Med.* **2021**, *63*, 181–190. [CrossRef]
67. Ferrante, G.; Mollicone, D.; Cazzato, S.; Lombardi, E.; Pifferi, M.; Turchetta, A.; Tancredi, G.; La Grutta, S. COVID-19 pandemic and reduced physical activity: Is there an impact on healthy and asthmatic children? *Front. Pediatr.* **2021**, *9*, 695703. [CrossRef]

buildings

Article

A Study on the Measurement of Unregulated Pollutants in Korean Residential Environments

Hyuntae Kim [1,*], Taewoo Kim [2] and Sihwan Lee [3]

1 Department of Architectural Design and Engineering, Yamaguchi University, 2-16-1 Tokiwa-dai, Ube 755-8611, Japan
2 EBS (Environmental Building Safety) E&C, 257-18 Deahyeon-dong, Buk-gu, Daegu Metropolitan 41569, Korea; kimsiyul0125@gmail.com
3 Department of Architecture, Shinshu University, 4-17-1 Wakasato, Nagano 380-8553, Japan; shany@shinshu-u.ac.jp
* Correspondence: hyuntae@yamaguchi-u.ac.jp

Abstract: This study investigated the pollution caused by unregulated chemical substances in Korean residential environments. A TA tube was used for indoor air collection, and Gas Chromatography–Mass Spectrometry was used for the analysis of chemical substances. According to the results of this study, 13 substances out of the 16 analyzed chemicals were detected and, among them, the concentrations of phenol, α-pinene, and limonene within the indoor air were high. The average concentration of phenol was 32.7 μg/m^3. α-pinene and limonene were detected, of which the highest concentrations were as 598.2 μg/m^3 and 652.5 μg/m^3, respectively. The maximum concentrations of these three substances exceeded the levels of the lowest concentration of interest. Notably, α-pinene and limonene were released from the wood itself. Wood has been widely used indoors as a natural building material and as furniture. Therefore, it was considered that this was the reason for the high the concentrations of the two substances in indoor air. However, we do not argue that the usage of wood should be reduced because of the results obtained in this study. Instead, we suggest that it is important to reduce the emissions of α-pinene and limonene through the processing of the wood, extending its drying period, and determining the most appropriate time of use.

Keywords: sick house syndrome; indoor air quality; volatile organic compounds; pollutants; chemical substances

Citation: Kim, H.; Kim, T.; Lee, S. A Study on the Measurement of Unregulated Pollutants in Korean Residential Environments. *Buildings* **2022**, *12*, 243. https://doi.org/10.3390/buildings12020243

Academic Editors: Ashok Kumar, M Amirul I Khan, Alejandro Moreno Rangel and Michał Piasecki

Received: 28 January 2022
Accepted: 16 February 2022
Published: 19 February 2022

1. Introduction

In Korea, sick house syndrome has been a significant issue since the 1990s owing to the chemical contamination of indoor air [1–3]. Modern-day people spend more than 90% of their time indoors, and indoor air quality can affect their health, comfort, and intellectual productivity [4–6]. Volatile organic compounds (VOCs) such as formaldehyde, benzene, and toluene are representative chemicals that contaminate indoor air [7–10]. Hazardous chemicals in the living environment are emitted from interior finishes, such as wallpaper, flooring, and paint, and household items, such as televisions, sofas, and closets [11–13]. In addition, indoor heating appliances and smoking by occupants can further deteriorate the indoor air quality [14–16]. As the social interest in indoor pollutants has increased, in 2003, the Ministry of Environment of Korea implemented the indoor air quality management act for new apartment complexes and, in 2005, the guidelines for indoor air quality for new apartment complexes were published [17,18]. Furthermore, the presence of a mechanical ventilation system was mandated to ensure indoor ventilation. In the case of formaldehyde, the Healthy Building Mark (HB Mark) is displayed according to the amount of emission to empower consumers or construction workers to select low-emission building materials [19]. In December 2010, the Ministry of Land, Infrastructure and Transport in Korea (2010) announced, and has since enforced, construction standards for clean and healthy houses [20]. The aim of this policy was to solve sick house syndrome. However, despite the establishment of guidelines for improving indoor air quality and new revisions of construction standards, residents have recently complained about indoor air quality. Residents are concerned about the contamination of indoor air by unregulated chemicals as the use of alternative chemicals and new building materials increases [21,22].

Therefore, this study measured the concentrations of unregulated pollutant chemicals in Korean houses to analyze new indoor pollutants that could cause sick house syndrome.

2. Method

2.1. Houses to Be Measured and Air Collection

Table 1 presents an overview of the houses to be measured. Table 2 lists the finishing materials and singularities in the houses. In this study, eleven houses were measured: seven apartment houses in Daegu, three houses for apartments in Busan, and one apartment in Andong City. The targeted houses were evaluated for indoor air quality at the request of the residents and construction companies. In Korea, for apartment houses with more than 100 households, it is required to make the results of the indoor air quality measurements known, and the construction method incorporating the HB Mark is applied only to apartment houses with more than 500 households. The A to G houses measured in Daegu are houses that are not regulated by the Korean government for the improvement of indoor air quality (non-regulated house: Non-RH). However, the four houses measured in both Busan and Andong were built using a construction method that included the indoor air quality improvement method proposed by the Korean government (regulated house: RH). In accordance with the official experimental method promulgated by the South Korean Ministry of Environment (2003), the indoor air quality for each house was measured [17]. Before collecting indoor air, all doors and windows contacted with the outside air were opened. In addition, all internal doors and furniture doors were opened, and the house was left to ventilate for 30 min. Thereafter, all the windows and doors connected to the outside were closed, while the furniture doors and the lower kitchen sink cupboards were left open. The house was left in this state for 5 h. During this 5 h period in which the house was sealed, indoor air was sampled for 30 min under this condition. The air-sampling pump used was a SIBATA (Japan) MP-Σ30H. The VOCs were sampled using a Tenax TA tube. The indoor air sampling was performed at the center of the room, 1.2 m from the floor. A travel blank (TB) was used to confirm the contamination of the sampler.

Table 1. The overview of the houses.

<table>
<tr><th>City</th><th>Sample Name</th><th>Floor Area (m^2)</th><th>Measuring Position</th><th>Ventilation</th><th>Completion Date</th><th>Measurement Period</th></tr>
<tr><td rowspan="7">Daegu (Non-RH)</td><td>A</td><td>22.3</td><td rowspan="7">Living room</td><td rowspan="11">On</td><td rowspan="3">15 April 2019</td><td rowspan="11">From 10 to 20 October 2020</td></tr>
<tr><td>B</td><td>20.3</td></tr>
<tr><td>C</td><td>39.0</td></tr>
<tr><td>D</td><td>32.6</td><td rowspan="4">13 May 2019</td></tr>
<tr><td>E</td><td>36.0</td></tr>
<tr><td>F</td><td>38.3</td></tr>
<tr><td>G</td><td>38.3</td></tr>
<tr><td rowspan="3">Pusan (RH)</td><td>A</td><td>65.5</td><td>Room</td><td rowspan="3">8 August 2018</td></tr>
<tr><td>B</td><td>59.4</td><td>Living room</td></tr>
<tr><td>C</td><td>82.5</td><td>Room</td></tr>
<tr><td>Andong (RH)</td><td>D</td><td>105.6</td><td>Living room</td><td>15 May 2018</td></tr>
</table>

Table 2. Finishing materials and singularities in the house.

City	Sample Name	Materials			Resident	Remarks
		Wall	Floor	Ceiling		
Daegu	A	Wallpaper (PVC)	PVC sheet	The finishing material of the ceiling is a same as the wallpaper	Before the occupant moves in	Furniture, sinks, and dining tables are laid out (synthetic wood products)
	B					
	C					
	D					
	E					
	F					
	G					
Pusan	A	Wallpaper (silk)	Wooden flooring		2 residents	Wooden bookshelf, artificial leather sofa
	B				2 residents	Wooden dining table, artificial leather sofa
	C				3 residents	Wooden dining table, artificial leather sofa
Andong	D				1 resident	Wooden desk and bookshelf, wooden dining table, artificial leather sofa

2.2. Measured Substances

Saito reported on the frequency and concentrations of unregulated chemicals in houses, and mentioned that some chemicals are associated with sick house syndrome [21,22]. Therefore, in this study, we decided to select and measure chemicals with high detection frequencies and high concentrations that were mentioned in previous studies. In this study, 16 chemicals were analyzed. A Tenax TA tube containing an adsorbent was used to collect the air in the room. The chemical analysis system consists of an Automatic Thermal Desorption (ATD) mechanism that heats the TA tube, and a Gas Chromatography–Mass Spectrometer (GC/MS) for the qualitative and quantitative analysis of chemicals. The ATD device desorbs the chemicals collected in the TA tube, and the desorbed chemicals are injected into the column. Depending on the temperature of the GC oven and the kinds of column, each chemical is separated, enabling the qualitative analysis of the chemical.

The temperature range of the GC oven is from 35 to 250 °C. The temperature change of the GC oven is increased by 15 °C per minute from 35 °C to 95 °C; by 2.5 °C per minute from 95 °C to 105 °C; and by 5 °C per minute from 105 °C to 250 °C. The column selectively delays each chemical and separates it according to the difference in arrival time to the detector. The column used in this study was HP-VOC 60 m × 0.32 mm, df = 1.8 μm. The change in the GC oven temperature served to separate the mixed chemicals inside the column. The detection limit was <5 ng. Table 3 shows the conditions of the GC/MS analysis.

Table 3. The conditions of GC/MS.

Automatic Thermal Desorption	PerkinElner Turbo Matrix ATD
Desorption temp. (Time)	260 °C (10 min)
Second desorption temp. (Time)	5 °C → 280 °C (45 min)
Gas Chromatography–Mass Spectrometry	Agilent GC/MS 6890N/5973inert
Chromatographic column	HP-VOC 60 m × 0.32 mm, df = 1.8 μm
GC oven temp.	35 °C (2 min) → 15 °C/min → 95 °C → 2.5 °C/min→105 °C → 5 °C/min → 250 °C (5 min)
Split ratio	7:1
MS analysis mode	SCAN
MS range	m/z 35 (low) – 550 (high)
Ion source temp.	250 °C

3. Results

3.1. Concentration of Unregulated Chemicals

Figure 1 show the concentrations of chemical substances measured in the air. In this study, the concentration range of acetone in the air was 31.0–83.4 μg/m^3 and the average value was 58.8 μg/m^3. The average concentration of 2-butanone was 279.4 μg/m^3 and the highest concentration was 402.5 μg/m^3, which was found in House B in Daegu. The concentration of 2-ethyl-1-hexanol was in the range of 15.3–163.5 μg/m^3 and the results demonstrated that the concentration of this material differed significantly depending on the housing. The average concentration of 2-ethyl-1-hexanol was 128.8 μg/m^3. The concentrations of Texanol and TXIB within the indoor air were 1.1–1.8 μg/m^3 and <1.0 μg/m^3, respectively, which were low. The concentration of 2-(2-butoxyethoxy) ethanol was in the range of 2.0–6.1 μg/m^3 and its average concentration was 3.9 μg/m^3. The average concentration of phenol was 32.7 μg/m^3 and it ranged from 7.9 to 50.2 μg/m^3, showing differences in concentration depending on the housing. The concentration of α-pinene in terpenes was in the range of 16.4–598.2 μg/m^3 and the D house in Daegu had the highest concentration. The average concentration of α-pinene was 317.2 μg/m^3. The average concentration of limonene was 414.1 μg/m^3 and the range was 120.4–652.5 μg/m^3. The concentration of camphene among terpenes was in the range of 1.1–4.2 μg/m^3 and its average concentration was 2.5 μg/m^3. Notably, the concentration of 3-caren was found to be at a very low concentration of <1.0 μg/m^3. The concentration of dichloromethane was detected in the range of 8.7–67.2 μg/m^3 and its average concentration was 3.1 μg/m^3. The results showed that the concentration of methylcyclohexane was in the range of 8.78–67.2 μg/m^3 and its average concentration was 45.9 μg/m^3. The concentration of tridecane was in the range of 1.2–6.1 μg/m^3 and its average concentration was 4.2 μg/m^3. Lastly, the concentration of 1,2,4-trimethylbenzene was in the range of 1.4–4.6 μg/m^3 and its average concentration was 2.9 μg/m^3. The concentration of p-cymene was <1.0 μg/m^3.

3.2. Indoor Air Quality Evaluation

Table 4 presents a comparison between the measurement results and the lowest concentration of interest (LCI). The LCIs within indoor air were determined in a European theoretical R&D cooperation [23]. The LCI value is defined as the minimum concentration that irritates organs such as the skin and eyes in humans. Because the unregulated chemical substances measured in this study do not have guidelines for indoor air quality, the measurement results of this study were compared with the LCI values. Among the 16 chemicals measured in this study, the substances exceeding the LCI value were phenol, α-pinene, and limonene. The average concentration of phenol was 1.637 times its LCI, and the maximum concentration of phenol was measured to be 2.510 times higher than its LCI. The maximum concentration of α-pinene and limonene were 2.39 and 2.18 times higher than their LCIs, respectively. The average concentration of α-pinene and limonene were 1.269 and 1.380 times higher than their LCIs, respectively. In contrast, the maximum concentrations of other chemicals were assessed to be 0.01–0.4 times lower than their LCIs. The maximum concentration of Texanol, TXIB, 3-caren, di-chloromethane, methylcyclohexane, tridecane, and p-cymene were found to be 0.008 times their LCI concentrations.

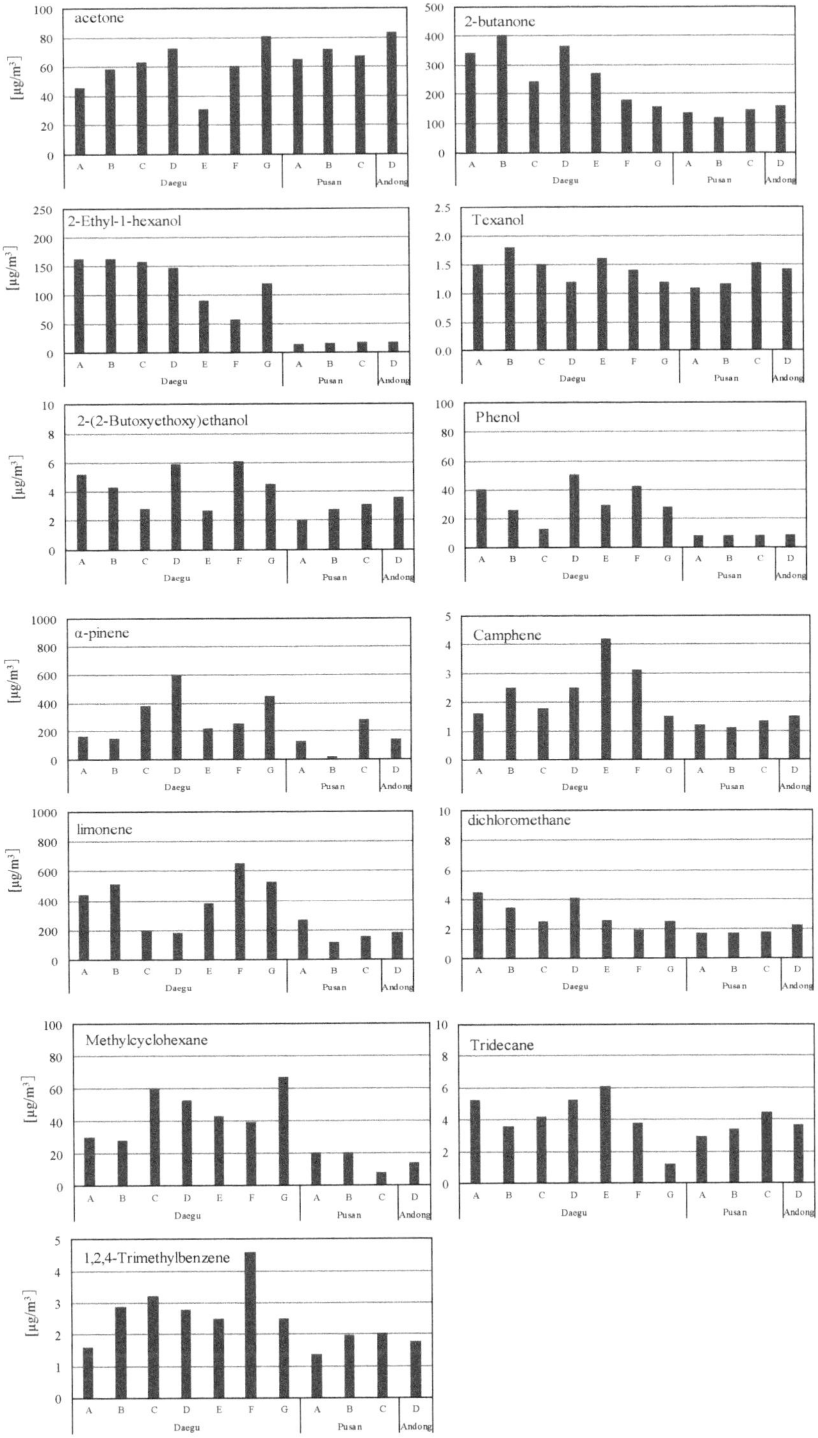

Figure 1. The concentrations of chemical substances measured in the air.

Table 4. Comparison between measurement results and LCI (lowest concentration of interest).

Chemicals	Average (μg/m^3)	Max (μg/m^3) *	LCI (μg/m^3) **	Reference	Average/LCI	Max/LCI
Acetone	58.8	83.4	400	Danish EPA, 2003 [24]	0.147	0.208
2-Butanone	279.4	402.5	1000	Danish EPA, 2003 [24]	0.279	0.403
2-Ethyl-1-hexanol	128.8	163.5	1000	Danish EPA, 2003 [24]	0.129	0.164
Texanol	1.5	1.8	1000	Hensen et al., 2001 [25]	0.001	0.002
TXIB	-	-	450	AgBB, 2015 [26]	-	-
2-(2-Butoxyethoxy)ethanol	4.5	6.1	120	Hensen et al., 2001 [25]	0.038	0.051
Phenol	32.7	50.2	20	Hensen et al., 2001 [25]	1.637	2.510
α-pinene	317.2	598.2	250	Danish EPA, 2003 [24]	1.269	2.393
3-Caren	-	-	250	Hensen et al., 2001 [25]	-	-
Limonene	414.1	652.5	300	Danish EPA, 2003 [24]	1.380	2.175
Camphene	2.5	4.2	250	Danish EPA, 2003 [24]	0.010	0.017
Dichloromethane	3.1	4.5	1220	Danish EPA, 2003 [24]	0.003	0.004
Methylcyclohexane	45.9	67.2	8000	Danish EPA, 2003 [24]	0.006	0.008
Tridecane	4.2	6.1	2000	Danish EPA, 2003 [24]	0.002	0.003
1,2,4-Trimethylbenzene	2.9	4.6	500	Hensen et al., 2001 [25]	0.006	0.009
p-cymene	-	-	550	Hensen et al., 2001 [25]	-	-

*: Maximum concentration in this study, **: lowest concentration of interest.

4. Discussion

According to the results of this study, 13 of the 16 chemicals analyzed were detected. The chemicals that exceeded their LCI levels were phenol, α-pinene, and limonene.

Phenol is widely used in many industries for various purposes. Phenol is a commonly used disinfectant and has been proven to be an effective antibacterial, antifungal, and antiviral substance. In addition, it is also used in the wood industry as a preservative to protect the wood from infestations of microorganisms such as bacteria and mold [27,28]. Phenol is produced during the thermal decomposition of organic substances. Thus, it is a constituent of motor vehicle exhaust gases, wood smoke, cigarette smoke, and smoked foods. In the general human, approximately two-thirds of phenol intake may be from air exposure [29].

According to the results of this study, phenol concentration in the air was high in the houses measured in the Daegu area. What is important to note is that within the houses in Daegu, the sinks, tables, and furniture were made of synthetic wood. Although formalin was widely used as an antimicrobial agent in wood building finishes and wooden furniture, its use declined after formaldehyde was included in air quality guidelines. Therefore, it is considered that phenol is likely to be used as a substitute for formalin. In the houses measured in the Daegu area, it was not considered that phenol was generated from the activities of daily life, such as cooking, because the residents have not yet moved in.

It is well known that α-pinene and limonene are substances that are emitted from wood [30]. In this study, α-pinene and limonene were detected at high concentrations. These two chemicals belong to the class of terpenes and have been reported to cause eye irritation and respiratory problems [31,32]. For α-pinene, 4 out of 11 houses exceeded the LCI values and for limonene, 5 out of 11 houses exceeded the LCI values. In particular, the concentrations of α-pinene and limonene were found to be high in houses using synthetic wood furniture. However, the concentrations from houses with wooden furniture and wooden flooring did not exceed the LCI levels. The most probable reason for this is that the houses in Busan and Andong that had wooden furniture have been around for more than two years from the date of construction, and the furniture was also purchased more than two years ago. However, about a year has passed since the construction of the houses in the Daegu area and the residents have not moved in.

Approximately 20 years have passed since the Korean government promulgated the indoor air quality guidelines to improve indoor air quality. Recently, the concentration of VOCs, such as formaldehyde, toluene, styrene, and benzene, within the air in the general residential environment was found to be remarkably low. However, as the use of alternative chemicals and vinyl chloride-based interior finishing materials has increased, indoor contamination of unregulated chemicals has become a concern.

In particular, phthalate is a representative contaminant of plastics, as they are the plasticizers used in plastic products [33,34]. The plasticizer emitted from the interior finishing material attaches to household dust and interior surfaces, and it is reportedly related to atopic dermatitis and asthma in children [35–37].

Therefore, in recent years, there has been a trend in the use of synthetic wood and wood as interior finishing materials to reduce the amount of plastic products used indoors. The same is also true for furniture. This study showed that the α-pinene and limonene emitted from wood were measured at high concentrations indoors. In spite of this, the amount of wood used indoors has been increased in the construction market.

This does not sμggest that we should reduce the amount of wood used indoors; instead, we propose using wood more safely indoors. As shown in this study, even if the floor finishing material is wood and the furniture is made of wood, the air concentrations of α-pinene and limonene are sometimes measured as low. This result is thoμght to be related to the construction period and the period of use of the furniture. If the processing and drying period of wood are adjusted, the amount of terpenes emitted from the wood can be reduced [38] and, even if the amount of wood used indoors increases, the air quality will not be greatly affected.

5. Conclusions

This study evaluated the contamination of unregulated chemicals in Korean houses. Of the 16 analyzed chemicals, 13 unregulated chemicals were detected. Among them, the average concentrations of phenol (32.7 $\mu g/m^3$), α-pinene (317.2 $\mu g/m^3$), and limonene (414.1 $\mu g/m^3$) were higher than their LCI concentrations, and the maximum concentrations of chemicals were found to be more than twice their LCI levels. According to this study, these chemicals should be noted as new pollutants present in the air within a house. However, althoμgh α-pinene and limonene are emitted from wood, there is no need to limit the use of wood indoors. Instead, this study sμggests reducing the amount of chemical substances emitted from wood throμgh the processing method and drying period of the wood, which would be the ways to use wood more safely indoors.

Author Contributions: The three authors contributed equally to this research. Conceptualization, H.K. and T.K.; methodology, H.K., T.K. and S.L.; validation, T.K. and S.L.; Analysis, H.K.; investigation, T.K.; data curation, T.K. and S.L.; writing—original draft preparation, H.K.; writing—review and editing, T.K.; visualization, S.L.; project administration, H.K.; funding acquisition, H.K. All authors have read and agreed to the published version of the manuscript.

Funding: This research was funded by KAKENHI, Grant-in-Aid for Scientific Research(C)20K04809.

Institutional Review Board Statement: Not applicable.

Informed Consent Statement: Not applicable.

Data Availability Statement: The data presented in this study are available on request from the corresponding author.

Acknowledgments: Thanks to the people who participated in the measurement. Additionally, I would like to express my gratitude to H.Tanaka of MC Evolve Technologies Corporation, who analyzed the chemical substances.

Conflicts of Interest: The authors declare no conflict of interest.

References

1. Molhave, L. Volatile organic compounds, indoor air quality and health. *Indoor Air* **1991**, *1*, 357–376. [CrossRef]
2. Lee, Y.; Kim, C. A Field Survey on Indoor Air Quality of the Existing Apartment House. *J. Archit. Inst. Korea Plan. Des.* **2004**, *20*, 327–334.
3. Yu, H.; Park, J.; Rhee, E. A Study on the Emission Characteristic of Formaldehyde and TVOC from Indoor Finishing Materials. *J. Archit. Inst. Korea Plan. Des.* **2005**, *21*, 141–149.
4. Klepeis, N.E.; Nelson, W.C.; Ott, W.R.; Robinson, J.P.; Tsang, A.M.; Switzer, P.; Behar, J.V.; Hern, S.C.; Engelmann, W.H. The national human activity pattern survey (NHAPS): A resource for assessing exposure to environmental pollutants. *J. Expo. Sci. Environ. Epidemiol.* **2001**, *11*, 231–252. [CrossRef] [PubMed]
5. Salthammer, T.; Mentese, S.; Marutzky, R. Formaldehyde in the indoor environment. *Chem. Rev.* **2010**, *110*, 2536–2572. [CrossRef] [PubMed]
6. Wolkoff, P.; Nielsen, G.D. Organic compounds in indoor air e their relevance for perceived indoor air quality? *Atmos. Environ.* **2010**, *35*, 4407–4417. [CrossRef]
7. Zhu, J.P.; Newhook, R.; Marro, L.; Chan, C.C. Selected volatile organic compounds in residential air in the city of Ottawa, Canada. *Environ. Sci. Technol.* **2005**, *39*, 3964–3971. [CrossRef]
8. Park, J.S.; Ikeda, K. Exposure to mixtures of organic compounds in homes in Japan. *Indoor Air* **2004**, *14*, 413–420. [CrossRef]
9. Lai, H.K.; Kendall, M.; Ferrier, H.; Lindup, I.; Alm, S.; Hanninen, O.; Jantunen, M.; Mathys, P.; Colvile, R.; Ashmore, M.R.; et al. Personal exposures and microenvironment concentration of PM2.5, VOC, NO_2 and CO in Oxford UK. *Atmos. Environ.* **2004**, *38*, 6399–6410. [CrossRef]
10. Kim, Y.M.; Harrad, S.; Harrison, R.M. Concentration and sources of VOCs in urban domestic and public microenvironments. *Environ. Sci. Technol.* **2001**, *35*, 997–1004. [CrossRef]
11. Guo, H.; Murray, F.; Wilkinson, S. Evaluation of total volatile organic compounds emissions form adhesives based on chamber test. *J. Air Waste Manag. Assoc.* **2000**, *50*, 199–206. [CrossRef] [PubMed]
12. Plaisance, H.; Blondel, A.; Desauziers, V.; Mcho, P. Hierarchical cluster analysis of carbonyl compounds emission profiles from building and furnitrur materials. *Build. Environ.* **2014**, *75*, 40–45. [CrossRef]
13. Ye, W.; Little, J.C.; Won, D.Y.; Zhang, X. Screening-level estimates of indoor exposure to volatile organic compounds emitted form building materials. *Build. Environ.* **2014**, *75*, 58–66. [CrossRef]
14. Gou, H.; Kwok, N.H.; Cheng, H.R.; Lee, S.C.; Hung, W.T.; Li, Y.S. Formaldehyde and volatile organic compounds in Hong Kong homes: Concentration and impact factors. *Indoor Air* **2009**, *19*, 206–217.
15. Garrett, M.H.; Hooper, M.A.; Hooper, B.M. Formaldehyde in Australian homes: Levels and sources. *Clean Air Environ. Qual.* **1997**, *31*, 28–32.
16. Edwards, R.D.; Jurvelin, J.; Saarela, K.; Jantunen, M. VOC concentrations measured in personal samples and residential indoor, outdoor and work place microenvironments in EXPLIS-Helsinki, Finland. *Atmos. Environ.* **2001**, *35*, 4531–4543. [CrossRef]
17. Ministry Environment, Korea: Indoor Air Quality Management Act. 2003. Available online: http://me.go.kr/home/web/main.do (accessed on 5 May 2018).
18. Ministry Environment, Korea: Indoor Air Quality Management Act (Revised Version). 2005. Available online: http://www.Kaca.or.kr/ (accessed on 5 May 2018).
19. Healthy Building Material, Korea Air Cleaning Association, Korea. 2005. Available online: http://www.Kaca.or.kr/ (accessed on 5 May 2018).
20. Ministry of Land, Infrastructure and Transport, Korea. 2010. Available online: http://www.molit.go.kr/ (accessed on 10 July 2018).
21. Saito, I.; Onuki, A.; Todaka, E.; Nakaoka, H.; Hosaka, M.; Ogata, A. Recent trends in indoor air pollution: Health risks from unregulated chemicals. *Jpn. J. Risk Anal.* **2011**, *21*, 91–100.
22. Onuki, A.; Saito, I.; Tada, T.; Fukuda, M.; Kurita, M.; Ogata, A. Trends in Indoor Air Chemicals Detected at High Concentrations in Newly Built Houses. *Ann. Rep. Tokyo Metr. Inst. Public Health* **2009**, *60*, 245–251.
23. Europen Collaborative Action (ECA). *Urban Air, Indoor Environment and Human Exposure, Harmonisation Framework for Health Based Evaluation of Indoor Emissions from Construction Products in the European Union Using the EU-LCI Concept*; Report No. 29; Publications Office of the European Union: Luxembourg City, Luxembourg, 2013.
24. Danish Environmental Protection Agency. Survey of Chemical Compounds in Consumer Products, Survey no. 36, Survey, Emission and Evaluation of Volatile Organic Chemicals in Printed Matter. 2003. Available online: https://eng.mst.dk/media/mst/69119/36.pdf#search=%27Danish+Environmental+Protection+Agency+%282003%29+Svey+of+chemical+compounds+in+consumer+products%2C+Survey+no.+36%2C+Survey%2C+emission+and+evaluation+of+volatile+organic+chemicals+in+printed+matter.%27 (accessed on 9 May 2019).

25. Hensen, L.; Larsen, A.; Molhave, L.; Hansen, M.K.; Kundsen, B. Health evaluation of volatile organic compound (VOC) emissions from wood and wood-based materials. *Arch. Environ. Health* **2001**, *56*, 419–432.
26. AgBB. Ausschuss zur Gesundheitlichen Bewertung voc Bauproduckten (Committee for Health-Related Evaluation of Building Products), Updated List of LCI Values 2015 in Part 3. 2015. Available online: https://www.umweltbundesamt.de/sites/default/files/medien/355/dokumente/agbb_evaluation_scheme_2015.pdf (accessed on 9 May 2019).
27. Uses of Phenol. Available online: https://www.vedantu.com/chemistry/uses-of-phenol (accessed on 9 December 2021).
28. Nielsen, G.D.; Hansen, L.F.; Nexø, B.A.; Poulsen, O.M. Indoor Air Guideline Levels for Phenol and Butylated Hydroxytoluene (BHT). *Indoor Air* **1998**, *5*, 25–36. [CrossRef]
29. WHO. Phenol. In *International Programme on Chemical Safety (Environmental Health Criteria 161)*; World Health Organization: Geneva, Switzerland, 1994.
30. Tohmura, S.; Miyamoto, K.; Inoue, A.; Chiba, Y. Measurement of volatile organic compounds emissions from laminas for the glue-laminated timber and domestic solid wood stored long term. *Bull. FFPRI* **2005**, *4*, 145–155. (In Japanese)
31. Molhave, L.; Kjaergaard, S.K.; Hempel-jorgensen, A.; Juto, J.E.; Andersson, K.; Stridh, G.; Falk, J. The Eye Irritation and Odor Potencies of Four Terpenes which are Major Constituents of the Emissions of VOCs from Nordic SoftWoods. *Indoor Air* **2000**, *10*, 315–318. [CrossRef]
32. Filipsson, A.F. Short term inhalation exposure to turpentine: Toxicokinetics and acute effects in men. *Occup. Environ. Med.* **1996**, *53*, 100–105. [CrossRef] [PubMed]
33. Abb, M.; Heinrich, T.; Sorkau, E.; Lorenz, W. Phthalates in house dust. *Environ. Int.* **2009**, *35*, 965–970. [CrossRef]
34. Becker, K.; Seiwert, M.; Angerer, J.; Heger, W.; Koch, H.M.; Nagorka, R.; Rosskamp, E.; Schluter, C.; Seifert, B.; Ullrich, D. DEHP metabolites in urine of children and DEHP in house dust. *Int. J. Hyg. Environ. Health* **2004**, *207*, 409–417. [CrossRef] [PubMed]
35. Bergh, C.; Torgrip, R.; Emenius, G.; Östman, C. Organophosphate and phthalate esters in air and settled dust—A multi-location indoor study. *Indoor Air* **2010**, *21*, 67–76. [CrossRef] [PubMed]
36. Bonvallot, N.; Mandin, C.; Mercier, F.; Le Bot, B.; Glorennec, P. Health ranking of ingested semi-volatile organic compounds in house dust. *Indoor Air* **2010**, *20*, 458–472. [CrossRef]
37. Mínguez, R.; Montero, J.M.; Fernández-Avilés, G. Measuring the impact of pollution on property prices in Madrid: Objective versus subjective pollution indicators in spatial models. *J. Geogr. Syst.* **2013**, *15*, 169–191. [CrossRef]
38. Eri, M. Temporal changes in volatile compounds in the indoor air of a laboratory finished with Cryptomeria japonica interior materials. *Bull. FFPRI* **2019**, *18*, 15–25.

buildings

MDPI

Article

Performance of Modern Passive Stack Ventilation in a Retrofitted Nordic Apartment Building

Ilia Kravchenko [1,*], Risto Kosonen [1,2,3], Juha Jokisalo [1,3] and Simo Kilpeläinen [1]

1 Department of Mechanical Engineering, School of Engineering, Aalto University, 02150 Espoo, Finland; risto.kosonen@aalto.fi (R.K.); juha.jokisalo@aalto.fi (J.J.); simo.kilpelainen@aalto.fi (S.K.)
2 Department of HVAC, College of Urban Construction, Nanjing Tech University, Nanjing 211800, China
3 Smart City Center of Excellence, TalTech, 19086 Tallinn, Estonia
* Correspondence: ilia.kravchenko@aalto.fi

Abstract: The paper analyses the performance of a five-storey apartment building equipped with modern passive stack ventilation in Nordic conditions. The passive stack ventilation system was retrofitted in 2019, and novel self-regulating air inlet devices with filters were equipped. The building was simulated with IDA ICE software, where the model of the self-regulating terminal units was developed using manufacturer product data. Several case scenarios were created to analyze the effects of poor maintenance, improved airtightness, and window opening on the system performance. For the analysis, one-room and three-room apartments on the second and fifth floors have been chosen. The CO_2 concentration and indoor air temperature were analyzed and compared with EN 16798-1 standard guidelines. The results show a significant effect of poor maintenance and possibility to open windows on the CO_2 concentration. The results also show a trend for the one-room apartments to overheat despite having a higher air change rate than the three-room apartments. The three-room apartments tolerate over-heating, although they are much more sensitive to poor maintenance. Furthermore, the apartments on the fifth floor are even more sensitive to poor maintenance, and three-room apartments there showed warning levels of CO_2. Improving the envelope airtightness does not benefit the IAQ of the apartments.

Keywords: natural ventilation; Nordic climate; apartment building; building overheating; indoor climate; retrofitting

Citation: Kravchenko, I.; Kosonen, R.; Jokisalo, J.; Kilpeläinen, S. Performance of Modern Passive Stack Ventilation in a Retrofitted Nordic Apartment Building. *Buildings* **2022**, *12*, 96. https://doi.org/10.3390/buildings12020096

Academic Editors: Ashok Kumar, M. Amirul I. Khan, Alejandro Moreno Rangel and Michał Piasecki

Received: 29 November 2021
Accepted: 13 January 2022
Published: 20 January 2022

1. Introduction

The general function of the building ventilation system is to provide occupants with enough fresh air while maintaining high energy efficiency. According to the WHO, IAQ is one of the most important determinants of human health and well-being, thus playing a significant role in the indoor environment of the building [1]. In the European Union (EU), most countries have their national building codes and normative documentation for the building design, which are binding [2]. The preferable indoor air quality and airflow rates are presented in the EU directives, binding for EU countries and standards. They are presented in such documents as Energy performance of buildings directive with levels of Energy performance Certification, EN 16798-1 standard in general, and EN 15214 in specific for the IAQ (indoor air quality) [3–5]. Most recommendations and buildings codes consider the minimum airflow rate, temperature level and CO_2 concentration. In Finland, the building stock ventilation construction and design requirements are provided by the Ministry of Environment [3,6,7]. The documents consider new and retrofitted buildings separately as buildings of different ages present the stock [8].

Mainly, in Finland, the residential building stock is presented by 85% of all buildings. Blocks of flats represent only 4% of this number. However, they account for approximately 30% of the total floor area of the residential building stock and around 1.3 million occupants for the buildings with four floors or higher [9]. The buildings constructed before the 1950s are mostly equipped with passive stack ventilation. After the 1960s and until the 2000s, apartment buildings were typically equipped with mechanical exhaust ventilation thanks to the reliable and predictable airflow rates. New apartment buildings are mostly equipped with balanced mechanical ventilation [10].

The new buildings are required to follow strict heat losses standards, calculated with the compensation principle [7]. Although, starting from 2018, the requirements have changed, making it possible to utilize natural ventilation systems in buildings in certain conditions. After renovation and retrofitting, if a ventilation system is changed in an old building, it should have at least 45% heat recovery. However, if only the envelope is retrofitted, the ventilation system could remain the same [10,11]. Additionally, in the case of protected buildings, energy performance requirements are not applied instead of following the standard requirements for major renovation often require separate permission for retrofitting from the Finnish Heritage Agency. In practice, it creates a building stock equipped with natural ventilation presented with a passive stack ventilation system that operates in Nordic conditions.

Overall, natural ventilation utilizes the wind driving forces and thermal buoyancy forces to provide airflow [12]. The basic wind-induced ventilation concept is windows opening ventilation with single or crossflow. This approach is widely used in detached houses and apartment buildings in warm climates [13–15]. However, these systems are likely to create draughts and are not applicable in cold climates. Wind towers and wind-catchers have been introduced to further the advancement of technology in cold climates. This approach gives a centralized source of airflow, which may be distributed and used to create systems with heat recovery and regulated airflow rate. These systems have limitations applied to the residential apartment buildings though, such as building height, floor number and local weather conditions [13,16].

On the other hand, natural ventilation can also be realized by thermally induced ventilation. The passive stack ventilation systems often present a basic ventilation strategy of this type. This approach is widely used in the cold climate to create underpressure in the apartments, thus enabling ventilation by infiltration through the envelope. However, these systems are strongly dependent on the outdoor conditions and the indoor-outdoor temperature difference [17]. The advancement of this technology includes solar chimneys and double skin facades. The solar chimneys create a centralized air distribution that is also controllable. However, this technology requires a significant amount of solar radiation throughout the year [18–20]. The double-skin facades create buoyancy-driven airflow between internal and external envelopes or between external and internal glazing. This airflow may be controlled and utilized for heat recovery. These systems are energy-efficient but sophisticated and mainly utilized in office buildings [21–23].

In practice, old buildings are usually equipped with passive stack ventilation systems with windows opening ventilation for the warm period of the year [24]. Some of these buildings are also equipped with self-regulating inlet devices. The inlet devices maintain the designed airflow rate by different means: indoor-outdoor pressure difference, outdoor temperature, or manually controlling the slot size [25,26]. The devices with pressure control show a reliable constant airflow rate in laboratory measurements [27]. Component performance field studies for warm and mild climates show a predictable performance for cases with a 10 Pa pressure difference or higher, thus, the airflow characteristics depend on the opening degree of the slot [28]. The system simulation studies of different types of buildings with mechanical exhaust ventilation and passive stack ventilation with self-regulating inlet devices in Belgium indicate poor IAQ conditions for low-pressure indoor to outdoor difference and possible draft issues [29]. The field studies with occupant surveys in Portugal assessed the IAQ in social buildings with partly natural ventilation, introduced by self-regulated inlets. It is reported that the average air change rate is 0.6–0.7 ACH and thermal comfort, presented with PMV and PPD in class B [4,30]. However, it is also reported that self-regulated inlets had been sealed in 40% of apartments due to draft issues and cold sensations during the winter [31]. Further laboratory device testing and investigation showed malfunction of pressure-control inlets due to the membrane, leading to an inconsistent airflow rate that differs from manufacturer data [32]. Another field study in Porto of 40 social residential buildings showed an air change rate level of 0.35 ACH in winter, best-case scenario, and around 0.1 ACH in August, in the worst-case scenario. Some of the inlets were also sealed by the occupants [33]. A study in the UK has identified that, for a significant period of time, the supply of outdoor air via the inlet devices will not provide a Category A according to the UK building regulation [30] perceived indoor air quality index [34].

In the Nordic climate, the interest in implementing such devices is presented in retrofitting protected or heritage buildings. These buildings have limited or no access to the retrofit of the envelope and ventilation system. Some retrofitted apartment multi-storey buildings in Finland are equipped with self-regulating inlets with outdoor temperature control to preserve a natural passive stack ventilation system. The ventilation system is designed for the nominal conditions; however, natural ventilation performance depends on the outdoor conditions, and yearly performance has not been assessed. Some studies have investigated the performance of the self-regulated inlet devices in cold climate via CFD analysis [35,36]; yet, no studies regarding the building ventilation system performance in Nordic climate were found. Another investigated performance of slot-controlled or pressure-controlled inlet devices, although the self-regulating inlet device with outdoor temperature control, which works on reducing the inlet area when the outdoor temperature decreases, was not assessed or simulated in the literature.

The paper novelty comes from the performance assessment of a multi-storey apartment building with natural ventilation retrofitted with self-regulated air inlets in Nordic climate. The building presents old heritage and protected building stock with limited or no access to the ventilation system reconstruction, demanding to be retrofitted to perform according to the EN energy and IAQ standards [37,38]. The importance of renovation and decarbonization of old stock buildings also empathizes with the recent European renovation wave strategy [39]. Natural ventilation systems performance depends on outdoor and weather conditions and may significantly vary during the year, making it essential to make a simulation to meet the requirements. The building performance simulation reflects various cases with the effect of poor maintenance, different retrofit strategies such as the implementation of shading and improved envelope airtightness, and effect of buildings user behaviour. Such a ventilation system has individual filters for each apartment, making maintenance demanding. The poor maintenance cases investigate the influence of dirty inlet device filter, passive stack duct, and a combination of those. The different airtightness cases describe the influence of envelope retrofitting. The air movement is also provided by infiltration and exfiltration through the building envelope; thus, the airtightness of the building might also influence the ventilation system performance. The occupant behaviour cases describe different schedules for opening windows and doors as the occupants operate doors, possibly creating additional airflow resistance. The research evaluates the impact of these factors on the system performance, along with weather conditions and building height. In this study, a building model was created in IDA ICE with a custom component to describe the temperature-dependent self-regulating inlet. The IAQ parameters were calculated and evaluated concerning requirements and legislation. The internal airflows were also calculated for various periods and assessed. The main research question is if the ventilation system with modern passive stack ventilation has sufficient performance in a multi-storey building in the Nordic climate.

2. Materials and Methods

2.1. Target Values

The chosen parameters reflect such metrics as CO_2—the direct IAQ indicator and reflection of the EN standards, temperature—thermal comfort and overheating indicator, internal airflow and air change rate as an indicator of IAQ, internal airflow patterns and reflection pf EN standards. The target values used in this paper are based on national Finnish building codes, legislations and European standards EN 16798-1 [38] and EN 15251 [37] for the IAQ parameters, the CO_2 concentration in residential apartments in specific.

The requirements forced by the Ministry of the Environment define overheating in the living spaces of the buildings as apartments being more than 150 °Ch over 27 °C [7]. This requirement applies to the simulated indoor temperature from June to August in the design phase of the new building, and the simulation input data required by the building code are used. In this paper, this rule is used to evaluate overheating risk and thermal comfort. However, it is not applicable to fulfil this requirement due to the different building code input data. Additionally, the requirement by the Ministry of Social Affairs and Health of Finland for all the existing residential buildings or other living spaces is 30 °C as the maximum health-related temperature for the elderly people who are cared for in the residential living spaces and 32 °C as the overall maximum indoor air temperature [40].

The guidelines suggested by EN 15251 are applied for CO_2 concentration analysis. The CO_2 concentration is presented for the I to IV indoor air categories with a base concentration assumed to be 430 ppm [41]. The categories from I to III present acceptable CO_2 levels, also referring to the apartment airflow rates. The IV category presents all other possible cases allowed in the apartments only for a limited period of the year.

All the data are presented in hourly mean values. The degree hours are also calculated with hourly mean values.

2.2. Building Description

For the purpose of analysis, an apartment building with passive stack ventilation in Southern Finland, Helsinki, has been chosen. The building was constructed in 1951 and recently renovated during 2016–2018. The building is located close to the city centre and is sheltered from direct wind by an adjacent apartment building. During the renovation, it was equipped with self-regulating air inlet devices with filters. The building consists of 5 floors and have 600 m^2 of net floor area. The ground floor is non-residential. The four residential floors have the same apartment and room layout, shown in Figure 1.

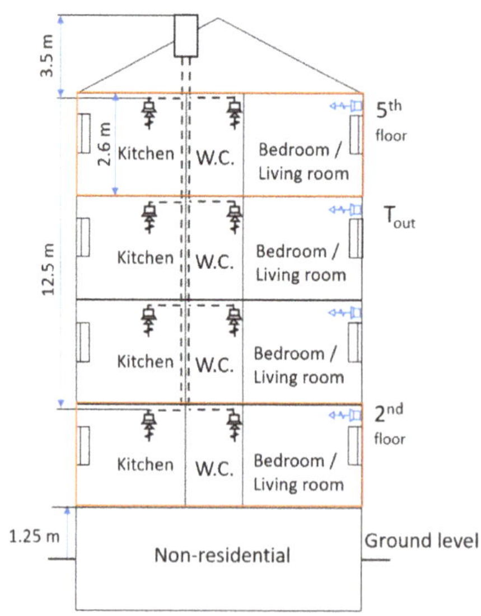

Figure 1. The building natural passive stack ventilation system design with openable windows and self-regulating inlet devices with an outdoor temperature-dependent airflow rate.

Three-room and one-room apartments on the second and fifth floor in one staircase have been chosen for the analysis and presented in Figure 2.

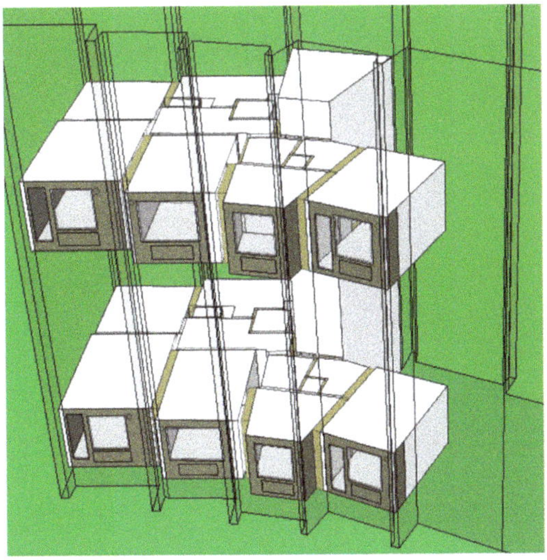

Figure 2. The building simulation model for the three and one-room apartments on the second and fifth floors connected with stairwell.

The outdoor air in apartments is supplied into bedrooms and living rooms through the inlet devices and the envelope. The separated exhaust stack ducts are located in the kitchen and WC. The apartment room layout and ventilation design are presented in Figure 3.

The envelope properties, window properties and other building structure properties are set according to the common practice of the construction year and shown in Table 1. The load-bearing structures of the building are massive concrete, external walls are two rows of burnt bricks with insulation layers, internal walls between the apartments are brick walls, and internal walls between rooms are lightweight structures with an air gap. The envelope airtightness was set according to the building year for the reference case, and the air leakage rate (n_{50}) equals 2.4 L/h at a pressure difference of 50 Pa [24].

The internal doors have a gap at the floor level of 2 cm. The windows are 2 panes glazed with a U-value of 2 W/m^{2}K and are equipped with integrated shading with blinds between panels. The window blinds are manually controlled according to the occupation profile and the intensity of solar radiation (>100 W/m^2). In three-room apartments, all windows besides the ones in the kitchen are openable. In one-room apartments, all windows are openable. The openable windows area is 10% of a window.

The water radiators carry out space heating with a dimensioning temperature of 70/40 °C, and the heat distribution efficiency is 80%. The design powers are 100 W/floor-m^2 on the top floor and 60 W/floor-m^2 on the middle floor. The temperature setpoint of space heating is 21 °C in the apartments. In the staircase and basement floor, the setpoint of space heating is 17 °C. The annual net heating demand of domestic hot water (DHW) is 35 kWh/m^2 per heated net floor area. It is assumed that DHW consumption is constant with time. Heat losses of the DHW circuit are 0.56 W/m^2, and 50% of the heat losses were assumed to end up as internal heat gains in the zones.

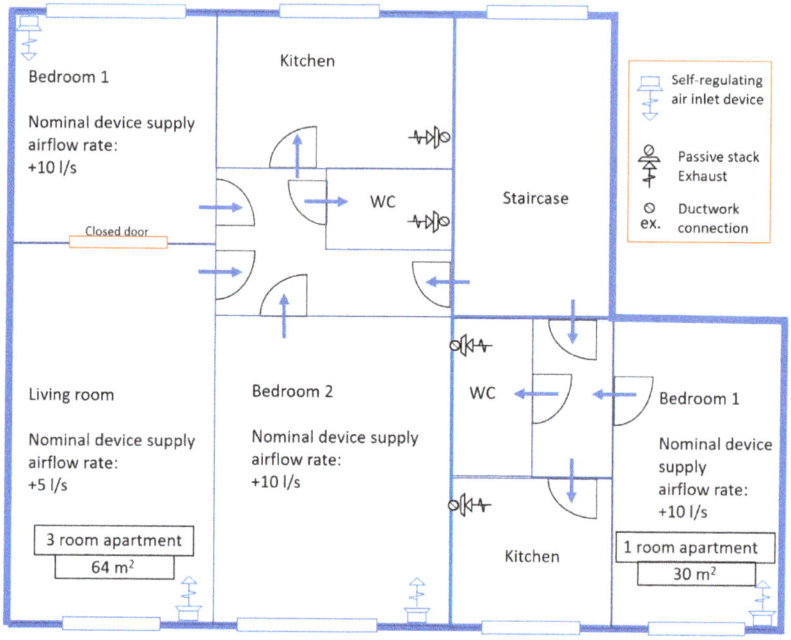

Figure 3. The building floor level ventilation system design and airflow rates at nominal conditions of 5 Pa pressure difference over the inlet device and outdoor temperature of 15 °C.

Table 1. The structural building details and properties of windows.

Description	Building Details
U-values, (W/m^{2}K)	
Roof	0.5
Floor	0.5
External walls	0.5
Entrance doors	1.1
Apartment doors	2.2
Windows properties	
U-value, (W/m^{2}K)	2
Total solar heat transmittance (g-value)	0.44
Direct solar transmittance (ST)	0.72
Integrated shading	Blinds
External shading	No

2.3. Inlet Device

The self-regulating inlet devices are installed in the living rooms and bedrooms of the apartments. The inlet device regulates airflow based on the outdoor temperature. The minimum opening is 4 mm, and the maximum is 16 mm for −5 °C and lower, and +15 °C and higher, respectively, and the settings are linear. The inlet device flow characteristics are presented in Figure 4. The bedrooms are equipped with a 160 mm diameter inlet device with a nominal setting of 9.3 L/s at a pressure difference of 5 Pa. The living rooms are equipped with 100 mm diameter inlet devices with a nominal setting of 5.1 L/s at a pressure difference of 5 Pa. The flow characteristics are presented in Table 2.

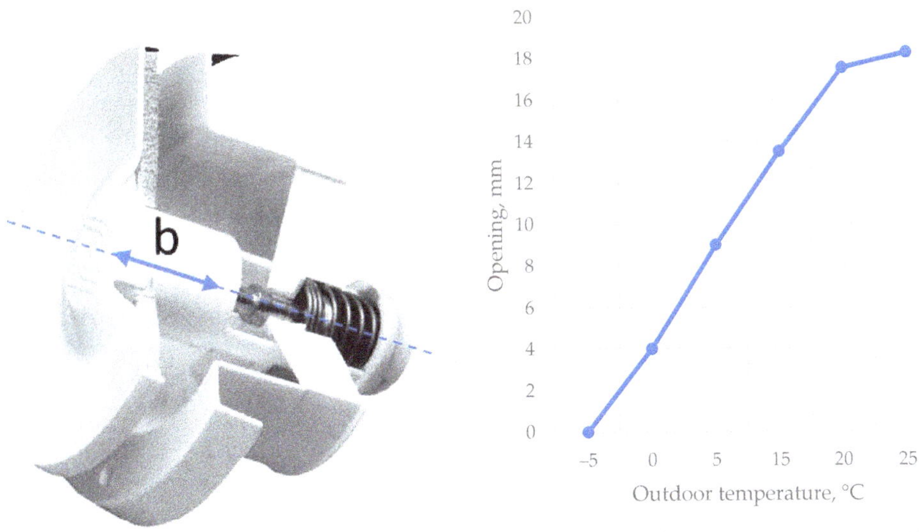

(**a**) (**b**)

Figure 4. The inlet device product scheme (**a**); The inlet device opening as a function of outdoor temperature (**b**).

Table 2. The inlet device airflow rate at different pressure differences and opening degree. Nominal conditions 5 Pa, 15 °C outdoor air temperature.

	Airflow Rate, L/s							
	Living Room Device				**Bedroom Device**			
Opening, b, mm	**Pressure Difference, Pa**							
	5	10	20	30	5	10	20	30
4	3.2	2.9	7.5	9.5	4.5	6.6	9.5	13
8	4.5	6.9	11	13	7	11	16	21
12	4.9	7.5	12	14	8.5	13	20	25
16	5.1 *	7.8	12	15	9.3 *	14	22	28

* nominal conditions 5 Pa, 15 °C outdoor air temperature.

2.4. The Building Usage

Household equipment's total annual electricity consumption is 21.0 kWh/m^2 per heated net floor area [7]. The appliances are used every day between 9:00 and 22:00. The total annual electricity consumption of indoor lighting is 7.9 kWh/m^2, per the building's total heated net floor area [7]. The electric lighting power is assumed to be evenly distributed by the floor area of all the simulated zones in the apartments and by the floor area of the staircase. The usage time of the lights is between 21:00 and 23:00 from May to August and 7:00–9:00 and 15:00–23:00 from September to April [10].

- The occupational patterns for the rooms and the apartment occupant number are presented in Table 3.

Table 3. The apartment occupancy and occupancy patterns.

Apartment	Occupancy	Bedroom 1	Bedroom 2	Living Room	Kitchen
Three-room	4	22.00–9.00 2 Occ.	22.00–9.00 2 Occ.	9.00–22.00 2 Occ.	9.00–22.00 2 Occ.
One-room	1	22.00–9.00 1 Occ.			9.00–22.00 1 Occ.

- The windows opening schedule is set according to the script, that during the cold period, from September to April, the windows are closed. The windows are opened from May to August if the outdoor temperature exceeds 12 °C, and indoor temperature exceeds 22 °C.
- The internal doors of the bathrooms or WCs are always closed, but the other internal doors inside the apartments are always opened.
- The apartments' occupant activity level is 1.2 MET.

2.5. Weather Data

The weather data are presented with typical climatological conditions at the Helsinki-Vantaa weather station in southern Finland for the 2012 reference year [42,43]. The data consist of hourly outdoor air temperature, relative humidity, direct and diffused insolation, wind speed and direction. The temperature and wind speed are presented in Figure 5. Heating degree days at indoor temperature +17 °C annually are 3952 °Kd in the reference year.

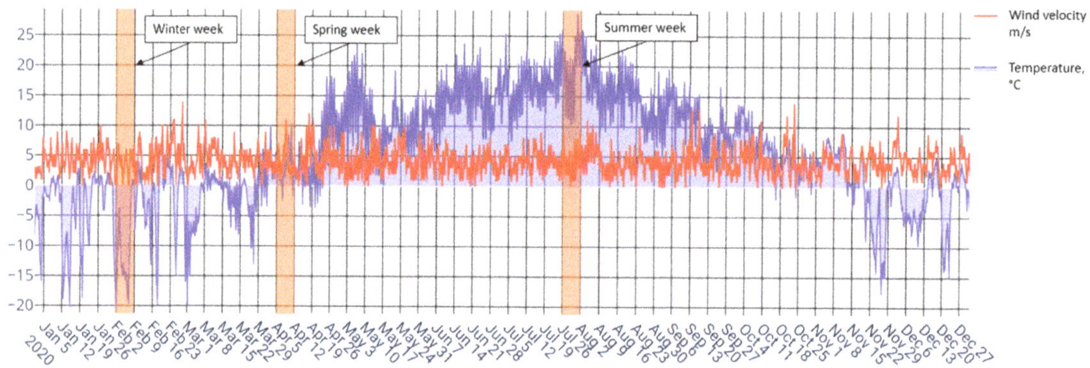

Figure 5. The yearly outdoor temperature and wind velocity of the reference year with chosen example weeks.

For the purpose of the air change rate and airflow rate analyses, three weeks have been chosen. The week with the lowest outdoor temperature in winter, a week with outdoor temperature close to average 2 °C and high average wind velocity in spring, and the week with the highest outdoor temperature in summer. The outdoor conditions for chosen weeks are presented in Table 4.

Table 4. The example weeks outdoor temperature and wind data.

Week		Maximum	Minimum	Average
Winter	Temperature, °C	1.1	−19.7	−9.3
	Wind velocity, m/s	7	1	3.5
Spring	Temperature, °C	7.8	−3.6	2.4
	Wind velocity, m/s	12	0	5.3
Summer	Temperature, °C	28.8	13.1	20.1
	Wind velocity, m/s	9	0	3.6

2.6. IDA ICE Simulation Tool

The model of the building has been created with the IDA ICE dynamic building simulation tool [42,44]. The software allows the modelling of multi-zone buildings and provides simultaneous dynamic simulation of heat transfer and airflows, considering flows between zones, building envelope and windows. It calculates the interactions between building structures, HVAC systems, operational and occupancy schedules of the building, and outdoor climate conditions. The infiltration airflows are calculated by wind pressure on each façade combined with zones stack effects.

2.6.1. Façade Pressure Calculation

Wind pressure distribution around the house is simulated using the normal assumption in building engineering that the wind flow is horizontal and an atmospheric boundary layer is neutral without vertical airflow. The wind conditions of the environment were approximated using the wind profile equation reported in [34], see Equation (1).

Wind pressure on facades corresponds to the LBL model wind profile:

$$U(h) = U_m \cdot k \cdot \left(\frac{h}{h_m}\right)^a, \tag{1}$$

where $U(h)$ is the wind speed at height h (m/s), U_m is the wind speed measured on open ground at the weather station (m/s), h is the height from the surface of the ground (m), h_m is the height of the measurement equipment (10 m), and parameters k and a are terrain-dependent constants.

The simulated building is located in a typical Finnish city center area with closely built houses where the height of adjacent houses is approximately the same as the simulated one.

However, this study simplified the calculation of wind conditions, and wind pressure coefficients were not measured nor simulated.

The values of the wind pressure coefficients are approximated values for low-rise buildings surrounded by obstacles equal to the height and size of the house. The shape of the building being studied is more complicated, so the simulated wind pressure distribution around the building was also simplified.

The wind pressure outside the building facades P_w is determined by Equation (2):

$$P_w = c_p \cdot \frac{1}{2} \rho_{out} \cdot U^2, \tag{2}$$

where ρ_{out} is the outdoor air density (kg/m^3), C_p is the wind pressure coefficient, and U is the local wind velocity defined by Equation (1).

Because of the square dependence of the wind velocity in Equation (2), wind velocity has a more significant effect on wind pressure than the value of the wind pressure coefficient. The local outside surface pressure P_s on the building facades is:

$$P_s = P_{out} - \rho_{out} \cdot g \cdot h + P_w, \tag{3}$$

where P_{out} is the outdoor air pressure at ground level (Pa), ρ_{out} is the outdoor air density (kg/m^3), and g is the acceleration of gravity (m/s^2).

The pressure difference between the zone and outdoor air is calculated as:

$$\Delta P = P_{in} - \rho_{in} \cdot g \cdot h_{in} - P_s, \tag{4}$$

where P_{in} is the indoor air pressure at floor level (Pa), ρ_{in} is the indoor air density (kg/m^3), and h_{in} is the height from floor level (m).

2.6.2. Internal Flows Calculation

IDA ICE calculates the internal flows for each zone, where large vertical openings such as an open door between the zones are simulated as bi-directional flows. The vertical flow profile in the opening depends on the density differences between the adjusted zones. If the densities are equal, the flow profile is flat. Otherwise, it is slanted. In the case of a flat velocity profile, the air mass flow between the zones is calculated with the standard orifice flow equation:

$$Q = C_d \cdot A \sqrt{2\rho \cdot \Delta P}, \tag{5}$$

where C_d is a discharge coefficient and A is the area of the opening (m^2). In the case of a slanted profile, the airflow between the zones is simultaneously bi-directional.

- The windows are also presented with bi-directional flow openings and have 0.65 discharge coefficient, and 10% of those openable are for the mean of airflow calculation.
- The envelope cracks (leakage) are presented as external area infiltration distributed based on the power law. The exfiltration and infiltration are separated.
- The internal doors have a 2 cm gap for air movement. The apartment entrance door has the mail slot, which is a crack with a k coefficient equal to 9.3×10^{-4} and power-law exponent 0.7 [45].
- The model for the internal nodes of the simulation model is fully mixed for the concentration calculation, such as CO_2 level.

2.6.3. Passive Stack

The passive stack ventilation is implemented with the standard IDA ICE chimney model with stacks of different heights according to the floor. The chimney model considers the inlet and outlet loss coefficient, duct roughness, duct shape and height. The model calculates bi-directional flow.

2.6.4. Inlet Device

The self-regulating inlet device was created as a custom model based on the infiltration model with temperature-dependent power-law k-factor and exponent equal 0.5. The model has a simultaneous single direction flow.

The k-values for the inlet device and filter were calculated from the manufacturer product data for designed airflows. The following equation was used for the volumetric airflow rate:

$$\mathrm{q_v} = \mathrm{k} \cdot \sqrt{\Delta p}, \tag{6}$$

where $\mathrm{q_v}$ is volumetric airflow rate and Δp is component pressure drop.

The k-value has been calculated for the given inlet device positions and linearly interpolated between the data points. The k-value has been coupled with outdoor temperature and presented as a function in Figure 6.

The calculated function for the bedroom and living room inlet devices has been used in the simulation model to calculate the airflow according to the pressure difference and outdoor temperature. Dirty filters were simulated by decreasing k-values twice, assuming that the filter had been working for the year without maintenance [46].

2.7. *The Simulation Case Description*

The CO_2 level during the year and indoor air temperature during the summer have been chosen to assess the IAQ. The CO_2 level is used as an indirect indicator for the room and personal airflow rate and compared against standards [7,10]. The indoor air temperature has been used to assess the influence of the airflow rate in apartments and occupant personal conditions.

The apartments on the second and fifth floors were chosen to represent the influence of the height on the stack effect. One and three-room apartments were selected to represent the influence of different floor areas and inlet supply ventilation system configuration.

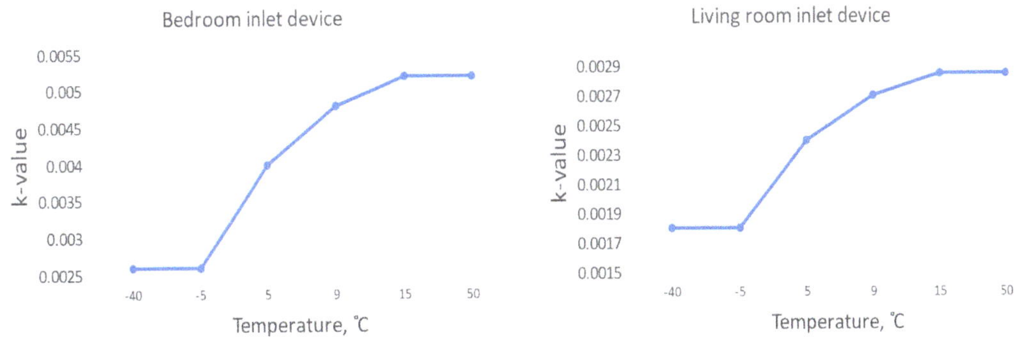

(**a**) (**b**)

Figure 6. The inlet device flow characteristics via k-value against outdoor temperature: (**a**) bedroom inlet device; (**b**) living room inlet device.

The three time periods have been chosen to address the most critical weather conditions for the passive stack ventilation: the coldest week during the winter, a week with an average outdoor temperature of 2 °C combined with the highest average wind during spring and a week with warmest outdoor air temperature. The results during the cold week present the influence of a significant pressure difference. The spring conditions represent the case with a low pressure difference and the absence of additional windows opening ventilation. The summer case has the lowest pressure difference and influence of additional windows opening ventilation. The apartment air change rates have been calculated to present the apartment airflow rates for the chosen time. For the reference case, internal airflows and their direction have also been calculated.

A range of cases, descriptions, and abbreviations have been created to assess the chosen parameters, shown in Tables 5 and 6.

Table 5. The simulation case scenarios, name and abbreviation cross-dependency.

Abbreviation	Description
Ref.	Reference case. Similar to best case, but bedroom doors are closed (20 mm slot below the door) during the night
Best	Best case. Any external or internal factor does not decrease performance
M1	Maintenance issue: filter loaded (pressure drop is higher in 1.4 times compare to reference case)
M2	Similar to M1, but stack ducts are dirty. (Exhaust pressure drop is higher in 1.4 times)
M3	Similar to M2, but the higher envelope airtightness. (from n_{50} 2.4 L/h to 1.5 L/h)
M4	Maintenance issues, high envelope airtightness and no windows shading (g = 0.39 blinds, g = 0.55 without blinds)
M5	Maintenance issues, high envelope airtightness, no windows opening and shading
M6	Maintenance issues, high envelope airtightness, no windows opening and shading, all apartments doors are closed

Table 6. The building simulation case scenarios.

Case Scenario	Bedroom Door	Bathroom Door	Inlet Device	Stack Duct	Airtightness n_{50}, L/h	Windows	Windows Opening	
						Shading	Summer	Winter
Ref.	Closed, Night	Opened	Clean	Clean	2.4	Yes	Always, if >12 °C	30 min. before sleep
Best	Opened	Opened	Clean	Clean	2.4	Yes	Same	Same
M1	Closed, Night	Closed	Dirty	Clean	2.4	Yes	Same	Same
M2	Closed, Night	Closed	Dirty	Dirty	2.4	Yes	Same	Same
M3	Closed, Night	Closed	Dirty	Dirty	1.5	Yes	Same	Same
M4	Closed, Night	Closed	Dirty	Dirty	1.5	No	Same	Same
M5	Closed, Night	Closed	Dirty	Dirty	1.5	No	No	Same
M6	Closed	Closed	Dirty	Dirty	1.5	No	No	No

The reference case represents the case where the inlet devices and passive stack duct are clean, and only the bedroom doors are closed at night. The windows shading is realized with blinds and operated according to the solar insolation. The windows are closed for the cold period from September to April for most of the day and open for half an hour, 22.00–22.30. In the summertime, windows are always opened if the outdoor temperature is higher than 12 °C and indoor higher than 22 °C, Table 6. The stack duct has the summed pressure loss coefficient of passive stack equal to 15. In the best-case scenario, all the doors are always opened.

The cases with dirty inlet device filters (M1) and passive stack ducts (M2) are created to represent poor maintenance cases, where the filters and duct are not serviced for more than 1 year. [46] The dirty filter is described as in the reference case presented in inlet device characteristics but with half the standard k-value. The stack duct has the summed pressure loss coefficient of the passive stack increased to 40. In these cases, the roles of the inlet device and the passive stack are assessed. The case with improved airtightness (M3) represents a building with better envelope insulation, and thus higher airtightness of 1.5 L/h to assess the influence of the infiltration airflow change on the indoor conditions. The case with no windows shading (M4) represents no integrated blinds between glazing. The cases with non-openable windows (M5) describe the ventilation only via infiltration and inlet devices, and represent the scenario where windows are not operated for some reason, such as occupant inability to do it. The worst-case scenario (M6) describes the case with closed doors due to the occupant's possible preference or draught issues.

3. Results

3.1. Apartment Indoor Temperature Overheating Analysis Results

The apartment overheating was assessed based on the indoor air temperature results. The results are presented for three-room and one-room apartments on the second and fifth floor to consider the size of apartments and height factor influences. The results are shown for the summer period, June to August, as figures, duration curves, and tables with degree hours, in Figures 7 and 8 and Tables 7 and 8, respectively. The results are presented first for the three-room apartments and then for one-room apartments for each described case. The colours for the figures are used consistently throughout the paper to show the correlations.

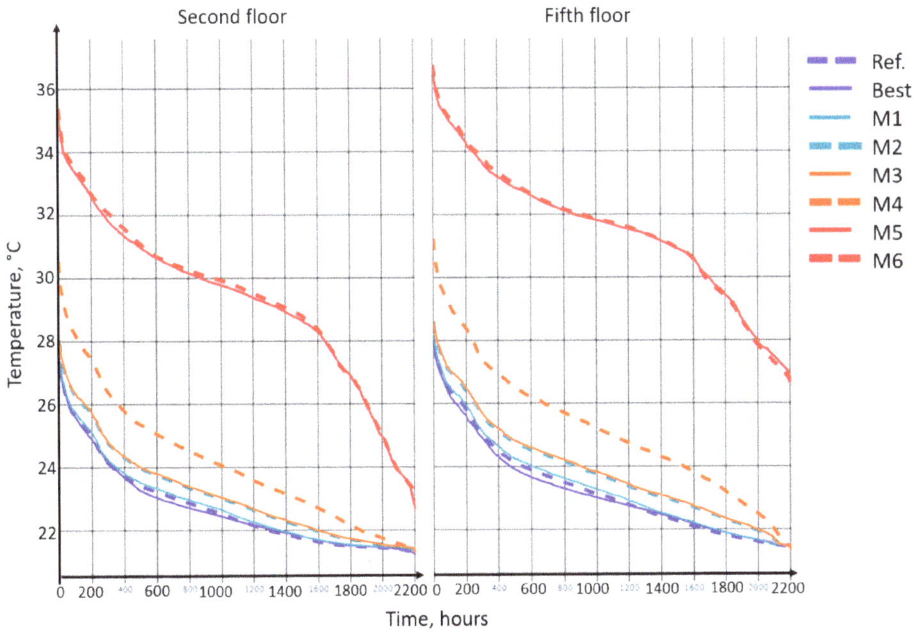

Figure 7. The indoor air temperature duration curves for the three-room apartments on the second and fifth floors from June to August.

The simulation shows the significant influence of the poor maintenance and ability to open the windows on the overheating possibility. The indoor air temperatures in the three-room apartments on the second and fifth floors are shown in Table 7 and in Figure 7. The reference case, best case, and cases with poor maintenance (M1, M2) show acceptable performance on both floors. The case with no integrated window blinds (M4) shows a warning performance level on the second floor and is unacceptable for new buildings on the fifth floor with more than 150 °Ch above 27 °C. The cases with no window opening (M5, M6) show a poor level of performance with most hours spent above 27 °C and around 300 °Ch above 32 °C for the first floor. For the fifth floor, more than 1000 °Ch are spent above 32 °C, which is above health legislation [40].

Overall, the higher floor shows lower performance due to more insolation, and results indicate lower airflow rates in the apartments.

The indoor air temperatures in the one-room apartments on the second and fifth floors are shown in Table 8 and in Figure 8. The results have the same trend as three-room apartments with indoor air overheating in the cases with no windows shading (M4) and non-openable windows (M5, M6). Smaller apartments have higher indoor air temperatures during the summer and are more likely to overheat, resulting in a dangerous level of performance with most hours spent above 32 °C and more than 1000 °Ch and 3800 °Ch for the first and fifth floor in the cases with no window opening (M5, M6). Time spent above 32 °C is an overall health warning level and 30 °C is a health risk for the elderly people.

3.2. The Indoor Air Quality Results

The results are presented for three-room and one-room apartments on the second and fifth floors. The results are presented separately for the winter and summer periods to present the influence of the opening window ventilation and to make the results comparable to the overheating analysis. The winter period is from January to April, and the summer period is from May to August to consider the heating period.

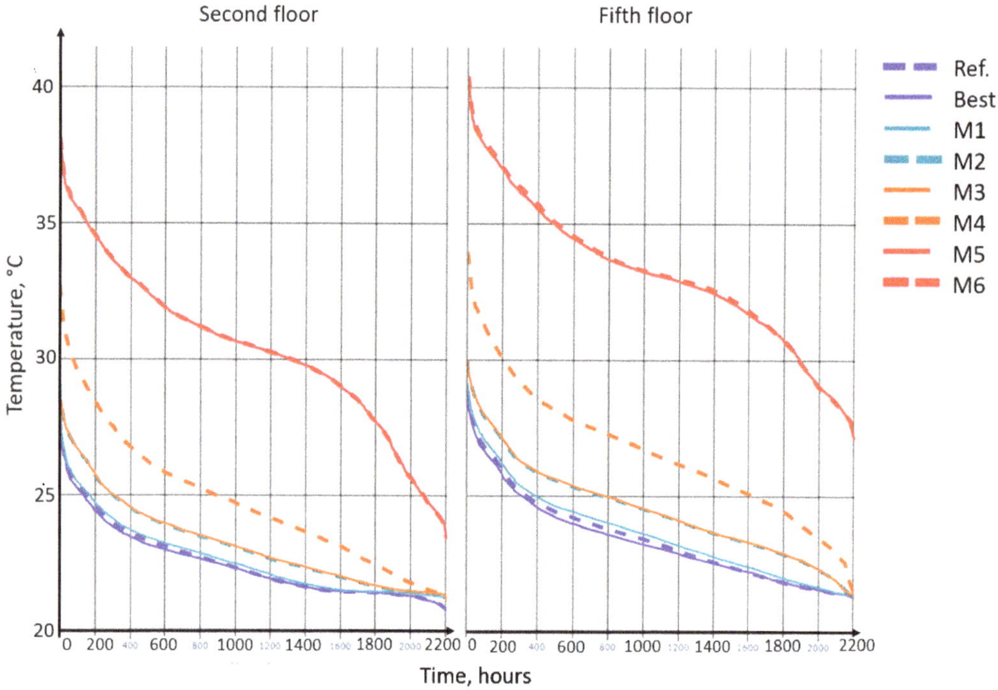

Figure 8. The indoor air temperature duration curves for the one-room apartments on the second and fifth floors from June to August.

Table 7. The three-room apartment on the second and fifth floor overheating results—number of degree hours above 27 °C, 30 °C and 32 °C during the year.

Second Floor	**Degree Hours, °Ch**		
	27	**30**	**32**
Ref.	2	0	0
Best	2	0	0
M1	4	0	0
M2	17	0	0
M3	19	0	0
M4	286	2	0
M5	5956	1366	324
M6	6185	1484	366
Fifth Floor			
Ref.	13	0	0
Best	19	0	0
M1	26	0	0
M2	56	0	0
M3	64	0	0
M4	581	14	0
M5	11,066	4130	1196
M6	11,088	4246	1282

Table 8. The one-room apartment on the second and fifth floor overheating results—number of degree hours over 27 °C, 30 °C and 32 °C during the year.

Second Floor	Degree hours, °Ch		
	27	30	27
Ref.	2	0	0
Best	4	0	0
M1	7	0	0
M2	47	0	0
M3	49	0	0
M4	676	71	5
M5	7957	2958	1159
M6	7971	2970	1167
Fifth floor			
Ref.	41	0	0
Best	54	0	0
M1	79	0	0
M2	215	0	0
M3	227	0	0
M4	2328	298	35
M5	15,814	7898	3887
M6	15,987	8083	4047

3.2.1. Apartment Bedroom Average CO_2 Concentration Analysis Results

The CO_2 concentration in the three-room apartments on the second floor is shown in Table 9 and Figure 9. In winter, in the best-case scenario, the occupants spend more than 40% of the time in indoor air categories II and III and in I [37] for the rest, and the concentration is around 720 ppm on average. The reference case shows a significant effect of the occupant and door schedules, transitioning to more than 50% in the II and III categories and 890 ppm on average. Cases with maintenance issues (M1, M2) show the effects of dirty inlet device filter and passive stack duct, further deteriorating the IAQ to 25% and 35% at the IV category for the dirty filter and its combination with stack duct, with the concentrations at 960 ppm and 1200 ppm on average. High airtightness (M3) and non-openable window (M4) cases show the worst performance, with an average of around 45% of the time in the IV category and 1350 ppm.

Table 9. The three-room apartment on the second floor CO_2 level results. Percentage of hours in each indoor air quality category (I–IV) during the year.

Case	Winter (January–May)					Summer (June–August)				
	I, %	II, %	III, %	IV, %	Average, ppm	I, %	II, %	III, %	IV, %	Average, ppm
Ref.	47.1	18.4	34.1	0.5	890	73.2	10.9	12.1	3.8	720
Best	59.8	36.8	3.4	0.0	720	77.8	17.0	5.2	0.0	670
M1	32.4	19.7	22.0	25.9	960	71.8	10.6	6.3	11.3	760
M2	20.4	10.3	26.3	43.0	1200	67.6	11.9	6.4	14.1	860
M3	15.2	7.5	23.1	54.2	1350	66.0	12.8	5.6	15.7	900
M4	15.1	7.6	23.1	54.2	1350	65.0	13.5	5.9	15.7	910
M5	15.4	7.5	23.4	53.8	1350	7.5	6.7	10.6	75.3	1630

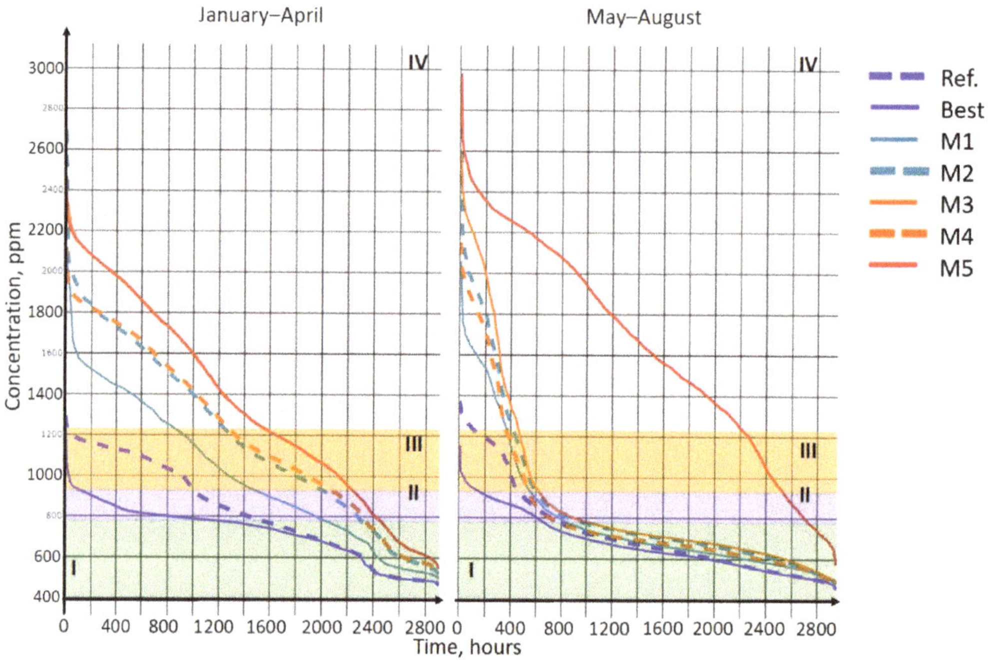

Figure 9. The duration curves of CO_2 level in the three-room apartment on the second floor for different cases for winter and summer with indoor air quality reference levels.

In summer, the additional opening ventilation significantly improves cases with maintenance issues, with only around 12% and 13% of the time spent in the IV category and about 670 ppm on average. The case with high airtightness (M3) shows the same performance as the previous ones. The case with non-openable windows (M5) show the worst performance, most of the time in the IV category and around 1600 ppm on average.

The CO_2 concentration in the three-room apartments on the fifth floor has the same trend as on the first floor, although the average level is much higher, as shown in Table 10 and Figure 10. Compared to the first floor, occupants spend more time in the III and IV category and only around 20% and 10% in I and II in reference, best and M1 cases. The average concentrations are around 1000 ppm. Other cases in winter (M2–M5) are presented only in the time spent in II, but mostly in III and IV categories with about 4%, 10% and 85%, respectively, with average concentrations of about 2400 ppm.

Table 10. The three-room apartment on the fifth floor IAQ results. Time spent in each indoor air category in percent.

Case	Winter (January–May)					Summer (June–August)				
	I, %	II, %	III, %	IV, %	Average, ppm	I, %	II, %	III, %	IV, %	Average, ppm
Ref.	19.1	10.6	25.5	44.8	1300	69.0	11.1	5.4	14.6	870
Best	23.6	16.8	49.7	10.0	950	75.7	7.5	12.5	4.3	750
M1	15.6	8.7	21.3	54.4	1450	65.4	13.1	5.4	16.0	950
M2	1.7	4.8	10.7	82.8	2300	52.6	23.0	6.1	18.3	1070
M3	0.3	2.3	10.2	87.1	2400	48.6	25.7	6.4	19.2	1100
M4	0.3	2.2	10.3	87.1	2400	48.6	25.5	6.5	19.3	1150
M5	0.3	2.2	10.4	87.1	2400	0.0	0.2	3.1	96.7	2600

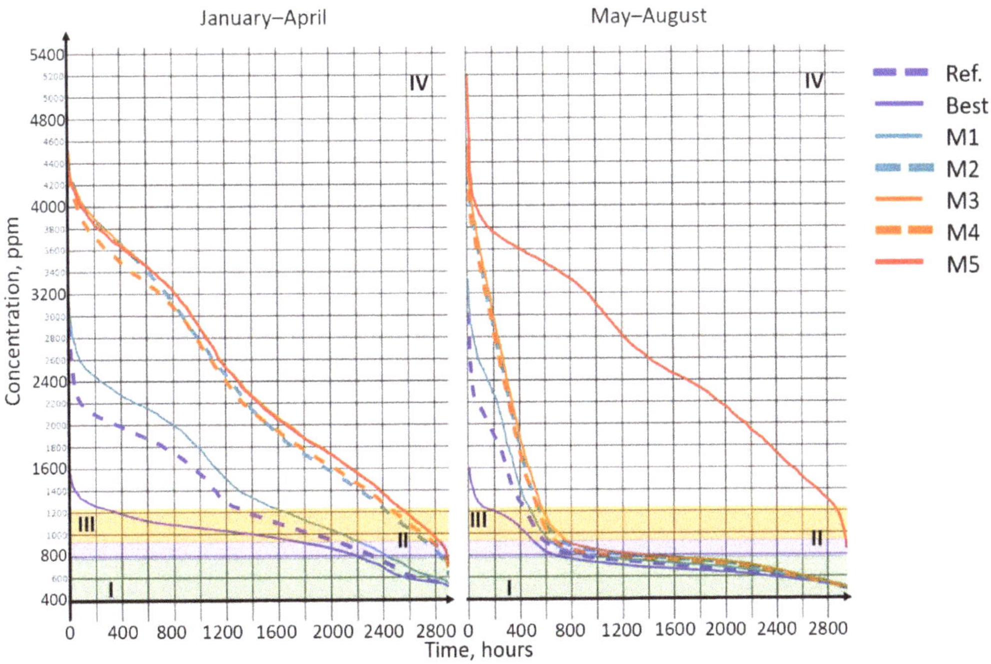

Figure 10. The duration curves of CO_2 level in the three-room apartment on the fifth floor for different cases for winter and summer periods with indoor air quality reference levels.

In summer, the additional opening ventilation significantly affects cases with openable windows (Ref., Best, M1–M4) showing better performance, with only around 16% and 18% of the time in the IV category and about 1000 ppm on average. Although, the case with non-openable windows (M5) shows the worse performance, with most of the time in the IV category and around 2600 ppm on average as the stack effect is lower in summer and the stack duct length in fifth floor apartments is also about three times shorter.

The CO_2 concentration in the one-room apartments on the second floor is shown in Table 11 and Figure 11. Overall, in winter, most of the time is spent in the I and II categories. In the best, reference and case with dirty inlet device filter (M1), at around 100% of time spent in the I category. All other cases have comparable performance with around 60% and 30% in the I and II categories with 700 ppm on average.

Table 11. The one-room apartment on the second floor IAQ results. Time spent in each indoor air category in percent.

Case	Winter (January–May)					Summer (June–August)				
	I, %	II, %	III, %	IV, %	Average, ppm	I, %	II, %	III, %	IV, %	Average, ppm
Ref.	100.0	0.0	0.0	0.0	560	96.6	3.4	0.0	0.0	560
Best	100.0	0.0	0.0	0.0	570	96.8	3.2	0.0	0.0	570
M1	98.6	1.3	0.2	0.0	600	93.3	6.4	0.3	0.0	570
M2	72.6	26.2	1.2	0.0	680	86.7	8.4	4.8	0.0	620
M3	57.4	32.5	10.1	0.0	740	85.5	5.6	8.9	0.0	630
M4	57.4	32.4	10.2	0.0	745	85.5	5.7	8.8	0.0	625
M5	57.1	31.8	11.1	0.0	740	42.0	28.3	28.5	1.2	820

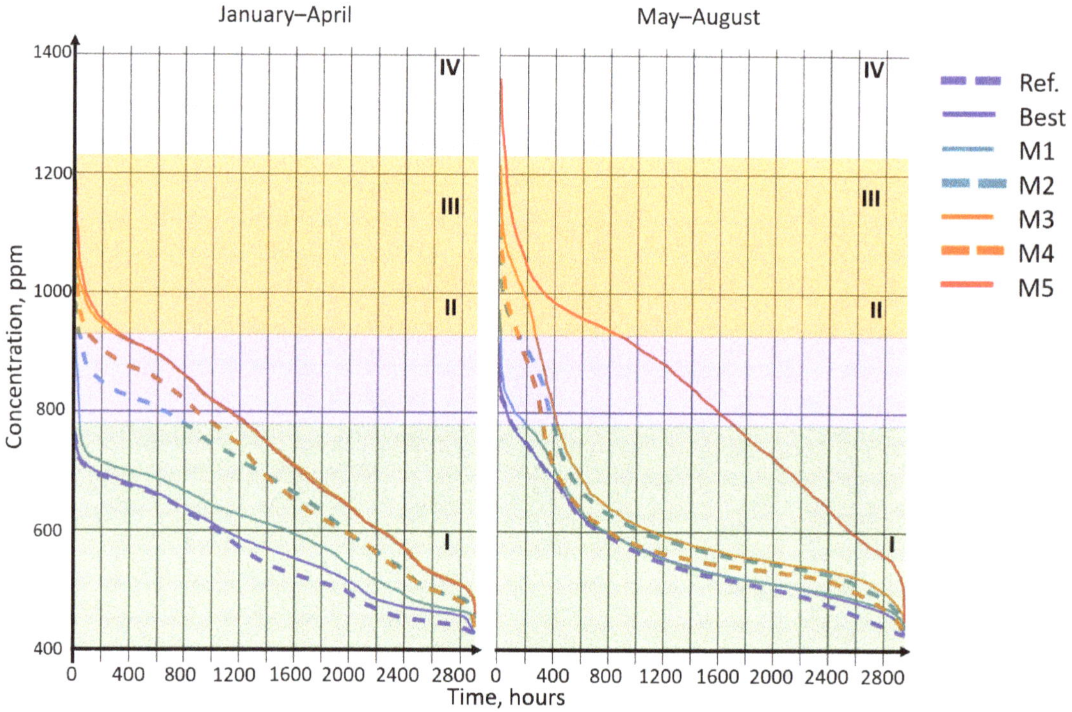

Figure 11. The duration curves of CO_2 level in the one-room apartment on the second floor for different cases for winter and summer with indoor air quality reference levels.

In summer, the performance has the same trends as in the three-room apartments. The average time spent in the I category for all cases slightly decreased for the best reference and case with a dirty inlet device filter (M1). However, more maintenance issues (M2) and improved envelope airtightness (M3) showed better performance due to the additional airflow through the windows. The performance of the worst-case scenario is around 20%, 30% and 50% at the III, II, and I categories and indicates the significance of the additional airflow through the windows.

The CO_2 concentration in the one-room apartments on the fifth floor has the same trend as on the first floor and the same, as three-room apartments on the fifth floor. Overall, the average level is between three-room apartments on the first and fifth floor. The results are shown in Figure 12 and Table 12.

In the best case, around 90% of the time is spent in the I category in winter. The rest of the time is spent in the II category. The average CO_2 concentration is 650 ppm. The reference case shows a significant effect of the occupant and door schedules, transitioning to more than 25% in the IV category and 790 ppm on average. Case with dirty inlet device filter (M1) shows further deterioration of the IAQ to around 25% in the IV category. The combination of dirty inlet filter and stack duct (M2) shows mostly the same performance as with additional combination with high airtightness (M3) and non-openable windows (M5) with around 45% time in IV category and 1470 ppm on average. The worst-case (M5) with non-openable windows shows the worst performance with 45% in the IV category.

In the summer case, the additional opening ventilation significantly affects all cases, showing better performance. The best reference and cases with maintenance issues (M1, M2) show around 80% in the I and II categories with only around 2%, 4%, 12%, and 13% of the time in the IV category for reference case, cases with maintenance issues (M1, M2) and case high airtightness (M3). The case with non-openable windows (M5) shows the worst performance with 50% in the IV category.

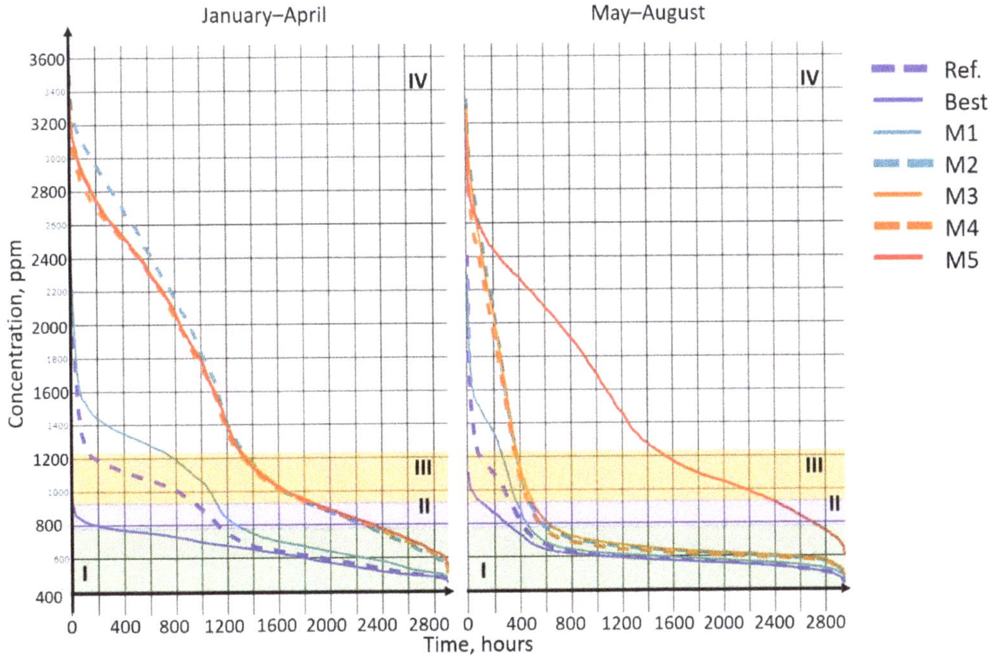

Figure 12. The duration curves of CO_2 level in the one-room apartment on the fifth floor for different cases for winter and summer with indoor air quality reference levels.

Table 12. The one-room apartment on the fifth floor IAQ results. Time spent in each indoor air category in percent.

Case	Winter (January–May)					Summer (June–August)				
	I, %	II, %	III, %	IV, %	Average, ppm	I, %	II, %	III, %	IV, %	Average, ppm
Ref.	60.7	6.6	28.0	4.7	790	85.8	3.4	8.5	2.3	650
Best	89.0	10.8	0.2	0.0	650	89.2	7.8	3.0	0.0	610
M1	54.6	7.0	13.3	25.1	900	84.2	3.3	4.0	8.5	700
M2	20.5	17.1	16.3	46.1	1500	79.9	4.2	3.5	12.5	845
M3	17.8	17.9	18.8	45.5	1470	78.3	4.9	4.0	12.7	850
M4	17.8	17.8	18.9	45.5	1490	78	4.9	4.2	12.8	860
M5	18.3	17.8	19.0	44.9	1470	7.4	12.3	30.4	50.0	1450

3.2.2. Apartment Internal Airflow and Air Change Analysis Results

The results for the internal airflow rate and air change rates for the apartments are presented in Figure 13 and Table 13. The airflow and air change rates are average during the chosen weeks in winter, spring and summer. The nominal air change rate shows rate at 15 °C as a nominal conditions. In figures, arrows represent the average airflow direction through envelope and windows and between the rooms through doors. Additionally, the mail slot is taken into consideration as a connection to the stairwell. Tables show the average airflow rate for each room. Table 13 shows air change rates for the reference case, for the cases with poor maintenance and the worst-case scenario to show the overall influence of factors on the air change rates of the apartments. The ventilation air change rate was calculated for the exhaust airflow rate through the passive stack. The total air change rate was calculated for the exhaust airflow rate through the passive stack, envelope and windows, considering all outcoming airflow rates.

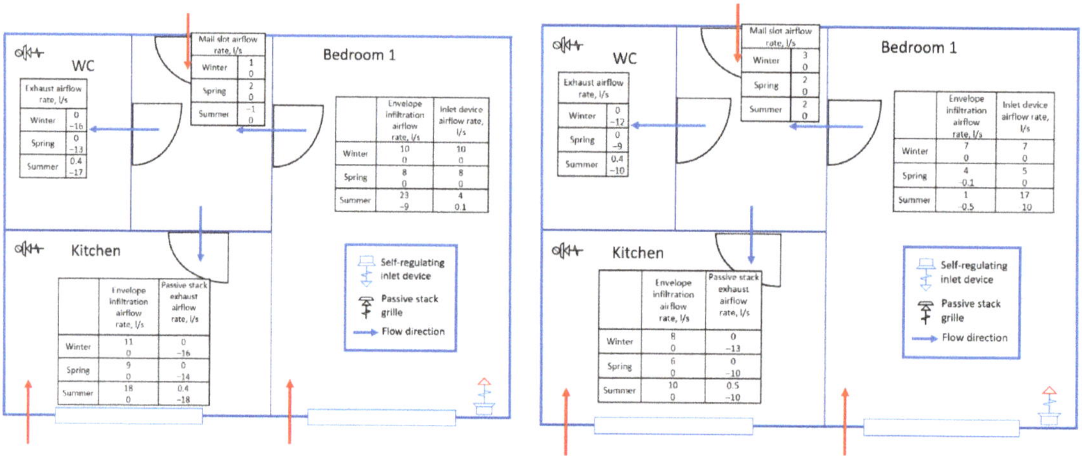

(**a**) (**b**)

Figure 13. The building simulation airflow directions pattern and rate values for the one-room apartments on the second floor (**a**); And on the fifth floor (**b**), where red arrows are external airflows and blue are internal.

Table 13. Apartment average ventilation and total air change rates for the second and fifth floor apartments during the example weeks.

Apartment Type	Season	Reference		M1		M2		M3		M5	
		Vent *	Total *	Vent	Total	Vent	Total	Vent	Total	Vent	Total
One-room, second floor	Winter	0.38	0.38	0.35	0.35	0.26	0.26	0.23	0.23	0.21	0.21
	Spring	0.32 *	0.32	0.3	0.3	0.21	0.21	0.18	0.18	0.15	0.15
	Summer	0.31	0.52	0.3	0.5	0.19	0.27	0.18	0.26	0.15	0.15
One-room, fifth floor	Winter	0.32	0.32	0.3	0.3	0.24	0.24	0.22	0.22	0.2	0.2
	Spring	0.3	0.3	0.26	0.26	0.19	0.19	0.17	0.17	0.13	0.13
	Summer	0.23	0.35	0.2	0.32	0.13	0.27	0.13	0.27	0.1	0.1
Three-room, second floor	Winter	0.28	0.28	0.27	0.27	0.14	0.14	0.12	0.14	0.1	0.12
	Spring	0.23	0.23	0.23	0.23	0.11	0.11	0.11	0.11	0.1	0.1
	Summer	0.21	0.36	0.21	0.37	0.08	0.3	0.08	0.3	0.08	0.1
Three-room, fifth floor	Winter	0.23	0.23	0.2	0.2	0.11	0.12	0.1	0.12	0.1	0.1
	Spring	0.15	0.15	0.12	0.12	0.09	0.09	0.1	0.1	0.1	0.1
	Summer	0.13	0.26	0.1	0.26	0.05	0.26	0.05	0.26	0.05	0.1

* nominal airflow rate.

Results show the trend for the apartments air change rate. The apartments on the second floor have a higher air change rate of around 15% than apartments on the fifth floor due to the higher buoyancy effect. The ventilation air change rate deteriorates from winter to summer in all cases in percentage from 20% to 50% compared to winter cases. The total ventilation air change rate deteriorates from winter to spring around 20% compared to the winter case. The total air change rate is highest in summer due to the additional airflow through windows opening, around 20% higher than the winter case.

The one-room apartment on the fifth floor shows the highest air change rates across the apartments. However, cases show increasing deterioration from reference to the worst case at around 15%, 30%, 40% and 50% between summer and spring ventilation air change, respectively. The combination of maintenance issues shows the most significant relative effect on the air change rate. In summer, the trend is the same with 5%, 23%, 29% and 30% reductions, respectively.

The one-room apartment on the fifth floor shows less significant relative deterioration from reference case to worst case. Although, the overall air change rate is much lower. The deterioration is around 6%, 25%, 31%, and 31% for the summer case. The air change rate plummets in the spring by about 13%, 37%, 43%, and 47%, respectively. The combination of maintenance issues shows the most significant relative effect on the air change rate. In summer the trend is the same with 5%, 23%, 29% and 30% reductions.

The three-room apartment on the second floor shows a lower air change rate than both one-room apartments. Additionally, the deterioration trend from reference to worst case stays the same with around 4%, 50%, 57%, and 64% for summer. The air change rate is the same for reference case and M1 in the spring but plummets by about 52%, 57%, and 57%, respectively. The dirty inlet filter and passive stack duct combination (M2) shows the most significant relative effect on the air change rate. The trend is the same in summer with no change for the M1 case and 62% for the rest, respectively.

The three-room apartment on the fifth floor shows the lowest air change rate across the simulated apartments. The overall trend is the same. However, the case with a dirty inlet device filter also affects the results. The simulation shows deterioration from reference case to worst case of around 13%, 52%, 57% and 57% for summer. In the spring, the air change rate plummets by about 20%, 40%, 33% and 33%, respectively. The combination of maintenance issues shows the most significant relative effect on the air change rate. In summer the trend is the same with 23% for the M1 case and 62% and for the rest, respectively.

The apartment airflow rate in the one-room apartments on the fifth floor is shown in Figure 14. Due to the vertical location differences of second and fifth floors the airflow rate is lower by around 20%. The infiltration airflow rate in the bedroom is mostly equal to the inlet device airflow rate in winter and spring cases. In summer, the windows opening ventilation combined with infiltration accounts for around 80% of outdoor airflow.

The lowest apartment total supply airflow rates are presented during the springtime on both floors, with 27 L/s and 17 L/s for the second and fifth floors, respectively. In winter, the apartment total airflow rate is around 32 L/s and 25 L/s. The total apartment and supply airflows are the highest in summer, around 45 L/s and 28 L/s, respectively. During the summer, the reversed airflow may occur due to the apartment overheating. This also indicates a low apartment airflow rate in that period. Although, a low average reverse airflow rate indicates that it is a rare occurrence.

The apartment airflow rate in the three-room apartments has the same trend as in one-room apartments and shown in Figure 14, with the fifth floor lower by around 30% than the second floor due to the vertical position difference. The infiltration airflow rate in the bedroom is also almost equal to the inlet device airflow rate in winter and spring cases. In summer, the windows opening ventilation combined with infiltration accounts for around 75% of supply airflow.

The lowest apartment total supply airflow rates are presented during the springtime on both floors, with 44 L/s and 27 L/s for the second and fifth floors, respectively. In winter, the apartment total airflow rate is around 50 L/s and 42 L/s. The total supply airflow is the highest in summer, around 79 L/s and 72 L/s, respectively.

During the summer, the reversed airflow is also presented due to the apartment overheating. This also indicates a low apartment airflow rate in that period. Although, low average reverse airflow rate indicates that it is a rare occurrence.

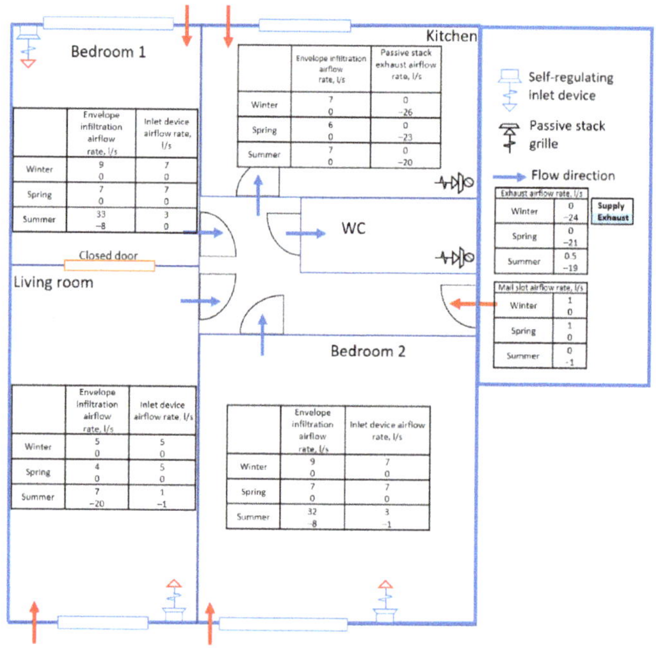

(a)

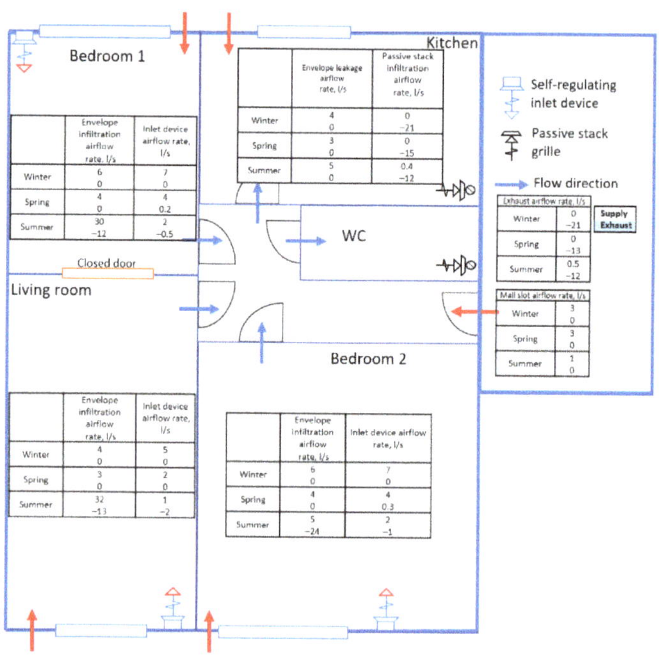

(b)

Figure 14. The building simulation airflow directions pattern and airflow rates for the three-room apartments on the second floor (**a**); And fifth floor (**b**), where red arrows are external airflows and blue are internal.

4. Discussion

Apartment retrofitting requires a simple but efficient solution to provide adequate IAQ, energy performance, and retrofit costs. It is particularly important for protected or heritage buildings with natural passive stack ventilation and no or limited access to the building envelope or ventilation system changes. One of the solutions is the implementation of self-regulating inlet devices to preserve the initial ventilation system and envelope and provide designed airflow rates and low costs as it is commonly assumed that natural ventilation does not have much maintenance. However, modern self-regulating inlet devices have filters that require at least yearly maintenance, which should be done by the service company or by occupants. The results clearly show that maintenance of the modern passive stack system with openable apartment windows is essential. These results are to consider, as if it is the occupant responsibility to do maintenance, it might be a challenge doing that without much experience. On the other hand, if the service company does it, it requires labour and the ability to visit apartments to be carried out. Additionally, the maintenance of the passive stack duct should be carefully planned to prevent its clogging.

It is also crucial to avoid overheating in the cases of a group of vulnerable people, such as elderly people who have openable windows but cannot operate them. Otherwise, the apartment temperature exceeds 30 °C, which is a health risk for elderly people. In some cases, the temperature exceeds 32 °C, which is a health limit for other occupants.

The three-room and one-room apartments, both equipped with the same exhaust system, consist of two passive stacks in the bathroom and kitchen. The difference is the number of rooms with inlet devices and an external surface for infiltration, thus lowering system resistance. In general, it means that three-room apartments are more sensible for the passive stack ventilation system poor maintenance than one-room apartments. Therefore, three-room apartments on the fifth floor with a low buoyancy effect show a CO_2 level higher than 4000 ppm. On the other hand, improved airtightness in such apartments does not benefit the ventilation system and IAQ performance.

It is presented in the simulation of the reference case that the CO_2 level in one-room apartments is lower than in three-room apartments. However, they are much more likely to overheat. Although, this is partly mitigated by the fact that the air movement rate in a one-room apartment is higher, creating more pleasant indoor thermal conditions.

In cases with poor maintenance, with dirty inlet devices and passive stack, the most crucial effect is shown on the fifth-floor apartments for the CO_2 level, which rises due to the significantly lower passive stack exhaust rates. The case with improved airtightness restricts infiltration and exfiltration airflow rate in all the apartments. It leads to significant overheating in the one-room apartments with an indoor air temperature of 30 °C and higher. The additional airflow rate of the windows opening ventilation shows a crucial effect with a much lower CO_2 level in summer. However, the window opening ventilation has its limitation due to the outdoor airborne and noise pollution, and it is preferable not to be utilized in the cities with high population density, near roads and traffic lines.

The limitations of the study are mostly presented with physical model limitations and case-specific input data. This simulation analysis assesses the average airflow and air change rates calculated via hourly average outdoor conditions. However, the momentary airflow rate may be significantly different. The building simulation model considers building design and structure, device parameters, occupant behaviour, and lighting and heating schedule, but it still has some limitations. The simulation model is created with separate nodes for each room, but each node represents the entire room. All the nodes are calculated to be in balance. The distribution of the parameters within each node is calculated only for the boundary elements, such as inlets, doors and windows. As the distribution in each node, room, is even as for the mixed model, the calculated values are average, but local values are needed to analyze draught. This means that cold draughts, airflow patterns etc., may be calculated indirectly and may significantly change the occupant thermal comfort sensations. The case-specific input is presented with the Nordic climate weather and outdoor conditions. The façade wind pressure coefficients and building structure materials were assumed according to the building age. Furthermore, the inlet device model is created based on the design manufacturer data, representing its theoretical performance and placed according to the building documentation. The pressure drop in filters and stack ducts in cases of poor maintenance has been assumed based on literature. The case building is presented with five floors; thus, the simulation results for high-rise buildings might differ due to the significant effect of the wind pressure.

The simulation results of ACH may be compared against previous experimental studies of passive stack ventilation. The study was conducted in the warm climate of Portugal and showed a good correlation. The average air change rate was 0.6–0.7 ACH with window opening ventilation [31] and the air change level of 0.35 ACH in winter, best-case scenario, and around 0.1 ACH in August, in the worst-case scenario for the cases without opening ventilation [33]. Additionally, the results agree with previous field studies in Nordic climate, Helsinki, where the mean air-exchange rates in apartments had a high variation (average 0.6 L/h, range 0.1–1.2 L/h) [47]. The ASHRAE minimum value of 0.35 L/h was not achieved in 28% of all dwellings, and the average air change rate in the naturally ventilated apartments is 0.64 L/h [47]. Some previous studies assessed the CO_2 in the cold climate, Beijing, in bedrooms, concluding the necessity of additional windows opening ventilation. The maximum CO_2 level was observed at around 4000 to 5000 ppm [48].

Natural ventilation advancements present the trend of making systems less dependent on outdoor weather conditions and having reliable and constant airflow rates. In practice, one of the most demanding paths is the building stock retrofit, which requires high IAQ, but simple solutions, presented with such devices as self-controlled air inlets or passive stack outlets and wise windows opening strategies. The results and highlighted points may be considered in the renovation design for the buildings with passive stack ventilation in the Nordic conditions to ensure good IAQ and prevent apartment overheating, especially in homes of vulnerable groups of people.

5. Conclusions

The regulations and standards are developed to ensure high indoor environment quality in the building stock, and that the classification of the IAQ parameters reflects the desirable level in residential buildings. In practice, the lowest level considers the effect of health; thus, renovation and retrofit of the old buildings should aim to provide a high IAQ level. The paper analyses the performance of a retrofitted five-storey apartment building equipped with modern passive stack ventilation in Nordic conditions. The passive stack ventilation system was retrofitted in 2018, and novel self-regulating air inlet devices with filters were equipped. The building was simulated with IDA ICE software, where the model of the self-regulating inlet devices was developed using manufacturer product data. Several case scenarios were created to analyze the effect of poor maintenance, improved airtightness, and window opening on the system performance. For the analysis, one-room and three-room apartments on the second and fifth floors were chosen. The CO_2 levels and indoor air temperature were analyzed and compared with EN 16798-1 to assess the IAQ. The results are separated for the winter and summer to show the influence of additional airflow from opening ventilation. The apartment air change rate and internal airflow patterns were assessed and compared case by case.

The results show a trend for the one-room apartment to overheat, despite having a higher air change rate than the three-room apartments. The three-room apartments tolerate overheating, although they are much more sensible considering the poor maintenance. Improving the envelope airtightness does not benefit the IAQ of the apartments. The results show a significant effect of poor maintenance and window opening possibility on the CO_2 concentration. Furthermore, the apartments on the fifth floor are more sensitive to poor maintenance, and three-room apartments situated there showed warning levels of CO_2. The case with non-openable windows showed more than 150 °Ch over 32 °C in all apartments.

Filter replacement is essential for the desired operation of the modern passive stack ventilation system. Additionally, the maintenance of the passive stack duct should be carefully planned to prevent its clogging. It is crucial to prevent overheating due to windows being left closed. Otherwise, the temperature in the apartments can reach above 32 °C, which is a health risk.

The results and highlighted points are crucial as the protected and heritage buildings with natural ventilation and limited or no access to the envelope or ventilation system reconstruction require retrofit to meet current building codes requirements. The results may be applied to retrofit the buildings with passive stack ventilation in the Nordic conditions to ensure good IAQ and prevent apartment overheating, especially in the homes of vulnerable groups of people.

Author Contributions: Conceptualization, I.K., R.K., J.J., S.K.; methodology, I.K., J.J., R.K.; software, I.K., J.J.; validation, I.K., J.J., S.K.; formal analysis, I.K.; investigation, I.K., J.J.; resources, I.K.; data curation, I.K.; writing—original draft preparation, I.K.; writing—review and editing, R.K., J.J., S.K.; visualization, I.K.; supervision, R.K.; project administration, R.K.; funding acquisition, R.K., J.J. All authors have read and agreed to the published version of the manuscript.

Funding: This research was funded by HEATCLIM (Heat and health in the changing climate, Grant No. 329306) funded by the Academy of Finland within the CLIHE (Climate change and health) program. SUREFIT (Sustainable solutions for affordable retrofit of domestic buildings) funded by the European Union (Horizon 2020 program, Grant No. 894511).

Institutional Review Board Statement: Not applicable.

Informed Consent Statement: Not applicable.

Acknowledgments: The authors would like to acknowledge Mika Vuolle from Equa Simulation Finland Ltd. for developing the inlet device model, IDA ICE software support and cooperation.

Conflicts of Interest: The authors declare no conflict of interest.

References

1. World Health Organization. *The World Health Report 2000: Health Systems: Improving Performance*; WHO: Geneva, Switzerland, 2000; ISBN 978-92-4-156198-3.
2. Olesen, B.W. Indoor Environment Criteria for Design and Calculation of Energy Performance of Buildings EN15251. In Proceedings of the 6th International Conference on Indoor Air Quality, Ventialtion & Energy Conservation in Buildings: Sustainable Build Environment, Sendai, Japan, 28–31 October 2007.
3. Brelih, N.; Seppanen, O. Ventilation Rates and IAQ in European Standards and National Regulations. In Proceedings of the 32nd AIVC Conference and 1st TightVent Conference, Brussels, Belgium, 12–13 October 2011.
4. Fernbas Energy Performance of Buildings Directive. Available online: https://ec.europa.eu/energy/topics/energy-efficiency/energy-efficient-buildings/energy-performance-buildings-directive_en (accessed on 5 November 2020).
5. Dimitroulopoulou, C. Ventilation in European Dwellings: A Review. *Build. Environ.* **2012**, *47*, 109–125. [CrossRef]
6. The National Building Code of Finland. Available online: https://ym.fi/en/the-national-building-code-of-finland (accessed on 11 November 2020).
7. Ministry of the Environment (Finland). *Ministry of Environment Decree (1010/2017) on the Energy Performance of the New Building*; Ministry of the Environment: Helsinki, Finland, 2018.
8. Ahola, M.; Säteri, J.; Sariola, L. Revised Finnish Classification of Indoor Climate 2018. *E3S Web Conf.* **2019**, *111*, 02017. [CrossRef]
9. Rämö, A. Statistics Finland—Building Stock 2019. Available online: http://www.stat.fi/til/rakke/2019/rakke_2019_2020-05-27_kat_002_en.html (accessed on 5 November 2020).
10. Department of Built Environment, Ministry of the Environment (Finland). *National Building Code of Finland. Part D2. Indoor Climate and Ventilation of Buildings Regulations and Guidelines*; Department of Built Environment, Ministry of the Environment (Finland): Helsinki, Finland, 2012.
11. International Energy Agency. *Ministry of the Environment Decree (4/13, Amendment 2/17) on Improving the Energy Performance of Buildings Undergoing Renovation or Alteration*; International Energy Agency: Paris, France, 2013.
12. Nazaroff, W.W. Residential Air-Change Rates: A Critical Review. *Indoor Air* **2021**, *31*, 282–313. [CrossRef] [PubMed]
13. Liddament, M.; Axley, J.; Heiselberg, P.; Li, Y.; Stathopoulos, T. Achieving Natural and Hybrid Ventilation in Practice. *Int. J. Vent.* **2006**, *5*, 115–130. [CrossRef]
14. Gou, Z.; Gamage, W.; Lau, S.S.-Y.; Lau, S.S.-Y. An Investigation of Thermal Comfort and Adaptive Behaviors in Naturally Ventilated Residential Buildings in Tropical Climates: A Pilot Study. *Buildings* **2018**, *8*, 5. [CrossRef]

15. Saif, J.; Wright, A.; Khattak, S.; Elfadli, K. Keeping Cool in the Desert: Using Wind Catchers for Improved Thermal Comfort and Indoor Air Quality at Half the Energy. *Buildings* **2021**, *11*, 100. [CrossRef]
16. Calautit, J.K.; O'Connor, D.; Hughes, B.R. A Natural Ventilation Wind Tower with Heat Pipe Heat Recovery for Cold Climates. *Renew. Energy* **2016**, *87*, 1088–1104. [CrossRef]
17. Gong, J.; Hang, J. Buoyancy-Driven Natural Ventilation in One Storey Connected with an Atrium. *Int. J. Vent.* **2018**, *18*, 281–302. [CrossRef]
18. Hussain, S.; Oosthuizen, P.H. Numerical Investigations of Buoyancy-Driven Natural Ventilation in a Simple Atrium Building and Its Effect on the Thermal Comfort Conditions. *Appl. Therm. Eng.* **2012**, *40*, 358–372. [CrossRef]
19. Khanal, R.; Lei, C. Solar Chimney—A Passive Strategy for Natural Ventilation. *Energy Build.* **2011**, *43*, 1811–1819. [CrossRef]
20. Salata, F.; Alippi, C.; Tarsitano, A.; Golasi, I.; Coppi, M. A First Approach to Natural Thermoventilation of Residential Buildings through Ventilation Chimneys Supplied by Solar Ponds. *Sustainability* **2015**, *7*, 9649–9663. [CrossRef]
21. Barbosa, S.; Ip, K. Perspectives of Double Skin Façades for Naturally Ventilated Buildings: A Review. *Renew. Sustain. Energy Rev.* **2014**, *40*, 1019–1029. [CrossRef]
22. Kim, Y.-M.; Kim, S.-Y.; Shin, S.-W.; Sohn, J.-Y. Contribution of Natural Ventilation in a Double Skin Envelope to Heating Load Reduction in Winter. *Build. Environ.* **2009**, *44*, 2236–2244. [CrossRef]
23. Hsu, H.-H.; Chiang, W.-H.; Huang, J.-S. Hybrid Ventilation in an Air-Conditioned Office Building with a Multistory Atrium for Thermal Comfort: A Practical Case Study. *Buildings* **2021**, *11*, 625. [CrossRef]
24. Vinha, J.; Manelius, E.; Korpi, M.; Salminen, K.; Kurnitski, J.; Kiviste, M.; Laukkarinen, A. Airtightness of Residential Buildings in Finland. *Build. Environ.* **2015**, *93*, 128–140. [CrossRef]
25. Biler, A.; Unlu Tavil, A.; Su, Y.; Khan, N. A Review of Performance Specifications and Studies of Trickle Vents. *Buildings* **2018**, *8*, 152. [CrossRef]
26. Choi, Y.; Song, D. How to Quantify Natural Ventilation Rate of Single-Sided Ventilation with Trickle Ventilator? *Build. Environ.* **2020**, *181*, 107119. [CrossRef]
27. Karava, P.; Stathopoulos, T.; Athienitis, A.K. Investigation of the Performance of Trickle Ventilators. *Build. Environ.* **2003**, *38*, 981–993. [CrossRef]
28. Willems, L.; Janssens, A. Performance Prediction of Dwelling Ventilation with Self-Regulating Air Inlets. In Proceedings of the 26th AIVC Conference: Ventilation in Relation to the Energy Performance of Buildings, Brussels, Belgium, 21–23 September 2005; pp. 197–202.
29. Janssens, A.; Willems, L.; Laverge, J. Performance Evaluation of Residential Ventilation Systems Based on Multi-Zone Ventilation Models. In Proceedings of the 4th International Building Physics Conference: Energy Efficiency and New Approaches, Istanbul, Turkey, 15–18 June 2009; 7p.
30. Building Regulation—GOV.UK. Available online: https://www.gov.uk/housing-local-and-community/building-regulation (accessed on 3 August 2021).
31. Pinto, M.; Freitas, V.; Viegas, J.; Matias, L. Residential Hybrid Ventilation Systems in Portugal: Experimental Characterization. In Proceedings of the 8th International Conference and Exhibition on Healthy Buildings 2006, Lisbon, Portugal, 1–8 June 2006; Volume 4, pp. 357–362.
32. Pinto, M.; Viegas, J.; de Freitas, V.P. Air Permeability Measurements of Dwellings and Building Components in Portugal. *Build. Environ.* **2011**, *46*, 2480–2489. [CrossRef]
33. Ramos, N.M.M.; Almeida, R.M.S.F.; Curado, A.; Pereira, P.F.; Manuel, S.; Maia, J. Airtightness and Ventilation in a Mild Climate Country Rehabilitated Social Housing Buildings—What Users Want and What They Get. *Build. Environ.* **2015**, *92*, 97–110. [CrossRef]
34. Ward, I.C. The Potential Impact of the New (UK) Building Regulations on the Provision of Natural Ventilation in Dwellings—A Case Study of Low Energy Social Housing. *Int. J. Vent.* **2008**, *7*, 77–88. [CrossRef]
35. Neve, J.D.; Denys, S.; Pieters, J.G.; Pollet, I.; Denul, J. CFD Analysis of the Effect of Self-Regulating Devices on the Distribution of Naturally Supplied Air. In Proceedings of the 26th AIVC Conference: Ventilation in Relation to the Energy Performance of Buildings, Brussels, Belgium, 21–23 September 2005; 6p.
36. Arendt, K.; Krzaczek, M. Co-Simulation Strategy of Transient CFD and Heat Transfer in Building Thermal Envelope Based on Calibrated Heat Transfer Coefficients. *Int. J. Therm. Sci.* **2014**, *85*, 1–11. [CrossRef]
37. *Indoor Environmental Input Parameters for Design and Assessment of Energy Performance of Buildings Addressing Indoor Air Quality, Thermal Environment, Lighting and Acoustics*; EN 15251:2007; European Committee for Standardization: Brussels, Belgium, 2007.
38. *Energy Performance of Buildings—Ventilation for Buildings—Part 1: Indoor Environmental Input Parameters for Design and Assessment of Energy Performance of Buildings Addressing Indoor Air Quality, Thermal Environment, Lighting and Acoustics*; EN 16798-1:2019; European Committee for Standardization: Brussels, Belgium, 2019.
39. Renovation and Decarbonisation of Buildings. Available online: https://ec.europa.eu/commission/presscorner/detail/en/ip_21_6683 (accessed on 29 December 2021).
40. Ministry of Social Affairs and Health (Finland). *35. Decree (525/2015) of the Ministry of Social Affairs and Health on Health-related Conditions of Housing and Other Residential Buildings and Qualification Requirements for Third-party Experts*; Ministry of Social Affairs and Health (Finland): Helsinki, Finland, 2015.

41. Observations in Finland—Finnish Meteorological Institute. Available online: https://en.ilmatieteenlaitos.fi/observations-in-finland (accessed on 22 June 2021).
42. Validation & Certifications—Simulation Software | EQUA. Available online: https://www.equa.se/en/ida-ice/validation-certifications (accessed on 22 June 2021).
43. Kalamees, T.; Jylhä, K.; Tietäväinen, H.; Jokisalo, J.; Ilomets, S.; Hyvönen, R.; Saku, S. Development of Weighting Factors for Climate Variables for Selecting the Energy Reference Year According to the EN ISO 15927-4 Standard. *Energy Build.* **2012**, *47*, 53–60. [CrossRef]
44. Kontonasiou, E. Analysis of Indoor Air Quality & Thermal Comfort Parameters in Building Regulations in 8 Member States. In Proceedings of the 36th AIVC Conference "Effective Ventilation in High Performance Buildings", Madrid, Spain, 23–24 September 2015; 10p.
45. Jokisalo, J.; Kurnitski, J.; Vuolle, M.; Torkki, A. Performance of Balanced Ventilation with Heat Recovery in Residential Buildings in a Cold Climate. *Int. J. Vent.* **2003**, *2*, 223–236. [CrossRef]
46. REHVA Guidebook 29. Available online: https://www.rehva.eu/hvac-guidebook-repository/rehva-guidebook-29 (accessed on 7 July 2021).
47. Ruotsalainen, R.; Ronnberg, R.; Sateri, J.; Majanen, A.; Seppanen, O.; Jaakkola, J.J.K. Indoor Climate and the Performance of Ventilation in Finnish Residences. *Indoor Air* **1992**, *2*, 137–145. [CrossRef]
48. Lei, Z.; Liu, C.; Wang, L.; Li, N. Effect of Natural Ventilation on Indoor Air Quality and Thermal Comfort in Dormitory during Winter. *Build. Environ.* **2017**, *125*, 240–247. [CrossRef]

International Journal of
Environmental Research and Public Health

MDPI

Article

A Time-Varying Model for Predicting Formaldehyde Emission Rates in Homes

Haoran Zhao *, Iain S. Walker, Michael D. Sohn and Brennan Less

Residential Building Systems Group and Indoor Environment Group, Lawrence Berkeley National Laboratory, Berkeley, CA 94720, USA; iswalker@lbl.gov (I.S.W.); mdsohn@lbl.gov (M.D.S.); bdless@lbl.gov (B.L.)
* Correspondence: haoranzhao@lbl.gov; Tel.: +1-(312)-804-8091

Abstract: Recent studies have succeeded in relating emissions of various volatile organic compounds to material mass diffusion transfer using detailed empirical characteristics of each of the individual emitting materials. While significant, the resulting models are often scenario specific and/or require a host of individual component parameters to estimate emission rates. This study developed an approach to estimate aggregated emissions rates based on a wide number of field measurements. We used a multi-parameter regression model based on previous mass transfer models to predict formaldehyde emission rate for a whole dwelling using field-measured, time-resolved formaldehyde concentrations, air exchange rates, and indoor environmental parameters in 63 California single-family houses built between 2011 and 2017. The resulting model provides time-varying formaldehyde emission rates, normalized by floor area, for each study home, assuming a well-mixed mass balance transport model of the home, and a well-mixed layer transport model of indoor surfaces. The surface layer model asserts an equilibrium concentration within the surface layer of the emitted materials that is a function of temperature and *RH*; the dwelling ventilation rate serves as a surrogate for indoor concentration. We also developed a more generic emission model that is suitable for broad prediction of emission for a population of buildings. This model is also based on measurements aggregated from 27 homes from the same study. We showed that errors in predicting household formaldehyde concentrations using this approach were substantially less than those using a traditional constant emission rate model, despite requiring less unique building information.

Keywords: formaldehyde; indoor air quality; emission rate; new homes; field measured data; temperature; humidity; modeling; simulation

Citation: Zhao, H.; Walker, I.S.; Sohn, M.D.; Less, B. A Time-Varying Model for Predicting Formaldehyde Emission Rates in Homes. *Int. J. Environ. Res. Public Health* **2022**, *19*, 6603. https://doi.org/10.3390/ijerph19116603

Academic Editors: Paul B. Tchounwou, Ashok Kumar, Michał Piasecki, M Amirul I Khan and Alejandro Moreno Rangel

Received: 30 March 2022
Accepted: 26 May 2022
Published: 28 May 2022

1. Introduction

Formaldehyde emission rates have most commonly been estimated as fixed values based on materials and house characteristics that are invariant with temperature, humidity or air change rate [1,2]. However, previous field measurements and modeling studies have shown that these environmental factors influence indoor formaldehyde emissions. The objective of this study was to develop an improved calculation procedure to estimate the emission rate of formaldehyde for modeling indoor air quality in residential buildings. Rather than a fixed emission rate, we developed an emission rate model that varies in time depending on environmental parameters. The model-development procedure was based on using measured field data to estimate emission rates and to correlate the emission rate with various commonly known indoor parameters: temperature, humidity, ventilation rate, and floor area. The intent was that the emission rate estimates could be used to determine formaldehyde concentrations in indoor air in homes under dynamic environmental and ventilation conditions. Some previous studies have used similar physical models, but were based on coefficients from test chamber samples rather than emissions in real homes requiring considerable assumptions, to convert emissions from samples to emissions from all the sources in a home. In order to remove these assumptions, the current study used measured data from a group of homes to investigate home-to-home emission rate variability. The value of accurate, time-varying emission estimates for formaldehyde in dwellings is that we can improve our ability to predict changes in formaldehyde exposures associated with changes in the building code, dwelling ventilation rates or controls.

Estimation of formaldehyde concentrations in homes is important, because indoor exposures are associated with substantial public health burdens, as quantified by Disability Adjusted Life Years (DALYs) [3]. Formaldehyde is found in many common building materials, such as engineered wood products, cabinetry, and flooring. Acute exposure to formaldehyde can cause nose, eye, and throat irritation [4,5]. Indoor chronic exposure to formaldehyde can cause respiratory symptoms and cancer [6,7].

Previous studies have found that formaldehyde concentrations in new and existing residences routinely exceed health relevant thresholds. In a study of 105 California homes built in 2002–2005 [8], formaldehyde concentrations measured over 24-h exceeded the California Office of Environmental Health Hazards Assessment (OEHHA) chronic and 8-h reference exposure levels of 9 $\mu g/m^3$ (7.3 ppb) [9] in 98% of homes, and exceeded the World Health Organization 30-min exposure guideline of 0.1 mg/m^3 [4] in 5% of the homes. In a more recent study in California of newly built homes with low-emitting materials, weekly average formaldehyde concentrations exceeded the California OEHHA chronic and 8-h reference exposure levels in all 68 homes [10]. In another large-scale study of 352 existing California homes, the average indoor formaldehyde concentration was lower (14 $\mu g/m^3$), but 95% homes still exceeded the California OEHHA chronic and 8-h reference exposure levels [11]. In a study investigating 398 existing US homes, the mean indoor formaldehyde concentration was 21.6 $\mu g/m^3$ [12]. Two recent surveys conducted in Canada found formaldehyde concentrations (averaged over 24-h) exceeded the Health Canada residential indoor air quality 8-h exposure guideline of 50 $\mu g/m^3$ [13] in 16 out of 59 homes (27%) in Prince Edward Island [14], and in 11 out of 96 homes (11%) in Quebec City [15].

There are two key engineering control measures for limiting formaldehyde concentrations in residences: source control through use of low-emitting materials and ventilation with outside air.

Formaldehyde emissions from engineered wood products were first regulated in the US by the State of California beginning in 2007. National regulations based on the California requirements (Formaldehyde Standards for Composite Wood Products Act of 2010—Code of Federal Regulations 40 CFR Part 770) [16] were legislated in 2010 and came into force in March of 2019. These standards limit formaldehyde emissions by prescribing maximum allowable equilibrium concentrations measured in laboratory chamber tests of product samples under standard conditions. The effectiveness of these regulations in reducing formaldehyde concentrations has been demonstrated in field studies [17]. However, the emission rates are not measured or regulated directly by the standard. The actual emission rate of the emitting materials in homes is dominated by the maximum allowable equilibrium concentration, but also affected by environmental conditions, such as temperature and relative humidity, which will be described in the later sections. The whole house equilibrium concentration is highly variable because the type and quantity of the materials in homes remain unknown. Thus, the model we developed in this study will focus on a specific group of homes with low- emitting materials. The whole house equilibrium concentration was estimated as a coefficient to represent house to house variance.

Ventilation with outside air can reduce the concentration of formaldehyde in residences via dilution and removal. Quantitative studies have demonstrated how formaldehyde concentrations decrease as air change rates increase cross-sectionally for populations of homes [17–20]. Based on formaldehyde emission factors, one study estimated that an air change rate (ACH) of 0.5 h^{-1} would maintain formaldehyde concentrations below 50 ppb in typical new North American houses [21]. A study in Canadian homes found that an ACH of 0.35 h^{-1} appears sufficient to ensure a formaldehyde concentration lower than the 50 $\mu g/m^3$ Health Canada guideline in most homes [15].

Increasing ventilation rate would increase the concentration gradient between material air surface layer and the room air, leading to an increment of whole house formaldehyde emission rate, as suggested by previous studies [17,22–26]. Specifically, ventilation has been shown to increase formaldehyde emissions, while still providing a net-reduction in indoor concentrations. Hult et al. reported measurements in nine new homes in which they systematically achieved three different ventilation rates [17]. As ventilation rates were increased, they compared observed reductions in formaldehyde concentrations versus expected reductions based a fixed emission rate assumption. They found that up to 60% of the benefit of increased ventilation (assuming fixed emissions) was lost due to corresponding increases in formaldehyde emission rates. Liu et al. performed a time-resolved assessment of VOC emission rates (including formaldehyde) in a Northern California residence, and they found that emission rates increased with household ventilation rates and with temperature [25]. Offermann et al. tested three ventilation rates in a CA home (0.21, 0.41 and 0.64 h^{-1}), and observed formaldehyde emissions increase from 17 to 24 to 31 $\mu g/m^3/h$ [26].

Several studies have measured changes in formaldehyde concentrations associated with temperature and humidity conditions, from which changes in emission rates are inferred. Andersen et al. measured an increase in temperature of 7 °C doubled the formaldehyde equilibrium concentration in a chamber and the change of 40% relative humidity also doubled the formaldehyde concentration [27]. Salthammer et al. measured an increase of 6 $\mu g/m^3$ per Celsius degree increase in temperature and 2 $\mu g/m^3$ for every 1% increase in relative humidity [19]. Poppendieck et al. found almost a factor of 2.6 increase in VOCs for an 8 °C increase in temperature [22]. Another study measured four homes during winter and summer and found changes of about three to five ppb per °C [23]. A study measuring formaldehyde concentrations in environmental chamber tests [28] found formaldehyde concentrations were positively correlated with temperature and absolute humidity, but were poorly correlated with relative humidity.

Studies using material mass diffusion transfer analytical models to predict the volatile organic compound (VOC) emission rates from multiple building materials have demonstrated that VOC emission rates are dominated by three factors: the initial emittable concentration (C_0), a mass diffusion coefficient for the compound in building materials (D_m), and the material-air partition coefficient (K_p) [29–31]. Chamber studies have shown that K_p and D_m are strongly influenced by temperature [32–34] and C_o is driven by both temperature and humidity [35]. By including the factors mentioned above, previous studies have used measured emission rates of material samples from test chambers to determine the parameters for mass diffusion transfer (C_0, D_m, and K_p), and, in turn, to develop physics-based emission models to predict the emission rate for materials, such as a particleboard, plywood paneling, or hard wood piece with UF coating [29–31]. The studies investigating physical models have provided referenced parameters for estimating the mass transfer and the relationship between these parameters and environmental conditions. However, to utilize the chamber measured parameters to predict a whole house emission rate, the quantities of each type of emitting materials in the house need to be characterized, including structural materials, furniture, cabinetry, and other indoor sources. For example, in a previous case study in an unfurnished net-zero house [36], the investigator characterized the surface area of the emitting surfaces and determined the corresponding mass transfer dynamic parameters (C_0, D_m, and K_p) from previous chamber studies. The whole house VOC emission rate was estimated using a physics-based model combined with measured temperature and humidity. A similar study by Bourdin et al. used a simplified surface mass transfer model to estimate formaldehyde emission rate in a classroom [37]. The mass transfer coefficient (D_m) was estimated using an empirical equation and the concentration at the surface layer of each type of material was measured in a chamber. With an accurately measured surface area of each piece of emitting material in the room, the dynamic formaldehyde emission rate was estimated. Generally, it is very difficult and impractical to measure the required input data for the physics-based models for each emitting material in each home. The characterization of emitting materials in real homes during field test is impracticable due to limit amount of time, specifically the mixture of quantities and material types present in any given home.

Data-driven approaches, such as partial linear regression, machine learning, and deep learning, have been previously developed to predict indoor air pollutant concentrations such as CO_2 and $PM_{2.5}$ [38]. Those data-drive approaches were expanded for predicting formaldehyde emission rate and/or concentrations for certain materials in the chamber or a whole building in recent studies. Akyüz et al. presented an implantation of artificial neural networks (ANN) for modeling the formaldehyde emission from particleboard based on manufacturing variables, including wood-glue moisture content, density of board, and pressing temperature [39]. Ouaret et al. developed an approach using Fourier transform and two nonlinear model: threshold autoregressive (TAR) and Chaos dynamics models to forecast the formaldehyde concentration 12 h ahead in a regularly occupied office with diurnal pattern [40]. Zhang et al. recently applied an artificial neural networks (ANN) approach to predict gas-phase VOC concentrations from four kinds of furniture in a chamber [41]. The ANN approach used VOC concentration at the previous timestep, temperature, relative humidity, and ventilation rate as inputs for training the model, and the method was validated by predicting predict VOC concentrations for different environmental conditions. Zhang et al. also developed another approach using deep learning model and tested it in an occupied classroom [42]. Similarly, Mohammadshirazi et al. also used a LSTM deep learning approach to predict formaldehyde concentration in an occupied office based on historical measured data [43] and compared to other three forecasting models: rolling average, Random Forest, and Gradient Boosting. The data-driven methods do not require detailed mass transfer parameters of the emitting materials, but the approaches typically need massive data for training and the approaches have not been applied to any residential buildings, where the environmental and occupancy pattern are more complex than commercial buildings. In addition, it is unknown how well these models trained for an individual building or room would predict emission rates or concentrations in other spaces. In our study we want to develop a model that could be applied beyond an individual home where the measurements were made. Therefore, we developed an empirical model derived from physics-based model in order to bypass characterizing mass transfer parameters as well as involving the emission rate variability due to environmental conditions.

In indoor environments, formaldehyde mass transport from building materials has been modeled by assuming the concentration in a thin layer of air near the emitting material (C_{eq}) is in equilibrium with the contaminant concentration in the surface layer of the storage medium ($C_{material}$). $C_{material}$ remains constant because internal transport within the material is rapid enough to replenish the surface layer as it emits into the air above the surface. At any given moment, the formaldehyde emission is governed by transport from air surface layer to bulk air at a constant rate (k), as shown in Equation (1) [17,31,44–46].

$$E = k(C_{eq} - C_{in})A_m \quad (1)$$

where E is the whole-house formaldehyde emission rate (µg/s) at certain temperature and humidity; C_{eq} is the concentration within the air surface layer, which is equal to the bulk air concentration when the ventilation rate is zero (µg/m^3) at that condition; C_{in} is the concentration in the bulk air (µg/m^3) (i.e., the indoor formaldehyde concentration); k is the mass transfer constant (m/s); and A_m is the effective surface area of the emitting materials indoors (m^2). The values of k, C_{eq}, and C_{in} are treated as whole-house values that include all the emitting surfaces in the home. This simplified concentration-dependent emission model has been validated in chamber studies [44,45], and the implications of indoor formaldehyde concentration on emission rate were discussed in a previous study [46]. Under this model, the changes in temperature and humidity will influence C_{eq}, which has been investigated in previous studies [27,47,48]. The indoor air exchange rate will influence C_{in}. Changes of indoor temperature and air velocity caused by changing air change rate will also influence the mass transfer rate (k), but this is assumed to be negligible in this study, because the variations of indoor temperature and surface air velocity are small.

The focus of this paper is to develop a simplified emission model for predicting formaldehyde emission rates in homes that vary with the key variables explored above. This is a top-down approach that does not rely on the availability of highly specific details about emitting materials in each home. Instead, we focused on estimating whole-house emission rates across a group of sample homes using three predictor variables: temperature, humidity, and air change rate. We used field measured, time-resolved formaldehyde concentrations together with coincident temperature and relative humidity in 63 California single-family homes built in 2011–2017 with low-emitting materials (i.e., materials regulated by the California Air Resources Board). Estimates of time-resolved ventilation rates were used in a mass balance to estimate the time-varying formaldehyde emission rates. A multivariate regression was used to develop a predictive model for emission rate as a function of temperature, humidity, and air change rate. The resulting emission model was evaluated by using it to predict the concentrations in the same homes used to generate the emission model, and then comparing the resulting predicted concentrations against those measured in the field. This evaluation was performed for individual model coefficients specific to each home, as well as for coefficients averaged over the cohort of homes.

2. Materials and Methods

2.1. Data Collection Overview

The data used to estimate formaldehyde emission rates were collected from a recent field study of ventilation and indoor air quality in new California homes. The Healthy, Efficient New Gas Homes (HENGH) study [49] collected data in 2016–2018 in 70 single-family, detached houses that were constructed between 2011 and 2017. These homes were built using composite wood products required in California to have low formaldehyde emissions. All homes had dwelling unit mechanical ventilation systems installed to meet state building code requirements. The homes also had natural gas cooking appliances with venting range hoods and bathroom exhaust fans. Each home was monitored for a six-to-nine-day period. Residents were asked to keep windows closed and the dwelling unit mechanical ventilation system operating. This allowed us to make good estimates of the ventilation rate, because the homes were dominated by the air flow through mechanical ventilation systems, for which airflows and operation were measured and recorded in the study. We included estimates of natural infiltration, based on air leakage tests of the homes, local weather conditions (from the nearest publicly available weather station) and the enhanced ventilation model from ASHRAE Handbook of Fundamentals [50] and Walker and Wilson [51]. The total ventilation rate combining the mechanical fan and natural infiltration flows was determined using the superposition method from ASHRAE Standard 62.2 and a previous study [52].

Measurements in each home included time-integrated indoor and outdoor formaldehyde concentrations, and additional time-resolved measurements were made indoors. The outdoor formaldehyde concentrations were measured using SKC Umex-100 passive samplers at each site to obtain an average concentration for the whole monitoring period. The time-resolved indoor formaldehyde concentrations were measured at 30-min or 60-min intervals using Shinyei/Graywolf FM-801 photoelectric photometry meters deployed in the living rooms and master bedrooms in most of the homes. The averaged indoor concentrations calculated using the real-time meters were compared against UMEx-100 passive samplers deployed at the same location with same duration in 66 test homes that had both types of measurements. Results showed considerable scattering between co-located real-time formaldehyde meters and passive samplers, as shown in Figure 1. The weekly averaged indoor concentrations measured by real-time meters compared to the passive samplers, had a negative bias of 2% and root mean square difference (RMSE) of 6.9 $\mu g/m^3$. The temperature and relative humidity were also measured in the living rooms and master bedrooms in these houses using ExTech CO_2 monitors at 1-min intervals.

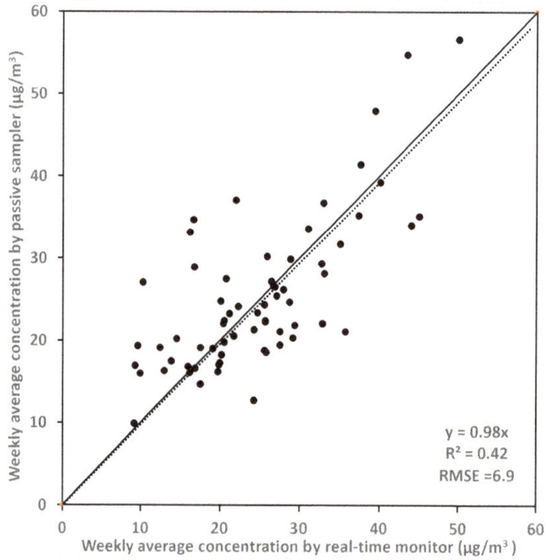

Figure 1. Weekly averaged formaldehyde concentrations measured by passive samplers and real-time monitors in 66 test houses, concentrations were averaged from both master bedroom and living room.

The airflows of bath and laundry exhaust fans in each home were measured using a TEC Exhaust Fan Flow Meter. Range hood airflows were measured using a balanced-pressure flow hood method using a TEC Minneapolis Duct Blaster [53]. The operation of these fans was monitored at 1-min intervals using a logging anemometer (Digisense WD-20250-22) placed at the air inlet or using a motor on-off logger (Onset HOBO UX90-004) placed close to the motor. The air leakage of the building envelope and the forced air heating/cooling system were measured with the DeltaQ test (ASTM-E1554-2013, Method A) using a TEC Minneapolis Blower Door System with DG-700 digital manometer. The test also quantifies air leakage of the forced air heating/cooling system to outside of the living space under normal operating conditions. Building envelope air leakage was converted to air changes per hour at 50 Pa indoor-outdoor pressure difference (ACH_{50}) using the estimated home volume. Not all of the 70 homes in the original study were included in the analysis. Two houses had instrumentation failure, four homes did not have measured envelope air leakage (so we could not estimate air change rates), and one did not have temperature or relative humidity (*RH*) measured, leaving 63 homes to be evaluated.

2.2. Time-Resolved Formaldehyde Emission Rate Calculation

For a well-mixed home, a mass balance can be used to describe the indoor formaldehyde concentrations, as shown in Equation (2). A discretized version of Equation (2) is shown in Equation (3).

$$\frac{dCin}{dt} = aCout - aCin + \frac{E}{V} \tag{2}$$

$$E_t = \frac{V}{dt}(Cin_{t+1} - Cin_t) + a_t Cin_t V - a_t V Cout \tag{3}$$

where E_t is the formaldehyde net emission rate at the time step (μg/s); dt is the time step (1 h = 3600 s); Cin_t and Cin_{t+1} are formaldehyde concentrations at this time step and one-time step after (μg/m^3); $Cout$ is the average outdoor formaldehyde concentration (μg/m^3); V is the total volume of the house (m^3); and a_t is the air exchange rate (AER) (1/s). Indoor formaldehyde is both absorbed as well as emitted (in a reversible way) by building surfaces [54], therefore, in our method, the time-resolved emission rates in each home were the net-emission rate, representing both desorption and absorption processes. For most of the time, the net-emission was positive, because the combined emission and desorption were much larger than adsorption.

A key assumption of this approach is that we can use a single concentration for the whole home, and that the concentration is conditional to the whole home ventilation rates in our calculations. To investigate the validity of this approach, the well-mixed condition for formaldehyde in the test houses was evaluated by comparing the weekly average formaldehyde concentrations measured in the master bedroom and in the living room of each home, as shown in Figure 2. A linear regression fit was performed to the weekly averaged concentrations, showing reasonable correlation (R-squared of 0.64, a slope of 1.05 and an intercept of 2.4 μg/m^3). The RMSE was 7.1 μg/m^3. Given the instrument accuracy is 4.9 μg/m^3 (4 ppb) or 10% of the reading (whichever is larger), these results indicate that the assumption of uniform formaldehyde concentrations was reasonable overall, but the situation varies home-by-home. We also calculated the absolute difference of the hourly measured formaldehyde concentrations between the master bedroom and living room at each home. The average absolute difference across all homes was 5.3 μg/m^3 (4.3 ppb), which is close to the instrument accuracy. The mean absolute differences between bedroom and living room were larger than the instrument accuracy in 21 homes. Of these 21 homes, 19 had two-stories. These results indicate that our assumption of uniform concentration within a home is generally acceptable.

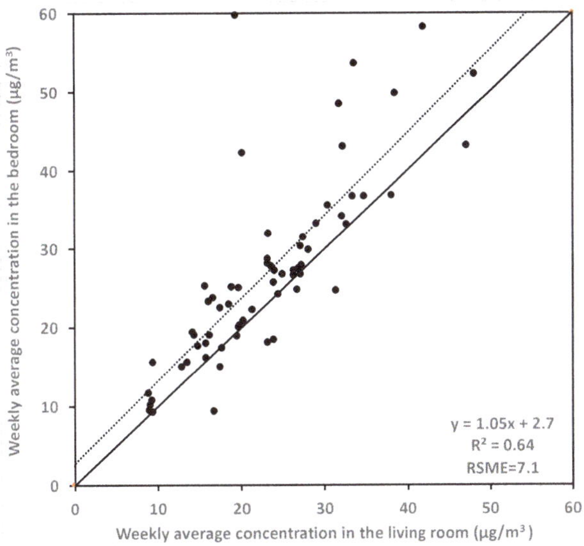

Figure 2. Weekly averaged formaldehyde concentrations measured in the master bedroom and living room in 63 test houses with both locations measured.

These concentrations are lower than those measured in new California homes built in 2002–2005 in a similar study [8], where the mean indoor concentration was 43 μg/m^3. They are also lower than the formaldehyde concentrations measured in studies from more than ten years ago, such as 32.2 μg/m^3 from 162 French homes [55] and about 30 μg/m^3 from 96 Canadian homes [15]. Possible reasons for the lower concentrations in this set of homes is that the sample homes were all built with lower-emitting materials and mechanical ventilation as required by California building regulations.

2.3. Predictors for Formaldehyde Emission Rate

Formaldehyde is emitted from building materials, fittings, and furnishings, therefore, the emission rate scales with the quantities of these elements in a home. To be useful for future modeling purposes, the emission rates need to be normalized to account for this. A direct approach is to assume that the quantity of emitting materials scales with floor area/volume and to use floor area to normalize the emission rates. It might be that this is not an exact correlation, because the sources of formaldehyde may not scale exactly with floor area. For example, a larger house might not have proportionally more furnishings, cabinetry, etc. Furthermore, formaldehyde emissions are associated with effective surface area that is emitting formaldehyde, and the formaldehyde content of the materials present in the home varies greatly between homes. For the purposes of this study, we performed a simple analysis to verify that normalizing by floor area is a reasonable assumption, which is discussed in the results section.

Previous studies have demonstrated that C_{eq} varies with temperature and relative humidity [48]. The temperature and RH varied within each home during the sampling period. These parameters also varied cross-sectionally, since the homes were sampled in different seasons, had different thermostat setpoints, different occupancies, and other changes that would impact temperature and RH. In order to account for the impacts of temperature and RH on the emission rate, an empirical mathematical equation from Myers [48] was used to normalize the equilibrium formaldehyde concentration to a value (C_{st}) at reference condition (i.e., 25 °C, 50% RH), as shown in Equation (4).

$$C_{eq} = C_{st} \exp\left[A\left(\frac{1}{T} - \frac{1}{298}\right)\right] \times [1 + B(RH - 50)] \quad (4)$$

For indoor environments when the variation of temperature is small, a simple linear form is often used:

$$C_{eq} = C_{st}[1 + A(T - 25)] \times [1 + B(RH - 50)] \quad (5)$$

Applying Equation (5) to Equation (1), the time-varying concentration-dependent emission model corelated with temperature and relative humidity is shown in Equation (6).

$$\frac{E_t}{A_f} = kL\{C_{st}[1 + A(T_t - 25)] \times [1 + B(RH_t - 50)] - Cin_t\} \times H \quad (6)$$

where A, B, and C_{st} are the fitted parameters. L is the effective emitting material loading rate in the house (A_m/V, m^2/m^3). T_t and RH_t are the average temperature and relative humidity of the rooms with a formaldehyde monitor (in this case, the living room and a bedroom of each home) at the time step. Et and Cint are the emission rate and indoor formaldehyde concentration at the time step. A_f is the floor area and H is the ceiling height. We did try using the Equation (6) and the field measured hourly formaldehyde concentrations to develop our model but the performance of this model to estimate time-resolved concentrations was dissatisfying. A main problem with this approach was that it used the concentration from a previous time step to estimate the emission rate for the current time step because the current concentration is unknown. To improve the modeling accuracy for predicting time-resolved concentrations, we developed an approach to use hourly air exchange rate as a surrogate for the concentration in the bulk room air, which has been used in previous studies [14,38–40].

In our measured data, the indoor formaldehyde concentrations were sampled hourly, and the differences between consecutive hours (i.e., $Cin_{t+1} - Cin_t$) were typically very small. Similarly, the temperature and RH varied slowly with time. Air exchange rate could change suddenly due to mechanical ventilation operation, but the duration of the fan usage was typically short, leading the hourly variation of the total air exchange rate to be relatively small. Therefore, we assume that the measured formaldehyde concentration at each hour can be considered to be a pseudo-steady-state concentration under the corresponding temperature, RH, and AER conditions. The calculated hourly emission rate was, therefore, also a pseudo-steady-state emission rate. For a given well-mixed home, the steady-state indoor concentration (Cin_{ss}) under certain temperature, relative humidity, and air exchange conditions can be expressed using Equation (7).

$$Cin_{ss} = Cout + \frac{E}{aV} \tag{7}$$

Replacing Equation (1) with a pseudo-steady-state emission rate and concentration yields Equation (8).

$$E = (C_{eq} - Cout)\frac{akL}{a + kL}V \tag{8}$$

In our measured data, the average outdoor formaldehyde concentration is 2.2 μg/m^3. This suggests the outdoor term is an order of magnitude smaller than the indoor term. Ignoring the outdoor term and combining with Equation (5), the hourly pseudo-steady-state emission rate was correlated to the hourly average measured temperature, *RH* with modeling coefficients (*A* and *B*) and equilibrium concentration at reference condition (C_{st}) through a multi-parameter model, along with hourly air exchange rates, mass transport coefficient, and loading rate as other independent inputs (Equation (9)).

$$\frac{E_t}{A_f} = \frac{C_{st} \times (1 + A(T_t - 25))(1 + B(RH_t - 50))}{\frac{1}{a_t} + \frac{1}{kL}} \times H \tag{9}$$

In the analysis of the measured data, we used one-hour averages for all the measured parameters and corresponding one-hour averaged emission rates calculated using Equation (3). This avoided the issue generated by small step changes in some parameters—such as air change rate—from one time-step to another. The one-hour pseudo-steady-state emission rate may not be appropriate in some homes settings due to sudden changes in AER, temperature, and humidity caused by occupancy activities or mechanical equipment operation. Such cases resulted in "outlier" emission rates at the time-step with sudden changes. To eliminate these sudden large changes in emission rate, we examined an option that excluded the hourly emission rates that were greater than the 95th percentile and smaller than the 5th percentile for each home prior to fitting the regression model in Equation (9). We also investigated an approach that applied an eight-hour running average to the measured formaldehyde concentration, air exchange rate, temperature and *RH*. Given the average air exchange rate across all homes was 0.35 h^{-1} and the ventilation was the only effective loss term for indoor formaldehyde, a home would generally achieve steady-state within about eight hours after any changes in emission and ventilation. The multi-parameter regressions were compared using the running 8-h and 1-h inputs. The approach was used to check whether hourly emission rates could be assumed to be pseudo-steady-state.

The constant *kL* is the product of the transport coefficient *k* and the loading factor *L*. Measurements of loading factor *L* from another study [56] were found to be relatively stable, ranging from 0.5 to 1 m^2/m^3, and the *k* value ranged from 0.011 to 3.6 m/h. Based on measurements in single-family and mobile homes, Myers reported *k* between 0.19 and 2.7 m/h [45]. Homes likely contain a range of formaldehyde-containing materials, but the fastest timescales (higher *kL*) will tend to dominate the effective value for a home [46]. In our model, we use the average value from Sherman and Hult which reported *kL* values from 0.05 to 0.62 in nine low-emitting US houses (most in California) with average of 0.29/h^{-1} [46]. We did attempt to also include *kL* as a fitted parameter in our model, but this resulted in unstable model values, with large variations in *kL* that also drove large changes in the other three coefficients that were out of the range of common building materials reported by Myers. This is likely caused by limited data in each home, where we only have a small range of temperature, *RH*, and AER, resulting in least square regression results with large uncertainties. Due to this result, we chose to fix the value of *kL* based on those found in the literature described above.

A multi-parameter, least square non-linear regression fit was applied to Equation (9) for each house. The independent inputs of the regression fit were the measured temperature, *RH* and air exchange rate, either by hourly step or 8-h running average. The *kL* was assumed constant. The dependent input of the regression was the floor area normalized emission rate for each home, either by hourly step or 8-h running average. The regression fits resulted in 63 sets of least squares fitted coefficients: A, B, and C_{st} for each home. We have considered multiple statistical approaches used in the previous studies for indoor air quality model evaluation [57,58]. The commonly-used parameters for model performance evaluation include standard deviation of observations and predictions, least square slope and intercept regression statistics, Quantile–Quantile (Q-Q) plots, etc. By considering all of the statistical approaches, two criteria were selected to carefully evaluate the predictor sets:

1. The degree of correlation and the remaining errors from the empirical multi-parameter model for predicting the *emission rate*, which were identified by calculating the r-squared and root mean square error (RMSE) for each regression;
2. The accuracy and consistency of the predicted emission rate for estimating *indoor formaldehyde concentration*, which was evaluated by comparing the measured time-resolved formaldehyde concentrations (C_{in}) in each home versus the estimated concentration (Cin_{est}) calculated using the regression model's time-varying emission rate predicted by temperature, relative humidity, and air change rates at the corresponding time step, as shown in Equation (10).

$$Cin_{est,t+1} = Cin_{est,t} + \left(\frac{E_{est,t}}{V} - a_t Cin_{est,t} + a_t Cout \right) dt \tag{10}$$

where $Cin_{est,t}$ is the estimated formaldehyde concentration at current time; $Cin_{est,t+1}$ is the predicted concentration for next time step; $E_{est,t}$ is the emission rate predicted using the three coefficients for each home; and dt is the length of the time step (one-hour in this case). The accuracy of the prediction was evaluated by calculating the Normalized Root Mean Square errors (NRMSE) for all the measurements (where N is the number of measurements, typically 160 over the week of testing for each home), as shown in Equation (11).

$$Normalized\ RMS\ Error\ (\%) = \frac{\sqrt[2]{\sum_0^N \frac{(Cin_t - Cin_{est,t})^2}{N}}}{\overline{Cin}} \tag{11}$$

3. Results and Discussion

We begin by describing the emission rate estimates produced from our calculation procedure, and we compare these against previously reported measurements. Next, we present a summary of the regression models used to estimate emission rates and the accuracy of the predicted concentrations using those same emission estimates in each home. Finally, a generalized regression model is presented that combines the model parameter coefficients from each individual study home into a generic model for future modeling efforts.

3.1. Emission Rate Estimation

The mean emission rate across the 63 houses calculated using Equation (3) was 1.3 µg/s with a standard deviation of 0.6 µg/s. The distribution of weekly averaged emission rates ranked by emission rate for each home is shown Figure 3. The distribution is fairly uniform between 1 and 3 µg/s, with no significant grouping at any particular emission rate. This indicates a wide range of formaldehyde sources in these homes, even though they represent a very specific subset of homes because they were selected to be new, single-family homes from California that should be compliant with State standard requiring low formaldehyde emission products to be used in their construction.

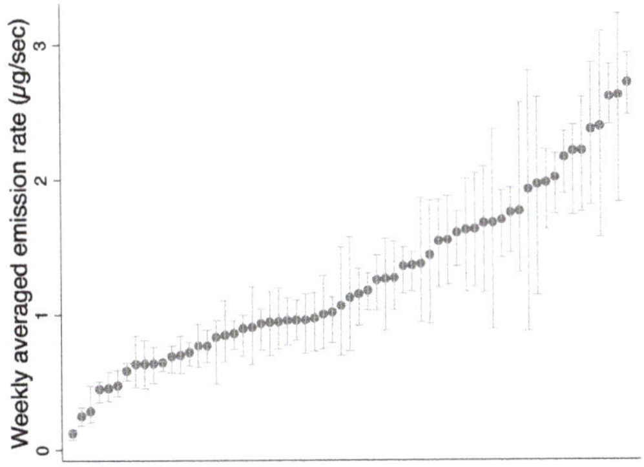

Figure 3. Weekly average formaldehyde emission rate (marker) for 63 new California single-family homes; shading area presents the 25th and 75th of the hourly emission rate for each home, x-axis rank ordered by average emission rate.

It may be useful to normalize emission rates by floor area to account for differences in emission rates for different sized homes. There is a weak general trend that emission rate increased with floor area in the study homes, with a Spearman correlation rank of 0.34 (p-value < 0.01) and Pearson rank of 0.31 (p-value = 0.016). This suggests that normalizing the emission rate by floor area can slightly improve emission rate estimates.

The distribution of floor area normalized emission rates is shown in Figure 4 with a mean (±s.d.) of 19.6 ± 10.4 µg/h/m^2. The value is comparable to the emission rate calculated using the concentration measured by co-located passive samplers, that had a mean of 17.4 µg/h/m^2. This is greater than the emission rate of 6.7 µg/h/m^2 previously reported in a home designed and constructed to be low-emitting [22], but it is lower than the mean emission rate of 23 µg/h/m^2 measured in 13 homes in another study intended to have low-emitting materials [17]. It is also lower than the average emission rate of 29 µg/h/m^2 reported by a previous study in 99 California homes built prior to formaldehyde emission limits for building materials and that generally did not have mechanical ventilation [8]. The value is also much lower than those in older studies, such as Hodgson et al., who reported emission rates of 45 µg/h/m^2 for manufactured homes [59].

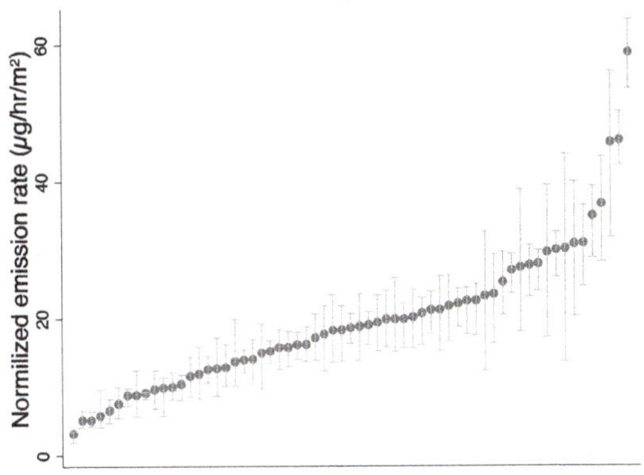

Figure 4. Distribution of weekly averaged formaldehyde emission rate (marker) normalized by floor area; shading area presents the 25th and 75th of the hourly normalized emission rate for each home, x-axis rank ordered by average normalized emission rate.

3.2. Formaldehyde Emission Rate Model and Concentration Prediction

We carefully reviewed the 63 sets of regression coefficients, and we noticed that some homes had regression coefficients of $A < 0$ or $B < 0$. We consider these to be non-physical results, because emission rates should positively correlate with temperature and *RH* according to previous studies. Table 1 summarizes the degree of correlation and the remaining errors from the multi-parameter models (r-squared and relative RMSE of the regression fits), comparing the model-predicted emission rates against those derived from the measured data. Table 1 also summarizes the accuracy and consistency of the predicted emission rates for estimating indoor formaldehyde concentrations, which are shown as the normalized RMS errors between estimated indoor formaldehyde concentrations using the predicted emission rate and the measured concentrations. Two variations on the regression models were assessed: (1) applying an eight-hour running average to the measured data, and (2) excluding hourly emission rates outside of the 5th–95th percentile range. Both of these variations improved the fitness of the multi-parameter regression, with higher r-squared values and lower relative RMSE. The improvements are expected, because both approaches intentionally eliminate the outliers of the hourly emission rate and/or decrease the noise in the data used for the regression.

Table 1. Summary of regression performance results.

	Evaluation Criteria	1-h Average	8-h Moving Window Running Average	Use Hourly Emission Rate within 5th to 95th Percentile
Number of homes with valid coefficients		39	41	41
For predicting emission rates	R-square [Mean Median (Min–Max)]	0.88 0.91 (0.40–0.98)	0.97 0.98 (0.89–0.99)	0.94 0.96 (0.66–0.99)
	RMSE (%) [Mean Median (Min–Max)]	29% 27% (12%–81%)	15% 12% (6%–43%)	20% 19% (8%–44%)
For estimating indoor concentrations using predicted emission rates	NRMSE % [Mean Median (Min–Max)]	13% 13% (6%–24%)	11% 9% (5%–22%) [1] 13% 12% (6%–26%) [2]	13% 13% (6%–25%)

[1] NRMSE between estimated 8-h running average indoor concentration and 8-h running average measured data.
[2] NRMSE between estimated hourly indoor concentration and hourly measured data.

While using running mean inputs and removing outliers improved emission rate predictions, they did not meaningfully improve the accuracy for estimating indoor concentrations. All three methods gave the similar results for estimating indoor concentrations using the predicted emission rates. This indicates that our original approach using one-hour average data and our assumption that the hourly emission rate was a pseudo-steady-state emission rate are reasonable.

For all three approaches, the formaldehyde concentration predictions were poor in some remaining homes. The reasons for this were unclear, but may include poor indoor mixing; unexpected ventilation (e.g., if windows or doors were opened); high emitting materials concentrated in one place (the area normalized emission assumption may not applicable); large variations in formaldehyde concentrations, temperature, *RH*, and AER between adjacent hours caused by occupant activity (the steady-state assumptions may not applicable); different loading rate and mass transport coefficients in some home (assumption of $kL = 0.29$ may not applicable); and other possible measurement errors for temperature, *RH* and AER. Illustrative examples of qualitatively poor and good predictions are shown in the time-series of measured and estimated formaldehyde concentrations in Figure 5a (poor predictions in home 46) and in Figure 5b (good predictions in home 31).

In Figure 5a, some very low formaldehyde concentrations were measured without any obvious changes in other parameters, such as the air exchange rate, which might be caused by window opening by occupants. In fact, actual concentrations in Home 46 appear to be positively correlated with the ventilation rate, such that increased outside airflow leads to higher indoor concentrations. This further supports the potential for errors in the ventilation rate calculation method for this home. The good prediction in Home 31 shows agreement in both the magnitude and timing of changes in the indoor formaldehyde concentrations, with notable short-term spikes in the ventilation rate followed by temporarily reduced formaldehyde concentrations.

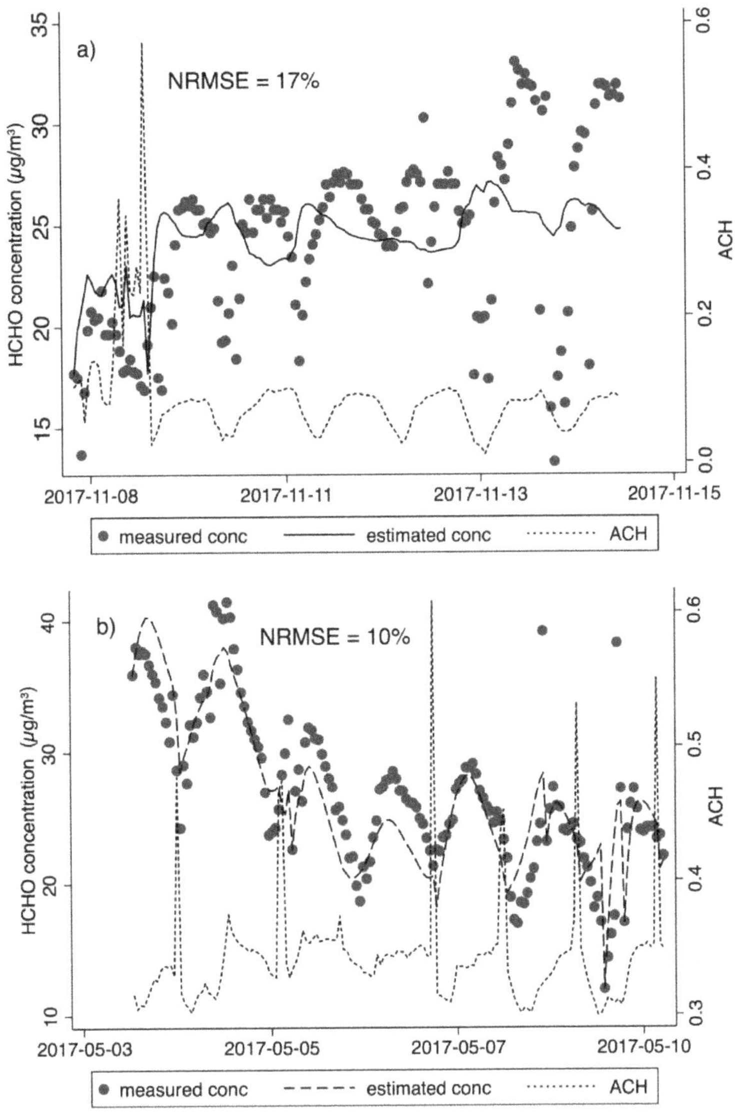

Figure 5. Examples of (**a**) a poor predictor and (**b**) a good predictor, by plotting time-resolved measured and estimated formaldehyde concentrations along with the air exchange rate per hour.

Our intent is to develop a working relationship that results in reasonable predictions of emission rates and the resulting indoor formaldehyde concentrations. Accordingly, we decided that the emission predictions that gave the poorest estimates on either emission rate or indoor concentration would not be used. Firstly, we removed a quarter of the homes with lowest r-square values from multi-parameter regression models using Equation (9). These homes were considered not applicable to the generalized multi-parameter regression model, because the emission rates were not well-correlated with indoor temperature, *RH*, or AER. Then, by calculating average relative difference using Equation (11) for each home, we removed the homes that had greater than 20% average relative difference, unless the average was affected by some extreme data points. This filtering process left 27 sets of estimates of predictors for the formaldehyde emission rate when using the original 1-h average approach, 27 sets for the 8-h running average approach and 26 sets for the approach excluding outliers. Most selected homes with good estimates were the same homes irrespective of the method used, but there were three to four selected homes may vary by approaches.

The estimated concentrations using the predicted emission rates based on house specific coefficients by one-hour average method for 27 selected homes with good estimators are compared to the measured formaldehyde concentrations in those same homes in Figure 6a. These results show an overall bias of prediction of less than 0.1% (slope = 0.9993). An RMSE of 3.2 μg/m^3 (2.5 ppb) and r-square of 0.88 indicate that the general prediction is consistent, and that the fitted coefficients are also reasonable at predicting the changes in concentration as the parameters vary. For comparison, we also plot estimated concentrations using a fixed weekly average emission rate of each home versus the measured concentrations in Figure 6b. The RMSE is substantially higher (8.6 vs. 3.2) and r-square is substantially lower (0.45 vs. 0.88) when using weekly averaged emission rates compared to the dynamic emission rates predicted by temperature, *RH*, and air exchange rates. Similar comparisons are performed for the method excluding outliners (Figure 6c,d), and method using 8-h running average (Figure 6e,f). Generally, all three methods show similar improvement in predicting indoor concentrations compared to single, fixed weekly average emission rates from each home. The methods using 8-h running averages and those excluding outliers slightly underestimated overall concentrations (slopes of 0.99 and 0.98). This is expected because both alternative methods filter out very high concentrations/emission rates before applying to the regression model, and the resulting coefficient estimators are more accurate for mid-range concentrations. We've considered multiple guidelines that have been used for indoor air quality model evaluation [57]. The ideal IAQ model should have the observed value and predicted value plotted along the 1:1 line, with relatively smaller MSE between observations and predictions. Thus, the original 1-hr average approach was selected for further analysis.

Our overall estimate of an area normalized emission rate model for a generic house was determined by averaging the A, B, C_{st} model coefficients for each of the selected homes. Coefficients were averaged together, because they were linearly correlated with the emission rate (i.e., the value of A for use in generic predictions is the average of the 27 values of A from the 27 homes). The resulting generic regression coefficients and variance in selected homes for each approach are shown in Table 2. The coefficients resulting from the regression model for temperature, *RH*, and equilibrium concentration are also compared to those in the previous studies. Overall, the coefficients we found from the selected homes are comparable to effects observed in previous studies.

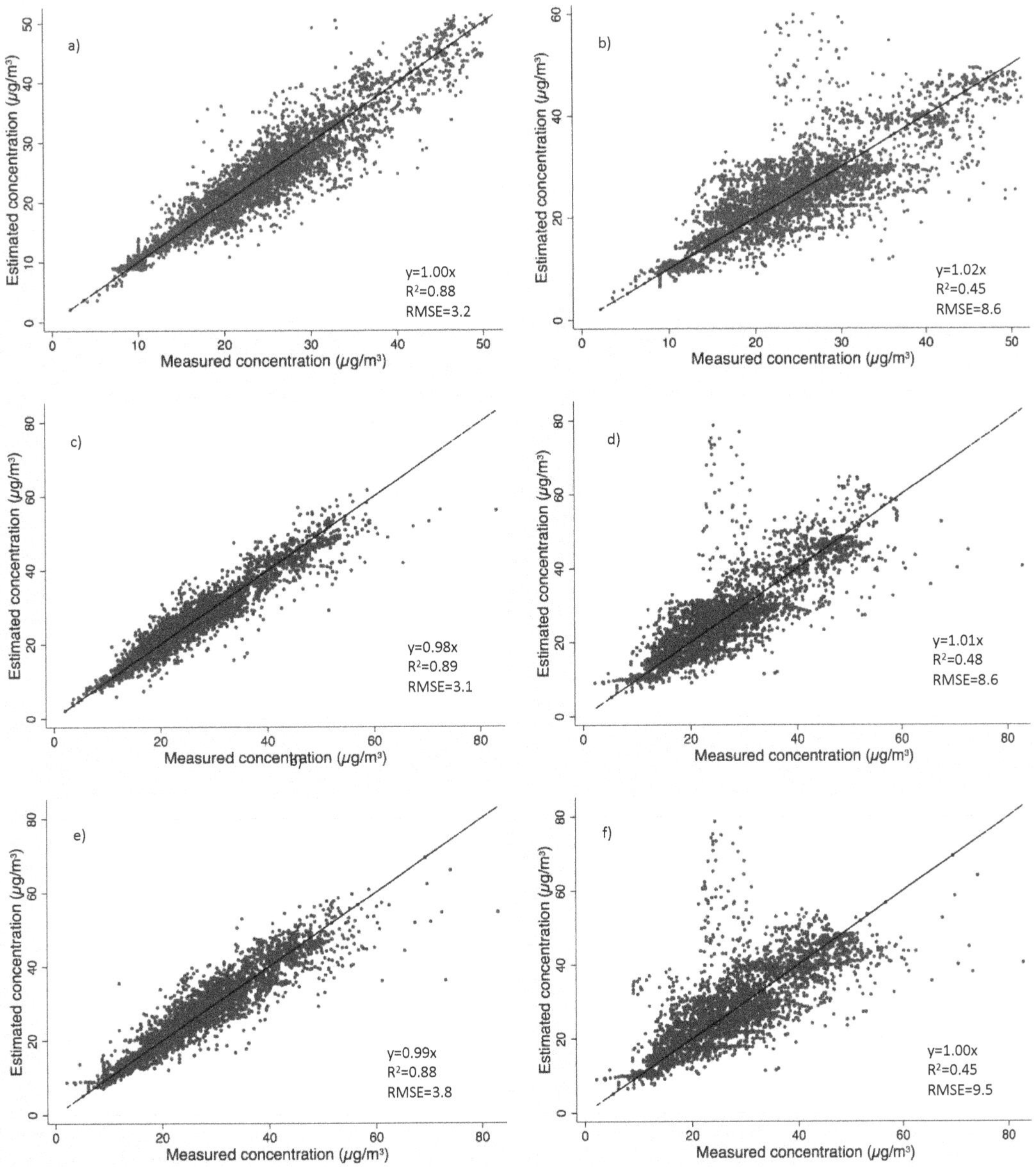

Figure 6. Predicted HCHO concentrations versus measured concentrations in selected houses using (**a**) emission rates predicted by the home-specific coefficients for each home using hourly averaged method, (**b**) corresponding constant emission rates by weekly average for each home using hourly averaged method, (**c**) emission rates predicted by the home-specific coefficients for each home using excluding outliner method, (**d**) corresponding constant emission rates by weekly average for each selected home using excluding outliner method, (**e**) emission rates predicted by the corresponding coefficients for each individual home using 8-hr average method, and (**f**) corresponding constant emission rates by weekly average for each selected home using 8-hr average method.

Table 2. Summary of regression coefficients in selected homes.

Method		1-Hour Average	8-Hour Running Average	Use Hourly Emission Rate within 5th to 95th Percentile	Reference Range from Previous Studies
Coefficient estimates [Mean Median (Min-Max)]	A (1/°C)	0.088 0.085 (0.015–0.253)	0.086 0.080 (0.005–0.230)	0.089 0.072 (0.007–0.203)	0.080 [27] 0.05–0.15 [48]
	B (1/RH%)	0.036 0.031 (0.009–0.076)	0.047 0.042 (0.014–0.100)	0.033 0.029 (0.006–0.078)	0.005–0.038 [48]
	Cst (μg/m^3)	72.9 74.8 (24.1–117.8)	70.8 70.7 (39.6–111.1)	64.1 66.1 (37.2–90.4)	41–118 [17] 23–985 [46]

An additional analysis was performed to evaluate the overall estimate of an area normalized emission rate model using the average A, B, C_{st} model coefficients. The estimated concentrations in 27 selected homes using the predicted emission rates based on averaged model coefficients (A, B, C_{st}) in Table 2 with 1-hr average method are compared to measured hourly concentrations in Figure 7a. Figure 7b shows the estimated concentrations using a single fixed floor area normalized emission rate that averaged across 27 selected homes (i.e., 23.6 μg/h/m^2) versus the measured hourly concentrations. Significant improvement is presented when using the proposed time-varying model with averaged coefficients, which gives an overall slope of 0.98, r-square value of 0.67 and a root mean square error of 5.6 μg/m^3 (3.9 ppb). While using an averaged fixed floor area normalized emission rate, the root mean square error between estimated and measured concentration is doubled, with a value of 11.6 μg/m^3 (9.3 ppb) with a poor r-square value of 0.06, though the overall slope is 0.99. The overall variation of time-resolved formaldehyde concentrations in a group of homes consists of three dimensions: (1) within-home variation due to environmental condition changes during the measured week; (2) cross-home variation due to house to house environmental condition (e.g., one home may have higher indoor humidity than the other, even though same emitting materials were furnished in the two home); and (3) cross-home variation due to different emitting materials across homes. Figure 7a used the proposed model with averaged model coefficients for the whole dataset that predicted the time-resolved concentration with emission rates to account for the temperature, humidity, and air change rate variability within home and cross homes. Conversely, the results in Figure 7b, which used a fixed floor area normalized emission rate to predict time-resolved concentrations for each home in the group, did not capture any temperature, humidity, and air change rate variations. Estimated concentrations by both approaches resulted in overall slopes close to one when comparing to measured values, which indicates that the time-averaged estimated concentrations for homes by either approach would show little difference compared to averaged measured concentrations. However, using a single average the floor area normalized emission rate for all homes omits the variations of emission rates due to environmental condition changes within a home and across homes, leading to larger differences when comparing to time-resolved hourly data. We note here that the overall fit in Figure 7a is worse than Figure 6 left panel, because we used a single set of model coefficients that averaged coefficients over 27 homes to predict the time-resolved concentrations for the whole group of houses. The variation that is caused by the difference emitting materials across homes was not accounted for, leading to the estimated values having great variation across the 1:1 line. Thus, this set of averaged model coefficient would preferably be used as a predictive/comparative tool in future modeling work, rather than as a forecasting model for a specific house.

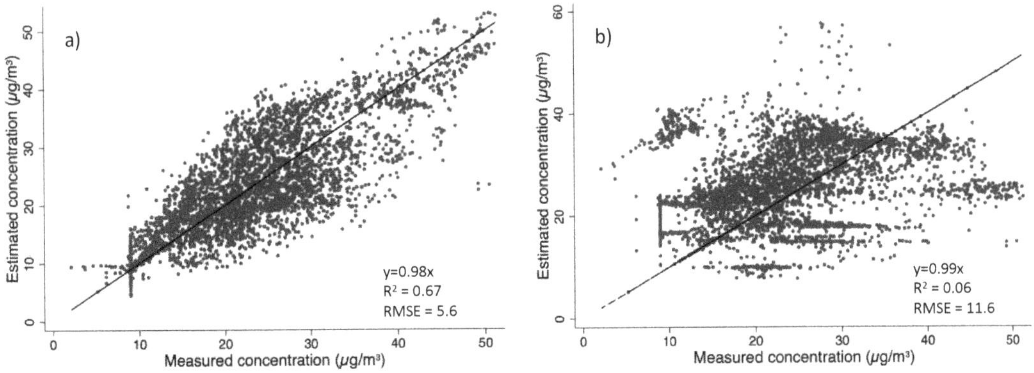

Figure 7. Predicted HCHO concentrations versus measured concentrations in 27 selected houses using (**a**) estimated emission rate by the proposed model with averaged coefficients across homes and (**b**) estimated emission rate by a traditional approach that using a fixed floor area normalized emission rate averaged across 27 homes.

4. Limitations

The most important limitation of this study is the unknown bias associated with the sample of homes used to estimate the emission rates compared with any particular home (or group of homes) one may want to model. The homes where the measurements were made were relatively newly constructed (built since 2011) in California, and they were required to use low-emitting products and install mechanical ventilation. This group of 27 homes cannot be assumed to represent conditions in all homes throughout the state, let alone the US. The average temperature, humidity, and air exchange rates across the sample of homes ranged from 18–27 °C, 28–63% and 0.08–1.14 h^{-1}. All regression results, therefore, must be regarded as exploratory and suggestive, and we caution their use beyond similar houses within similar environmental conditions. Our model can be improved by having a larger dataset of measurements in real homes. We are collecting more data in about 120 houses across the US. Future studies will refine the current model and improve the accuracy. The data-driven approaches will be also tested to compare the performance in real homes.

An additional source of potentially meaningful error in these emission rate estimates are the air exchange rates used to determine emission factors from measured concentrations. The air exchange rates were estimated from building leakage measurements, weather data and fan operation logging, and these estimates are subject to errors in accounting, measurement, and the models used to combine natural and mechanical flows. In addition, window and door operation cannot be ruled out as contributing to the measured concentrations, while not being reflected in air exchange rate estimates.

Finally, the accuracy of the time-resolved formaldehyde concentrations is an important source of error. Comparing one-week average concentrations for the real-time data used in this study to time averaging sensors showed across all test homes the RMSE was 6.9 $\mu g/m^3$. The error may be larger for measuring time resolved data.

5. Conclusions

The intent of this work was to develop a modeling approach to determine formaldehyde emission rates in dwellings that is suitable for estimating indoor formaldehyde concentrations based on variations in indoor temperature, humidity and air change rate. This study applied an empirical model based on previous study to correlate emission rates with temperature, relative humidity, and air change rate in 63 new houses in California. Compared to the approaches using physics-based models, the method herein does not require detailed model coefficients for every emitting material to predict a dynamic whole house formaldehyde emission rate. The proposed model also provides a simplified approach to investigate emission rate variability due to environmental condition changes for a group of reprehensive homes built with low-emitting materials. In total, 27 homes with acceptable regression results were selected with resulting uncertainty in the predicted indoor formaldehyde concentrations of about 3.2 μg/m^3 (13%). These results indicate that the simplified functional form and parameterization of the emission rate prediction is a reasonable approach. Obvious accuracy improvement was found for predicting indoor formaldehyde concentrations using the derived emission rate models, compared to using constant emission rates averaged weekly for each individual house. We caution that this likely would not be the case if this model were used to predict concentrations in any individual home, rather than using it as a predictive/comparative tool.

Author Contributions: Conceptualization, I.S.W.; methodology, H.Z., I.S.W., and M.D.S.; validation, H.Z., I.S.W., and B.L.; formal analysis, H.Z.; investigation, H.Z., I.S.W., and M.D.S.; resources, I.S.W.; data curation, H.Z.; writing—original draft preparation, H.Z.; writing—review and editing, I.S.W., M.D.S., and B.L.; visualization, H.Z. and B.L.; supervision, I.S.W.; funding acquisition, I.S.W. All authors have read and agreed to the published version of the manuscript.

Funding: This research was funded by the California Energy Commission through Contract PIR-14-007 and the U.S. Department of Energy Building America Program via Contract DE-AC02-9 05CH11231.

Institutional Review Board Statement: The field study contributing data to this research were approved by LBNL's institutional review board following US government regulations for research involving human subjects; the house study was protocol 318H003 approved 5/12/2015 and the apartment study was protocol 280H013 approved 11/19/2018.

Informed Consent Statement: Informed consent was obtained from all subjects involved in the study.

Conflicts of Interest: The authors declare no conflict of interest.

References

1. Salthammer, T.; Mentese, S.; Marutzky, R. Formaldehyde in the Indoor Environment. *Chem. Rev.* **2010**, *110*, 2536–2572. [CrossRef] [PubMed]
2. Kelly, T.J.; Smith, D.L.; Satola, J. Emission Rates of Formaldehyde from Materials and Consumer Products Found in California Homes. *Environ. Sci. Technol.* **1999**, *33*, 81–88. [CrossRef]
3. Logue, J.M.; Price, P.N.; Sherman, M.H.; Singer, B.C. A Method to Estimate the Chronic Health Impact of Air Pollutants in US Residences. *Environ. Health Perspect.* **2012**, *120*, 216–222. [CrossRef] [PubMed]
4. WHO. *Who Guidelines for Indoor Air Quality: Selected Pollutants*; World Health Organization: Copenhagen, Denmark, 2010; ISBN 978-92-890-0213-4.
5. Lang, I.; Bruckner, T.; Triebig, G. Formaldehyde and Chemosensory Irritation in Humans: A Controlled Human Exposure Study. *Regul. Toxicol. Pharmacol.* **2008**, *50*, 23–36. [CrossRef]
6. McGwin, G.; Lienert, J.; Kennedy, J.I. Formaldehyde Exposure and Asthma in Children: A Systematic Review. *Environ. Health Perspect.* **2010**, *118*, 313–317. [CrossRef]
7. IARC Formaldehyde, 2-Butoxyethanol and 1-Tert-Butoxypropan-2-Ol. In *IARC Monographs on the Evaluation of Carcinogenic Risks to Humans*; International Agency for Research on Cancer: Lyon, France, 2006; ISBN 978-92-832-1288-1.
8. Offermann, F.J. *Ventilation and Indoor Air Quality in New Homes*; California Energy Commission and California Air Resources Board: Sacramento, CA, USA, 2009.
9. OEHHA OEHHA Acute, 8-Hour and Chronic Reference Exposure Level (REL) Summary. Available online: https://oehha.ca.gov/air/general-info/oehha-acute-8-hour-and-chronic-reference-exposure-level-rel-summary (accessed on 26 January 2021).
10. Singer, B.C.; Chan, W.R.; Kim, Y.; Offermann, F.J.; Walker, I.S. Indoor Air Quality in California Homes with Code-required Mechanical Ventilation. *Indoor Air* **2020**, *30*, 885–899. [CrossRef]
11. Mullen, N.A.; Li, J.; Russell, M.L.; Spears, M.; Less, B.D.; Singer, B.C. Results of the California Healthy Homes Indoor Air Quality Study of 2011-2013: Impact of Natural Gas Appliances on Air Pollutant Concentrations. *Indoor Air* **2016**, *26*, 231–245. [CrossRef]
12. Weisel, C.P.; Zhang, J.; Turpin, B.J.; Morandi, M.T.; Colome, S.; Stock, T.H.; Spektor, D.M.; Korn, L.; Winer, A.M.; Kwon, J.; et al. Relationships of Indoor, Outdoor, and Personal Air (RIOPA). Part I. Collection Methods and Descriptive Analyses. *Res. Rep. Health Eff. Inst.* **2005**, 1–107; discussion 109–127.

13. Health Canada Residential Indoor Air Quality Guideline: Formaldehyde. Available online: https://www.canada.ca/en/health-canada/services/publications/healthy-living/residential-indoor-air-quality-guideline-formaldehyde.html (accessed on 26 January 2021).
14. Gilbert, N.L.; Gauvin, D.; Guay, M.; Heroux, M.E.; Dupuis, G.; Legris, M.; Chan, C.C.; Dietz, R.N.; Levesque, B. Housing Characteristics and Indoor Concentrations of Nitrogen Dioxide and Formaldehyde in Quebec City, Canada. *Environ. Res.* **2006**, *102*, 1–8. [CrossRef]
15. Gilbert, N.L.; Guay, M.; Gauvin, D.; Dietz, R.N.; Chan, C.C.; Lévesque, B. Air Change Rate and Concentration of Formaldehyde in Residential Indoor Air. *Atmos. Environ.* **2008**, *42*, 2424–2428. [CrossRef]
16. 15 U.S.C. 2697(d). 40 CFR 770 - Formaldehyde Standards for Composite Wood Products. 2018. Available online: https://www.ecfr.gov/current/title-40/chapter-I/subchapter-R/part-770 (accessed on 29 March 2022).
17. Hult, E.L.; Willem, H.; Price, P.N.; Hotchi, T.; Russell, M.L.; Singer, B.C. Formaldehyde and Acetaldehyde Exposure Mitigation in US Residences: In-Home Measurements of Ventilation Control and Source Control. *Indoor Air* **2015**, *25*, 523–535. [CrossRef] [PubMed]
18. Burman, E.; Stamp, S. Trade-Offs between Ventilation Rates and Formaldehyde Concentrations in New-Build Dwellings in the UK. In Proceedings of the 40th AIVC–8th TightVent & 6th Venticool Conference, AIVC (Air Infiltration and Ventilation Centre), Ghent, Belgium, 15 October 2019; Volume 40.
19. Salthammer, T.; Fuhrmann, F.; Kaufhold, S.; Meyer, B.; Schwarz, A. Effects of Climatic Parameters on Formaldehyde Concentrations in Indoor Air. *Indoor Air* **1995**, *5*, 120–128. [CrossRef]
20. Van der Wal, J.F. Formaldehyde Measurements in Dutch Houses, Schools and Offices in the Years 1977–1980. *Atmos. Environ. (1967)* **1982**, *16*, 2471–2478. [CrossRef]
21. Sherman, M.H.; Hodgson, A.T. Formaldehyde as a Basis for Residential Ventilation Rates: Formaldehyde as a Basis for Residential Ventilation Rates. *Indoor Air* **2004**, *14*, 2–8. [CrossRef] [PubMed]
22. Poppendieck, D.G.; Ng, L.C.; Persily, A.K.; Hodgson, A.T. Long Term Air Quality Monitoring in a Net-Zero Energy Residence Designed with Low Emitting Interior Products. *Build. Environ.* **2015**, *94*, 33–42. [CrossRef]
23. Huangfu, Y.; Lima, N.M.; O'Keeffe, P.T.; Kirk, W.M.; Lamb, B.K.; Walden, V.P.; Jobson, B.T. Whole-House Emission Rates and Loss Coefficients of Formaldehyde and Other Volatile Organic Compounds as a Function of the Air Change Rate. *Environ. Sci. Technol.* **2020**, *54*, 2143–2151. [CrossRef]
24. Willem, H.; Hult, E.L.; Hotchi, T.; Russell, M.L.; Maddalena, R.L.; Singer, B.C. *Ventilation Control of Volatile Organic Compounds in New US Homes: Results of a Controlled Field Study in Nine Residential Units*; Lawrence Berkeely National Laboratory: Berkeley, CA, USA, 2013.
25. Liu, Y.; Misztal, P.K.; Xiong, J.; Tian, Y.; Arata, C.; Weber, R.J.; Nazaroff, W.W.; Goldstein, A.H. Characterizing Sources and Emissions of Volatile Organic Compounds in a Northern California Residence Using Space- and Time-Resolved Measurements. *Indoor Air* **2019**, *29*, 630–644. [CrossRef]
26. Offermann, F.J.; Hodgson, A.T. Emission Rates of Volatile Organic Compounds in New Homes. In *Proceedings of the Indoor Air: Proceedings of the 12th International Conference on Indoor Air Quality and Climate, Austin, TX, USA, 5–10 June 2011*; pp. 5–10.
27. Andersen, I.B.; Lundqvist, G.R.; Mølhave, L. Indoor Air Pollution Due to Chipboard Used as a Construction Material. *Atmos. Environ. (1967)* **1975**, *9*, 1121–1127. [CrossRef]
28. Liang, W.; Yang, S.; Yang, X. Long-Term Formaldehyde Emissions from Medium-Density Fiberboard in a Full-Scale Experimental Room: Emission Characteristics and the Effects of Temperature and Humidity. *Environ. Sci. Technol.* **2015**, *49*, 10349–10356. [CrossRef]
29. Little, J.C.; Hodgson, A.T.; Gadgil, A.J. Modeling Emissions of Volatile Organic Compounds from New Carpets. *Atmos. Environ.* **1994**, *28*, 227–234. [CrossRef]
30. Cox, S.S.; Little, J.C.; Hodgson, A.T. Predicting the Emission Rate of Volatile Organic Compounds from Vinyl Flooring. *Environ. Sci. Technol.* **2002**, *36*, 709–714. [CrossRef] [PubMed]
31. Huang, H.; Haghighat, F. Modelling of Volatile Organic Compounds Emission from Dry Building Materials. *Build. Environ.* **2002**, *37*, 1127–1138. [CrossRef]
32. Zhang, Y.; Luo, X.; Wang, X.; Qian, K.; Zhao, R. Influence of Temperature on Formaldehyde Emission Parameters of Dry Building Materials. *Atmos. Environ.* **2007**, *41*, 3203–3216. [CrossRef]
33. Deng, Q.; Yang, X.; Zhang, J. Study on a New Correlation between Diffusion Coefficient and Temperature in Porous Building Materials. *Atmos. Environ.* **2009**, *43*, 2080–2083. [CrossRef]
34. Wang, Y.; Wang, H.; Tan, Y.; Liu, J.; Wang, K.; Ji, W.; Sun, L.; Yu, X.; Zhao, J.; Xu, B.; et al. Measurement of the Key Parameters of VOC Emissions from Wooden Furniture, and the Impact of Temperature. *Atmos. Environ.* **2021**, *259*, 118510. [CrossRef]
35. Liang, W.; Lv, M.; Yang, X. The Combined Effects of Temperature and Humidity on Initial Emittable Formaldehyde Concentration of a Medium-Density Fiberboard. *Build. Environ.* **2016**, *98*, 80–88. [CrossRef]
36. Jonge, K.D.; Laverge, J. Modeling Dynamic Behavior of Volatile Organic Compounds in a Zero Energy Building. *Int. J. Vent.* **2020**, *20*, 193–203. [CrossRef]
37. Bourdin, D.; Mocho, P.; Desauziers, V.; Plaisance, H. Formaldehyde Emission Behavior of Building Materials: On-Site Measurements and Modeling Approach to Predict Indoor Air Pollution. *J. Hazard. Mater.* **2014**, *280*, 164–173. [CrossRef]

38. Wei, W.; Ramalho, O.; Malingre, L.; Sivanantham, S.; Little, J.C.; Mandin, C. Machine Learning and Statistical Models for Predicting Indoor Air Quality. *Indoor Air* **2019**, *29*, 704–726. [CrossRef]
39. Akyüz, İ.; Özşahin, Ş.; Tiryaki, S.; Aydın, A. An Application of Artificial Neural Networks for Modeling Formaldehyde Emission Based on Process Parameters in Particleboard Manufacturing Process. *Clean Technol. Environ. Policy* **2017**, *19*, 1449–1458. [CrossRef]
40. Ouaret, R.; Ionescu, A.; Petrehus, V.; Candau, Y.; Ramalho, O. Spectral Band Decomposition Combined with Nonlinear Models: Application to Indoor Formaldehyde Concentration Forecasting. *Stoch. Environ. Res. Risk Assess.* **2018**, *32*, 985–997. [CrossRef]
41. Zhang, R.; Wang, H.; Tan, Y.; Zhang, M.; Zhang, X.; Wang, K.; Ji, W.; Sun, L.; Yu, X.; Zhao, J.; et al. Using a Machine Learning Approach to Predict the Emission Characteristics of VOCs from Furniture. *Build. Environ.* **2021**, *196*, 107786. [CrossRef]
42. Zhang, R.; Tan, Y.; Wang, Y.; Wang, H.; Zhang, M.; Liu, J.; Xiong, J. Predicting the Concentrations of VOCs in a Controlled Chamber and an Occupied Classroom via a Deep Learning Approach. *Build. Environ.* **2022**, *207*, 108525. [CrossRef]
43. Mohammadshirazi, A.; Kalkhorani, V.A.; Humes, J.; Speno, B.; Rike, J.; Ramnath, R.; Clark, J.D. Predicting Airborne Pollutant Concentrations and Events in a Commercial Building Using Low-Cost Pollutant Sensors and Machine Learning: A Case Study. *Build. Environ.* **2022**, *213*, 108833. [CrossRef]
44. Sparks, L.E.; Tichenor, B.A.; Chang, J.; Guo, Z. Gas-Phase Mass Transfer Model for Predicting Volatile Organic Compound (Voc) Emission Rates from Indoor Pollutant Sources. *Indoor Air* **1996**, *6*, 31–40. [CrossRef]
45. Myers, G.E. Effect of Ventilation Rate and Board Loading on Formaldehyde Concentration: A Critical Review of the Literature. *For. Prod. Research* **1984**, *34*, 59–68.
46. Sherman, M.H.; Hult, E.L. Impacts of Contaminant Storage on Indoor Air Quality: Model Development. *Atmos. Environ.* **2013**, *72*, 41–49. [CrossRef]
47. Silberstein, S.; Grot, R.A.; Ishiguro, K.; Mulligan, J.L. Validation of Models for Predicting Formaldehyde Concentrations in Residences Due to Pressed-Wood Products. *JAPCA* **1988**, *38*, 1403–1411. [CrossRef]
48. Myers, G.E. The Effects of Temperature and Humidity on Formaldehyde Emission from UF-Bonded Boards: A Literature Critique. *For. Prod. J.* **1985**, *35*, 20–31.
49. Chan, W.R.; Kim, Y.-S.; Less, B.D.; Singer, B.C.; Walker, I.S. *Ventilation and Indoor Air Quality in New California Homes with Gas Appliances and Mechanical Ventilation*; Lawrence Berkeley National Laboratory: Berkeley, CA, USA, 2019.
50. ASHRAE. *ASHRAE Handbook of Fundamentals*; American Society of Heating, Refrigerating and Air-Conditioning Engineers, Inc.: Atlanta, GA, USA, 2017; ISBN 978-1-939200-58-7.
51. Walker, I.S.; Wilson, D.J. Field Validation of Equations for Stack and Wind Driven Air Infiltration Calculations. *ASHRAE HVACR Res. J.* **1998**, *4*, 119–140. [CrossRef]
52. Hurel, N.; Sherman, M.H.; Walker, I.S. Sub-Additivity in Combining Infiltration with Mechanical Ventilation for Single Zone Buildings. *Build. Environ.* **2016**, *98*, 89–97. [CrossRef]
53. Walker, I.S.; Wray, C.P.; Dickerhoff, D.J.; Sherman, M.H. *Evaluation of Flow Hood Measurements for Residential Register Flows*; Lawrence Berkeley National Laboratory: Berkeley, CA, USA, 2001.
54. Mendez, M.; Blond, N.; Blondeau, P.; Schoemaecker, C.; Hauglustaine, D.A. Assessment of the Impact of Oxidation Processes on Indoor Air Pollution Using the New Time-Resolved INCA-Indoor Model. *Atmos. Environ.* **2015**, *122*, 521–530. [CrossRef]
55. Marchand, C.; Le Calvé, S.; Mirabel, P.; Glasser, N.; Casset, A.; Schneider, N.; de Blay, F. Concentrations and Determinants of Gaseous Aldehydes in 162 Homes in Strasbourg (France). *Atmos. Environ.* **2008**, *42*, 505–516. [CrossRef]
56. Hodgson, A.T.; Ming, K.Y.; Singer, B.C. *Quantifying Object and Material Surface Areas in Residences*; Ernest Orlando Lawrence Berkeley National Laboratory: Berkeley, CA, USA, 2005.
57. Kadiyala, A.; Kumar, A. Evaluation of Indoor Air Quality Models with the Ranked Statistical Performance Measures Using Available Software. *Environ. Prog. Sustain. Energy* **2012**, *31*, 170–175. [CrossRef]
58. Kadiyala, A.; Kumar, A. *Guidelines for Operational Evaluation of Air Quality Models*; Lambert Academic Publishing GmbH & Co.: Saarbrücken, Germany, 2012.
59. Hodgson, A.T.; Rudd, A.F.; Beal, D.; Chandra, S. Volatile Organic Compound Concentrations and Emission Rates in New Manufactured and Site-Built Houses: VOC Concentrations and Emission Rates in New Manufactured and Site-Built Houses. *Indoor Air* **2000**, *10*, 178–192. [CrossRef]

buildings

MDPI

Article

Model to Balance an Acceptable Radon Level Indoors

Torben Valdbjørn Rasmussen * and Thomas Cornelius

Department of Civil Engineering and Construction Management, BUILD, Aalborg University, A.C. Meyers Vænge 15, 2450 Copenhagen, Denmark; tcb@build.aau.dk
* Correspondence: tvr@build.aau.dk

Abstract: A theoretical model is presented for balancing an acceptable radon concentration in indoor air. The infiltration of radon from the ground to the indoor air can be controlled by barriers or by lowering the air pressure at the lower zone of the ground slab. Indoor air with a radon concentration higher than that of outdoor air can further be controlled through the effective dilution of indoor air with outdoor air. The theory estimates the allowed radon infiltration from the ground to balance radon at an acceptable level indoors for a given ventilation rate, considering the radon contribution to the indoor air from indoor materials, building materials and the interior. A method using this theory is presented, identifying the necessary airtightness required for a radon barrier to balance the acceptable radon concentration for a building. Barriers include commercially used system solutions, such as bitumen-based radon blockers, wet-room membranes, reinforced fixed mortar pastes, and polyethene membranes. An acceptable indoor radon concentration of between 100 and 300 Bq/m^3 in indoor air is used. Barriers are evaluated by their ability to prevent soil gas penetration from the ground in combination with their effect on the building durability, as barriers may create a far more vulnerable building.

Keywords: model; radon; soil gas; indoor materials; penetration; ventilation; indoor air quality

Citation: Rasmussen, T.V.; Cornelius, T. Model to Balance an Acceptable Radon Level Indoors. *Buildings* **2022**, *12*, 447. https://doi.org/10.3390/buildings12040447

Academic Editors: Ashok Kumar, Amirul I Khan, Alejandro Moreno-Rangel and Michał Piasecki

Received: 28 February 2022
Accepted: 31 March 2022
Published: 5 April 2022

Publisher's Note: MDPI stays neutral with regard to jurisdictional claims in published maps and institutional affiliations.

1. Introduction

Radon-222 develops from the radioactive decay of radium-226 and has a half-life of 3.8 days. This gas seeps through the soil into buildings to interfere with radon derived from the atmosphere and building materials. If not diluted with outdoor air through ventilation, much higher human exposure levels can occur indoors than outdoors [1,2]. Thus, radon affects occupants through the indoor climate.

Radium is a decay product of uranium. Radium is a solid as uranium. Since uranium is one of the most common radioactive elements on Earth, radon will be present on Earth long into the future despite its short half-life.

The World Health Organization (WHO) recommends that states introduce requirements for the maximum radiation concentration from natural indoor-air sources. After determining that radon is responsible for 3% to 14% of lung cancer cases, the WHO recommended these requirements, depending on the average radon exposure in various countries [3]. The results indicate that radon is the second-leading cause of lung cancer (smoking tobacco is still the primary cause). Therefore, it is crucial to prevent radon from penetrating buildings. Since 2010, Danish building regulations have required that buildings be constructed to ensure that indoor radon levels remain below 100 Bq/m^3 [4].

The radon level indoors in Danish dwellings built before 2018 is 105 Bq/m^3. For dwellings built before 1995, the radon level is 106 Bq/m^3. For dwellings built between 1996 and 2009, the radon level is 93 Bq/m^3, and for dwellings built between 2010 and 2018, the radon level is 58 Bq/m^3. Approximately 9% of dwellings built before 2018 have a radon level above 200 Bq/m^3. In addition, 41% have a radon level above 100 Bq/m^3 [5]. In comparison, the radon level in dwellings in Finland is 96 Bq/m^3, in Sweden 108 Bq/m^3 and in Norway 60 Bq/m^3. In addition, the radon level in Germany is 50 Bq/m^3, in France

66 Bq/m^3 and in England 20 Bq/m^3, [6]. In Sweden, Norway and Finland, the limit value for radon levels in newly built buildings is 200 Bq/m^3. Norway requires that buildings for permanent residence must be able to activate measures to reduce the radon level, if the radon level exceeds 100 Bq/m^3. In England (England, Wales, Scotland and Ireland) the authorities apply an action level of 200 Bq/m^3 and a target level of 100 Bq/m^3. In Germany, the radon level in a workplace must not exceed 300 Bq/m^3 [7]. For other buildings, there is no requirement for the radon level in the indoor air [8]. However, new buildings should be planned and constructed so that the radon level does not exceed 100 Bq/m^3.

Infiltration of radon from the ground to the indoor air can be prevented by barriers, such as membranes, or by lowering the air pressure at the lower zone of the ground slab or combining them.

Radon originates from the ground. Soil gas penetrates from the ground underneath a building and is the primary radon source in indoor air [9]. However, building materials can also contribute to the radon concentration in indoor air if they contain radium or the chemical elements uranium and thorium (e.g., granite and alum shale). The radon contributions to the indoor air from building materials used indoors are seldomly considered in balancing the radon concentration. Outdoor air and the atmosphere contain a low concentration of radon because the soil gas is diluted when reaching the ground surface.

When using barriers as a system solution to prevent radon from penetrating buildings, it is crucial to determine the airtightness of such barriers. Moreover, the barrier must be sufficiently airtight and have airtight joints at the corners, across floor-level changes, around barrier-penetrating pipes and against floor drains.

This paper presents a theoretical model for balancing an acceptable radon concentration in indoor air for a typical single-family building construction. The presented theory theoretically estimates the allowed radon infiltration from the ground to balance the radon at an acceptable level indoors for a given ventilation rate, considering the radon contribution to the indoor air from indoor materials, such as building materials and the interior.

However, the choice of a radon barrier must be made consistently with an acceptable change in the building physics. Using a barrier to prevent radon gas penetration from soil often causes a change in the building physics related to the moisture level in the building materials from the rising soil moisture.

Ideally, the indoor radon concentration is lowered to a balanced level that meets the national building regulations. However, for existing buildings, a higher indoor radon concentration might be considered acceptable, considering the expense of preventing a rise in the soil moisture level. Therefore, a barrier must be evaluated by its ability to prevent soil gas penetration from the ground and its influence on the overall moisture level in the affected building materials.

This paper demonstrates the theory used in practice to balance the indoor radon concentration at an acceptable level, using several different radon barriers, which were evaluated as single-system solutions. The barriers include system solutions based on various materials, such as bitumen-based radon blockers, wet-room membranes, reinforced fixed mortar pastes, and mortar and polyethene membranes.

The barriers were tested using a modified version of the NBI 167/02 radon membrane airtightness test method [10], which determines the airtightness of a radon barrier used as a system solution. The assessment method was modified by providing a digital stirring and control system and introducing equipment to determine the overall mean air-pressure difference over the barrier. Barriers were identified to balance the indoor radon concentration between 100 and 300 Bq/m^3 for a ventilation rate of between 0.5 and 4 h^{-1}. For these findings, the model considered a low initial radon contribution from indoor materials of around 40 Bq/m^3 and higher contributions of around 1000 Bq/m^3. Barriers managed the radon exposure from the ground of up to 800,000 Bq/m^3 in the soil gas.

2. Balancing Radon Indoors

Indoor-air infiltration of radon from the ground must be prevented, and the radon that reaches the indoor air must be diluted to reach a balance of an acceptable radon concentration or a radon concentration at a lower level. An efficient way to avoid radon infiltration in a building is by making the ground slab airtight and lowering the air pressure at the lower zone of the ground slab, either as individual measures or by combining the two measures. If resulting in a higher radon concentration than that of the outdoor air, radon in the indoor air can be diluted with outdoor air and ventilated.

Methods to balance the indoor radon concentration comprise a combination of the three design criteria shown in Figure 1:

1. Making the ground slab airtight;
2. Lowering the air pressure at the lower zone of the ground slab;
3. Effectively diluting indoor air with outdoor air.

The indoor radon concentration can be balanced at an acceptable level using this method [11]. However, in contrast to new buildings, the three design criteria may not be implementable to influence the indoor radon concentration sufficiently for already-constructed buildings.

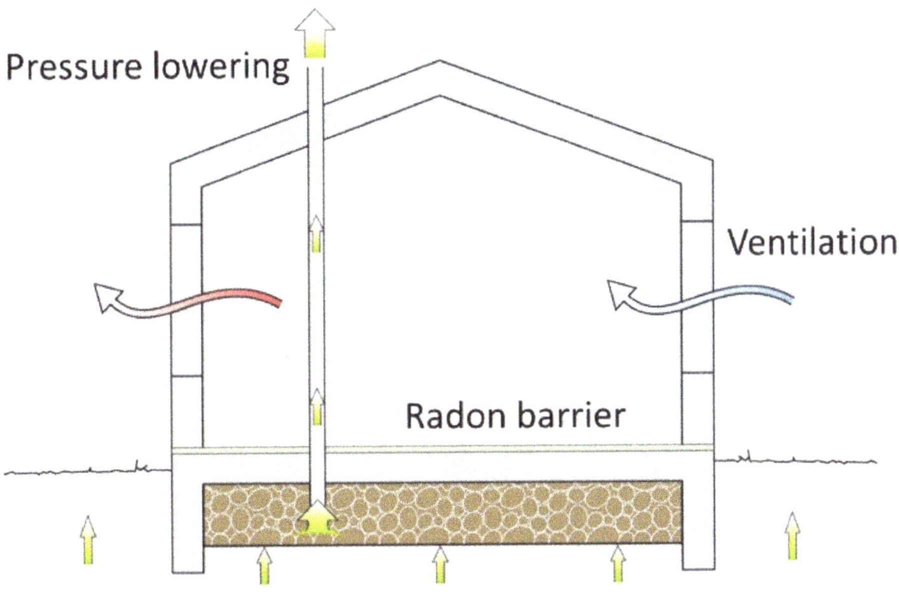

Figure 1. Design criteria to control the radon penetration and radon concentration in indoor air: 1. radon barrier—establishing a barrier preventing soil gas from penetrating from the ground; 2. pressure lowering—lowering the air pressure in the lower zone of the ground slab; and 3. ventilation—diluting indoor air with outdoor air.

3. Model for Balancing Radon Indoors

The theoretical model is based on a description of a detached single-family house with a ground area denoted by A, a ceiling height h and an air-change rate q. The indoor air is diluted with outdoor air with a radon concentration denoted by r and an indoor-air radon concentration denoted by R, as shown in Figure 2. Soil gas and the contribution from building materials and the interior are assumed to increase the indoor-air radon concentration. Therefore, the maximum penetration of soil gas with radon content (R_g)

and contribution from indoor materials (R_m) to maintain an acceptable indoor radon concentration were found using the equilibrium equation.

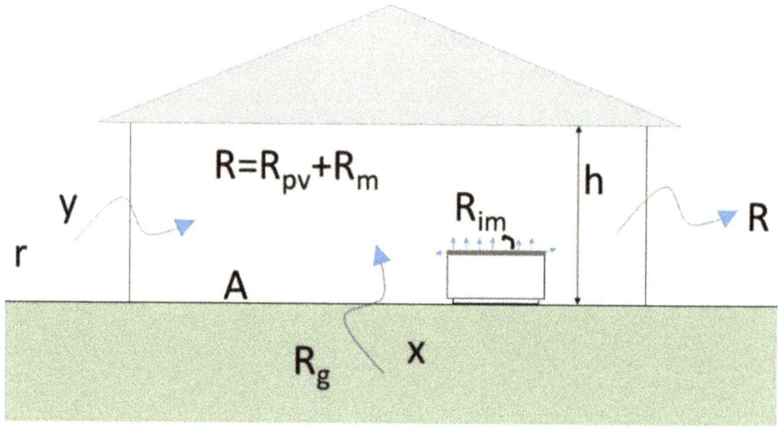

Figure 2. The equilibrium equation describes the equilibrium between the constant radon concentration in the indoor air (R), and the radon supply from soil gas (R_g), exterior air (r) and indoor materials (R_{im}) for a constant air-pressure difference between the interior and exterior over time.

Assuming the air-pressure difference between the interior and exterior of the building is constant over time, the equilibrium equation describes the static equilibrium of all internal and external system forces [12]. In the static case, the equilibrium equation is as follows:

$$K \cdot u = F, \quad (1)$$

where K denotes the stiffness matrix of the system, u is the vector with nodal displacements and F represents external forces.

The equilibrium equation describes the equilibrium between the constant radon concentration in the indoor air and the radon supply from soil gas, exterior air and indoor materials. The soil gas and exterior air are both assumed to have a constant but different radon concentrations. The contribution from indoor materials is assumed to follow the dilution equation. The radon contribution from indoor materials contributes to the indoor radon concentration and depends on the ventilation rate. The contribution to the indoor radon concentration from indoor materials reduces by 50% when the ventilation rate doubles. The equilibrium is given by Equations (2)–(4):

$$q \cdot A \cdot h \cdot R_{pv} = y \cdot r + x \cdot R_g, \quad (2)$$

where the indoor-air radon content, denoted as R, is the result of the radon contribution from soil gas, outdoor air (R_{pv}) and indoor materials (R_m):

$$R = R_{pv} + R_m. \quad (3)$$

The radon contribution from indoor materials (R_m) is described by the function F, where the contribution declines with the ventilation rate following the dilution equation:

$$R_m = F\,(R_{im}, q), \quad (4)$$

where R_{im} is the initial radon contribution from indoor materials. The radon content in the air outlet equals the indoor-air radon content provided from the three supply sources: the outdoor air, soil gas and indoor materials.

The equilibrium equation also describes the equilibrium between the indoor-air volume ventilated out of the building and the air supply volume needed from the soil gas and exterior air to stabilize the air-pressure difference over the building envelope over time. The equilibrium is given by Equation (5):

$$x + y = q \cdot A \cdot h. \tag{5}$$

The variables x and y are the only undefined variables in these equations (i.e., in Equations (2) and (5)). The air supply from the ventilation and the penetrating soil gas is equal to the building air outlet.

4. Quantifying the Contribution of Indoor Materials

The radon contribution from indoor materials is well known [13]. The contribution to the indoor-air radon content is related to the specific materials used in a building, contributing to the indoor radon concentration if the materials contain radium or the chemical elements uranium and thorium (e.g., granite and alum shale). The radon contribution to the indoor radon concentration from building materials is seldomly significant in well-ventilated buildings. However, if an acceptable indoor-air level of radon concentration is as low as 100 Bq/m^3, or even lower, radon contributions from less polluting sources must be considered.

The contribution from indoor materials is theoretically described in this paper by the function F, where the contribution declines with the ventilation rate. The radon concentration from indoor materials is described by an initial contribution (R_{im}) that declines by 50% every time the ventilation rate is doubled, following the dilution equation [14].

The initial contribution (R_{im}) from indoor materials (R_m) must be defined. The presented theory defines the initial radon contribution to the indoor-air radon concentration and considers the contribution related to a very low air change q of 0.1 times per hour, as illustrated in Figure 3 and Table 1.

Table 1. Decline in the radon contribution to the indoor-air radon concentration from indoor materials. q is the air change per hour.

q (h^{-1})	R_m (Bq/m^3)			
0.01	400.00	1000.00	5000.00	10,000.00
0.05	80.00	200.00	1000.00	2000.00
0.10 [1]	40.00	100.00	500.00	1000.00
0.20	20.00	50.00	250.00	500.00
0.40	10.00	25.00	125.00	250.00
0.80	5.00	12.50	62.50	125.00
1.60	2.50	6.25	31.25	62.50
3.20	1.25	3.13	15.63	31.23
6.40	0.63	1.56	7.81	15.63
12.80	0.31	0.78	3.91	7.81

[1] R_m is calculated for several different ventilation rates ranging from 0.01 h^{-1} to 12.8 h^{-1}. Initial radon contributions (R_{im}) of 40, 100, 500 and 1000 Bq/m^3 are shown. The initial radon contribution (R_{im}) is defined at the air change q equal to 0.1 times per hour.

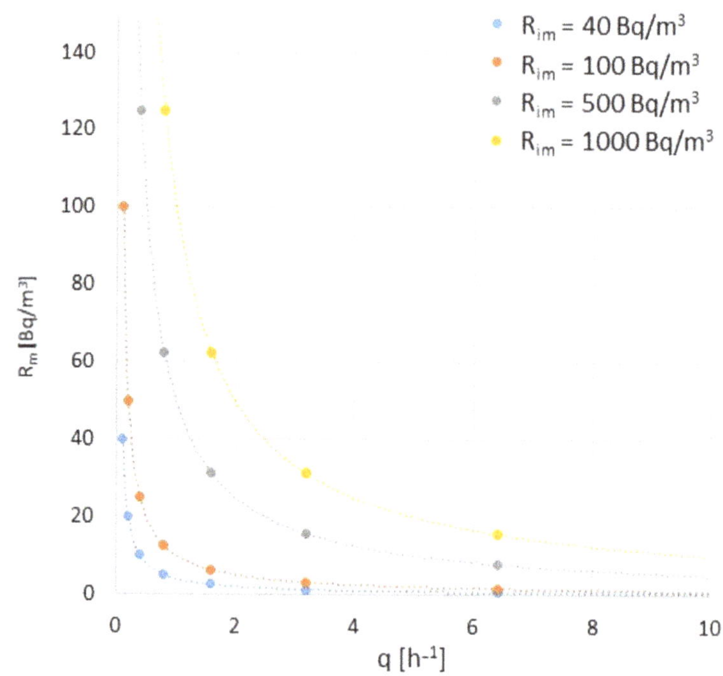

Figure 3. Radon contribution to the indoor-air radon concentration from indoor materials (R_m) described by the function F where the contribution declines by 50% every time the ventilation rate doubles, taking its starting contribution as the initial contribution (R_{im}) at an air-change rate q of 0.1 times per hour.

Although a ventilation rate of 0.1 h^{-1} is low, field studies show measurements of the ventilation rates in new detached single-family houses to be as low as 0.07 h^{-1} [15].

5. Balancing Radon Indoors

The presented theory can be used to determine the related values and requirements for the radon penetration from soil gas, the radon contribution from indoor materials and the radon concentration in outdoor air. The theory can also determine the ventilation rate to balance radon in indoor air at an acceptable level for a specific detached single-family house.

For a detached single-family house, the maximum penetration of soil gas to maintain an acceptable indoor radon concentration of 100 Bq/m^3 was determined for several radon exposures from soil gas. The radon concentration in soil gas varied from less than 1000 to 150,000 Bq/m^3. The ground area of the house was 100 m^2 with a ceiling height of 2.5 m. The air-change rate was 0.5 h^{-1} to maintain an acceptable indoor environment, equivalent to changing all the indoor air every two hours.

The initial radon contribution from indoor materials to the indoor radon concentration (R_{im}) was 40 Bq/m^3, resulting in a radon contribution of 8 Bq/m^3 from indoor materials (R_m) to the indoor radon concentration (Figure 3 and Table 1). Indoor air was diluted with outdoor air with a radon concentration of 5 Bq/m^3. The requirements to balance an acceptable indoor radon concentration R of 100 Bq/m^3 for the penetration of soil gas containing radon are listed in Figure 4.

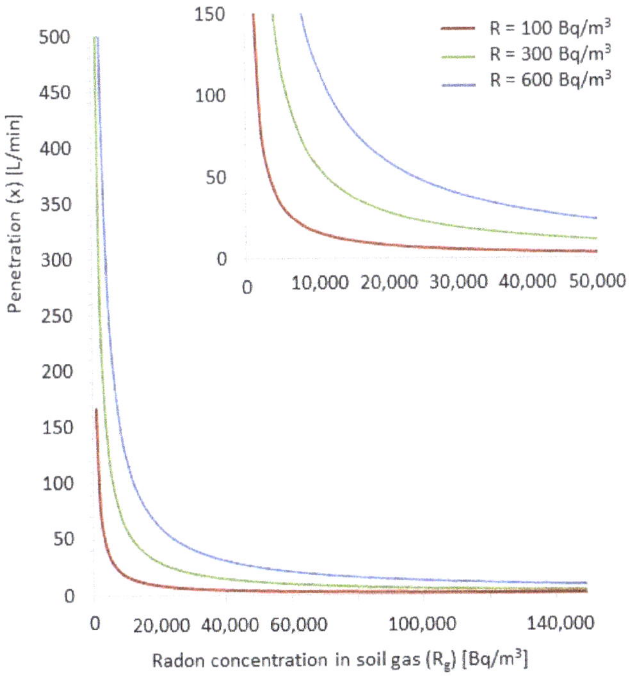

Figure 4. Soil gas penetration, balancing an acceptable radon concentration in indoor air of 100, 300, and 600 Bq/m^3. Soil gas contains radon. Indoor air was diluted with outdoor air. Outdoor air contains 5 Bq/m^3 radon. The air-change rate was 0.5 h^{-1}. The initial radon contribution from indoor materials (R_{im}) was 40 Bq/m^3, providing a radon contribution from indoor materials (R_m) of 8 Bq/m^3 to the radon indoor-air concentration. The house has a ground area of 100 m^2 and a ceiling height of 2.5 m.

Additionally, Figure 4 illustrates that the soil gas penetration for the same detached single-family house can increase to balance an acceptable radon indoor-air concentration R of 300 and 600 Bq/m^3. Penetration was calculated in liters per minute. Less soil gas may penetrate the indoor air through the ground slab to balance an acceptable radon indoor-air level of 100, 300 and 600 Bq/m^3 to increase the radon concentration in the soil gas. To reach a balance at a higher level of an acceptable radon concentration in the indoor air, a larger amount of radon penetrates indoor air through the ground slab, either through the increased penetration of soil gas or a higher radon concentration in the soil gas.

When balancing an acceptable indoor radon concentration of 100 Bq/m^3 for a house, the maximum penetration of soil gas was found for several radon exposures from soil gas and for several initial radon contributions from indoor materials (R_{im}) with air-change rates of 0.5, 1.06 and 2.11 h^{-1}. For the initial radon contribution from indoor materials (R_{im}) of 237 Bq/m^3, an indoor radon concentration R of 100 Bq/m^3 can be balanced and kept with an air-change rate of 0.5 h^{-1} if soil gas penetration containing radon is avoided. To further increase the initial radon contributions from indoor materials, the air-change rate must be increased to balance indoor radon at a concentration of 100 Bq/m^3, still avoiding soil gas penetration containing radon. For the initial radon contribution from indoor materials of 500 Bq/m^3, an air-change rate of 1.06 h^{-1} is needed. For an initial radon contribution from indoor materials of 1000 Bq/m^3, an air-change rate of 2.11 h^{-1} is needed for balance at an acceptable radon indoor-air concentration R of 100 Bq/m^3 (Figure 5). The ground slab must be airtight, and measures must be taken to lower the air pressure at its lower zone to avoid soil gas penetration of the indoor air through the ground slab of a detached single-family house.

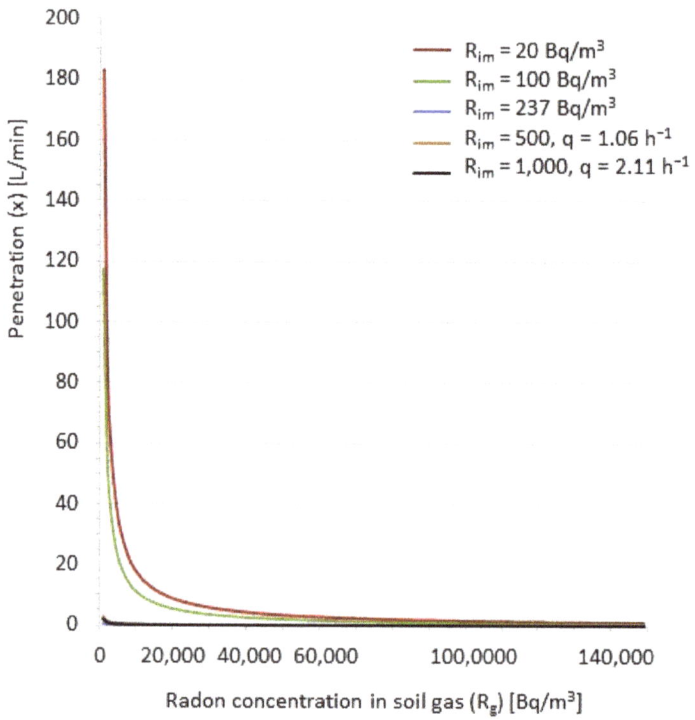

Figure 5. The allowed soil gas penetration with a given radon concentration balancing the radon indoor-air concentration at 100 Bq/m^3 with increased initial radon contributions from indoor materials and an air-change rate starting from 20 Bq/m^3 and 0.5 h^{-1}, respectively.

6. Controlling Soil Gas Penetration

Controlling the radon concentration via soil gas penetration through the ground slab is a key parameter for balancing the radon indoor-air concentration at an acceptable level. Measures that make the ground slab airtight or lower the air pressure at the lower zone of the ground slab can be used individually or combined. Making the ground slab airtight increases the effect of a pressure-lowering measurement at the lower slab zone. A measure reducing radon penetration to a predefined level can be reached using a barrier. The barrier choice depends on its ability to reduce infiltration. Ten radon barriers used as system solutions were tested with the modified version of the NBI 167/02 radon membrane, the airtightness test method [10], which determines the airtightness of a radon barrier used as a system solution.

6.1. Barriers

Ten barriers were tested as system solutions, which are denoted as Systems A through J, as shown in Table 2.

Table 2. Barrier systems tested.

System	Contents
A	A fixed mortar paste combined with acrylic sealant, also used as a wet-room membrane.
B	A firm bitumen-based radon blocker combined with a two-component floating sealant.
C	A reinforced fixed mortar paste combined with acrylic sealant.
D	A one-component floating membrane combined with edge reinforcements, epoxy and elastic pipe collars.
E	A two-component fixed mortar paste combined with edge reinforcements, epoxy and elastic pipe collars.
F	A foil system consisting of nonwovens filled with a two-component fixed mortar paste combined with edge reinforcements, epoxy and elastic pipe collars.
G	A polyethene membrane with solid tape joints, acrylic primer and elastic pipe collars.
H	A polyethene membrane with solid tape joints, acrylic adhesive, acrylic primer and elastic pipe collars.
I	A noise-reducing aluminum foil-coated subflooring with aluminum butyl tape joints, primer and elastic pipe collars.
J	A noise-reducing aluminum foil-coated subflooring with aluminum butyl tape joints, primer, elastic pipe collars and a one-component flow membrane.

Figure 6 illustrates mounting the test material inside the mock-up for System B. System B is a firm bitumen-based radon blocker combined with a two-component floating sealant. Figure 7 displays the mounting of the two-component fixed mortar paste combined with edge reinforcements, epoxy and elastic pipe collars, denoted as System E.

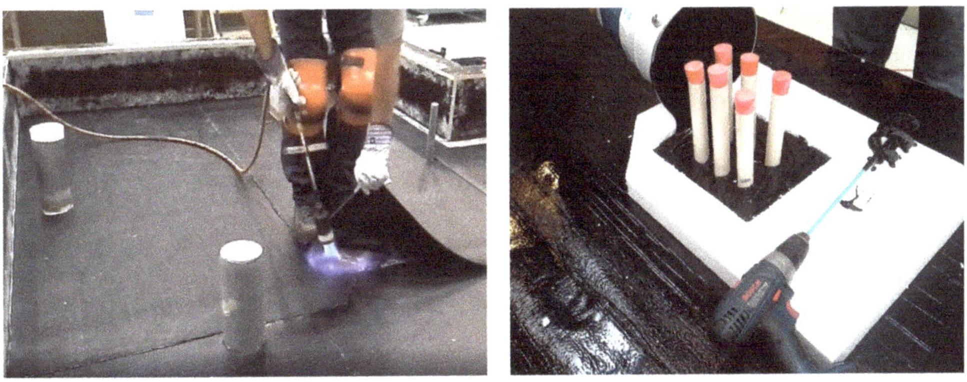

(a) (b)

Figure 6. Mounting the test material inside the mock-up for System B, which is a firm bitumen-based radon blocker (**a**) combined with a two-component floating sealant (**b**).

The barriers were used as delivered, and the manufacturer mounted them inside the mock-up. The tests started 40 h after mounting the barrier to ensure a stress-free barrier and joints. The tests set no specific requirements for the indoor climate at the testing laboratory. However, the laboratory climate should be a dry tempered room with a temperature between 17 °C and 25 °C with relative humidity between 15% and 65%.

Figure 7. Mounting the test material inside the mock-up for System E, which is a two-component fixed mortar paste combined with edge reinforcements, epoxy and elastic pipe collars.

6.2. Test of Air Infiltration

The test determines the air penetration through a material evaluated for suitability as a radon barrier. The test evaluates how well a barrier prevents soil gas with radon from penetrating the indoor air. The barrier was mounted inside a mock-up, providing a stable basis with penetrating pipes, an elevation, and narrow-angled and wide-angled corners. The airtightness of the barrier was determined as the air penetration through the barrier and its joints for a difference in air pressure of 30 Pa, denoted as q_{30}. The difference in air pressure over the barrier is the difference in the air pressure between the air inside the mock-up (designed as a box) and in the surrounding test laboratory.

6.3. Measurement Setup

The test was conducted by mounting the test material inside a mock-up. After molding the test material, the mock-up was filled with pressure-firm thermal insulation using mineral wool. On top of the firm insulation, a test-material layer was mounted to seal the mock-up volume that holds the firm insulation enveloped by the test material. The constant airflow from the sealed mock-up was measured. The airflow provides a constant air-pressure difference.

6.4. Equipment

The barrier was mounted in a mock-up of laminated wooden boards 3.0 m long and wide and 0.3 m high with a notch of 1.0 by 1.0 m, with changed floor levels, penetrating pipes and floor drains (Figure 8). The air was extracted from the volume using a fan. The cavity of the mock-up was filled with pressure-firm thermal insulation material and enveloped by the test barrier material. The coherent airflow values and difference in air pressure between the air inside the mock-up and the surrounding test laboratory were systematically measured and logged.

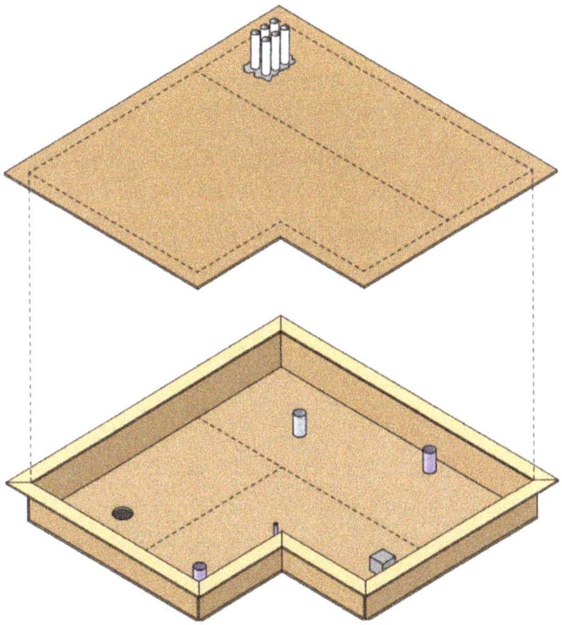

Figure 8. Sketch of mock-up measuring the barrier airtightness.

Using the program TECLOC3 from BlowerDoor Gmbh, the data were logged by connecting a (1) computer to a unit measuring the pressure difference and (2) a fan. The fan was a Minneapolis micro leakage meter, type FD E51-767, which measured the airflow between 0.09 and 79 m^3h^{-1}. The fan was mounted on a disc with a circular hole to measure the airflow. Individual discs were mounted, and each had a circular hole of 3.8, 8.0, 20 or 45 mm. A computer controlled the fan to extract the air from the mock-up volume and measure the airflow, introducing predetermined differences in air pressure between the volume within the mock-up and the air in the surrounding test laboratory.

The mean value of the difference in air pressure between the volume within the mock-up and the air in the surrounding test laboratory was determined using five air-pressure difference measurement units mounted on the top layer of the test material. These units were used to calibrate the airflow pressure measurements because the air pressure within the mock-up was not homogeneously distributed.

Adding air infiltration through well-defined openings was necessary to measure the airtightness of the barriers with very low airflow in the lower ranges of the capacity of the micro leakage meter. The well-defined openings were added using discs with a 7, 10, 14 or 20 mm diameter. The airflow through the well-defined opening was subtracted from the measured airflow during data processing.

6.5. Processing Results

The airflow was measured at four air-pressure levels of 30, 50, 70 and 90 Pa controlled by the air-pressure measuring equipment mounted over the barrier system. At each pressure level, four measurements were performed using four different well-defined openings. For all 16 measurements, the opening areas, the individual air-pressure differences in the five air-pressure difference measurement units, and the airflow through the suction point were measured. The measurements were used to calculate the airflow in liters per minute for a 30-Pa mean pressure difference, denoted as q_{30}, over the barrier system, where q_{30} was determined for the individual barrier systems.

The airflow for a 30-Pa mean pressure difference over the barrier system comprises the soil gas penetration for a one-floor building with a ground area of 100 m^2 with a difference in air pressure over the building envelope of 1 to 4 Pa [4,9,10,16]. The highest allowed soil gas penetrations with a radon concentration not exceeding an acceptable level in the indoor air of 100, 200 and 300 Bq/m^3 were determined. Soil gas penetration was determined as the intersection between the air balance indoors, given by the air-change rate and an acceptable radon concentration from Equations (2) and (3), an initial radon contribution from indoor materials of 40 Bq/m^3 and the penetration of soil gas, q_{30}. For the calculations, indoor air was assumed to be diluted with outdoor air with a radon concentration of 5 Bq/m^3 [17]. Additionally, the air-change rate in the building was set at 0.5 h^{-1} [18]. Figure 9 presents the soil gas determination with a radon concentration not exceeding acceptable indoor-air levels of 100, 200 and 300 Bq/m^3 for the System B and E barriers.

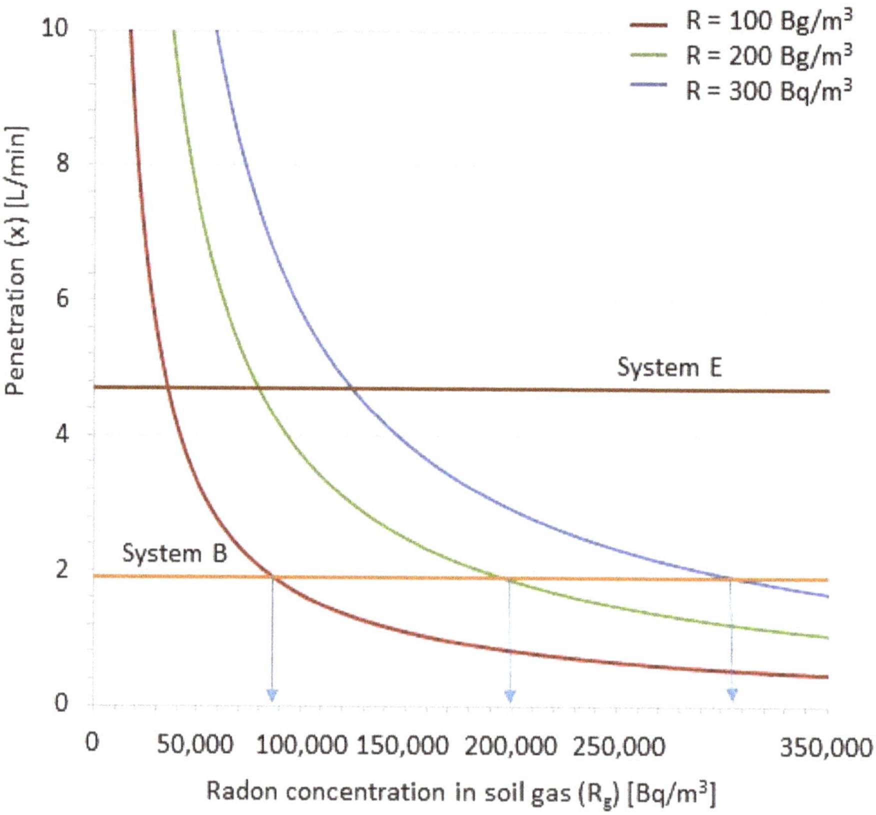

Figure 9. Radon barriers for System B and E, where the intersection between the horizontal line indicating the measured airtightness and the curves for reaching an acceptable radon indoor-air level of 100, 200 and 300 Bq/m^3 provides the critical radon concentration in soil gas.

Figure 10 displays the soil gas determination with a radon concentration not exceeding an acceptable level in indoor air of 100 Bq/m^3 for an air-change rate of 0.5, 1.0, 2.0 and 4.0 h^{-1} for the System B and E barriers.

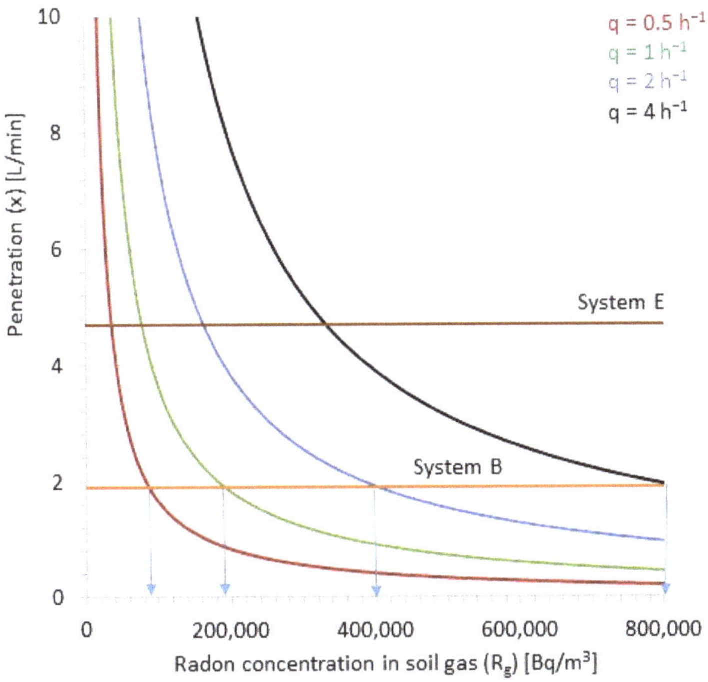

Figure 10. Radon barriers for System B and E, where the intersection between the horizontal line measuring the airtightness and the curves for the air-change rates provides the radon concentration in soil gas.

7. Results

The penetration rates and radon concentration in soil gas (Table 3) should not exceed 100, 200 and 300 Bq/m^3 to reach an acceptable radon concentration in indoor air. For Table 3, the air-change rate was 0.5 h^{-1}, and the initial radon contributions from indoor materials (R_{im}) was 40 Bq/m^3. Moreover, the penetration rates and radon concentration in soil gas to not exceed 100 Bq/m^3 are listed in Table 4, where the air-change rates were 0.5, 1.0, 2.0 and 4.0 h^{-1}, and the initial radon contribution from indoor materials (R_{im}) was 40 Bq/m^3.

Table 3. Maximum soil gas penetration to reach an indoor radon concentration of 100, 200 and 300 Bq/m^3 for System A to J barriers. The air-change rate was 0.5 h^{-1}, and the initial radon contribution from indoor materials (R_{im}) was 40 Bq/m^3. The airflow penetration rate (q_{30}) defines how well a barrier prevents soil gas penetration.

Barrier System	Airflow, Penetration Rate (q_{30}) (L/min)	R_g in Soil Gas		
		100 (Bq/m^3)	200 (Bq/m^3)	300 (Bq/m^3)
A	12.0	13,500	31,000	48,500
B	1.9	86,600	196,200	305,800
C	29.0	5700	12,900	20,100
D	4.0	34,400	77,600	121,000
E	4.7	35,000	79,400	123,700
F	12.6	13,000	29,500	46,000
G	132.0	1400	2800	4400
H	8.9	18,500	42,000	65,700
I	63.9	2600	5900	9100
J	16.6	9800	22,500	35,000

Table 4. Maximum soil gas penetration to reach an indoor-air radon concentration of 100 Bq/m^3 for System A to J barriers. The air-change rate was 0.5, 1.0, 2.0 and 4.0 h^{-1}, and the initial radon contribution from indoor materials (R_{im}) was 40 Bq/m^3. The airflow penetration rate (q_{30}) defines how well a barrier prevents soil gas penetration.

Barrier System	Airflow, Penetration Rate (q_{30}) (L/min)	R_g in Soil Gas			
		q = 0.5 (h^{-1})	q = 1.0 (h^{-1})	q = 2.0 (h^{-1})	q = 4.0 (h^{-1})
A	12.0	13,500	30,500	63,500	129,000
B	1.9	86,600	190,800	399,000	817,000
C	29.0	5700	12,500	26,200	53,500
D	4.8	34,400	75,500	158,000	323,000
E	4.7	35,000	77,200	161,300	330,000
F	12.6	13,000	29,000	60,500	123,000
G	132.0	1400	2700	5800	11,800
H	8.9	18,500	40,500	85,500	174,200
I	63.9	2600	5600	11,800	24,200
J	16.6	9800	22,000	45,500	94,000

8. Moisture Challenges

A radon barrier can easily be applied during building construction, creating a barrier to increase the ground slap airtightness within or above the ground slab. The barrier can even be mounted in the ground below the slab. This barrier can be applied in numerous ways with suitable fixation onto the materials and surfaces, combined with a moisture barrier that prevents ground moisture from reaching constructions above the foundation or the basement interior. Applying a radon barrier to an already-constructed building can affect the durability of the building, especially for heritage buildings, because measures may create a far more vulnerable building and change its robustness to withstanding moisture and user behavior.

The influence and change in moisture load and content of other building components and constructions must be considered when deciding on a radon barrier mounted on the ground slab or basement wall and floor. Thus, the changed water vapor diffusion and resulting rise in soil moisture load may create a more vulnerable building after mounting a radon barrier for construction. Special attention must be focused on the risk of mold growth, for example, in an air cavity behind a radon barrier that is not bonded to the underlayment.

Through diffusion, radon can penetrate the ground slab or basement wall and floor. The ability of gases, vapors and other minor molecules to penetrate the ground slab, basement wall and floor by diffusion depends on the individual permeability of the ground slab, basement wall and floor.

Diffusion through concrete is considered limited. Fixed mortar paste can reduce diffusion but cannot prevent penetration by diffusion. As the ability to limit diffusion is related to the density of the fixed mortar paste and the thickness of the mortar paste layer, even minor cracks can increase diffusion [19].

Investigations have found that radon diffusion through a typical concrete slab of 150 mm in thickness without cracks contributes to indoor radon by approximately 15 to 20 Bq/m^3. For these investigations, an air-change rate of 0.5 h^{-1} was provided in the building, and the radon content in the soil gas was 500,000 Bq/m^3 [20].

In Denmark, the general radon content in soil gas is substantially lower, approximately 50,000 Bq/m^3 [21]. In this case, the contribution by radon diffusion into the indoor air is substantially lower at approximately 2 Bq/m^3.

Radon penetration through the ground slab, basement wall and floor by diffusion in buildings today represents a limited contribution to the overall indoor-air radon content, and the primary source is soil gas from the ground. However, a high indoor-air radon content can be observed in indoor air where the air-change rate is lower than 0.5 h^{-1} due to the accumulation of radon from indoor materials.

9. Discussion

Soil gas penetrating through the ground slab is the primary source of radon in indoor air in most cases [11]. However, the contribution from indoor materials may affect the indoor-air radon content, resulting in an unacceptable level. Therefore, the (1) geological composition of the ground on which a building is situated, (2) radon concentration in soil gas, (3) soil gas penetration through the ground slab, (4) contribution from indoor materials and (5) air-change rate are used to set the indoor radon concentration level. Radon seeps into a building through soil gas penetration through cracks or other ground construction openings [22] and indoor materials. Therefore, it is essential to control soil gas penetration and balance the radon concentration indoors through ventilation.

Establishing a barrier that prevents soil gas penetration from the ground is an efficient way to prevent radon penetration. By avoiding soil gas penetration and lowering the air pressure in the lower zone of the ground slab, a barrier provides a more effective solution, providing a far better possibility of providing an air-change rate of 0.5 h^{-1} that balances the indoor radon concentration at an acceptable level. However, when combining the three mentioned design criteria, (1) making the ground slab airtight, (2) lowering the air pressure at the lower zone of the ground slab and (3) effectively diluting the indoor air with outdoor air, the radon concentration in indoor air can be robustly balanced and maintained at an acceptable level. If the air pressure in the lower zone of the ground slab cannot be lowered, the radon barrier choice is crucial for soil gas penetrating the indoor air.

The presented theory aids in combining the radon barrier choice and related necessary ventilation rate of the indoor air to balance the radon at an acceptable indoor concentration. The theory estimates the allowed radon infiltration from the ground to balance the radon at an acceptable indoor level for a given ventilation rate, considering the radon contribution to the indoor air from indoor materials. However, the moisture-level change in the building components must be considered when choosing the most suitable radon barrier, which depends on individual building physics.

The requirement for the airtightness of a radon barrier, the penetration rate (q_{30}), can be determined from the radon concentration in soil gas underneath a building. In certain cases, a diffusion-tight radon barrier can be used, and in others, a diffusion-open barrier is preferred. The barrier choice depends on the moisture level after mounting. It is crucial to choose a sufficiently airtight radon barrier to meet the requirements while contributing to the building physics.

From the theoretical processing of the test results combined with the radon contribution from indoor materials and the indoor-air ventilation rates, a radon barrier can be chosen based on the indoor radon concentration being balanced at an acceptable level and the radon content in the soil gas underneath a building. The theoretical processing demonstrates that, for an initial radon contribution from indoor materials (R_{im}) of up to 237 Bq/m^3, an acceptable indoor radon concentration of 100 Bq/m^3 can be achieved with an air-change rate of 0.5 h^{-1}, controlling the soil gas penetration. However, at a radon contribution from materials of 237 Bq/m^3, soil gas penetration containing radon must be avoided. An increased initial radon contribution from indoor materials means an increased ventilation rate is needed, balancing an acceptable indoor radon concentration of 100 Bq/m^3. The ventilation rates of 1.06 and 2.11 h^{-1} are needed for radon contributions from indoor materials of 500 and 1000 Bq/m^3, respectively, balancing an acceptable indoor radon concentration of 100 Bq/m^3 and avoiding soil gas penetration containing radon. Hence, in this study, the radon contribution from indoor materials was determined as the initial contribution at a ventilation rate of 0.1 h^{-1}. Avoiding soil gas penetration into the indoor air through the ground slab requires combined measures, including making the ground slab airtight and lowering the air pressure at the lower zone of the ground slab to a level that is even lower than the air pressure above the ground slab [23].

The theoretical test results indicate that the radon barrier in System B with the penetration rate (q_{30}) of 1.9 L/min can balance an acceptable radon concentration in indoor air that is less than or equal to 100 Bq/m^3 in a building on soil with a radon concentration of less than or equal to 86,600 Bq/m^3. If the soil gas contains a concentration of between 86,600 and 305,800 Bq/m^3, an acceptable indoor radon concentration can be balanced between 100 and 300 Bq/m^3. For theoretical processing, it was assumed that indoor air was diluted with outdoor air with a radon concentration of 5 Bq/m^3 at an air-change rate of 0.5 h^{-1} and an initial radon contribution from indoor materials of 40 Bq/m^3. However, by increasing the air-change rate to 1, 2, or 4 h^{-1}, an acceptable radon concentration in indoor air could be kept balanced at 100 Bq/m^3 or less in a building on soil with a radon concentration of 190,800, 399,000 and 817,000 Bq/m^3, respectively.

In terms of the testing barriers, it is vital to be aware of how the joints perform. These concerns are based on the performance of Systems G and H and Systems I and J, which are alike except for how the joints perform.

10. Conclusions

A model for theoretically balancing the radon concentration in indoor air was presented. The theory estimates the allowed radon infiltration from the ground to balance the radon at an acceptable indoor level for a given ventilation rate considering the radon contribution to the indoor air from indoor materials, such as building materials and the interior. The theory is useful for a typical building construction for a single-family house. Furthermore, the paper presents a theoretical processing method to balance the radon concentration indoors by combining the results from an improved testing method for determining the airtightness of a radon barrier assessed as a system solution [10]. Moreover, if appearing in the indoor air, a radon concentration above that of the outdoor air can be lowered by diluting the indoor air using outdoor air and ventilation. The model also demonstrates how the radon contribution from indoor materials influences the measures balancing the radon concentration indoor at an acceptable level.

Using the theoretical processing of the results determining the airtightness of the radon barriers as system solutions made it possible to choose a radon barrier with an acceptable radon concentration in indoor air and soil gas underneath a building with the ventilation rate and radon exposure from indoor materials. However, the acceptable radon concentration in indoor air could be compromised because a suitable radon barrier depends on the moisture-level change in the building after mounting the radon barrier. A radon barrier must contribute to the building physics, creating a more robust building. Further, the needed ventilation rate to achieve an acceptable radon concentration in indoor air could compromise the energy performance of the building.

The presented theory and theoretical processing method assumed that only soil gas, indoor materials and the atmosphere contain radon and that soil gas and indoor materials are the radon sources in indoor air. However, the contribution to the radon concentration in indoor air from indoor building materials is seldom significant. The contribution from indoor building materials is included in the theory, as materials contribute radon if they contain radium or the chemical elements uranium and thorium (e.g., granite and alum shale).

Author Contributions: Conceptualization, methodology, validation, formal analysis, investigation, data curation, writing—original draft preparation, writing—review and editing, project administration and funding acquisition: T.V.R.; visualization and lab tests: T.C. All authors have read and agreed to the published version of the manuscript.

Funding: This research was funded by the Realdania a philanthropic association, with the mission of improving quality of life and benefitting the common good by improving the built environment. Its focus is on solving challenges in Danish society in cooperation with the government, the municipalities, foundations, associations, private businesses and local, voluntary enthusiasts.

Institutional Review Board Statement: Not applicable.

Informed Consent Statement: Not applicable.

Data Availability Statement: Data are reported in Danish: Rasmussen, T.V. og Buch-Hansen, T.C. (2018). SBI-rapport; Nr. 2018:06. Egnede membransystemer til radonsikring: vurdering af ti membransystemer. 1. udg.: Statens Byggeforskningsinstitut, Aalborg Universitet. København. 28 s. (SBi-Report; No. 2018:06: Membranes for radon protection of buildings; in Danish). Danish Building Research Institute-Aalborg University. Copenhagen. Denmark. The test method is described in Danish: Rasmussen, Torben Valdbjørn & Buch-Hansen, Thomas Cornelius. (2016). Airtightsenes of radon barrier: Testmethod (Lufttæthed af materialer til radonsikring: Testmetode). (SBi, Vol. 2016:21). 1. ed. Copenhagen: SBi. 27 p.

Conflicts of Interest: The authors declare no conflict of interest.

References

1. Nazaroff, W.W. Radon transport from soil to air. *Rev. Geophys.* **1992**, *30*, 137–160. [CrossRef]
2. Brunekreef, B.; Holgate, S.T. Air pollution and health. *Lancet* **2002**, *360*, 1233–1242. [CrossRef]
3. Zeeb, H.; Shannoun, F. (Eds.) *WHO Handbook on Indoor Radon: A Public Health Perspective*; World Health Organization: Geneva, Switzerland, 2009.
4. Danish Enterprise and Construction Authority. Danish Building Regulations. *Dan. Build. Regul.* **2010**, *1*.
5. Rasmussen, T.V. *Comply of Radon Protection in Homes*; SBi-Report; No. 2019:07; Danish Building Research Institute, Aalborg University: Copenhagen, Denmark, 2019. (In Danish)
6. Available online: http://www.stuk.fi/sateilyymparistossa/radon/sv_FI/pitoisuudet/ (accessed on 8 February 2022).
7. Available online: http://www.bgbl.de/xaver/bgbl/start.xav?startbk=Bundesanzeiger_BGBl&jumpTo=bgbl117s1966.pdf (accessed on 8 February 2022).
8. Available online: https://lfu.rlp.de/de/arbeits-und-immissionsschutz/radoninformationen/ (accessed on 8 February 2022).
9. Rasmussen, T.V. Design criteria for achieving acceptable indoor radon concentration. *Int. J. Civ. Environ. Struct. Constr. Archit. Eng.* **2016**, *10*, 268–273.
10. Rasmussen, T.V.; Cornelius, T. Radon barrier: Method of testing airtightness (2nd ed.). In Proceedings of the 11th Nordic Symposium on Building Physics (NSB2017) 2017, Trondheim, Norway, 11–14 June 2017.
11. Rasmussen, T.V. SBi-Instructions 233, 2nd ed.; In *Measures Preventing Radon to Penetrate into New Buildings*, Danish Building Research Institute, Aalborg University: Hørsholm, Denmark, 2010; 44p. (In Danish)
12. Kyosev, Y.K. The finite element method (FEM) and its application to textile technology. In *Simulation in Textile Technology*; Woodhead Publishing: Sawston, UK, 2012. [CrossRef]
13. Al-Hamarneh Ibrahim, F. Radiological hazards for marble, granite and ceramic tiles used in buildings in Riyadh, Saudi Arabia. *Environ. Earth Sci.* **2017**, *76*, 1–10. [CrossRef]
14. Knudsen, H.N.; Kjaer, U.D.; Nielsen, P.A.; Wolkoff, P. Sensory and chemical characterization of VOC emissions from building products: Impact of concentration and air velocity. *Atmos. Environ.* **1999**, *33*, 1217–1230. [CrossRef]
15. Jensen, R.B.; Gunnarsen, L. *SBi-Report 2009:12. Concentration of Radon in Detached Single-Family Houses*; Building Research Institute Aalborg University: Hørsholm, Denmark, 2008. (In Danish)
16. SINTEF Byggforsk. NBI 167/02, Radon Membrane: Test of Airtightness; February 2016. Norge: SINTEF Byggforsk. Available online: http://www.byggforsk.no (accessed on 8 February 2022).
17. Rasmussen, T.V. *SBi-Instructions 270: Measuring Radon in Buildings*; Danish Building Research Institute, Aalborg University: Copenhagen, Denmark, 2018. (In Danish)
18. Transport, Building and Housing Agency. Danish Building Regulations 2018. Available online: https://bygningsreglementet.dk/ (accessed on 7 February 2022).
19. Font Guiteras, L. *Radon Generation, Entry and Accumulation Indoors*; Universitat Autònoma de Barcelona: Barcelona, Spain, 1997. Available online: http://www.tdr.cesca.es/tdx/tdx_uab/tesis/available/tdx-0506108-225143//lfg1de2.pdf (accessed on 8 February 2022).
20. Clavensjö, B.; Åkerblom, G. *The Book of Radon: Preventing Measures in New Buildings in Sweedish*; (Radonboken: Förebyggande åtgärder i nya byggnader); Formas: Stockholm, Sweden, 2004.
21. Danish Health Authority. Available online: www.sst.dk (accessed on 7 February 2022).
22. Danish Transport and Construction Agency. *Radon and Single-Family House*; Transport and Construction Agency: Copenhagen, Denmark, 2007. (In Danish)
23. Rasmussen, T.V. Novel radon sub-slab suctioning system. *Open Constr. Build. Technol. J.* **2013**, *7*, 13–19. [CrossRef]

atmosphere

Article

Modeling the Airborne Transmission of SARS-CoV-2 in Public Transport

Christina Matheis [1,*], Victor Norrefeldt [1], Harald Will [1], Tobias Herrmann [2], Ben Noethlichs [2], Michael Eckhardt [3], André Stiebritz [3], Mattias Jansson [3] and Martin Schön [3]

[1] Department of Energy Efficiency and Indoor Climate, Fraunhofer Institute for Building Physics IBP, Fraunhoferstr. 10, 83626 Valley, Germany; victor.norrefeldt@ibp.fraunhofer.de (V.N.); harald.will@ibp.fraunhofer.de (H.W.)

[2] IFB (Institute for Railway Technology), Carnotstr. 6, 10587 Berlin, Germany; he@bahntechnik.de (T.H.); bn@bahntechnik.de (B.N.)

[3] Alstom, Am Rathenaupark 1, 16761 Hennigsdorf, Germany; michael.eckhardt@alstomgroup.com (M.E.); andre.stiebritz@alstomgroup.com (A.S.); mattias.jansson@alstomgroup.com (M.J.); martin.schoen@alstomgroup.com (M.S.)

* Correspondence: christina.matheis@ibp.fraunhofer.de

Abstract: This study presents the transmission of SARS-CoV-2 in the main types of public transport vehicles and stations to comparatively assess the relative theoretical risk of infection of travelers. The presented approach benchmarks different measures to reduce potential exposure in public transport and compares the relative risk between different means of transport and situations encountered. Hence, a profound base for the selection of measures by operators, travelers and staff is provided. Zonal modeling is used as the simulation method to estimate the exposure to passengers in the immediate vicinity as well as farther away from the infected person. The level of exposure to passengers depends on parameters such as the duration of stay and travel profile, as well as the ventilation situation and the wearing of different types of masks. The effectiveness of technical and behavioral measures to minimize the infection risk is comparatively evaluated. Putting on FFP2 (N95) masks and refraining from loud speech decreases the inhaled viral load by over 99%. The results show that technical measures, such as filtering the recirculated air, primarily benefit passengers who are a few rows away from the infected person by reducing exposure 84–91%, whereas near-field exposure is only reduced by 30–69%. An exception is exposure in streetcars, which in the near-field is 17% higher due to the reduced air volume caused by the filter. Thus, it can be confirmed that the prevailing measures in public transport protect passengers from a high theoretical infection risk. At stations, the high airflows and the large air volume result in very low exposures (negligible compared to the remaining means of transport) provided that distance between travelers is kept. The comparison of typical means of transport indicates that the inhaled quanta dose depends primarily on the duration of stay in the vehicles and only secondarily on the ventilation of the vehicles. Due to the zonal modeling approach, it can also be shown that the position of infected person relative to the other passengers is decisive in assessing the risk of infection.

Keywords: simulation; zonal modeling; SARS-CoV-2; public transport; airborne transmission; risk assessment

Citation: Matheis, C.; Norrefeldt, V.; Will, H.; Herrmann, T.; Noethlichs, B.; Eckhardt, M.; Stiebritz, A.; Jansson, M.; Schön, M. Modeling the Airborne Transmission of SARS-CoV-2 in Public Transport. *Atmosphere* **2022**, *13*, 389. https://doi.org/10.3390/atmos13030389

Academic Editors: Ashok Kumar, Amirul Khan, Alejandro Moreno Rangel and Michał Piasecki

Received: 18 January 2022
Accepted: 23 February 2022
Published: 25 February 2022

1. Introduction

During the spread of SARS-CoV-2, it was found that transmission occurs primarily by virus-bearing particles [1–5]—consider the following three routes of transmission for SARS-CoV-2:

1. Direct transmission by droplets >5 µm containing the virus emitted by an infected person.
2. Transmission by respiratory droplets and aerosols (<5 µm) that contain the virus and can remain suspended in the air for an extended time and travel greater distances.

3. Transmission by direct contact with the virus through contact with an infected person or through direct contact with contaminated surfaces.

The difference between droplets and aerosols is the particle size or physical properties. While larger particles (>5 µm) sink to the ground more quickly, the smaller aerosols can remain in the air for a longer time and thus disperse in enclosed spaces. For example, a 5 µm aerosol takes 33 min to sink to ground from 1.5 m in resting air. Whether and how long droplets and aerosols remain suspended in the air depends on various factors such as temperature and humidity [2,6].

In the context of the SARS-CoV-2 pandemic, ways to minimize the risk of infection are constantly being sought. A minimum distance of 1.5 m from another person is recommended to minimize the likelihood of coming into contact with virus-containing droplets from a person infected with SARS-CoV-2 [7]. Partly because these distances cannot be maintained during rush hour, many people have health concerns about using public transportation. Despite implemented hygiene concepts, this has led to a significant decline in passenger numbers. Statistical data in the number of sold tickets in Germany reveal a decrease of 40–70% of passengers after the outbreak of SARS-CoV-2 in 2020 [8]. To counteract this effect, the effectiveness of current protective measures, as already elaborated in [9], is to be examined by means of simulations.

In [10], it is also shown that there is a great demand for research in the transport sector worldwide to counteract this effect. This includes some publications on infections with SARS-CoV-2 in public transport in USA, China, Japan and UK [10]. For example, in a Chinese study, a variety of protection measures in public transportation are developed, ranging from institutional requirements to personal protection and knowledge promotion [11]. However, the effect can only be confirmed in general terms. The authors of [12] conduct a systematic literature review on transmission in trains and buses and conclude that an empirical definition of the risk of infection is lacking observational data. Therefore, a model-based estimation of the risk based on the interior air, the travel duration and the passenger density is considered a beneficial approach. In [13], elaborate CFD flow simulations are performed in a car to determine infection risk. It is found that zero-dimensional approaches have limited applicability for an adequate assessment of risk in confined spaces, and that multidimensional approaches are necessary to represent complex fluid dynamics. The detailed consideration, however, does not allow the results to be transferred to other means of transport [13]. An approach to risk assessment in transportation based on simple geometry and the assumption of an ideally mixed space is shown in [14]. Nevertheless, these methods do not allow for a detailed comparison of all occupied areas in public transport taking into account airflows. In an experimental study on a train, [15] concludes that the carriage is not well mixed over its length but rather along its height and width. Hence, the location of a possibly infectious passenger is crucial for the infection risk, and a purely well-mixed assumption is not valid. Similar to these findings, virus exposure is considered locally resolved. The calculated exposures provide the basis for assessing the risk of airborne transmission of SARS-CoV-2 in public transportation and for evaluation of measures and recommendations. Here, the focus lies in understanding the dispersion of SARS-CoV-2 in indoor air and quantifying it assuming a SARS-CoV-2 infected passenger is on a train, bus or in a train station. Scenarios are simulated with adherence to the behavioral recommendations, such as wearing masks, avoiding speech and maintaining distances. The influence of ventilation in respect to fresh air rates and filtration efficiencies will also be investigated. With regard to a return to normality, scenarios without these measures are also considered.

A represented selection of the most important vehicle types of German public transport is being taken into account: long-distance trains and long-distance buses, regional trains, suburban trains, city trains and subway trains, streetcars and city buses. Furthermore, stations and stops are modeled both above and below ground. For model validation, CO_2 measurements were used as field measurements in public transport, from which fresh air volumes can be back-calculated and verified against manufacturer data. In a previously performed literature study, typical vehicle categories, information on possibilities and limitations of the system technology, information on aerosol dispersion, data on passenger numbers before and after start of the pandemic and documented transmissions of SARS-CoV-2 in public transport were determined and used for the simulations [16]. Through this approach, the gap can be closed between cited measurements or simulations for specific coaches and ventilation situations and the broad overview of meta-studies.

2. Materials and Methods

The applied modeling methodology is based on a zonal model, which is used to describe the indoor airflow [17]. In the model, a passenger infected with SARS-CoV-2 is inserted as a source. Starting from this, the dispersion behavior in different trains, buses and station types is determined. The main features of the modeling approach are presented below.

2.1. Zonal Model

The "Indoor Environment Simulation Suite" is a toolbox of different sub-models for the rapid simulation of indoor climate. The core of this toolbox is the "Velocity Propagating Zonal Model" (VEPZO) [17], which in many cases is a superior alternative to complex computational fluid dynamics (CFD) simulations. A trade-off between computational effort and level of detail of the result is chosen. It uses similar mathematical theories but divides the space into only 100 to 1000 volume zones [17]. Especially for considerations such as temperature and concentration fields in the interior, zonal modeling can achieve informative value similar to the detailed CFD simulations, but at lower computational cost. Therefore, the zonal modeling approach can be used for parametric studies. The model has been developed in the multi-physics modeling language Modelica [18], and the commercial software Dymola is used for solving of the model equations.

The VEPZO volume model implements the conservation of scalar quantities, such as mass, heat and tracer gas and particle/aerosol concentrations. Neighboring zones are connected by flow models in which the amount of exchanged air is calculated. By arranging the volume and flow models in three dimensions, space is represented zonally (Figure 1) to predict temperature, mass and airflow distribution.

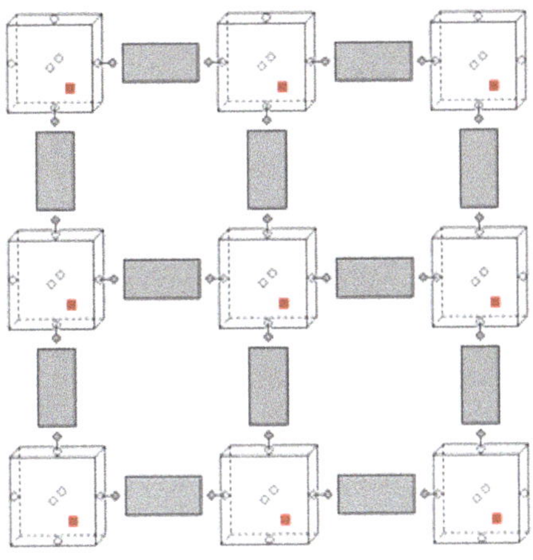

Figure 1. Schematic 2D representation of a zonal model: subdivision of the space into zones (cubes) connected by flow models (grey).

A detailed description of the zonal approach comprising the flow and volume models can be found in [17]. In the volume model, the equations for conservation of mass, heat and tracer gases are set up. For mass conservation, the air volumes flowing across the six zonal boundaries (right, left, front, back, down and up) are added. In a steady state, the sum of all inflowing and outflowing air quantities is zero. For heat conservation, the internal loads and the enthalpies flowing across the zone boundaries are summarized in Equation (1) [17]. This results in the transient profile of the enthalpy. The temperature can be determined via the equations of the state of the air:

$$V_i \cdot \rho_i \cdot \dot{h}_i = \sum_{j=1}^{6} \dot{m}_j \cdot h_{i/j} + \sum \dot{Q}_{Source} \tag{1}$$

where V_i, ρ_i, $\dot{h}_i$ is volume, density and enthalpy change of zone i; $\dot{m}_j$ is mass flow from the adjacent zone (positive: inflowing, negative: outflowing); $h_{i/j}$ is enthalpy of zone i or j, depending on flow direction; $\dot{Q}_{Source}$ is heat flow from sources, e.g., heat emission from persons, convective exchange with enclosing surfaces, etc.

The conservation equations for tracer gases, particles and aerosols in the air are implemented analogously to enthalpy conservation. Since emitted human viral particles have been shown to be capable of remaining airborne for extended periods [19], deposition was not considered in the simulation. This approach is considered conservative. In common zonal models, the airflow between two zones is calculated using the Bernoulli equation. In the VEPZO model, however, the acceleration of the flow in the flow paths is calculated in order to avoid the numerically unstable square root function of velocity vs. pressure difference. To model the losses of the flow, a viscous term is introduced. The flow model takes into account the air fluxes between the neighboring zones and calculates the mass flow to be exchanged via the pressure, momentum, height difference and the viscous loss term. The effective viscosity is a calibration parameter of the model, and it has been concluded that 0.001 provides good results [17]. To calculate the flow velocity, Equation (2) sums up the forces acting on the flow path and determines the resulting acceleration of the flow. The equation underlying the flow path is shown for the x-coordinate but is correspondingly valid for the other Cartesian coordinates:

$$\dot{u} = -\frac{\Delta p_{i,j} + \Delta\left(u^2\right)_{i,j} + g \cdot \Delta z_{i,j}}{\Delta x} + \frac{\mu}{\rho} \cdot \left(\frac{\Delta \frac{\partial u}{\partial y}}{\Delta y} + \frac{\Delta \frac{\partial u}{\partial z}}{\Delta z} \right) \tag{2}$$

where $\dot{u}$ is acceleration of air in the x-direction (in the steady state 0); $\Delta p_{i,j}$, $\Delta\left(u^2\right)_{i,j}$ and $\Delta z_{i,j}$ are pressure difference, difference of velocity squares and height difference, respectively, between zones i and j; g is 9.81 m/s^2; ρ is density of flowing air; μ is calibration parameter for effective viscosity (0.001).

2.2. Model Development and Evaluation

The Thermal Model Generation Tool is a self-developed tool used for model generation [20]. Starting from a geometry file of the simulated interior, the zoning in x-, y- and z-directions is defined, and the location of flow sources and sinks as well as heat loads are determined. The tool then automatically generates the Modelica source code of the zonal model. After defining the source intensities and the thermal resistances of enclosures, the exported model is ready for simulation. The described workflow is shown in Figure 2.

The airborne exposure to potentially infectious material inside vehicles and at stations was evaluated in particular. To represent the airborne SARS-CoV-2 spread, the so-called quanta notion was used. This is a description of the amount of virus emitted by a person infected with SARS-CoV-2 and is based on [21,22]. By definition, a vulnerable person has a 63% risk of getting infected after inhaling the dose of one quanta. This definition was set out for the initial SARS-CoV-2 virus, to the best of our knowledge, how mutations change this rate is not defined. The advantage of this approach is that, regardless the dominant mutation of SARS-CoV-2 or any other airborne infectious disease, the general conclusions on protective means and their efficiency remain valid. Therefore, the theoretical risk assessment in this study is based on the inhaled quanta-dose. The calculated quanta concentration is exported as a result for each individual zone and presented as a numerical value. In addition, the concentration predicted in simulation is deposited as a color gradient, as shown in Figure 3, from green (from 0 mili-quanta/m^3) to yellow (at 20 mili-quanta/m^3) to red (from 50 quanta/m^3).

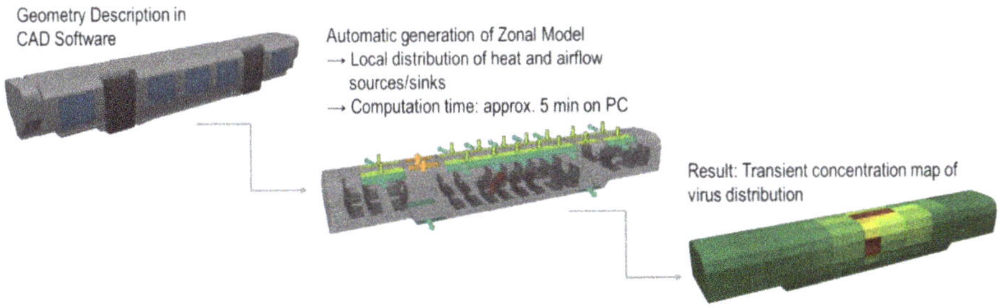

Figure 2. Indoor Environment Simulation Suite (IESS) workflow.

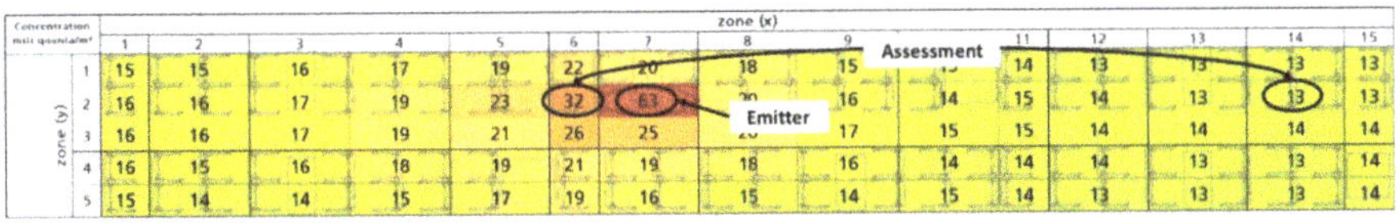

Figure 3. Example of evaluation/representation of the simulation: shown is the concentration in mili-quanta/m^3 in a section through the compartment at breathing height.

The inhaled dose at selected locations is determined by integrating the concentration over the residence time, weighted by the respiratory volume and the protective effect of masks, as shown in Equation (3). The neighboring zone of the emitter with the highest concentration (max. dose) and a zone far away from the emitter (min. dose) are evaluated in each case. As a measure for the dose, the mili-quanta is used, where 1000 mili-quanta correspond to one quanta.

$$Dose = \dot{V}_{Breathing} \cdot f_{Mask} \cdot \int_{t_{start}}^{t_{end}} c_i(t) dt \quad (3)$$

where $\dot{V}_{Breathing}$ is breathing volume, here 540 L/h (light, sedentary work, [23]); f_{Mask} is self-protection effect depending on mask type (Section 2.3 Boundary Conditions); $c_i(t)$ is time-resolved course of concentration in the evaluated zone i; t_{start} and t_{end} are start and end of exposure, respectively.

2.3. *Boundary Conditions*

2.3.1. Viral Load

In the following, a theoretical risk of infection is assumed for everyone present in the vehicles without knowledge of personal risk factors. To assess whether an infectious human should be modeled by aerosol, particle or quanta emission rates, a comparison in Figure 4 was performed [16].

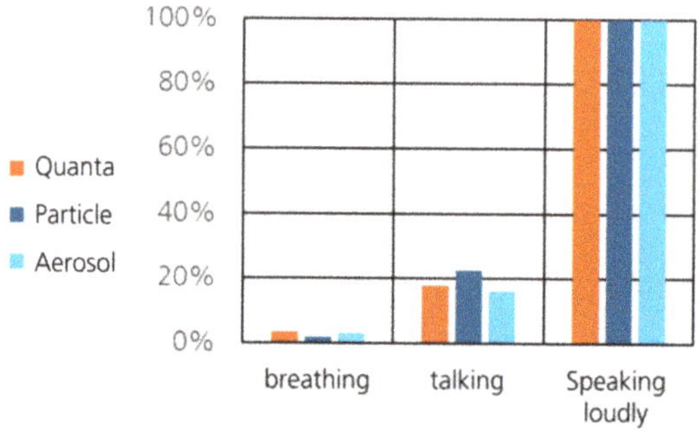

Figure 4. Relative comparison of approaches to describe the emitter as a quanta, particulate or aerosol source.

Speaking loudly corresponds to 100%. Depending on the observation, breathing equals 2–4% of the emissivity of speaking loudly and talking equivalent to 16–23%. Thus, an approximately constant gradation between activity levels is expected independent of the selected source term. The relative proportions between breathing, talking and speaking loudly are quite close (Table 1). That is, regardless of how the source is modeled, the relative outcome between the different activity levels remains similar.

Table 1. Comparison of the source description of the emitter.

	Quanta		Particle		Aerosol	
Literature	[24]	[21,22]	[25]	[26]	[23]	[27]
Breathing	2.3 quanta/h	Double logarithmic plots and information on percentiles	0.1 particle/s	Normal: 14–71 particle/L	0.0018 mL/m^3	Online calculator, based on [23], use of a stochastic approach for risk assessment.
Talking	11.4 quanta/h		1.2 particle/s		0.0096 mL/m^3	
Speaking Loudly	65.1 quanta/h		5.3 particle/s Max.: 17 particle/s		0.06 mL/m^3	
Super Emitter	factor 10^2		660–3230 p/L (factor 10^2)	660–3230 p/L (factor 10^2)	no	
Assessment	Introduced specifically for SARS-CoV-2 Allows super emitter assessment Theoretical risk assessment		Reference literature is not SARS-CoV-2 specific. Divergent data on super emitters.		No information on super emitters. Theoretical risk assessment derived, specifically introduced for SARS-CoV-2.	

The quanta doses recorded in different scenarios are compared with the assumption that a higher dose intake always leads to a higher risk. The emission strength is given in quanta/h for different activity levels. An Excel calculation tool [24] fixed the following listed mean emission rates:

1. Breathing: 2.3 quanta/h
2. Talking: 11.4 quanta/h
3. Speaking loudly: 65.1 quanta/h

These values are implemented as a unidirectional source in the model.

2.3.2. CO_2 Emission

For model validation against in situ measurements, it was necessary to use an airborne tracer that is commonly found in transport vehicles. CO_2 is a reliable tracer gas emitted by passengers and thus allows, together with the passenger count, an estimation of the fresh airflow rate supplied to the cabin. To measure the CO_2 concentration in transport means, a Rotronic CP11, 0–5000 ppm with accuracy of $\pm$30 ppm/$\pm$5% was used. Passengers were accurately counted where feasible (especially in long-haul transport) or estimated (e.g., quarter filled, half full, especially in local transport). For model validation an emission rate of 18 L/h is assumed per passenger [28].

2.3.3. Masks

Wearing masks is considered an effective measure to reduce the spread of SARS-CoV-2. A recent review [29] also recommended the wearing of masks in public places. Therefore, the following three mask types were included in simulations:

1. without mask
2. mouth-nose protection (MNP) and homemade masks
3. FFP2-mask

In each case, the simulation of mask types includes the protective effect during exhalation (i.e., a percentage reduction in the source term) and the protective effect during inhalation (i.e., a reduction in the absorbed dose). Average values for the mask types are considered in the simulations as given in Table 2, however, a higher protective effect [24,30] can be achieved with correct handling. To compare the three different mask types, it is assumed that everyone in the vehicle or on the station wears the same mask type.

Table 2. Reduction effect through masks [31].

Mask Type	Reduction Exhalation	Reduction Inhalation
without	0%	0%
(MNP) or homemade mask	50%	30%
FFP2 (N95) mask	90%	90%

2.3.4. Ventilation

Depending on the operational condition, different modes of ventilation are implemented in the models. Generally, the supply air in public transport is a mixture of fresh air, which is free of SARS-CoV-2 pathogens, and recirculated air, with the viral load of the return air of the vehicle. Typical filters used today on trains are not of sufficient quality for viral particles. In the case studies, hypothetical filter implementations were considered, taking into account that changing the filter to HEPA in an existing system will lead to reduced flow. In the model, the filter is described as a sink with a certain efficiency, i.e., the viral load downstream is reduced by a factor from the upstream load. The magnitude of flow reduction and realistically achievable filter efficiencies was provided by experts within the research group. Any filtering and purification devices reduce the pathogen concentration in the recirculated air by a certain percentage. For example, if a filtering effect of 80% is assumed, the recirculated air in the model will have a residual pathogen concentration of 20% compared to the exhausted air.

In addition, the air exchange through the open doors is implemented in the model. The main driver for this is the temperature difference between the interior and the outside air. When the door is opened, this causes cool air to enter the cabin through the lower area of the door, while warmer air leaves the cabin through the upper area. The formulas for temperature-driven air exchange at a rectangular opening are derived from [32].

$$\dot{V}_{door} = \frac{1}{3} \cdot C_D \cdot B \cdot \sqrt{\frac{\Delta T \cdot g \cdot H^3}{T_m}} \tag{4}$$

where $\dot{V}_{door}$ is volume flow through the open door; B is width; H is height; ΔT is temperature difference; T_m is mean temperature; g = 9.81 m/s^2; C_D = pressure loss coefficient.

C_D is the pressure loss coefficient and ultimately describes the flow resistance of the door opening. As a typical, conservative assumption, the value of C_D is considered as 0.4. The indoor temperature of 23 °C, the outdoor temperature of 16.6 °C for the summer and 9.1 °C for winter (Germany-wide average) is assumed [33]. The outdoor temperature in the subway tunnel was estimated to be 15 °C based on measurement (27 January 2021, Munich, Sendlinger Tor subway station). The airflow calculated by Equation (4) during the door opening times serves as input for a ventilation source in the model.

Openable windows were not modeled. Since the infection situation is most critical in winter, windows are usually closed at this time of year for comfort and energy efficiency reasons. If a window is opened in practice, additional air exchange takes place, which results in a lower risk of infection. The simulations thus correspond to a worst-case scenario. In addition, their shape varies greatly, and the actual opening is difficult to model in practice.

2.3.5. Partition Walls

Partition walls as flow obstacles are implemented in the model by reducing the cross-section area of the geometrically closest flow path. In the case of an airtight partition, the corresponding flow path and thus the air exchange between the affected, neighboring zones are removed from the model. Thus, seat surfaces and backrests that affect the airflow are considered in the model.

2.3.6. Occupancy Density

The occupancy density is used as a parameter for heat release in the interior. For air conditioning and ventilation systems operated in fixed-volume flow mode, the occupancy density does not influence the supply airflowrate. In demand-controlled systems (e.g., the high-speed train ICE), the fresh air volume adjusts to the occupancy. For the passenger density at the stations, it is assumed that there is a train on each side of the platform. The number of people is therefore made up of the passengers who get on or off both trains at the same time. A typical capacity utilization of the trains in pandemic periods was applied [16]. Simulations focus on the airborne spread of infectious matter, hence it is intrinsically assumed that the distance between passengers is large enough to inhibit direct particle transmission.

2.4. *Determination of Train, Bus and Station Types*

In order to make a representative selection of train types, a survey was carried out on the number and characteristics of the train stock in Germany [16]. Furthermore, the selection was based on the availability of operational data and the possibility to conduct validation measurements on the modeled vehicles. Table 3 shows the selected types and the criteria by which these types where chosen. In cases where no detailed data on ventilation were available, data from these measurements were used and determined using CO_2 balancing equations.

Table 3. Representative trains, buses and stations based on research and statistical analysis.

Means of Transport	Type	Selection Criterion	Literature
Long-Distance Train	ICE high-capacity train	Most common type	[34–36]
Regional Train/Local Traffic	multiple-unit train TALENT 2/3 (Bombardier Transportation)	Very common type, Detailed data basis	[34–36]
Subway/Light Rail Vehicles	Munich subway (A series) Munich subway (C series)	Most common length (15 to 30 m) Future increase in frequency expected	[37]
Tram/Streetcar	Flexity Berlin (Bombardier Transportation)	Most common length (30 m)	[37–40]
Suburban Train	TALENT 2 (Bombardier Transportation)	Typical vehicle dimensions, Detailed data basis	-
City Bus	12 m Bus	Most common type, Length	[40]
Long-Distance Bus	FDH2 bus	Possibility of in situ measurements	[41]
Station	Subway platform in low position with central platform, station concourse of terminus station (half-open)	Most common platform type for subway, limiting case (underground)	

If similar ventilation systems are installed for the train types not considered here, the simulated results can also be transferred to these. For this purpose, the fresh and recirculated air volumes, the form of air injection and the driving cycle must be compared with the input data used here.

As an estimate of whether the distance of 1.5 m can be maintained to exclude transmission by large particles, the maximum occupancy density possible for this purpose is determined. A circle of 1.5 m diameter requires an area of 1.76 m^2. It corresponds to a maximum occupancy density of 0.56 passengers/m^2, neglecting areas that cannot be used by passengers. The number of passengers for the considered means of transport in the pre-pandemic phase was ascertained from German operator data [42–48] and statistical information [8]. The reduction of travelers during the pandemic was determined from [16]. In general, it can be assumed that the minimum distance of 1.5 m can only be maintained in selected cases, such as in low-occupancy vehicles at night or on secondary routes. For this reason, it is deemed necessary to wear a medical mask or mouth-nose protection (MNP). Both terms are used synonymously in the following. Additionally, simulation cases with stronger-filtering FFP2 masks were included to take into account that some regions impose this type of mask.

3. Simulation

In the simulation, it is assumed that an infected person is present in the transport vehicle or on the platform. Based on this, the exposure in the near field and in the wider environment of the emitter is calculated. The virus is assumed to be airborne. Pathogen transmission through surfaces (smear infection) is not modeled because findings consistently show only low levels of viral load on surfaces [16].

The simulation study included eight different means of public transport and two types of train stations, with the typical travel time determined for the respective means of transport. The typical maximum time spent on the platform (8 to 35 min) was taken from [49]. The models and corresponding input data were validated with existing manufacturer data or by CO_2 measurements. In each case, the evaluation is performed concerning the activity (breathing, talking and loud speaking) of the SARS-CoV-2 infected passenger and by mask type (without mask, MNP and FFP2). Then the influence of air filtration and the amount of fresh air is considered. In addition, the heating and cooling scenarios in the respective means of transport are examined to observe a possible influence on the airflow pattern. The effect on exposure of introducing compartments in comparison to the saloon coach was also investigated.

3.1. *Input Data*

For zonal modeling, the geometry of the selected means of transport are divided into small zones. Depending on the geometry and interior design, 8–17 zones in the x-direction (longitudinal) and 4–5 zones in the y-direction were created. The height is divided into five zones in each case (cf. Figure 5). In comparison, the zones in the models of stations are significantly larger to represent areas shown in Figure 6. The zones surrounding the emitter are 5 m long in their largest extension.

In heating mode, the air is supplied mainly through the floor area and is extracted through the ceiling. In cooling mode, air is supplied from the ceiling (cf. Figure 5). This results in different flow characteristics in the coaches. Depending on the train type, recirculation air is aspired in a dedicated outlet or from the exhaust air ducting. According to the operators, no distinction is made between heating and cooling cases in buses and tramways.

Figure 5. Zonal model of the ICE 4 with sources and sinks for heating (**top**) and cooling (**bottom**) mode: light green arrows, supply air; dark green arrows, exhaust air; red-marked person, emitter.

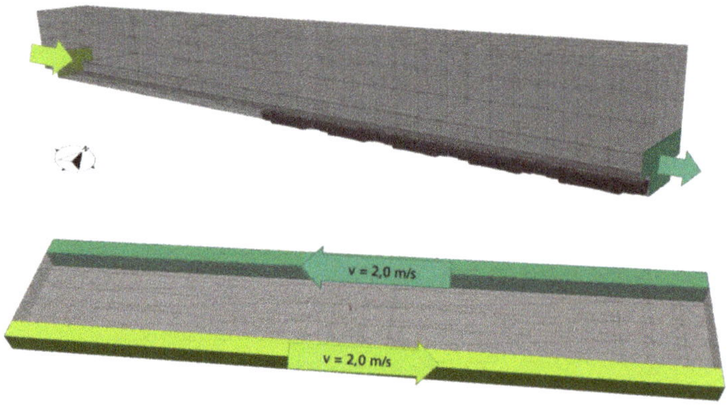

Figure 6. Simulation models of the train hall section (**top**) and an underground station using the example of Munich Central Station and the Odeonsplatz (U3/U6 subway station) in Munich (**bottom**).

For the train station hall, two cases were considered as flow boundary conditions. One case is characterized by the mean wind speed from the direction NW to SW at 3.3 m/s according to reference weather data in Munich [33]; the other case is purely thermally driven, with an assumed temperature difference of 1 K. This is an assumption. However, it is expected that waste heat from trains, lighting and passengers, as well as solar heat input may well lead to an increase in temperature in the building. The formula according to [32] was again used to determine the resulting airflowrate. For the evaluation of a subway station, a mean flow velocity through the two tunnel tubes of 2 m/s was assumed as a boundary condition. This value is the time average of any flows created by the stack effect and the piston ventilation effect that incoming trains have (Z. Kebdani, personal communication, 5 February 2021) [50].

To consider the effects of door opening in the simulations, travel profiles for the various means of transport were derived (Table 4):

Table 4. Typical travel profiles and durations of stay in the different means of transport and stations.

Means of Transport	Stop Time	Travel Time between Stations	Total Travel Duration	Literature
Long-Distance Train	negligible	2.5 h	2.5 h	Measurement period during validation
Regional Train/Local Traffic	52 s (1 door)	295 s	98 min	Research on travel and stop times
Subway/Light Rail Vehicles	25 s (3 doors)	72 s	29.5 min	Research on travel and stop times [48,51]
Tram/Streetcar	17 s (2 doors)	65 s	25 min	Research on travel and stop times
Suburban Train	36 s (2 doors)	127 s	77 min	Research on travel and stop times
City Bus	12 s (2 doors)	70 s	21.5 min	Research on travel and stop times
Long-Distance Bus	negligible	2.5 h	2.5 h	Comparability with long-distance train
Stations	-	-	12–35 min (depending on reason for travel and time of day)	[49]

3.2. Validation

The models were validated using measured CO_2 concentrations from field measurements. For example, measurement was carried out on the Munich–Erfurt route in an ICE 4 to validate the long-distance train (Figure 7). Shortly before Erfurt, the trains pass through a tunnel, where the fresh air supply is interrupted to avoid the pressure surge in the cabin. Figure 7 shows the measured (black, dashed) and simulated (black, solid) CO_2 concentration. Overall, there is good agreement between simulation and measurement, with a maximum deviation of about 150 ppm at time 60 min. Later, it was found that there is also a tunnel at that time, shortly before Nuremberg, which could lead to the measured CO_2 peak.

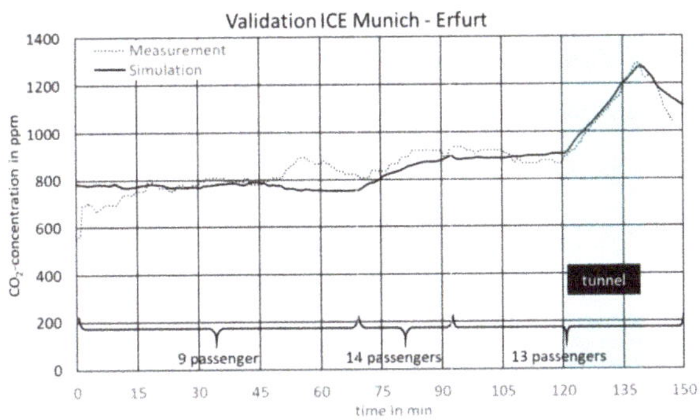

Figure 7. Comparison of measured and simulated CO_2 concentration on Munich–Erfurt route in an ICE 4.

The validation of the remaining models was performed similarly to the long-distance train. The occupancy in the means of transport during the measurements was estimated based on recordings of the measurement team. The actual amount of fresh air was determined based on CO_2 measurements and occupancy. The validation of the zonal model of the regional train and the suburban railroad was carried out based on extensive flow simulations by the manufacturer, Bombardier Transportation. It could be shown in all models that the zonal simulation approach used here is suitable to represent the temperature distribution and thus the indoor climate in the train. For the validation of the above-ground station, CO_2 concentration was measured at the Munich Central Station. However, the measured values were so close to the outside air that a meaningful validation is impossible.

3.3. *Main Results of Flow Simulations*

The activity levels of breathing, speaking and speaking loudly, without a mask or with a MNP or FFP2 mask were considered. A concentration profile was created for each simulation. Figure 8 shows an example of the concentration distribution in the horizontal section at head height (approx. 1.1 m) of an ICE large-capacity coach for the case of a speaking infected passenger in the case of HVAC heating at 50% occupancy. It is clear that around the emitter (zone marked with a red oval), there is a higher concentration of up to 32 mili-quanta/m^3, while farther away in the wagon it is 13 to 19 mili-quanta/m^3. The reason for the presence of some infectious material in the distant field is the shape of recirculated air because of the ventilation in the coach.

Concentration in mili-quanta/m³	zone (x)														
zone (y)	1	2	3	4	5	6	7	8	9	10	11	12	13	14	15
1	15	15	16	17	19	22	20	18	15	13	14	13	13	13	13
2	16	16	17	19	23	32	63	20	16	14	15	14	13	13	13
3	16	16	17	19	21	26	25	20	17	15	15	14	14	14	14
4	16	15	16	18	19	21	19	18	16	14	14	14	13	13	14
5	15	14	14	15	17	19	16	15	14	15	14	13	13	13	14

Figure 8. Example of concentration distribution in mili-quanta per m^3 for the case "HVAC heating, 50% occupancy, talking, without mask" in ICE.

Integrating the concentration from Equation (3) throughout the trip yields the determined inhaled dose. For each simulated case, the minimum dose farther away and the maximum dose at the seats adjacent to the infected passenger are evaluated.

Figure 9 represents the results of minimum and maximum inhaling of infectious material in different speaking and mask wearing scenarios after 2.5 h in an ICE. Without wearing masks, the maximum doses are columns 1, 2 and 3 for breathing, speaking and loud speaking, respectively. The worst-case scenario of loud speaking is considered for MNP and FFP2 masks, where the maximum doses are columns 4 and 5, respectively. For the FFP2 mask, the massive reduction in values is due to pathogen filtering during both exhalation and inhalation. These ratios are valid for all types of transport means and stations.

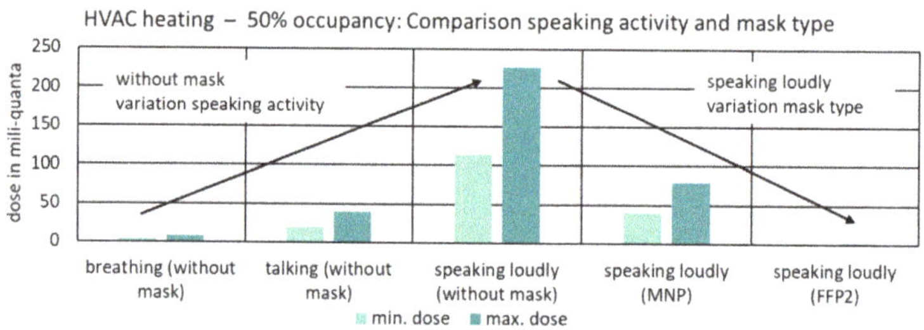

Figure 9. Comparison of inhaled dose in mili-quanta after 2.5 h in ICE with an infected person during different activities (breathing, talking or speaking loudly) of the emitter and with different mask types (none, MNP or FFP2): min. dose, minimum dose absorbed farther away from the emitter; max. dose, maximum exposure that is absorbed close to the emitter.

A comparison of the different ventilation scenarios shows in all means of transport that a similar maximum dose is reached in the vicinity of the emitter with the same supply air quantities. Farther away from the infected person, however, the minimum dose increases as the proportion of outdoor air decreases. The Figure 10 shows the inhaled doses at different ventilation rates as an example case for the ICE. Here, for example, a demand-driven reduction in the fresh air rate from 1500 m^3/h to 500 m^3/h due to lower occupancy results in a 3.4-fold increase in exposure farther away. In contrast, ventilation with pure, fresh air leads to a 90% reduction in exposure farther away from the emitter.

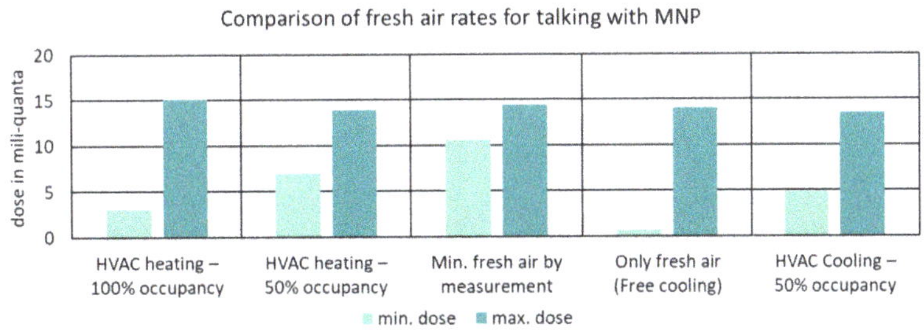

Figure 10. Influence of fresh air and recirculated airflowrate on the amount of exposure for the ICE: min. dose, minimum dose absorbed farther away from the emitter; max. dose, maximum exposure that is absorbed close to the emitter.

For the consideration of recirculating filtered air, a filter effectiveness of 80% towards SARS-CoV-2 was assumed in accordance with the current state of technology. As a result of the increased pressure drop across the filter, there is an assumed reduction in air volumes of 10%. Figure 11 shows the reduction of the exposure due to filtration.

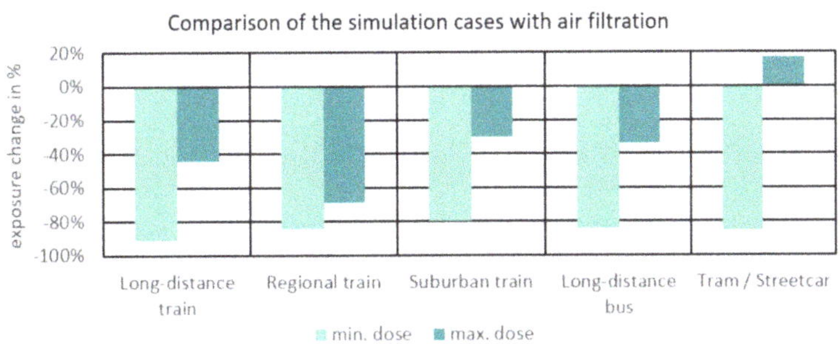

Figure 11. Influence of filtering on the amount of exposure: min. dose, minimum dose absorbed farther away from the emitter; max. dose, maximum exposure that is absorbed close to the emitter.

In the areas farther away from the infected person, the reduction of the inhaled quanta amount is between 80% and 90% in all cases. In the close-up area, the supply of fresh air has a significant influence on the quanta concentration in the air. The better the area is ventilated, the more the emissions can be diluted and the concentration decreases. In the case of streetcar ventilation, at 34%, the proportion of recirculated air is the lowest in comparison with the other vehicles. Here, the main effect is the lower amount of supply air in case of filtering in the close range of the infected person. The emissions are less diluted, resulting in an increase of the quanta dose in the vicinity.

Table 5 presents the inhaled dose for breathing activity of the emitter in the different means of transport. When speaking loudly, the values from Table 6 are obtained. For the comparison of the individual means of transport, the worst-case heating scenario with minimum fresh air supply was selected. In the case of the train station hall, the unfavorable case of thermal-buoyancy-driven flow by a 1 K temperature difference is chosen for comparison.

Table 5. Absorbed dose in mili-quanta when breathing at close proximity (max. dose) or farther away from the emitter (min. dose) for the assumed durations of stay.

	Without Mask		With MNP		With FFP2-Mask	
	Min. Dose	**Max. Dose**	**Min. Dose**	**Max. Dose**	**Min. Dose**	**Max. Dose**
Long-Distance Train (2.5 h)	6.09	8.33	2.13	2.96	0.06	0.08
Regional Train/Local Traffic (98 min)	0.97	3.01	0.34	1.05	0.01	0.03
Old/New Subways (29.5 min)	0.07/0.03	1.52/1.52	0.02/0.01	0.53/0.53	0.00/0.00	0.02/0.02
Tram/Streetcar (25 min)	0.16	0.87	0.05	0.30	0.00	0.01
Suburban Train (77 min)	0.30	0.96	0.10	0.33	0.00	0.01
City Bus (21.5 min)	0.41	3.16	0.14	1.10	0.00	0.03
Long-Distance Bus (2.5 h)	3.91	6.24	1.37	2.18	0.04	0.06
Train Station Hall (35 min)	0.00	0.09	0.00	0.03	0.00	0.00
Underground Station (8 min)	0.00	0.04	0.00	0.01	0.00	0.00

Table 6. Absorbed dose in mili-quanta when speaking loudly at close proximity (max. dose) or farther away from the emitter (min. dose) for the assumed durations of stay.

	Without Mask		With MNP		With FFP2-Mask	
	Min. Dose	**Max. Dose**	**Min. Dose**	**Max. Dose**	**Min. Dose**	**Max. Dose**
Long-Distance Train (2.5 h)	172.47	235.86	60.37	82.55	1.72	2.36
Regional Train/Local Traffic (98 min)	27.49	85.15	9.62	29.80	0.27	0.85
Old/New Subways (29.5 min)	2.01/0.74	43.12/42.95	0.70/0.26	15.09/15.03	0.02/0.01	0.43/0.43
Tram/Streetcar (25 min)	4.41	24.59	1.54	8.61	0.04	0.25
Suburban Train (77 min)	8.45	27.09	2.96	2.48	0.08	0.27
City Bus (21.5 min)	11.62	89.34	4.07	31.27	0.12	0.89
Long-Distance Bus (2.5 h)	110.60	176.64	38.71	61.82	1.11	1.77
Train Station Hall (35 min)	0.05	2.45	0.02	0.86	0.00	0.02
Underground Station (8 min)	0.01	1.10	0.00	0.38	0.00	0.01

3.4. Further Simulations

For a fully occupied long-distance train, the presence of an infected person in a compartment is investigated. For this purpose, walls were introduced in the model around the emitter's seating group. Due to pressure equalization, overflow is possible through joints or gaps, for example, through doors. It is assumed that a fraction of exhaust air from the compartment is supplied to the rest of the coach by the central air recirculation system. Figure 12 shows the concentration distribution when the emitter speaks loudly without a mask in a compartment. Compared with the large-capacity coach, the concentration peak is confined to the compartment. In the area outside the compartment, the recirculating air is the cause of dispersion, and a result similar to the large-capacity coach is obtained. Figure 13 compares the inhaled dose. Other passengers in the compartment are exposed to a dose almost two times higher than in the large-capacity coach. On the other hand, numerically, fewer persons are affected. The optimum protection for persons outside the compartment would theoretically be achieved by a decentralized air recirculation system, but this would mean that each compartment would need its own ventilation system.

Concentration in mili-quanta/m³		zone (x)														
		1	2	3	4	5	6	7	8	9	10	11	12	13	14	15
zone (y)	1	25	25	26	28	29	37	176	30	27	25	24	24	23	23	24
	2	26	26	27	30	29	41	446	34	29	27	25	25	24	24	24
	3	26	27	28	30	32	37	41	compartment		27	26	25	24	24	24
	4	26	26	27	29	31	33	31	33	29	26	25	25	24	24	24
	5	25	24	25	26	27	31	32	29	26	26	26	24	23	23	24

Figure 12. Concentration distribution in mili-quanta/m^3 for the case "Speaking loudly, without mask" in the ICE with compartment formation around the emitter.

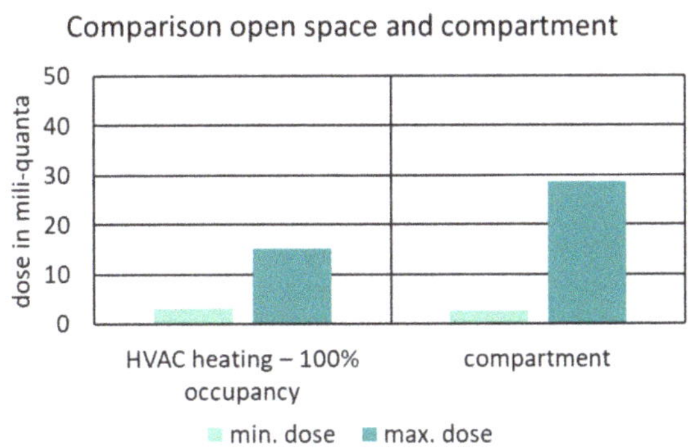

Figure 13. Comparison of the absorbed quanta dose in a large-capacity railcar (**left**) versus a compartment (**right**): min. dose, minimum dose absorbed farther away from the emitter; max. dose, maximum exposure that is absorbed close to the emitter.

3.5. Risk Assessment

In all cases, the highest protective effect is obtained by wearing an FFP2 mask by all passengers. This measure provides both good third-party protection and high self-protection. In addition, speaking loudly should be avoided. This represents another way of releasing as small an amount of infectious material as possible. Filtered recirculation reduces the emission load farther away from the emitter. In contrast, the load closer to the infected person decreases only slightly or may have a slightly higher concentration peak due to the associated reduction in airflow. Operation with pure fresh air at a lower total flowrate results in a higher concentration peak in the area of the emitter but reduces the exposure to passengers farther away. Since in reality the infected person remains unknown to fellow passengers, the highest possible level of self-protection is advisable for every passenger.

The comparison makes it clear that only the consistent use of an FFP2 mask can achieve values in the near and far range of the emitter in the lower range of the probability of infection with the original SARS-CoV-2 virus reported from the observational study. Speaking loudly significantly increases exposure by a factor of about 28 and thus indirectly increases the theoretical risk of infection. The recommendation to avoid loud talking in all public transport as a risk-reduction measure can be justified because it is expected that this also worsens the fit of the mask [52]. In addition, masks should only be removed as briefly as possible for eating or drinking. Technical measures, such as increasing the fresh air rate or recirculating filtered air limit the area of spread and thus reduce the risk of infection farther away from the emitter.

A direct derivation from the level of exposure to a possible medical risk from the quanta dose determined in each case is not considered possible. However, Ref. [53] gives indications on the risk of infection in Chinese high-speed trains in the period December 2019 to March 2020. The study also distinguishes between exposure in the close range of the emitter and in the more distant range. The assumption is made that the Chinese high-speed trains are ventilated in a basically similar way to the German ICE trains. Thus, the risk of infection in the ICE can at least be classified. Due to cultural customs, it can at best be assumed that people in Chinese trains speak quietly and never loudly. Whether the Chinese passengers were wearing MNP at the time and to what extent cannot be determined. However, wearing MNP in public transport was quite common in Asia even before the pandemic. Therefore, the comparison can only serve as an orientation. Another limitation is that the study refers to the original SARS-CoV-2 variant. Over time, however, the apparently more contagious mutations dominate the infections. With these assumptions and limitations, the probability of infection can be narrowed down for the original SARS-CoV-2 in such a way that the risk of infection lies in the range of 0.14% to 3.5% when 0.6 to 40 mili-quanta are inhaled. For this purpose, the dose range (Figure 14) between "Breathing without MNP" and "Talking with MNP" for the HVAC heating case with high occupancy was colored in the diagram.

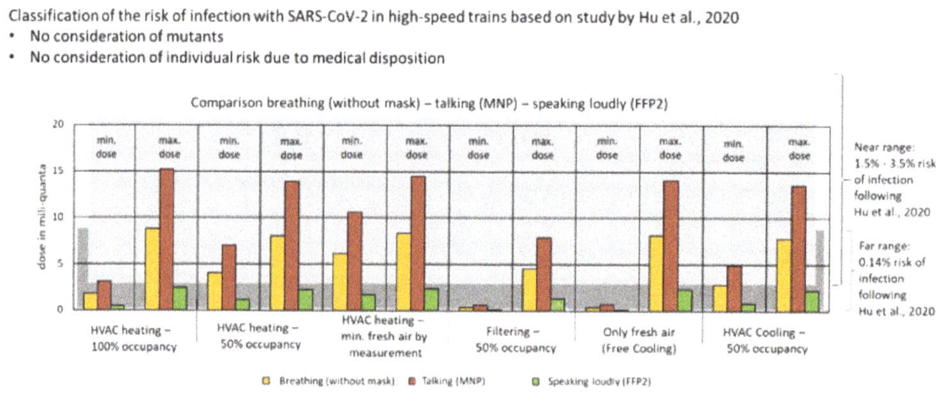

Figure 14. Comparison of the dose in mili-quanta determined in the simulation in the area farther away from the infected person compared to the determined probability of infection according to Hu et al. [53].

Assuming that the ventilation system is similar to the bus considered here, a comparison with documented contagions during bus trips indicates that a substantial risk of infection may exist. For example, during a 2.5 h bus ride, Ref. [54] described eight additional infections attributable to an infected person. The infected persons were both close to and farther away from the infected person. The authors of [55] investigated infections during a total 1 h 40 min pilgrimage of Buddhist believers in a bus. Here, 24 of 68 passengers later tested positive for SARS-CoV-2. Both studies indicate that the buses were ventilated with a recirculating air component. Since the studies consider individual cases, it is not possible to make a generalized estimate of risk, as is the case for high-speed trains [53]. The studies do not include averages over several journeys or information on journeys with infected persons without contagions. Moreover, it cannot be excluded that the index persons were super emitters, i.e., their emission is higher by a factor of 10–100 than assumed in the simulations shown here. Thus, the exposure for other passengers would also have been correspondingly higher. Nevertheless, the studies impressively show that contagions cannot be ruled out even for the scenarios simulated here.

4. Results

Potential exposure to SARS-CoV-2 via aerosols is detailed for each mode of transportation in Section 3. Figures 15–17 compare the cases "breathing without mask", "speaking with MNP" and "speaking loudly with FFP2". The respective times spent in vehicles were estimated due to the lack of available data (Table 4). For the selection, a reference ventilation case or cases actually measured in operation were selected.

Figure 15 shows that, particularly in means of transport with a high proportion of recirculated air, an increased quanta dose can also be absorbed farther away from the emitter (min. dose). Near the emitter, this also applies to means of transport without recirculation. Figure 16 demonstrates that the combination "talking with MNP" leads to an increased exposure compared to "Breathing without mask". Figure 17 shows that even speaking loudly with an FFP2 mask results in a lower dose than breathing without a mask.

A significant reduction of the dose and thus of the risk results from the use of MNP or FFP2 masks, as well as from not speaking loudly. Refraining from loud speech leads to a reduction of the quanta emission of about 80%. The consistent wearing of an FFP2 mask by all passengers causes a reduction of the inhaled dose of 99%. If passengers use MNP, the reduction is only 65%. The zonal modeling approach can also be used to show that the location of the infectious passenger in relation to others plays a major role for the spread and exposure.

In addition, discrepancies between expected and actual ventilation were found in some measurements. The reduced supply of fresh air leads to a significantly higher infection risk, especially in the vicinity of the infected person.

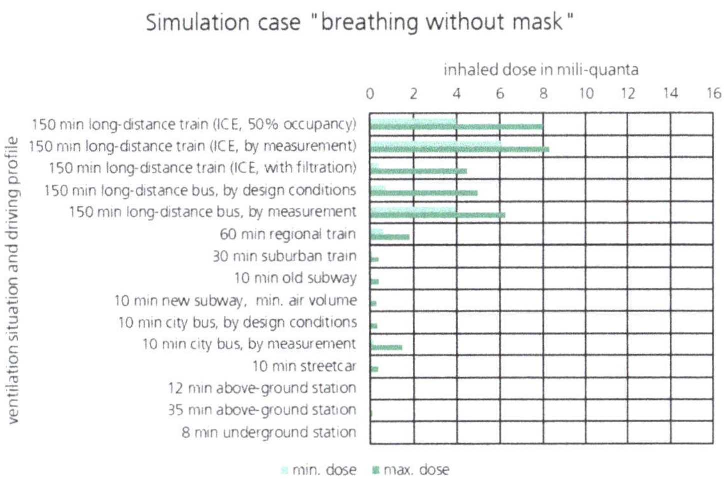

Figure 15. Comparison of typical means of transport considered for the case "breathing without mask": min. dose, minimum dose absorbed farther away from the emitter; max. dose, maximum exposure that is absorbed close to the emitter.

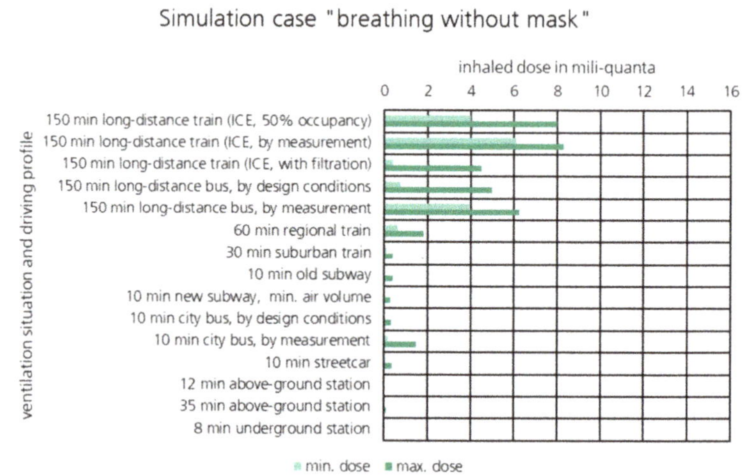

Figure 16. Comparison of typical means of transport considered for the case "Talking with MNP": min. dose, minimum dose absorbed farther away from the emitter; max. dose, maximum exposure that is absorbed close to the emitter.

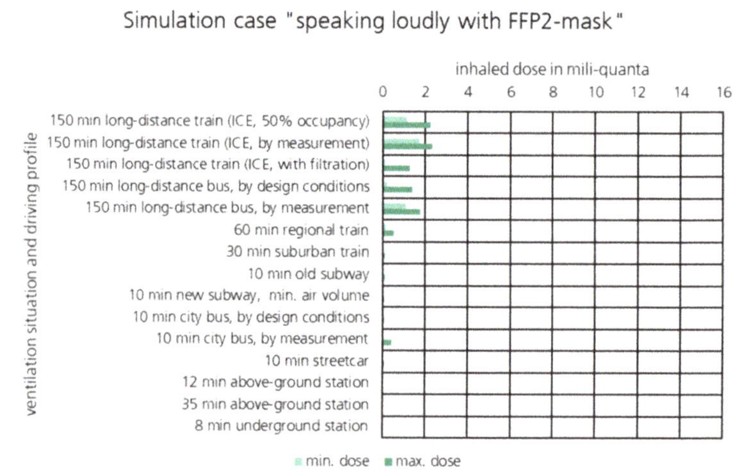

Figure 17. Comparison of typical means of transport considered for the case "Speaking loudly with FFP2": min. dose, minimum dose absorbed farther away from the emitter; max. dose, maximum exposure that is absorbed close to the emitter.

5. Discussion

This study deals with the risk of essentially airborne transmission of SARS-CoV-2 in public transport. The simulations allow the assessment of the potential exposure in the near and far field when travelling with an infected passenger. A direct conclusion from the exposure in a coach to a percentage risk, however, is not possible. An analogy comparison between the study from Hu et al. [53] on infections in Chinese high-speed trains and with the simulation results of the ICE from Section 3.3 provides at least an estimate. Through this analogy consideration, it is shown that there is also a risk of infection with SARS-CoV-2 when using rail- and road-passenger transport. This risk is different for different scenarios but can, to a large extent, be mitigated by technical measures such as recirculation air filtration, increased fresh airflow and by personal behavior such as mask wearing and refraining from loud speech. For example, the highest theoretical risk of infection are for routes with a longer duration, no masks and loud speaking, as determined based on the comparatively high quanta dose. More infectious mutations of the Sars-CoV-2 virus and the vaccination or infection of large fractions of the populations have, to some extent, outdated the risk assessed by Hu [53]; nevertheless, the general conclusions of this simulation study remain valid.

For the exposure calculations, the quanta approach was chosen because this term does not attempt to model, for example, the flight dynamics of particles. From these calculations, it is evident that a significantly lower dose is achieved on the platforms of the stations investigated compared to the interior of the respective means of transport. On the one hand, this can be attributed to the relatively short stay of only a few minutes and on the other hand to the good ventilation. In accordance with the current scientific literature (e.g., [56]), no higher theoretical risk of infection is found in outdoor areas, in this case in the area of the train station hall. Provided that the minimum distance can be maintained, it is, therefore, possible to dispense with the wearing of an MNP or an FFP2 mask in outdoor areas.

In the confined areas, and if the required minimum distance cannot be maintained, there is a theoretical risk of infection. In these cases, further measures should be taken to reduce the risk, e.g., wearing a mask to prevent direct droplet infection. FFP2 masks show a higher reduction in both emission and inhaling of infectious material compared with surgical MNP. For this reason, they are more suitable for both third-party and self-protection.

5.1. *Influence of Input Parameters*

It should be taken into account that the study described here investigates the mean emission of a SARS-CoV-2 infected person during different activities (breathing, talking or speaking loudly) and using different masks (none, MNP or FFP2/N95). Here, it is always assumed that all passengers wear the same type of mask for the entire trip. Mixtures of mask types give results between the cases considered. So, for example, if the emitter has an MNP and the person taking in the dose has an FFP2 mask, the dose taken in can be expected to be between the "MNP" case and the "FFP2" case.

There are reports of so-called super emitters, who emit up to 100 times more than a normal emitter [57]. In the simulation, this would likewise lead to a factor of 100 higher dose uptake. In the case of the reported infections in public transport, it is unknown whether these are due to "normal" or super emitters. The impact of a super emitter in this simulation would be a factor of 100 higher; the relative ratios of the measures to each other would be unaffected.

5.2. *Influence of Compliance*

The simulations assume full compliance of rules by the passengers, i.e., the rules for wearing MNP or FFP2 and refraining from loud speech. Obviously, unruly passengers would lead to a situation closer to the case of no-mask with elevated speech in terms of source intensity and/or infectious matter uptake.

5.3. *Influence of Occupancy*

One limitation of this study is that the actual risk of presence of one infected passenger is not known. Thus, even though intuitively a higher occupation will result in higher risk of presence of an infected passenger, this cannot be quantified. Therefore, in demand-controlled ventilation cases, the trade-off between higher occupancy reducing airborne transmission due to increased ventilation and the increased risk that one of the passengers actually is infected is not possible.

Due to the lack of quantification, the occupancy density in the sense of the probability of the presence of a passenger infected with SARS-CoV-2 as a risk factor is thus not evaluated in this study.

6. Conclusions

The study investigates the theoretical risk for infection with SARS-CoV-2 in public transport using dispersion modeling in different vehicles and train stations. The actions (breathing, talking and speaking loudly), as well as the preventive measures (masks, filtering recirculating air and fresh air operation), are used to determine the risk assessment based on the definition of an infected passenger in the model. It is shown that the risk is reduced most efficiently if loud speaking is avoided and a FFP2 (N95) mask is worn correctly. Only these two measures create a reduction of the virus load of over 99% for both those in the close range of the infected person and those farther away. Thus, the already known protective measures, such as keeping quiet and using masks, can be confirmed in this study. Technical measures, such as recirculating filtered air further reduce the exposure to other passengers in the close range by 30–69% and farther away in the same vehicle by 80–91% (except in the streetcar/tram, where near-field exposure is increased by 17% due to filter-related reduced airflow). Higher fresh air rates also lead to a decrease in exposures in the broader environment. The study shows that near-field exposure cannot be eliminated, no matter how good the ventilation is. However, the refurbishment of trains and buses with HEPA filters in the recirculation air would lead to a clear reduction of other passengers' exposure. In addition, operators should absolutely avoid decreasing fresh air ventilation rates during operation. More broadly, these findings show that local protection can only be achieved locally (mask wearing), whereas central protection (filtration) mainly is effective more distant from the source. Hence, future research and development should focus on how technical solutions could act locally, for example by using partitions or ionization for the supply air. Analysis of the space needed to comply with the distance rules reveals that the distances cannot be met inside the vehicles. Therefore, the mask requirement should remain in place to protect against transmission by droplets. Compared with the risk inside the means of transport, the exposure on the platforms of the stations is considered minor. Particularly on above-ground platforms and provided that the recommended minimum distance of 1.5 m can be consistently maintained, the wearing of an MNP/FFP2 mask is temporarily dispensable, or an interruption of the mask requirement is justifiable. The inhaled quanta doses in the various means of transport mainly depend on the time spent in the vehicles. The ventilation of the transport vehicles also has an impact but is subordinate to the time component.

Even though new mutations of the SARS-CoV-2 virus and the increased immunity of large fractions of the population have altered the initial risk of infection, the general conclusions in this paper are considered valid.

Author Contributions: Conceptualization, C.M., V.N. and H.W.; methodology, V.N.; software, C.M.; validation, C.M.; formal analysis, V.N.; investigation, C.M. and V.N.; resources, T.H., B.N., M.S., A.S., M.E. and M.J.; data curation, T.H., B.N., M.S., A.S., M.E. and M.J.; writing—original draft preparation, C.M.; writing—review and editing, C.M. and V.N.; visualization, C.M. and V.N.; supervision, H.W.; project administration, H.W.; funding acquisition, H.W. All authors have read and agreed to the published version of the manuscript.

Funding: This research was funded by Deutsches Zentrum für Schienenverkehrsforschung beim Eisenbahnbundesamt grant number 2020-33-S-1202.

Institutional Review Board Statement: Not applicable.

Informed Consent Statement: No applicable.

Acknowledgments: This study was commissioned by "German Center for Rail Transport Research (DZSF) at the Railroad Federal Office". The authors are responsible for the content of this publication.

Conflicts of Interest: The authors declare no conflict of interest.

References

1. Scheuch, G. Breathing Is Enough: For the Spread of Influenza Virus and SARS-CoV-2 by Breathing Only. *J. Aerosol Med. Pulm. Drug Deliv.* **2020**, *33*, 230–234. [CrossRef] [PubMed]
2. Wang, C.C.; Prather, K.A.; Sznitman, J.; Jimenez, J.L.; Lakdawala, S.S.; Tufekci, Z.; Marr, L.C. Airborne transmission of respiratory viruses. *Science* **2021**, *373*, 3–5. [CrossRef] [PubMed]
3. Harrison, A.G.; Lin, T.; Wang, P. Mechanisms of SARS-CoV-2 Transmission and Pathogenesis. *Trends Immunol.* **2020**, *41*, 1100–1115. [CrossRef] [PubMed]
4. Hadei, M.; Hopke, P.K.; Jonidi, A.; Shahsavani, A. A Letter about the Airborne Transmission of SARS-CoV-2 Based on the Current Evidence. *Aerosol Air Qual. Res.* **2020**, *20*, 911–914. [CrossRef]
5. Morawska, L.; Cao, J. Airborne transmission of SARS-CoV-2: The world should face the reality. *Environ. Int.* **2020**, *139*, 1–2. [CrossRef] [PubMed]
6. Nazari, A.; Jafari, M.; Rezaei, N.; Arash-Azad, S.; Talati, F.; Nejad-Rahim, R.; Taghizadeh-Hesary, F.; Taghizadeh-Hesary, F. Effects of High-speed Wind, Humidity, and Temperature on the Generation of a SARS-CoV-2 Aerosol; a Novel Point of View. *Aerosol Air Qual. Res.* **2021**, *21*, 200574. [CrossRef]
7. Gameiro Da Silva, M. An analysis of the transmission modes of COVID-19 in light of the concepts of Indoor Air Quality. *REHVA J.* **2020**, *3*, 46–54. [CrossRef]
8. Statistisches Bundesamt. Korrektur: 46% Weniger Fahrgäste im Fernverkehr mit Bussen und Bahnen im 1. Halbjahr. 2020. Available online: https://www.destatis.de/DE/Presse/Pressemitteilungen/2020/10/PD20_424_461.html (accessed on 9 February 2022).
9. Tirachini, A.; Cats, O. COVID-19 and Public Transportation: Current Assessment, Prospects, and Research Needs. *JPT* **2020**, *22*. [CrossRef]
10. Kutela, B.; Novat, N.; Langa, N. Exploring geographical distribution of transportation research themes related to COVID-19 using text network approach. *Sustain. Cities Soc.* **2021**, *67*, 102729. [CrossRef]
11. Shen, J.; Duan, H.; Zhang, B.; Wang, J.; Ji, J.S.; Wang, J.; Pan, L.; Wang, X.; Zhao, K.; Ying, B.; et al. Prevention and control of COVID-19 in public transportation: Experience from China. *Environ. Pollut.* **2020**, *266*, 115291. [CrossRef]
12. Heinrich, J.; Zhao, T.; Quartucci, C.; Herbig, B.; Nowak, D. SARS-CoV-2 Infektionen während Reisen mit Bahn und Bus. Ein systematisches Review epidemiologischer Studien. *Gesundh. Bundesverb. Arzte Offentlichen Gesundh.* **2021**, *83*, 581–592. [CrossRef] [PubMed]
13. Arpino, F.; Grossi, G.; Cortellessa, G.; Mikszewski, A.; Morawska, L.; Buonanno, G.; Stabile, L. Risk of SARS-CoV-2 in a car cabin assessed through 3D CFD simulations. *arXiv* **2022**, arXiv:2201.09958.
14. Park, J.; Kim, G. Risk of COVID-19 Infection in Public Transportation: The Development of a Model. *Int. J. Environ. Res. Public Health* **2021**, *18*, 12790. [CrossRef]
15. Woodward, H.; Fan, S.; Bhagat, R.K.; Dadonau, M.; Wykes, M.D.; Martin, E.; Hama, S.; Tiwari, A.; Dalziel, S.B.; Jones, R.L.; et al. Air Flow Experiments on a Train Carriage—Towards Understanding the Risk of Airborne Transmission. *Atmosphere* **2021**, *12*, 1267. [CrossRef]
16. Will, H.; Scherer, C.; Stratbücker, S.; Norrefeldt, V.; Matheis, C.; Reith, A.; Schwitalla, C.; de Boer, J.; Neves Pimenta, D.; Zaglauer, M.; et al. Risikoeinschätzung zur Ansteckungsgefahr mit COVID-19 im Schienenpersonen—Sowie im Straßenpersonennah- und -Fernverkehr. Berichte des Deutschen Zentrums für Schienenverkehrsforschung, Nr. 12, Dresden. 2021. Available online: https://www.dzsf.bund.de/SharedDocs/Textbausteine/DZSF/Forschungsberichte/Forschungsbericht_2021-12.html (accessed on 9 February 2022).
17. Norrefeldt, V.; Grün, G.; Sedlbauer, K. VEPZO—Velocity propagating zonal model for the estimation of the airflow pattern and temperature distribution in a confined space. *Build. Environ.* **2012**, *48*, 183–194. [CrossRef]
18. Modelica Association. Modelica. Available online: https://modelica.org/ (accessed on 7 February 2022).
19. Hartmann, A.; Lange, J.; Rotheudt, H.; Kriegel, M. Emissionsrate und Partikelgröße von Bioaerosolen beim Atmen, Sprechen und Husten. 2020. Available online: https://do.tu-berlin.de/bitstream/11303/11451/4/hartmann_etal_2020_de.pdf (accessed on 9 February 2022).
20. Pathak, A.; Norrefeldt, V.; Lemouedda, A.; Grün, G. The Modelica Thermal Model Generation Tool for Automated Creation of a Coupled Airflow, Radiation Model and Wall Model in Modelica. In Proceedings of the 10th International Modelica Conference, Lund, Sweden, 10–12 March 2014; Linköping University Electronic Press: Linköping, Sweden, 2014; pp. 115–124.
21. Buonanno, G.; Morawska, L.; Stabile, L. Quantitative assessment of the risk of airborne transmission of SARS-CoV-2 infection: Prospective and retrospective applications. *Environ. Int.* **2020**, *145*, 106–112. [CrossRef] [PubMed]
22. Buonanno, G.; Stabile, L.; Morawska, L. Estimation of airborne viral emission: Quanta emission rate of SARS-CoV-2 for infection risk assessment. *Environ. Int.* **2020**, *141*, 105794. [CrossRef]
23. Müller, D.; Rewitz, K.; Derwein, D.; Burgholz, T.M.; Schweiker, M.; Bardey, J.; Tappler, P. *Abschätzung des Infektionsrisikos durch Aerosolgebundene Viren in Belüfteten Räumen (2. Überarbeitete und Korrigierte Auflage)*; RWTH Aachen Uviersity: Aachen, Germany, 2021.
24. Jimenez, J.L. *SARS-CoV-2 Aerosol Transmission Estimator*; University of Colorado: Boulder, CO, USA, 2020.
25. Asadi, S.; Wexler, A.S.; Cappa, C.D.; Barreda, S.; Bouvier, N.M.; Ristenpart, W.D. Aerosol emission and superemission during human speech increase with voice loudness. *Sci Rep.* **2019**, *9*, 2348. [CrossRef] [PubMed]

26. Edwards, D.A.; Man, J.C.; Brand, P.; Katstra, J.P.; Sommerer, K.; Stone, H.A.; Nardell, E.; Scheuch, G. Inhaling to mitigate exhaled bioaerosols. *Proc. Natl. Acad. Sci. USA* **2004**, *101*, 17383–17388. [CrossRef]
27. RWTH Aachen University. RisiCo. Available online: https://risico.eonerc.rwth-aachen.de/ (accessed on 15 February 2022).
28. Lahrz, T.; Bischof, W.; Sagunski, H.; Baudisch, C.; Fromme, H.; Grams, H.; Gabrio, T.; Heinzow, B.; Müller, L. Gesundheitliche Bewertung von Kohlendioxid in der Innenraumluft. Mitteilungen der Ad-hoc-Arbeitsgruppe Innenraumrichtwerte der Innenraumlufthygiene-Kommission des Umweltbundesamtes und der Obersten Landesgesundheitsbehörden. *Bundesgesundheitsblatt Gesundh. Gesundh.* **2008**, *51*, 1358–1369. [CrossRef]
29. Howard, J.; Huang, A.; Li, Z.; Tufekci, Z.; Zdimal, V.; van der Westhuizen, H.-M.; Von Delft, A.; Price, A.; Fridman, L.; Tang, L.-H.; et al. An evidence review of face masks against COVID-19. *Proc. Natl. Acad. Sci. USA* **2021**, *118*. [CrossRef] [PubMed]
30. Grinshpun, S.A.; Haruta, H.; Eninger, R.M.; Reponen, T.; McKay, R.T.; Lee, S.-A. Performance of an N95 filtering facepiece particulate respirator and a surgical mask during human breathing: Two pathways for particle penetration. *J. Occup. Environ. Hyg.* **2009**, *6*, 593–603. [CrossRef] [PubMed]
31. Davies, A.; Thompson, K.-A.; Giri, K.; Kafatos, G.; Walker, J.; Bennett, A. Testing the efficacy of homemade masks: Would they protect in an influenza pandemic? *Disaster Med. Public Health Prep.* **2013**, *7*, 413–418. [CrossRef]
32. Nordquist, B. Vädring av Skolor—Ett Komplement till Normal Ventilation? Ph.D. Thesis, Department of Building Science, Lund Institute of Technology, Lund, Sweden, 1998.
33. Deutscher Wetterdienst. Testreferenzjahre (TRY). 2021. Available online: https://www.dwd.de/DE/leistungen/testreferenzjahre/testreferenzjahre.html (accessed on 9 February 2022).
34. Deutsche Bahn, AG. Daten & Fakten. 2019. Available online: https://assets.static-bahn.de/dam/jcr:1289cfc8-512e-42c3-a7e3-04302f1784c7/233600-311901.pdf (accessed on 9 February 2022).
35. Deutsche Bahn, AG. Kennzahlen der DB Regio nach Geschäftsbereichen. Available online: https://www.dbregio.de/wir/zahlen-daten-fakten (accessed on 9 February 2022).
36. Deutsche Bahn, AG. Züge im Fernverkehr: Zugtypen und Ihre Strecken: ICE 4. Available online: https://www.bahn.de/p/view/service/zug/fahrzeuge/zugtypen.shtml?dbkanal_007=L01_S01_D001_KIN_-rs-zug_NAVIGATION-fahrzeuge_LZ01 (accessed on 9 February 2022).
37. Schwandl, R. *Tram Atlas Deutschland 5*, 5th ed.; Revidierte Ausgabe; Robert Schwandl: Berlin, Germany, 2019; ISBN 9783936573602.
38. Maibaum, C.-A. Strassenbahn-Online. Available online: http://www.strassenbahn-online.de/ (accessed on 9 February 2022).
39. Esser, B. Tram-info. Available online: https://www.tram-info.de/ (accessed on 9 February 2022).
40. Verband Deutscher Verkehrsunternehmen VDV. VDV-Statistik & Jahresbericht. Available online: https://www.vdv.de/statistik-jahresbericht.aspx (accessed on 9 February 2022).
41. Stade, C. Gleispläne der Webseite gleisplanweb.de. Available online: https://gleisplanweb.eu/ (accessed on 9 February 2022).
42. Deutsche Bahn, AG. Produktmanagement ICE: Fahrzeuglexikon für den Fernverkehr. Available online: http://download-data.deutschebahn.com/static/datasets/fahrzeuglexikon/Fahrzeuglexikon_2017.pdf (accessed on 9 February 2022).
43. Siemens, A.G. Der Icx—Eine Neue Ära im Fernverkehr der Deutschen Bahn. Available online: https://docplayer.org/37850426-Siemens-com-mobility-der-icx-eine-neue-aera-im-fernverkehr-der-deutschen-bahn.html (accessed on 9 February 2022).
44. Scharff, S. Markteinführung des TALENT 3 mit Ausblick. In *Sonderheft Graz*; Statistisches Amt: Graz, Austria, 2017; p. 141.
45. Vlexx GmbH. Datenblatt Bombardier Talent 3. Available online: https://www.vlexx.de/ueber-uns/fahrzeugflotte/talent3/ (accessed on 9 February 2022).
46. EvoBus GmbH. Die Citaro Stadtbusse. *Technische Information*. Available online: https://www.mercedes-benz-bus.com/de_DE/buy/services-online/download-technical-brochures.html#content/headline_840766654_c (accessed on 9 February 2022).
47. HeiterBlick GmbH. TW3000 Hannover Datenblatt. Available online: https://www.heiterblick.de/fahrzeuge/hochflur/tw-3000/ (accessed on 9 February 2022).
48. Münchner Verkehrsgesellschaft mbH. Website der Münchner Verkehrsgesellschaft mbH (MVG). Available online: https://www.mvg.de/ (accessed on 9 February 2022).
49. Norta, M.; Valleé, D. Ein Verkehrsmittelwahlmodell für den Personenfernverkehr auf der Basis von Verkehrswiderständen. Ph.D. Thesis, University of Aachen, Aachen, Germany, 2012.
50. Kebdani, Z. Ventilation of subway stations. Personal communication, 2021.
51. DIN—Deutsches Institut für Normung e.V. *DIN EN 14750-1*; Bahnanwendungen—Luftbehandlung in Schienenfahrzeugen des Innerstädtischen und Regionalen Nahverkehrs—Teil 1: Behaglichkeitsparameter; Deutsches Institut für Normung: Berlin, Germany, 2006.
52. Schumann, L.; Lange, J.; Rotheudt, H.; Hartmann, A.; Kriegel, M. Experimentelle Untersuchung der Leckage und Abscheideleistung von typischen Mund-Nasen-Schutz und Mund-Nasen-Bedeckungen zum Schutz vor luftgetragenen Krankheitserregern, Berlin. 2020. Available online: https://www.depositonce.tu-berlin.de/handle/11303/11975 (accessed on 9 February 2022).
53. Hu, M.; Lin, H.; Wang, J.; Xu, C.; Tatem, A.J.; Meng, B.; Zhang, X.; Liu, Y.; Wang, P.; Wu, G.; et al. Risk of Coronavirus Disease 2019 Transmission in Train Passengers: An Epidemiological and Modeling Study. *Clin. Infect. Dis.* **2021**, *72*, 604–610. [CrossRef] [PubMed]

54. Luo, K.; Lei, Z.; Hai, Z.; Xiao, S.; Rui, J.; Yang, H.; Jing, X.; Wang, H.; Xie, Z.; Luo, P.; et al. Transmission of SARS-CoV-2 in Public Transportation Vehicles: A Case Study in Hunan Province, China. *Open Forum Infect. Dis.* **2020**, *7*, ofaa430. [CrossRef]
55. Shen, Y.; Li, C.; Dong, H.; Wang, Z.; Martinez, L.; Sun, Z.; Handel, A.; Chen, Z.; Chen, E.; Ebell, M.H.; et al. Community Outbreak Investigation of SARS-CoV-2 Transmission Among Bus Riders in Eastern China. *JAMA Intern. Med.* **2020**, *180*, 1665–1671. [CrossRef]
56. Qian, H.; Miao, T.; Liu, L.; Zheng, X.; Luo, D.; Li, Y. Indoor transmission of SARS-CoV-2. *Indoor Air* **2021**, *31*, 639–645. [CrossRef]
57. Moreno, T.; Pintó, R.M.; Bosch, A.; Moreno, N.; Alastuey, A.; Minguillón, M.C.; Anfruns-Estrada, E.; Guix, S.; Fuentes, C.; Buonanno, G.; et al. Tracing surface and airborne SARS-CoV-2 RNA inside public buses and subway trains. *Environ. Int.* **2021**, *147*, 106326. [CrossRef]

International Journal of
Environmental Research and Public Health

MDPI

Article

Mediating Factors Explaining the Associations between Solid Fuel Use and Self-Rated Health among Chinese Adults 65 Years and Older: A Structural Equation Modeling Approach

Qiutong Yu [1,2], Yuqing Cheng [1,2], Wei Li [1,2] and Genyong Zuo [1,2,*]

1 Centre for Health Management and Policy Research, School of Public Health, Cheeloo College of Medicine Shandong University, 44 Wen-Hua-Xi Road, Jinan 250012, China; yuqiutong@126.com (Q.Y.); yuqing686@163.com (Y.C.); liwei0830zjqz@163.com (W.L.)

2 NHC Key Laboratory of Health Economics and Policy Research, Shandong University, 44 Wen-Hua-Xi Road, Jinan 250012, China

* Correspondence: smartyong@sdu.edu.cn; Tel.: +86-0531-88382222 (ext. 8009)

Abstract: Exposure to indoor air pollution from cooking with solid fuel has been linked with the health of elderly people, although the pathway to their association is unclear. This study aimed to investigate the mediating effects between solid fuel use and self-rated health by using structural equation modeling (SEM) with the baseline data from Chinese Longitudinal Healthy Longevity Survey (CLHLS). We conducted a cross-sectional survey among 7831 elderly people aged >65 years from the CLHLS. SEM was used to analyze the pathways underlying solid fuel use and self-rated health. We estimated indirect effects of sleep quality ($\beta = -0.027$, SE = 0.006), cognitive abilities ($\beta = -0.006$, SE = 0.002), depressive symptoms ($\beta = -0.066$, SE = 0.007), systolic blood pressure ($\beta = 0.000$, SE = 0.000), and BMI ($\beta = -0.000$, SE = 0.000) on the association between solid fuel and the self-rated health using path analysis. Depressive symptoms emerged as the strongest mediator in the relationship between solid fuel use and self-rated health in the elderly. Interventions targeting sleep quality, cognitive abilities, depressive symptoms, systolic blood pressure, and BMI could greatly reduce the negative effects of solid fuel use on the health of the elderly population.

Keywords: household air pollution; solid fuel; self-rated health; structural equation modeling; elderly

Citation: Yu, Q.; Cheng, Y.; Li, W.; Zuo, G. Mediating Factors Explaining the Associations between Solid Fuel Use and Self-Rated Health among Chinese Adults 65 Years and Older: A Structural Equation Modeling Approach. *Int. J. Environ. Res. Public Health* **2022**, *19*, 6904. https://doi.org/10.3390/ijerph19116904

Academic Editors: Ashok Kumar, M Amirul I Khan, Alejandro Moreno Rangel and Michał Piasecki

Received: 1 May 2022
Accepted: 2 June 2022
Published: 5 June 2022

1. Introduction

The aging population in China has grown rapidly in the past few decades. According to the report of the seventh census in 2020, the population of those aged >60 years was 264.02 million, accounting for 18.70% of the total population, while the population of those aged >65 years was 190.64 million, accounting for 13.50% [1]. The Chinese population is approaching the depth of the aging stage. With the deepening of social aging in China, more attention should be paid to both physical and mental health problems in elderly people.

Approximately 490 million people in China are exposed to indoor air pollution from cooking with solid fuel, such as coal, charcoal, and wood [2]. The particulate matters produced by burning solid fuel, such as PM2.5, PM10, carbon monoxide, nitrogen dioxide, sulfur dioxide, or other volatile organic compounds [3], have a negative impact on the physical or mental health of elderly people [4–6]. Therefore, it is necessary to explore the effect of indoor air pollution caused by using solid fuel on the health of elderly people.

Previous studies have shown that the use of solid fuel seriously affected both the mental and the physical health of the elderly [5,7–11]. Many studies on middle-aged and elderly people have concluded that solid fuel use was significantly correlated with the health of elderly people, in terms of poor sleep quality [7], low cognitive function [8], high incidence of arthritis [12], high incidence of depression [5], and high incidence of hypertension [9,10]. In pathogenesis research, there is an increasing link between indoor air pollution and physical diseases from solid fuel [13]. The underlying mechanism is that solid fuel in the combustion chamber produces toxic volatile organic compounds (VOCs), which can easily turn into vapors and are involved in metabolic processes that lead to low cognitive function or an increased blood pressure [8,14,15]. However, all the abovementioned effects are single indicators of health measurement. Self-rated health is a comprehensive measurement indicator of health that can reflect the respondents' physiological state, their knowledge of this state, and their health expectations [16,17]. However, the association of solid fuel use with self-rated health in elderly people is unclear. Moreover, evidence on the effect of solid fuel use on the self-rated health of elderly people directly and indirectly through multiple mediators and the distinctive pathways, particularly in China, is lacking.

The available evidence suggests that people with long-term exposure to indoor air pollution from cooking with solid fuel are more likely to have poor sleep quality [7], high risk of depressive symptoms [5], low cognitive function [8], high blood pressure [9,10], and low body mass index (BMI) [11], which might result in poor self-rated health as mediators in the elderly. Therefore, structural equation modeling (SEM) was used to evaluate the total, direct, and indirect effects of exposure to indoor air pollution from cooking with solid fuel on the self-rated health in a mediation analysis and to assess the indirect effect within these distinctive paths.

This study aimed to investigate the mediating effects between solid fuel use and self-rated health using SEM with the baseline data from the Chinese Longitudinal Healthy Longevity Survey (CLHLS). Changing the fuel for cooking is a long-term project and may be costly, which may impose a huge financial burden on developing countries such as China. However, we can change the mediating factors to minimize the danger of solid fuel use to the health of the elderly, which could be of great help to achieve healthy aging in countries that are evolving into an aging society.

2. Materials and Methods

2.1. Setting and Participants

We used secondary data derived from the 2018 CLHLS, which has been a cohort project since 1998, to conduct a longitudinal population-based study of people aged >65 years in China. We used the 2018 CLHLS because it contained the latest data which best fit the current situation of China's aging society. Using the multistage stratified proportional probability sampling design, approximately 16,000 elderly people in urban and rural communities were randomly selected from 500 sample areas in 23 provinces, and 15,874 people were interviewed successfully. The biomedical ethics committee of Peking University approved the study, and all study participants signed an informed consent form. After excluding 95 participants who were younger than 65 years, 45 participants who "never cook", 51 participants who had technical problems, 2409 participants who refused to answer, 1103 participants who answered "not applicable", and 4340 participants who were unable to provide the data, 7831 individuals were finally included in the study (Figure 1).

2.2. Outcome Variables

Respondents were asked, "how do you feel about your health?", and, according to the five-point Likert scale, their health status was rated as "very good", "good", "fair", "poor", or "very poor". Self-rated health status has been identified as a reliable predictor of health and has been widely used in previous health studies conducted in China [18].

2.3. Exposure Variables

Respondents were asked, "what is the main source of cooking fuel in your family?", and those who answered "other" were excluded. We defined coal, charcoal, and wood as solid fuel, whereas solar energy, natural gas, induction cooker, and other electrical appliances were defined as clean fuel.

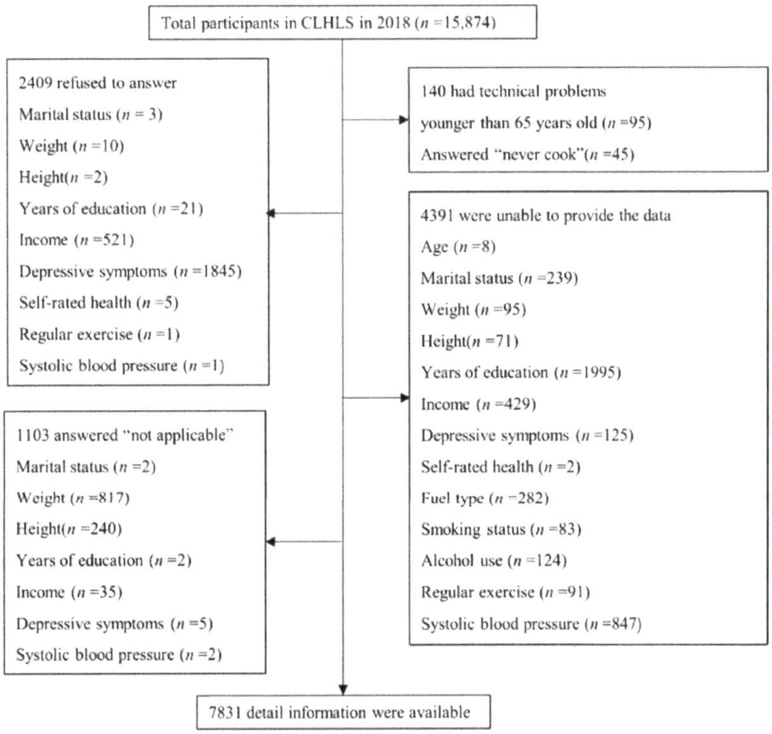

Figure 1. Study flowchart of participant selection (aged ≥65 years) from the Chinese Longitudinal Healthy Longevity Survey 2018 survey data. Abbreviation: CLHLS: Chinese Longitudinal Healthy Longevity Survey.

2.4. Mediators

Previous studies [5,7–11] have found that solid fuel use affects sleep quality, cognition abilities, depressive symptoms, blood pressure, and BMI. Respondents were asked "how is your sleep quality?" according to a five-point Likert scale, and sleep quality was rated as "very good", "good", "moderate", "poor", or "very poor". Blood pressure was the average of two measurements on the right arm of participants using a mercury sphygmomanometer after the participants had rested for 5 min. Body mass index was calculated as the weight in kilograms divided by the height in meters squared (kg/m^2).

Cognitive function was measured using the Chinese version of MMSE (the Mini Mental State Examination) [19]. The MMSE has been validated in previous studies for the Chinese elderly [20,21]. The correct answers were encoded as 1, while incorrect answers or "inapplicable" answers were encoded as 0. Then, we summed the cognitive scores of each participant. Higher cognitive scores indicated better cognitive function.

Depression was measured using the questions from the 10-item Center for Epidemiologic Studies Short Depression Scale (CES-D scale) [22], which has been translated and validated in previous studies for assessing cognitive levels in the Chinese elderly [23]. There are five levels of answers to all questions; we reverse-coded the positively oriented questions and recoded all responses as follows: "always" as 5, "often" as 4, "sometimes" as 3, "seldom" as 2, and "never" as 1. The depression scores of the participants were summed. Higher depression scores indicated greater depression severity.

2.5. Covariates

Notably, many studies have estimated the modification effects by sociodemographic factors and lifestyle behaviors when exploring the effects of household air pollution on the mediators in this paper [24,25]. Demographic characteristics including age (years), sex (female/male), and marital status (not married and married) were analyzed. The "not married" status included widowed, divorced, separated, or never married. Community location (urban/rural) and socioeconomic status, including education and family income, were also analyzed. Education was recoded into three levels (0 years/1–6 years/<6 years). Family income was recoded into three levels (>10,000 CNY, 10,000–50,000 CNY, and <50,000 CNY). Lifestyle behaviors including smoking status (not current/current), alcohol use (not current/current), and regular exercise (not current/current) were also evaluated [26].

2.6. Statistical Analysis

The chi-square test was used for dichotomous variables, including sex, marital status, community location, education years, household income, smoking status, alcohol use, physical activity, sleep quality, and self-rated health, and the t-test was used for continuous variables, including cognitive abilities, depressive symptoms, systolic blood pressure, and BMI between those who cook with solid fuel and those who cook with clean fuel.

Structural equation modeling (SEM) is a multivariate analytic technique. It is used to simultaneously assess multiple relationships among variables. SEM was used to conduct a formal mediation test and disaggregate the relationship between solid fuel use and self-rated health through causally defined indirect and direct pathways. SEM contains a series of multiple regression models, linear regression models for continuous outcomes, and logistic regression models for binary outcomes. The proportion of the total effect of solid fuel on self-rated health attributable to the mediators was calculated by dividing the ratio of the indirect effect through the mediated pathway by the ratio of the total effect. Estimation for SEM was performed using maximum likelihood. Three common measures were used to evaluate the fit indices of SEM: the root-mean-square error of approximation (RMSEA), comparative fit index (CFI), and Tucker–Lewis index (TLI). TLI and CFI values of 0.95 indicate a reasonably good fit [27]. An RMSEA value of 0.05–0.08 represents a moderate fit, while a value of 0.08–0.10 represents an acceptable fit [28]. All data were analyzed using Stata15.0.

3. Results

3.1. Basic Characteristics of the Participants

The characteristics of the study participants are shown in Table 1. Of the 7831 individuals, 2317 (29.59%) used solid fuel for cooking, and 5514 (70.41%) used clean fuel for cooking. Significant differences in sex, marital status, community location, education years, income, smoking status, alcohol use, physical activity, sleep quality, cognitive abilities, depressive symptoms, hypertension, BMI, and self-rated health were observed between individuals using solid fuel and those using clean fuel for cooking ($p < 0.05$). Participants who used clean fuel had higher socioeconomic indicators, in terms of both years of education and family income, than those using indoor solid fuel. Moreover, the proportions of individuals with current smoking (19.25% vs. 16.00%) and drinking (17.22% vs. 15.43%) habits were higher among individuals using solid fuel for cooking than among those using clean fuel. However, the proportion of individuals who engaged in physical activities was significantly higher among those using clean fuel for cooking (42.00% vs. 24.08%) than among those using solid fuel. Moreover, individuals using clean fuel for cooking reported better sleep quality, cognitive abilities, and self-rated health. Among those using solid fuel for cooking, the average systolic blood pressure was 141.07 mmHg.

Table 1. Characteristics of selected variables among the participants.

Variables	All (n = 7831)	Solid Fuel (n = 2317)	Clean Fuel (n = 5514)	p-Value
Age (years, mean, SD)	82.70 (11.28)	82.75 (11.22)	82.68 (11.31)	0.783
Sex (n, %)				0.024
Male	3682 (47.02)	1044 (45.06)	2638 (47.84)	
Female	4149 (52.98)	1273 (54.94)	2876 (52.16)	
Marital status (n, %)				0.024
Not married	3997 (51.04)	1137 (49.07)	2860 (51.87)	
Married	3834 (48.96)	1180 (50.93)	2654 (48.13)	
Community Location (n, %)				<0.001
Urban	4383 (55.97)	907 (39.15)	3476 (63.04)	
Rural	3448 (44.03)	1410 (60.85)	2038 (36.96)	
Education (n, %)	3407 (43.51)	1272 (54.90)	2135 (38.72)	<0.001
0	2451 (31.30)	421 (18.17)	2030 (36.82)	
1–6	1973 (25.19)	624 (26.93)	1349 (24.46)	
7–				<0.001
Income (n, %)	2105 (26.88)	1055 (45.53)	1050 (19.04)	
0–10,000	2633 (33.62)	884 (38.15)	1749 (31.72)	
10,000–50,000	3093 (39.05)	378 (16.31)	2715 (49.24)	
≥50,000				
Smoking status (n, %)				<0.001
Not current	6503 (83.04)	1871 (80.75)	4632 (84.00)	
Current	1328 (16.96)	446 (19.25)	882 (16.00)	
Alcohol use (n, %)				0.049
Not current	6581 (84.04)	1918 (82.78)	4663 (84.57)	
Current	1250 (15.96)	399 (17.22)	851 (15.43)	
Regular exercise (n, %)				<0.001
Not current	4957 (63.30)	1759 (75.92)	3198 (58.00)	
Current	2874 (36.70)	558 (24.08)	2316 (42.00)	
Sleep quality (n, %)				<0.001
Very poor	160 (2.04)	47 (2.03)	113 (2.05)	
Poor	926 (11.82)	301 (12.99)	625 (11.33)	
Moderate	2471 (31.55)	801 (34.57)	1670 (30.29)	
Good	2939 (37.53)	854 (36.86)	2085 (37.81)	
Very good	1335 (17.05)	314 (13.55)	1021 (18.52)	
Cognitive abilities (mean, SD)	20.44 (4.93)	19.90 (5.29)	20.67 (4.75)	<0.001
Depression symptoms (mean, SD)	22.87 (5.38)	24.05 (5.44)	22.37 (5.28)	<0.001
SBP [1] (mmHg, mean, SD)	139.50 (20.82)	141.07 (21.56)	138.84 (20.46)	<0.001
BMI (kg/m^2, mean, SD)	22.67 (4.36)	22.02 (3.92)	22.94 (4.50)	<0.001
Self-rated health (n, %)				<0.001
Very poor	63 (0.80)	27 (1.17)	36 (0.65)	
Poor	857 (10.94)	299 (12.90)	558 (10.12)	
Fair	2969 (37.91)	949 (40.96)	2020 (36.63)	
Good	2892 (36.93)	813 (35.09)	2079 (37.70)	
Very good	1050 (13.41)	229 (9.88)	821 (14.89)	

[1] SBP, systolic blood pressure; BMI, body mass index; SD, standard deviation.

3.2. Structural Equation Model

Structural equation modeling is a multivariate analytic technique used to simultaneously assess multiple relationships among variables. As shown in Figure 2, we performed SEM with a good fit to the data (RMSEA = 0.045, CFI = 0.970, TLI = 0.829), showing that the model fit quite well after adjusting for age, sex, marital status, community location, education years, household income, smoking status, alcohol use, and physical activity. To determine the extent of the impact of solid fuel, sleep quality, cognitive abilities, depressive symptoms, systolic blood pressure, and BMI on the self-rated health of the elderly people in the path model, a standardized path coefficient of the SEM was estimated (Table 2). The total indirect effect of solid fuel use for self-rated health was −0.146 ($p < 0.001$). A significant direct effect of the use of solid fuel on self-rated health (β = −0.041, S.E. = 0.020), with indirect effects accounting for most of the total effects, was identified.

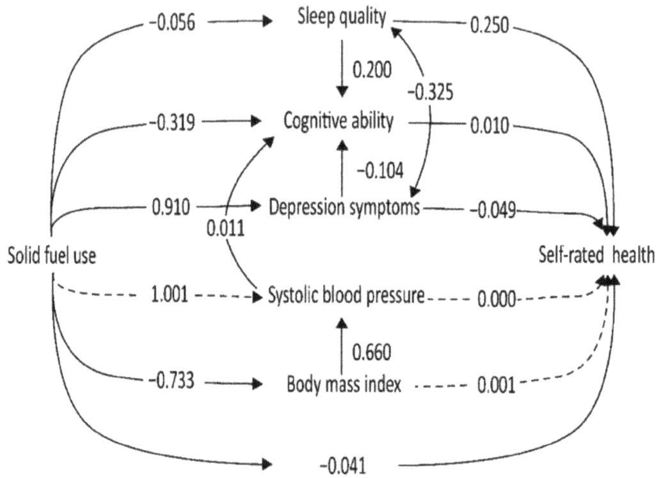

Figure 2. Pathways between solid fuel, mediators, and self-rated health, according to the Chinese Longitudinal Healthy Longevity Survey, 2018. Structural equation modeling was performed among Chinese older adults over 65 years old. The model was adjusted for age, sex, marital status, community location, education years, household income, smoking status, alcohol use, and physical exercise. Dashed lines denote insignificant pathways between solid fuel, mediators, and self-rated health, while solid lines denote significant pathways between solid fuel, mediators, and self-rated health.

Table 2. Direct, indirect, and total effects of solid fuel use on self-rated health.

Pathways	β [1]	SE	*p*-Value
Direct effects			
Solid fuel→sleep quality	−0.056	0.026	0.030
Solid fuel→cognitive abilities	−0.319	0.111	0.004
Solid fuel→depression symptoms	0.910	0.138	<0.001
Solid fuel→ systolic blood pressure	1.001	0.556	0.068
Solid fuel→body mass index	−0.733	0.111	<0.001
Solid fuel→self-rated health	−0.041	0.020	0.037
Sleep quality→self-rated health	0.250	0.009	<0.001
Cognitive abilities→self-rated health	0.010	0.002	<0.001
Depression symptoms→self-rated health	−0.049	0.002	<0.001
Systolic blood pressure→self-rated health	0.000	0.000	0.876
Body mass index→self-rated health	0.001	0.002	0.599
Indirect effects			
Solid fuel→sleep quality→self-rated health	−0.013	0.006	0.030
Solid fuel→cognitive symptoms→self-rated health	−0.003	0.001	0.011
Solid fuel→depression symptoms→self-rated health	−0.045	0.007	<0.001
Solid fuel→systolic blood pressure→self-rated health	0.000	0.000	0.0877
Solid fuel→body mass index→self-rated health	−0.001	0.002	0.600
Total effects			
Solid fuel→self-rated health	−0.107	0.022	<0.001

[1] β, coefficient; SE, standard error.

Table 2 shows that sleep quality (β = 0.250), cognitive ability (β = −0.010), and depression (β = −0.049) had a direct influence on self-rated health ($p < 0.005$). The result from SEM indicated that using solid fuel exhibited a direct effect on sleep quality (β = −0.056), cognitive ability (β = −0.319), depression (β=0.910), and BMI (β = −0.733). However, we did not find that systolic blood pressure ($p = 0.876$) and BMI ($p = 0.876$) were significantly associated with self-rated health, nor did we find that solid fuel was significantly associated with systolic blood pressure. Moreover, SEM is used either to assess the total effect (i.e., direct and indirect effects) of a treatment or exposure on an outcome in the mediation analysis or to assess a specific indirect effect with those complex paths. First, a significant negative indirect effect of solid fuel use on self-rated health via sleep quality was observed ($\beta = -0.013$, SE = 0.006). Second, cognitive abilities were also found to be a mediator between solid fuel use and self-rated health ($\beta = -0.003$, SE = 0.001). Third, a significant negative indirect effect of solid fuel on self-rated health via depressive symptoms ($\beta = -0.045$, SE = 0.007) was also observed. Additionally, the indirect effects of systolic blood pressure on self-rated health, as well as those of body mass index on self-rated health, were not detected in the model involving solid fuel exposure and self-rated health (all $p > 0.05$).

4. Discussion

4.1. Main Findings

In this cross-sectional study, we focused on assessing the potential mediating factors for the relationships between solid fuel use and self-rated health. Exposure to solid fuel was found to have a direct contribution to the decreased score of self-rated health. Moreover, we observed that exposure to solid fuel was significantly associated with a decreased score of self-rated health, and this linkage was mediated by sleep quality, cognitive ability, and depression symptoms. These effects remained significant even after controlling for confounders such as sociodemographic factors and lifestyle behaviors.

4.2. Available Evidence on the Association of Solid Fuel with Self-Rated Health

We found that the direct effect of solid fuel use on self-rated health was -0.044 ($p < 0.001$). Previous studies have demonstrated that solid fuels can affect physical health measures such as blood pressure, BMI, cognition, and mental health measures such as sleep quality and depression status. However, the dependent variables used in these studies were all single health indicators evaluating a specific aspect of the health of an individual. Nevertheless, by constructing a structural equation model, we found that solid fuel can affect the above single health indicators, thereby affecting the comprehensive indicators of personal health, because self-rated health can reflect people's physical and mental health. Therefore, screening and management of these disorders in older adults with heavy use of solid fuels is necessary.

4.3. Depression Was the Strongest Mediator of the Relationship between Solid Fuel Use and Self-Rated Health

The results showed that individuals using solid fuel had greater depression severity ($\beta = 0.893$), and depression symptoms emerged as the strongest mediator of the relationship between solid fuel and self-rated health rather than sleep quality and cognitive ability. However, we only found three similar studies exploring the association between solid fuel and depression whose findings were consistent with our results that individuals using solid fuel were at a higher risk of depression [5,29,30]. Moreover, regarding household air pollution, there is an increasing link between mental diseases and household air pollutants. This study contributes to the limited literature on the association between solid fuel and poor sleep quality in the elderly. Our results indicated that using solid fuel was significantly associated with poor sleep quality, even after accounting for a wide range of covariates, including sociodemographic factors, lifestyle behaviors, and presence of chronic diseases. Our findings were in line with previous findings [31,32]. However, limited evidence is available on the association between mental diseases and household air pollutants in pathogenesis research. One possible reason is that solid fuel combustion produces much higher levels of various gaseous pollutants than clean fuel and may increase the risk of developing mental disorders such as depression and poor sleep quality through pathways such as cerebrovascular damage, oxidative stress, neuroinflammation, or neurodegeneration [33,34].

4.4. Cognition as the Protective Factor Linking Systolic Blood Pressure to Self-Rated Health

An indirect path linking solid fuel and self-rated health was identified through cognitive abilities, although the other mediators including systolic blood pressure and BMI were not found to be associated with self-rated health. Our findings suggested that people who use solid fuel for cooking had lower cognitive abilities ($\beta = -0.319$, SE = 0.111). Several studies in China contributed to the literature on the association between solid fuel and poor cognitive ability in the elderly. Recent evidence from a study in China found that solid fuel use was significantly associated with mental health and cognitive ability in middle-aged and older adults [8]. There were also studies that further showed the potentially harmful effects of household air pollution exposure on other aspect of memory. A follow-up study showed that solid fuel use was associated with a greater decline in cognitive score, mostly in the episodic memory and visuo-construction dimensions [35]. Another prospective analysis found a significant adverse impact on cognitive abilities, especially short-term memory and mathematical reasoning. These results demonstrated that using solid fuel poses a health threat to elderly people [36].

4.5. Strengths and Limitations

This study had several strengths. Firstly, this study specified the pathways of the relationship between solid fuel use and self-rated health of the elderly. Secondly, self-rated health was not only considered a comprehensive measurement indicator of health, but also used as a predictor of morbidity and mortality [37]. This study's results can help achieve primary and secondary prevention and improve the health of the elderly by stopping the use of solid fuel. Lastly, our study included 500 sample areas in 23 provinces in China, which gives our findings strong external validity for the Chinese society. Moreover, the findings were robust across the study regions, demographic characteristics, and lifestyle behaviors.

However, a major drawback should be noted. The assessment of self-rated health in our study was based on only one self-reported question, and this may not provide exactly accurate information compared with a structured interview tool. Other limitations should also be mentioned. Firstly, constrained by the CLHLS data, we were unable to derive information on whether the individuals were responsible for cooking, types of cooking in childhood, and time spent cooking with indoor solid fuel; additionally, indoor air pollution exposure may vary by family and personal characteristics [38]. Secondly, the results of this cross-sectional study may not explain the underlying mechanisms of the relationship between solid fuel use and self-rated health. The underlying mechanisms may need to be investigated in large prospective cohort studies. Thirdly, the relationship of mediators including sleep quality, cognitive ability, depression, systolic blood pressure, and BMI with solid fuel use has been confirmed in previous studies. Other diseases or pathophysiological indicators that may be caused by the use of solid fuel, which have not been proven, can be explored in future studies.

5. Conclusions

Sleep quality, cognitive abilities, and depressive symptoms partially contributed to the association between solid fuel use and self-rated health. However, systolic blood pressure and BMI were not found to be directly associated with self-rated health. Among these mediators, depression was the strongest mediator of the relationship between solid fuel use and self-rated health. Our results demonstrated that using solid fuel poses a health threat for elderly people. Replacing solid fuel with clean fuel may be an important way to improve self-rated health of elderly people. Regarding this, priority should be giving to those with significant solid fuel exposure.

Author Contributions: Q.Y., writing—original draft; Y.C., data curation; W.L., formal analysis; G.Z., writing—review and editing. All authors have read and agreed to the published version of the manuscript.

Funding: This research was funded by the National Natural Science Foundation of China (No. 71774102).

Institutional Review Board Statement: The study was conducted in accordance with the Declaration of Helsinki and approved by the Ethical Review Committee of Peking University (IRB00001052–13074).

Informed Consent Statement: Informed consent was obtained from all subjects involved in the study. Written informed consent was obtained from the patients to publish this paper.

Data Availability Statement: Data are available on the open research data service platform of Peking University. Data for this study were sourced from the Chinese Longitudinal Healthy Longevity Survey (CLHLS) and are available at https://opendata.pku.edu.cn (accessed on 1 January 2022).

Acknowledgments: The authors thank the Chinese Longitudinal Healthy Longevity Survey team for providing data.

Conflicts of Interest: The authors declare no conflict of interest.

References

1. National Bureau of Statistics of the People's Republic of China Interpretation of the Seventh National Census Communiqué. Available online: http://www.stats.gov.cn/tjsj/sjjd/202105/t20210512_1817336.html (accessed on 17 November 2021).
2. Tang, X.; Liao, H. Energy poverty and solid fuels use in rural China: Analysis based on national population census. *Energy Sustain. Dev.* **2014**, *23*, 122–129. [CrossRef]
3. Wang, L.; Xiang, Z.; Stevanovic, S.; Ristovski, Z.; Salimi, F.; Gao, J.; Wang, H.; Li, L. Role of Chinese cooking emissions on ambient air quality and human health. *Sci. Total Environ.* **2017**, *589*, 173–181. [CrossRef] [PubMed]
4. Cao, L.; Zhai, D.; Kuang, M.; Xia, Y. Indoor air pollution and frailty: A cross-sectional and follow-up study among older Chinese adults. *Environ. Res.* **2021**, *204*, 112006. [CrossRef]
5. Shao, J.; Ge, T.; Liu, Y.; Zhao, Z.; Xia, Y. Longitudinal associations between household solid fuel use and depression in middle-aged and older Chinese population: A cohort study. *Ecotoxicol. Env. Saf.* **2021**, *209*, 111833. [CrossRef] [PubMed]
6. Balidemaj, F.; Isaxon, C.; Abera, A.; Malmqvist, E. Indoor Air Pollution Exposure of Women in Adama, Ethiopia, and Assessment of Disease Burden Attributable to Risk Factor. *Int. J. Env. Res. Public Health* **2021**, *18*, 9859. [CrossRef]
7. Yu, H. Solid Fuel-Related Indoor Air Pollution And Poor Sleep Quality In Adults Aged 45 Years And Older; A National Longitudinal Study in China. Master's Thesis, Yale, New Haven, CT, USA, January 2020.
8. Luo, Y.; Zhong, Y.; Pang, L.; Zhao, Y.; Liang, R.; Zheng, X. The effects of indoor air pollution from solid fuel use on cognitive function among middle-aged and older population in China. *Sci. Total Environ.* **2021**, *754*, 142460. [CrossRef] [PubMed]
9. Deng, Y.; Gao, Q.; Yang, D.; Hua, H.; Wang, N.; Ou, F.; Liu, R.; Wu, B.; Liu, Y. Association between biomass fuel use and risk of hypertension among Chinese older people: A cohort study. *Environ. Int.* **2020**, *138*, 105620. [CrossRef]
10. Lin, L.; Wang, H.H.; Liu, Y.; Lu, C.; Chen, W.; Guo, V.Y. Indoor solid fuel use for heating and cooking with blood pressure and hypertension: A cross-sectional study among middle-aged and older adults in China. *Indoor Air* **2021**, *31*, 2158–2166. [CrossRef]
11. Pan, M.; Gu, J.; Li, R.; Chen, H.; Liu, X.; Tu, R.; Chen, R.; Yu, S.; Mao, Z.; Huo, W.; et al. Independent and combined associations of solid-fuel use and smoking with obesity among rural Chinese adults. *Environ. Sci. Pollut. Res. Int.* **2021**, *28*, 33613–33622. [CrossRef]
12. Deng, Y.; Gao, Q.; Yang, T.; Wu, B.; Liu, Y.; Liu, R. Indoor solid fuel use and incident arthritis among middle-aged and older adults in rural China: A nationwide population-based cohort study. *Sci. Total Environ.* **2021**, *772*, 145395. [CrossRef]
13. Dutta, A.; Mukherjee, B.; Das, D.; Banerjee, A.; Ray, M.R. Hypertension with elevated levels of oxidized low-density lipoprotein and anticardiolipin antibody in the circulation of premenopausal Indian women chronically exposed to biomass smoke during cooking. *Indoor Air* **2011**, *21*, 165–176. [CrossRef] [PubMed]
14. Yu, Q.; Zuo, G. Relationship of indoor solid fuel use for cooking with blood pressure and hypertension among the elderly in China. *Environ. Sci. Pollut. Res.* **2022**, *2022*, 1–12. [CrossRef] [PubMed]
15. Sun, J.; Wang, J.; Shen, Z.; Huang, Y.; Zhang, Y.; Niu, X.; Cao, J.; Zhang, Q.; Xu, H.; Zhang, N.; et al. Volatile organic compounds from residential solid fuel burning in Guanzhong Plain, China: Source-related profiles and risks. *Chemosphere* **2019**, *221*, 184–192. [CrossRef] [PubMed]
16. Idler, E.L.; Benyamini, Y. Self-rated health and mortality: A review of twenty-seven community studies. *J. Health Soc. Behav.* **1997**, *38*, 21–37. [CrossRef] [PubMed]
17. Jylha, M. What is self-rated health and why does it predict mortality? Towards a unified conceptual model. *Soc. Sci. Med.* **2009**, *69*, 307–316. [CrossRef]
18. Chen, F.; Yang, Y.; Liu, G. Social Change and Socioeconomic Disparities in Health over the Life Course in China: A Cohort Analysis. *Am. Sociol. Rev.* **2010**, *75*, 126–150. [CrossRef]
19. Yi, Z.; Vaupel, J.W. Functional Capacity and Self-Evaluation of Health and Life of Oldest Old in China. *J. Soc. Issues* **2002**, *58*, 733–748. [CrossRef]
20. Zeng, Y.; Feng, Q.; Hesketh, T.; Christensen, K.; Vaupel, J.W. Survival, disabilities in activities of daily living, and physical and cognitive functioning among the oldest-old in China: A cohort study. *Lancet* **2017**, *389*, 1619–1629. [CrossRef]
21. Lv, X.; Li, W.; Ma, Y.; Chen, H.; Zeng, Y.; Yu, X.; Hofman, A.; Wang, H. Cognitive decline and mortality among community-dwelling Chinese older people. *BMC Med.* **2019**, *17*, 63. [CrossRef]

22. Andresen, E.M.; Malmgren, J.A.; Carter, W.B.; Patrick, D.L. Screening for Depression in Well Older Adults: Evaluation of a Short Form of the CES-D. *Am. J. Prev. Med.* **1994**, *10*, 77–84. [CrossRef]
23. Cheng, S.; Chan, A. The Center for Epidemiologic Studies Depression Scale in older Chinese: Thresholds for long and short forms. *Int. J. Geriatr. Psychiatry* **2010**, *20*, 465–470. [CrossRef] [PubMed]
24. Idler, E.; Cartwright, K. What Do We Rate When We Rate Our Health? Decomposing Age-related Contributions to Self-rated Health. *J. Health Soc. Behav.* **2018**, *59*, 74–93. [CrossRef] [PubMed]
25. Engberg, I.; Segerstedt, J.; Waller, G.; Wennberg, P.; Eliasson, M. Fatigue in the general population- associations to age, sex, socioeconomic status, physical activity, sitting time and self-rated health: The northern Sweden MONICA study 2014. *BMC Public Health* **2017**, *17*, 654. [CrossRef] [PubMed]
26. Meyer, O.L.; Castro-Schilo, L.; Aguilar-Gaxiola, S. Determinants of mental health and self-rated health: A model of socioeconomic status, neighborhood safety, and physical activity. *Am. J. Public Health* **2014**, *104*, 1734–1741. [CrossRef] [PubMed]
27. Hu, L.T.; Bentler, P.M. Cutoff criteria for fit indexes in covariance structure analysis: Conventional criteria versus new alternatives. *Struct. Equ. Model. A Multidiscip. J.* **1999**, *6*, 1–55. [CrossRef]
28. Porritt, J.M.; Sufi, F.; Barlow, A.; Baker, S.R. The role of illness beliefs and coping in the adjustment to dentine hypersensitivity. *J. Clin. Periodontol.* **2014**, *41*, 60–69. [CrossRef]
29. Li, C.; Zhou, Y.; Ding, L. Effects of long-term household air pollution exposure from solid fuel use on depression: Evidence from national longitudinal surveys from 2011 to 2018. *Environ. Pollut.* **2021**, *283*, 117350. [CrossRef]
30. Liu, Y.; Chen, X.; Yan, Z. Depression in the house: The effects of household air pollution from solid fuel use among the middle-aged and older population in China. *Sci. Total Environ.* **2020**, *703*, 134706. [CrossRef]
31. Yu, H.; Luo, J.; Chen, K.; Pollitt, K.J.G.; Liew, Z. Solid fuels use for cooking and sleep health in adults aged 45 years and older in China. *Sci. Rep.* **2021**, *11*, 13304. [CrossRef]
32. Chen, C.; Liu, G.G.; Sun, Y.; Gu, D.; Zhang, H.; Yang, H.; Lu, L.; Zhao, Y.; Yao, Y. Association between household fuel use and sleep quality in the oldest-old: Evidence from a propensity-score matched case-control study in Hainan, China. *Environ. Res.* **2020**, *191*, 110229. [CrossRef]
33. Siddharthan, T.; Grigsby, M.R.; Goodman, D.; Chowdhury, M.; Rubinstein, A.; Irazola, V.; Gutierrez, L.; Miranda, J.J.; Bernabe-Ortiz, A.; Alam, D.; et al. Association between Household Air Pollution Exposure and Chronic Obstructive Pulmonary Disease Outcomes in 13 Low- and Middle-Income Country Settings. *Am. J. Respir. Crit. Care Med.* **2018**, *197*, 611–620. [CrossRef] [PubMed]
34. Block, M.L.; Calderón-Garciduenas, L. Air pollution: Mechanisms of neuroinflammation and CNS disease. *Trends Neurosci.* **2009**, *32*, 506–516. [CrossRef]
35. Cao, L.; Zhao, Z.; Ji, C.; Xia, Y. Association between solid fuel use and cognitive impairment: A cross-sectional and follow-up study in a middle-aged and older Chinese population. *Environ. Int.* **2021**, *146*, 106251. [CrossRef] [PubMed]
36. Qiu, Y.; Yang, F.-A.; Lai, W. The impact of indoor air pollution on health outcomes and cognitive abilities: Empirical evidence from China. *Popul. Environ.* **2019**, *40*, 388–410. [CrossRef]
37. Kaplan, G.A.; Goldberg, D.E.; Everson, S.A.; Cohen, R.D.; Salonen, R.; Tuomilehto, J.; Salonen, J. Perceived Health Status and Morbidity and Mortality: Evidence from the Kuopio Ischaemic Heart Disease Risk Factor Study. *Int. J. Epidemiol.* **1996**, *25*, 259–265. [CrossRef] [PubMed]
38. Balakrishnan, K.; Ramaswamy, P.; Sambandam, S.; Thangavel, G.; Ghosh, S.; Johnson, P.; Mukhopadhyay, K.; Venugopal, V.; Thanasekaraan, V. Air pollution from household solid fuel combustion in India: An overview of exposure and health related information to inform health research priorities. *Glob. Health Action* **2011**, *4*, 1–9. [CrossRef] [PubMed]

atmosphere

Article

Investigation of Airflow Distribution and Contamination Control with Different Schemes in an Operating Room

Fujen Wang [1,*], Indra Permana [2], Dibakar Rakshit [3] and Bowo Yuli Prasetyo [4]

[1] Department of Refrigeration, Air Conditioning and Energy Engineering, National Chin-Yi University of Technology, Taichung 411, Taiwan
[2] Graduate Institute of Precision Manufacturing, National Chin-Yi University of Technology, Taichung 411, Taiwan; indra.refrigeration@gmail.com
[3] Department of Energy Science and Engineering, Indian Institute of Technology Delhi, New Delhi 110016, India; dibakar@iitd.ac.in
[4] Department of Refrigeration and Air Conditioning, Politeknik Negeri Bandung, Bandung 40559, Indonesia; bowo.yuliprasetyo@gmail.com
* Correspondence: fjwang@ncut.edu.tw; Tel.: +886-922-836-010

Abstract: Controlling contamination via proper airflow distribution in an operating room becomes vital to ensure the reliable surgery process. The heating, ventilation, and air conditioning (HVAC) systems significantly influence the operating room environment, including temperature, relative humidity, pressurization, particle counts, filtration, and ventilation rate. A full-scale operating room has been investigated extensively through field measurements and numerical analyses. Computational fluid dynamics (CFD) simulation was conducted and verified with the field measurement data. The simulation was analyzed with three different operating room schemes, including at-rest conditions (case 1), normal operational conditions with personnel (case 2), and actual conditions with personnel inside and some medical equipment blocking the return air (case 3). The concentration decay method was used to evaluate this study. The results revealed that the contamination concentration in case 1 could be diluted quickly with the average value of 404 ppm, whereas the concentration in case 2 slightly increased while performing a surgery with the average value of 420 ppm. The return air grilles in case 3, blocked by obstacles from some medical equipment, resulted in the average concentration value of 474 ppm. Other than that, the contaminant dilution could be obstructed dramatically, which revealed that proper and smooth airflow distribution is essential for contamination control. The ventilation efficiency of case 2 and case 3 dropped around 6% and 17.91% compared to case 1 in the unoccupied and ideal condition. Ventilation efficiency also decreased along with decreasing the air change rate per hour (ACH), while with increasing ACH, the ventilation efficiency in case 3 actually increased, approaching case 2 in the ideal condition.

Keywords: operating room; airflow distribution; contamination control; field measurement; computational fluid dynamics

Citation: Wang, F.; Permana, I.; Rakshit, D.; Prasetyo, B.Y. Investigation of Airflow Distribution and Contamination Control with Different Schemes in an Operating Room. *Atmosphere* **2021**, *12*, 1639. https://doi.org/10.3390/atmos12121639

Academic Editors: Ashok Kumar, M. Amirul I. Khan, Alejandro Moreno Rangel and Michał Piasecki

Received: 23 November 2021
Accepted: 5 December 2021
Published: 8 December 2021

1. Introduction

The critical area of any hospital is the operating room. Anything in the operating room can endanger a patient's life, such as a variety of bacteria and viruses [1]. Those contaminants can be transmitted through the air that can contaminate medical tools. This could be dangerous to a patient when the operating room staff members perform the procedure in the operating room [2]. HVAC systems provide comfort and sufficient quality air for patients and staff in the operating room. A comfortable and healthy environment is generally determined by temperature, humidity, and air velocity [3]. Therefore, in maintaining a clean and healthy environment for patients and healthcare workers, thermal comfort and indoor air quality requires a valid regulation. American Society of Heating, Refrigerating, and Air-Conditioning Engineers (ASHRAE) standard 170 [4] mentions directive notices in an operating room, including the number of air changes per hour, airflow distribution, room pressurization, and filtration. ASHRAE standard 62 [5] asserts that indoor pollutants can influence occupants' activities; carbon dioxide is an example of an indoor pollutant. The total carbon dioxide exposure in the room must be less than 1000 ppm: this will give health workers a comfortable and healthy condition to stay focused on the procedure. Shortness of breath, headaches, confusion, and other symptoms can occur in the room because of the high exposure to carbon dioxide.

Additionally, researchers have conducted many studies on changing the velocity of supply air to control contamination spread in the operating room. The relatively low speed in the operating room will affect the concentration of microbial carrier particles (MCP) and the room's deposition rate. This suggests that there may be a risk of microbiological contamination from exposed surfaces to areas of low velocities, such as under lights during surgical procedures [6]. Uniform vertical laminar airflow is established, and high cleanliness is achieved in the center of the room when the surgical lamp is arranged in two axes [7]. In addition, the movement of the particles in the operating room can be affected by the position of the surgical lightings, and it was also shown that higher supply velocity ($\geq$0.38 m/s) might affect the flow disturbance [8]. Current evidence has shown a positive relationship between the airborne concentration of bacteria-carrying particles (BCPs) in the operating room and the rate of infections. The accumulation of airborne BCPs under operating lighting poses a high risk of infection for patient safety [9]. In another study, four different supply air velocities (0.16, 0.24, 0.29, and 0.33 m/s), were investigated by Liu et al. [10]. A higher cleanliness level in the operating room can be ensured by supplying air velocities larger than 0.24 m/s. Meanwhile, when the supply air velocity increases to larger than 0.33 m/s, this will also increase bioaerosol deposition.

The air supply velocity must be optimally designed to match the energy consumption for energy saving. The HVAC system in the operating room is operated for 24 h throughout the year with intensive energy consumption [11]. The HVAC system in the operating room is operated under full load even when the room is unoccupied. Research has studied the operating room ventilation systems' best practice for energy efficiency, health, and safety [12]. Proper design, operation, and controls can reduce these costs by as much as 65% while ensuring a healthy and safe environment for the surgical team and the patient. Concerning energy saving, a preliminary study of numerical analysis has been carried out to evaluate the air velocity distribution and concentration contours while carrying out a ACH approach in an unoccupied operating room [13].

A variety of ventilation schemes have been developed for operating room use. Each has pros and cons and may be better suited than another for operations under certain conditions. The proper functioning of OR ventilation is also affected by external and internal disruptions. By applying CFD, the present study investigates the airflow and contaminant distribution in operating rooms under different conditions [14]. CFD simulation uses field measurements that are carried out as the pedestal parameters as boundary conditions [15]. In this study, CFD simulations were performed to discover the potential of HVAC systems to control air contamination, a comfortable environment for occupants, and the possibilities of energy-efficient approaches in the operating room. This simulation is based and verified on field data collection. Other than that, CFD simulation methods were also conducted in other research fields to predict and evaluate some systems in low cost and efficient ways. Zhiyi et al. [16] investigated ventilation performance in typical apartment buildings predicted by CFD in a multi-zone airflow model. The improvement in indoor air quality (IAQ) was also conducted by the measurement and CFD simulations that are shown as valid tools for IAQ indication [17]. In addition, CFD modeling of contaminant migration in a household gas furnace was investigated by Szczepanik-Scislo [18]. The results revealed that the location of the furnace could influence contaminant accumulation and migration. Such simulations can be an essential tool when designing a ventilation system concerning a furnace to improve the removal of dangerous substances.

With the intention of achieving a good environmental condition, the concentration decay method can be used to assess indoor ventilation efficiency. Tracer gas or particle experiments could be used in CFD methods. However, the pathogens as particles could be simplified without considering their biological characteristics, as most researchers have investigated [19]. Specific piecewise-linear techniques were applied to the concentration decay method to determine the ACH values for smaller time intervals. This is necessary because the plotted semi-logarithmic decay curve itself is not linear as the ventilation rate changes with time due to the changing buoyancy force [20]. Chung [21] used carbon dioxide (CO_2) as a pollutant to evaluate the efficiency of indoor ventilation. The tracer gas was injected into the room and mixed into the air; a decrease in tracer gas concentration was logged over a given period [22]. This study investigates the contamination control in different schemes to discover performance improvements carried out through comprehensive field measurement tests as well as numerical simulation analysis.

2. System Description

The operating room is generally categorized as a positively pressurized bio-cleanroom that ensures a critical environment for infection control concerns to comply with applicable standards and regulations. The dimension of the investigated operating room was at a length of 6.3 m, a width of 6.0 m, a height of 3.0 m, and a total area of 37.8 m^2. The function of this operating room was heart surgery. High-efficiency particulate air (HEPA) filtered the supply air with a total of 15 units located in the center of the ceiling. The operating room was classified into ISO 7 [23] with a maximum of particles per cubic meter at a size 0.5 μm is 352,000 or equal to the Federal Standard 209E [24] with a cleanliness level of 10,000 particles per cubic feet. The design specification of indoor environmental parameters in the investigated operating room included temperature of 22 ± 2 °C, relative humidity at 30–60%, and pressurization at 5 Pa. Figure 1 displays the HVAC system in the operating room, (a) filter in air handling unit (AHU) system to filter dirty air coming from the mixing air cabin, (b) cooling coil to cool down the temperature of the air with chilled water on the coil that comes from the process of cooling the water by the chiller, (c) heating coil for the process of heating and humidifying the air to fit with the design of the operating room, (d) fan to supply the air into the room, (e) HEPA filter to filter the air particles with the efficiency of HEPA filters over 99.97% (above 0.5 μm) so that the air entering the room becomes clean, (f) return air; the air coming from the room draughts to the AHU system and supplies the operating room.

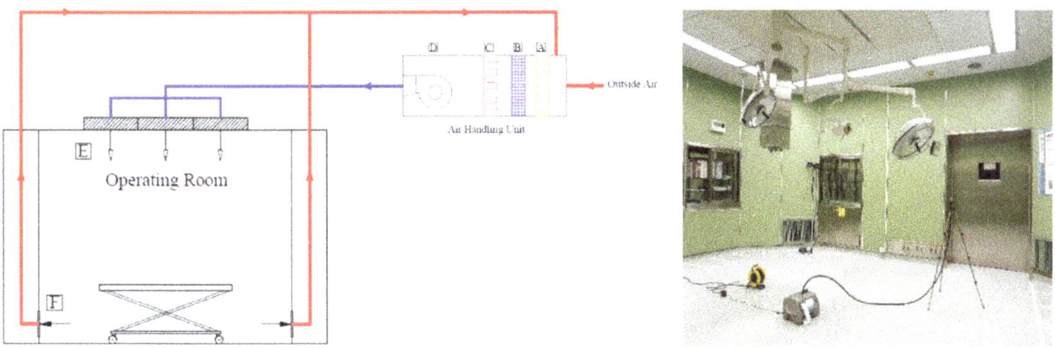

(a) (b)

Figure 1. The investigated operating room: (**a**) HVAC system; (**b**) snapshot.

3. Methodology

The proposed methodology of this research is illustrated in Figure 2. It generally consists of three steps: field measurement test, CFD simulation, and performance improvement strategy.

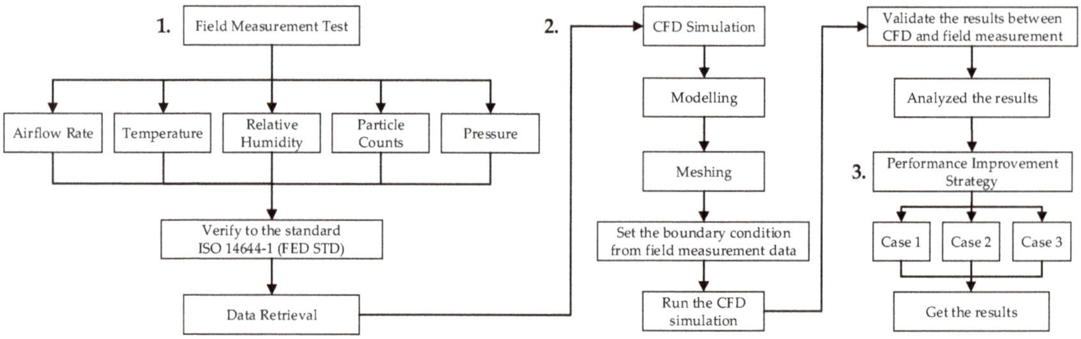

Figure 2. The proposed methodology framework.

3.1. *Field Measurement Tests*

This operating room requires a clean environment to prevent contamination in the room because the surgical process is sensitive to environmental parameters, including temperature, relative humidity, particles, and pressurization. The field measurement tests were conducted to examine the indoor environment parameters during an unoccupied period (at-rest). Parameters taken were airflow rate, pressurization, particle counts, temperature, and relative humidity. The apparatus tests for field measurement were as follows (1) Airflow rate: a TSI model PH-731 was employed to measure the airflow rate of each HEPA in cubic meter per hour. (2) Particle counter was used to count particles in the air of an operating room. Finding out the number of particles in the room was carried out using Met One 3413, and it was measured at the height of 1.2 m above the floor within a one minute recording. (3) Temperature and relative humidity in the room are very influential on objects in a room. TSI model 9565P was used to find out the temperature and humidity value in this operating room, and it was measured at the height of 1.2 m above the floor with three times measurement. The detailed specification of the apparatus field measurement tests is shown in Table 1. Furthermore, the measurement data were validated with the results of numerical simulation. The results of this measurement data were used as the basic parameters for ensuring that the operating room is in accordance with the desired design.

Table 1. Apparatus for field measurement tests.

Parameters	Apparatus Model	Operative Range	Accuracy
Velocity, Pressure	TSI PH-731	0.125–12.5 (m/s) Differential ± 3735 pa	3% 2%
Particles	Met One 3413	0.3, 0.5, 1, 3, 5, 10 μm	5%
Temperature, Humidity	TSI 9565P	−10~60 (°C), 0–100 (%RH)	0.3 °C 3%RH

3.2. *CFD Simulation and Improvement Strategy*

CFD was conducted to investigate the airflow distribution and concentration of airborne particles. The operating room simulation was performed using the ANSYS Fluent software version 2020 R2 [25]. Three different operating room schemes were conducted in this study to determine the performance of the HVAC system and reduce the concentration of the contaminant. The geometry was created based on the actual size and situation in the operating room, as shown in Figure 3. The study aims to prevent bacteria or even fungi from entering the patient's body who is undergoing the surgical process. In addition, the analyses of environmental conditions are also considered. Various cases based on the different conditions are described below.

- Case 1: at-rest condition with no personnel and equipment inside the operating room.
- Case 2: operational condition with personnel inside performing a surgery.
- Case 3: actual condition with personnel inside and equipment blocking the return air.

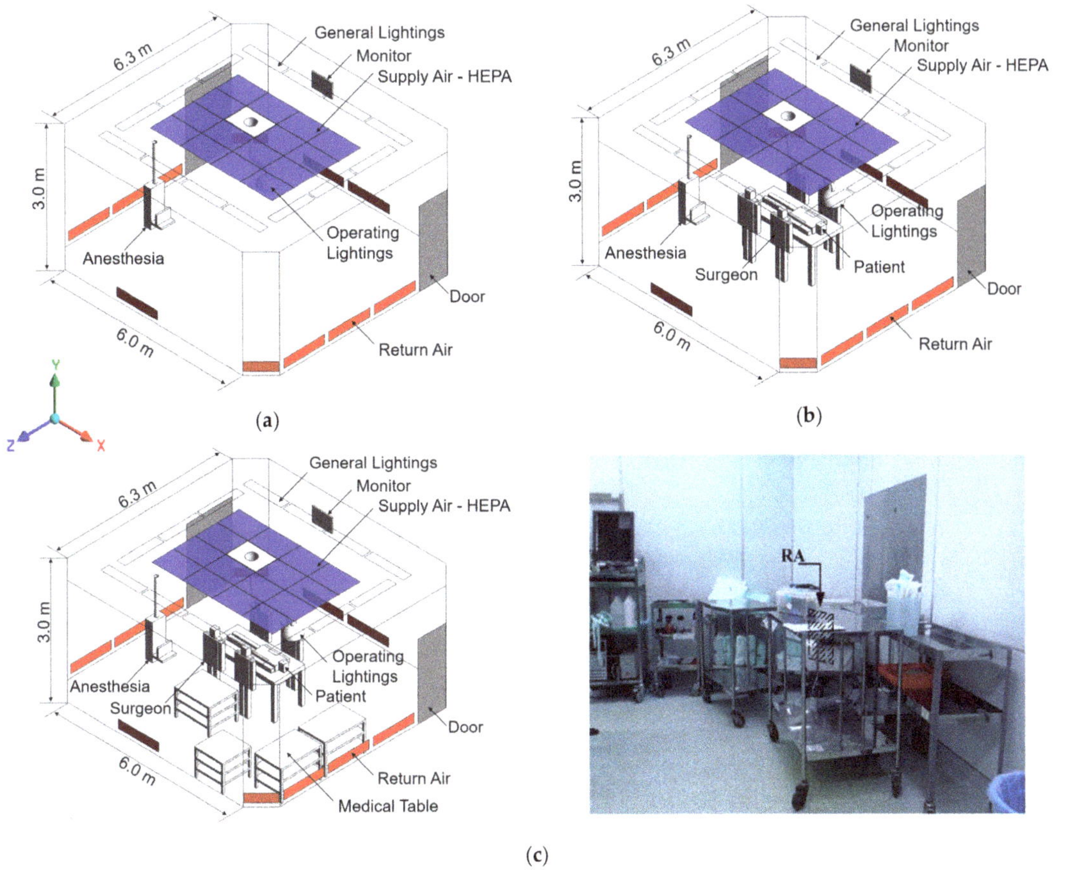

Figure 3. The geometry of the investigated operating room in three different schemes: (**a**) case 1: at-rest condition; (**b**) case 2: operational condition; (**c**) case 3: actual condition.

3.3. *Airflow Modelling and Boundary Conditions*

ANSYS Fluent provides several equations to solve the problems, including laminar and turbulent fluid flow problems, incompressible and compressible fluid, and other problems. In order to solve the flow and temperature fields of the problem, the equation for mass conservation, momentum, and energy is written as follows

$$\frac{\partial \rho}{\partial t} + \nabla\left(\rho \vec{v}\right) = S_m \tag{1}$$

$$\nabla = \frac{\partial}{\partial x}\vec{i} + \frac{\partial}{\partial x}\vec{j}\,\frac{\partial}{\partial x}\vec{k} \tag{2}$$

Equation (1) is the general form of mass conservation equation for incompressible and compressible flows. Where the t, ρ, $\vec{v}$, ∇ are time, density, velocity, gradient operator, respectively, and S_m is the mass added to the continuous phase from the dispersed second phase and any user-defined sources. ANSYS Fluent defined ∇ according to the cartesian coordinate in Equation (2).

Airflow turbulence simulation uses two simulation methods carried out in this study, transient and steady-state condition with the renormalization group (RNG) k-ε as the turbulence model. Transient conditions can be used to monitor the reduction in the concentration in the operating room with a simulation time of about 500 s with a time step of 50 s. The steady-state condition is used to validate the field measurement data for temperature and velocity. The iterative coupling calculation for this stage is solved by the SIMPLE (Semi-Implicit Method for Pressure Linked Equation) method. The numerical simulation was calculated until it reached the residual bellow 10^{-3} for the velocity and continuity, while energy residuals reached below 10^{-6} to produce more precise results. The general form of the RNG k-ε model governing equation is as follows

$$\frac{\partial (\rho\phi)}{\partial t} + \nabla\left(\rho\phi\vec{V}\right) = \nabla\left(\Gamma_\phi \nabla\phi\right) + S_\phi \tag{3}$$

where ρ is the density of air, $\vec{V}$ is the air velocity vector, ϕ represents each of the three components, Γ_ϕ is the effective diffusion coefficient of ϕ, and S_ϕ is the source term.

Lagrangian particle tracking was used for the simulation method of particle tracking. The bioaerosol was injected into the space with the discrete phase model and simulated transiently. The particle size was 1–5 µm with a median size of 2.5 µm with a density of 1000 kg/m^{3,} which is approximately equal to the density of water. It was simulated as spherical particles. The discrete phase for supply air and outlet air was set up with "escape" boundary conditions, while the remaining surfaces such as walls, medical equipment, etc., were set up with "trap" boundary conditions. Saffman lift force and thermophoretic force for the particle phase were used in this study. The equation is as follows.

$$\frac{du_{pi}}{dt} = \frac{18\mu}{\rho_p d_p^2}\frac{C_D Re}{24}\left(U_i - U_{pi}\right) + g_i\left(1 - \frac{\rho}{\rho_p}\right) + F_{ai} \tag{4}$$

where U_i and U_{pi} are the velocities of the fluid and particles, respectively; μ is the molecular viscosity of the fluid; ρ and ρ_p are the densities of the fluid and particles, respectively; d_p is the diameter of the particles; Re is the particle Reynolds number; C_D is the drag coefficient; g_i is the gravitational acceleration in the i direction; F_{ai} is the additional force exerted on the particles.

A tracer gas method was carried out in this study, with simplified pathogen or particles without considering biological characteristics. Carbon dioxide (CO_2) was selected as a pollutant to assess indoor ventilation efficiency and environmental conditions in the operating room with different models and conditions. The boundary conditions of numerical simulation are shown in Table 2. The CO_2 concentration in the outdoor atmosphere is about 400 ppm, which will be used as the concentration value for supplying air from HEPA [26]. The recommended indoor CO_2 concentrations should be maintained at or below 1000 ppm [27]. The exhaled air from patient and personnel are set with a concentration of around 38,000 ppm [28]. Heat flux generated from each patient and surgeon are at 17.45 W/m^2 and 33.55 W/m^2, respectively [29]. The walls and door were assumed to be adiabatic, which have no heat transfer.

Table 2. The boundary condition for numerical simulations.

Parameter	Type	Value
Supply Air	Velocity Inlet Discrete phase: escape	Velocity: 0.298 m/s Temperature: 20.2 °C Concentration: 400 ppm
Return Air	Pressure Outlet Discrete phase: trap	Temperature: 25 °C Pressure: +10.6 Pa
CO_2 Concentration	Velocity Inlet	Velocity Inlet: 0.18 m/s Exhale: 38,000 ppm [29]
Bioaerosol	DPM: Injection	Velocity: 1.5 m/s Flowrate: 0.17 kg/s Particle Size: 1–5 μm, median 2.5 μm
Patient	Wall	Heatflux: 17.45 W/m^2 [30]
Surgeon	Wall	Heatflux: 33.55 W/m^2 [30]
General Lightings	Wall	Heatflux: 288 W/m^2 [30]
Operating Lightings	Wall	Heatflux: 320 W/m^2 [30]

3.4. Grid Independence Test and Validation

The parameters could change the level of accuracy during the simulation process [30]. Increasing the number of mesh elements influences the accuracy of the simulation results. However, this requires a long time and sufficient resources. The grid independence test and validation of the simulation are illustrated in Figure 4. Three different meshes with 894,474, 1,543,686, and 2,303,385 were generated and simulated to obtain the optimal number of elements that can meet the appropriate meshing process. Furthermore, the grid independence test was validated for accuracy with the field measurement data of temperature and velocity. There were seven temperature measurement points in the field measurements, and then compared with the numerical simulation results. The velocity data were analyzed from the height of 0 m to 3 m. The type of mesh that is closest to the measurement data is 2,303,285 elements. However, it required sufficient resources and time. Therefore, considering the number of 1,543,686 elements with an error of less than 10% could be optimum for the subsequent simulation.

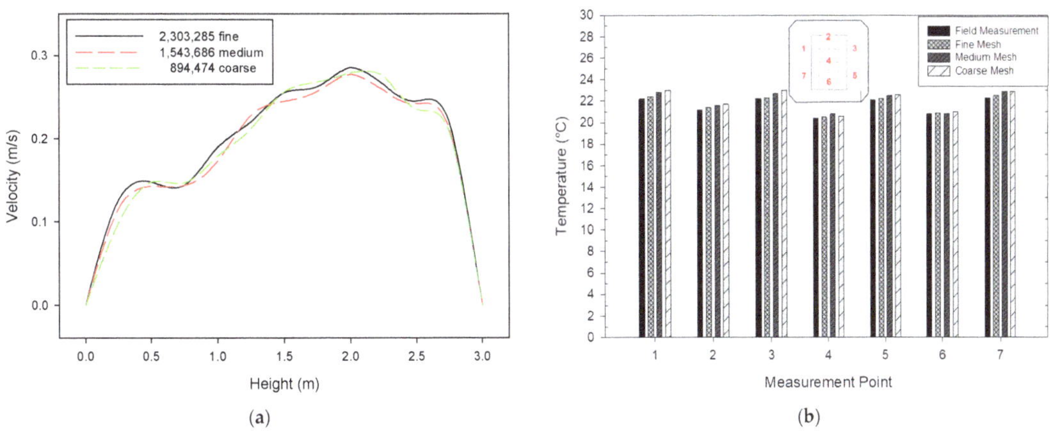

Figure 4. Grid independence test and validation of the measurement and simulation. (**a**) Grid independence test; (**b**) Validation.

4. Results and Discussion

4.1. Experimental Results

Field measurement tests were conducted in at-rest occupancy state conditions, and the results were also retrieved in accordance with the operating room standards. The results can represent the operating room quality with the data parameters: ventilation rate, temperature, relative humidity, pressurization, and particle counts. The measurement results revealed that the total air change per hour in this operating room was 22 ACH, which qualifies to the operating room design based on ASHRAE Standard 170 with a minimum of 20 ACH. The other indoor environmental parameters met good agreement with the standard: temperature average of 21.6 °C, relative humidity of 51.4% (shown in Figure 5), and pressurization of 10.6 Pa. The operating room is classified as ISO 7 (class 10,000). According to the field measurement results, particles at size 0.5 μm were counted less than the standard of 352,000 particles/m^3, and also the particles at size 5 μm were counted less than 2900 particles/m^3. The field measurement points of 2, 4, and 6 are located under the supply HEPA filter, resulting in a lower temperature and fewer particles in contrast to the outer HEPA location.

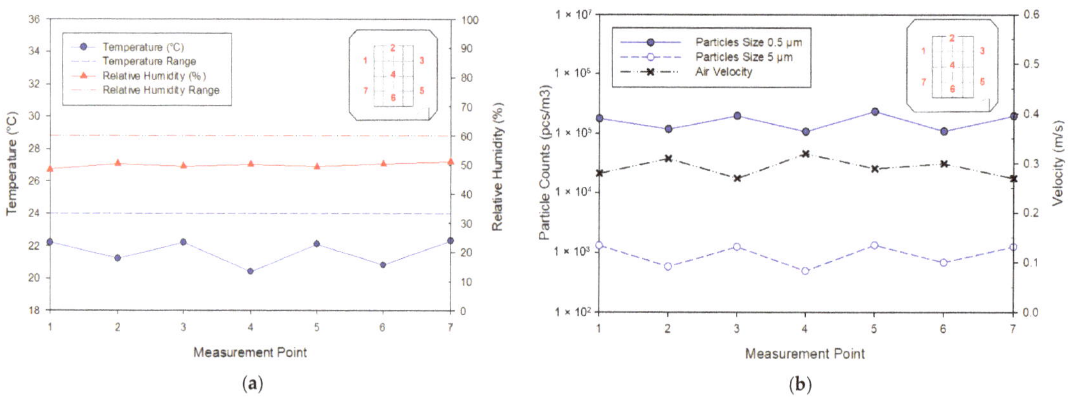

Figure 5. Field measurement test results, (**a**) temperature and relative humidity, (**b**) particle counts and air velocity.

4.2. Airflow Pattern Distribution

The airflow distribution in these three different cases needs to be reviewed in more detail. This will certainly affect the flow of clean air supplied by the HVAC system through the HEPA filter to reduce the amount of contamination in the operating room. Figure 6 shows the airflow distribution in different schemes. The airflow in case 1 can spread eventually in the room. In contrast to case 2, the addition of patients, personnel, and medical staff in a critical area becomes very influential in the airflow spread. Some airflow that hits the surface of the human body will cause the variation of velocity. Not only that but the airflow also does not appropriately spread at the bottom of the patient's bed. This is caused by the obstruction of airflow. Overall, the airflow in the room for case 2 can be well distributed, although it has not reached the entire room properly. The HVAC system recirculates the air in the operating room through the return air grilles. Case 3 shows the importance of paying attention to the airflow direction in the room blocked by the medical trolley. Putting a trolley near the return air grille causes the air suction process in the operating room to obstruct. The airflow collides on the top surface of the trolley and makes the air flow in a reverse direction. The air is more turbulent in the room. Therefore, airflow has difficulty reaching areas outside of the critical zone.

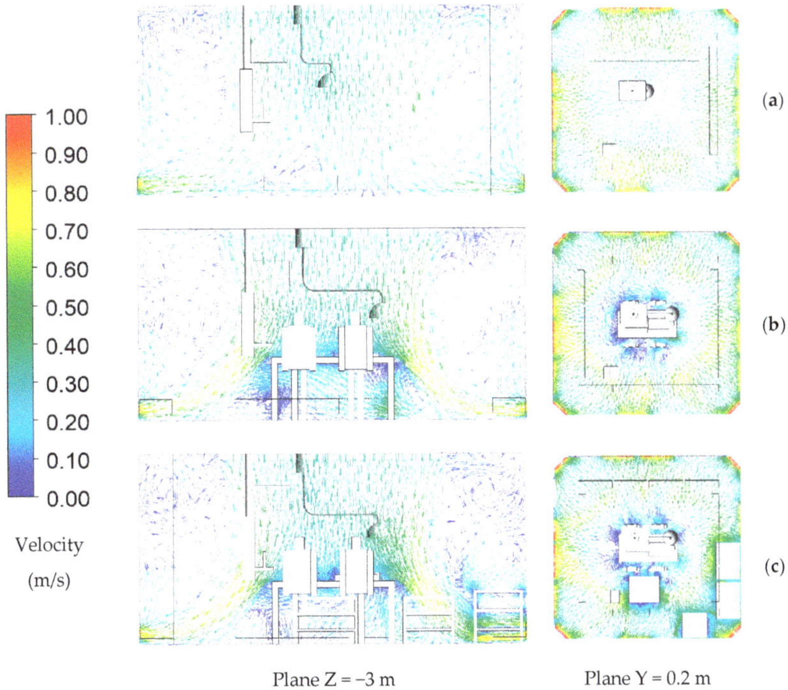

Figure 6. The airflow distribution in different schemes: (**a**) case 1: at-rest condition; (**b**) case 2: operational condition; (**c**) case 3: actual condition.

4.3. Contamination Removal Analyses in Different Cases

Different cases certainly have different results of concentration. Case 1 analyzes the performance of the HVAC system to reduce the amount of contamination during at-rest conditions. Furthermore, the identification was made in case 2 by adding occupants as a source of contamination in the operating room. Most likely, the amount of contamination is no longer the same as in case 1. However, conditions in the room are not always ideal conditions. Sometimes, health workers put surgical equipment anywhere and, therefore, could block the path of air return. Therefore, case 3 should be examined more comprehensively to determine whether there is a difference from the other cases.

The airflow in the operating room also has a function to dilute contamination. CO_2 was assumed as a source of contamination in the operating room. Figure 7 shows the concentration profile in three different cases. Contamination in case 1 has a low concentration because the contamination could be diluted quickly, and also clean air is evenly distributed in the room (Figure 7a). Case 1 shows a decrease in contamination and is more efficient compared to other cases. This is because the operating room in case 1 was unoccupied and without any medical equipment. In contrast, in case 2, additional patient and surgery personnel generated some contaminants. Concentration increases in case 2 due to the addition of occupants placed in the middle of the room (critical zone) so that the airflow flowing in the room is slightly obstructed (Figure 7b). The air that spreads in the room has a concentration of air exhaled from the patient and surgery personnel. The cross-section from that figure shows the highest concentration is in the ceiling because airflow cannot reach that part. With the object near the air return, it means the dilution of concentration in the room is inhibited so that the concentration in the room is higher than in other cases. In case 3, it can be clearly seen that the top of the trolley has a high concentration value (Figure 7c). The clean airflow causes this area to be obstructed by the object. The results show the differences between the schemes given in the rooms in case 1, case 2, and case 3.

In the final condition, case 1 has the lowest concentration level of 404 ppm, case 2 has an average concentration of 420 ppm, and case 3 has a higher concentration than other cases of 474 ppm. This analysis shows that using the ventilation rate of 22 ACH can efficiently reduce contamination in the different operating room cases.

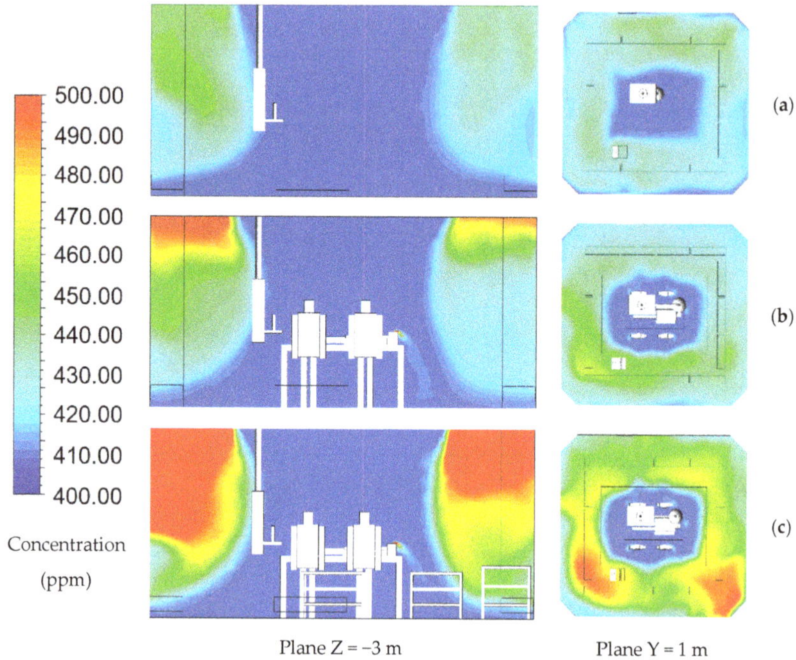

Figure 7. The concentration profile in different schemes: (**a**) case 1: at-rest condition; (**b**) case 2: operational condition; (**c**) case 3: actual condition.

4.4. Effect of Ventilation Rate on the Operating Room Concentration

The ventilation rate certainly affects the amount of higher or lower concentrations in the operating room. Lower ventilation rates can result in energy savings but concentrations may increase. In contrast, increased ventilation rates produce fewer particles in the operating room but require more energy. Therefore, the optimal ventilation rate must be adjusted to match the energy consumption and concentration. Increasing the ventilation rate does not always result in a lower concentration, but air pattern distribution is one of the essential things. This study investigated an obstruction near the return air grilles by some medical trolleys, resulting in more turbulent airflow patterns. The increase and decrease in ACH number were carried out in this study with 15 ACH, 22 ACH, and 29 ACH, respectively.

Figure 8 illustrates the concentration contamination decay in different schemes that were monitored for 500 s. The results revealed that the air distribution spread eventually in the operating room for case 1 and case 2 with 22 ACH and could remove the contamination. For case 3, objects near the return air grilles made the concentration higher than the others. The average concentration in the operating room with 22 ACH was 474 ppm. Compared to ideal conditions, the result is higher when the medical equipment is located in the wrong area that could obstruct the airflow. In addition, studies with increasing ventilation rates were also carried out in order to result in lower concentrations. The results revealed that when ventilation rates increased to 29 ACH, the concentration became lower and could be reduced to 446 ppm. The concentration is close to case 2 when the operating room is in ideal conditions (no obstruction in the return air grilles).

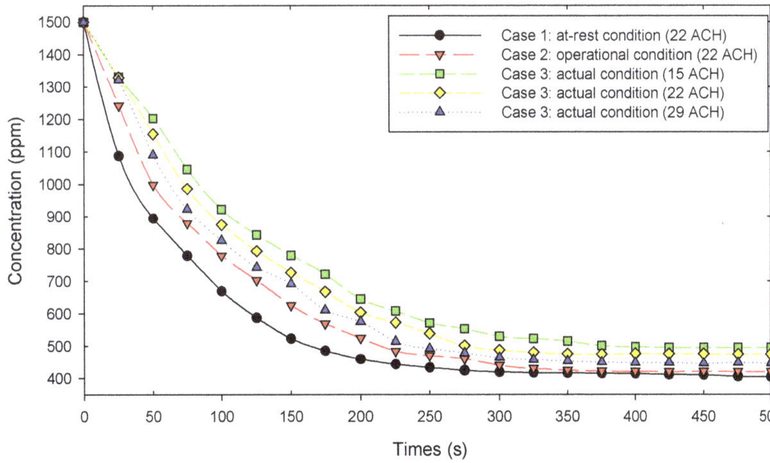

Figure 8. Concentration decay effect in different schemes.

In order to have some energy saving, the reduction in ventilation rates was conducted in this study with 15 ACH. The average concentration in the room increased along with the reduction in the velocity inlet. The average concentration was 495 ppm. The lack of air distribution causes the dilution of concentration in the area to be inhibited. Reducing the ventilation rates or velocity of air supply entering the room cannot be tried by guessing the numbers because velocity is closely related to airflow and the dilution of contamination. Hence, velocity reduction also has a limit. The ventilation rate reduction could be possible for the operating room with at-rest (unoccupied) and ideal conditions.

4.5. Ventilation Efficiency

Ventilation efficiency is the ratio between the contaminant concentration in the occupied spaces and the concentration in the outlet air. It measures how effectively the air present in a space is replaced by fresh air from the ventilation system [31]. The ventilation efficiency is expressed by the Equation (1)

$$\varepsilon = \frac{C_e - C_s}{(C) - C_s} \times 100\% \quad (5)$$

where ε is ventilation efficiency, Ce is pollutant concentration at the outlet air, Cs is pollutant concentration at supply, and (C) is the average pollutant concentration in the room.

The ventilation efficiency results are shown in Table 3. The results revealed that case 1 has the highest efficiency because of no concentration generated inside the operating room, while case 2 and case 3 decreased due to the additional personnel inside the operating room and the blocked return air grilles, resulting in lower ventilation efficiency.

Table 3. Ventilation efficiency results.

Case Study	C (ppm)	Cs (ppm)	Ce (ppm)	Ventilation Efficiency (%)
Case 1 (22 ACH)	404	400	403.7	92.50
Case 2 (22 ACH)	420	400	417.3	86.50
Case 3 (22 ACH)	474	400	455.2	74.59
Case 3 (15 ACH)	495	400	465.5	68.95
Case 3 (29 ACH)	446	400	438.1	82.83

4.6. Bioaerosol Flow Path Model

Several things that can affect the distribution of bacteria-carrying particles (BPCs) are occupancy state condition, ventilation rates, and operating room design and condition. In this study, two different operating room conditions were investigated during the ideal and actual conditions. The bioaerosol particles were injected into the space from the exact location. Particle sizes were 1–5 μm and median 2.5 μm. The particles were released for the same amount of time in the simulation. Figure 9 illustrates the results of the different particles birth time of 50 and 300 s in two different conditions.

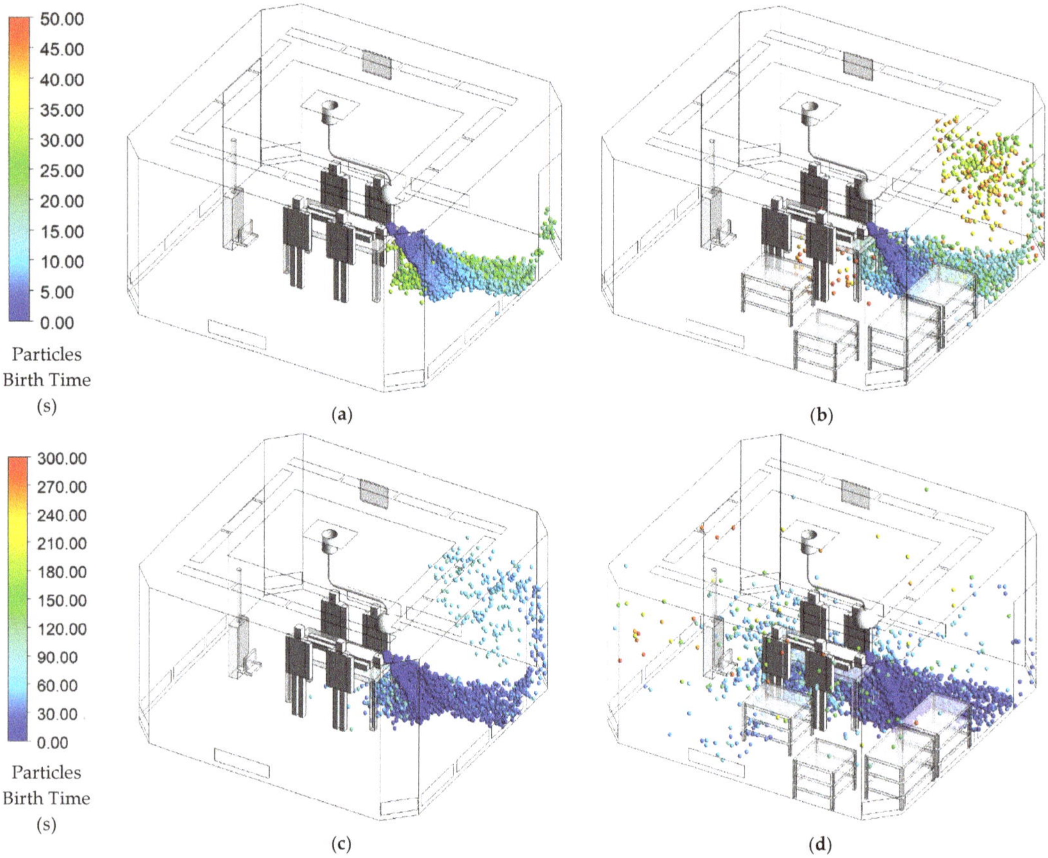

Figure 9. Distribution of bioaerosol particles in the operating room. (**a**) case 2: particle birth at 50 s; (**b**) case 3: particle birth at 50 s; (**c**) case 2: particle birth at 300 s; (**d**) particle birth at 300 s.

The model carried out in the ideal condition presents a good flow path of the bioaerosol particles model. Particles' birth time nodes at 50 s could be faster diluted through the outlet air (Figure 9a). Along with the time period, the airflow distribution could carry the particles reaching almost the ceiling corner (Figure 9c). In addition, the different conditions were conducted to know the effect of the actual condition in the operating room. The placement of the medical equipment was located blocking the outlet air. The bioaerosol particles were injected. The particles spread to the upper corner of the operating room when simulated for 50 s of particles' birth time, as shown in Figure 9b. It also had deposition particles below the surgical table. The medical table location affects the air pattern and obstructs the removal flow path to the return air grilles. Considering not to put the medical equipment near the outlet air grilles could make for better particles' removal.

4.7. Pressurization

In order to maintain the quality of the air in the operating room, it should have sufficient clean air supplied to dilute and remove the airborne contamination generated within the room. Pressurization is critical to the proper functioning of the cleanroom. Thus, the contamination can be prevented during the surgery process. Figure 10 depicts the results of the pressurization in a different scheme. The field measurement was conducted with the pressurization at 10.6 Pa, compared to the numerical simulation with the pressurization of 10.8 Pa, which has been validated, and the results were close to the experimental results. The design specification of the pressure is 5 Pa, and excessive design air supply creates high pressure. This study was conducted in three different models and different ventilation rates. Case 1 had a pressure of 10.8 Pa, followed by case 2 with 11.1 Pa, and case 3 with 10.9 Pa. The difference model conditions in the operating room did not show a significant change in the results of room pressurization. In addition, the different ventilation rates in case 3 made a quite significant change compared to the existing design. The results of operating room pressurization with ventilation rates at 15 ACH, 22 ACH, and 29 ACH were 9.2 Pa, 10.9 Pa, and 13.6 Pa, respectively. Increasing the ventilation rates makes the pressurization higher, but when it decreases, it is still larger than the design requirement minimum at 5 Pa.

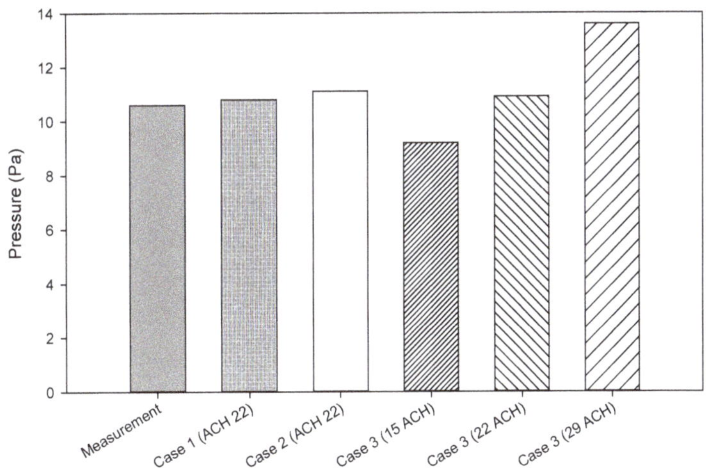

Figure 10. Pressurization effect with different schemes.

5. Conclusions

This research investigates indoor environmental parameters for the operating room through field measurement tests. CFD simulations were also conducted to investigate and analyze the operating room performance in different schemes. The conclusions are as follows:

- The experimental data were retrieved during unoccupied conditions (at-rest), and this condition reached the design specification following ASHRAE 170 standard and ISO 14644.
- The results of concentration contamination and bioaerosol flow path revealed that case 1 presents a good airflow distribution and less particle concentration when unoccupied with the average concentration value of 404 ppm, while case 2 generated a higher concentration while performing a surgery with an average concentration value of

420 ppm. Then, some medical equipment blocked the outlet air in case 3, resulting in the highest concentration with an average concentration value of 474 ppm.

- Increasing the ventilation rates could result in a lower concentration. Increasing ventilation rates does not always present a good concentration dilution, but the air distribution pattern could also affect it. Some medical equipment is recommended not to block the outlet air grilles for dilution purposes. The average concentration in case 3 with different ventilation rates: 15 ACH, 22 ACH, and 29 ACH were 495 ppm, 474 ppm, and 446 ppm, respectively.
- According to case 1, the ventilation efficiency in case 2 and case 3 dropped around 6% and 17.91%, respectively. Ventilation efficiency also decreased along with decreasing ACH, while with increasing ACH, the ventilation efficiency in the case 3 actual condition increased, approaching case 2 in an ideal condition.
- The blocked return air also affected the bioaerosol distribution that could not be directly removed or diluted through the outlet. It could obstruct the flow path resulting in the airflow distribution that could carry the particles reaching almost the ceiling corner, and even deposited in behind the surgical table.
- The reduction in ventilation could increase the concentration inside the room and would not be possible to implement when the operating room is performing surgery. The reduction also has a limitation that should be met with the design requirements such as temperature, relative humidity, pressurization, and particle counts. It could be implemented during the unoccupied state condition to achieve energy saving.

Author Contributions: Conceptualization, F.W., I.P. and D.R.; Data curation, I.P. and B.Y.P.; Formal analysis, I.P., D.R. and B.Y.P.; Investigation, F.W., I.P. and B.Y.P.; Methodology, I.P.; Validation, I.P.; Visualization, I.P.; Writing—original draft, I.P.; Writing—review and editing, F.W. and D.R. All authors have read and agreed to the published version of the manuscript.

Funding: This study was supported by the Ministry of Science and Technology under the grant no. MOST 109-2622-E-167-002-CC3.

Institutional Review Board Statement: Not applicable.

Informed Consent Statement: Not applicable.

Conflicts of Interest: The authors declare no conflict of interest.

References

1. Guo, L. Implementation of a risk management plan in a hospital operating room. *Int. J. Nurs. Sci.* **2015**, *2*, 348–354. [CrossRef]
2. Munoz-Price, L.S.; Birnbach, D.J.; Lubarsky, D.A.; Arheart, K.L.; Fajardo-Aquino, Y.; Rosalsky, M.; Cleary, T.; DePascale, D.; Coro, G.; Namias, N.; et al. Decreasing operating room environmental pathogen contamination through improved cleaning practice. *Infec. Cont. Hosp. Epidemiol.* **2012**, *33*, 897–904. [CrossRef] [PubMed]
3. Koenigshofer, D.; Likhonin, P. HVAC Systems in Hospitals. Engineered Systems Magazine. 2017. Available online: https://www.esmagazine.com/articles/98525-hvac-systems-in-hospitals (accessed on 6 August 2021).
4. ANSI/ASHRAE/ASHE Standard 170. *Ventilation of Health Care Facilities*; American Society of Heating, Refrigerating, and Air-Conditioning Engineers, Inc.: Atlanta, GA, USA, 2017.
5. ANSI/ASHRAE/ASHE Standard 62.1. *Ventilation and Acceptable Indoor Air Quality*; American Society of Heating, Refrigerating, and Air-Conditioning Engineers, Inc.: Atlanta, GA, USA, 2019.
6. Aganovic, A.; Cao, G.; Stenstad, L.I.; Skogås, J.G. Impact of surgical lights on the velocity distribution and airborne contamination level in an operating room with laminar airflow system. *Build. Environ.* **2017**, *126*, 42–53. [CrossRef]
7. Kai, T.; Ayagaki, N.; Setoguchi, H. Influence of the arrangement of surgical light axes on the air environment in operating rooms. *J. Healthc. Eng.* **2019**, *2019*, 4861273. [CrossRef]
8. Chow, T.T.; Lin, Z.; Bai, W. The integrated effect of medical lamp position and diffuser discharge velocity on ultra-clean ventilation performance in an operating theatre. *Indoor Built Environ.* **2006**, *15*, 315–331. [CrossRef]
9. Sadeghian, P.; Wang, C.; Duwig, C.; Sadrizadeh, S. Impact of surgical lamp design on the risk of surgical site infections in operating rooms with mixing and unidirectional airflow ventilation: A numerical study. *J. Build. Eng.* **2020**, *31*, 101423. [CrossRef]
10. Liu, Z.; Zhang, M.; Cao, G.; Tang, S.; Liu, H.; Wang, L. Influence of air supply velocity and room temperature conditions on bioaerosols distribution in a class I operating room. *Build. Environ.* **2021**, *204*, 108116. [CrossRef]
11. Wang, F.J.; Lai, C.M.; Cheng, T.J.; Liu, Z.Y. Performance evaluation of indoor environment parameters for an unoccupied operating room. *ASHRAE Trans.* **2011**, *117*, 557–564.

12. Jarvis, I.; Vahabi, F. Operating Room Ventilation Systems Best Practices Guide for Energy Efficiency, Health and Safety. A Greening Healthcare Research Project. 2017. Available online: https://www.enerlife.com/wp-content/uploads/2017/06/Enerlife-OR-Ventilation-Best-Practices-Guide-April-2017.pdf (accessed on 14 July 2021).
13. Wang, F.J.; Hung, J.; Chen, Y.; Hsu, C. Performance evaluation for operation rooms by numerical simulation and field measurement. *Int. J. Vent.* **2017**, *16*, 189–199. [CrossRef]
14. Wang, C. Ventilation Performance in Operating Rooms: A Numerical Assessment. Doctoral Thesis, KTH Architecture and The Built Environment, Stockholm, Sweden, 2019.
15. Bombač, M.; Novak, G.; Mlačnik, J.; Četina, M. Extensive field measurements of flow in vertical slot fishway as data for validation of numerical simulations. *Ecolog. Eng.* **2015**, *84*, 476–484. [CrossRef]
16. Zhang, Z.; Wei, Y.; Tianwen, W.; Yonghan, L.; Yawen, Z.; Guoqiang, Z. Potential of cross-ventilation channels in an ideal typical apartment building predicted by CFD and multi-zone airflow model. *J.Build. Eng.* **2021**, *44*, 103408.
17. Szczepanik-Scislo, N.; Antonowicz, A.; Scislo, L. PIV measurement and CFD simulations of an air terminal device with a dynamically adapting geometry. *Appl. Sci.* **2019**, *1*, 1–9. [CrossRef]
18. Szczepanik-Scislo, N.; Scislo, L. Comparison of CFD and Multizone Modeling from Contaminant Migration from a Household Gas Furnace. *Atmosphere* **2021**, *12*, 79. [CrossRef]
19. Peng, S.; Chen, Q.; Liu, E. The role of computational fluid dynamics tools on investigation of pathogen transmission: Prevention and control. *Sci. Total Environ.* **2020**, *31*, 142090. [CrossRef]
20. Van Hooff, T.; Blocken, B. CFD evaluation of natural ventilation of indoor environments by the concentration decay method: CO2 gas dispersion from a semi-enclosed stadium. *Build. Environ.* **2013**, *61*, 1–17. [CrossRef]
21. Chung, K.C.; Hsu, S.P. Effect of ventilation pattern on room air and contaminant distribution. *Build. Environ.* **2001**, *36*, 989–998. [CrossRef]
22. Cui, S.; Cohen, M.; Stabat, P.; Marchio, D. CO_2 tracer gas concentration decay method for measuring air change rate. *Build. Environ.* **2015**, *84*, 162–169. [CrossRef]
23. ISO 14644-1. *Cleanroom and Associated Controlled Environments-Part 1: Classification of Air Cleanliness by Particle Concentration*; Vernier: Geneva, Switzerland, 2015.
24. U.S. General Services Administration Federal Standard 209E. *Airborne Particulate Cleanliness Classes in Cleanrooms and Clean Zones*; General Services Administration: Washington, DC, USA, 1992.
25. ANSYS. Ansys Fluent, Workbench 2020 R2. Available online: https://www.scribd.com/document/478910198/ANSYS-Fluent-Tutorial-Guide-2020-R2-pdf (accessed on 6 March 2021).
26. Minnesota Department of Health United States. Carbon Dioxide (CO_2). Available online: https://www.health.state.mn.us/communities/environment/air/toxins/co2.html (accessed on 15 June 2021).
27. Moreno-Rangel, A.; Musau, F.; Sharpe, T.; McGill, G. Indoor Air Quality Assessment of Latin America's First Passivhaus Home. *Atmosphere* **2021**, *12*, 1477. [CrossRef]
28. Shih, Y.C.; Chiu, C.C.; Wang, O. Dynamic airflow simulation within an isolation room. *Build. Environ.* **2007**, *42*, 3194–3209. [CrossRef] [PubMed]
29. Brohus, H.; Balling, K.D.; Jeppesen, D. Influence of movements on contaminant transport in an operating room. *Indoor Air.* **2006**, *16*, 356–372. [CrossRef] [PubMed]
30. Suresh, K.; Regalla, S.P. Effect of mesh parameters in finite element simulation of single point incremental sheet forming process. *Proc. Mat. Sci.* **2014**, *6*, 376–382. [CrossRef]
31. Sandberg, M. What is ventilation efficiency? *Build. Environ.* **1981**, *16*, 123–135. [CrossRef]

buildings

MDPI

Article

A Performance-Based Window Design and Evaluation Model for Naturally Ventilated Offices

Hardi K. Abdullah [1,*] and Halil Z. Alibaba [2]

1 Department of Architecture, College of Engineering, Salahaddin University-Erbil, Erbil 44001, Iraq
2 Department of Architecture, Faculty of Architecture, Eastern Mediterranean University, Famagusta 99628, Cyprus; halil.alibaba@emu.edu.tr
* Correspondence: hardi.abdullah@su.edu.krd

Abstract: This study proposes a performance-based window design model for optimised natural ventilation potential by reducing the level of indoor carbon dioxide (CO_2) concentration and improving thermal comfort, consequently minimising supplementary heating/cooling loads. The model consists of several stages: (1) Knowledge acquisition, (2) establishing a relationship between window design and natural ventilation, (3) identifying performance criteria and the design of experiments (DOE), (4) conducting performance-based dynamic simulations, (5) evaluation of findings, and (6) making informed design decisions. The study also proposed an evaluation method by which assessments of indoor CO_2 concentration and adaptive thermal comfort are performed using the threshold suggested by the World Health Organisation (WHO, Geneva, Switzerland) and the acceptability categories of the British/European standard BS EN 15251:2007. The proposed model was applied to a single office inspired by the staff offices at the Department of Architecture, Eastern Mediterranean University, Famagusta, North Cyprus. The findings show that the developed model of performance-based window design enables the handling of various window design variables along with different performance criteria to determine the near-optimal window design alternatives for effective natural ventilation (NV) and mixed-mode (MM) offices. This model can guide architects in making informed decisions in the early stages of office window design.

Keywords: window design; natural ventilation; indoor air quality; indoor CO_2 concentration; adaptive thermal comfort; performance-based design

Citation: Abdullah, H.K.; Alibaba, H.Z. A Performance-Based Window Design and Evaluation Model for Naturally Ventilated Offices. *Buildings* **2022**, *12*, 1141. https://doi.org/10.3390/buildings12081141

Academic Editor: Xi Chen

Received: 11 July 2022
Accepted: 29 July 2022
Published: 1 August 2022

1. Introduction

Air movement for habitable spaces has an important impact on perceived indoor air quality [1]. Studies claim that air tightening within an occupied zone may result in complaints of unsatisfactory indoor air, particularly in air-conditioned (AC) spaces. Recent field studies suggest that elevated airspeed can achieve thermal comfort even at higher temperatures and improve perceived indoor air quality [2].

The importance of indoor air quality (IAQ) is reflected in the increased number of researchers studying various aspects of this topic. Due to the increasing demand for energy-saving and energy-efficient buildings, research into IAQ requires adopting various passive alternatives. In recent studies, the utilisation of natural ventilation to remove indoor pollutants and maintain indoor air quality, along with the indoor thermal comfort of various building types, has been challenged [3]. However, past attempts examined one goal at a time (e.g., indoor air quality, thermal comfort, energy consumption, productivity, etc.) and assessed the ideal environmental conditions for optimising that single target. The findings of previous studies recommend conflicting objectives and emphasise the need to pursue a more integrative approach to indoor environmental quality (IEQ) by tackling more than one criterion simultaneously [1].

Natural ventilation through window openings is the most common means to deliver fresh air indoors [4]. An effective method for maintaining indoor air quality and thermal comfort is window openings controlled by building occupants. It has been proven that window-based NV can profitably replace mechanical ventilation, as well as ventilative cooling techniques using windows, and it can be harvested during free-running periods instead of using AC systems [5]. Therefore, a significant amount of energy consumption and carbon dioxide emissions can be reduced [6,7].

These discussions often note that window design has a strong relationship with NV performance regardless of the building type. Evidently, window design is an early decision for architects, who need adequate knowledge supported by quantitative data and experiments concerning airflow and heat transfer in buildings [8]. This study attempts to bridge the gaps in window design, natural ventilation, indoor air quality, and thermal comfort in a holistic, performance-based design approach that can guide architects in early design decisions.

1.1. Aim and Objectives of the Study

An appropriate window design can maximise the free-running period and thus save a considerable amount of energy and reduce CO_2 emissions. Thus, architects need to understand the elements of window design decisions in terms of NV performance. The primary aim of this study is to develop a performance-based window design model that can optimise natural ventilation performance in terms of reduced indoor CO_2 concentration and supplementary heating/cooling loads, as well as improved ventilation rates and thermal comfort in NV and MM offices.

Accordingly, the objectives of the study are:

- To develop a performance-based window design model for early window design in terms of natural ventilation performance;
- To develop an evaluation model for assessing the findings of the model;
- To test the developed model using a case application;
- To identify the most influential window design parameters and their optimal levels with respect to each selected criterion;
- To demonstrate the trade-off selection method for window design variables among multiple conflicting performance criteria.

1.2. Architectural Considerations for Natural Ventilation

The relationship of natural ventilation with a building is developed using various aspects of architectural design, which Kleiven [9] defined as characteristic elements in his concept of a "natural ventilation system". The decisions on these aspects are mainly made in the early architectural design process, including site selection (building location), planning, landscaping, building form, and envelope-related components [10].

Overall, building envelope elements have a greater impact on natural ventilation performance [11] due to the fact that most of these components are directly related to natural ventilation design, such as openings, shadings, orientation, thermal mass, etc. This study focuses on the effects of the building envelope, particularly those of window design on natural ventilation performance; thus, more details are provided on these topics.

1.3. Window Design Parameters

The glazed envelope is located at the opening of the building's façade and provides a visual connection between the outdoor environment and the indoor spaces. In addition to providing aesthetic value and a view to the outside, windows are the most critical components that affect building performance in terms of indoor air quality, natural ventilation, thermal comfort, daylight, visual comfort, and, essentially, energy performance. According to state-of-the-art research in the reviewed literature, including but not limited to [12–18], the most important window design variables identified are: size, orientation, type, opening, shape, position, separation, glazing, frame, and the availability of shading.

The impact of the window-to-wall ratio on different building performance goals has been studied more frequently, such as in the cases of [19–24]. The reviewed studies report that window size has a significant impact on natural ventilation conditions [25] and indoor environmental quality [26]. An investigation of windows located at the east and west orientations in a hot–humid climate showed that a 25% WWR provided better indoor thermal comfort conditions than a 50% WWR [27]. According to building regulations in North Cyprus, the minimum window size is defined as a 10% window-to-floor area ratio [28]. However, the question of whether this window size is sufficient to sustain the indoor air and thermal conditions of naturally ventilated offices needs to be answered.

Window orientation is considered a significant design parameter in terms of wind direction and solar radiation. A suitably placed window in a specific wall orientation can maximise ventilative cooling potential and minimise direct solar radiation, which is highly important in warm and hot climates. Therefore, window orientation is one of the critical energy-efficient design decisions that influence building envelope energy performance. The results of one study [29] investigating the effect of orientation and envelope insulation appliances found an up to 43% reduction in the resulting cooling load. Researchers [27] conducted an experimental study in a hot–humid climate; they reported that rooms with east-orientated windows had less thermal comfort hours than west-oriented windows in the case of 50% WWR, while both rooms performed similarly when they had a 25% WWR. The optimum window size depends on the window orientation and weather conditions; for instance, WWRs ranging from 10–70% are suggested for different window orientations and climates in Iran, where the difference between the minimum and maximum energy consumption rate is between 20–100% in its hot–humid climate [30].

Window type and natural ventilation are closely related to each other. The basic window types, performance ratings, and glossary of window-related terms are described in the AAMA/NWWDA/CSA 101/I.S.2/A440-08—North American Fenestration Standard/Specification for Windows, Doors, and Skylights [31]. Wang and Chen [32] investigated the impact of different window types, namely, casement, awning, and hopper windows, on single-sided natural ventilation with different opening angles using computational fluid dynamics (CFD) as an airflow prediction method. The findings suggest that the impact of the window type on the ventilation rate varied with the wind direction, whereby the windows and the turbulence effect created different flow patterns. These conclusions were also reported by a similar study [33]. Another study [34] evaluated the influence of different window types on ventilation performance in the residential buildings of Hong Kong using air change per hour (ACH) to quantify natural ventilation. The authors claimed that casement windows are the most effective design solutions, followed by awnings and sliding windows, in that order. It has been reported that casement windows are preferable in warm months, while hopper windows are preferable in cold months for both single-sided and cross ventilation [35]. Moreover, the natural ventilation performance of hopper windows also improves with a different opening angle [36], while the discharge coefficients of casement and hopper windows do not vary significantly [35]. Casement windows allow higher airflows for windward conditions compared to hopper and awning windows; however, hopper windows perform better in terms of overall airflow rates for all wind directions due to fewer obstructions [37].

In naturally ventilated buildings, window-opening behaviour significantly affects indoor air quality, thermal comfort, and energy consumption [38,39]. Closed windows increase the concentration of indoor particles (e.g., $PM_{2.5}$) emitted by indoor particle sources [40]. Window-opening behaviour relies on both subjective sensations, particularly physiology and psychology, and objective factors, which include indoor air and thermal comfort; thus, it is subjected to a fair degree of randomness and uncertainty [41]. It has been found that the duration of window-opening in warm climates is significantly higher than in cold climates, especially during working hours (9:00–17:00) on weekdays, even in residential apartments [42]. Researchers [38,41] identified the major variables in determining the probability of window-opening as the level of indoor CO_2 concentration and outdoor temperature. Furthermore, window-opening prediction models and occupant behaviour have recently come under consideration [43,44], including questions concerning the reliability of simulation tools in handling this matter [45,46]. A few studies claim that occupant-controlled window operation leads to insufficient natural ventilation performance; instead, they recommend automated ventilation control schemes [47–50].

Window shape (or window aspect ratio) is another important parameter that can affect the flow pattern of air indoors. The commonly used window shapes are rectangular (vertical or horizontal) and square shapes. One study [15] tested a number of vertical and horizontal rectangles and square windows with cross ventilation. The square window performed better than both the vertical rectangle and horizontal rectangle windows.

Opening position (or window location) is considered a significant factor that can affect the indoor airflow pattern. Shetabivash [13] studied the effect of various window positions and configurations on natural cross ventilation performance. The window positions the study investigated included placing the windows at the top and bottom of a room in opposite directions (windward and leeward sides). When the windows were placed at the same level but near the bottom of the wall, this presented the least effective scenario. However, window positions perpendicular to each other can improve natural cross ventilation performance [16]. Ventilation flow rate also depends on window separation in a way that low separation (S′~0.1)—aperture separation scaled by building width (S′)—can boost single-sided natural ventilation performance, while a larger separation ($S' > \frac{1}{2}$) inhibits the realisation of this added benefit [51].

A window's thermal performance is typically a function of the glazing, frame, and perimeter details, with the overall goal of achieving the most effective natural ventilation (in the case of openable windows) to maintain IAQ and TC, as well as the best possible daylight transmission with the least heat transmission (e.g., heat gain and heat loss). Overall, glazing thermal performance relies on controlling the level of radiative heat transfer, which is mostly transferred through solar radiation and longwave infrared radiation [52]. One of the most effective ways of improving window thermal performance is the use of low-E coatings on the glass pane. Window frame conductivity is a function of the frame material, geometry, and use of thermal breaks inside the frames. Aluminium, vinyl (PVC), wood, and fibreglass are the common materials used for window frames in the building construction industry.

External window shade is another envelope component that is mainly applied to envelope openings. It is a form of solar control that can be utilised to optimise the amount of solar gain and daylight entering a building. Therefore, it can reduce energy use and, eventually, CO_2 emissions. Window shade has a significant influence on the thermal and visual comfort of occupants, protecting them from overheating and glare. Numerous studies focus on the role of window shades on the energy usage, thermal comfort, and visual performance of buildings [20,22,53–56]. Overall, well-thought-out window parameters (including window size, orientation, and shades) lead to a significant improvement in natural ventilation conditions and thermal comfort, increasing the airspeed by six times and reducing the air temperature by 2.5% [12]. The most effective way to realise the full potential of natural ventilation in the Mediterranean climate is to determine the appropriate window-to-wall area for optimal thermal performance, the appropriate material for glazed windows, and the right shading devices when deciding on the building envelope so that the reliance on active systems is minimized [55].

2. The Proposed Model of Window Design and Evaluation Relative to Natural Ventilation Performance

2.1. Rationale of the Proposed Model

Architectural design is an iterative process of understanding, exploration, and validation in which design assumptions are continuously modified and assessed against the intended performance criteria. Using iterations, designers have the ability to go back and forth through the cyclical process until the design solution achieves a lower risk of failure. Therefore, architects need comprehensive frameworks to explore and evaluate their early design decisions, which eventually affect the upcoming design stages, construction stage, and post-occupancy building performance. The concept of the proposed model originated from a performance-based design approach within the digital design process. In the PBD paradigm, "performance" is defined as "the desirability of the confluence between form and function in a given context" [57]. Unlike generative design (another approach to the digital design process), in the PBD paradigm, the computer does not generate design solutions but "acts as a partner with the designer during the design process" [58]. Hence, a performance-based design approach facilitates structuring the architectural design process to enable architects to make informed decisions in the early design stages [58,59].

Numerous studies have investigated the impact of window design on indoor environmental conditions [11–17,23–27,30,32,34–41,43–49,51,60,61]. Certainly, these attempts confirm the crucial role of window design on occupant health, comfort, and productivity, especially in naturally ventilated buildings. The concept of proposing a comprehensive, performance-based window design model is intended to provide architects with informative feedback about potential design decisions aimed at simultaneously improving IAQ and TC performance. Another significance of the proposed model is that it overcomes the limitations of previous methods in terms of reducing the required time and effort by adopting a practical approach in conducting a minimal number of experiments, called Taguchi design of experiments, to determine the impact of each design parameter on the performance criteria. For reference, in the case of eight parameters, each with three levels (3^8), the full factorial design method requires 6561 runs to test all combinations; in contrast, only 18 runs are necessary (less than 3%) for the Taguchi orthogonal arrays used in the proposed model. In addition, the proposed model facilitates the trade-off selection of design solutions among multiple objective functions as an alternative to the assumed optimal solution for a particular criterion.

2.2. *Components of the Proposed Model*

The proposed model is a performance-based model encompassing procedural methods aimed at ensuring architects make educated decisions early on in the design stage concerning office envelope design, particularly window- and NV-related design parameters. The major stages include (1) knowledge acquisition, (2) establishing a relationship between window design and natural ventilation, (3) identifying performance criteria and the design of experiments (DOE), (4) conducting performance-based dynamic simulations, (5) the evaluation of findings, and (6) making informed design decisions.

2.2.1. Knowledge Acquisition

To start any architectural design process, the predesign stages involve data collection and knowledge acquisition about the project and its requirements. Therefore, the first stage of the proposed model is referred to as the "knowledge acquisition" of the space under design, such as the building location, information about the context and environment, and the building type and function, as well as relative local or international building regulations and codes. These pieces of information serve as design constraints, not variables, and should be considered by designers in defining design parameters in the proposed model.

2.2.2. Establishing a Relationship between Window Design and Natural Ventilation

A well-designed window paves the way for efficient NV performance to improve indoor air, occupant thermal comfort, and, consequently, a reduction in the use of mechanical ventilation and cooling [25]. In addition, airflow rate, windspeed, and indoor temperature are directly proportional to the various window design variables [60,61].

This stage combines the design of envelope-related components and a natural ventilation strategy. The model concentrates on the design of wall glazing in relation to NV performance within early building envelope design; nevertheless, other envelope-related design parameters can also be studied using the proposed model. Natural ventilation types (i.e., wind-driven and buoyancy-driven) and classifications (i.e., single-sided and cross ventilation) are defined by the window design parameters, for which the amount of airflow that enters and leaves the space is determined accordingly. Therefore, this stage establishes a relationship between window design and natural ventilation by developing a correlation between various parameters affecting the ventilation rates and, consequently, indoor air and thermal conditions.

2.2.3. Design of Experiments and Identifying Performance Criteria

Design of experiment is proposed as an alternative to full factorial design (FFD), in which the number of necessary experiments can be minimised to a reasonable amount while obtaining all the required information about the sensitivity of the design variables under study. Among the available DOE methods, this study suggests the use of the "Taguchi orthogonal arrays" method [62] as a standard method of experimental design. Furthermore, the data analyses include the analysis of variance (ANOVA) approach and the signal-to-noise (S/N) ratio [63]. Using this performance-based model, architects can select intended environmental performance objectives in the domains of indoor environmental quality and energy efficiency goals. However, in this model, the considered performance criteria are limited to ventilation rates, the indoor CO_2 concentration level, and occupant comfort.

2.2.4. Performance-Based Dynamic Simulations

The British/European standard 15251:2007 recommends "whole year computer simulations" as a reliable method to study and evaluate the indoor environment and energy performance of new and existing buildings. Studies on computer modelling and simulations have shown that computer simulations play a vital role in building design, influencing resident comfort and energy performance by helping to solve building performance issues [64]. Computer simulations of energy modelling require substantial knowledge about the physical and operational characteristics of the building, as well as precise input data on the building and climate. During the application of the proposed model, any validated simulation software can be used, such as computational fluid dynamics tools. In this study, Tas Engineering software version 9.4.4—developed by Environmental Design Solutions Limited (EDSL) [65]—was used to conduct the computational dynamic thermal simulations and fulfil this stage of the study.

2.2.5. Evaluation and Decision-Making

This stage covers the evaluation of the analytical and numerical findings from simulation experiments, on the basis of which informed decisions can be made. The evaluation method comprises the assessment of each measurement indicator of the selected performance criteria, namely ventilation rate, carbon dioxide concentration, thermal comfort, and supplementary heating/cooling loads using a relevant and recommended calculated indicator. Following the evaluation of findings and data analysis, architects can make informed decisions, taking into account whether they are satisfied with the performance of the initial design or the evaluated results, and suggest improvements through the modification of envelope-related parameters, particularly wall glazing variables and NV design. Accordingly, the framework of the proposed model is developed and illustrated in Figure 1.

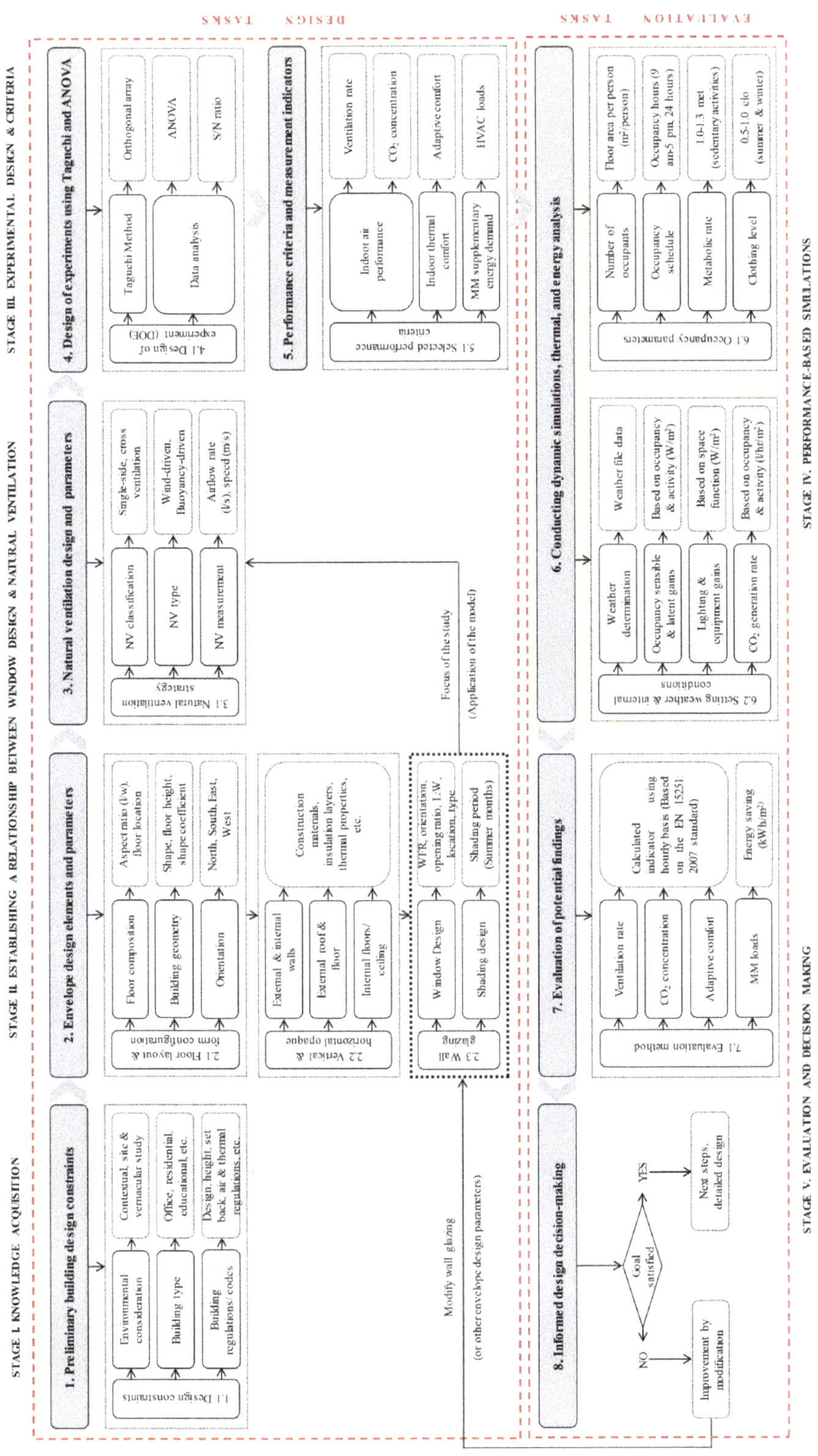

Figure 1. The framework of the proposed model.

2.3. Evaluation Method of the Findings

The BS EN 15251:2007 standard in Annex I (see Table 1) contains a classification of indoor environmental assessments based on building status [66]. The developed model addresses the early design of office spaces by assessing the impact of various architectural design variables on the indoor environment, as well as the energy performance of a mixed-mode strategy (if applicable). Consequently, it applies a year-round hourly dynamic computer simulation based on the classification method suggested in the BS EN 15251:2007 standard. The objective is to guide decision-making in the early design phases and apply building performance simulation (BPS) at the outset of the design process in a PBD approach. The effectiveness of window design and its implications for NV performance were assessed in terms of the ventilative cooling potential for IAQ and TC and the additional HVAC load needed to maintain indoor environmental conditions when natural ventilation proved insufficient due to extreme weather conditions.

Table 1. Classification of methods used for indoor environmental assessment [66].

Category	Evaluation Method	Building Status
a	Criteria used for energy calculations (design indicators)	New buildings
b	Whole-year computer simulations of the indoor environment and energy performance (calculated indicators)	New and existing buildings
c	Long-term measurement of selected parameters for the indoor environment (measurements)	Existing buildings
d	Subjective responses from occupants (questionnaire)	Existing buildings

According to the BS EN 15251:2007 standard [66], the "calculated indicators of indoor environment method include the (1) simple indicator, (2) hourly criteria, (3) degree hours criteria, and (4) overall thermal comfort criteria (weighted PMV criteria)". The hourly criteria indicator was adopted in this study, which allows building performance to be assessed based on the percentage of time (%) and/or number of hours (h) during which the intended criteria were met.

This research is limited to examining and evaluating the performance of window-based natural ventilation in diluting indoor carbon dioxide and maintaining acceptable indoor air and thermal comfort for the building occupants. Hence, the considered measurement criteria are the ventilation rate and CO_2 level, thus assessing indoor air performance and predicting the thermal sensation of occupants using the adaptive comfort model to evaluate indoor thermal comfort in free-running buildings while also lowering HVAC loads in mixed-mode spaces. The evaluation model for assessing the potential findings from the proposed model is illustrated in Figure 2.

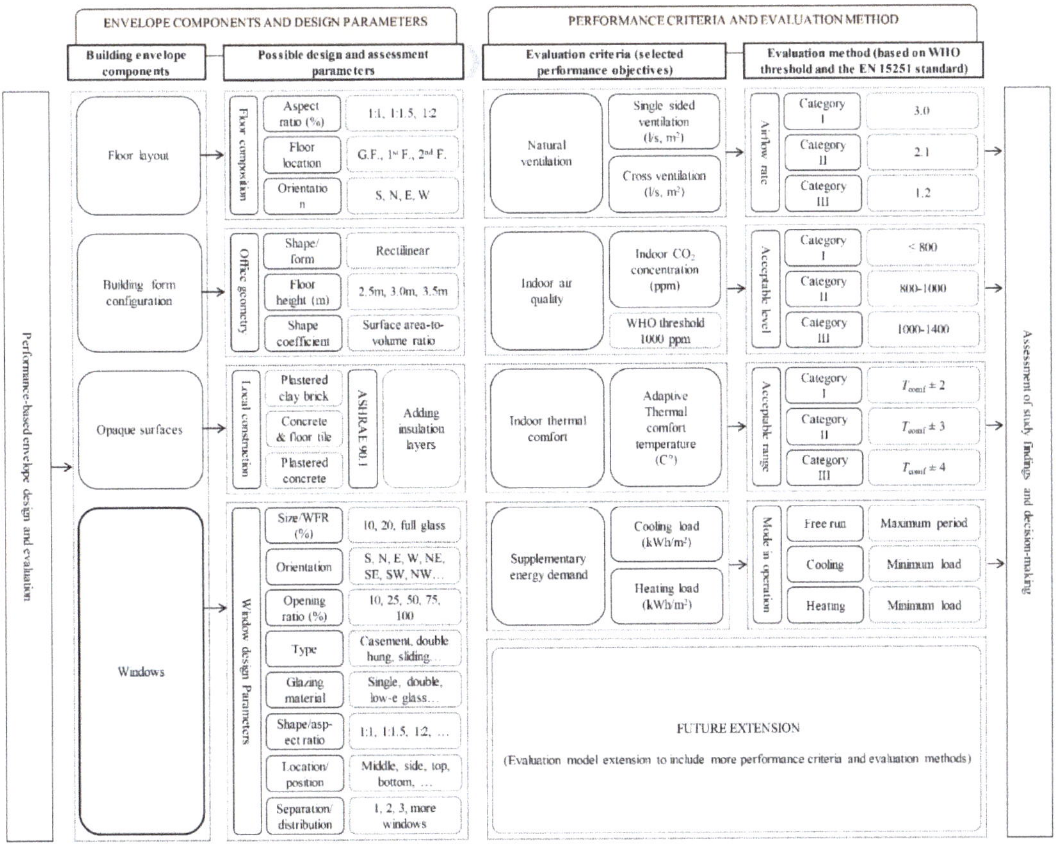

Figure 2. Evaluation model used to assess findings from the proposed window design model.

2.3.1. Assessment of Indoor Air Performance

The assessment of indoor air is limited to ventilation rates and carbon dioxide levels. Other common measurements of IAQ include concentrations of formaldehyde (HCHO) and volatile organic compounds (VOCs), which were not considered in this study. The concentration of carbon dioxide in an indoor space is often a reliable indicator of the quality of the space. CO_2 concentration has also been used in previous studies to evaluate the ventilation performance of indoor spaces using the "gas tracer method" in field experiments or through dynamic building simulations. The benchmark limits of acceptable carbon dioxide concentrations in indoor spaces are defined by multiple standards and guidelines, including: the WHO [67], ASHRAE 62.1 [68], BS EN 15251 [66], and EN 13779 [69] standards. The World Health Organisation [67] recommends 1000 ppm as the upper limit of CO_2 concentration, after which higher concentration levels are an indication of poor ventilation, significantly increasing the likelihood of indoor air quality problems and resulting in sick building syndrome [70].

In the same vein, the BS EN 15251:2007 standard [66] classifies indoor CO_2 levels into different categories. The ASHRAE 62.1 standard similarly endorses the 1000 ppm threshold specified by the WHO, which is within the Category II range of indoor carbon dioxide concentration specified by the BS EN 15251:2007 standard. The 1000 ppm threshold recommended by the WHO was utilised in this study to evaluate the natural ventilation performance of different types of offices. Table 2 outlines the various standards addressing the level of indoor carbon dioxide concentration.

Table 2. Indoor carbon dioxide concentration thresholds defined by relative standards.

Standard	CO_2 Concentration (ppm)	Method
WHO	1000 ppm	Threshold
ASHRAE 62.1	1100 ppm	Threshold
BS EN 15251:2007	900 ppm, 1200 ppm	Category II, III

2.3.2. Assessment of Ventilation Rates

Natural ventilation efficiency can be evaluated based on the amount of fresh air delivered to indoor spaces from the outdoor environment. The airflow rate can be evaluated through the relevant standards for determining the acceptability of indoor air quality and ventilation rates, including the ASHRAE 62.1 [68], BS EN 15251 [66], and EN 13779 [69] standards. The minimum ventilation rates outlined in these standards are determined based on the type of building, occupancy, and/or floor area. The breathing zone outdoor airflow (V_{bz}) in the ASHRAE 62.1 standard is calculated using Equation (1). Similarly, the BS EN 15251:2007 uses Equation (2) to calculate the overall ventilation rates (q_{tot}) for indoor spaces based on the building emission ventilation rates (q_B). It is noteworthy that, despite the fact that both standards adopt similar logics, they do not necessarily produce identical outputs. The ventilation rate calculation method suggested in the BS EN 15251:2007 standard was utilised in the proposed evaluation model. Table 3 outlines the recommended ventilation rates for office spaces. It is worth mentioning that the ventilation rate for smoking was omitted due to the prohibition on smoking in offices.

$$V_{bz} = R_p \cdot P_z + R_a \cdot A_z \quad (1)$$

where R_p is the airflow rate per person (L/s·pers), P_z is the number of occupants, R_a is airflow per unit area (L/s·m^2), and A_z is the zone floor air (m^2).

$$q_{tot} = n \cdot q_p + A \cdot q_B \quad (2)$$

where q_{tot} is the total ventilation rate of the space (L/s), n is the number of occupants, q_p is the airflow rate per person (L/s·pers), A is the zone floor air (m^2), and q_B is the airflow rate for building emissions (L/s·m^2).

Table 3. Ventilation rates (L/s·m^2) for non-low polluted offices defined by the BS EN 15251 standard [66].

Building Type	Category	Occupancy Density (m^2/pers)	Ventilation Rate (L/s·m^2)		
			Occupancy (q_p)	Building Pollution (q_B)	Total (q_{tot})
Office	I	10	1.0	2.0	3.0
	II	10	0.7	1.4	2.1
	III	10	0.4	0.8	1.2

2.3.3. Assessment of Indoor Thermal Comfort

Indoor thermal comfort is another significant performance criterion that needs to be evaluated when assessing IEQ, especially in warm and hot climates. As stated in the previous sections, the scope of this research is limited to NV—including mixed-mode—buildings; therefore, to achieve more reliable results, the most precise and suitable thermal comfort model should be employed. Fanger's PMV and PPD model [71] is widely used to assess the thermal comfort status of airconditioned spaces, although some researchers claim that the PMV and PPD method overestimates the percentage of occupant discomfort in hot and warm conditions for naturally ventilated spaces [72]. Furthermore, field studies have proved that the adaptive thermal comfort model is better suited to addressing the thermal comfort of users in free-running and MM buildings, owing to the fact that this method takes into account human adaptation mechanisms as a reaction to changes in the outdoor environment [1,73].

The field studies under review take a negative position regarding the classification of the MM system with respect to AC buildings in current thermal comfort standards (i.e., ASHRAE 55 and BS EN 15251), arguing instead that natural ventilation is in use for most of the occupied hours in office spaces. Natural ventilation is described as being synonymous with free-running buildings in the aforementioned thermal comfort standards, for which the adaptive thermal comfort model has been developed using information generated by a variety of field studies. Recent field surveys have found that occupant thermal sensations in NV and MM buildings are better represented using the adaptive model relative to the PMV/PPD model, which does not adequately account for the various ways in which residents can adapt to variations in outdoor weather conditions. Furthermore, adaptive thermal comfort can also be used in conducting climate change impact studies on mixed-mode office spaces [74].

In mixed-mode buildings, indoor thermal comfort involves NV and AC systems, which can be assessed individually using the adaptive and steady-state thermal comfort models, respectively. This study implements an adaptive method to quantify occupant thermal sensations in terms of being comfortable or not in a given period, thereby evaluating the space based on acceptable adaptive model comfort ranges suggested by the relative standards. The British/European adaptive comfort model, stated in the BS EN 15251:2007 standard [66], is used on account of its being less restrictive when explaining the model's applicability conditions compared to the American adaptive model (i.e., ASHRAE 55).

However, because this study focuses on the potential benefits of natural ventilation in office spaces (as a free-running building or under a mixed-mode strategy), the evaluation of indoor thermal comfort is limited to the natural ventilation period by the adaptive thermal comfort of the BS EN 15251:2007 standard shown in Equation (3). The optimal indoor operative temperature is defined relative to an exponentially weighted outdoor running mean temperature, which is calculated for the previous 7–30 days using Equation (4). Depending on the value of constant α, the significance of the resulting temperatures declines over time. The three categories defined in the standard are I ($T_o \pm 2$), II ($T_o \pm 3$), and III ($T_o \pm 4$), respectively representing high, normal (for new buildings), and moderate (for existing buildings) expectations. Table 4 reports the details of the adaptive thermal comfort model of both the American (ASHRAE 55) and British/European (BS EN 15251) standards. Based on the upper and lower limits of the intended category, the number of comfort hours during the occupancy period can be utilised as an indicator in evaluating the thermal comfort performance of a design scenario, and it is formulated by the BS EN 15251:2007 standard as follows:

$$T_o = 0.33 \cdot T_{rm} + 18.8 \quad (3)$$

$$T_{rm} = (1-\alpha)T_{od-1} + \alpha T_{od-2} + \alpha^2 T_{od-3} + \alpha^3 T4\ldots, \quad (4)$$

where T_o is the indoor optimal operative temperature (°C); T_{rm} stands for the exponentially weighted running mean temperature (°C) for the last 7–30 days; α represents a constant between 0 and 1; and T_{od-1} is the daily mean outdoor temperature for the day before, the day before that (T_{od-2}), the day before that (T_{od-3}), and so on.

The significance of the temperatures declines over time, with the speed of decay depending on the value of the constant, α. The equation developers suggested $\alpha = 0.8$ as an appropriate value according to their SCAT database [75].

Table 4. The differences between American and British/European standards for an adaptive thermal comfort model.

Standard	Adaptive Comfort Formula	Category	Comfort Range (°C)		Expectations
			Upper	Lower	
ASHRAE 55 (American)	$T_{comf} = 0.31 \cdot T_{ref} + 17.8$	90% 80%	$T_{comf}+2.5$ $T_{comf}+3.5$	$T_{comf}-2.5$ $T_{comf}-3.5$	High Normal
BS EN 15251 (British/European)	$T_{comf} = 0.33 \cdot T_{rm} + 18.8$	I II III	$T_{comf}+2$ $T_{comf}+3$ $T_{comf}+4$	$T_{comf}-2$ $T_{comf}-3$ $T_{comf}-4$	High Normal Moderate

2.3.4. Assessment of Heating, Ventilation, and Airconditioning Loads

The aim of the mixed-mode strategy is to realise the full potential of natural ventilation using operable windows and maintain the quality of indoor thermal performance by utilising supplementary heating, ventilation, and air-conditioning (HVAC) in extreme weather conditions. This results in significant energy savings, along with a reduction in GHG emissions.

Natural ventilation is typically used in a hot or warm climate when the outdoor temperature ranges between 20 °C to 24 °C [76]. To amplify the impact of ventilative cooling and ensure compliance with the occupants' window-opening preferences, as outlined in the adaptive thermal comfort model, NV operation can be predicted or, alternatively, designed based on automation. Such an automated design will allow the windows to start opening when the indoor air temperature is at 21 °C and fully open when this rises to 24 °C. Practically speaking, the building management system (BMS) will need to be integrated with the necessary control mechanism [76,77].

To reduce the chance of overcooling, the operation of window openings conforms to the cooling/heating temperature ranges suggested by the BS EN 15251:2007 standard for a particular category, such as Category II for normal expectations, as shown in Table 5. The maximum temperature required for cooling in AC spaces is 26 °C, while the minimum indoor temperature for heating is 20 °C. However, occupants in naturally ventilated buildings are able to adapt to a wider range of temperatures relative to the outdoor temperature using a variety of adaptive behaviours [78]. The operation of air-conditioning within the mixed-mode system is regulated by the minimum heating temperature setpoint for Category II (20 °C), while the cooling temperature setpoint is defined by the Category II upper limit of the European adaptive model, as shown in Equation (5). For reference, cooling begins when the outdoor running mean temperature is 30 °C and the indoor operative temperature reaches 31.7 °C.

$$T_{o,u-ii} = 0.33 \cdot T_{rm} + 21.8 \quad (5)$$

Table 5. Heating and cooling temperature ranges for hourly calculation in Category II of the BS EN 15251:2007 standard [66].

Space Type	Metabolic Rate (met)	Clothing Level (clo)	Heating Temp Range (°C)	Cooling Temp Range (°C)
Office (cellular and open-plan)	Sedentary activity (~1.2 met)	Winter (~1.0 clo) Summer (~0.5 clo)	20.0–24.0	23.0–26.0

Lastly, the annual comfort hours provided by natural ventilation (free-running period) are represented by the number of hours when the indoor operative temperature is within the acceptability limits of the adaptive model. Thermal satisfaction can be provided for the remaining office working hours (discomfort period) through mechanical air-conditioning in the mixed-mode system. The total HVAC load of the air-conditioning period is calculated for each design alternative. A comparative study for a particular design solution can be conducted to contrast the performances of the mixed-mode system and full air-conditioning based on the heating and cooling temperature ranges, as defined in Table 5. Therefore, the assessment of HVAC in MM offices is based on maximising the free-running period (only NV in operation) and minimising the AC period using the number of hours, in which a specific mode is in operation during office working hours (occupation), as the calculated indicator.

2.4. Validation of the Model Using Ventilative Cooling Methods

Developed by the National Institute of Standards and Technology (NIST) [79] and further advanced in the International Energy Agency (IEA) Annex 62 [80] framework, the ventilative cooling (VC) method is used in validating natural ventilation performance in comparison to the comfort hours forecasted by the dynamic building simulation. The prevalence of this method is partly due to the growing interest in energy-efficient buildings and reducing greenhouse gas emissions. The VC method is useful for evaluating the potential benefits of natural ventilation during early design stages by accounting for internal heat gains (i.e., lighting, occupancy, solar radiation gains, and equipment gains), the thermal properties of the building envelope, and the airflow rate required to maintain IAQ and TC based on the relevant standards and regulations. Based on local climatic conditions, such an analysis is particularly useful for designer decision-making as it relates to the configuration of the building envelope and layout.

The algorithm used by the model considers the intended thermal comfort criteria and processes annual climatic conditions on an hourly basis. The model is derived from the energy balance of a well-mixed single zone, accepting that the accumulation term of the energy balance could be insignificant in the event that either the space's thermal mass is negligible or the internal temperature is maintained at a relatively constant level. In such an instance, the steady state model defines the thermal response of the zone based on an approximation of the particular climate's ventilative cooling potential, calculated using Equation (6).

$$T_{o-hbp} = T_{i-hsp} - \frac{q_i}{\dot{m}p_{min}} \tag{6}$$

where T_{o-hbp} is the heating balance point temperature (°C), T_{i-hsp} is the internal heating setpoint temperature (°C), q_i is the total internal and solar heat gains (W/m^2), $\dot{m}_{min}$ is the minimum required mass flow rate (kg/s), c_p is air capacity (J/kg·K), $\sum UA$ is envelope thermal conductance (w/K), U is average U-value of the envelope (W/m^2·K), and A is the area of the envelope exposed to outdoor conditions (m^2).

According to this method, heating must be introduced when the outdoor air temperature falls below a certain level in order to preserve the indoor air temperature at a required internal heating setpoint temperature ($T_{i\text{-}hsp}$), which is determined by the heating balance point temperature ($T_{o\text{-}hbp}$). Direct ventilative cooling can be introduced when the outdoor temperature is higher than the heating balance point temperature as a means to counterbalance internal heat gains and maintain IAQ and TC within the required range. However, the utility of VC diminishes when the outdoor temperature is at or below $T_{o\text{-}hbp}$, although acceptable and healthy indoor air requires the provision of the minimum required ventilation rate suggested by the relevant standards, including BS EN 15251:2007 and ASHRAE 62.1.

In AC buildings, the steady-state values constitute the minimum and maximum $T_{i\text{-}hsp}$, taking into consideration the building type, such as the indoor temperature ranges suggested for cooling and heating in office spaces, as previously outlined in Table 5. However, the development of the adaptive comfort model progresses relative to variations in outdoor temperature; consequently, the acceptability limits (ASHRAE 55) or categories (BS EN 15251) for adaptive comfort are used to calculate $T_{i\text{-}hsp}$. As was pointed out earlier, Category II (for new buildings) of adaptive thermal comfort forms the primary focus of this study, the conditions for which are also applied to the analysis of ventilative cooling.

To compare the results of both the VC method and the dynamic simulations, it is necessary to calculate the amount of direct ventilative cooling resulting from an increase in the airflow rate. This can guarantee comfort conditions when the outdoor temperature falls inside the limits set for the comfort zone temperature, taking into consideration the temperature range of the particular category (i.e., Category II of the BS EN 15251 standard). If we accept that conductive losses that occur in the warm months are relatively small compared to the internal gains (i.e., $\sum UA\ (T_{i\text{-}max} - T_{o\text{-}db}) < q_i$), the ventilation rate required for the provision of thermal comfort can be calculated using Equation (7).

$$\dot{m}_{cool} = T_{i-hsp} - \frac{q_i}{c_p(To - db_{i-max})} \tag{7}$$

where $T_{i\text{-max}}$ is the upper limit temperature of Category II (calculated by Equation (5) and $T_{o\text{-}db}$ is the outdoor dry bulb temperature.

3. Model Application: Window Design of a Single Office with Single-Sided Natural Ventilation

3.1. Knowledge Acquisition

In this study, a hypothesised single office with single-sided natural ventilation was proposed, inspired by the academic staff offices at the Department of Architecture, Faculty of Architecture, Eastern Mediterranean University, Famagusta, North Cyprus. The application of various open-plan offices with cross ventilation can be found in [81]. The office floor area is 16.8 m^2, and the floor aspect ratio was taken to be 1:1 (4.1 m × 4.1 m). The clear ceiling height was fixed at 3 m in accordance with the normal floor-to-ceiling height recommended in local building codes and regulations [28]. To examine the effect of an exclusively window-based NV design on the predefined performance criteria, the layout and form configuration, as well as the properties of the vertical and horizontal opaque features, were fixed in all design scenarios. These offices are designed to accommodate just one person; however, the provided space is often used by two persons, or even more, in some situations for a limited period. In this research, it was assumed that two occupants use the space during office hours (i.e., 9 am to 5 pm). Therefore, the floor area per person exceeds the suggested 10 m^2 per user in single offices [66,82], resulting in elevated internal heat gains and, eventually, higher CO_2 releases from occupants.

Due to the size of single offices, the majority of cases utilising such office designs have only one wall with an external condition or exposed to the outdoor environment. Hence, there might be a limit to the amount of fresh air permitted into the indoor space through a window (or windows) from this particular external wall, which is known as single-sided natural ventilation. It is worth mentioning that in North Cyprus, the minimum ratio of the WFR is 10%, and the minimum provided window-opening area is 5% or half of the minimum WFR [28].

3.2. Establishing a Relationship between Window Design and Natural Ventilation

The considered window design variables included window size, orientation, type, glazing property, aspect ratio, location, and shading availability. The levels of window size were 10%, 20%, 30%, and 50% (e.g., an approximately fully glazed external wall) window-to-floor area. The window orientations studied were north, south, east, and west, while the remaining available orientations were excluded. As explained in the previous sections, there are various types of windows relative to their operation. Of these, four common types were investigated in the present study, namely: casement, sliding, double-hung, and single-hung. The selected window types offer different natural ventilation scenarios depending on the driving forces of the NV, such as wind-driven and buoyancy effects. The glazing property is considered one of the most sensitive parameters affecting window performance in terms of indoor thermal comfort. Single-pane glass, double glass, double glass with low emissivity (low-E) coating, and triple glass with low-E coating were tested as various levels of glazing properties. The window aspect ratios of 1:1 (square shape) and 1:2 (rectangle shape), as well as the location of the window placement (i.e., middle or side) in the wall, were other studied variables and their particular levels were taken into account. The availability of shading is another studied parameter that can have a significant influence on window performance. Different design scenarios with either fully shaded windows during office hours or no shading mechanisms were examined as parameter levels to determine the role of shading in the summer period. Shading can be provided using any external or internal means, vegetation, solar shading devices, internal curtains, etc. In this research, external shading devices using horizontal fins (for south-oriented windows) or vertical fins (for east- and west-oriented windows) were implemented. The fins were designed in a way such that they can prevent excessive solar gains during office working hours in the warm months, specifically, May, June, July, August, and September.

The hypothesised office for a single-office design comprises a single thermal zone, which is located on the ground floor. The wall containing the window was defined as an external wall, whereas the other walls were assumed to be internal walls, and the ceiling was also considered an internal surface. Table 6 summarises the construction specifications used in the building performance simulations. The selection of materials and their properties were identical to the case study office building (determined by field observations), representing common construction systems in the study location (determined by studying local building construction guidelines). However, the glazing material was considered one of the window design variables in order to test different compositions.

Table 6. The construction materials and their U-values.

Construction	Description/Thickness	U-Value (W/m^2·°C)
External wall	Light-weight plaster (25 mm), clay brick wall (250 mm), light-weight plaster (25 mm)	0.39
Internal wall	Light-weight plaster (25 mm) and clay brick wall (100 mm), light-weight plaster (25 mm)	0.66
Ceiling/Floor	Ceiling tiles (15 mm), air gap (200 mm), reinforced concrete (150 mm), concrete screed (50 mm), floor wood tiles (10 mm)	1.0
Ground floor	Floor wood tiles (10 mm), concrete screed (50 mm), reinforced concrete (150 mm), crushed stone (75 mm), soil (1000 mm)	0.28
Single glass	4 mm clear float glass	5.75 (Gv = 0.85)
Double glass	4 mm clear float glass, 10 mm air, 4 mm clear float glass	2.96 (Gv = 0.75)
Double glass, low-E	6 mm SG planilux clear, 12 mm air, 6 mm SG cool-lite neutral	1.64 (Gv = 0.35)
Triple glass, low-E	6 mm SG planitherm low-E, 12 mm argon, 6 mm SG cool-lite blue TS 120, 12 mm argon, 6 mm clear float glass	1.0 (Gv = 0.24)
Window frame	3 mm aluminium, 50 mm air, 3 mm aluminium	1.450

3.3. DOE and Selection of Performance Criteria

Table 7 outlines the studied window design parameters and their considered levels. Based on the number of design parameters and their levels, the most appropriate Taguchi orthogonal array is *L*16 (4^4 2^3) for which the Taguchi-based DOE suggests sixteen experiments to understand the whole study as well as the effect of each variable on the intended performance objectives. Thus, Table 8 reports the required design scenarios and the specific levels of each factor.

Table 7. The studied single-office window design variables and their levels.

Level	Parameter (A)	Parameter (B)	Parameter (C)	Parameter (D)	Parameter (E)	Parameter (F)	Parameter (G)
	Size (WFR)	Orientation	Type	Glazing	Aspect Ratio	Location	Shading
1	10%	North	Casement	Single-pane	1:1	Middle	Yes
2	20%	East	Sliding	Double glass	1:2	Side	No
3	30%	South	Double-hung	Double low-E	-	-	-
4	50%	West	Single-hung	Triple low-E	-	-	-

Table 8. Simulation design scenarios based on the Taguchi *L*16 (4^4 2^3) standard orthogonal array.

Simulation Experiments	Factorial Levels							Performance Values
	Parameter (A)	Parameter (B)	Parameter (C)	Parameter (D)	Parameter (E)	Parameter (F)	Parameter (G)	
1	1	1	1	1	1	1	2	P1
2	1	2	2	2	1	2	1	P2
3	1	3	3	3	2	1	1	P3
4	1	4	4	4	2	2	2	P4
5	2	1	2	3	2	2	2	P5
6	2	2	1	4	2	1	1	P6
7	2	3	4	1	1	2	1	P7
8	2	4	3	2	1	1	2	P8
9	3	1	3	4	1	2	1	P9
10	3	2	4	3	1	1	2	P10
11	3	3	1	2	2	2	2	P11
12	3	4	2	1	2	1	1	P12
13	4	1	4	2	2	1	1	P13
14	4	2	3	1	2	2	2	P14
15	4	3	2	4	1	1	2	P15
16	4	4	1	3	1	2	1	P16

Using analysis of variance, the effect of the design parameters on the intended performance criteria was evaluated, including the DF, the SSV, the SSTO, the MSV, the MSE, and factor effectiveness. The S/N ratio was used to identify the near-optimal level combinations of the design variables through a logarithmic transformation of the mean square deviation, where the signal-to-noise ratio of larger-is-better was employed for performance criteria related to NV, and smaller-is-better was applied for supplementary AC loads.

The intended measurement criteria for assessing window design in relation to NV performance were the airflow rates, CO_2 concentration, adaptive thermal comfort, and mixed-mode loads. The calculated indicator for the NV-related measurements was the number of hours in which the criteria were met. That is, the total number of hours at which airflow rate and adaptive comfort are within Category II of the BS EN 15251:2007 standard and the number of hours in which the CO_2 concentration level is equal to or less than the WHO threshold of 1000 ppm. Furthermore, the number of electricity loads (kWh/m^2) required to maintain indoor thermal conditions when NV is not adequate was calculated to evaluate MM air-conditioning loads.

3.4. *Performance-Based Simulation*

3.4.1. Setting Weather Data

The international climate zone classification provided in ANSI/ASHRAE/IES 90.1-2019 [83] and the Köppen–Geiger climate system [84] classify Famagusta (35.1149° N, 33.9192° E) weather under warm–humid or the Csa: Mediterranean climate, respectively. This climate is characterised by cold, rainy, rather changeable winters and dry, hot summers in which July and January are the warmest and coldest months of the year, as described in Figure 3. Figures 4 and 5 show the monthly average diurnal temperature swing and global horizontal radiation and the wind rose of the study location, respectively.

The moderate climate of Famagusta facilitates the adoption of the mixed-mode system to preserve IAQ and TC conditions, which maximises the use of natural ventilation and energy-saving potential. The International Weather for Energy Calculations (IWEC) [85] offers typical metrological year (TMY) hourly datasets, which can be used for dynamic computational simulations. For verification purposes, the TMY datasets were compared to hourly weather data for 2019, measured by an official local metrological office. The comparison indicated the relative consistency and accuracy of the TMY datasets, which represent real conditions.

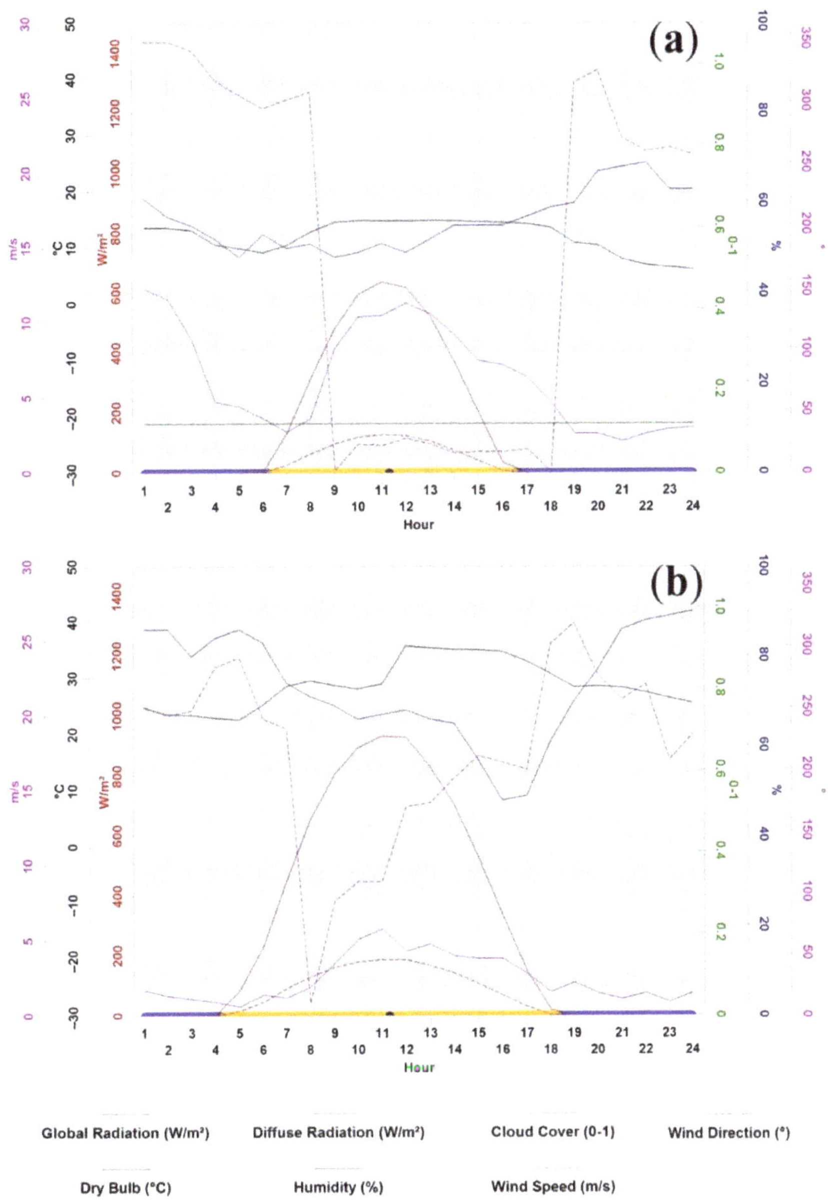

Figure 3. Famagusta climate characteristics on (**a**) 21st January and (**b**) 21st July.

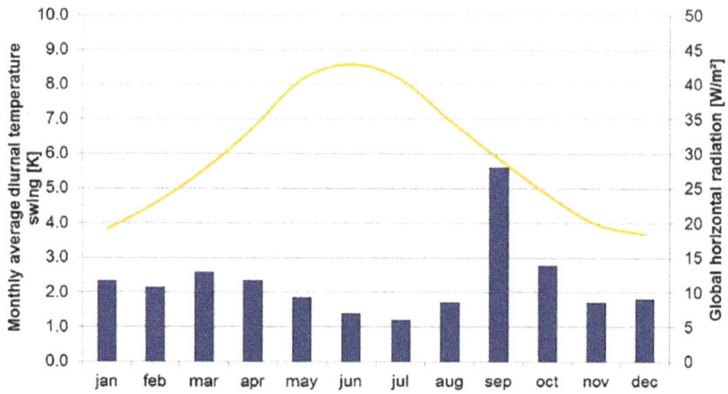

Figure 4. Monthly average diurnal temperature swing and global horizontal radiation.

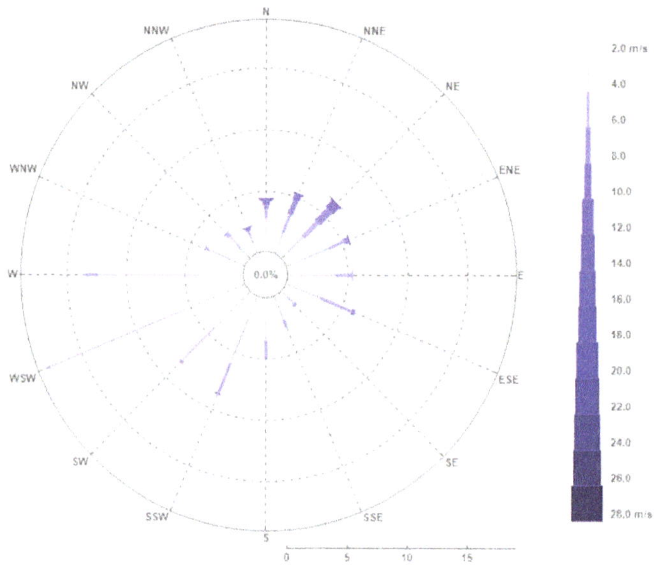

Figure 5. Wind speed and wind directions in Famagusta.

3.4.2. Benchmark Values for Internal Heat Gains and Schedules

The empirical-based benchmark values suggested by the Chartered Institution of Building Services Engineers (CIBSE) Guide A: Environmental Design [82] were employed to define the internal heat gains of the single thermal zone (office space); refer to Table 9. For occupancy, electrical equipment, and 500 lux artificial light schedules, the internal gains of the highest possible scenario (k = 1.0) were accounted for, corresponding to 45.0 W/m^2, the average total internal heat gain (Q_{int}). Finally, 0.3 ach was set for infiltration, and in order to determine only natural ventilation potential, no mechanical ventilation was assigned to the mixed-mode system.

The ASHRAE 55 standard [86] and ASHRAE standard [87] predict a metabolic rate of 1.2 met for office activities (e.g., sedentary and light office work), which corresponds to 125.7 W/person. Based on the Du Bois method [88], an average-sized adult releases 0.0052 L/s carbon dioxide, which is described in the ASHRAE 62.1 standard (ventilation for acceptable indoor air quality) [68]. In accordance with the 8.4 m^2 office area per person in this specific case study, the total CO_2 generation rate was 2.22 l/h/m^2.

Table 9. Schedules and loads assigned to calculate internal heat gains for the study of a single office.

Building Type		Office
Operation time	Time	09:00–17:00
	Hours/day	8.0
	Days/week	5.0
Occupancy	Usage rate (0–1 *k*)	1.0
	Metabolic rate (met)	1.2
	Density (m^2/pers)	8.4
	Total (W/m^2)	15.0
Lighting	Usage rate (0–1 *k*)	1.0
	Power (W/m^2)	12.0
Equipment	Usage rate (0–1 *k*)	1.0
	Power (W/m^2)	18.0

4. Results and Discussion

4.1. Impact of Window Design Variables on the Studied Performance Criteria

To appraise the window design variables and their respective levels, the annual acceptable hours, specified in the category ranges, for ventilation rate, carbon dioxide concentration, and adaptive thermal comfort were calculated. In addition, the annual air-conditioning loads for each design experiment, defined by the Taguchi *L*16 (4^4 2^3) orthogonal array, was measured and are displayed in Table 10 and Figure 6.

The sixteen representative runs indicate that scenarios 15 and 11 provide more acceptable comfort hours in terms of the ventilation rate, CO_2, and thermal comfort compared to other simulated cases. In scenario 15, airflow rates were inside Category II for about 1573 occupancy hours (75.3%), carbon dioxide less than 1000 ppm was recorded for 1740 h (83.3%), and thermal comfort was within the Category II range of adaptive comfort for 1391 h (66.6%). The initial interpretation for this case could be the suitability of a larger window size, which provides more fresh air and ambient air-cooling potential, particularly when the window is placed at a southern orientation. In contrast, for example, these combinations required a higher energy demand for mechanical cooling (14.7 kWh/m^2) than scenario 9 (12.9 kWh/m^2), which means that larger window sizes contribute to a higher internal heat gain by allowing for a greater amount of solar radiation, particularly when solar shading does not exist.

Table 10. The total annual acceptable hours for VR, CO_2, and TC, as well as air-conditioning loads for the set of the Taguchi *L*16 (4^4 2^3) simulation scenarios.

Design Cases	Design Parameters							Measured Performance Criteria			
	Size (WFR)	Window Orientation	Window Type	Glazing Property	Aspect Ratio	Window Location	External Shading	VR (h)	CO_2 (h)	TC (h)	AC Load (kWh/m^2)
1	10	N	Casement	Single g.	1:1	Middle	No	644	1044	923	18.1
2	10	E	Sliding	Double g.	1:1	Side	Yes	412	954	894	21.5
3	10	S	D-hung	D. low-E	1:2	Middle	Yes	745	1200	1034	15.3
4	10	W	S-hung	Triple g.	1:2	Side	No	429	982	976	18.8
5	20	N	Sliding	D. low-E	1:2	Side	No	1016	1298	987	14.6
6	20	E	Casement	Triple g.	1:2	Middle	Yes	1037	1331	1020	15.7
7	20	S	S-hung	Single g.	1:1	Side	Yes	952	1382	1251	18.1
8	20	W	D-hung	Double g.	1:1	Middle	No	1094	1362	1072	21.4
9	30	N	D-hung	Triple g.	1:1	Side	Yes	1171	1422	1020	12.9
10	30	E	S-hung	D. low-E	1:1	Middle	No	1090	1312	1076	21.5
11	30	S	Casement	Double g.	1:2	Side	No	1514	1634	1189	21.2
12	30	W	Sliding	Single g.	1:2	Middle	Yes	1138	1373	954	22.2
13	50	N	S-hung	Double g.	1:2	Middle	Yes	1151	1359	976	20.1
14	50	E	D-hung	Single g.	1:2	Side	No	1224	1442	1086	50.1
15	50	S	Sliding	Triple g.	1:1	Middle	No	1573	1740	1391	14.7
16	50	W	Casement	D. low-E	1:1	Side	Yes	1277	1498	1033	17.3

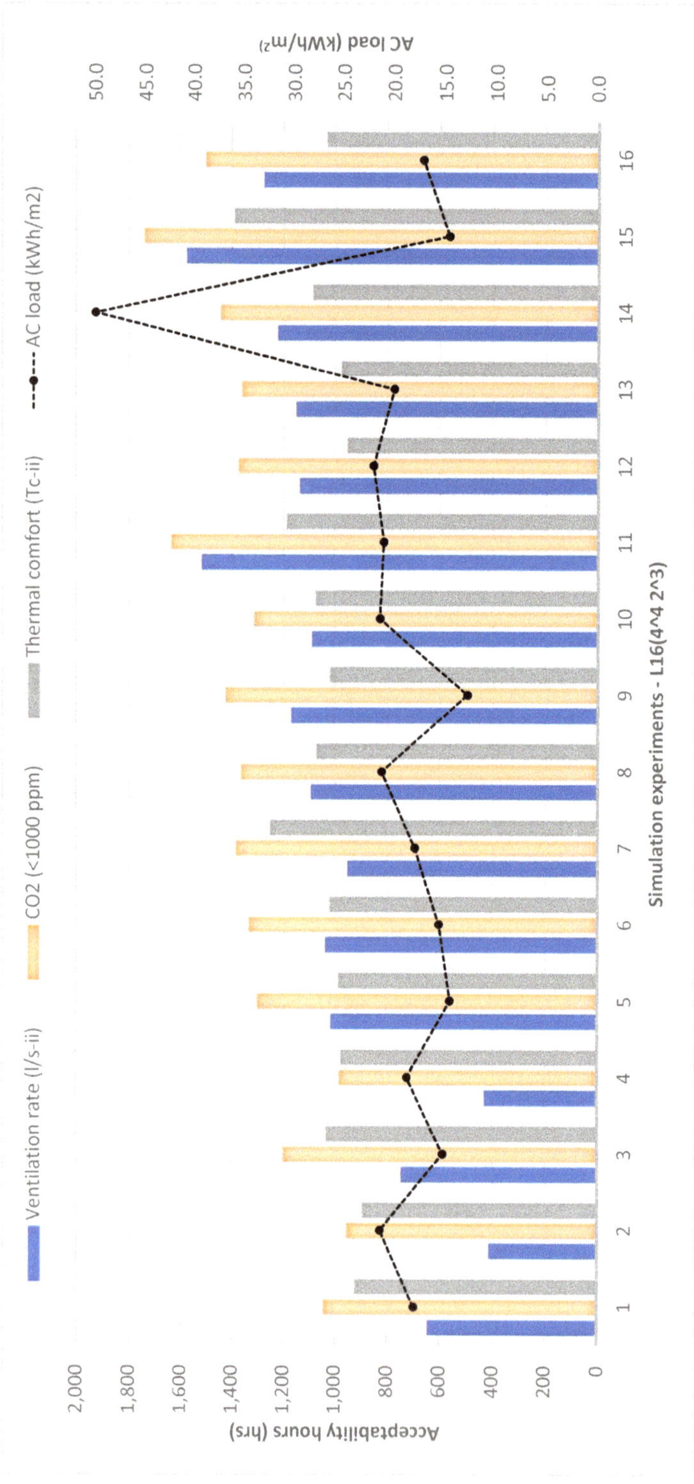

Figure 6. Annual acceptability hours of the VR, CO_2 and TC, and AC loads for the 16-simulation runs suggested by the Taguchi *L16* (4^4 2^3) orthogonal array.

Using the analysis of variance method, the factor effect (percentage contributions) of the window design variables were perceived, as outlined in Tables 11–14. It can be concluded that window size has the highest impact on airflow and CO_2 concentration at 81.59% and 73.54%, respectively, followed by the window orientation and type. Moreover, the window aspect ratio and location have the least influence on the studied performance objectives, for which the factor effect does not surpass 1.1% in any cases.

Contrarily, the factor effect of the window design parameters indicates different patterns when the acceptability hours of the adaptive thermal comfort are considered: window orientation comes in first at 58.12%, followed by window size (24.25%) and shading (6.85%). The air-conditioning load needed to maintain indoor thermal conditions is highly affected by glazing property (29.36%), window orientation (26.52%), window size (14.79%), window type (11.44%), and the availability of external shading devices or other useful shading means (8.09%). Thus, the role of solar radiation is crucial to indoor thermal comfort, as well as AC loads, particularly in the absence of solar shading. Window location and aspect ratio have a lesser influence compared to other design variables, in which the percentages of contribution were calculated at 3.72% and 6.08%, respectively.

Table 11. Factor effect percentages to acceptable hours of VR.

Factor	DF	SSV	MSV	Effect	Rank
Size	3	1355593	451864	81.59%	1
Orientation	3	155118	51706	9.33%	2
Type	3	96306	32102	5.80%	3
Glazing	3	9242	3081	0.56%	6
Aspect ratio	1	105	105	0.01%	7
Location	1	14221	14221	0.86%	5
Shading	1	30713	30713	1.85%	4
Residual error	0				
Total	15	1661296		100%	

Table 12. Factor effect percentages to acceptable hours of CO_2.

Factor	DF	SSV	MSV	Effect	Rank
Size	3	498977	166326	73.54%	1
Orientation	3	133147	44382	19.62%	2
Type	3	32188	10729	4.74%	3
Glazing	3	7457	2486	1.10%	4
Aspect ratio	1	564	564	0.08%	7
Location	1	743	743	0.11%	6
Shading	1	5439	5439	0.80%	5
Residual error	0				
Total	15	678515		100%	

Table 13. Factor effect percentages to acceptable hours of adaptive TC.

Factor	DF	SSV	MSV	Effect	Rank
Size	3	59416	19805.4	24.25%	2
Orientation	3	142395	47465.1	58.12%	1
Type	3	1651	550.4	0.67 %	6
Glazing	3	12756	4252.1	5.21%	4
Aspect ratio	1	11990	11990	4.89%	5
Location	1	6	6	0.00%	7
Shading	1	16770	16770	6.85%	3
Residual error	0				
Total	15	244986		100%	

Table 14. Factor effect percentages to AC loads.

Factor	DF	SSV	MSV	Effect	Rank
Size	3	159.83	53.27	14.79%	3
Orientation	3	286.47	95.49	26.52%	2
Type	3	123.61	41.20	11.44%	4
Glazing	3	317.15	105.71	29.36%	1
Aspect ratio	1	65.65	65.65	6.08%	6
Location	1	40.23	40.23	3.72%	7
Shading	1	87.38	87.38	8.09%	5
Residual error	0				
Total	15	1080.32		100%	

After determining the percentage contributions of each design parameter using the ANOVA approach, the signal-to-noise ratio method was then used to identify the most appropriate factor levels, thus obtaining the near-optimal design scenarios that can support early design decision-making.

4.2. *Identifying Optimal Design Alternative*

Using the signal-to-noise ratio method, the most significant level combinations of each design parameter were determined, which represent a near-optimal design scenario. Although this level combination does not necessarily correspond to the optimal case, as discrete levels of the parameters were implied in the analysis.

Figure 7 shows the S/N ratios for the tested design variable levels relative to each intended performance criterion. Figure 7a–c is based on the signal-to-noise of greater-is-better, while Figure 7d applies smaller-is-better. By observing Figure 7a,b, it can be seen that the optimal level combinations for both ventilation rate and CO_2 performance are almost similar, specifically for the factors that represent the most influential variables, confirming the direct proportionality relationship between the amount of delivered airflow and indoor air pollutants. For **ventilation rate** performance, the optimal level combinations are as follows:

- Larger window size (more opening area) (i.e., 50% WFR);
- South orientation;
- Casement or double-hung windows;
- Double glass with low-E coating;
- Longitudinal windows (i.e., an aspect ratio of 1:2) rather than square windows;
- Window located in the middle of the wall;
- No shading devices because external shadings may prevent wind from entering the space.

Concerning **carbon dioxide concentration**, similar level combinations are preferred, except for the glazing property and aspect ratio, in which triple glazing and square windows show better results for the performance of this criterion. By looking at the S/N ratio plot of **thermal comfort**, shown in Figure 7c, the selection of optimal level combinations is as follows:

- Large-sized window (i.e., 50% WFR), noting that 20% WFR performs better than 30% WFR;
- Southern window orientation offers far better thermal comfort acceptance compared to other orientations;
- Double-hung or sliding window types;
- Triple glass or low-E coated double glass;
- Square windows (i.e., an aspect ratio of 1:1);
- Window located in one side of the wall rather than the middle; however, this variable does not make a considerable difference in adaptive comfort;
- The availability of solar shading contributes to better indoor thermal conditions, especially in the case of higher-glazing U-values.

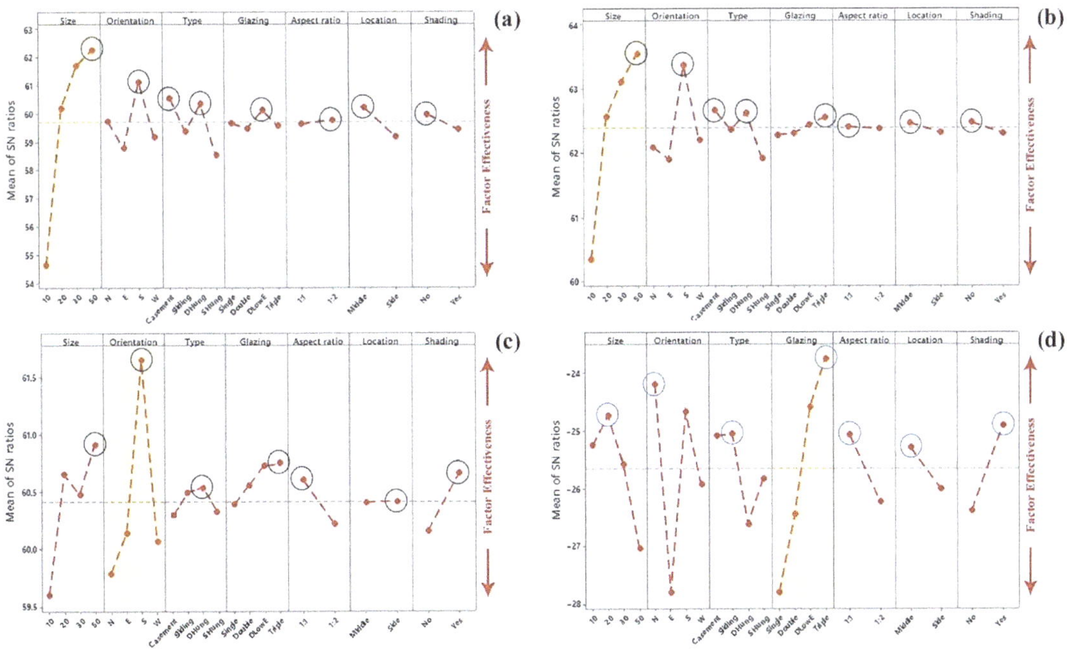

Figure 7. Signal-to-noise (S/N) ratio plots showing the effectiveness of each parameter and optimal factorial levels for (**a**) ventilative rate, (**b**) CO_2 concentration, (**c**) adaptive thermal comfort, and (**d**) AC loads.

The S/N ratio plot of the studied variable levels relative to the performance of **mechanical air-conditioning loads**, shown in Figure 7d, indicates significant differences compared to the performance of the rest of the criteria. Discovered by analysis of variance, the most influential variable was glazing property, followed by window orientation and size. The optimal level combinations include:

- Small to medium window size (e.g., 10% WFR to 20% WFR);
- Northern orientation or southern orientation;
- Sliding or casement;
- Triple glass, followed by double glass with low-E coating;
- Square windows;
- Window located in the middle of the wall;
- The presence of an external shading device.

4.3. Trade-off Selection Based on Near-Optimal Level Combinations

In the multi-objective optimisation approach, the near-optimal level combinations are prescribed by selecting trade-offs between distinct objective functions. Consequently, the most effective level combinations (trade-offs) and their overall performance results for each criterion are outlined in Table 15, followed by their visual illustration in Figure 8.

Based on the S/N ratio results, the trade-off window orientation is south-facing windows with square shapes placed in the middle of external walls. Offices with small windows normally require less energy demand; however, larger-sized windows were found to be the most appropriate scenarios when consciously designed by considering optimal factorial level combinations. For reference, trade-off options 1 and 6 had the same window design features, but a larger-sized window (50% WFR) was assigned to the former, and a smaller window (20% WFR) was provided for the latter; thus, the MM supplementary loads were recorded at 11.66 kWh/m^2 and 12.94 kWh/m^2, respectively. Consequently, the larger-sized window can be a considerably more energy-efficient solution by 10.4% compared to the 20% WFR. In addition, large windows can have a better outside view and aesthetic appearance, while visual comfort risks can be eliminated or lowered using a novel solar shading design.

Table 15. Results of the trade-off design solutions for different window design parameters.

Trade-off Cases	Design Parameters							Measured Performance Criteria			
	Size (WFR)	Window Orientation	Window Type	Glazing Property	Aspect Ratio	Window Location	External Shading	VR (h)	CO_2 (h)	TC (h)	AC Load (kWh/m^2)
1	50	S	D-hung	D. low-E	1:1	Middle	Yes	1511	1749	1466	11.66
2	50	S	Sliding	D. low-E	1:1	Middle	Yes	1502	1746	1451	11.85
3	50	S	Casement	D. low-E	1:1	Middle	Yes	1501	1748	1379	12.41
4	50	S	S-hung	D. low-E	1:1	Middle	Yes	1396	1632	1374	14.96
5	50	S	Casement	Triple g.	1:1	Middle	No	1586	1751	1398	14.56
6	20	S	D-hung	D. low-E	1:1	Middle	Yes	1125	1441	1194	12.94

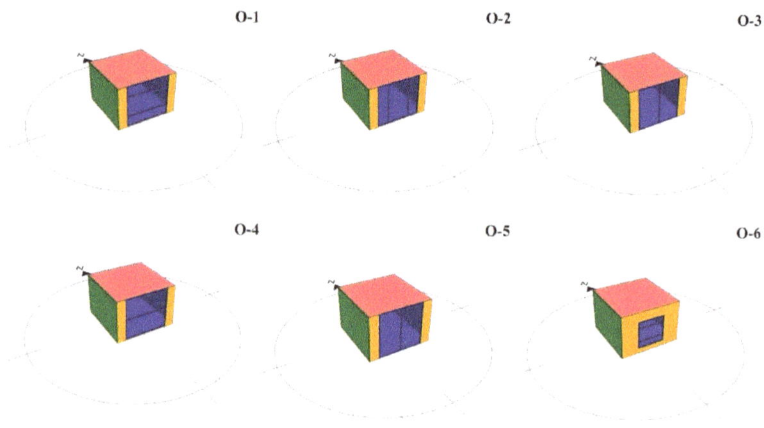

Figure 8. The selected trade-off options for a detailed study of the intended performance criteria.

The same window design characteristics were applied to options 1 through 4, although window types varied. Double-hung windows offer the best possible results for each performance criteria, followed by sliding, casement, and single-hung windows. Such a window design, with trade-off option 1 attributes, provides 72.3% of occupancy hours inside Category II ventilation rates, an 83.7% CO_2 concentration level below the WHO threshold (1000 ppm), and a 70.2% adaptive comfort Category II, and it maintains indoor conditions for 29.8% of hours; altogether, an annual AC load of 11.66 kWh/m^2 is needed. Since double-hung and sliding windows allow effective air circulation, particularly in both the wind-driven and buoyancy effects, natural ventilation might occur through double-hung windows. These results are tangible evidence that needs to be considered by architects when making early decisions concerning the window design of offices in the Mediterranean region and similar climatic conditions.

Shading negatively affects NV performance relative to VR and CO_2 concentration performance, as can be seen in trade-off option 5, which performs better than the previous design scenarios. Nevertheless, solar shading improves indoor thermal comfort and reduces AC loads. In this situation, a double glass window with low-E coating can be more profitable than triple glass. Conversely, if shading does not exist, a triple glass window is essential if high-performance offices are intended.

4.4. Results of Airflow Rates

Table 15 reports the total annual number of hours at which the ventilation rates, for both occupancy and building pollution, were higher than the lower limit of Category II (VR $\geq$ 2.1) for the selected trade-off designs. Despite the constant window size (50% of floor area) and other window design features (apart from window type) assigned to scenarios for trade-off options 1–4, the double-hung window provided more acceptability hours (1511 h) of VR than sliding (1502 h), casement (1501 h), and single-hung (1398 h) windows. Therefore, double-hung windows facilitate effective NV to allow fresh air to enter the space, while sliding and casement windows perform similarly relative to airflow rates.

The optimal design solutions for each of the double-hung, sliding, casement, and single-hung windows offer 72.3%, 71.9%, 71.8%, and 66.8% Category II ventilation rate hours annually during office working hours. Due to cold outdoor conditions, which keep windows closed most of the time, January and February recorded lower airflows than the threshold. Therefore, a minimum airflow rate for acceptable indoor air quality needs to be provided using mechanical ventilation, or alternatively, windows should be opened regularly for a short time to replace exhausted indoor air. In general, the window aspect ratio had a minimal impact on the airflow performance; nevertheless, longitudinal (e.g., rectangle) windows were found to be better than the square shape.

Figure 9 shows the monthly ventilation rates for the trade-off designs selected through the analysis of variance and signal-to-noise ratio approach, in which the double-hung, sliding, and casement windows can accomplish Category II minimum amounts of ventilation rates for all months except January and February using the proposed window-opening scheme and MM cut-off temperature. By comparing the VR of trade-off option 3 to trade-off option 5, one can see that external solar shading (in this case, horizontal fins) reduces the NV potential for the airflow rate by 4.8%, but it can simultaneously enhance ambient air's ventilative cooling potential. The amount of VR reaches 10 L/s·m^2 in the spring and autumn months, when windows are open during most of the occupancy hours; thus, the ventilative cooling potential of ambient air facilitates passive cooling. Finally, the small-sized window, namely, 20% WFR, offers 1235 h of Category II VR, 29.2% less effective in bringing fresh air indoors compared to the same window design inputs in the large window (i.e., 50% WFR).

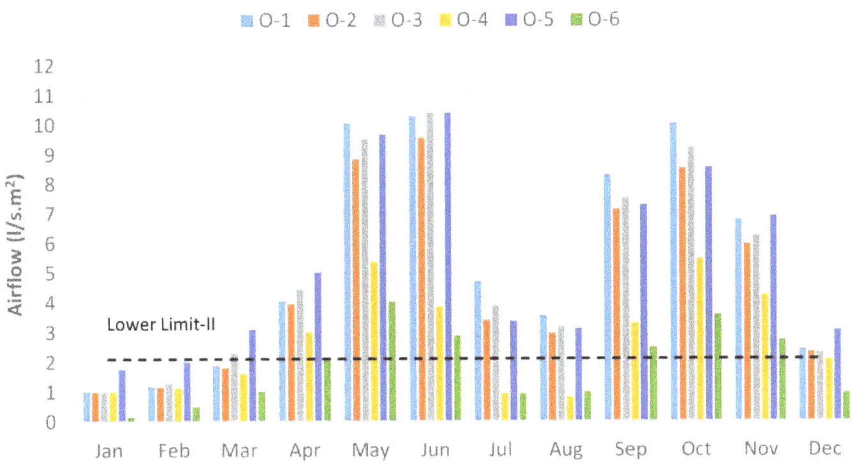

Figure 9. Monthly airflow rates for the studied trade-off design scenarios.

4.5. Results of Carbon Dioxide Concentration

The number of hours for which the level of CO_2 concentration is below 1000 ppm during occupancy time is presented in Table 15. The shaded double-hung window (50% WFR) provides around 1749 h out of 2088 h per annum, corresponding to approximately 83.7% of the time. Moreover, sliding, and casement windows offer approximately 83%, while the single-hung window provides 78.1% of the office hours within the CO_2 threshold. The mixed-mode cut-off temperature of 31.7 °C closed the windows during the harsh summer days, which resulted in increased CO_2 concentration. In the warm and cool periods, the average carbon dioxide concentration was below the WHO threshold. However, when the windows are closed during office working hours, the level of CO_2 concentration exceeded the recommended threshold. For example, CO_2 concentration rose to over 1400 ppm in July and August when the office window was closed all the time due to hot outside temperatures, regardless of the window type, as shown in Figure 10.

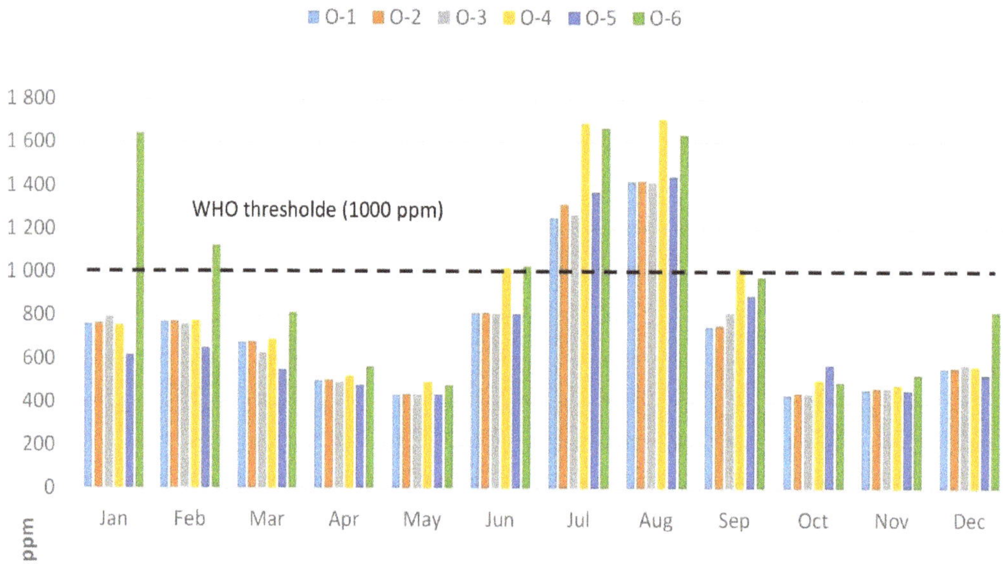

Figure 10. The level of carbon dioxide concentration for the studied trade-off scenarios.

Different window types offered similar results in terms of indoor CO_2 concentration. Conversely, window size had a significant effect on the level of carbon dioxide concentration; for instance, a 20% WFR can only provide 69.0% (1441 h) compared to the same scenarios for a large-sized window (83.7%). In addition to a high indoor concentration in the warm months, a small-sized window can cause health-related problems in the cold months. Overall, larger window sizes, with greater opening fractions, allow more airflow to enter indoors, which can lower the level of CO_2. The availability of solar shading does not make a considerable difference in regard to CO_2 contamination, such as in the case of trade-off options 1 and 5.

4.6. Results of Adaptive Thermal Comfort

In this research, the potential of natural ventilation alone for thermal comfort was studied and reported, and TC during air-conditioning hours was excluded. In other words, the discomfort hours require the operation of mechanical air-conditioning within the MM system. By looking at Figure 11, specifically trade-off options 1–5, the total annual number of comfort hours through NV reaches 90%, meaning that the NV strategy can provide acceptable comfort conditions for nearly all the occupancy time in the cold period. In the other words, these months constitute a free-running period. In June and September, it can cover approximately 40% to 60% of the office working time. However, the minimum number of comfort hours can be found during July (less than 10%) and August (less than 15%) in the summer. Therefore, the AC mode should be working most of the time during July and August compared to the other months.

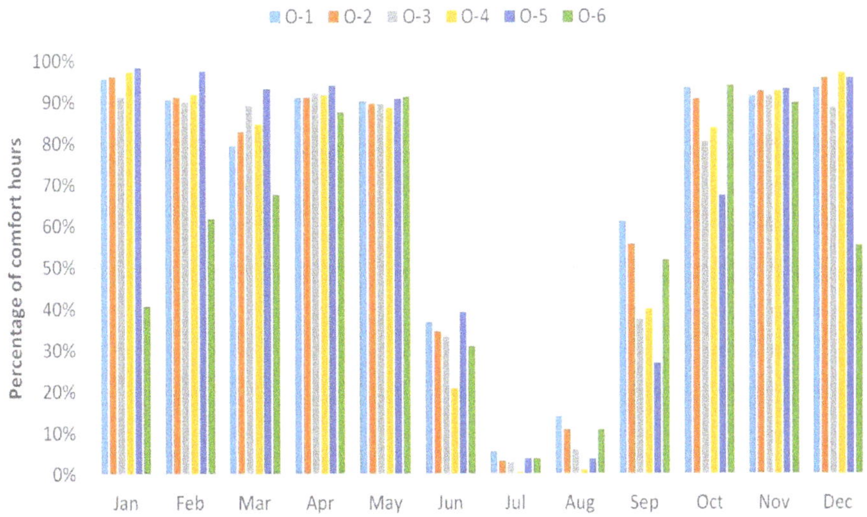

Figure 11. Monthly percentages of comfort hours based on the Category II adaptive comfort limits for the studied trade-off design scenarios.

Nearly all window types with double glass coated with low-E and shading offer similar thermal comfort hours—for reference: double-hung, 70.2%; sliding, 69.5%; casement, 66.04%; and single-hung, 65.8%. In addition, triple glass without shading can offer identical results with a small difference, such as with a casement window at 66.9%. However, a small-sized window (i.e., 20%) can only provide 57.2% comfort hours during office occupancy time. Window location does not have a significant effect on indoor thermal comfort, while a window with an aspect ratio of 1:1 performs better than a window with a 1:2 proportion. Figure 12 illustrates the scatter plot of hourly indoor operative temperature in accordance with an outdoor running mean temperature for each month, employing the Category II upper and lower limits of the BS EN 15251:2007 standard for the optimal design scenarios: (a) O-1 and (b) O-6 (large and small windows, respectively). The hours appearing in between both limits represent the acceptable thermal comfort hours for Category II. The hours exceeding the upper limit correspond to the "too warm" hours in the summertime, particularly in July and August, while those below the lower limit are "too cool" hours in the winter occupancy time.

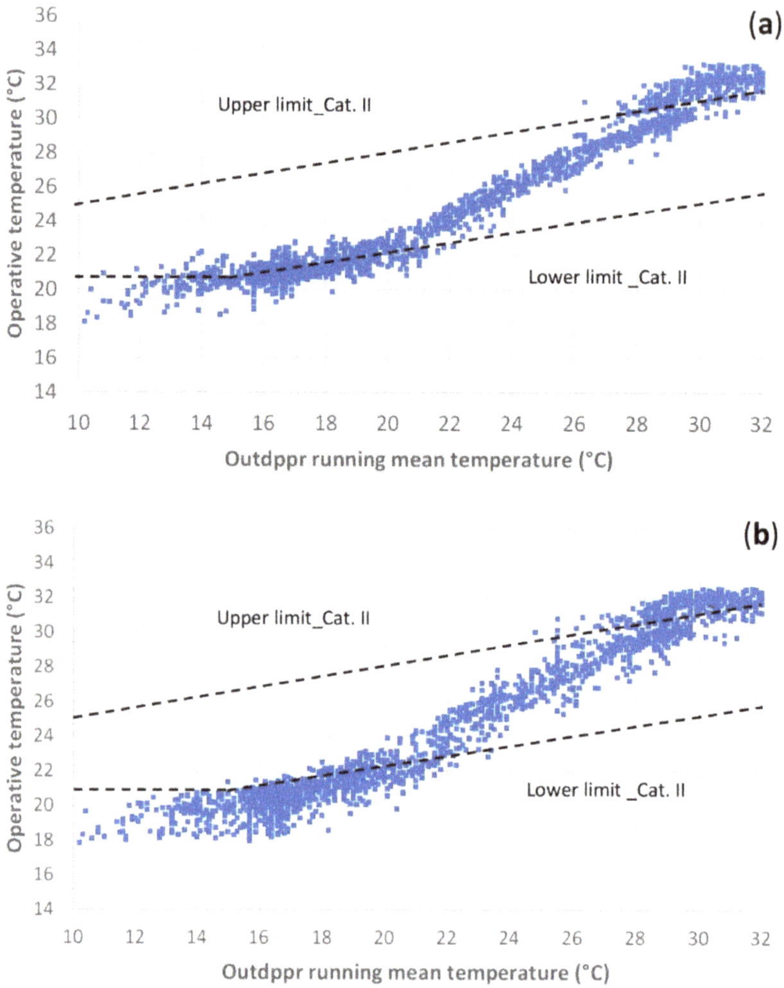

Figure 12. Hourly indoor operative temperature for the adaptive comfort Category II in the case of (**a**) O-1 50% WFR and (**b**) O-6 20% WFR.

4.7. Air Conditioning Loads of the Mixed-Mode Strategy and a Fully Airconditioned Case

The operation of air-conditioning within the mixed-mode system began when the indoor operative temperature was higher than 31.7 °C in the warm period or lower than 20 °C in the cool period. These approximately correspond to the upper and lower boundary limits of Category II in the British/European adaptive comfort standards. All the design variables affect AC loads as well as different factorial levels. Generally, the north façade receives a lesser solar ratio; thus, a lesser amount of air-conditioning loads will be required, especially in the absence of solar shading in the cases of the other window orientations that receive more annual solar radiation. Hence, the S/N ratio showed that smaller windows might spend less on MM air-conditioning compared to unshaded large-sized windows.

Large windows (i.e., 50% WFR) with double-hung, sliding, or single-hung properties are more energy-efficient solutions than windows with size a 20% window-to-floor ratio, as well as with respect to the other studied criteria. A 50% WFR with a double-hung shaded square window located in the middle of the wall and double glass low-E utilises 11.66 kWh/m^2 annually, whereas a 20% WFR, having the same design variables as the large-sized window, needs a 12.94 kWh/m^2 AC load per annum. However, a large-sized shaded casement window with double glass low-E seems to be an inefficient window type in relation to AC load, requiring 14.94 kWh/m^2 annually, which is even more than the unshaded casement window with triple glass (14.56 kWh/m^2). When a designer does not apply a solar shading device, a high-performance window property (e.g., triple glass) must be used to achieve results nearly equal to a shaded window with a higher glazing U-value. Regardless of the window size, glazing property, location, or proportion, windows in southern and the northern external walls constitute the most efficient window orientations; therefore, these windows allow a greater amount of natural ventilation to be harnessed, thus facilitating less dependence on active AC systems.

The monthly air-conditioning loads for trade-off design scenarios are presented in Figure 13. High outdoor running mean temperatures cause elevated indoor operative temperatures in July and August, in which the Category II upper limit, 31.7 °C (cooling setpoint), is surpassed during most office working hours; thus, the maximum AC loads were recorded in these months. In nearly all the design scenarios, the cool period represents the free-running (no mechanical systems in operation) months, while in the rest of the months, both the natural ventilation and air-conditioning modes of the mixed-mode system were alternated. Unshaded high-performance windows (trade-off option 5) and shaded small-sized windows (trade-off option 6) utilise a small amount of AC load in the cool months. Conversely, if the air-conditioning is controlled by the adaptive comfort upper and lower limits of a particular category, the results might not be identical to the previous cases. This study used constant cooling and heating setpoints for the activation of AC; this was due to the limitations of the current dynamic simulation software. In this case, the results of the "comfort hours" indicator can better define the free-running hours. Overall, double-hung and sliding windows are more efficient window types than single-hung and casement windows, respectively.

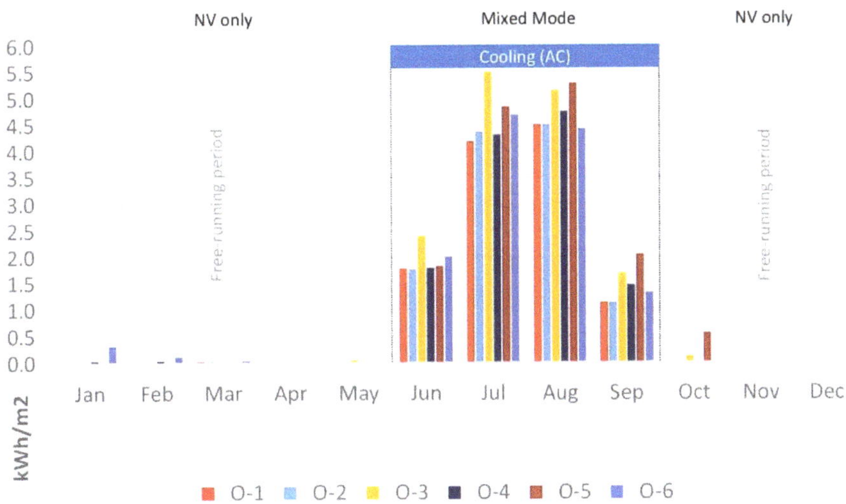

Figure 13. Monthly AC loads for the trade-off design scenarios.

In order to assess the performance of the mixed-mode system against a fully air-conditioned scenario, the air-conditioning loads of the O-1 trade-off design were compared to an identical design case with a fully AC system, using 20 °C and 26 °C for the heating and cooling temperatures, respectively, as suggested in Category II of the BS EN 15251:2007 standard, illustrated in Figure 14. In July and August, the fully AC scenario used more than 11.0 kWh/m^2, nearly 7.0 kWh/m^2 more compared to the MM system. In the heating season, particularly January, February, and March, both MM and AC systems performed similarly due to assigning the same heating setpoint temperature (i.e., 20 °C) to both systems, although the fully AC system consumed more energy. The total annual cooling and heating loads for the fully AC and MM cases were 56.63 and 11.66 kWh/m^2, respectively. Accordingly, the mixed-mode system can reduce cooling and heating loads by 79.41% compared to a fully AC cellular office, taking into account the design specifications of the O-1 trade-off design in the climatic conditions of Famagusta, North Cyprus. An almost similar reduction in air-conditioning loads was also observed in the results of a field study [77], in which the mixed-mode office consumed less than a quarter of the energy required by a similar fully air-conditioned space; a nearly 45% reduction was reported in another study [7].

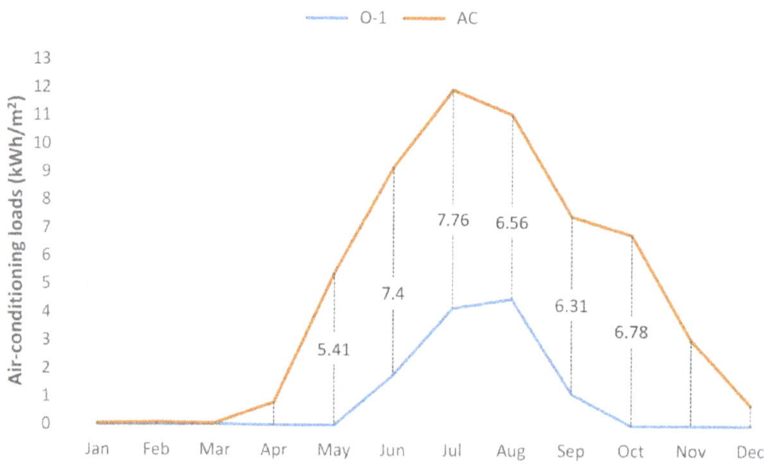

Figure 14. Monthly AC loads for the O-1 design scenario in mixed-mode and fully AC systems.

5. Conclusions

This study presented a performance-based window design and evaluation model for NV and MM offices. The applicability of the proposed model was tested on the window design of a naturally ventilated single office with additional cooling and heating (mixed-mode conditioning) in a Mediterranean climate. Multiple window design variables and levels were assessed using the Taguchi orthogonal array, ANOVA analysis, and S/N ratio approach, which are suggested in the model. The investigations included the study of window size, orientation, window type, glazing property, aspect ratio, location, and window shading in relation to the potential of NV to achieve acceptable indoor air and thermal comfort with significantly reduced air conditioning loads using a mixed-mode strategy. Suggested in the model stages, an hourly dynamic simulation method was utilised to measure the CO_2 concentration levels, airflow rate, adaptive thermal comfort, and cooling/heating loads, taking the hours in which a specific criterion was satisfied as the calculated indicator. The analysis of variance results revealed the effectiveness of each variable on the selected performance criteria, as stated below.

5.1. Contribution of Window Design Parameters to Airflow Rate and CO_2 Concentration

- Window size was in the first rank or scored the highest percentage of contribution (81.59% and 73.54%, respectively), followed by window orientation and type.

5.2. Contribution of Window Design Parameters to Adaptive Thermal Comfort

- Window orientation plays a vital role in providing comfortable indoor conditions, with a percentage of contribution of 58.12%. Window orientation is significantly correlated with the position of the sun and the direction of the wind, determining the amount of air and solar radiation permitted into the space.

5.3. Contribution of Window Design Parameters to the Supplementary Air Conditioning Loads

- The supplementary AC load required to retain indoor thermal conditions when NV is not sufficient is highly influenced by the window's glazing property (or U-value), for which the percentage of contribution was recorded at 29.36%.
- Window orientation, size, type, and external shading are the most significant parameters affecting the energy-efficient MM office, with their individual factor effectiveness calculated as 26.52%, 14.79%, 11.44%, and 8.09%, respectively.

Accordingly, trade-off designs with near-optimal combinations were selected and further studied. The outcome of the O-1 trade-off design revealed that the ventilation rate met the minimum VR $\geq$ 2.1 for approximately 72.3% of the annual office working hours. The level of CO_2 concentration did not exceed the 1000 ppm threshold for 83.7% of the time. The indoor operative temperature was within the Category II temperature ranges of the adaptive comfort approximately 70.2% of the occupancy time, constituting the free-running period, while air-conditioning was required for the remainder of the time to sustain indoor thermal comfort conditions, requiring 11.66 kWh/m^2. Up to 90% of the office working hours in January, February, March, April, May, October, November, and December constitute the free-running period based on the number of comfort hours designated by the BS EN 15251 standard adaptive model.

Conversely, as a result of the elevated outdoor air temperature, ventilative cooling could only offer 5–15% adaptive comfort hours in July and August, as well as 40–60% in June and September. Nonetheless, the mixed-mode system resulted in a 79.41% reduction in cooling/heating loads relative to a fully air-conditioned scenario, considering the conditions of this study. The reduction in air-conditioning loads is also similar to the results reported by a reviewed field study.

Author Contributions: Conceptualization, H.K.A. and H.Z.A.; methodology, H.K.A.; software, H.K.A.; validation, H.K.A. and H.Z.A.; formal analysis, H.K.A.; investigation, H.K.A.; resources, H.Z.A.; data curation, H.K.A.; writing—original draft preparation, H.K.A.; writing—review and editing, H.K.A. and H.Z.A.; visualization, H.K.A.; supervision, H.Z.A.; project administration, H.Z.A.; funding acquisition, H.Z.A. All authors have read and agreed to the published version of the manuscript.

Funding: This research received no external funding.

Institutional Review Board Statement: Not applicable.

Informed Consent Statement: Not applicable.

Data Availability Statement: Not applicable.

Conflicts of Interest: The authors declare no conflict of interest.

References

1. DeDear, R.J.; Brager, G.S. Thermal Comfort in Naturally Ventilated Buildings: Revisions to ASHRAE Standard 55. *Energy Build.* **2002**, *34*, 549–561. [CrossRef]
2. Fang, L.; Wargocki, P.; Witterseh, T.; Clausen, G.; Fanger, P.O. Field Study on the Impact of Temperature, Humidity and Ventilation on Perceived Air Quality. In Proceedings of the Indoor Air, Edinburgh, Scotland, 8–13 August 1999; pp. 107–112.
3. Jia, L.-R.; Han, J.; Chen, X.; Li, Q.-Y.; Lee, C.-C.; Fung, Y.-H. Interaction between Thermal Comfort, Indoor Air Quality and Ventilation Energy Consumption of Educational Buildings: A Comprehensive Review. *Buildings* **2021**, *11*, 591. [CrossRef]
4. Larsen, T.S.; Heiselberg, P. Single-Sided Natural Ventilation Driven by Wind Pressure and Temperature Difference. *Energy Build.* **2008**, *40*, 1031–1040. [CrossRef]

5. Abdullah, H.K.; Alibaba, H.Z. Towards Nearly Zero-Energy Buildings: The Potential of Photovoltaic-Integrated Shading Devices To Achieve Autonomous Solar Electricity and Acceptable Thermal Comfort in Naturally-Ventilated Office Spaces. In Proceedings of the 16th International Conference on Clean Energy, Philadelphia, PA, USA, 9–11 May 2018; Eastern Mediterranean University: Famagusta, North Cyprus, 2018; pp. 1–11.
6. Mora-pérez, M.; Guillen-guillamón, I.; López-patiño, G.; López-jiménez, P.A. Natural Ventilation Building Design Approach in Mediterranean Regions—A Case Study at the Valencian Coastal Regional Scale (Spain). *Sustainability* **2016**, *8*, 855. [CrossRef]
7. Duan, Z.; Sun, Y.; Wang, M.; Hu, R.; Dong, X. Evaluation of Mixed-Mode Ventilation Thermal Performance and Energy Saving Potential from Retrofitting a Beijing Office Building. *Buildings* **2022**, *12*, 793. [CrossRef]
8. Zhai, Z.; El Mankibi, M.; Zoubir, A. Review of Natural Ventilation Models. *Energy Procedia* **2015**, *78*, 2700–2705. [CrossRef]
9. Kleiven, T. *Natural Ventilation in Buildings: Architectural Concepts, Consequences and Possibilities*; Norwegian University of Science and Technology: Trondheim, Norway, 2003.
10. Tran, T. *Optimization of Natural Ventilation Design in Hot and Humid Climates Using Building Energy Simulation*; University of Hawai'i: Honolulu, HI, USA, 2013.
11. Inanici, M.N.; Demirbilek, F.N. Thermal Performance Optimization of Building Aspect Ratio and South Window Size in Five Cities Having Different Climatic Characteristics of Turkey. *Build. Environ.* **2000**, *35*, 41–52. [CrossRef]
12. Elshafei, G.; Negm, A.; Bady, M.; Suzuki, M.; Ibrahim, M.G. Numerical and Experimental Investigations of the Impacts of Window Parameters on Indoor Natural Ventilation in a Residential Building. *Energy Build.* **2017**, *141*, 321–332. [CrossRef]
13. Shetabivash, H. Investigation of Opening Position and Shape on the Natural Cross Ventilation. *Energy Build.* **2015**, *93*, 1–15. [CrossRef]
14. Stavrakakis, G.M.; Zervas, P.L.; Sarimveis, H.; Markatos, N.C. Optimization of Window-Openings Design for Thermal Comfort in Naturally Ventilated Buildings. *Appl. Math. Model.* **2012**, *36*, 193–211. [CrossRef]
15. Yin, W.; Zhang, G.; Yang, W.; Wang, X. Natural Ventilation Potential Model Considering Solution Multiplicity, Window Opening Percentage, Air Velocity and Humidity in China. *Build. Environ.* **2010**, *45*, 338–344. [CrossRef]
16. Gao, C.F.; Lee, W.L. Evaluating the Influence of Openings Configuration on Natural Ventilation Performance of Residential Units in Hong Kong. *Build. Environ.* **2011**, *46*, 961–969. [CrossRef]
17. Roetzel, A.; Tsangrassoulis, A.; Dietrich, U.; Busching, S. A Review of Occupant Control on Natural Ventilation. *Renew. Sustain. Energy Rev.* **2010**, *14*, 1001–1013. [CrossRef]
18. Albatayneh, A. Optimising the Parameters of a Building Envelope in the East Mediterranean Saharan, Cool Climate Zone. *Buildings* **2021**, *11*, 43. [CrossRef]
19. Fadzil, S.F.S.; Abdullah, A.; Harun, W.M.W. The Impact of Varied Orientation and Wall Window Ratio (WWR) To Daylight Distribution in Residental Rooms. In Proceedings of the CIBW 107 International Symposium on Construction in Developing Economies: Commonalities Among Diversities, Penang, Malaysia, 5–7 October 2009; pp. 478–486.
20. Wagdy, A.; Sherif, A.; Sabry, H.; Arafa, R.; Mashaly, I. Daylighting Simulation for the Configuration of External Sun-Breakers on South Oriented Windows of Hospital Patient Rooms under a Clear Desert Sky. *Sol. Energy* **2017**, *149*, 164–175. [CrossRef]
21. AlAnzi, A.; Seo, D.; Krarti, M. Impact of Building Shape on Thermal Performance of Office Buildings in Kuwait. *Energy Convers. Manag.* **2009**, *50*, 822–828. [CrossRef]
22. Pedrini, A.; Vilar De Carvalho, J.P. Analysis of Daylight Performance in Classrooms in Humid and Hot Climate. In Proceedings of the 30th International PLEA Conference, Gujarat, India, 16–18 December 2014; CEPT University: Ahmedabad, India, 2014; pp. 1–10.
23. Aflaki, A.; Mahyuddin, N.; Al-Cheikh Mahmoud, Z.; Baharum, M.R. A Review on Natural Ventilation Applications through Building Façade Components and Ventilation Openings in Tropical Climates. *Energy Build.* **2015**, *101*, 153–162. [CrossRef]
24. Alibaba, H.Z. Determination of Optimum Window to External Wall Ratio for Offices in a Hot and Humid Climate. *Sustainability* **2016**, *8*, 187. [CrossRef]
25. Sacht, H.; Lukiantchuki, M.A. Windows Size and the Performance of Natural Ventilation. *Procedia Eng.* **2017**, *196*, 972–979. [CrossRef]
26. Huang, K.; Feng, G.; Li, H.; Yu, S. Opening Window Issue of Residential Buildings in Winter in North China: A Case Study in Shenyang. *Energy Build.* **2014**, *84*, 567–574. [CrossRef]
27. Al-Tamimi, N.A.M.; Syed Fadzil, S.F.; Wan Harun, W.M. The Effects of Orientation, Ventilation, and Varied WWR on the Thermal Performance of Residential Rooms in the Tropics. *J. Sustain. Dev.* **2011**, *4*, 142. [CrossRef]
28. KTMMOB Chapter 96 Regulation: The Streets and Buildings Regulation. Available online: http://www.mimarlarodasi.org/tr/mevzuat/fasil-96-duzenleme/ (accessed on 21 May 2019).
29. Rilling, D.; Han Siang, S.; Hui Siang, S. Thermal Simulation as Design Tool for Residential Buildings in Southeast Asia. *J. Alam Bina* **2007**, *9*, 45–54.
30. Shaeri, J.; Habibi, A.; Yaghoubi, M.; Chokhachian, A. The Optimum Window-to-Wall Ratio in Office Buildings for Hot-Humid, Hot-Dry, and Cold Climates in Iran. *Environments* **2019**, *6*, 45. [CrossRef]
31. NAFS. *AAMA/NWWDA/CSA 101/I.S.2/A440-08—North. American Fenestration Standard/Specification for Windows, Doors, and Skylights*; NAFS: Schaumburg, IL, USA, 2008.
32. Wang, H.; Chen, Q. Modeling of the Impact of Different Window Types on Single-Sided Natural Ventilation. *Energy Procedia* **2015**, *78*, 1549–1555. [CrossRef]

33. Gough, H.L.; Barlow, J.F.; Luo, Z.; King, M.F.; Halios, C.H.; Grimmond, C.S.B. Evaluating Single-Sided Natural Ventilation Models against Full-Scale Idealised Measurements: Impact of Wind Direction and Turbulence. *Build. Environ.* **2020**, *170*, 106556. [CrossRef]
34. Liu, T.; Lee, W.L. Using Response Surface Regression Method to Evaluate the Influence of Window Types on Ventilation Performance of Hong Kong Residential Buildings. *Build. Environ.* **2019**, *154*, 167–181. [CrossRef]
35. Heiselberg, P.; Svidt, K.; Nielsen, P.V. Characteristics of Airflow from Open Windows. *Build. Environ.* **2001**, *36*, 859–869. [CrossRef]
36. Yang, C.; Shi, H.; Yang, X.; Zhao, B. Research on Flow Resistance Characteristics with Different Window/Door Opening Angles. *HVAC R Res.* **2010**, *16*, 813–824. [CrossRef]
37. Wang, H.; Karava, P.; Chen, Q. Development of Simple Semiempirical Models for Calculating Airflow through Hopper, Awning, and Casement Windows for Single-Sided Natural Ventilation. *Energy Build.* **2015**, *96*, 373–384. [CrossRef]
38. Andersen, R.; Fabi, V.; Toftum, J.; Corgnati, S.P.; Olesen, B.W. Window Opening Behaviour Modelled from Measurements in Danish Dwellings. *Build. Environ.* **2013**, *69*, 101–113. [CrossRef]
39. Rodrigues, A.M.; Santos, M.; Gomes, M.G.; Duarte, R. Impact of Natural Ventilation on the Thermal and Energy Performance of Buildings in a Mediterranean Climate. *Buildings* **2019**, *9*, 123. [CrossRef]
40. Xiao, Y.; Wang, L.; Yu, M.; Liu, H.; Liu, J. Effects of Source Emission and Window Opening on Winter Indoor Particle Concentrations in the Severe Cold Region of China. *Build. Environ.* **2018**, *144*, 23–33. [CrossRef]
41. Li, N.; Li, J.; Fan, R.; Jia, H. Probability of Occupant Operation of Windows during Transition Seasons in Office Buildings. *Renew. Energy* **2015**, *73*, 84–91. [CrossRef]
42. Lai, H.K.; Kendall, M.; Ferrier, H.; Lindup, I.; Alm, S.; Hänninen, O.; Jantunen, M.; Mathys, P.; Colvile, R.; Ashmore, M.R.; et al. Personal Exposures and Microenvironment Concentrations of PM2.5, VOC, NO2and CO in Oxford, UK. *Atmos. Environ.* **2004**, *38*, 6399–6410. [CrossRef]
43. Deme Belafi, Z.; Naspi, F.; Arnesano, M.; Reith, A.; Revel, G.M. Investigation on Window Opening and Closing Behavior in Schools through Measurements and Surveys: A Case Study in Budapest. *Build. Environ.* **2018**, *143*, 523–531. [CrossRef]
44. Markovic, R.; Grintal, E.; Wölki, D.; Frisch, J.; van Treeck, C. Window Opening Model Using Deep Learning Methods. *Build. Environ.* **2018**, *145*, 319–329. [CrossRef]
45. Stazi, F.; Naspi, F.; Ulpiani, G.; Di Perna, C. Indoor Air Quality and Thermal Comfort Optimization in Classrooms Developing an Automatic System for Windows Opening and Closing. *Energy Build.* **2017**, *139*, 732–746. [CrossRef]
46. Tahmasebi, F.; Mahdavi, A. An Inquiry into the Reliability of Window Operation Models in Building Performance Simulation. *Build. Environ.* **2016**, *105*, 343–357. [CrossRef]
47. Dhalluin, A.; Limam, K. Comparison of Natural and Hybrid Ventilation Strategies Used in Classrooms in Terms of Indoor Environmental Quality, Comfort and Energy Savings. *Indoor Built Environ.* **2012**, *23*, 527–542. [CrossRef]
48. Psomas, T.; Fiorentini, M.; Kokogiannakis, G.; Heiselberg, P. Ventilative Cooling through Automated Window Opening Control Systems to Address Thermal Discomfort Risk during the Summer Period: Framework, Simulation and Parametric Analysis. *Energy Build.* **2017**, *153*, 18–30. [CrossRef]
49. Sorgato, M.J.; Melo, A.P.; Lamberts, R. The Effect of Window Opening Ventilation Control on Residential Building Energy Consumption. *Energy Build.* **2016**, *133*, 1–13. [CrossRef]
50. Chen, C.-P.; Hwang, R.-L.; Liu, W.; Shih, W.-M.; Chang, S.-Y. The Influence of Air-Conditioning Managerial Scheme in Hybrid-Ventilated Classrooms on Students' Thermal Perception. *Indoor Built Environ.* **2015**, *24*, 761–770. [CrossRef]
51. Daish, N.C.; Carrilho da Graça, G.; Linden, P.F.; Banks, D. Impact of Aperture Separation on Wind-Driven Single-Sided Natural Ventilation. *Build. Environ.* **2016**, *108*, 122–134. [CrossRef]
52. Vigener, N.; Brown, M.A. Whole Building Desing Guide. Available online: https://www.wbdg.org/guides-specifications/building-envelope-design-guide (accessed on 18 November 2021).
53. Ercan, B.; Elias-Ozkan, S.T. Performance-Based Parametric Design Explorations: A Method for Generating Appropriate Building Components. *Des. Stud.* **2015**, *38*, 33–53. [CrossRef]
54. Lavin, C.; Fiorito, F. Optimization of an External Perforated Screen for Improved Daylighting and Thermal Performance of an Office Space. *Procedia Eng.* **2017**, *180*, 571–581.
55. Mirrahimi, S.; Mohamed, M.F.; Haw, L.C.; Ibrahim, N.L.N.; Yusoff, W.F.M.; Aflaki, A. The Effect of Building Envelope on the Thermal Comfort and Energy Saving for High-Rise Buildings in Hot-Humid Climate. *Renew. Sustain. Energy Rev.* **2016**, *53*, 1508–1519. [CrossRef]
56. Miran, F.D.; Abdullah, H.K. Evaluation of the Optimal Solar Shading Devices for Enhancing Daylight Performance of School Building (A Case Study of Semi-Arid Climate—Erbil City). *ZANCO J. Pure Appl. Sci.* **2016**, *28*, 580–598.
57. Kalay, Y.E. Performance-Based Design. *SFPE Handb. Fire Prot. Eng. Fifth Ed.* **1999**, *8*, 395–409. [CrossRef]
58. Gagne, J. *An Interactive Performance-Based Expert System for Daylighting in Architectural Design*; Massachusetts Institute of Technology: Cambridge, MA, USA, 2011.
59. Petersen, S.; Svendsen, S. Method and Simulation Program Informed Decisions in the Early Stages of Building Design. *Energy Build.* **2010**, *42*, 1113–1119. [CrossRef]
60. Abdullah, H.K.; Alibaba, H.Z. Window Design of Naturally Ventilated Offices in the Mediterranean Climate in Terms of CO_2 and Thermal Comfort Performance. *Sustainability* **2020**, *12*, 473. [CrossRef]
61. Aldawoud, A. Windows Design for Maximum Cross-Ventilation in Buildings. *Adv. Build. energy Res.* **2017**, *11*, 67–86. [CrossRef]

62. Taguchi, G.; Yokoyama, Y. *Taguchi Methods: Design of Experiments*; American Supplier Institute: Dearborn, MI, USA, 1994.
63. Roy, R.K. *A Primer on the Taguchi Method Dearborn*; Society of Manufacturing Engineer: Southfield, MI, USA, 2010.
64. Nimlyat, P.S.; Dassah, E. Computer Simulations In Buildings: Implications For Building Energy Performance. *IOSR J. Eng.* **2014**, *4*, 56–62. [CrossRef]
65. *EDSL TAS Engineering (Computer Software)*, v.9.5.0; Envieonmental Desing Solutions Ltd.: Stony Stratford, UK, 2019.
66. *EN 15251*; BS EN 15251—Indoor Environmental Input Parameters for Design and Assessment of Energy Performance of Buildings Addressing Indoor Air Quality, Thermal Environment. Lighting and Acoustics. British Standards Institution (BSI): London, UK, 2007.
67. WHO. *Air Quality Guidelines for Europe*, 2nd ed.; European Series, No. 91; World Health Organization Regional Office for Europe: Copenhagen, Denmark, 2000; ISBN 92 890 1358 3.
68. *ASHRAE*; ANSI/ASHRAE Standard 62.1—Ventilation for Acceptable Indoor Air Quality. American National Standard Institute (ANSI) and American Society of Heating, Refrigerating, and Air-Conditioning Engineers (ASHRAE): Atlanta, GA, USA, 2019.
69. *BS EN 13779*; BS EN 13779—Ventilation for Non-Residential Buildings—Performance Requirements for Ventilation and Room-Conditioning Systems. British Standards Institution (BSI): London, UK, 2007.
70. Erdman, C.A.; Steiner, K.C.; Apte, M.A. Indoor Carbon Dioxide Concentrations and Sick Building Syndrome Symptoms in the Base Study Revisited: Analyses of the 100 Building Dataset. *Indoor Air* **2002**, 443–448.
71. Fanger, P.O. *Thermal Comfort*; Danish Technical Press: Copenhagen, Denmark, 1970.
72. Nguyen, A.T.; Singh, M.K.; Reiter, S. An Adaptive Thermal Comfort Model for Hot Humid South-East Asia. *Build. Environ.* **2012**, *56*, 291–300. [CrossRef]
73. Humphreys, M.A.; Nicol, J.F.; Raja, I.A. Field Studies of Indoor Thermal Comfort and the Progress of the Adaptive Approach. *Adv. Build. Energy Res.* **2007**, *1*, 55–88. [CrossRef]
74. de Wilde, P.; Tian, W. The Role of Adaptive Thermal Comfort in the Prediction of the Thermal Performance of a Modern Mixed-Mode Office Building in the UK under Climate Change. *J. Build. Perform. Simul.* **2010**, *3*, 87–101. [CrossRef]
75. Nicol, F.; Humphreys, M. Derivation of the Adaptive Equations for Thermal Comfort in Free-Running Buildings in European Standard EN15251. *Build. Environ.* **2010**, *45*, 11–17. [CrossRef]
76. Deng, X.; Tan, Z. Numerical Analysis of Local Thermal Comfort in a Plan Office under Natural Ventilation. *Indoor Built Environ.* **2020**, *29*, 972–986. [CrossRef]
77. Rowe, D. A Study of a Mixed Mode Environment in 25 Cellular Offices at the University of Sydney. *Int. J. Vent.* **2003**, *1*, 53–64. [CrossRef]
78. Halawa, E.; Van Hoof, J. The Adaptive Approach to Thermal Comfort: A Critical Overview. *Energy Build.* **2012**, *51*, 101–110. [CrossRef]
79. Emmerich, S.J.; Polidoro, B.; Axley, J.W. Impact of Adaptive Thermal Comfort on Climatic Suitability of Natural Ventilation in Office Buildings. *Energy Build.* **2011**, *43*, 2101–2107. [CrossRef]
80. Belleri, A.; Avantaggiato, M.; Psomas, T.; Heiselberg, P. Evaluation Tool of Climate Potential for Ventilative Cooling. *Int. J. Vent.* **2018**, *17*, 196–208. [CrossRef]
81. Abdullah, H.K.; Alibaba, H.Z. Open-Plan Office Design for Improved Natural Ventilation and Reduced Mixed Mode Supplementary Loads. *Indoor Built Environ.* **2020**, *0*, 1–23. [CrossRef]
82. CIBSE. *Guide A: Environmental Design*; The Chartered Institution of Building Services Engineers (CIBSE): London, UK, 2015.
83. ASHRAE. *ANSI/ASHRAE Standard 90.1—Energy Standard for Buildings Except Low-Rise Residential Buildings*; American National Standard Institute (ANSI) and American Society of Heating, Refrigerating and Air-Conditioning Engineers (ASHRAE): Atlanta, GA, USA, 2016.
84. Kottek, M.; Grieser, J.; Beck, C.; Rudolf, B.; Rubel, F. World Map of the Köppen-Geiger Climate Classification Updated. *Meteorol. Z.* **2006**, *15*, 259–263. [CrossRef]
85. ASHRAE. *International Weather for Energy Calculations (IWEC Weather Files) User's Manual and CD-ROM*; ASHRAE: Atlanta, GA, USA, 2001.
86. *ASHRAE*; ANSI/ASHRAE Standard 55—Thermal Environmental Conditions for Human Occupancy. American National Standard Institute (ANSI) and American Society of Heating, Refrigerating and Air-Conditioning Engineers (ASHRAE): Atlanta, GA, USA, 2017.
87. ASHRAE. *ASHRAE Handbook: Fundamentals*; American Society of Heating, Refrigerating and Air-Conditioning Engineers: Atlanta, GA, USA, 2013.
88. Du Bois, D.; Du Bois, E.F. A Formula to Estimate the Approximate Surface Area If Height and Weight Be Known. *Arch. Intern. Med.* **1916**, *17*, 863–871. [CrossRef]

atmosphere

MDPI

Article

Impact of Preventive Measures on Subjective Symptoms and Antigen Sensitization against Japanese Cedar, Cypress Pollen and House Dust Mites in Patients with Allergic Rhinitis: A Retrospective Analysis in the COVID-19 Era

Takashi Oda [1], Fumiaki Maeda [1], Sachio Takeno [1,*], Yuri Tsuru [1], Chie Ishikawa [1], Takashi Ishino [1], Kota Takemoto [1], Takao Hamamoto [1], Tsutomu Ueda [1], Tomohiro Kawasumi [1], Hiroshi Iwamoto [2], Kazunori Kubota [3], Yoshio Nakao [4] and Masaru Kunimoto [1,5]

[1] Department of Otorhinolaryngology, Head and Neck Surgery, Graduate School of Biomedical Sciences, Hiroshima University, Hiroshima 734-8551, Japan; odataka@hiroshima-u.ac.jp (T.O.); fumi0721@hiroshima-u.ac.jp (F.M.); yuri14@hiroshima-u.ac.jp (Y.T.); chie0324@hiroshima-u.ac.jp (C.I.); tishino@hiroshima-u.ac.jp (T.I.); kota61@hiroshima-u.ac.jp (K.T.); takao0320@hiroshima-u.ac.jp (T.H.); uedatsu@hiroshima-u.ac.jp (T.U.); d193690@hiroshima-u.ac.jp (T.K.); makunimoto@kunimoto-orl.com (M.K.)

[2] Department of Molecular and Internal Medicine, Graduate School of Biomedical and Health Sciences, Hiroshima University, Hiroshima 734-8551, Japan; hir@hiroshima-u.ac.jp

[3] Kubota ENT and Allergy Clinic, Hiroshima 731-5141, Japan; kazunokubota@gmail.com

[4] Nakao ENT and Allergy Clinic, Hiroshima 730-0823, Japan; titarou0810@yahoo.co.jp

[5] Kunimoto ENT Clinic, Hiroshima 731-3164, Japan

* Correspondence: takeno@hiroshima-u.ac.jp

Citation: Oda, T.; Maeda, F.; Takeno, S.; Tsuru, Y.; Ishikawa, C.; Ishino, T.; Takemoto, K.; Hamamoto, T.; Ueda, T.; Kawasumi, T.; et al. Impact of Preventive Measures on Subjective Symptoms and Antigen Sensitization against Japanese Cedar, Cypress Pollen and House Dust Mites in Patients with Allergic Rhinitis: A Retrospective Analysis in the COVID-19 Era. *Atmosphere* **2022**, *13*, 1000. https://doi.org/10.3390/atmos13071000

Academic Editors: Ashok Kumar, Amirul I Khan, Alejandro Moreno-Rangel and Michał Piasecki

Received: 1 June 2022
Accepted: 20 June 2022
Published: 21 June 2022

Abstract: For >2 years, Japan's government has been urging the populace to take countermeasures to prevent COVID-19, including mask wearing. We examined whether these preventive behaviors have affected the rate and degree of sensitization against pollen and house dust antigens in patients with allergic rhinitis. We retrospectively surveyed 2565 patients who had undergone allergy blood testing during the period 2015–2021. We subdivided this period into eras based on the COVID-19 pandemic: the pre-COVID (2015–2019, n = 1879) and COVID (2020–2021, n = 686) eras. The positive rates for Japanese cedar and cypress in the 40–59-year-olds and those for house dust in the 20–39-year-olds were significantly reduced in the COVID era versus those in the pre-COVID era. Each group's mean antigen-specific CAP scores decreased significantly from the 1st to 2nd era: from 1.98 to 1.57 for cedar ($p < 0.01$), 1.42 to 0.95 for cypress ($p < 0.05$), and 2.86 to 2.07 for house dust ($p < 0.01$). Our survey of the patients' clinical records indicates that 47.5% of the pollinosis patients reported improvement in nasal symptoms after the three seasons of pollen dispersion in the COVID era. Japan's quarantine policies designed to combat the spread of COVID-19 thus coincide with pivotal measures to alleviate allergic reactions.

Keywords: allergic rhinitis; face mask; COVID-19; house dust mite; Japanese cedar pollen; Japanese cypress pollen; preventive behavior; subjective symptoms

1. Introduction

Coronavirus disease 2019 (COVID-19) is an ongoing pandemic infection caused by severe acute respiratory syndrome coronavirus 2 (SARS-CoV-2) [1]. For over 2 years, Japan's government has urged the populace to take countermeasures to prevent COVID-19, with guidance such as "wear a mask", "wash your hands frequently", and "stay home and avoid the 3Cs outside (crowded places, close contact settings, and closed spaces)" [2]. These measures have helped suppress respiratory viral infections and the risk of asthma exacerbations [3]. We hypothesized that these preventive behaviors may also have affected the severity of nasal symptoms and the rate and degree of sensitization against common antigens among patients with allergic rhinitis (AR) in Japan. We conducted a retrospective survey of the data of 2565 patients who showed allergic symptoms and had undergone allergy blood testing during the period from 2015 to 2021. We subdivided the period into two eras based on the outbreak of the COVID-19 pandemic in Japan: the pre-COVID-19 era (2015–2019) and the COVID-19 era (2020–2021). The patients' data in the two eras were compared based on four age groups: 0–19, 20–39, 40–59, and ≥60 years old. We also conducted a survey to investigate changes in the patients' social behaviors and subjective nasal symptoms after the start of the COVID-19 pandemic.

Allergic rhinitis (AR) can be classified into seasonal allergic rhinitis (SAR) and perennial allergic rhinitis (PAR). Japanese cedar/cypress and house dust mites are major causative antigens for SAR and PAR, respectively [4], and the numbers of individuals in Japan with SAR or PAR both increased markedly in the pre-COVID-19 era. The results of a nationwide epidemiological survey conducted in 2019 revealed the presence of cedar pollinosis in 38.8% of the respondents compared with 16.2% in 1998 and 26.5% in 2008 [5]. The presence of PAR has also shown gradual increases from 18.7% in 1998 to 23.4% in 2008 and 24.5% in 2019 [4].

The elimination and avoidance of antigens are pivotal measures to alleviate allergic reactions, and these measures coincide with quarantine policies designed to combat the spread of COVID-19 [4,6,7]. We have found no prior study that specifically assessed the impact of anti-COVID-19 measures on AR patients in Japan based on both objective and subjective parameters.

2. Materials and Methods

2.1. Patient Enrollment and Pollen Counts

We retrospectively analyzed the data of 2565 patients who showed allergic symptoms and had allergy blood tests against common antigens at Hiroshima University Hospital during the years 2015–2021. The antigens included Japanese cedar pollens (*Cryptomeria japonica*), Japanese cypress pollens (*Chamaecyparis obtusa*), and house dust mites (*Dermatophagoides pteronyssinus*). The patients' antigen-specific IgE levels were determined by the ImmunoCAP™ Specific IgE system (ThermoFisher Scientific, Waltham, MA, USA). The blood tests are sandwich tests in which the solid phase of specific antigens ensures binding of all relevant antibodies, providing a uniquely high binding capacity. The CAP score system is graded as follows: 0, ≤0.34 UA/mL; 1, 0.35–0.69 UA/mL; 2, 0.70–3.49 UA/mL; 3, 3.50–17.4 UA/mL; 4,17.5–49.9 UA/mL; 5, 50.0–99.9 UA/mL; 6, ≥100 UA/mL. The CAP-RAST scores ≥2 are regarded as positive, 1 as borderline, and 0 as negative, respectively. The diagnosis of AR was based on the combination of the CAP score ≥2 and the presence of nasal symptoms such as sneezing, nasal discharge, and nasal congestion [4].

We divided the study period 2015–2021 into two eras based on the outbreak of the COVID-19 pandemic in Japan: the pre-COVID (2015–2019) and COVID (2020–2021) eras. We compared patients in the two eras classified into four age groups: 0–19, 20–39, 40–59, and ≥60 years old. The proportion and distribution of patients with positive ImmunoCAP scores were determined for each age group, and we compared the differences in these scores between the two eras.

In addition, to assess the possible changes in the patients' social behaviors and subjective allergic symptoms after the start of the COVID-19 pandemic, we analyzed the clinical records of pollinosis patients who visited the above-mentioned hospital or related ENT clinics (led by KK, YN and KM) in Hiroshima City after the onset of the COVID-19 pandemic. The records included whether the patient (1) had engaged in limited outdoor behaviors in accord with social regulations, i.e., wearing a mask, and (2) reported improvement in his or her nasal and ocular symptoms in the pollinosis seasons after the change in social behaviors.

The degree of pollen dispersion was monitored annually by a gravitational pollen sampler on the roof of the Hiroshima University Hospital. The cypress and cedar pollen counts were determined daily by staining with Calberla solution from 15 January to 31 May each year.

This study was performed in accordance with the Declaration of Helsinki, with approval from the Hiroshima University School of Medicine Institutional Review Board (approval no. E-1738; approval date: 4 September 2019).

2.2. Statistical Analyses

The Kruskal–Wallis and Mann–Whitney U test were used for between-group comparisons. Fisher's exact test was used to compare qualitative data. p-values < 0.05 were considered significant. JMP Pro ver. 14 (SAS, Cary, NC, USA) was used for the analyses.

3. Results

3.1. Changes in the Proportions of SAR and PAR Patients

A total of 1879 patients in the pre-COVID era and 686 patients in the COVID era were enrolled (Table 1). There were no significant differences in the age or gender distributions between the two eras. The pollen counts and dispersion periods of cedar and cypress fluctuated annually, due mainly to weather conditions in the previous summer. The amounts of mean season cedar pollens and the mean dispersion periods of cypress pollens tended to increase during the COVID era, but no significant between-era differences in these values were observed (Mann–Whitney U test, $p = 0.6985$ for cedar pollen counts and $p = 0.0506$ for cypress dispersion periods) (Table 2). We also collected information on the air pollutant levels in Hiroshima City that exert adverse effects on allergic symptoms [8] (Table 2). The mean levels of particulate matter (PM) 2.5 and related gaseous materials (SO_2 and NOx) tended to improve in the COVID era, but a significant between-era difference was not observed (Mann–Whitney U test).

Table 1. Demographics of the study population, air pollutants, and pollen dispersion in Hiroshima City.

		Pre-COVID-19 Era (2015–2019)	COVID-19 Era (2020–2021)
Patient, n (male/female)	Age, yrs.		
	0–19	522 (316/206)	200 (124/76)
	20–39	268 (137/131)	95 (48/47)
	40–59	421 (223/198)	164 (79/85)
	$\geq$60	668 (347/321)	227 (130/97)
Antigen-positive, n	Cedar/cypress	999 (523/476)	361 (181/180)
	House dust	667 (389/278)	195 (108/87)

Table 2. Comparison of pollen dispersion counts and periods, and air pollutants in Hiroshima City.

		Pre-COVID-19 Era (2015–2019)	COVID-19 Era (2020–2021)
Mean season pollen counts, /cm^2 (range)	Cedar	4749.8 (1982–10,194)	7542.8 (3403–11,682)
	Cypress	2812.8 (449–7051)	1788.1 (1764–1812)
Mean pollen dispersion period, days (range)	Cedar	45.0 (36–56)	48.5 (43–54)
	Cypress	28.6 (20–37)	56.0 (48–64)
Mean air pollutant level (range)	$PM_{2.5}$, µg/m^3	12.56 (11.1–13.7)	11.6 (10–13.2)
	SO_2 and NOx, ppm	0.0136 (0.012–0.015)	0.0115 (0.011–0.012)

Figure 1 illustrates the time-course changes in the proportion of patients with positive ImmunoCAP scores ($\geq$2) from 2015 to 2021. In the SAR patients, the positive rates for both cedar and cypress in the 40–59-year-olds were significantly reduced in the COVID era compared with those in the pre-COVID era (Figure 1a,b). In this age group, the mean positive rates decreased significantly from 63.2% to 51.4% for cedar ($p < 0.05$) and from 53.7% to 31.0% for cypress ($p < 0.01$). The positivity tended to be lower for both antigens in 2021 compared with 2020. No similar significant between-era differences existed in the other age groups. In the PAR patients, the positive rates for house dust in the 20–39-year-olds were significantly reduced in the COVID era compared with those in the pre-COVID era (Figure 1c). In this age group, the mean positive rates decreased significantly from 70.5% to 47.8% ($p < 0.01$). We further compared positive antigen rates of the patients between the two eras stratified by 10-year-olds generation, gender and CAP scores for each antigen (Table 3). The positive rates in the pre-COVID era for the antigens in each generation were compatible with those by previously published data in 2006 and 2016 [9]. A significant decrease in the positive rates for both SAR and PAR was observed in the generations of COVID-19 era that corresponded to the results shown in Figure 1. No significant differences were detected in the gender proportions between the two eras.

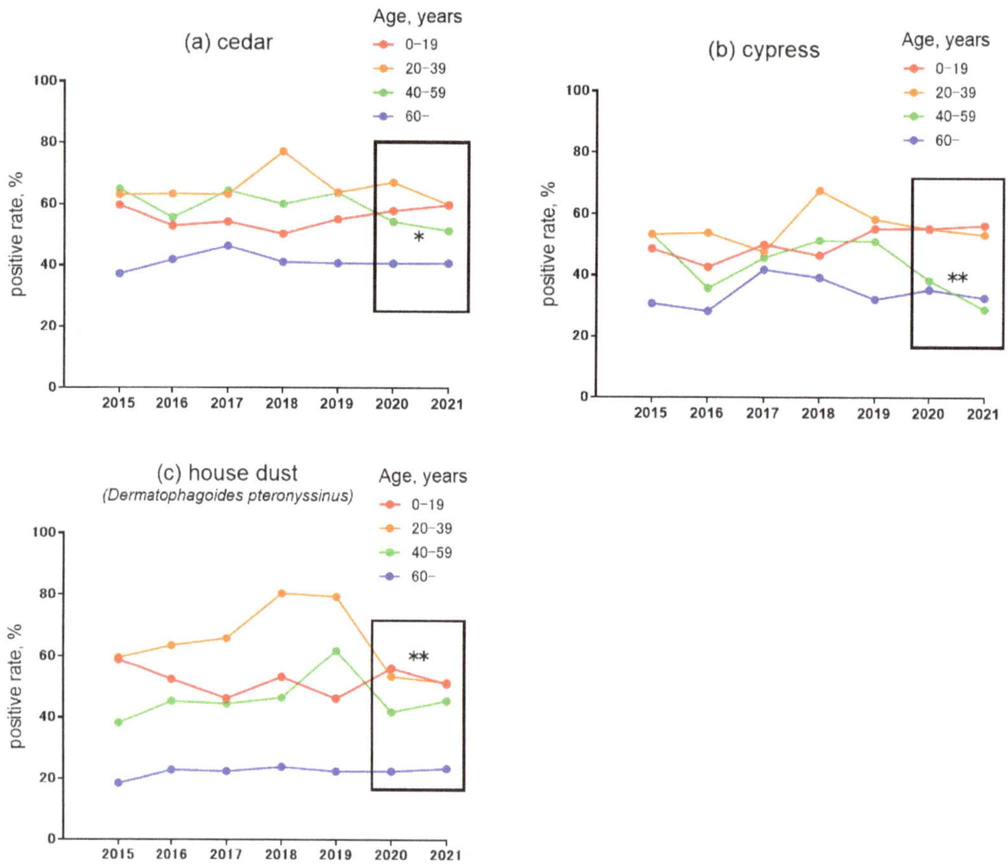

Figure 1. Changes in the positive antigen rate against (**a**) cedar, (**b**) cypress, and (**c**) house dust mites for each age group before and after the COVID-19 outbreak. * $p < 0.05$, ** $p < 0.01$, Fisher's exact test.

3.2. Changes in the CAP Scores for Pollens and House Dust

We also examined the CAP score for the responsible antigens in each age group between the pre-COVID and COVID eras. The results are consistent with those of the antigen proportion rates. Seasonal AR patients in the 40–59-year-old group showed a significant reduction in CAP scores in the COVID era compared with those in the pre-COVID era (Figure 2). The mean CAP scores decreased from 1.98 to 1.57 for cedar ($p < 0.01$) and from 1.42 to 0.95 for cypress ($p < 0.05$). No similar significant differences were identified in the other age groups. In the PAR patients, the 20–39-year-old group showed a significant reduction in CAP scores in the COVID era versus those in the pre-COVID era (Figure 3). The mean CAP scores for house dust decreased from 2.86 to 2.07 ($p < 0.01$).

Table 3. Comparison of positive antigen rates of the patients between the two eras stratified by 10-year-old generation and CAP scores for each antigen.

			Pre-COVID-19 Era (2015–2019)						□
Patient, %			**Cedar**			**Cypress**			**House Dust**
CAP Score	2–3	≥4	Total (Male/Female)	2–3	≥4	Total (Male/Female)	2–3	≥4	Total (Male/Female)
Age, years									
0–9	18.5	31.5	50.1 (51.9/44.5)	23.9	19	42.9 (43.7/41.5)	12.6	28.2	40.9 (50.8/24.3)
10–19	23	39.5	62.6 (62.7/62.5)	28.7	30.1	58.9 (59.2/58.5)	14.7	51.9	66.6 (72.4/60)
20–29	29.6	36.3	65.9 (71/60)	39.2	20.6	59.8 (63.4/55.5)	26.3	50.8	77.1 (80.3/73.6)
30–39	35.6	30.3	65.9 (70/62.5)	29.2	22.9	52.1 (57.1/48.1)	29.2	35	64.2 (71.9/57.1)
40–49	41.7	21.1	62.7 (62.76/62.7)	38.7	9.3	54.6 (61.3/45.1)	32.6	26	59.3 (65.5/51.2)
50–59	45.4	18.2	63.6 (60.4/66.1)	43.3	9.4	48.6 (44.4/57.5)	24.7	14.6	39.4 (40.6/38.3)
60–69	34.9	12.6	47.5 (47.5/47.5)	33.9	4.3	38.2 (32.2/44.4)	21.8	6.4	28.2 (30.7/25.3)
70–79	28.6	10.7	39.3 (38.7/40)	32.1	5	37.1 (38/36.2)	14.8	3.6	18.4 (20.4/16.1)
80–	21.6	4.5	26.1 (31.7/21.3)	24.4	0	24.4 (33.3/16.7)	10.3	5.7	16.1 (17.1/15.2)
□					COVID-19 Era (2020–2021)				
Patient, %			Cedar			Cypress			House Dust
CAP Score	2–3	≥4	Total (Male/Female)	2–3	≥4	Total (Male/Female)	2–3	≥4	Total (Male/Female)
Age, years									
0–9	12.9	37	50 (49.2/52.1)	25.9	16.8	42.8 (40.4/48.2)	19.7	26.7	46.4 (48.7/43.3)
10–19	24.4	45.3	69.7 (70.0/69.0)	41	33.9	75 (57.5/71.8)	21.5	39.2	60.7 (58.6/63.6)
20–29	28.3	35.8	64.1 (64/64.2)	27.7	27.7	55.5 (50/66.6)	15.3	38.4	53.8 (50/56.5) **
30–39	41.8	18.6	60.4 (55/65.2)	41.3	3.4	44.8 (38.4/50)	23.3	16.6	40 (46.6/33.3) *
40–49	42.8	11.9	54.7 (57.8/52.1) †	28.3	5.6	33.9 (31/37.5) **	34.9	20.6	55.5 (43.5/52.9)
50–59	37.6	10.5	48.2 (40.5/54.1) *	28.5	0	28.6 (30.3/26.6) **	19.4	13.4	32.8 (44.8/23.6)
60–69	41	3.6	44.6 (45.1/43.7)	22.7	0	22.7 (24/22.2) *	18.3	5	23.3 (29.7/13)
70–79	33	13.2	46.2 (41.6/52.1)	37.2	1.6	38.3 (31/45.1)	24.4	1.1	25.5 (28/22.5)
80–	16.2	2.7	18.9 (10.5/27.8)	21.4	0	25 (22.2/20)	11.5	0	11.5 (7.1/16.6)

† $p = 0.125$, * $p < 0.05$, ** $p < 0.01$ versus the corresponding groups of the pre-COVID era.

3.3. Changes in Subjective Nasal Symptoms after the Start of the COVID-19 Pandemic

Figure 4 illustrates the changes in the patients' social behaviors and reported subjective allergic symptoms after the start of the COVID-19 pandemic, based on survey of their clinical records. We collected records from 122 patients with cedar/cypress pollinosis based on a positive CAP score. Their mean age was 42.3 years, with 49 males and 73 females. Regarding outdoor behaviors compared with before the COVID-19 pandemic, almost 90% of patients (111/122) reported that they always wore masks when out in public, in accordance with the Government's request. The proportions of patients who reported improvement in nasal symptoms and ocular symptoms after the start of the COVID era were 47.5% (58/122) and 30.3% (37/122), respectively; the nasal symptom improvement rate is significantly higher than that of ocular symptoms ($p < 0.01$).

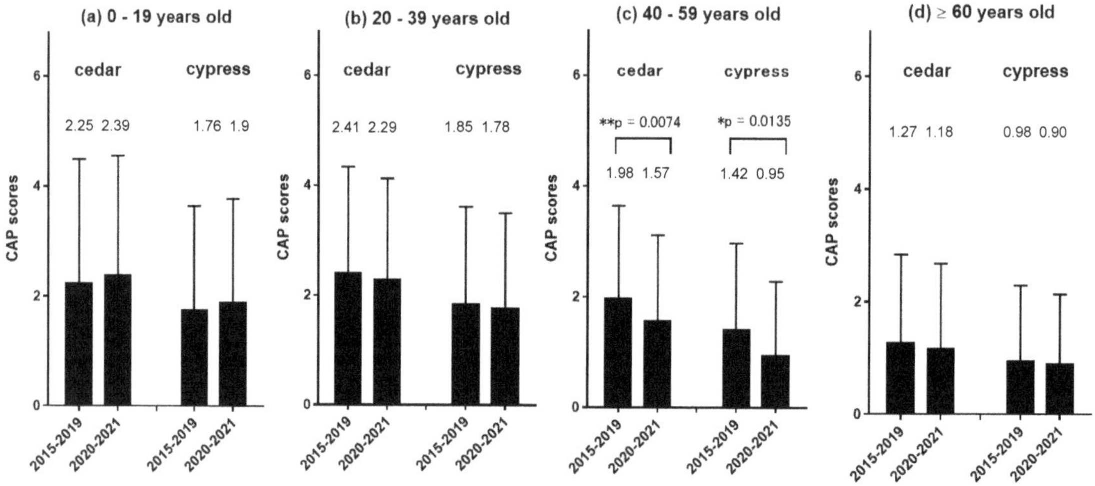

Figure 2. Comparison of CAP scores for cedar and cypress in each age group between the pre-COVID-19 (2015–2019) and COVID-19 (2020–2021) eras. (**a**) 0–19, (**b**) 20–39, (**c**) 40–59, (**d**) ≥60 years old groups. The data are mean ± SD (error bars). * $p < 0.05$, ** $p < 0.01$.

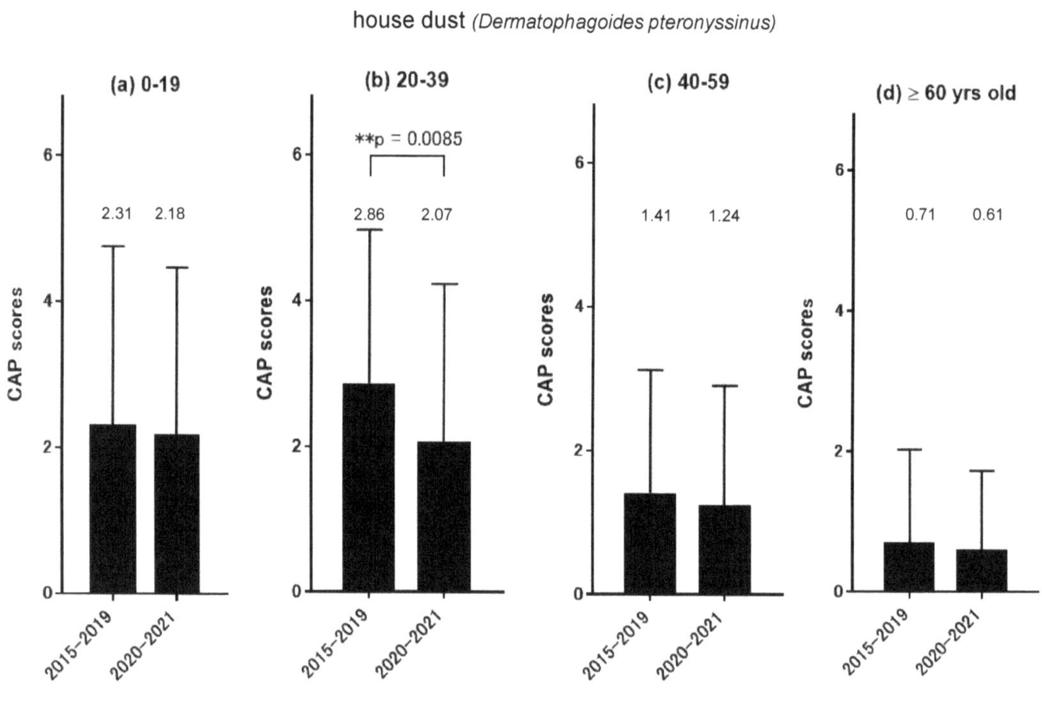

Figure 3. Comparison of CAP scores for house dust in each age group between the pre-COVID-19 (2015–2019) and COVID-19 (2020–2021) eras. (**a**) 0–19, (**b**) 20–39, (**c**) 40–59, (**d**) ≥60 years old groups. The data are mean ± SD (error bars). ** $p < 0.01$.

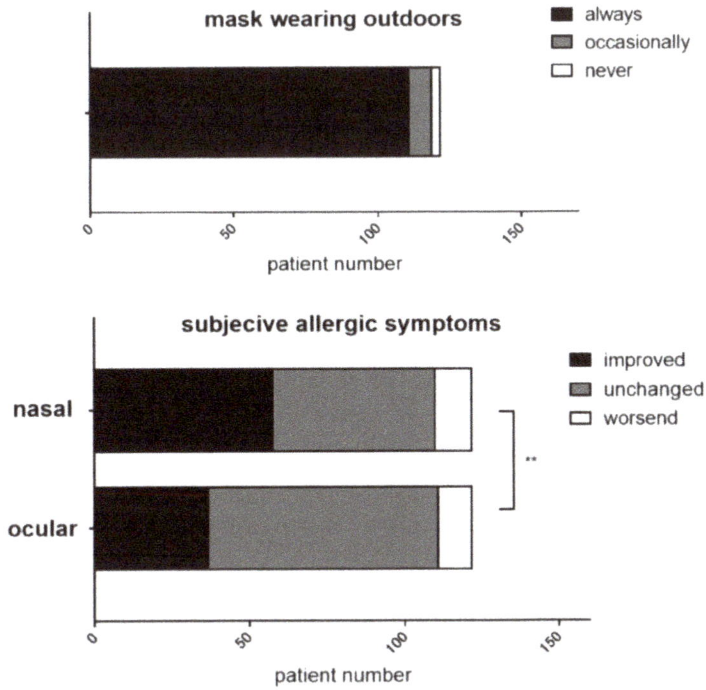

Figure 4. Changes in the social behaviors and the severity of subjective allergic symptoms after the start of the COVID-19 pandemic. Clinical records were surveyed from 122 cedar/cypress pollinosis patients who visited the hospital/clinics from April to May in 2022. ** $p < 0.01$, Fisher's exact test.

4. Discussion

Environmental variations induced by industrialization and climate change partially explain the increases in the prevalence and severity of allergic disease. The prevalence of cedar/cypress pollinosis and that of house dust mite-induced PAR continue to show increasing trends in Japan, accompanied by environmental and circumstantial increases in antigen exposure [4,8]. During the post-World War II period 1946–1980, approx. 20% of Hiroshima prefecture's land area (1660 km^2) was planted with cedar or cypress forests in compliance with a massive national afforestation policy designed to secure timber and maintain land preservation. The resulting increased exposure to pollens among younger individuals has been reported to have led to early sensitization to pollen antigens [10].

Each year during the Japanese cedar pollen-dispersion season (February to April), followed by that of Japanese cypress (April to May), a large number of pollinosis patients experience severe nasal and ocular symptoms. Because Japanese cypress pollens contain several components that cross-react with cedar pollens, about 70% of pollinosis patients suffer the symptom burdens from both types of trees. A severe affliction due to cedar and cypress pollens is also attributable to the nature of the pollens' dispersion, i.e., their large quantities and long (nearly 100-km) airborne distances [11].

As a quantitative test, CAP scoring enables monitoring of the development and severity of allergic diseases [12]. In sensitized pollinosis patients, antigen-specific IgE levels are strongly affected by the amount and periods of cedar or cypress pollen exposure [8,13]. These patients' CAP scores rise after they experience larger amounts and/or longer periods of pollen exposure, and their scores remain high through to the next season. We recently reported the trends in pollen dispersion and their possible relationship with the degree of antigen sensitization against cedar and cypress pollens from 2001 to 2018 in the same single-institution setting [14]. Our present analyses revealed that the proportion of patients with positive CAP scores for both cedar and cypress increased continually over the past 18 years, with the increase rate of the cypress CAP scores more prominent at 25%. These results indicate that the levels of pollen dispersion have provided sufficient exposure to maintain antigen sensitization during daily activities before the COVID-19 outbreak in Japan. In contrast, the preventive measures during the COVID-19 pandemic period appear to have attenuated the potential pollen sensitization. Inhaled airborne allergens such as pollen (10–100 μm) and house-dust mite feces (10–40 μm) play a significant role in triggering IgE-mediated immunologic responses in typical allergic rhinitis symptoms [4].

Our present findings indicate that both the positive rates and the mean CAP scores for both cedar and cypress in the 40–59-year-old group of SAR patients decreased significantly in the COVID era, i.e., 2020 and 2021. The improvement of these objective parameters could be attributable to the potential contribution of wearing non-woven surgical masks that can filter particles > 3 μm [15]. The scrupulous nature of Japanese citizens, who have agreed to change their outdoor behaviors as requested by the Government, is likely to have reinforced the protective effects. Our analyses considered environment factors such as air pollutants, which have adverse effects on allergic symptoms; the analyses revealed no significant difference in the mean annual levels of $PM_{2.5}$ and related gaseous materials (SO_2 and NOx) between the pre-COVID and COVID eras.

The present findings are in line with the recent reports in other countries describing a reduction in the subjective burden of screened nasal symptoms that are due to seasonal or perennial allergic rhinitis after the adoption of anti-COVID-19 measures [6,7,16]. Mengi et al. evaluated the use of face masks on AR symptoms in 50 pollen allergy patients who were compulsorily using face masks due to the COVID-19 pandemic in Turkey [6]. They found that the rate of participants with severe-moderate nasal symptoms decreased significantly during the pandemic with the use of face masks, from 92% (46/50) to 56% (28/50), and the corresponding rate of ocular symptoms decreased significantly from 60% (30 patients) to 32% (16 patients). An investigation conducted in Northern Italy examined the effects of quarantine and face-masking policies on nasal and ocular symptoms in a pool of 124 patients suffering from ragweed allergy [16], and the results demonstrated that the overall burden of oculorhinitis decreased significantly during the 2020 ragweed season. Reductions in the use of the common anti-allergic medications, such as oral antihistamines and nasal steroids, were also observed. To assess the impact of face masks on subjective AR symptoms, Dror et al. analyzed the data of a multicenter questionnaire distributed in 2020 for 2 weeks to hospital nurses in Israel, and they reported reductions in AR symptoms [7]. Our present findings also showed that 70% of the SAR patients described an improvement in nasal symptoms after the three seasons of pollen dispersion in the COVID era. Together the above-cited results highlight the potential benefit of face masks for AR patients.

Several reasons have been proposed in relation to the worldwide increase in PAR caused by house dust mites. The exacerbation factors include global warming as well as the increased time spent indoors with air conditioning inside higher and more airtight residences [17,18]. In the present study's PAR patients, a significant decrease occurred in the positive rates and the mean CAP scores for house dust in the 20–39-year-olds after the outbreak of COVID. In this sense, the elimination and avoidance of mite antigens are pivotal measures to alleviate allergic reaction. They coincide with official quarantine policies designed to combat the spread of COVID-19, i.e., mask-wearing and improved or frequent ventilation of indoor spaces [2].

Our patients in the 40- to 59-year-old age group of SAR patients and those in the 20- to 39-year-old PAR group showed significant reductions in positive rates and CAP scores in the COVID-19 era. There are possible explanations for the differences between the age groups. The prevalence of Japanese cedar pollinosis is most common among middle-aged individuals, especially 40–49-year-olds, whose morbidity rate is up to 40%. In contrast, house dust mite allergy is prevalent mainly among younger individuals, i.e., 20–39-year-olds [4,5]. Yonekura et al. reported that SAR induced by cedar pollen took chronic courses in the majority of middle-aged patients [19]. The prevalence of cedar pollinosis in Chiba, Japan increased over 10 years from 1995 to 2005 probably due to a high level of pollen exposure. It is thus likely that preventive behaviors would manifest their inhibitory effects in these corresponding age groups.

Another possibility is that the individuals in these generations tend to be more amenable to social infection-avoidance behaviors such as remote indoor working and restrictions on outdoor activities as well as mask-wearing and hand-washing [20]. In any case, the importance of determining the reason(s) for the age-group differences should be acknowledged, as the possible relationship between lifestyle habits and associated exposure routes might have non-negligible effects on the present outcomes worldwide.

This study has several limitations. It was cross-sectional and based on a regional sample collection. A causal relationship between the two eras cannot be directly determined. We did not include information on the severity of nasal and ocular symptoms of the subjects that correspond directly to CAP scores. A direct relationship between the subjects' lifestyle and associated exposure routes was not clarified. Possible important factors that determine the age-group differences should be further assessed, including lifestyle habits and associated exposure frequencies. Further studies on a larger scale and with control groups are also necessary to elucidate the effects of personal protective equipment.

At the time of writing the manuscript (18 June 2022), Japan's government still enforces mask-wearing to the citizens and applies other virus-related preventive rules. However, acknowledgement of increased vaccination certificates and changes in genome shifts to omicron variants with mild virulent forms might lift regulation guidelines on how to prevent the spread of the coronavirus. In this sense, our data presented herein would be of value as the reference.

In conclusion, the COVID-19 pandemic has provided an opportunity to assess the effects against allergen exposure to pollens and other air pollutants. Our findings suggest that appropriate COVID-preventive actions are important and effective measures as reflected by the decreased allergic parameters (both objective and subjective) in the Japanese population investigated herein.

Author Contributions: Conceptualization, T.O. and S.T.; methodology, T.O., S.T. and H.I.; validation, S.T. and T.H.; formal analysis, T.O. and S.T.; investigation, T.O., F.M. and S.T.; data curation, F.M., Y.T., C.I., T.I., T.K., K.T., K.K., Y.N. and M.K.; writing—original draft preparation, T.O. and F.M.; writing—review and editing, S.T.; visualization, T.O. and F.M.; supervision, S.T. and T.U.; project administration, S.T. and H.I.; funding acquisition, S.T. All authors have read and agreed to the published version of the manuscript.

Funding: This research was funded partly by a grant from the Japan Society for the Promotion of Science KAKENHI: 22K09668 and a Health Labor Sciences Research grant: 21FC1013.

Institutional Review Board Statement: This study was performed in accordance with the Declaration of Helsinki, with approval from the Institutional Review Board at the Hiroshima University School of Medicine (approval no. E-1738; approval date: 4 September 2019).

Informed Consent Statement: Informed consent was obtained from all participants involved in the study.

Data Availability Statement: The data presented in this study are available on reasonable request from the corresponding author.

Acknowledgments: We thank Yukako Okamoto for the technical assistance.

Conflicts of Interest: The authors declared no potential conflict of interest with respect to the research, authorship, and/or publication of this article.

References

1. Wu, F.; Zhao, S.; Yu, B.; Chen, Y.M.; Wang, W.; Song, Z.G.; Hu, Y.; Tao, Z.W.; Tian, J.H.; Pei, Y.Y.; et al. A new coronavirus associated with human respiratory disease in China. *Nature* **2020**, *579*, 265–269. [CrossRef] [PubMed]
2. Ministry of Health, Labour and Welfare (MHLW). Current situation in Japan of Coronavirus (COVID-19). Available online: https://www.mhlw.go.jp/stf/covid-19/kokunainohasseijoukyou_00006.html (accessed on 23 February 2022).
3. Bun, S.; Kishimoto, K.; Shin, J.H.; Maekawa, T.; Takada, D.; Morishita, T.; Kunisawa, S.; Imanaka, Y. Impact of the COVID-19 pandemic on asthma exacerbations in children: A multi-center survey using an administrative database in Japan. *Allergol. Int.* **2021**, *70*, 489–491. [CrossRef] [PubMed]
4. Okubo, K.; Kurono, Y.; Ichimura, K.; Enomoto, T.; Okamoto, Y.; Kawauchi, H.; Suzaki, H.; Fujieda, S.; Masuyama, K.; Japanese Society of Allergology. Japanese guidelines for allergic rhinitis 2020. *Allergol. Int.* **2020**, *69*, 331–345. [CrossRef] [PubMed]
5. Matsubara, A.; Sakashita, M.; Gotoh, M.; Kawashima, K.; Matsuoka, T.; Kondo, S.; Yamada, T.; Takeno, S.; Takeuchi, K.; Urashima, M.; et al. Epidemiological survey of allergic rhinitis in Japan 2019. *J. Otolaryngol. Jpn.* **2020**, *123*, 485–490. (In Japanese) [CrossRef]
6. Mengi, E.; Kara, C.O.; Alptürk, U.; Topuz, B. The effect of face mask usage on the allergic rhinitis symptoms in patients with pollen allergy during the covid-19 pandemic. *Am. J. Otolaryngol.* **2022**, *43*, 103206. [CrossRef] [PubMed]
7. Dror, A.A.; Eisenbach, N.; Marshak, T.; Layous, E.; Zigron, A.; Shivatzki, S.; Morozov, N.G.; Taiber, S.; Alon, E.E.; Ronen, O.; et al. Reduction of allergic rhinitis symptoms with face mask usage during the COVID-19 pandemic. *J. Allergy Clin. Immunol. Pract.* **2020**, *8*, 3590–3593. [CrossRef] [PubMed]
8. Air Pollutant Levels in Hiroshima Prefecture. Available online: https://www.pref.hiroshima.lg.jp/eco/e/kanshi/ (accessed on 30 May 2022).
9. Sakashita, M.; Tsutsumiuchi, T.; Kubo, S.; Tokunaga, T.; Takabayashi, T.; Imoto, Y.; Kato, Y.; Yoshida, K.; Kimura, Y.; Kato, Y.; et al. Comparison of sensitization and prevalence of Japanese cedar pollen and mite-induced perennial allergic rhinitis between 2006 and 2016 in hospital workers in Japan. *Allergol. Int.* **2021**, *70*, 89–95. [CrossRef] [PubMed]
10. Urashima, M.; Asaka, D.; Endo, T.; Omae, S.; Sugimoto, N.; Takaishi, S.; Mitsuyoshi, R.; Nakayama, T.; Nagakura, H.; Endo, T.; et al. Japanese cedar pollinosis in Tokyo residents born after massive national afforestation policy. *Allergy* **2018**, *73*, 2395–2397. [CrossRef] [PubMed]
11. Yamada, T.; Saito, H.; Fujieda, S. Present state of Japanese cedar pollinosis: The national affliction. *J. Allergy Clin. Immunol.* **2014**, *133*, 632–639.e5. [CrossRef] [PubMed]
12. Lambert, C.; Sarrat, A.; Bienvenu, F.; Brabant, S.; Nicaise-Roland, P.; Alyanakian, M.A.; Apoil, P.A.; Capron, C.; Couderc, R.; Evrard, B.; et al. The importance of EN ISO 15189 accreditation of allergen-specific IgE determination for reliable in vitro allergy diagnosis. *Allergy* **2015**, *70*, 180–186. [CrossRef] [PubMed]
13. Okawa, T.; Konno, A.; Yamakoshi, T.; Numata, T.; Terada, N.; Shima, M. Analysis of natural history of Japanese cedar pollinosis. *Int. Arch. Allergy Immunol.* **2003**, *131*, 39–45. [CrossRef] [PubMed]
14. Itoh, S.; Horibe, Y.; Takeno, S.; Takahara, D.; Takemoto, K.; Sasaki, A.; Kono, T.; Taruya, T.; Ishino, T.; Hamamoto, T.; et al. Changes in the level of dispersion and the degree of antigen sensitization of Japanese cedar and cypress pollen in allergic rhinitis patients in Hiroshima prefecture. *Pract. Oto-Rhino-Laryngol.* **2020**, *113*, 481–486. (In Japanese) [CrossRef]
15. Oberg, T.; Brosseau, L.M. Surgical mask filter and fit performance. *Am. J. Infect. Control* **2008**, *36*, 276–282. [CrossRef] [PubMed]
16. Dubini, M.; Robotti, C.; Benazzo, M.; Rivolta, F. Impact of quarantine and face masks on ragweed-induced oculorhinitis during the COVID-19 pandemic in Northern Italy. *Int. Forum. Allergy Rhinol.* **2021**, *12*, 220–222. [CrossRef] [PubMed]
17. Acevedo, N.; Zakzuk, J.; Caraballo, L. House dust mite allergy under changing environments. *Allergy Asthma Immunol. Res.* **2019**, *11*, 450–469. [CrossRef] [PubMed]
18. d'Alessandro, M.; Bergantini, L.; Perrone, A.; Cameli, P.; Beltrami, V.; Alderighi, L.; Pini, L.; Bargagli, E.; Saletti, M. House Dust Mite Allergy and the Der p1 Conundrum: A Literature Review and Case Series. *Allergies* **2021**, *1*, 8. [CrossRef]
19. Yonekura, S.; Okamoto, Y.; Horiguchi, S.; Sakurai, D.; Chazono, H.; Hanazawa, T.; Okawa, T.; Aoki, S.; Konno, A. Effects of aging on the natural history of seasonal allergic rhinitis in middle-aged subjects in South chiba, Japan. *Int. Arch. Allergy Immunol.* **2012**, *157*, 73–80. [CrossRef] [PubMed]
20. Nishijima, C.; Miyagawa, N.; Tsuboyama-Kasaoka, N.; Chiba, T.; Miyachi, M. Association between lifestyle changes and at-home hours during and after the state of emergency due to the COVID-19 pandemic in Japan. *Nutrients* **2021**, *13*, 2698. [CrossRef] [PubMed]

International Journal of
Environmental Research and Public Health

MDPI

Article

Evaluation of Typical Volatile Organic Compounds Levels in New Vehicles under Static and Driving Conditions

Ruihua Guo [1], Xiaofeng Zhu [1], Zuogang Zhu [1], Jianhai Sun [2], Yongzhen Li [1,*], Wencheng Hu [1] and Shichuan Tang [1,*]

1 Institute of Urban Safety and Environmental Science, Beijing Academy of Science and Technology, Beijing 100054, China; guoruihua1988@163.com (R.G.); zxf_402@163.com (X.Z.); zzg20022000@163.com (Z.Z.); hwc@bmilp.com (W.H.)
2 State Key Laboratory of Transducer Technology, Aerospace Information Research Institute, Chinese Academy of Sciences, Beijing 100194, China; sunjh@aircas.ac.cn
* Correspondence: yongzhen_l@sina.com (Y.L.); tsc@bmilp.com (S.T.)

Abstract: In modern societies, the air quality in vehicles has received extensive attention because a lot of time is spent within the indoor air compartment of vehicles. In order to further understand the level of air quality under different conditions in new vehicles, the vehicle interior air quality (VIAQ) in new vehicles with three different brands was investigated under static and driving conditions, respectively. Air sampling and analysis are conducted under the requirement of HJ/T 400-2007. Static vehicle tests demonstrate that with the increasing of vehicle interior air temperature in sunshine conditions, a higher concentration and different types of volatile organic compounds (VOCs) release from the interior materials than that in the environment test chamber, including alkanes, alcohols, ketones, benzenes, alkenes, aldehydes, esters and naphthalene. Driving vehicle tests demonstrate that the concentration of VOCs and total VOCs (TVOC) inside vehicles exposed to high temperatures will be reduced to the same level as that in the environment test chamber after a period of driving. The air pollutants mainly include alkanes and aromatic hydrocarbons. However, the change trends of VOCs and TVOC vary under different conditions according to various kinds of factors, such as vehicle model, driving speed, air exchange rate, temperature, and types of substance with different boiling points inside the vehicles.

Keywords: vehicle interior air quality; volatile organic compounds; new vehicles; static conditions; driving conditions

Citation: Guo, R.; Zhu, X.; Zhu, Z.; Sun, J.; Li, Y.; Hu, W.; Tang, S. Evaluation of Typical Volatile Organic Compounds Levels in New Vehicles under Static and Driving Conditions. *Int. J. Environ. Res. Public Health* **2022**, *19*, 7048. https://doi.org/10.3390/ijerph19127048

Academic Editors: Ashok Kumar, M Amirul I Khan, Alejandro Moreno Rangel and Michał Piasecki

Received: 25 April 2022
Accepted: 5 June 2022
Published: 9 June 2022

1. Introduction

Social concerns over indoor-air quality extend not only to the indoor-air environment of newly built apartment houses but also to that of vehicles [1,2]. In modern societies, as a result of urban sprawl, a vehicle cabin has been recognized as a part of the living environment because people are spending increased time in vehicles than ever before during business, shopping, recreation or travel activities [3–6]. Unfortunately, harmful volatile organic compounds (VOCs), such as benzene, toluene, ethylbenzene, xylenes, styrene, butyl acetate, and undecane, etc., exist in vehicular cabins, which deteriorate vehicle interior air quality (VIAQ) and threaten the health of drivers/passengers [7–14].

The vehicle interior pollution results from the emission of interior furnishing materials and the infiltration of engine exhausts and other exterior environmental pollutants [15–17]. In a vehicle cabin, the concentration of VOCs may be higher in comparison to concentrations found in public or private buildings [18–20], which may vary in time and are dependent on the interior temperature, humidity, ventilation, vehicle age and other parameters [21–23]. Wensing [24] proved that the concentrations of in-vehicle total volatile organic compounds (TVOC) decrease exponentially over a 40-day period from 35~120 mg/m^3 to 10~30 mg/m^3. Yoshida and Matsunaga [25] also demonstrated that the TVOC concentration decreased from over 10 mg/m^3 to 200 µg/m^3 during the first three years after delivery. The investigation carried out by Grabbs also found that TVOC levels inside new vehicles decreased by more than 90% during a three-week test period [26]. The concentrations of most VOCs declined over time, but increased with increasing interior temperature [27]. Increasing temperature encourages higher desorption of VOCs from interior materials, and the amount of VOCs in vehicles is higher during the summer than during the winter [28]. During vehicle operation, air pollutants originating from interior materials are reduced as more and more VOCs initially captured from interior materials are eventually removed by ventilation [28]. However, heavy traffic problems result in poor air quality in the city, and subsequently cause more serious in-vehicle air pollution problems [29]. Vehicle interior benzene concentrations range from 10~20 µg/m^3 during freeway travel to 150 µg/m^3 in heavy urban traffic [30]. VOCs in new vehicles are usually measured under static conditions, in which the air exchange rate is very low (1~3 h^{-1}) [31]. However, under other operating conditions, such as setting the fan to fresh air (closing windows), the air exchange rate in the vehicle will increase (13.3~26.1 h^{-1}), thus reducing the level of air pollutants in the vehicle [27].

In this study, in order to further understand the level of air quality under different conditions in new vehicles, the concentrations and types of typical VOCs are measured and identified under the static (parked in environment test chamber and in sunshine, vehicle's engine is off) and driving conditions, respectively. Additionally, the limits specified in Chinese national guidelines for air quality assessment of passenger cars (GB/T 27630-2011) [32] are cited for comparison with the concentrations of typical VOCs.

2. Experimental Methods

2.1. Vehicicles under Study and Their Pretreatment

The vehicles under study included three brands (Brand A, B, C) of vehicles from different manufacturers, which were all newly domestically produced vehicles in China (tested less than 28 ± five days from their date of production). There were three different models in vehicles of Brand A (A1, A2, A3) and B (B1, B2, B3) respectively, and one model in vehicles of Brand C (C1). The number (n) of vehicles of each model in Brand A, B and C were one (labeled as A1-1, A2-1, A3-1), two (labeled as B1-1, B1-2, B2-1, B2-2, B3-1, B3-2) and six (labeled as C1-1, C1-2, C1-3, C1-4, C1-5, C1-6) (Table 1). All vehicles were well maintained and in good operating condition. None of the vehicles had fuel leakages or any mechanical problems. The covering films, such as plastic film, on the surfaces of the vehicles' trim materials were ripped off. The passenger compartments were completely free of cigarette smoke and deodorizers. Details of interior materials of all vehicles are presented in Table 1.

Table 1. Vehicles under study and corresponding test conditions.

Tested Vehicles			n	Interior Materials			Test Conditions		
							Static Conditions		Driving Conditions
				Seat	Carpet	Interior	Environment Test Chamber	Sunshine Condition	
Brand A	A1	A1-1	1	Leather	Fabric	Plastic	Section 2.2.1	Section 2.2.2	-
	A2	A2-1	1	Fabric					
	A3	A3-1	1	Leather					
Brand B	B1	B1-1	2	Leather	Fabric	Plastic	Section 2.2.1	Closed exposure for 1 h, no sampling	40 km/h
		B1-2							
	B2	B2-1	2					Closed exposure for 1 h, no sampling	40 km/h
		B2-2							
	B3	B3-1	2					Closed exposure for 4 h, no sampling	40 km/h
		B3-2							

Table 1. *Cont.*

Tested Vehicles			n	Interior Materials			Test Conditions		
							Static Conditions		Driving Conditions
				Seat	Carpet	Interior	Environment Test Chamber	Sunshine Condition	
Brand C	C1	C1-1	4	Leather	Fabric	Plastic	Section 2.2.1	-	50 km/h
		C1-2							
		C1-3							
		C1-4							
		C1-5	2					Closed exposure for 2 h, no sampling	50 km/h
		C1-6							

2.2. Sampling Process under Static Conditions

Under static conditions, the air exchange between the interior and exterior environment of vehicles was significantly reduced when all windows and doors of vehicles were closed. In the case that the concentrations of air pollutants outside of vehicles were very low, VIAQ mainly depended on the amount of VOCs released from vehicle interior sources. That was, the amount of harmful substances released from vehicle interior trims could reflect the situation of vehicle interior air pollution. In this study, the static state was first chosen as the test state of the vehicles, and the vehicle interior air samples were collected in the environment test chamber and in sunshine condition respectively. Standard sampling and analytical methods were used in this experiment.

2.2.1. Vehicle Test Protocol in Environment Test Chamber

As many factors could affect concentrations of VOCs in vehicles, an environment test chamber with a volume of 100 m^3 was utilized in this experiment, which could provide stable and accurate control of the required temperature, relative humidity (%RH), and airflow velocity, according to set parameters. The air in the chamber was purified by activated carbon filters to reduce the influence of background VOCs on VIAQ. The interior surface of the chamber was constructed with stainless steel, which could minimize adsorption and emission of VOCs [29].

The test protocols utilized with the vehicles (Brand A~C) when sampling the interior air were as follows [33]: (a) The vehicle was moved (the engine was off) to the environment test chamber, and then the chamber's door was closed. (b) The environmental conditions in the chamber were adjusted according to the set parameters and kept for the whole test duration: environment temperature: 25.0 ± 1.0 °C; relative humidity: $50\% \pm 10\%$; airflow velocity: ≤ 0.3 m/s; background toluene and formaldehyde concentration: ≤ 0.02 mg/m^3; background TVOC concentration: ≤ 0.1 mg/m^3. The vehicle was aired by opening the windows and doors for 8 h to make a good mixture inside and outside of the vehicle, and then the vehicle was left closed for 16 h, assuming it could reach a steady state pollutant concentration in this period.

The sampling position inside the vehicle was set at head height in the middle of the front two headrests to simulate the height of the driver's breathing zone. Teflon tubing was used as the sampling line, which was led outside the vehicle from the upper corner of the vehicle's door, and the length between the sampling device and the sampling location was 2 m. In this way, the sampling process could be done outside the vehicle, thus eliminating the influence of the operator activities on the testing results. In-chamber air samples as background samples were also collected simultaneously. The sampling position in the chamber was within a range of 0.5 m from the test vehicle and at the same height with that in the vehicle. During the whole test procedure, temperature and relative humidity in the chamber were recorded to satisfy the required parameters [29,33].

2.2.2. Vehicle Test Protocol in Sunshine Condition

After the test in the environment test chamber, the vehicles of Brand A were moved outside of the chamber and parked under direct sunlight between 10:00 a.m. and 3:00 p.m. on a sunny and windless day in summer. The ambient temperature during the process of sun exposure should be in the range of 35~37 °C, which could make in-vehicle air temperature increase quickly. In the course of experiments, the Telfon tubing and sensor probe of the thermometer and hygrometer were fixed at the predetermined sampling point (Section 2.2.1), which could auto-monitor and record the temperature and relative humidity inside the vehicles. The tested vehicles were left closed for 4 h (A1-1, A2-1, A3-1) and then the samples of the vehicle's interior air were collected. The background concentrations of toluene, formaldehyde and TVOC in ambient air should meet the same requirements as in the environment test chamber (Section 2.2.1). Air samples outside the vehicles were collected for blank analysis simultaneously, and the sampling position was within a range of 0.5 m from the test vehicle and at the same height with that in the vehicle.

2.3. *Sampling Process under Driving Conditions*

After the test in the environment test chamber, the vehicles of Brand B and C were moved to the outside of the chamber and were tested on the vehicle proving ground according to the driving test conditions shown in Table 1. Similarly, a sunny and windless day in summer was chosen as the sampling day, and the background concentrations of toluene, formaldehyde and TVOC in ambient air should meet the same requirements as those in the environment test chamber (Section 2.2.1). The windows and vents of the vehicles were kept closed for the entire test procedure. The air conditioner in the vehicle was turned on and set to internal circulation, and the temperature was adjusted to 25 °C. Under driving conditions, since the in-vehicle air samples couldn't be collected outside the vehicle, it was necessary to bring the sampling device into the vehicle for sampling. The sampling points were arranged strictly according to the requirements of that in static conditions. The sampling workers entering the vehicle had to wear masks and foot covers to reduce the influence of the external air pollutants on the air quality of the tested vehicles. The sampling time began when the driver and sampling workers entered the tested vehicle and turned on the air conditioner in the vehicle (recorded as 0 min). The work from entering the vehicle to when sampling started should be completed within 1 min. The in-vehicle air samples of 0~30 min and 60~90 min were collected with a sampling duration of 30 min. The ambient air samples on the vehicle proving ground as background samples were also collected simultaneously, and the sampling position was at the same height as the sampling position in the vehicle during driving.

2.4. *Air Sampling and Analysis*

Air sampling and analysis was conducted under the requirement of HJ/T400-2007 [33]. In-vehicle VOC emissions (C_6–C_{16}) were taken by active sampling using controlled flow pumps at a rate of 100 mL/min for 30 min onto a stainless steel tube packed with Tenax TA. The samples obtained were stored at 4 °C and were protected from light in a refrigerator until analysis. The thermal desorption-gas chromatography/mass spectrometry (TD-GC/MS) was employed for identification and quantification of in-vehicle VOC emissions. The collected VOCs were thermally desorbed at 270 °C for 3 min. The desorbed compounds were cryogenically focused in a cold trap at −30 °C. After focusing, the trap underwent rapid heating to 280 °C to volatilize the compounds into a GC capillary column through a fused-silicaline heated at 250 °C. The desorbed compounds were identified from the mass spectral data by using the US National Institute of Standards and Technology (NIST). The standard curves were produced with the mixed standard solutions, which were composed of only 9 VOCs, such as benzene, toluene, ethylbenzene, p-xylene, m-xylene, o-xylene, styrene, butyl acetate, and undecane. The identifications of these 9 VOCs were confirmed by their respective chromatographic retention time, and their quantifications were based on a multipoint external standard curve. The response factor of toluene was utilized for quantification of other VOCs and TVOC [22,29].

Aldehydes and ketones in the vehicles were sampled by active sampling using controlled flow pumps at a rate of 400 mL/min for 30 min onto an adsorption tube coated with 2,4-dinitrophenylhydrazine (DNPH). The samples obtained were stored at 4 °C and protected from light in a refrigerator until analysis. Adsorbed aldehydes and ketones were extracted using acetonitrile (HPLC grade) and analyzed by high performance liquid chromatography (HPLC) using a UV detector (360 nm). The HPLC analysis was performed using acetonitrile/water elution (60%/40%, *v*/*v*) as a mobile phase at a flow rate of 1.0 mL/min, an injection volume of 25 μL, and a column temperature of 40 °C. The standard curves were produced with the mixed standard solutions, which were composed of 14 aldehydes and the DNPH derivatives of the ketones, such as formaldehyde-DNPH, acetaldehyde-DNPH, acrolein-DNPH, acetone-DNPH, propionaldehyde-DNPH, butenal-DNPH, butanone-DNPH, methacrolein-DNPH, butyraldehyde-DNPH, benzaldehyde-DNPH, valeraldehyde-DNPH, methylbenzaldehyde-DNPH, cyclohexanone-DNPH, and n-hexanal-DNPH. The identifications of these 14 aldehydes and ketones were confirmed by their respective chromatographic retention time, and their quantifications were based on a multipoint external standard curve.

3. Results and Discussion

3.1. Temperature and Relative Humidity in Vehicles of Brand A

The interior temperature and relative humidity in the tested vehicles remained constant in the environment test chamber. however, they were tested in sunny conditions, which would vary with external conditions, such as temperature, whether it was sunny or cloudy out, whether it was windy, etc. Thus, in order to increase the emission of VOCs from vehicle interior trims and reduce the air exchange rate inside and outside the vehicles to the greatest extent, a sunny and windless day in summer, as a "worst case" scenario, was chosen as the sampling day. For a better understanding of the temperature and relative humidity which could be reached inside the vehicles, temperature and relative humidity data inside the tested vehicles were recorded during enclosure and air sampling. As shown in Figure 1, in sunny conditions, the vehicles' interior air temperature ranged from 28.7 °C to 61.5 °C instead of remaining at 25 °C, and the relative humidity ranged from 11.8% to 26.1% instead of remaining at 50%. The temperature in the vehicle was inversely related to the relative humidity. Without the interference of external conditions, the longer the enclosure time, the higher the temperature in the car.

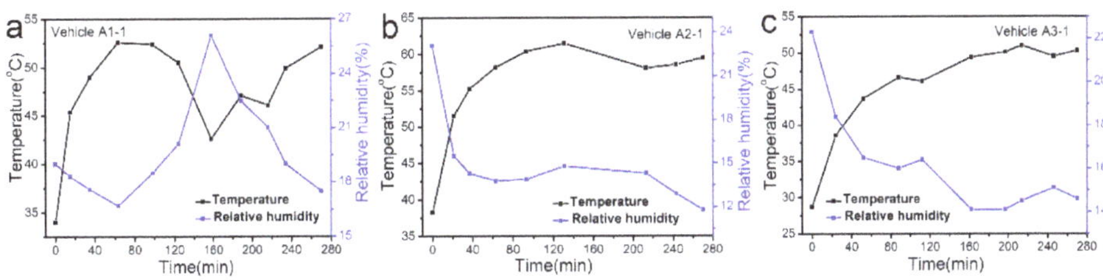

Figure 1. The changes in temperature and relative humidity in sunny conditions inside the vehicles of (**a**) A1-1, (**b**) A2-1 and (**c**) A3-1 during enclosure and air sampling.

3.2. Interior Concentration changes in Vehicles of Brand A

It had been commonly found that interior temperature was an especially important factor influencing the test results [22,29]. As shown in Figure 2, the ratios (C_S/C_E) of concentrations of the confirmed compounds and TVOC measured in Brand A in sunshine condition (C_S) to that in the environment test chamber (C_E) were greater than 1, indicating that the VOCs and TVOC pollution concentrations in the three model vehicles increased sharply when the temperature rose from 28.7 °C to 61.5 °C. In addition, as illustrated in

Figure 3, when the in-vehicle temperature was 25 °C (in the environment test chamber), the concentrations of the eight in-vehicle confirmed compounds were all lower than their respective limited values in the national standard GB/T 27630-2011. However, when in-vehicle temperature increased, the concentrations of formaldehyde, acetaldehyde, and acrolein in Vehicle A1-1 (Figure 3a) and that of styrene, formaldehyde, acetaldehyde, and acrolein in Vehicle A2-1 (Figure 3b) were 1.89, 1.92, 1.44, 1.40, 7.84, 2.1, and 1.76 times more than their corresponding limited values in the national standard GB/T 27630. Therefore, in-vehicle high temperature was helpful for the evaporation and off-gassing of more VOCs from vehicle interior trims, for the main reason that the release amount of such VOCs as organic solvents, adhesives and additives contained in the interior trim materials could increase more when in-vehicle temperature rose [34,35]. In addition, the reports also showed that the concentrations of VOCs in vehicle interiors increased in concert with the temperature [25,27,36]. Reducing in-vehicle temperature could slow down the VOC emissions from the vehicles' interior materials.

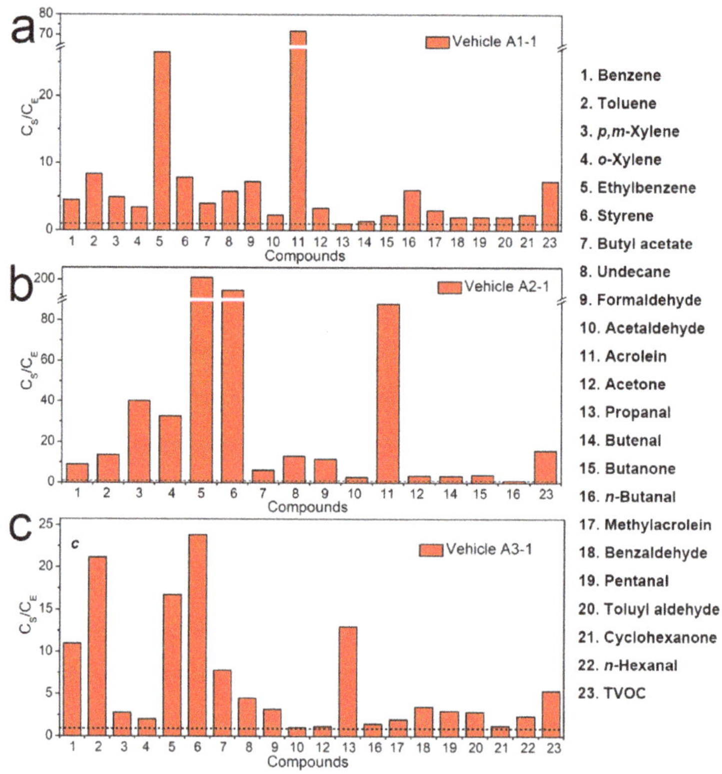

Figure 2. The ratios of concentrations of confirmed compounds and TVOC measured inside the (**a**) Vehicle A1-1, (**b**) Vehicle A2-1, (**c**) Vehicle A3-1 in sunshine condition (C_S) to that in the environment test chamber (C_E). The black short dash corresponds to a value of 1.

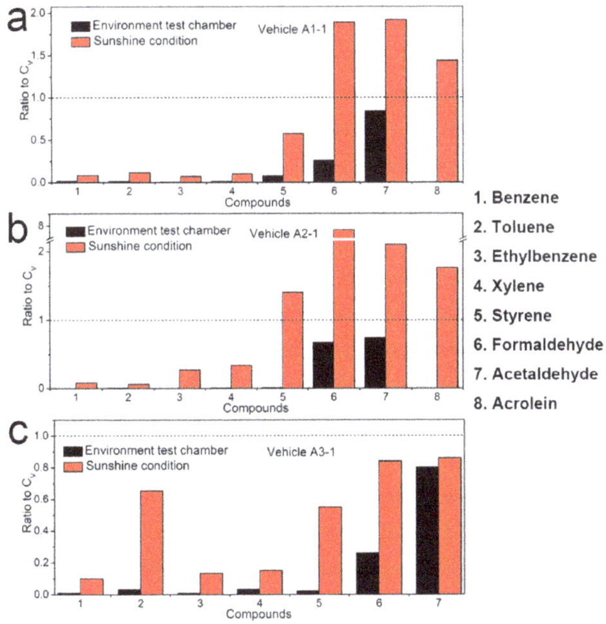

Figure 3. The ratios of concentrations of eight confirmed compounds measured inside (**a**) Vehicle A1-1, (**b**) Vehicle A2-1, (**c**) Vehicle A3-1 in the environment test chamber (C_E) with sunny outdoor conditions (C_S) to their corresponding limited values (C_V) of the national standard GB/T 27630, respectively. The black short dash corresponds to a value of 1.

3.3. Interior VOC Type changes in Vehicles of Brand A

Table 2 shows the types of the top 18 VOCs, excluding benzene, toluene, xylene, ethylbenzene, styrene, butyl acetate and undecane, identified in interior air samples of Vehicle A1-1, Vehicle A2-1, Vehicle A3-1, and changes of VOC types under different static conditions. In general, the most alkanes were in the three vehicles under each test condition, but there were more alkanes in the environment test chamber than in the sunshine condition. While in the sunshine condition, there were more other types of compounds, such as alcohols, ketones, benzenes, alkenes, aldehydes, esters, than that in environment test chamber (shown in Table 2). This was because the exposure of the vehicles to direct sunlight in the sunshine condition could lead to interior temperatures up to 61.5 °C, therefore the surface temperatures of the interior materials would be higher, which could cause the volatilization of various chemical substances with different boiling points from the interior surfaces. Thus, the chemical composition and types of VOCs were changed under different static conditions. In conjunction with high temperature, the transmission of solar radiation through glass windows could induce photochemical reactions and the production of degradation of byproducts, which could also cause changes in the chemical composition and types of VOCs.

An environment with a high concentration of VOCs could pose a very large health hazard to drivers and passengers. However, considering that few drivers and passengers would stay in such high-temperature vehicles, it was necessary to further study the changes in the concentrations and types of VOCs in the vehicles under driving conditions when they were exposed to direct sunlight.

Table 2. Types of the top 18 VOCs identified in interior air samples of Brand A (excluding benzene, toluene, xylene, ethylbenzene, styrene, butyl acetate and undecane).

Tested Vehicles	Static Conditions	Number of Each Type Compounds							
		Alkanes	Alcohols	Ketones	Benzenes	Alkenes	Aldehydes	Esters	Naphthalene
Vehicle A1-1	Environment test chamber	14	2	1	0	1	0	0	0
	Sunshine condition	8	3	3	2	0	1	1	0
Vehicle A2-1	Environment test chamber	12	1	1	0	0	1	1	2
	Sunshine condition	11	1	2	1	0	0	2	1
Vehicle A3-1	Environment test chamber	14	1	1	1	0	0	0	1
	Sunshine condition	8	2	2	2	1	0	2	1

3.4. Interior Concentration changes in Vehicles of Brand B and C

To further evaluate the differences in VOC concentrations in the vehicles' interior, air samples were also collected under driving conditions. According to the test results, the concentrations of eight confirmed compounds inside the vehicles of Brand B and C in the environment test chamber were commensurate, and the TVOC concentrations inside Brand C were obviously higher than that of Brand B. In addition, the concentrations of eight confirmed compounds and TVOC inside Brand B and C in the environment test chamber (C_E) and under driving conditions ($C_{D(0–30min)}$, $C_{D(60–90min)}$) were also compared and discussed.

As shown in Figure 4, in general, the concentration changes of eight confirmed compounds inside six vehicles of Brand B were $C_{D(0–30min)} > C_{D(60–90min)} \geq C_E$. But there were some exceptions. Inside the vehicle B1–1, the concentration change of benzene was $C_{D(0–30min)} = C_{D(60–90min)} > C_E$, that of xylene was $C_{D(60–90min)} > C_{D(0–30min)} > C_E$, that of ethylbenzene and styrene were $C_{D(60–90min)} > C_{D(0–30min)} = C_E$, and that of acrolein was $C_E > C_{D(0–30min)} = C_{D(60–90min)}$. Inside the vehicle B1-2, the concentration change of formaldehyde was $C_{D(0–30min)} > C_{D(60–90min)} > C_E$, while that of other compounds were $C_E > C_{D(0–30min)} \geq C_{D(60–90min)}$. Inside the vehicle B2-1, the concentration change of styrene was $C_E > C_{D(0–30min)} = C_{D(60–90min)}$, and that of formaldehyde was $C_{D(0–30min)} > C_E > C_{D(60–90min)}$. Inside the vehicle B2-2, the concentration change of ethylbenzene was $C_E = C_{D(0–30min)} > C_{D(60–90min)}$. Inside the vehicle B3-1 and B3-2, the concentration change of acetaldehyde was $C_{D(0–30min)} > C_E > C_{D(60–90min)}$. Whereas, as shown in Figure 5, the change trends of concentrations inside six vehicles of Brand C were clearly different with that inside Brand B, which generally were $C_E > C_{D(0–30min)} > C_{D(60–90min)}$. But there were also some exceptions. Inside the vehicle C1-1, the concentration changes of toluene and formaldehyde were $C_{D(0–30min)} > C_E > C_{D(60–90min)}$. The concentration changes of acetaldehyde inside vehicle C1-2, that of formaldehyde and acetaldehyde inside C1-3 and that of toluene inside C1-4 were all $C_E > C_{D(60–90min)} > C_{D(0–30min)}$. Inside vehicle C1-4, the concentration change of xylene was $C_E > C_{D(0–30min)} = C_{D(60–90min)}$, that of acrolein was $C_{D(60–90min)} > C_E = C_{D(0–30min)}$. Similarly, as shown in Figure 6, the TVOC concentration changes inside the six vehicles of Brand B were all $C_{D(0–30min)} > C_{D(60–90min)} > C_E$, while that inside Brand C were $C_E > C_{D(0–30min)} > C_{D(60–90min)}$, which had the same trend as that of eight confirmed compounds.

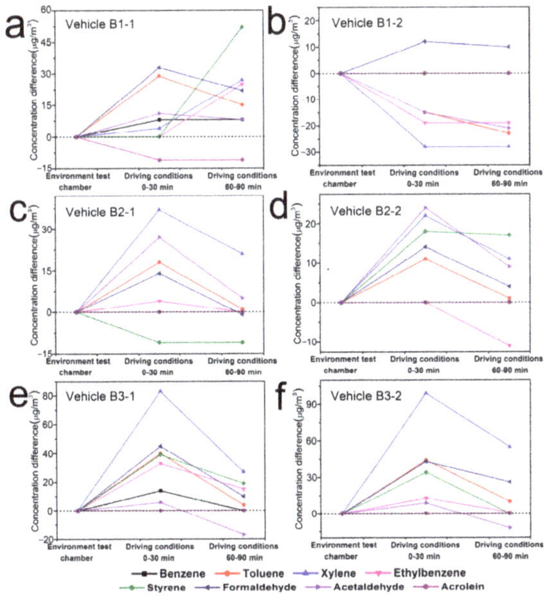

Figure 4. Concentration changes of eight confirmed compounds inside six vehicles of Brand B under different conditions ((**a**). Vehicle B1-1; (**b**). Vehicle B1-2; (**c**). Vehicle B2-1; (**d**). Vehicle B2-2; (**e**). Vehicle B3-1; (**f**). Vehicle B3-2). *Y*-axis indicates the concentration difference between $C_{D(0–30min)}$ and C_E, $C_{D(60–90min)}$ and C_E.

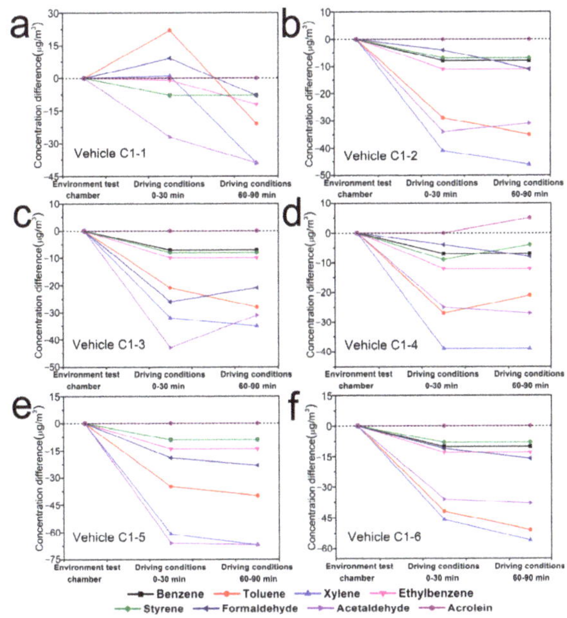

Figure 5. Concentration changes of eight confirmed compounds inside six vehicles of Brand C under different conditions ((**a**). Vehicle C1-1; (**b**). Vehicle C1-2; (**c**). Vehicle C1-3; (**d**). Vehicle C1-4; (**e**). Vehicle C1-5; (**f**). Vehicle C1-6)). *Y*-axis indicates the concentration difference between $C_{D(0–30min)}$ and C_E, $C_{D(60–90min)}$ and C_E.

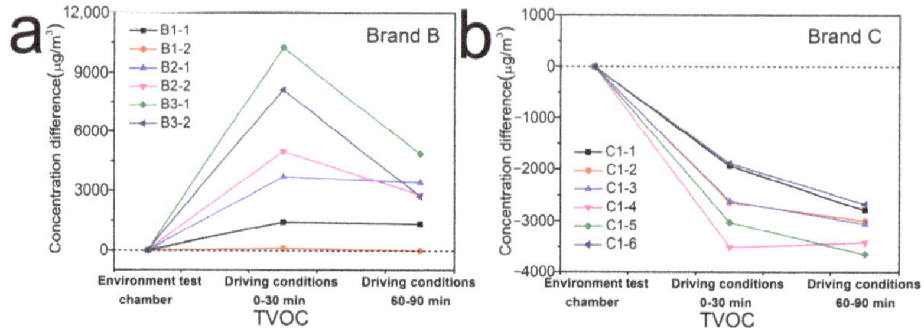

Figure 6. Concentration changes of TVOC inside six vehicles of (**a**) Brand B and (**b**) C under different conditions. *Y*-axis indicates the concentration difference between $C_{D(0\text{–}30min)}$ and C_E, $C_{D(60\text{–}90min)}$ and C_E.

As the air conditioning mode inside the tested vehicles was adjusted to internal circulation, and the infiltration air flow through joints and leaks in vehicle envelopes was the predominant airflow that could affect pollutant transportation inside vehicle cabins [17,37]. Under driving conditions, the vehicles ran at a certain speed, which could accelerate the air exchange inside and outside vehicles. Therefore, the concentration changes of VOCs and TVOC inside the vehicles should be $C_E > C_{D(0\text{–}30min)} > C_{D(60\text{–}90min)}$ in theory, which was consistent with the results tested inside the vehicles of Brand C. But based on the test results of Brand B, except for some substances inside the vehicle B1-1 and B1-2, $C_{D(0\text{–}30min)}$ were generally higher than C_E and $C_{D(60\text{–}90min)}$. That was because the six vehicles of Brand B were all parked and enclosed under direct sunlight (Table 1) before the experiments were carried out under driving conditions, which could accelerate volatilization of VOCs from vehicle interior trims due to the high temperature inside the vehicles. Therefore, it was reasonable that more pollutants were collected inside the vehicles of Brand B at the first 30 min under driving conditions than that in environment test chamber, even though the temperature was the same under these two conditions. However, although the vehicle C1-5 and C1-6 were also parked and enclosed under direct sunlight for 2 h before running on the vehicle proving ground, the $C_{D(0\text{–}30min)}$ of VOCs and TVOC were actually lower than their C_E. That was because different vehicle brands have different air exchange rates. And the higher speed of the vehicles of Brand C than that of Brand B could lead to the increase of the air exchange rate inside and outside Brand C on one hand, while on the other hand, there might be (no air sampling) less pollutants emitted from the interior trims of Brand C than that of Brand B under direct sunlight, and then the concentration of pollutants inside Brand C would decrease rapidly at a higher air exchange rate.

As the vehicles continued to run at a certain speed, the concentration of VOCs and TVOC inside the vehicles would decrease with time due to the air exchange inside and outside the vehicles. Thus, $C_{D(60\text{–}90min)}$ of VOCs and TVOC inside Brand B were less than their $C_{D(0\text{–}30min)}$. But the air exchange rate value determined whether a longer driving process was required to reduce the concentration of airborne pollutants in the vehicles to be consistent with or lower than that in the environment test chamber. According to the test results shown in Table 3, the $C_{D(60\text{–}90min)}$ of eight compounds and TVOC were 1.00~3.27 times and 0.99~7.93 times more than their C_E, demonstrating that after a period of driving, the concentrations of air pollutants inside the vehicles of Brand B were decreased to the same level with or close to that in the environment test chamber (Figures 4 and 6a). If the air conditioning mode was switched to external circulation (the concentration of ambient air pollutants should meet the requirements in Section 2.2.1), it would take a shorter time to reduce the concentration of air pollutants in the vehicles. The above results further indicated that the concentration values obtained by the standard method (in environment test chamber) were close to the actual exposure level for drivers and passengers.

Table 3. The ratios of $C_{D(60\text{–}90min)}$ and C_E of eight confirmed compounds and TVOC measured inside Brand B.

Compounds	$C_{D(60\text{–}90min)}/C_E$					
	B1-1	**B1-2**	**B2-1**	**B2-2**	**B3-1**	**B3-2**
Benzene	/	/	/	/	/	/
Toluene	1.71	/	1.06	1.07	1.21	1.56
Xylene	1.55	/	1.81	1.46	1.77	/
Ethylbenzene	3.27	/	1.00	/	/	1.09
Styrene	/	/	/	2.00	/	/
Formaldehyde	1.73	1.28	0.98	1.09	1.23	2.44
Acetaldehyde	1.4	0.46	1.15	1.30	0.67	0.71
Acrolein	/	/	/	/	/	/
TVOC	5.05	0.99	3.57	3.38	7.93	3.40

"/" means that the value of C_E was not detected.

3.5. Interior VOC Type changes in Vehicles of Brand B and C

The difference in the types and boiling points of VOCs inside the vehicles of Brand B and C would also lead to the difference in the trend of TVOC concentration changes inside these vehicles in actual driving conditions. It would take a longer driving time to reduce the TVOC concentration inside these vehicles to a level that was consistent with or lower than that in the environment test chamber.

Tables 4 and 5 showed types of the top 10 VOCs identified inside the vehicles of Brand B and C, and changes of VOCs types under different test conditions. For the vehicles of Brand B, alkanes were the main pollutants. But for the two vehicles of each model in Brand B, there was no difference in the VOC types under different conditions. Whereas inside the vehicles of Brand C, benzenes and alkanes were the main pollutants. But in the environment test chamber, there were more benzenes and less alkanes than that in driving conditions. In addition to the effect of temperature on the air quality inside the vehicles, air exchange rate inside and outside the vehicles was also the factor influencing the VOCs types.

Table 4. Types of the top 10 VOCs identified in interior air samples of Brand B.

Tested Vehicles	Test Conditions	Number of Each Type Compounds		
		Alkanes	**Alcohols**	**Alkenes**
Vehicle B1-1Vehicle B1-2	Environment test chamber Driving condition (0–30 min) Driving condition (60–90 min)	8	2	0
Vehicle B2-1Vehicle B2-2	Environment test chamber Driving condition (0–30 min) Driving condition (60–90 min)	10	0	0
Vehicle B3-1Vehicle B3-2	Environment test chamber Driving condition (0–30 min) Driving condition (60–90 min)	9	0	1

Table 5. Types of the top 10 VOCs identified in interior air samples of Brand C.

Tested Vehicles	Test Conditions	Number of Each Type Compounds					
		Benzenes	**Alkanes**	**Alcohols**	**Alkenes**	**Esters**	**Others**
Vehicle C1-1	Environment test chamber	8	2	0	0	0	0
	Driving conditions (0–30 min)	6	4	0	0	0	1
	Driving conditions (60–90 min)	4	6	0	0	0	1

Table 5. *Cont.*

Tested Vehicles	Test Conditions	Number of Each Type Compounds					
		Benzenes	Alkanes	Alcohols	Alkenes	Esters	Others
Vehicle C1-2	Environment test chamber	7	2	0	0	0	0
	Driving conditions (0–30 min)	4	4	1	0	0	1
	Driving conditions (60–90 min)	5	5	0	0	0	1
Vehicle C1-3	Environment test chamber	6	2	0	0	1	1
	Driving conditions (0–30 min)	3	2	0	1	0	4
	Driving conditions (60–90 min)	6	4	0	0	0	0
Vehicle C1-4	Environment test chamber	7	2	0	0	1	0
	Driving conditions (0–30 min)	4	6	0	0	0	1
	Driving conditions (60–90 min)	4	5	0	0	0	1
Vehicle C1-5	Environment test chamber	8	2	0	0	0	0
	Driving conditions (0–30 min)	5	5	0	0	0	1
	Driving conditions (60–90 min)	4	6	0	0	0	1
Vehicle C1-6	Environment test chamber	7	2	0	0	0	0
	Driving conditions (0–30 min)	4	5	0	0	0	1
	Driving conditions (60–90 min)	5	5	0	0	0	1

4. Conclusions

The following conclusions can be drawn through the comparison and discussion of the quantitative and qualitative analysis results of VOCs in the vehicle interior air of Brand A~C under different conditions:

(1) The in-vehicle high temperature in the sunshine condition causes higher concentrations and more different types of VOCs released from the interior materials with different boiling points of VOCs than that in environment test chamber. In the vehicles of Brand A, more alkanes were identified in the environment test chamber, while more other types of compounds, such as alcohols, ketones, benzenes, and esters, were identified in the sunshine condition. In the vehicles of Brand C, there are aromatic hydrocarbons and alkanes, and the number of aromatic hydrocarbons is slightly more than that of alkanes. While in Brand B, there are mainly alkanes without aromatic hydrocarbons. Therefore, the drivers and passengers should ventilate their vehicles and turn on the air conditioner to cool down the interior before using a vehicle exposed to the sunshine.

(2) Because of different in-vehicle temperatures, driving speeds, air exchange rates, and types of substances with different boiling points inside the vehicles, the change trends of eight typical organic pollutants and TVOC concentrations in the air of Brand B and C tested vehicles under different conditions are also different, namely:

The vehicles of Brand B: $C_{D(0–30min)} > C_{D(60–90min)} \geq C_E$,

The vehicles of Brand C: $C_E > C_{D(0–30min)} > C_{D(60–90min)}$.

The existence of individual exceptions is not excluded.

(3) There are no requirements with regard to the limited values and measurement methods for VIAQ under high temperature in the national standard GB/T 27630 and HJ/T 400. However, according to the results in this study, the concentrations of eight typical organic compounds inside the vehicles exposed to high temperature after a period of driving will be reduced to the same level as or tend to that in the environmental chamber test, indicating that the results of standard test methods are close to the actual driving exposure level. However, due to the variety of pollutants, it takes a longer time for the TVOC concentration to reduce to the same level as that in the environmental chamber test.

Author Contributions: Conceptualization, R.G. and Z.Z.; data curation, R.G. and Y.L.; formal analysis, R.G.; funding acquisition, R.G., X.Z. and Y.L.; investigation, R.G. and J.S.; methodology, R.G.; validation, R.G., X.Z., Z.Z. and Y.L.; visualization, R.G. and X.Z.; writing—original draft preparation, R.G.; resources, Z.Z., W.H. and S.T.; writing—review and editing, Z.Z. and Y.L.; supervision, R.G. and S.T.; All authors have read and agreed to the published version of the manuscript.

Funding: This research was funded by the BJAST Budding Talent Program (BGS202101), National Natural Science Foundation of China (No. 61874012) and Beijing Natural Science Foundation (No. 3224063).

Institutional Review Board Statement: Not applicable.

Informed Consent Statement: Not applicable.

Conflicts of Interest: The authors declare that they have no conflict of interest.

Nomenclature

VIAQ	vehicle interior air quality
VOCs	volatile organic compounds
TVOC	total volatile organic compounds
C_S	concentrations of VOCs and TVOC measured inside the vehicles in sunshine condition
C_E	concentrations of VOCs and TVOC measured inside the vehicles in environment test chamber
C_V	the limited values of VOCs specified in the standard GB/T 27630-2011
$C_{D(0\text{–}30min)}$	concentrations of VOCs and TVOC measured inside the vehicles under driving conditions of 0–30 min
$C_{D(60\text{–}90min)}$	concentrations of VOCs and TVOC measured inside the vehicles under driving conditions of 60–90 min

References

1. Seo, J.; Choi, Y. Estimation of the air quality of a vehicle interior: The effect of the ratio of fresh air to recirculated air from a heating, ventilation and air-conditioning system. *J. Automob. Eng.* **2013**, *227*, 1162–1172. [CrossRef]
2. Moreno, T.; Pacitto, A.; Fernández, A.; Amato, F.; Marco, E.; Grimalt, J.O. Vehicle interior air quality conditions when travelling by taxi. *Environ. Res.* **2019**, *172*, 529–542. [CrossRef]
3. Müller, D.; Klingelhöfer, D.; Uibel, S.; Groneberg, D.A. Car indoor air pollution-analysis of potential sources. *J. Occup. Med. Toxicol.* **2011**, *6*, 33. [CrossRef]
4. Klepeis, N.E.; Nelson, W.C.; Ott, W.R.; Robinson, J.P.; Tsang, A.M.; Switzer, P.; Behar, J.V.; Hern, S.C.; Engelmann, W.H. The national human activity pattern survey (NHAPS): A resource for assessing exposure to environmental pollutants. *J. Expo. Anal. Env. Epid.* **2001**, *11*, 231–252. [CrossRef]
5. Yoshida, T.; Matsunaga, I.; Tomioka, K.; Kumagai, S. Interior air pollution in automotive cabins by volatile organic compounds diffusing from interior materials: II. Influence of manufacturer, specifications and usage status on air pollution, and estimation of sir pollution levels in initial phases of delivery as a new car. *Indoor Built Environ.* **2006**, *15*, 445–462.
6. Dudzińska, M.R. Volatile organic compounds in private cars and public vehicles. *Rocz. Ochr. Sr.* **2011**, *13*, 101–116.
7. Dettmer, K.; Engewald, W. Adsorbent materials commonly used in air analysis for adsorptive enrichment and thermal desorption of volatile organic compounds. *Anal. Bioanal. Chem.* **2002**, *373*, 490–500. [CrossRef]
8. Idris, S.A.; Robertson, C.; Morris, M.A.; Gibson, L.T. A comparative study of selected sorbents for sampling of aromatic VOCs from indoor air. *Anal. Methods* **2010**, *2*, 1803–1809. [CrossRef]
9. Geiss, O.; Tirendi, S.; Barrero-Moreno, J.; Kotzias, D. Investigation of volatile organic compounds and phthalates present in the cabin air of used private cars. *Environ. Int.* **2009**, *35*, 1188–1195. [CrossRef]
10. Rahman, M.M.; Kim, K.H. Exposure to hazardous volatile pollutants back diffusing from automobile exhaust systems. *J. Hazard. Mater.* **2012**, *241–242*, 267–278. [CrossRef]
11. Li, S.; Chen, S.; Zhu, L.; Chen, X.; Yao, C.; Shen, X. Concentrations and risk assessment of selected monoaromatic hydrocarbons in buses and bus stations of Hangzhou, China. *Sci. Total Environ.* **2009**, *407*, 2004–2011. [CrossRef]
12. Faber, J.; Brodzik, K.; Gołda-Kopek, A.; Łomankiewicz, D. Benzene, toluene and xylenes levels in new and used vehicles of the same model. *J. Environ. Sci.* **2013**, *25*, 2324–2330. [CrossRef]
13. Schupp, T.; Bolt, H.M.; Jaeckh, R.; Hengstler, J.G. Benzene and its methyl-derivatives: Derivation of maximum exposure levels in automobiles. *Toxicol. Lett.* **2006**, *160*, 93–104. [CrossRef]
14. Chan, L.Y.; Lau, W.L.; Wang, X.M.; Tang, J.H. Preliminary measurements of aromatic VOCs in public transportation modes in Guangzou, China. *Environ. Int.* **2003**, *29*, 429–435. [CrossRef]
15. Jo, W.K.; Park, K.H. Concentration of volatile organic compounds in the passengers side and the back seat of automobiles. *J. Expo. Anal. Env. Epid.* **1999**, *9*, 217–227. [CrossRef]

16. Yoshida, T.; Matsunaga, I.; Tomioka, K.; Kumagai, S. Interior air pollution in automotive cabins by volatile organic compounds diffusing from interior materials: I. survey of 101 types of Japanese domestically produced cars for private use. *Indoor Built Environ.* **2006**, *15*, 425–444.
17. Xu, B.; Chen, X. Air quality inside motor vehicles' cabins: A review. *Indoor Built. Environ.* **2016**, *27*, 1–14. [CrossRef]
18. Mandalakis, M.; Stephanou, E.G.; Horii, Y.; Kannan, K. Emerging contaminants in car interiors: Evaluating the impact of airborne PBDEs and PBDD/Fs. *Environ. Sci. Technol.* **2008**, *42*, 6431–6436. [CrossRef]
19. Riediker, M.; Williams, R.; Devlin, R.; Griggs, T.; Bromberg, P. Exposure to particulate matter, volatile organic compounds, and other air pollutants inside patrol cars. *Environ. Sci. Technol.* **2003**, *37*, 2084–2093. [CrossRef]
20. Ilgen, E.; Levsen, K.; Angerer, J.; Schneider, P.; Wichmann, H.E. Aromatic hydrocarbons in the atmospheric environment. Part III: Personal monitoring. *Atmos. Environ.* **2001**, *35*, 1265–1279.
21. Zhang, G.; Li, T.; Luo, M.; Liu, J.; Liu, Z.; Bai, Y. Air pollution in the microenvironment of parked new cars. *Build. Environ.* **2008**, *43*, 315–319. [CrossRef]
22. Chen, X.; Feng, L.; Luo, H.; Cheng, H. Analyses on influencing factors of airborne VOCs pollution in taxi cabins. *Environ. Sci. Pollut. R.* **2014**, *21*, 12868–12882. [CrossRef] [PubMed]
23. Faber, J.; Brodzik, K.; Łomankiewicz, D.; Golda-Kopek, A.; Nowak, J.; Świątek, A. Temperature influence on air quality inside cabin of conditioned car. *Combust. Engines* **2012**, *149*, 49–56. [CrossRef]
24. Wensing, M. Standard test methods for the determination of VOCs and SOVCs in automobile interiors. In *Organic Indoor Air Pollutants*, 2nd ed.; Salthammer, T., Uhde, E., Eds.; Wiley-VCH: Weinheim, Germany, 2009; Chapter 7; pp. 147–164.
25. Yoshida, T.; Matsunaga, I. A case study on identification of air-borne organic compounds and time courses of their concentrations in the cabin of a new car for private use. *Environ. Int.* **2006**, *32*, 58–79. [CrossRef] [PubMed]
26. Grabbs, J.S.; Corsi, R.L.; Torres, V.M. Volatile organic compounds in new automobiles: Screening assessment. *J. Environ. Eng.* **2000**, *126*, 974–977. [CrossRef]
27. Chien, Y.C. Variations in amounts and potential sources of volatile organic chemicals in new cars. *Sci. Total Environ.* **2007**, *382*, 228–239. [CrossRef] [PubMed]
28. Brodzik, K.; Faber, J.; Lomankiewiez, D. In-vehicle VOCs composition of unconditioned newly produced cars. *J. Environ. Sci.* **2014**, *26*, 1052–1061. [CrossRef]
29. You, K.W.; Ge, Y.S.; Hu, B.; Ning, Z.W.; Zhao, S.T.; Zhang, Y.N.; Xie, P. Measurement of in-vehicle volatile organic compounds under static conditions. *J. Environ. Sci.* **2007**, *19*, 1208–1213. [CrossRef]
30. Duffy, B.L.; Nelson, P.F. Exposure to benzene, 1,3-butadiene and carbon monoxide in the cabins of moving motor vehicles. In Proceedings of the 13th International Clean Air and Environment Conference, Adelaide, Australia, 22–25 September 1996; Clean Air Society of Australia and New Zealand: Melbourne, Australia, 1996; pp. 195–200.
31. Chan, C.; Spengler, J.; Özkaynak, H. Commuter exposures to VOCs in Boston, Massachusetts. *J. Air Waste Manag.* **1991**, *41*, 1594–1600. [CrossRef]
32. *GB/T 27630-2011*; Guideline for Air Quality Assessment of Passenger Car. Standards Press of China: Beijing, China, 2011.
33. *HJ/T 400-2007*; Determination of Volatile Organic Compounds and Carbonyl Compounds in Cabin of Vehicles. Environmental Protection Industry Standard of China: Beijing, China, 2007.
34. Chen, X.; Zhang, G.; Zhang, Q.; Chen, H. Mass concentrations of BTEX inside air environment of buses in Changsha, China. *Build. Environ.* **2011**, *46*, 421–427. [CrossRef]
35. Parra, M.A.; Elustondo, D.; Bermejo, R.; Santamaria, J.M. Exposure to volatile organic compounds (VOC) in public buses of Pamplona, Northern Spain. *Sci. Total Environ.* **2008**, *404*, 18–25. [CrossRef] [PubMed]
36. Fedoruk, M.J.; Kerger, B.D. Measurement of volatile organic compounds inside automobiles. *J. Expo. Anal. Env. Epid.* **2003**, *13*, 31–41. [CrossRef] [PubMed]
37. Guo, R.; Sun, H.; Song, Y.; Hu, B.; Zhu, Z.; Lin, Y. Research progress on influencing factors of air quality in vehicle cabins. *Chin. J. Automot. Eng.* **2019**, *9*, 79–88.

International Journal of
Environmental Research and Public Health

MDPI

Article

Volatile Organic Compounds in Finnish Office Environments in 2010–2019 and Their Relevance to Adverse Health Effects

Kaisa Wallenius *, Hanna Hovi, Jouko Remes, Selma Mahiout and Tuula Liukkonen

Finnish Institute of Occupational Health, P.O. Box 40, FI-00032 Työterveyslaitos, Finland; hanna.hovi@ttl.fi (H.H.); jouko.remes@ttl.fi (J.R.); selma.mahiout@ttl.fi (S.M.); tuula.liukkonen@ttl.fi (T.L.)
* Correspondence: kaisa.wallenius@ttl.fi

Abstract: We gathered recent (2010–2019) data on the VOC and formaldehyde levels in Finnish non-industrial indoor work environments. The data comprised 9789 VOC and 1711 formaldehyde samples collected from the indoor air of offices, schools, kindergartens, and healthcare offices. We assessed the health risks by comparing the measured concentrations to the health-based RW I/II and EU-LCI reference values. The concentrations of individual VOCs and formaldehyde in these work environments were generally very low and posed no health risks. Total VOC concentration (TVOC) as well as concentrations of several individual compounds, including aromatic compounds, alkanes, 2-ethyl-1-hexanol, and formaldehyde, showed clearly decreasing trends. In contrast, several aldehydes, acids, and a few other compounds showed increasing trends. However, the increasing trends did not seem to affect the higher ends of the distributions, as the 95th percentile values remained fairly stable or decreased over the years. The VOC patterns in the environments of the offices, schools, kindergartens, and healthcare offices varied, probably reflecting the differences in typical activities and the use of materials. However, we do not expect these differences to be relevant to health outcomes.

Keywords: indoor air quality; VOC; formaldehyde; office; health risk; trend

Citation: Wallenius, K.; Hovi, H.; Remes, J.; Mahiout, S.; Liukkonen, T. Volatile Organic Compounds in Finnish Office Environments in 2010–2019 and Their Relevance to Adverse Health Effects. *Int. J. Environ. Res. Public Health* **2022**, *19*, 4411. https://doi.org/10.3390/ijerph19074411

Academic Editors: Ashok Kumar, M Amirul I Khan, Alejandro Moreno Rangel and Michał Piasecki

Received: 17 February 2022
Accepted: 24 March 2022
Published: 6 April 2022

1. Introduction

Volatile organic compounds (VOCs) are a versatile group of chemical compounds that are present both indoors and outdoors. Indoor air has a greater variety of different VOCs than outdoor air, and the concentrations of these compounds are typically higher indoors than outdoors [1–4]. The differences in the composition of indoor and outdoor air derive from greater human impact, a larger surface area to volume ratio, and lower levels of light and oxidising agents indoors [5]. Typical groups of the organic compounds present in indoor air are alkanes, terpenes, aromatic hydrocarbons, and aldehydes [4,6].

The spatial and temporal variation of volatile compounds in indoor environments is great. This variation is governed by both natural and man-made sources of emissions both indoors and outdoors. Indoor emission sources include building and interior materials, technical systems and equipment, buildings' occupants, and a large variety of chemicals, products, and materials used and produced by occupants in different activities. The main outdoor emission sources are traffic and industrial processes. VOC levels are impacted by the seasons [3,7] and the geographic locations of building [6–9]. The long-term chemical composition of indoor environments changes as new technologies and materials are developed [10–12].

Concerns over possible health risks related to VOC emissions in the indoor air are prevalent. Many VOCs and formaldehyde are known to be hazardous and to pose health risks in high concentrations in, for example, industrial work environments. The same does not necessarily apply to non-industrial environments if the concentrations remain below levels that induce health hazards.

The aim of the study was to (1) compile recent measurement data on the levels of VOCs and formaldehyde in offices and similar non-industrial indoor work environments in Finland and (2) to evaluate the health relevance of these. We also extended the study to analyse trends during the study period (2010–2019) and to inspect the differences between the environments of offices, schools, kindergartens, and healthcare offices.

To analyse the VOCs, we used the definition and analytical procedure described in the ISO 16000-6:2011 standard, which defines VOCs as substances that elute between n-hexane and n-hexadecane under defined chromatographic conditions. To analyse formaldehyde, which belongs to very volatile organic compounds (VVOC), we used an ISO 16000-3:2011-based analytical procedure.

2. Materials and Methods

2.1. Description of Data

The data of this study comprised results from indoor air samples of VOCs and formaldehyde from Finnish offices and similar non-industrial work environments analysed at the laboratory of the Finnish Institute of Occupational Health (FIOH) between January 2010 and December 2019. The total number of samples to measure VOCs was 9789, collected from offices (3872 samples), schools (3583 samples), kindergartens (727 samples), and healthcare offices (1607 samples). Healthcare offices were office-like spaces in healthcare premises where patients were not treated. The total number of samples for measuring formaldehyde was 1711, collected from offices (521 samples), schools (938 samples), kindergartens (68 samples), and healthcare offices (184 samples). The yearly distributions of VOC and formaldehyde samples are presented in Table 1.

Table 1. The yearly numbers of VOC (**a**) and formaldehyde (**b**) samples collected from office, school, kindergarten, and healthcare office environments.

(**a**) VOC samples.

Year	Office	School	Kindergarten	Healthcare Office
2010	384	253	52	119
2011	416	310	68	182
2012	333	298	67	295
2013	385	309	69	190
2014	447	344	102	105
2015	313	163	42	99
2016	324	489	81	195
2017	379	548	87	139
2018	446	449	90	144
2019	445	420	69	139

(**b**) Formaldehyde samples.

Year	Office	School	Kindergarten	Healthcare Office
2010	19	14	5	6
2011	47	37	7	14
2012	72	37	5	26
2013	35	42	5	28
2014	58	95	6	7
2015	73	79	9	19
2016	38	182	10	10

Table 1. *Cont.*

Year	Office	School	Kindergarten	Healthcare Office
2017	57	131	10	25
2018	77	208	5	39
2019	45	113	6	10

The sampling was performed by experts from a multitude of consultant engineering offices (customers of FIOH's analytical laboratory) as part of indoor air services, without a systematic monitoring programme. The samples were collected from occupied buildings during all seasons and from different parts of Finland. Winter (December, January, February) and spring (March, April, May) seasons accounted for approximately 60% (30% each) of all the VOC samples collected, whereas summer (June, July, August) and autumn (September, October, November) were less active sampling seasons with the shares of 15% summer and 24% autumn. Similar to VOCs, the seasonal distribution of formaldehyde samples was 32% winter, 27% spring, 17% summer, and 25% autumn.

The majority of the samples were collected from buildings with suspected indoor air-quality problems. In the buildings in which VOCs were measured, the suspected problems did not necessarily concern VOC pollution. In contrast, formaldehyde was measured in buildings in which the suspected problems specifically concerned formaldehyde. The laboratory did not record the age, the renovation status, or technical characteristics of the buildings, but we assume that the studied premises represent well the relatively homogenous Finnish building stock of public and office buildings built in 1960–2000. The vast majority of public and office buildings in Finland are equipped with mechanical supply and exhaust ventilation. The average number of samples per one sampling occasion (forming one laboratory assignment) was 3.1 for VOC (3167 sampling occasions) and 3.3 for formaldehyde (520 sampling occasions). The samples from single sampling occasions were mainly collected from one building but from different rooms. Thus, the number of sampling occasions gives a rough estimate of the number of sampled buildings.

2.2. Sampling and Analysing VOCs

The VOCs were sampled and analysed in accordance with the ISO 16000-6:2011 standard. The samples were collected in Tenax TA or Tenax TA/Carbograph 5 TD tubes from central room locations 1–1.5 m above floor level, mainly (99.5%) by active sampling (pump). Diffusive sampling was used for approximately 0.5% of the samples. We analysed the samples using thermal desorption and GC/MS. The compounds were identified by comparing them to pure reference substances and/or the Wiley or NIST mass spectral databases. FIOH's laboratory has approximately 150 different compounds calibrated with their own response factors. Calibrated compounds cover most of the common compounds in indoor air. Some individual compounds that are not frequently identified or quantified from samples, and some mixtures, such as higher boiling alcohols or hydrocarbon mixtures, are quantitated as toluene equivalents because reference compounds are not available. All the individual compounds whose results are presented in this article were quantified with substance-specific responses. The total concentration of volatile organic compounds (TVOC) was determined for each sample as a toluene-equivalent concentration. TVOC was determined as the area in the chromatogram between the n-hexane and n-hexadecane, including both substances.

FIOH's laboratory has ISO 17025 accreditation. The laboratory provided detailed sampling instructions and calibrated sampling equipment for the experts who performed sampling. The recommended sampling volume in active sampling was 7–12 dm^3. Typical sampling volume was 9 dm^3, which is equal to 45 or 90 min of sampling time. Diffusive sampling times were 2 to 4 weeks. The laboratory evaluated sampling volumes and times for every sample.

2.3. Sampling and Analysing Formaldehyde

Formaldehyde was sampled and analysed in accordance with the ISO 16000-3:2011 and the ISO 16000-4:2011 standards. The samples were collected in 2,4-dinitrophenylhydrazine (DNPH)-coated silica gel cartridges (Sep-Pak® DNPH-Silica Plus Short Cartridge) using active sampling (91%) or in DNPH-coated passive samplers (UMEx 100 Passive Sampler for formaldehyde) using diffusive sampling (9%). The DNPH derivate of formaldehyde was desorbed using acetonitrile and then analysed with a high-performance liquid chromatography (HPLC) that contained a UV detector. Formaldehyde was identified and quantitated with reference compounds.

The laboratory provided detailed sampling instructions and calibrated sampling equipment for the experts who performed sampling. Recommended sampling volume in active sampling was 100 dm^3, which is equal to 100 min of sampling time. Diffusive sampling time was 24 h. The laboratory evaluated sampling volumes and times for every sample.

2.4. Statistical Methods

First, we calculated the frequencies of the different analytes. Frequency indicates the percentage of samples whose results exceed the limit of quantitation (LOQ). To describe the distribution of the variables, we calculated the 50th percentile (median, Md), 90th percentile (P90), 95th percentile (P95), and 99th percentile (P99), first covering all the samples and then separately for different indoor environments and different years (2010–2019). For percentiles, we calculated the 95% confidence intervals based on normal distribution.

The association between the frequency of the different measures in the different types of environments was analysed using log-binomial regression analysis. The office was used as a reference group. We dichotomised the values such that <LOQ values were 0, and ≥LOQ values were 1. In log-binomial regression analyses, we compared percentages (value 1) separately school/kindergarten/healthcare offices to offices' percentages. We calculated the crude risk ratios (RR) and their 95% confidence intervals and made no adjustments.

We analysed the frequency and concentration trends of each compound. The frequency trend was tested using Somer's D test, in which the input data were binomial (measurement result either ≥LOQ or <LOQ). The concentration trend was tested using Somer's D test, in which the input data comprised all the measured concentration values. Here, measurement results that were <LOQ were replaced by a concentration value of LOQ/2. Statistically significant trends were evaluated using the Z value. This statistic is used to test the null hypothesis, according to which no trend exists. A positive Z indicates an increasing trend in a time-series, while a negative Z indicates a decreasing trend. We used the SPSS and SAS statistical software packages for our calculations.

2.5. Health Risk Assessment

Health-based RW I/II and EU-LCI values were used to evaluate the possible health risks of VOCs and formaldehyde at the concentration levels measured. Both reference values have been set by experts using epidemiological and toxicological data. We primarily used the RW I/II values. If the RW values were not available, we used the European EU-LCI values if they were available.

The German RW I and II values [13,14] are reference values for indoor air-quality assessment that are set to cover the entire population and long-term exposure. In Germany, they are used in assessment of indoor air quality in homes, offices, schools, and other public spaces. The RW II values represent concentration levels that may cause adverse health effects for individuals who are sensitive due to their health status, for example, if they are exposed to these concentration levels for extended periods of time. The RW I values represent concentration levels which, in the light of current knowledge, do not cause adverse health effects even in cases of lifetime exposure.

The EU-LCI values (LCI, Lowest Concentration of Interest) are intended for assessing the safety of construction products regarding the potential health risks posed by inhaling emissions from new products [15]. The values aim to prevent health risks and cover the lifetime exposure of the entire population. They therefore represent concentration levels that, in the light of current knowledge, are considered unlikely to cause adverse health effects even in the long term. However, the EU-LCI values are not intended for use as reference values for assessing indoor air quality; they are for assessing building material emissions under experimental conditions. Nonetheless, as they were derived using the principles of toxicological hazard assessments, we considered them adequate for use in our study as indicative reference values when RW values were not available.

Health risk assessment was performed by calculating risk characterisation ratios (RCRs; [16]) for the 42 most frequently detected VOCs. The calculations were made by dividing the 99th percentile (P99) of the measurements by the above-mentioned health-based reference values. The RCRs were considered to indicate a potential health risk if they exceeded 1.

3. Results

3.1. Statistics of Entire Ten-Year Data

Around 400 different analytes (single compounds or mixtures that cannot be separated by the measurement protocol) were detected and quantitated at least once in the ten-year VOC data, which consisted of 9789 air samples. Formaldehyde data collected and analysed using a different procedure from that used for VOC during the same study period consisted of 1711 air samples. The LOQ for different compounds ranged between 0.3 and 1 μg/m^3. The number of VOCs that had a frequency of ≥10% was 42. Table 2a presents the descriptive statistics of these 42 VOCs and the TVOC sum variable. Table 2b presents the corresponding statistics for the formaldehyde measurements. In addition to the measurement data, Table 2 is supplemented with up-to-date health-based reference values (EU-LCI, RW I, and RW II) for respective compounds if available.

The median values of the 42 most common VOCs were mostly below the respective LOQ: only 12 compounds had a frequency greater than 50% (Table 2a). P90 values were typically only slightly above the respective LOQ: 0.5–3 μg/m^3. The largest P90 value was observed for 1,2-propanediol, at 7 μg/m^3. P95 values ranged from 0.6 μg/m^3 (octane) to 13 μg/m^3 (1,2-propanediol). P99 values ranged from 1 μg/m^3 (octane, nonane) to 45 μg/m^3 (1,2-propanediol). The maximum values were tenfold to hundredfold larger than the P99 values for most of the compounds. The maximum values ranged from 12 μg/m^3 (octane) to 1110 μg/m^3 (xylenes p, m).

None of the RCRs, representing possible health risks, exceeded 1 when the P99 values of the 42 common VOCs were compared with their respective RW I, RW II, and EU-LCI values; all P99 values were well below their respective health-based reference values (Table 2a). The highest RCR compared to the RW I values, 0.75, was found for 1,2-propanediol.

No RW I/II or EU-LCI values exist for the alkanes nonane, octane, and 2,2,4,6,6-pentamethylheptane. All their P99 values (1–6 μg/m^3) remained notably below the EU-LCI value of heptane (15,000 μg/m^3), which belongs to the same group of alkanes. Based on the similar chemical properties and health hazard profiles of all these four alkanes, we can assume that this reference value would probably be in the same range as their own EU-LCI values. No RW I/II or EU-LCI values are available for benzene, but the UBA derived risk-related guide values for carcinogenic substances in indoor air [13]. The risk-related value for benzene is 4.5 μg/m^3 (preliminary value), which is above the P99 value of 3.0 μg/m^3 [14].

The maximum values of several of the 42 most common VOCs exceeded their RW I values. The maximum values for xylenes, 1,2-propanediol, 2-(2-ethoxyethoxy)ethanol, and phenoxyethanol also exceeded the RW II and/or EU-LCI values. In addition, the maximum value of benzene exceeded its risk-related value.

The TVOC sum variable has no health-based reference values. The health relevance of TVOC can only be meaningfully evaluated if the components of the total concentration are known.

Table 2. Statistics of the most frequent VOCs (**a**), formaldehyde (**b**), and selected infrequent VOCs (**c**), in air samples collected from Finnish office and similar non-industrial indoor environments in 2010–2019. Health-based reference values (RW I, RW II, and EU-LCI) are presented for comparison if available. LOQ values of different groups of compounds are approximate.

(**a**) Statistics of 42 most frequently detected VOCs in air samples collected from Finnish office and similar non-industrial indoor environments in 2010–2019. Bottom line presents TVOC sum variable statistics. VOCs were sampled and analysed in accordance with ISO 16000-6:2011.

Group	Analyte	CAS	All Samples $n = 9789$ (From Offices, 3872; Schools, 3583; Kindergartens, 727; and Healthcare Offices, 1607 Samples)						Health-Based Reference Values	
			Frequency in Samples 2010–2019 (>LOQ)	Md (μg/m^3)	P90 (μg/m^3)	P95 (μg/m^3)	P99 (μg/m^3)	Max (μg/m^3)	RW I/II (μg/m^3)	EU-LCI (μg/m^3)
Alkanes LOQ = 0.3–0.5 μg/m^3	Heptane	142-82-5	15%	<LOQ	0.5	0.9	3.0	110	–	15,000
	Nonane	111-84-2	13%	<LOQ	0.4	0.7	1.0	35	–	–
	Octane	111-65-9	13%	<LOQ	0.4	0.6	1.0	12	–	–
	2,2,4,6,6-Pentamethylheptane	13475-82-6	11%	<LOQ	0.4	1.0	6.0	260	–	–
Aromatic hydrocarbons LOQ = 0.5 μg/m^3	Benzene	71-43-2	65%	0.5	1.0	2.0	3.0	31	– [1]	–
	Ethylbenzene	100-41-4	23%	<LOQ	0.7	1.0	4.0	380	200/2000 [1]	850
	1,2,4-Trimethyl-benzene	95-63-6	15%	<LOQ	0.5	0.8	2.0	62	400/4000	450
	Xylenes (p, m)	108-38-3, 106-42-3	60%	0.5	2.0	3.0	12	1110	100/800 [2]	500 [1]
	Xylene (o)	95-47-6	27%	<LOQ	0.8	1.0	5.0	370	100/800 [2]	500 [3]
	Toluene	108-88-3	81%	0.7	3.0	5.0	17	620	300/3000 [2]	2900
Terpenes LOQ = 0.5 μg/m^3	3-Carene	498-15-7	32%	<LOQ	2.0	3.0	10	620	200/2000	1500
	Limonene	138-86-3, 5989-27-5, 5989-54-8	25%	<LOQ	1.0	3.0	14	1020	1000/10,000	5000
	α-Pinene	80-56-8	64%	0.7	4.0	8.0	24	250	200/2000	2500
	β-Pinene	127-91-3	10%	<LOQ	<LOQ	0.7	2.0	16	200/2000	1400
Alcohols LOQ = 0.5 μg/m^3 except for 1,2-propanediol 0.8–1 μg/m^3	Benzyl alcohol	100-51-6	19%	<LOQ	0.9	2.0	13	170	400/4000	440
	1-Butanol	71-36-3	73%	0.7	3.0	5.0	13	790	700/2000	3000
	2-Ethyl-1-hexanol	104-76-7	64%	0.6	3.0	7.0	21	230	100/1000 [1]	300
	2-Methyl-1-propanol	78-83-1	21%	<LOQ	0.8	1.0	4.0	180	–	11,000
	1,2-Propanediol	57-55-6	56%	0.8	7.0	13	45	720	60/600	2100

Table 2. *Cont.*

Group	Analyte	CAS	All Samples n = 9789 (From Offices, 3872; Schools, 3583; Kindergartens, 727; and Healthcare Offices, 1607 Samples)						Health-Based Reference Values	
			Frequency in Samples 2010–2019 (>LOQ)	Md (µg/m^3)	P90 (µg/m^3)	P95 (µg/m^3)	P99 (µg/m^3)	Max (µg/m^3)	RW I/II (µg/m^3)	EU-LCI (µg/m^3)
Phenols LOQ = 0.5 µg/m^3	Phenol	108-95-2	20%	<LOQ	0.8	1.0	4.0	40	20/200	70
Alcohol and phenol ethers LOQ = 0.5–1 µg/m^3	2-(2-Butoxy ethoxy)ethanol	112-34-5	17%	<LOQ	2.0	3.0	11	97	400/2000 [4]	350
	2-Butoxyethanol	111-76-2	19%	<LOQ	0.8	2.0	8.0	140	100/1000	1600
	2-(2-Ethoxyethoxy) ethanol	111-90-0	21%	<LOQ	2.0	4.0	25	730	700/2000 [4]	350
	2-Phenoxyethanol	122-99-6	22%	<LOQ	0.9	2.0	5.0	110	30/100	60
	1-Methoxy-2-propanol	107-98-2	14%	<LOQ	0.7	1.0	6.0	370	1000/10,000	7900
Aldehydes LOQ = 0.5 µg/m^3	Benzaldehyde	100-52-7	78%	1.0	2.0	3.0	5.0	76	20/200 [4]	–
	Decanal	112-31-2	62%	0.7	2.0	3.0	5.0	19	100/2000	900
	Hexanal	66-25-1	56%	0.6	3.0	5.0	14	310	100/2000	900
	Heptanal	111-71-7	17%	<LOQ	0.6	0.9	2.0	20	100/2000	900
	Nonanal	124-19-6	80%	1.0	4.0	6.0	11	75	100/2000	900
	Octanal	124-13-0	38%	<LOQ	1.0	1.0	3.0	36	100/2000	900
	Pentanal	110-62-3	32%	<LOQ	1.0	2.0	4.0	96	100/2000	800
Ketones LOQ = 0.5 µg/m^3	Acetophenone	98-86-2	23%	<LOQ	0.7	0.9	2.0	25	–	490
Acids LOQ = 0.5–1 µg/m^3	Hexanoic acid	142-62-1	39%	<LOQ	5.0	7.0	14	330	–	2100
	Pentanoic acid	109-52-4	12%	<LOQ	0.6	2.0	4.0	98	–	2100
	Propinoic acid	79-09-4	19%	<LOQ	2.0	3.0	8.0	110	–	1500
Esters LOQ = 0.3–0.5 µg/m^3	n-Butyl acetate	123-86-4	14%	<LOQ	0.6	1.0	5.0	150	–	4800
	2-(2-Butoxy ethoxy)ethyl acetate	124-17-4	10%	<LOQ	0.3	1.0	6.0	72	–	850
	Ethyl acetate	141-78-6	14%	<LOQ	0.7	2.0	8.0	450	600/6000	–
	Texanol	25265-77-4	23%	<LOQ	1.0	3.0	15	320	–	850
	TXIB	6846-50-0	23%	<LOQ	2.0	3.0	10	100	–	1300

Table 2. *Cont.*

Group	Analyte	CAS	All Samples n = 9789 (From Offices, 3872; Schools, 3583; Kindergartens, 727; and Healthcare Offices, 1607 Samples)						Health-Based Reference Values	
			Frequency in Samples 2010–2019 (>LOQ)	Md (µg/m^3)	P90 (µg/m^3)	P95 (µg/m^3)	P99 (µg/m^3)	Max (µg/m^3)	RW I/II (µg/m^3)	EU-LCI (µg/m^3)
Si-compounds LOQ = 0.5 µg/m^3	Decamethylcyclo-pentasiloxane	541-02-6	72%	1.0	6.0	11	33	680	100/1000	pending
TVOC			100%	30	90	137	290	4700	–	–

(**b**) Statistics of formaldehyde in air samples collected from Finnish office and similar non-industrial indoor environments in 2010–2019. Formaldehyde was sampled and analysed in accordance with ISO 16000-3:2011.

Analyte	CAS	All Samples n = 1711 (From Offices, 521; Schools, 938; Kindergartens, 68; and Healthcare Offices, 184 Samples)						Health-Based Reference Values	
		Frequency in Samples 2010–2019 (>LOQ)	Md (µg/m^3)	P90 (µg/m^3)	P95 (µg/m^3)	P99 (µg/m^3)	Max (µg/m^3)	RW I/II (µg/m^3)	EU-LCI (µg/m^3)
Formaldehyde LOQ = 1 µg/m^3	50-00-0	94%	3.8	12	18	46	88	100/-	100

(c) Statistics of selected VOCs with frequency of <10% in ten-year VOC data collected from Finnish office and similar non-industrial indoor environments in 2010–2019. VOCs were sampled and analysed in accordance with ISO 16000-6:2011.

Analyte	CAS	All Samples n = 9789 (From Offices, 3872; Schools, 3583; Kindergartens, 727; and Healthcare Offices, 1607 Samples)			Health-Based Reference Values	
		Frequency in Samples 2010–2019 (>LOQ)	P99 (µg/m^3)	Max (µg/m^3)	RW I/II (µg/m^3)	EU-LCI (µg/m^3)
Carbon tetrachloride	56-23-5	1.0%	<LOQ	12	–	pending
Chloroform	67-66-3	0.4%	<LOQ	9	–	–

Table 2. *Cont.*

		All Samples n = 9789 (From Offices, 3872; Schools, 3583; Kindergartens, 727; and Healthcare Offices, 1607 Samples)			Health-Based Reference Values	
Analyte	**CAS**	**Frequency in Samples 2010–2019 (>LOQ)**	**P99 (µg/m³)**	**Max (µg/m³)**	**RW I/II (µg/m³)**	**EU-LCI (µg/m³)**
1,4-Dichlorobenzene	106-46-7	0.03%	<LOQ	0.7	–	150
Trichloroethene	79-01-6	0.4%	<LOQ	10	– [5]	–
Tetrachloroethene	127-18-4	1.1%	0.4	170	100/1000	80
Styrene	100-42-5	5.7%	1.0	18	30/300	250

[1] Risk-related guide values for carcinogenic substances in indoor air: benzene preliminary value 4.5 µg/m³ [14]; [2] as total guide values C7–C8 alkylbenzenes [14]; [3] LCI value of 500 µg/m³ is common for all three xylene isomers (o, m, p) and their mixtures [15]; [4] preliminary value [14]. [5] Risk-related guide values for carcinogenic substances in indoor air: trichloroethene 20 µg/m³ [14].

The formaldehyde results revealed a shape of distribution that was different from most of the VOCs (Table 2b). For formaldehyde, the gap between P99 and the maximum values was notably smaller, and the proportion of the results that fell below the LOQ was also smaller than that for most VOCs. The formaldehyde data represented buildings/indoor locations that indoor air specialists anticipated to be at risk of elevated formaldehyde concentrations. Therefore, it is likely that in this sample of buildings, formaldehyde occurred more frequently and in higher concentrations than among the normal population of this type of building. Still, the maximum concentration of formaldehyde measured was also below the respective health-based RWI and EU-LCI reference values.

The majority of all the VOCs detected during the ten year-study period were present in less than 10% of the samples. These infrequent VOCs represented a wide variety of different organic compounds. Chlorinated and other VOCs, which are often studied and reported in scientific publications due to their related health concerns, were selected from the data mass and are presented in Table 2c. These chlorinated VOCs were detected very rarely in the ten-year VOC data. The frequency of aromatic styrene was also fairly low. The P99 values of carbon tetrachloride, chloroform, 1,4-dichlorobenzene, and trichloroethene were below the limit of quantitation. The P99 values for tetrachloroethene (0.4 $\mu g/m^3$) and styrene (1.0 $\mu g/m^3$) in turn were far below their RW I and EU-LCI values. It should be noted that Tenax TA has a rather low breakthrough volume for halogenated compounds, such as carbon tetrachloride, trichloroethene, and chloroform, so their concentrations are approximate.

3.2. Differences between Indoor Environments

Table 3a shows the differences between the four studied indoor environment types in terms of the frequency and P95 values of the 42 most common VOCs and the TVOC sum variable. Table 3b presents the corresponding information on formaldehyde. The comparison of environments was based on P95 values instead of medians or other lower percentiles because medians of most individual VOCs were below LOQ in all environments, and many of the P90 values were only slightly above LOQ. Geometric or arithmetic means were also regarded as unfit for this data due to the high percentages of measurement results below LOQ. Median and P90 values are presented as additional information for TVOC and formaldehyde, where they have informative value.

The alkanes heptane, nonane, and octane were detected more frequently in the offices (freq. 17–18%) than in the other studied indoor environments (freq. 10–13%), whereas 2,2,4,6,6-pentamethylheptane was more frequently found in healthcare offices (freq. 16%) than elsewhere (freq. 10%). The P95 values were ≤ 2 $\mu g/m^3$ for all alkanes in all the environments. The differences between the P95 values in the offices and other environments were minor but mainly statistically significant.

Aromatic VOCs, namely benzene, ethylbenzene, 1,2,4-trimethylbenzene, xylenes (p, m, o), toluene, and benzaldehyde (presented under the aldehyde group), were more frequent in the office environments than in the other studied environments. For most of the aromatic compounds presented, the lowest frequencies were measured in the kindergartens. For example, xylenes (p, m) had a frequency of 69% in the offices and 47% in the kindergartens. Despite notable differences in frequency, the differences between the P95 values of the aromatics in the environments were small. The highest P95 values in the aromatic group were observed for toluene: 4–5 $\mu g/m^3$.

Terpenes 3-carene and α-pinene were more frequent in the kindergartens than in the other environments, whereas limonene was the most frequent in the office environment. The lowest frequencies of terpenes were typically observed in the healthcare office environment. The differences between the P95 values were small although mainly statistically significant between office and other environments. The highest P95 values within the terpene group were observed for α-pinene: 6–9 $\mu g/m^3$.

Table 3. Comparison of office environment with school, kindergarten, and healthcare office environments with regard to VOCs (**a**) and formaldehyde (**b**). Statistically significant ($p < 0.05$) differences are marked with an asterisk (*).

(**a**) Comparison of office environment (shaded with gray) with school, kindergarten, and healthcare office environments in terms of frequency and P95 values of the 42 most frequently detected VOCs. Bottom line presents TVOC sum variable statistics.

Group	Analyte	CAS		Office $n = 3872$	School $n = 3583$	Kindergarten $n = 727$	Healthcare Office $n = 1607$
Alkanes LOQ = 0.3–0.5 μg/m^3	Heptane	142-82-5	Frequency	18%	13% *	11% *	12% *
			P95 (μg/m^3)	1.0	0.8 *	0.7 *	0.9 *
	Nonane	111-84-2	Frequency	17%	11% *	6% *	11% *
			P95 (μg/m^3)	0.8	0.6 *	0.5 *	0.6 *
	Octane	111-65-9	Frequency	17%	10% *	12% *	10% *
			P95 (μg/m^3)	0.7	0.5 *	0.6 *	0.5 *
	2,2,4,6,6-Pentamethylheptane	13475-82-6	Frequency	10%	10%	10%	16% *
			P95 (μg/m^3)	1.0	1.0	1.0	2.0 *
Aromatic hydrocarbons LOQ = 0.5 μg/m^3	Benzene	71-43-2	Frequency	68%	63% *	67%	59% *
			P95 (μg/m^3)	2.0	2.0	2.0	1.6 *
	Ethylbenzene	100-41-4	Frequency	28%	22% *	18% *	18% *
			P95 (μg/m^3)	1.0	1.0	0.8 *	1.0
	1,2,4-Trimethylbenzene	95-63-6	Frequency	18%	14% *	9% *	12% *
			P95 (μg/m^3)	0.8	0.8	0.6 *	0.9 *
	Xylenes (p, m)	108-38-3, 106-42-3	Frequency	69%	55% *	47% *	55% *
			P95 (μg/m^3)	3.0	4.0 *	2.0 *	3.0
	Xylene (o)	95-47-6	Frequency	32%	25% *	18% *	22% *
			P95 (μg/m^3)	1.0	2.0 *	0.9 *	1.0
	Toluene	108-88-3	Frequency	87%	77% *	79% *	79% *
			P95 (μg/m^3)	5.0	4.0 *	5.0	4.0 *
Terpenes LOQ = 0.5 μg/m^3	3-Carene	498-15-7	Frequency	31%	33%	42% *	28% *
			P95 (μg/m^3)	3.0	4.0 *	3.0	2.0 *
	Limonene	138-86-3, 5989-27-5, 5989-54-8	Frequency	33%	19% *	24% *	20% *
			P95 (μg/m^3)	3.4	2.0 *	3.0 *	2.0 *

Table 3. *Cont.*

Group	Analyte	CAS		Office n = 3872	School n = 3583	Kindergarten n = 727	Healthcare Office n = 1607
	α-Pinene	80-56-8	Frequency	65%	62% *	76% *	60% *
	β-Pinene	127-91-3	Frequency	10%	10%	10%	8% *
			P95 (μg/m^3)	0.7	0.7	0.7 *	0.5 *
Alcohols LOQ = 0.5 μg/m^3 except for 1,2-propanediol 0.8–1 μg/m^3	Benzyl alcohol	100-51-6	Frequency	19%	20%	18%	15% *
			P95 (μg/m^3)	2.0	3.0 *	1.0 *	1.0 *
	1-Butanol	71-36-3	Frequency	77%	71% *	75%	68% *
			P95 (μg/m^3)	4.0	5.0 *	5.6 *	5.0 *
	2-Ethyl-1-hexanol	104-76-7	Frequency	65%	62% *	67%	68% *
			P95 (μg/m^3)	7.0	6.0 *	6.0 *	8.0 *
	2-Methyl-1-propanol	78-83-1	Frequency	24%	20% *	20% *	18% *
			P95 (μg/m^3)	1.0	1.0	2.0 *	1.0
	1,2-Propanediol	57-55-6	Frequency	60%	51% *	63%	53% *
			P95 (μg/m^3)	13	12 *	14 *	13
Phenols LOQ = 0.5 μg/m^3	Phenol	108-95-2	Frequency	22%	18% *	17% *	21%
			P95 (μg/m^3)	1.0	1.0	1.0	1.0
Alcohol and phenol ethers LOQ = 0.5–1 μg/m^3	2-(2-Butoxy ethoxy)ethanol	112-34-5	Frequency	18%	18%	16%	14% *
			P95 (μg/m^3)	3.0	4.0 *	3.0	3.0
	2-Butoxyethanol	111-76-2	Frequency	20%	19%	19%	12% *
			P95 (μg/m^3)	2.0	2.0	2.0	1.0 *
	2-(2-Ethoxyethoxy)ethanol	111-90-0	Frequency	21%	24% *	23%	10% *
			P95 (μg/m^3)	4.0	7.0 *	5.0 *	1.0 *
	2-Phenoxyethanol	122-99-6	Frequency	22%	21%	24%	21%
			P95 (μg/m^3)	1.0	2.0 *	2.0 *	2.0 *
	1-Methoxy-2-propanol	107-98-2	Frequency	14%	17% *	15%	9% *
			P95 (μg/m^3)	1.0	2.0 *	2.0 *	1.0

Table 3. *Cont.*

Group	Analyte	CAS		Office $n = 3872$	School $n = 3583$	Kindergarten $n = 727$	Healthcare Office $n = 1607$
Aldehydes LOQ = 0.5 μg/m^3	Benzaldehyde	100-52-7	Frequency	80%	77% *	78%	77% *
			P95 (μg/m^3)	3.0	3.0	3.0	2.0 *
	Decanal	112-31-2	Frequency	60%	61%	71% *	66% *
			P95 (μg/m^3)	3.0	3.0	4.0 *	4.0 *
	Hexanal	66-25-1	Frequency	54%	55%	79% *	50% *
			P95 (μg/m^3)	5.0	6.0 *	8.0 *	4.0 *
	Heptanal	111-71-7	Frequency	16%	17%	31% *	13% *
			P95 (μg/m^3)	0.8	0.9 *	1.0 *	0.7 *
	Nonanal	124-19-6	Frequency	77%	80% *	93% *	81% *
			P95 (μg/m^3)	5.0	6.0 *	11 *	5.0
	Octanal	124-13-0	Frequency	39%	36% *	49% *	34% *
			P95 (μg/m^3)	1.0	1.0	2.0 *	1.0
	Pentanal	110-62-3	Frequency	33%	30% *	44% *	25% *
			P95 (μg/m^3)	2.0	2.0	3.0 *	1.0 *
Ketones LOQ = 0.5 μg/m^3	Acetophenone	98-86-2	Frequency	21%	25% *	23%	24% *
			P95 (μg/m^3)	0.8	0.9 *	0.8 *	1.0 *
Acids LOQ = 0.5–1 μg/m^3	Hexanoic acid	142-62-1	Frequency	44%	38% *	43%	31% *
			P95 (μg/m^3)	8.0	7.0 *	8.0	5.0 *
	Pentanoic acid	109-52-4	Frequency	15%	11% *	13%	8% *
			P95 (μg/m^3)	2.0	1.0 *	2.0	0.8 *
	Propinoic acid	79-09-4	Frequency	23%	18% *	20%	12% *
			P95 (μg/m^3)	4.0	3.0 *	4.0	2.0 *
Esters LOQ = 0.3–0.5 μg/m^3	n-Butyl acetate	123-86-4	Frequency	15%	13% *	20% *	11% *
			P95 (μg/m^3)	1.0	1.0	2.0 *	0.9 *
	2-(2-Butoxy ethoxy)ethyl acetate	124-17-4	Frequency	12%	9% *	11%	8% *
			P95 (μg/m^3)	1.0	1.0	1.0	0.8 *
	Ethyl acetate	141-78-6	Frequency	16%	13% *	14%	14%
			P95 (μg/m^3)	2.0	1.0 *	2.0	2.0

Table 3. *Cont.*

Group	Analyte	CAS		Office n = 3872	School n = 3583	Kindergarten n = 727	Healthcare Office n = 1607
	Texanol	25265-77-4	Frequency	22%	26% *	24%	17% *
			P95 (μg/m^3)	3.0	5.0 *	3.0	2.0 *
	TXIB	6846-50-0	Frequency	21%	20%	57% *	19%
			P95 (μg/m^3)	3.0	2.0 *	6.0 *	3.0
Si-compounds LOQ = 0.5 μg/m^3	Decamethylcyclo-pentasiloxane	541-02-6	Frequency	76%	65% *	70% *	76%
			P95 (μg/m^3)	13	9.0 *	12 *	12 *
TVOC			Frequency	100%	100%	100%	100%
			Md (μg/m^3)	30	20 *	30	23 *
			P90 (μg/m^3)	90	90	100 *	90
			P95 (μg/m^3)	140	130 *	136 *	130 *

(**b**) Comparison of office environment to school, kindergarten, and healthcare office environments with regard to frequency and percentile values of formaldehyde.

Analyte	CAS		Office n = 521	School n = 938	Kindergarten n = 68	Healthcare Office n = 184
Formaldehyde LOQ = 1 μg/m^3	50-00-0	Frequency	95%	93%	96%	91%
		Md (μg/m^3)	5	3 *	4	4
		P90 (μg/m^3)	18	10 *	14 *	13 *
		P95 (μg/m^3)	25	14 *	20 *	17 *

Alcohols generally had the lowest frequencies in the healthcare offices, but the differences between the environments were small. Alcohol ethers and phenol ethers also had the lowest frequencies in the healthcare offices, but their differences to other environments were more prominent. The only representative of the phenol group, namely phenol, had the lowest frequency in the kindergartens, but the differences between the environments were small. The P95 concentrations of alcohols, phenols, alcohol ethers, and phenol ethers were generally rather similar in all the environments. The biggest difference between the P95 concentrations in the different environments was observed for 2-(2-ethoxyethoxy)ethanol and ranged from 1 $\mu g/m^3$ (healthcare office) to 7 $\mu g/m^3$ (school). The highest P95 concentrations within these VOC groups were observed for 1,2-propanediol: 12–14 $\mu g/m^3$.

Apart from aromatic benzaldehyde, the VOCs in the aldehyde group, namely decanal, hexanal, heptanal, nonanal, octanal, and pentanal, had notably higher frequencies in the kindergartens than in the other environments. The P95 concentrations of aliphatic aldehydes were also systematically slightly higher in the kindergartens than in the other environments. The greatest difference observed in P95 values was for nonanal, with a P95 of 11 $\mu g/m^3$ in the kindergartens and 5–6 $\mu g/m^3$ in the other environments.

The only representative of the ketone group, namely acetophenone, had rather similar frequencies (range 21–25%) and P95 concentrations (range 0.8–1 $\mu g/m^3$) in all the studied environments.

The three carboxylic acids presented under the acids group, namely hexanoic acid, pentanoic acid, and propionic acid, had the highest frequencies in the office environment and the lowest frequencies in the healthcare offices. The P95 values of acids were also slightly lower in the healthcare offices than in the other environments. The largest difference between the P95 values was seen in hexanoic acid, with a P95 value of 5 $\mu g/m^3$ in the healthcare offices and 7–8 $\mu g/m^3$ in the other environments.

As regards esters, healthcare office environment displayed generally the lowest frequencies, whereas the environments with the highest frequencies varied. The kindergarten environment stood out with a substantially higher TXIB frequency (57%) than in any other environments (19–21%). n-butyl acetate also displayed a notably higher frequency (20%) in the kindergartens than in the other environments (11–15%). The differences between the frequencies of the other esters in the environments were small. TXIB had the largest difference in P95 values, with a P95 value of 6 $\mu g/m^3$ in the kindergartens and 2–3 $\mu g/m^3$ in the other environments.

The only representative of Si-compounds, namely decamethylcyclopentasiloxane, displayed rather high frequencies (65–76%) in all the environments. Its P95 concentration ranged from 9 $\mu g/m^3$ in the school environments to 12–13 $\mu g/m^3$ in the other environments.

The total sum of the VOCs was rather similar in the different environments, as demonstrated by the TVOC median, P90, and P95 values in Table 3a.

The frequency of formaldehyde was over 90% in all the studied environments (Table 3b). The P95 values of formaldehyde ranged from 14 $\mu g/m^3$ (school) to 25 $\mu g/m^3$ (office). Similarly, the lowest median and P90 values of formaldehyde were observed in the schools and the highest in the offices.

3.3. Trends

The total concentration of VOCs (TVOC) showed a strongly decreasing trend over the ten-year study period, 2010–2019. The shift in TVOC distribution is graphically presented in Figure 1. Table 4a presents the annual statistics of the 42 most common VOCs and the TVOC sum variable. Table 4b shows the corresponding information on formaldehyde. For each compound, we analysed the trends of both frequency (i.e., the share of quantifiable measurement results) and concentration. Statistically significant ($p < 0.0001$) trends are indicated by downward and upward arrows. The Z values shown below the arrow symbols indicate the direction and steepness of the trend.

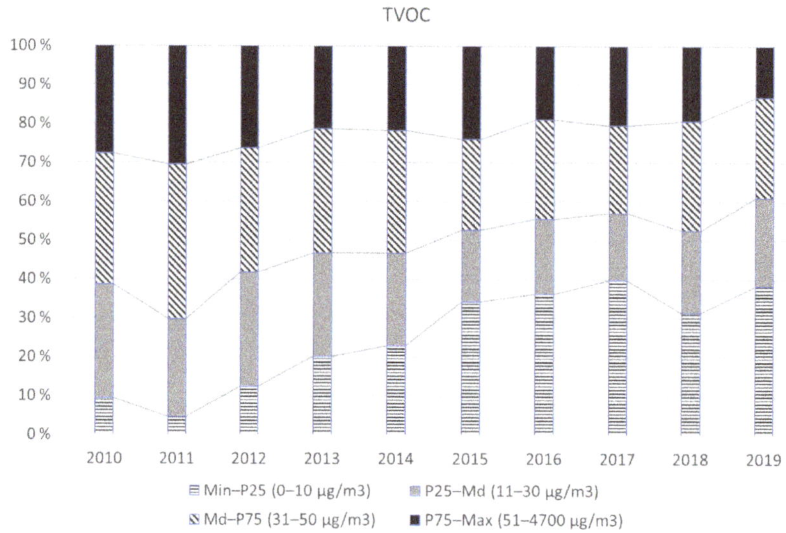

Figure 1. The shift in TVOC distribution in 2010–2019. The four different colour patterns represent the four quarters between the data points of Min, P25, Md, P75, and Max of the ten-year TVOC data (n = 9789). It can be seen from the graph that the share of the first quarter (Min–P25) increased and that the share of the top quarter (P75–Max) decreased during the study period.

The frequency and concentration trends of all four alkanes were clearly decreasing. This means that they have become rarer findings and that their concentration levels decreased during the ten-year study period. The most prominent decreases in frequency were observed for nonane and octane, which had 24% frequency in 2010 but only 4–5% frequency in 2019. The P95 values of the alkanes decreased during the study period although they were already minor ($\leq$1 µg/m^3) at the beginning of the study period.

Like those of the alkanes, the frequency and concentration trends of aromatic hydrocarbons were either strongly or moderately decreasing. The most prominent decrease in frequency was observed for benzene, which was present in quantifiable concentrations in nearly all the samples (98%) in 2010 but in only half of the samples (49%) in 2019. The frequency of xylenes (p, m) and ethylbenzene also fell considerably, from 84% to 52% and from 47% to 18%, respectively. These decreasing trends were reflected at the higher ends of the distributions, as demonstrated by the gradual decreases in the P95 concentrations of aromatic compounds.

Both the frequency and concentration of terpenes 3-carene and β-pinene showed slightly increasing trends. However, this was not reflected in their P95 values, which remained fairly stable over the years. The terpenes limonene and α-pinene showed no concentration trends, and α-pinene had only a very slightly increasing frequency trend. Interestingly, the P95 values of limonene decreased gradually from 5–6 µg/m^3 to around 2 µg/m^3 during the study period although there was no overall concentration or frequency trend.

Apart from 2-ethyl-1-hexanol, the alcohol compounds displayed a slightly increasing frequency trend and either no concentration trend or a slightly increasing concentration trend. In contrast, 2-ethyl-1-hexanol displayed clearly decreasing frequency and concentration trends. The P95 values of alcohols varied annually but no obvious decreases or increases were observed over the ten years.

Table 4. Annual statistics of VOCs (**a**) and formaldehyde (**b**) during the ten-year study period 2010–2019. Frequency trend was tested using Somer's D test, where input data were binomial (measurement result either >LOQ or <LOQ). Concentration trend was tested using Somer's D test, where input data comprised all measured concentration values. Here, measurement results that were <LOQ were replaced by a concentration value LOQ/2. Trends indicated by downward or upward arrow symbol were statistically significant ($p < 0.0001$) and had $|Z| \geq 4$. Z values shown below arrow symbols indicate direction and steepness of trend.

(**a**) Annual frequency and P95 values of the 42 most common VOCs during the ten-year study period 2010–2019. For TVOC presented on the bottom line, median, and P90 values are also shown.

Group	Analyte CAS	Trend (freq.) Z	Trend (conc.) Z	Year	2010 $n = 807$	2011 $n = 971$	2012 $n = 975$	2013 $n = 977$	2014 $n = 995$	2015 $n = 620$	2016 $n = 1089$	2017 $n = 1153$	2018 $n = 1129$	2019 $n = 1073$
Alkanes	Heptane	↘	↘	Frequency	20%	20%	22%	16%	12%	13%	12%	9%	11%	13%
	142-82-5	−10	−10	P95 (µg/m^3)	1.0	1.0	2.0	1.0	0.8	0.8	0.6	0.5	0.6	0.7
	Nonane	↘	↘	Frequency	24%	25%	23%	20%	15%	9%	5%	3%	6%	5%
	111-84-2	−23	−23	P95 (µg/m^3)	0.8	0.8	0.9	1.0	0.8	0.6	0.4	<LOQ	0.3	<LOQ
	Octane	↘	↘	Frequency	24%	32%	24%	15%	14%	5%	4%	3%	5%	4%
	111-65-9	−26	−26	P95 (µg/m^3)	0.8	0.8	0.8	0.7	0.7	0.4	<LOQ	<LOQ	<LOQ	<LOQ
	2,2,4,6,6-Pentam-ethylhep-tane	↘	↘	Frequency	13%	21%	20%	19%	9%	12%	8%	5%	6%	5%
	13475-82-6	−16	−16	P95 (µg/m^3)	1.0	4.0	2.0	2.0	0.7	0.7	0.6	<LOQ	0.4	0.4
Aromatic hydro-carbons	Benzene	↘	↘	Frequency	98%	89%	73%	70%	59%	52%	61%	49%	56%	49%
	71-43-2	−32	−33	P95 (µg/m^3)	2.0	2.0	2.0	1.0	1.0	1.0	1.0	1.0	1.0	1.0
	Ethylbenzene	↘	↘	Frequency	47%	36%	22%	21%	17%	24%	20%	14%	20%	18%
	100-41-4	−15	−15	P95 (µg/m^3)	1.6	1.0	2.0	2.0	0.9	3.0	1.0	0.7	1.0	0.8
	1,2,4-Trimethylbenzene	↘	↘	Frequency	31%	23%	13%	15%	9%	14%	17%	9%	11%	12%
	95-63-6	−11	−11	P95 (µg/m^3)	1.0	0.9	0.7	1.0	0.6	1.0	1.0	0.6	0.6	0.5
	Xylenes (p, m)	↘	↘	Frequency	84%	73%	66%	54%	53%	60%	58%	49%	60%	52%
	106-42-3 108-38-3	−15	−16	P95 (µg/m^3)	4.0	4.0	4.0	4.0	3.0	9.0	3.0	2.0	3.0	2.0

Table 4. *Cont.*

Group	Analyte CAS	Trend (freq.) Z	Trend (conc.) Z	Year	2010 n = 807	2011 n = 971	2012 n = 975	2013 n = 977	2014 n = 995	2015 n = 620	2016 n = 1089	2017 n = 1153	2018 n = 1129	2019 n = 1073
	Xylene (o)	↘	↘	Frequency	48%	38%	25%	24%	21%	26%	26%	17%	26%	22%
	95-47-6	−12	−11	P95 (μg/m^3)	2.0	1.0	1.0	2.0	1.0	4.0	1.0	1.0	1.0	1.0
	Toluene	↘	↘	Frequency	98%	90%	89%	83%	77%	76%	78%	71%	82%	75%
	108-88-3	−12	−19	P95 (μg/m^3)	6.0	4.4	6.0	7.0	4.0	5.0	4.0	3.0	3.0	4.0
Terpenes	3-Carene	↗	↗	Frequency	26%	24%	23%	29%	26%	37%	44%	39%	39%	36%
	498-15-7	+13	+12	P95 (μg/m^3)	2.0	2.0	2.0	4.0	3.0	4.0	4.0	3.0	4.0	3.0
	Limonene	-	-	Frequency	25%	29%	25%	22%	22%	26%	29%	25%	29%	25%
	138-86-3, 5989-27-5, 5989-54-8			P95 (μg/m^3)	5.0	6.0	3.0	2.0	3.0	2.0	2.0	2.0	2.0	2.0
	α-Pinene	↗	-	Frequency	65%	63%	57%	61%	61%	65%	67%	71%	68%	64%
	80-56-8	+4		P95 (μg/m^3)	7.0	7.0	7.0	10	8.0	9.0	8.0	9.0	9.0	6.0
	β-Pinene	↗	↗	Frequency	7%	5%	7%	11%	8%	12%	14%	11%	13%	12%
	127-91-3	+8	+8	P95 (μg/m^3)	0.7	0.4	0.5	0.7	0.7	0.7	0.7	0.6	0.8	0.7
Alcohols	Benzyl alcohol	↗	↗	Frequency	17%	11%	16%	19%	23%	22%	24%	20%	19%	19%
	100-51-6	+5	+4	P95 (μg/m^3)	3.0	1.0	1.2	2.0	3.0	5.0	4.0	2.3	1.0	2.0
	1-Butanol	↗	-	Frequency	81%	78%	71%	55%	72%	73%	70%	74%	80%	80%
	71-36-3	+5		P95 (μg/m^3)	5.0	5.0	4.0	5.0	5.0	5.0	5.0	6.0	4.0	3.0
	2-Ethyl-1-hexanol	↘	↘	Frequency	80%	67%	63%	60%	74%	59%	64%	60%	60%	59%
	104-76-7	−9	−15	P95 (μg/m^3)	5.0	9.0	9.0	6.0	4.0	5.0	4.0	7.0	4.0	13
	2-Methyl-1-propanol	↗	-	Frequency	26%	24%	16%	12%	14%	26%	29%	22%	24%	24%
	78-83-1	+4		P95 (μg/m^3)	1.6	1.0	1.0	1.0	1.0	2.0	2.0	1.0	2.0	1.0
	1,2-Propanediol	↗	-	Frequency	50%	50%	55%	55%	59%	64%	52%	52%	57%	66%
	57-55-6	+6		P95 (μg/m^3)	19	12	12	13	15	12	14	9.0	17	9.0

Table 4. *Cont.*

Group	Analyte CAS	Trend (freq.) Z	Trend (conc.) Z	Year	2010 $n = 807$	2011 $n = 971$	2012 $n = 975$	2013 $n = 977$	2014 $n = 995$	2015 $n = 620$	2016 $n = 1089$	2017 $n = 1153$	2018 $n = 1129$	2019 $n = 1073$
Phenols	Phenol 108-95-2	↗ +16	↗ +15	Frequency	18%	11%	11%	10%	12%	11%	34%	27%	26%	30%
				P95 (μg/m^3)	1.0	1.0	1.0	0.9	1.0	1.0	2.0	2.0	0.9	1.0
Alcohol and phenol ethers	2-(2-Butoxy ethoxy)ethanol 112-34-5	-	-	Frequency	14%	18%	17%	18%	21%	20%	19%	12%	17%	17%
				P95 (μg/m^3)	4.6	4.0	3.0	3.0	4.0	4.0	4.0	3.3	3.0	1.0
	2-Butoxyethanol 111-76-2	↗ +13	↗ +12	Frequency	8%	12%	13%	14%	16%	27%	26%	29%	23%	17%
				P95 (μg/m^3)	1.0	1.0	1.0	2.0	1.0	9.0	2.0	2.0	2.0	1.0
	2-(2-Ethoxy ethoxy)ethanol 111-90-0	↘ −5	↘ −6	Frequency	16%	22%	24%	27%	25%	23%	20%	13%	17%	17%
				P95 (μg/m^3)	6.0	4.4	7.0	9.0	5.0	5.0	5.0	2.0	2.0	2.0
	2-Phenoxyethanol 122-99-6	-	↘ −5	Frequency	13%	22%	26%	29%	22%	27%	25%	17%	19%	18%
				P95 (μg/m^3)	2.0	2.0	2.0	2.1	2.0	2.0	1.0	0.9	0.9	0.9
	1-Metoxy-2-propanol 107-98-2	-	-	Frequency	13%	15%	13%	16%	15%	16%	16%	13%	15%	13%
				P95 (μg/m^3)	2.0	2.0	1.0	2.0	1.2	3.0	1.0	1.0	1.0	1.0
Aldehydes	Benzaldehyde 100-52-7	↗ +23	↘ −9	Frequency	67%	58%	65%	76%	77%	86%	87%	87%	85%	90%
				P95 (μg/m^3)	4.0	3.0	3.0	3.0	3.0	3.0	3.0	3.0	2.0	2.0
	Decanal 112-31-2	↗ +20	-	Frequency	47%	48%	52%	53%	60%	72%	71%	64%	75%	75%
				P95 (μg/m^3)	4.0	4.0	4.0	3.0	4.0	3.0	2.0	2.0	2.0	3.0
	Hexanal 66-25-1	↗ +8	↗ +7	Frequency	49%	61%	50%	54%	52%	43%	55%	54%	66%	68%
				P95 (μg/m^3)	4.0	4.0	4.0	5.0	6.2	6.0	6.0	7.0	6.0	5.0
	Heptanal 111-71-7	↗ +9	↗ +8	Frequency	12%	20%	13%	14%	15%	12%	10%	13%	25%	31%
				P95 (μg/m^3)	0.9	1.0	0.8	0.9	0.9	0.8	0.7	0.8	0.8	0.8
	Nonanal 124-19-6	↗ +23	-	Frequency	60%	70%	70%	73%	75%	87%	90%	89%	90%	88%
				P95 (μg/m^3)	5.0	6.0	7.0	5.1	7.0	6.0	5.0	6.0	5.0	5.0

Table 4. *Cont.*

Group	Analyte CAS	Trend (freq.) Z	Trend (conc.) Z	Year	2010 $n = 807$	2011 $n = 971$	2012 $n = 975$	2013 $n = 977$	2014 $n = 995$	2015 $n = 620$	2016 $n = 1089$	2017 $n = 1153$	2018 $n = 1129$	2019 $n = 1073$
	Octanal	↗	-	Frequency	23%	50%	27%	28%	38%	35%	37%	37%	50%	45%
	124-13-0	+10		P95 (μg/m^3)	1.0	2.0	2.0	1.0	2.0	1.0	1.0	1.0	1.0	1.0
	Pentanal	↗	↗	Frequency	23%	27%	18%	20%	16%	39%	40%	38%	49%	44%
	110-62-3	+20	+16	P95 (μg/m^3)	2.0	2.0	1.0	2.0	2.0	2.0	2.0	2.0	2.0	2.0
Ketones	Acetophenone	↗	↗	Frequency	2%	8%	18%	31%	28%	15%	26%	25%	36%	31%
	98-86-2	+20	+18	P95 (μg/m^3)	<LOQ	0.7	1.0	1.0	1.0	0.8	0.8	0.8	0.9	0.8
Acids	Hexanoic acid	↗	↗	Frequency	21%	31%	22%	23%	28%	47%	51%	56%	51%	55%
	142-62-1	+27	+19	P95 (μg/m^3)	7.0	8.0	7.0	9.0	11	7.0	6.0	6.3	5.0	5.0
	Pentanoic acid	↗	↗	Frequency	8%	7%	3%	11%	10%	17%	17%	20%	16%	14%
	109-52-4	+12	+11	P95 (μg/m^3)	3.0	2.0	<LOQ	3.0	3.0	1.0	1.0	1.0	1.0	1.0
	Propionic acid	↗	↗	Frequency	10%	12%	6%	12%	6%	20%	21%	22%	28%	46%
	79-09-4	+24	+22	P95 (μg/m^3)	4.0	4.0	2.0	4.0	2.2	3.0	4.0	3.0	3.0	2.0
Esters	n-Butyl acetate	-	-	Frequency	15%	15%	12%	13%	16%	18%	12%	12%	17%	16%
	123-86-4			P95 (μg/m^3)	2.0	0.9	1.0	1.0	1.0	2.0	1.0	1.0	1.0	0.9
	2-(2-Butoxy ethoxy)ethyl acetate	↘	↘	Frequency	7%	10%	12%	10%	13%	12%	13%	9%	6%	6%
	124-17-4	−4	−5	P95 (μg/m^3)	1.0	2.0	1.0	1.1	2.0	0.8	1.0	0.9	0.5	0.5
	Ethyl acetate	↗	↗	Frequency	12%	15%	15%	9%	8%	16%	13%	14%	18%	23%
	141-78-6	+6	+6	P95 (μg/m^3)	2.0	2.0	2.0	1.0	1.0	2.0	2.0	2.0	2.0	2.0
	Texanol	↗	↗	Frequency	11%	17%	19%	22%	28%	28%	25%	27%	31%	20%
	25265-77-4	+9	+8	P95 (μg/m^3)	2.0	3.0	3.0	3.0	4.0	4.0	3.0	3.3	8.0	2.0
	TXIB	↗	-	Frequency	16%	19%	21%	24%	27%	23%	31%	20%	25%	22%
	6846-50-0	+4		P95 (μg/m^3)	3.0	4.0	2.0	3.0	5.0	4.0	3.0	2.0	2.0	2.0

Table 4. *Cont.*

Group	Analyte CAS	Trend (freq.) Z	Trend (conc.) Z	Year	2010 $n = 807$	2011 $n = 971$	2012 $n = 975$	2013 $n = 977$	2014 $n = 995$	2015 $n = 620$	2016 $n =$ 1089	2017 $n =$ 1153	2018 $n =$ 1129	2019 $n =$ 1073
Si-compounds	Decamethylcyclo-pentasiloxane 541-02-6	↗	↘	Frequency	57%	69%	75%	70%	70%	74%	73%	73%	76%	74%
		+7	−5	P95 (μg/m^3)	12	12	11	12	16	16	12	10	9.0	7.0
TVOC		-	↘	Frequency	100%	100%	100%	100%	100%	100%	100%	100%	100%	100%
			−20	Md (μg/m^3)	30	40	30	30	30	28	20	20	20	20
				P90 (μg/m^3)	100	100	100	90	100	130	80	80	80	70
				P95 (μg/m^3)	150	140	150	150	140	220	125	110	110	100

(**b**) Annual statistics of formaldehyde during the ten-year study period 2010–2019.

Analyte CAS	Trend (freq.)	Trend (conc.)	Year	2010 $n = 44$	2011 $n = 105$	2012 $n = 140$	2013 $n = 110$	2014 $n = 166$	2015 $n = 180$	2016 $n = 240$	2017 $n = 223$	2018 $n = 329$	2019 $n = 174$
Formaldehyde 50-00-0	-	↘	Frequency	100%	91%	96%	92%	89%	93%	94%	91%	95%	99%
			Md (μg/m^3)	9	10	5	4	3	4	4	3	4	3
		−6	P90 (μg/m^3)	25	26	15	14	11	11	10	10	12	9
			P95 (μg/m^3)	43	37	19	23	20	15	14	17	16	19

Phenol displayed moderately increasing frequency and concentration trends. However, its P95 concentration remained rather steady at around 1 μg/m^3 over the ten years.

Apart from 2-butoxyethanol, alcohol and phenol ethers displayed slightly decreasing frequency and concentration trends or none at all. The P95 concentrations of alcohol and phenol ethers slightly decreased during the study period. The frequency and concentration trends of 2-butoxyethanol were moderately increasing. However, the P95 concentration of 2-butoxyethanol did not increase over the ten years.

All seven aldehydes displayed increasing frequency trends during the study period, whereas the concentration trends varied. Interestingly, benzaldehyde displayed completely opposite frequency and concentration trends. This means that benzaldehyde is increasingly being detected but that its concentration level is decreasing. Despite some aldehydes showing a slightly increasing concentration trend, the P95 concentrations of aldehydes showed either a slightly decreasing trend or remained fairly stable over the ten years.

The ketone compound acetophenone displayed strongly increasing frequency and concentration trends. However, the P95 concentration of acetophenone stayed at ≤ 1 μg/m^3 throughout the study period.

Hexanoic, pentanoic and propionic acids showed similar trends of increasing frequency and concentration levels. However, the P95 concentrations of acids decreased during the study period.

Esters showed varying trends. 2-(2-Butoxy ethoxy)ethyl acetate displayed slightly decreasing frequency and concentration trends. n-Butyl acetate showed no significant trends. Ethyl acetate, Texanol, and TXIB displayed slightly increasing frequency trends from 11–16% to around 20%. We also found slightly increasing trends in the concentration levels of Texanol and TXIB. At the same time, the P95 values of all esters remained fairly stable over the ten years.

Decamethylcyclopentasiloxane showed a slightly increasing frequency trend, rising from around 60% to over 70%. At the same time, the concentration trend was slightly decreasing, and the P95 values of this Si-compound varied in the range of 7 to 16 μg/m^3, with no obvious trend.

Table 4b presents the annual statistics for formaldehyde. The frequency of formaldehyde displayed no trend, as it was high, 89–100%, every year. At the same time, the concentration level of formaldehyde showed a decreasing trend. The decrease in concentration was evident in all parts of the distribution, as demonstrated by the fall in the median, P90, and P95 values from 9 to 3 μg/m^3, from 25 to 9 μg/m^3, and from 43 to 19 μg/m^3, respectively.

4. Discussion

4.1. Indoor Air Concentrations of VOCs and Formaldehyde Are Generally Low and Pose No Health Risks

A large variety of volatile organic compounds originating from both indoor and outdoor sources are present in indoor environments. According to our ten-year VOC data collected in 2010–2019 in Finland, the most frequent VOCs in offices and similar non-industrial indoor environments are benzene, xylenes (p, m), toluene, α-pinene, 1-butanol, 2-ethyl-1-hexanol, 1,2-propanediol, benzaldehyde, hexanal, nonanal, and decamethylcyclopentasiloxane. These compounds were present in concentrations exceeding the respective LOQs (LOQ values varied 0.3–1 μg/m^3) in more than half of the 9789 samples collected in 2010–2019; i.e., these twelve compounds had a frequency over 50% in the total ten-year VOC data. Typical sources of these common VOCs are motor-vehicle emissions from outdoors (aromatic compounds), wood-based and other interior and construction materials (α-pinene, alcohols, aldehydes), water-dilutable glues and PVC materials (alcohols), detergents, fragrances, cosmetics (aldehydes, siloxanes), and food supplies (aldehydes).

Despite the VOC's multiple sources, the TVOC levels and the concentrations of single VOCs were generally low in comparison to previously published data on similar indoor environments [2,7,8,17]. However, the maximum values were generally bigger in our dataset than in other datasets, which is probably due to the notably bigger sample size of our study compared to the samples of others. The median, P90, P95, and P99 TVOC values in our ten-year dataset were 30, 90, 137, and 290 μg/m^3, respectively. This means that in over 99% of cases, TVOC concentration fell well below 400 μg/m^3, which is the TVOC reference value set by the Finnish Decree on Housing Health 545/2015. These concentration levels also fall into the stage one (out of five) hygienic guide value of $\leq$0.3 mg/m^3 set by the UBA for indoor air TVOC [13,14]. The UBA considers this first stage hygienically safe. Furthermore, the TVOC concentration levels displayed a clearly decreasing trend during the ten-year study period. In the last study year, 2019, the median, P90, P95, and P99 TVOC values were 20, 70, 100, and 215 μg/m^3, respectively.

Although the majority of VOC sampling was performed in buildings with suspected indoor air problems of some kind (not necessarily VOCs), we believe that the VOC levels measured in our study rather accurately represent those of a normal population of offices and similar non-industrial indoor environments in Finland. Considering the very low levels of VOCs measured in our large dataset, it appears obvious that VOCs are not currently a major concern in Finnish public and office buildings.

Unlike VOC measurements, the formaldehyde measurements (belonging to VVOCs) were targeted to buildings where elevated formaldehyde levels were expected. Nevertheless, the measured formaldehyde levels in our ten-year dataset were low in comparison to previously published data on similar indoor environments [2,7,8,17]. It is also noteworthy that the concentration level of formaldehyde displayed a clear decreasing trend during the ten-year period.

None of the RCRs calculated for the 99th percentile of the VOC and formaldehyde measurements exceeded 1 in comparison to the RW I values; the vast majority were far below this. Therefore, according to the current knowledge on their health hazards, the measured concentrations of these individual substances do not pose health risks. Several of the measured maximum values exceeded their respective RW I value, and a few also exceeded their RW II value. Such measurements originated from individual sampling locations, which should be further investigated.

Many VOCs can be smelled at low concentrations; their odours can be perceived as unpleasant and thus cause nuisance. However, they do not necessarily indicate a health risk, as odour thresholds can be considerably lower than the concentration levels that induce adverse health effects [18].

It should be noted that the occurrence of VOC mixtures was not studied in the dataset, and thus, the health risk assessment does not cover possible mixture effects. These could be relevant particularly for compounds that induce equivalent health hazards via the same action mechanism and would be an interesting topic for further research. However, considering the overall low levels of VOCs in the dataset in comparison to their respective health-based reference values, no immediate concern related to mixture effects is evident from these data.

4.2. Differences between VOC Patterns in Different Types of Indoor Environments Have No Practical Relevance

We inspected differences between offices, schools, kindergartens, and healthcare offices and found that these environments differed in terms of frequencies of several VOCs, whereas the differences between the P95 values were typically small. The office environment had a higher frequency of alkanes, aromatic hydrocarbons, and acids than the other environments. The kindergarten environment had a higher frequency of aldehydes, certain terpenes (α-pinene, 3-carene) and certain esters (TXIB, n-butyl acetate). The differences between the measured VOC patterns in these environments probably reflect the differences between their typical distances from busy roads, their typical activities, and the use of construction and interior materials, cleaning products, and utility articles.

Unlike VOCs, formaldehyde showed similar frequency, over 90%, in all the studied environments, whereas the concentration of formaldehyde ranged in a relatively large scale. The lowest median, P90, and P95 concentration values of formaldehyde were observed in the schools and the highest in the offices. As formaldehyde has a multitude of possible emission sources, e.g., traffic, construction materials, furniture, textiles, cosmetics, wood burning, cooking and oxidative reactions, it is difficult to try to explain the observed differences.

Despite the differences between VOC and formaldehyde patterns in these environments, all the measured concentrations were low in comparison with their respective health-based reference values, and therefore, we do not expect these differences to have any practical relevance for health outcomes.

4.3. Interpretation of VOC Trends Involves Uncertainties

The total VOC concentration, TVOC, calculated from each VOC sample in our dataset, showed a clearly decreasing trend during the study period, 2010–2019. Both increasing and decreasing trends were observed in individual compounds. Most notably, aromatic compounds and alkanes displayed systematic decreasing trends, whereas several aldehydes and acids showed increasing trends.

We analysed both frequency and concentration trends. The frequency trend reveals whether the frequency value, i.e., the percentage of results above LOQ, is rising or falling. However, the frequency trend does not prove that the concentration level trend is parallel. We found several examples of divergent frequency and concentration trends in our data. Benzaldehyde and decamethylcyclopentasiloxane showed completely opposite trends of increasing frequency and decreasing concentration. In other words, these two compounds were measured more frequently over the years but at the same time the measured concentrations became generally smaller. Formaldehyde showed no frequency trend but a decreasing concentration trend, whereas some VOCs, such as α-pinene and TXIB, showed slightly increasing frequency trend but no concentration trend. In most cases of increasing frequency trend, also the concentration trend was positive, although less prominent (smaller Z). This was true, for example, for several aldehydes, alcohols, and acids. Interestingly, P95 values tended to decrease or remain stable even in situations in which the concentration trend was increasing. In other words, several compounds were detected and quantified more frequently, but a larger share of the measurements were only slightly above the LOQ. One explanation for this phenomenon might be the increased detection and quantification of small peaks in VOC chromatograms due to decreased total VOC concentrations. The ISO 16000-6 standard requires at least two-thirds of the total TVOC area to be identified. This may lead, at low TVOC level, to quantification of very small concentrations that would be neglected with larger TVOC concentrations. Therefore, it is reasonable to view all increasing trends, especially increasing frequency trends, with caution. At the same time, it is important to keep in mind that increased use of textile carpets and epoxy and acrylic resins as well as novel products used in cleaning and personal hygiene might also partially explain some of the increasing trends observed during the study period.

Compared to increasing trends, decreasing trends have less uncertainties due to the increased detection of small peaks discussed above. Aromatic hydrocarbons showed equally strong decreasing frequency and concentration trends during the ten-year study period, 2010–2019. These compounds are mainly linked to fossil fuel combustion [19]. Therefore, we believe that the decreasing trends of aromatic hydrocarbons are mainly connected to better outdoor air quality due to, for example, an ongoing shift towards low-emission vehicles.

The decreasing trends of alkanes and formaldehyde are most likely connected to the increased use of low-emission building and interior materials. This positive development is probably due to the development and application of emission classification systems, the aim of which are to enhance the development and use of low-emission building materials and furniture. In Finland, M1-classification, developed and published for the first time in 1996, sets limit values for the emission of VOCs, formaldehyde, and ammonia as well as criteria for the acceptability of odour [20]. M1-classification is a voluntary labelling system for manufacturers, importers and exporters of building products. However, public property developers often demand the use of M1-certified products in their projects in Finland, thereby enhancing the development and usage of low-emission materials in buildings.

The decreasing frequency and concentration of 2-ethyl-1-hexanol is probably due to the development of non-phthalate plasticizers, which are increasingly being used in flooring materials.

5. Conclusions

This study presents a valuable dataset on VOCs and formaldehyde from an exceptionally large number of samples collected from offices and similar indoor environments over a decade in Finland. The data showed that indoor air concentrations of VOCs and formaldehyde in these environments are generally low and pose no health risks. The differences between VOC patterns in office, school, kindergarten, and healthcare office environments have no practical relevance to health outcomes. TVOC concentration showed a clear decreasing trend over the ten-year study period.

Author Contributions: Conceptualization, K.W., H.H., J.R., S.M. and T.L.; data curation, H.H. and J.R.; statistical analyses, J.R.; writing—original draft preparation, K.W.; writing—review and editing, K.W., H.H., J.R., S.M. and T.L.; project administration, T.L. All authors have read and agreed to the published version of the manuscript.

Funding: This study was funded by the Finnish Ministry of Social Affairs and Health as part of the Finnish Indoor Air and Health Programme 2018–2028.

Institutional Review Board Statement: Not applicable.

Informed Consent Statement: Not applicable.

Data Availability Statement: The raw data of this study are not publicly available because they are owned by a multitude of laboratory customers.

Acknowledgments: We thank Sirpa Rautiala, Pirjo Korenius, and Katri Leino for their expertise and fruitful discussions during the project. Tiina Santonen and Piia Taxell are acknowledged for their valuable comments, and we also thank the personnel of FIOH's analytical laboratory for analysing the VOC and formaldehyde samples. We are grateful to the numerous customers of FIOH's analytical laboratory for the collection and delivery of the VOC and formaldehyde samples of this study.

Conflicts of Interest: The authors declare no conflict of interest.

References

1. Edwards, R.D.; Jurvelin, J.; Koistinen, K.; Saarela, K.; Jantunen, M. VOC source identification from personal and residential indoor, outdoor and workplace microenvironment samples in EXPOLIS-Helsinki, Finland. *Atmos. Environ.* **2001**, *35*, 4829–4841. [CrossRef]
2. Geiss, O.; Giannopoulos, G.; Tirendi, S.; Barrero-Moreno, J.; Larsen, B.R.; Kotzias, D. The AIRMEX study—VOC measurements in public buildings and schools/kindergartens in eleven European cities: Statistical analysis of the data. *Atmos. Environ.* **2011**, *45*, 3676–3684. [CrossRef]
3. Paciencia, I.; Madureira, J.; Rufo, J.; Moreira, A.; Fernandes, E.d.O. A systematic review of evidence and implications of spatial and seasonal variations of volatile organic compounds (VOC) in indoor human environments. *J. Toxicol. Environ. Health B Crit. Rev.* **2016**, *19*, 47–64. [CrossRef] [PubMed]
4. Zhong, L.; Su, F.-C.; Batterman, S. Volatile Organic Compounds (VOCs) in Conventional and High Performance School Buildings in the U.S. *Int. J. Environ. Res. Public Health* **2017**, *14*, 100. [CrossRef] [PubMed]
5. Abbatt, J.P.D.; Wang, C. The atmospheric chemistry of indoor environments. *Environ. Sci. Process. Impacts* **2019**, *22*, 25–48. [CrossRef] [PubMed]
6. Spinazzè, A.; Campagnolo, D.; Cattaneo, A.; Urso, P.; Sakellaris, I.A.; Saraga, D.; Mandin, C.; Canha, N.; Mabilia, R.; Perreca, E.; et al. Indoor gaseous air pollutants determinants in office buildings—The OFFICAIR project. *Indoor Air* **2019**, *30*, 76–87. [CrossRef] [PubMed]
7. Mandin, C.; Trantallidi, M.; Cattaneo, A.; Canha, N.; Mihucz, V.G.; Szigeti, T.; Mabilia, R.; Perreca, E.; Spinazzè, A.; Fossati, S.; et al. Assessment of indoor air quality in office buildings across Europe—The OFFICAIR study. *Sci. Total Environ.* **2017**, *579*, 169–178. [CrossRef] [PubMed]

8. Baloch, R.M.; Maesano, C.N.; Christoffersen, J.; Banerjee, S.; Gabriel, M.; Csobod, É.; de Oliveira Fernandes, E.; Annesi-Maesano, I.; SINPHONIE Study Group. Indoor air pollution, physical and comfort parameters related to schoolchildren's health: Data from the European SINPHONIE study. *Sci. Total Environ.* **2020**, *739*, 139870. [CrossRef] [PubMed]
9. Sarigiannis, D.A.; Karakitsios, S.P.; Gotti, A.; Liakos, I.L.; Katsoyiannis, A. Exposure to major volatile organic compounds and carbonyls in European indoor environments and associated health risk. *Environ. Int.* **2011**, *37*, 743–765. [CrossRef] [PubMed]
10. Salthammer, T. Emerging indoor pollutants. *Int. J. Hyg. Environ. Health* **2020**, *224*, 113423. [CrossRef] [PubMed]
11. Sundell, J. Reflections on the history of indoor air science, focusing on the last 50 years. *Indoor Air* **2017**, *27*, 708–724. [CrossRef] [PubMed]
12. Weschler, C.J. Changes in indoor pollutants since the 1950s. *Atmos. Environ.* **2009**, *43*, 153–169. [CrossRef]
13. Fromme, H.; Debiak, M.; Sagunski, H.; Röhl, C.; Kraft, M.; Kolossa-Gehring, M. The German approach to regulate indoor air contaminants. *Int. J. Hyg. Environ. Health* **2019**, *222*, 347–354. [CrossRef] [PubMed]
14. Umweltbundesamt—UBA, German Committee on Indoor Guide Values. 2021. Available online: https://www.umweltbundesamt.de/en/topics/health/commissions-working-groups/german-committee-on-indoor-guide-values#guide-values-i-and-ii (accessed on 7 December 2021).
15. EU-LCI Working Group. EU-LCI Values. 2020. Available online: https://ec.europa.eu/growth/sectors/construction/eu-lci-subgroup_en (accessed on 7 December 2021).
16. ECHA. Guidance on Information Requirements and Chemical Safety Assessment. Part E: Risk Characterisation, Version 3.0. ECHA-2016-G-04-EN. 2016. Available online: https://echa.europa.eu/documents/10162/17224/information_requirements_part_e_en.pdf/ (accessed on 9 February 2022).
17. Madureira, J.; Paciência, I.; Rufo, J.; Ramos, E.; Barros, H.; Teixeira, J.P.; de Oliveira Fernandes, E. Indoor air quality in schools and its relationship with children's respiratory symptoms. *Atmos. Environ.* **2015**, *118*, 145–156. [CrossRef]
18. Greenberg, M.I.; Curtis, J.A.; Vearrier, D. The perception of odor is not a surrogate marker for chemical exposure: A review of factors influencing human odor perception. *Clin. Toxicol.* **2013**, *51*, 70–76. [CrossRef] [PubMed]
19. Campagnolo, D.; Saraga, D.E.; Cattaneo, A.; Spinazzè, A.; Mandin, C.; Mabilia, R.; Perreca, E.; Sakellaris, I.; Canha, N.; Mihucz, V.G.; et al. VOCs and aldehydes source identification in European office buildings—The OFFICAIR study. *Build. Environ.* **2017**, *115*, 18–24. [CrossRef]
20. M1 Classification for Low-Emission Building Materials. The Building Information Foundation RTS sr. 2021. Available online: https://cer.rts.fi/en/ (accessed on 7 December 2021).

environments MDPI

Article

Analysis of the Airflow Generated by Human Activity Using a Mobile Slipstream Measuring Device

Minkyeong Kim [1], Yongil Lee [2] and Duckshin Park [3,*]

[1] Railroad Test & Certification Division, Korea Railroad Research Institute, Uiwang 16105, Korea; mkkim15@krri.re.kr
[2] Environmental Monitoring Group, Han-River Basin Environmental Office, Hanam 12902, Korea; freego83@korea.kr
[3] Transportation Environmental Research Department, Korea Railroad Research Institute, Uiwang 16105, Korea
* Correspondence: dspark@krri.re.kr

Abstract: Human activities, including walking, generate an airflow, commonly known as the slipstream, which can disperse contaminants indoors and transmit infection to other individuals. It is important to understand the characteristics of airflow to prevent the dissemination of contaminants such as viruses. A cylinder of diameter 500 mm, which is the average shoulder width of an adult male, was installed in a motorcar and moved at a velocity of 1.2 m/s, which is the walking speed of an adult male. The velocity profile of the slipstream generated during this movement was measured by locating the sensor support at 0.15–2.0 m behind the cylinder. The wind velocity was set to 1.2 m/s to conduct the numerical analysis. The measurement data revealed the velocity profile of the space behind the cylinder, and a comparison of the numerical analysis and the measurement results indicate very similar u (measured velocity)/U (moving velocity) results, with a maximum difference of 0.066, confirming that the measured values were correctly estimated from the results of the numerical analysis.

Keywords: infectious viruses; indoor contaminants; mobile slipstream measuring instrument; cylinder; airflow

Citation: Kim, M.; Lee, Y.; Park, D. Analysis of the Airflow Generated by Human Activity Using a Mobile Slipstream Measuring Device. *Environments* **2021**, *8*, 97. https://doi.org/10.3390/environments8100097

Academic Editor: Ki-Hyun Kim

Received: 25 July 2021
Accepted: 21 September 2021
Published: 23 September 2021

1. Introduction

The severe acute respiratory syndrome epidemic that began in Hong Kong in 2003 reportedly spread widely through the air [1]. Middle East respiratory syndrome (MERS) was first reported in Saudi Arabia in 2012 and then spread worldwide, including Korea. Severe acute respiratory syndrome coronavirus 2 (COVID-19) was first detected in December 2019, in Wuhan City, Hubei Province, China, and then very quickly spread throughout other countries including Korea. Although the transmission pathway of MERS and other pathogens has not been identified with 100% certainty, it is presumed that it is transmitted via close contact among human beings [2]. In this case, the term "close contact" is defined as being within 2 m of another person, in a room with others, or in the care area of an infected person; it also includes direct contact with infectious secretions while not wearing appropriate personal protective equipment [2]. Airflow generated by human movements can accelerate the spread of various airborne materials, such as COVID-19 virus particles during the current pandemic [3–7].

Numerical analyses are used by many researchers to understand aerodynamic properties because the procedures have no spatial constraints. Regarding the dissemination of substances, airflow by heating, ventilation, and air conditioning systems have been reviewed [3–7]. The main factors in the diffusion of pollutants are the airflow generated by human breathing and body heat [8,9]. Liu et al. [8] numerically analyzed natural convection, and Martinho et al. [9] modeled an actual mannequin using 3D scans to analyze the airflow generated by body heat when the mannequin was placed in a sitting position indoors. In both studies, the results were compared with actual measurements. One study conducted a numerical analysis of airflow around the human body, taking into account the layer of air created by clothes [10]. The trajectory of particles exhaled by breathing was numerically analyzed according to the wind speed of the surrounding airflow [11]. Pollutant movement according to the airflow generated while passing through a door between a room and hallway was analyzed [12–15]. Simulations and numerical analyses have been performed using the speed of a moving person and the opening and closing of a door [16].

To evaluate the diffusion of pollutants, a study using a chamber was conducted. Zhang et al. [17] built a cabin with dimensions of 4.9 × 4.23 × 2.1 m in a chamber to evaluate the dissemination of contaminants in aircraft cabins. Experimental measurements and numerical simulations of airflow and contaminant transport were conducted in a "half occupied, twin-aisle cabin mockup". Poussou and Mazumdar [18] simulated an aircraft cabin using a small underwater tank and measured the variables using particle image velocimetry and planar laser-induced fluorescence. Contaminant propagation according to human movement in the aircraft cabin was analyzed [19]. Han et al. [20] built a test bed that could house actual-size mannequins and installed a wind velocity sensor to measure the velocity profile under different conditions. The airflow was measured using a warm mannequin and a mannequin with mobile parts moving at a velocity of 0.5–1.5 m/s. Milanowicz and Kedzior [21] modeled a human body falling from a height. Liu et al. [22] examined the airflow around a human body model in an enclosed space, examined changes in temperature and velocity, and simulated the transmission of infectious respiratory diseases.

Studies using mannequins have compared numerical analysis and measurement results, and confirmed particle diffusion [23,24]. In this study, a mobile slipstream measuring device was constructed to measure the velocity profile behind an object. The velocity profile behind a moving cylinder was measured directly, and a numerical analysis was performed to elucidate the airflow characteristics of the slipstream. In previous studies, no attempts were made to change the speed of the moving cylinder, or to detect changes in airflow by installing a flow rate sensor on the side of the cylinder.

Airflow is generated by human movements, which can affect the acceleration of the spread of various airborne materials, such as the COVID-19 virus, which is currently an important issue [3–7]. In this study, a moving cylinder was used to represent an adult male, and a constant walking pace was maintained. A regularly shaped cylinder of diameter 500 mm (average shoulder width of an adult male) was mounted on a motorcar and set to move at a velocity of 1.2 m/s (average walking velocity of humans). This cylinder approximates the movement of the human body. A flow rate sensor was installed on the back of the moving cylinder at different heights and distances to measure the change in airflow. In previous studies, no attempt was made to change the speed of a moving cylinder or to detect the changes in airflow by installing a flow rate sensor on the side of a cylinder. This would enable the changes in air flow around the cylinder to be determined during movement, and height and distance could be considered as variables. Studies of slipstreams have been conducted mainly in tunnels and laboratories. By performing a numerical analysis of the results of this study, the effects of the diffusion of air currents carrying air pollutants and viruses can be determined.

2. Materials and Methods

2.1. Experimental Equipment

A device measuring 3 m (W) × 35 m (L) × 2.5 m (H) was constructed to investigate the impact of the movement of an object on the slipstream in a large chamber. A rail was installed in the center of an indoor space to minimize the impact of the airflow. The mobile slipstream measuring device consisted of a rail, moving part, and sensor support (Patent-10-1517092). The rail consisted of a cylindrical aluminum pipe that helped the moving part, which was a specially constructed motorcar, to move seamlessly at adjustable velocities (Figure 1).

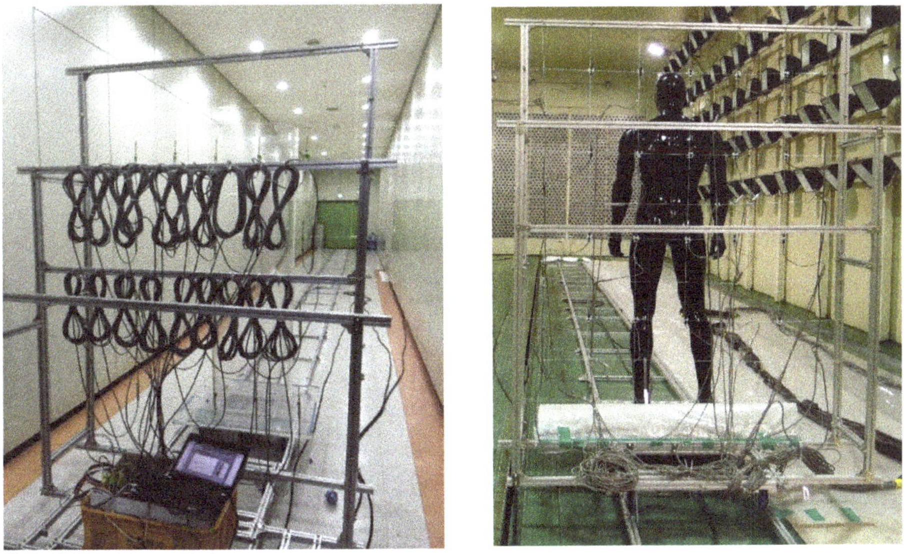

Figure 1. Testbed and sensor support.

A total of 20 wind velocity sensors (Model 0962-00, Kanomax, Andover, NJ, USA) were installed on the sensor support, with horizontal and vertical distances between sensors of 200 mm, as shown in Figure 2. The measuring range of the wind velocity sensors was 0.1–50 m/s, and the measurement error was ±0.1 m/s over the range 0–4.99 m/s. The relative wind speed was measured. The measured speed was subtracted from the human's moving speed to calculate the actual wind speed at each point.

$$U_r = U_h - U_m$$

Data were recorded every 0.1 s using a data logger (Model 1560, Kanomax, Suita, Japan). Table 1 shows the positioning of the sensors installed on the sensor support.

Table 1. Locations of wind velocity measurement sensors.

	Column B (X = −0.4 m)	Column C (X = −0.2 m)	Column D (X = 0.0 m)	Column E (X = 0.2 m)	Column F (X = 0.4 m)
2nd Height (Y = 1.8 m)	B2	C2	D2	E2	F2
4th Height (Y = 1.4 m)	B4	C4	D4	E4	F4
6th Height (Y = 1.0 m)	B6	C6	D6	E6	F6
8th Height (Y = 0.6 m)	B8	C8	D8	E8	F8

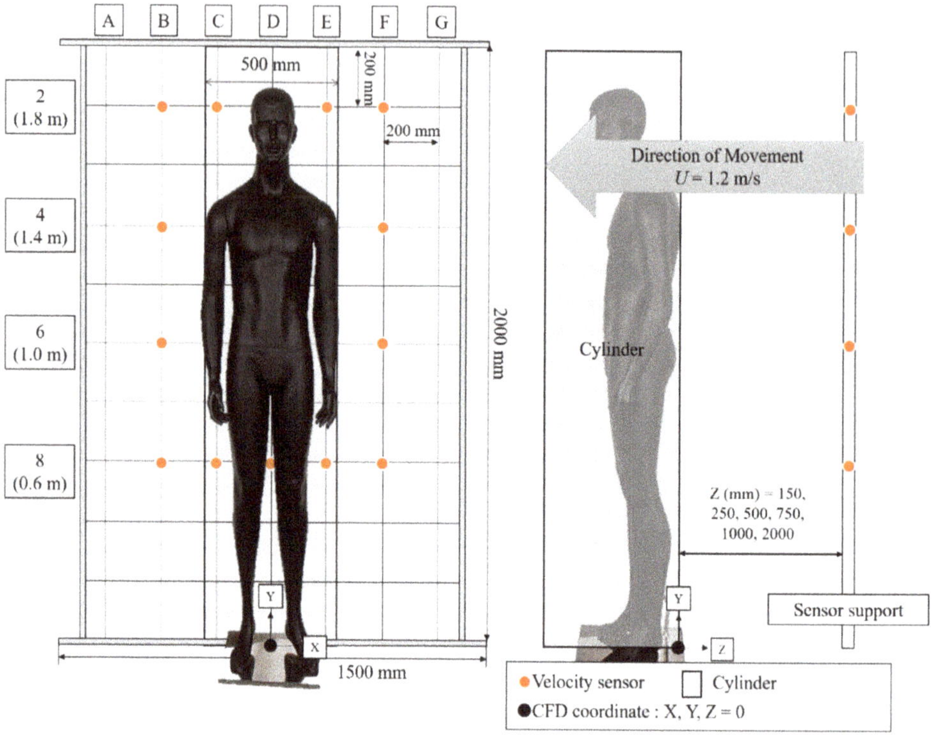

Figure 2. Schematic of the mobile wind velocity measurement system.

2.2. Experimental Methods

A normally shaped cylinder of diameter 500 mm, which is the average shoulder width of an adult male, was mounted on a motorcar and set to move at a velocity of 1.2 m/s. A running test was conducted five times, with a few pieces of corrugated cardboard placed in the empty spaces between the object and sensor support to flatten the bottom. Measurements were conducted at the rear of the cylinder after varying the sensor support position to 0.15, 0.25, 0.5, 0.75, 1, or 2 m. A numerical analysis was performed to evaluate the airflow of the cylinder slipstream. Fluent 17.7 software (Ansys Co., Canonsburg, PA, USA) was used to conduct the numerical analysis, and the test bed was modeled. The test bed dimensions were 3 m (W) × 2.5 m (H) × 10 m (L), and a cylinder of diameter 500 mm (2 m high) was placed at the center. Tetrahedral grids were placed in a tight formation around the cylinder and along the wall. A total of 354,330 nodes were generated in the flow field. The right, left, top, and bottom of the cylinder were specified as walls, and the no-slip condition was set. The front of the cylinder was specified as the inlet, and the wind velocity was set to 1.2 m/s (the walking speed of an adult male). The Reynolds number was 4.0×10^4. The rear surface was specified as the outlet and set to atmospheric conditions. A model built with the commercial code K-epsilon was used to solve the numerical analysis. The k-epsilon equation used in this study is as follows.

$$\mu_t = \frac{C_\mu \rho K^2}{\epsilon}$$

$$\rho\left(U_i \frac{\partial k}{\partial x_i}\right) = \frac{\partial}{\partial x_i}\left(\mu + \frac{\mu_t}{\sigma_k}\frac{\partial k}{\partial x_i}\right) + \mu_t\left(\frac{\partial U_i}{\partial x_j} + \frac{\partial U_j}{\partial x_i}\right)\frac{\partial U_i}{\partial x_j} - \rho\epsilon$$

$$\rho\left(U_i\frac{\partial \varepsilon}{\partial x_i}\right) = \frac{\partial}{\partial x_i}\left(\mu + \frac{\mu_t}{\sigma_\varepsilon}\frac{\partial \varepsilon}{\partial x_i}\right) + C_{\varepsilon 1}\frac{\varepsilon}{k}\left[\mu_t\left(\frac{\partial U_i}{\partial x_j} + \frac{\partial U_j}{\partial x_i}\right)\frac{\partial U_i}{\partial x_j}\right] - C_{\varepsilon 2\rho}\frac{\varepsilon^2}{k}$$

After a comparison of the results obtained using the cylinder, mannequin measurements were conducted using the same process.

3. Results and Discussion

3.1. Measurement Results

Each variable was measured five times using a mobile slipstream measuring device, and the average value was calculated. Figure 3 shows the measurement results at the 4th height position (Y = 1.4 m). In this case, Z was the distance between the cylinder and sensor support. The motor reached a speed of 1.2 m/s after 4 s and then continued at this velocity for approximately 8 s. The wind velocity approached the moving velocity of 1.2 m/s as Z increased. Although the change in wind velocity for rows B and F was not significant, the wind velocity near the sensor support was approximately 1.5 m/s, which was higher than the moving velocity of 1.2 m/s. The wind speed difference among rows B and F was not statistically significant according to non-parametric test results ($p > 0.05$). On the other hand, although the wind velocity varied greatly for rows C, D, and E according to the distance, the wind velocity near the sensor support was approximately 0.4 m/s, which was lower than the moving velocity of 1.2 m/s (Table 2).

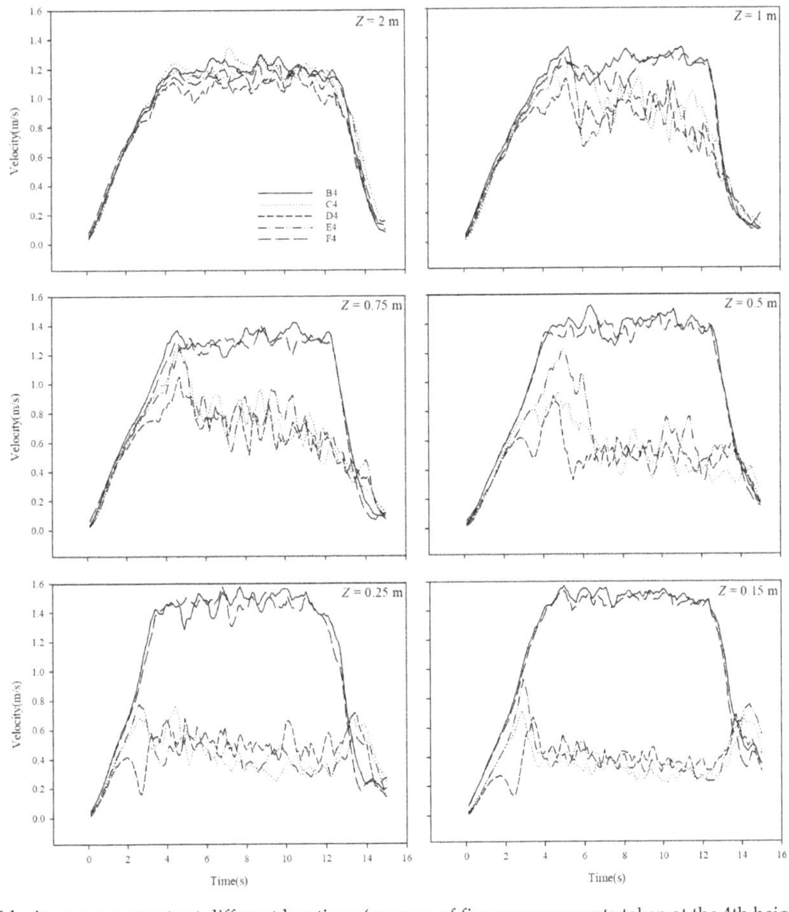

Figure 3. Velocity measurements at different locations (average of five measurements taken at the 4th height position).

Table 2. Wind velocity measurement results (average of five measurements taken at the 4th height position).

	Column B (X = −0.4 m)	Column C (X = −0.2 m)	Column D (X = 0.0 m)	Column E (X = 0.2 m)	Column F (X = 0.4 m)
Z = 2 m	0.944 ± 0.027	0.870 ± 0.049	0.788 ± 0.037	0.886 ± 0.030	0.877 ± 0.047
Z = 1 m	1.003 ± 0.032	0.527 ± 0.089	0.553 ± 0.092	0.690 ± 0.119	0.901 ± 0.031
Z = 0.75 m	1.034 ± 0.042	0.396 ± 0.074	0.442 ± 0.095	0.466 ± 0.158	0.963 ± 0.029
Z = 0.5 m	1.108 ± 0.034	0.2450 ± 0.044	0.244 ± 0.024	0.299 ± 0.027	0.943 ± 0.085
Z = 0.25 m	1.158 ± 0.043	0.384 ± 0.040	0.385 ± 0.041	0.313 ± 0.033	1.108 ± 0.064
Z = 0.15 m	1.188 ± 0.040	0.311 ± 0.043	0.354 ± 0.038	0.237 ± 0.052	1.159 ± 0.024

Figure 4 shows the measurement results at various sensor heights taken at a distance of 0.5 m between the cylinder and sensor support. Similar patterns were observed to the right and left of row D. Wind velocity decreased as the sensor height decreased, which appeared to be because there was no significant difference in distance between the second height position and the top of the cylinder, although the sensor at the second height position was positioned behind the cylinder. A similar trend was observed in previous studies as the wind speed varied according to the measurement height [23,24].

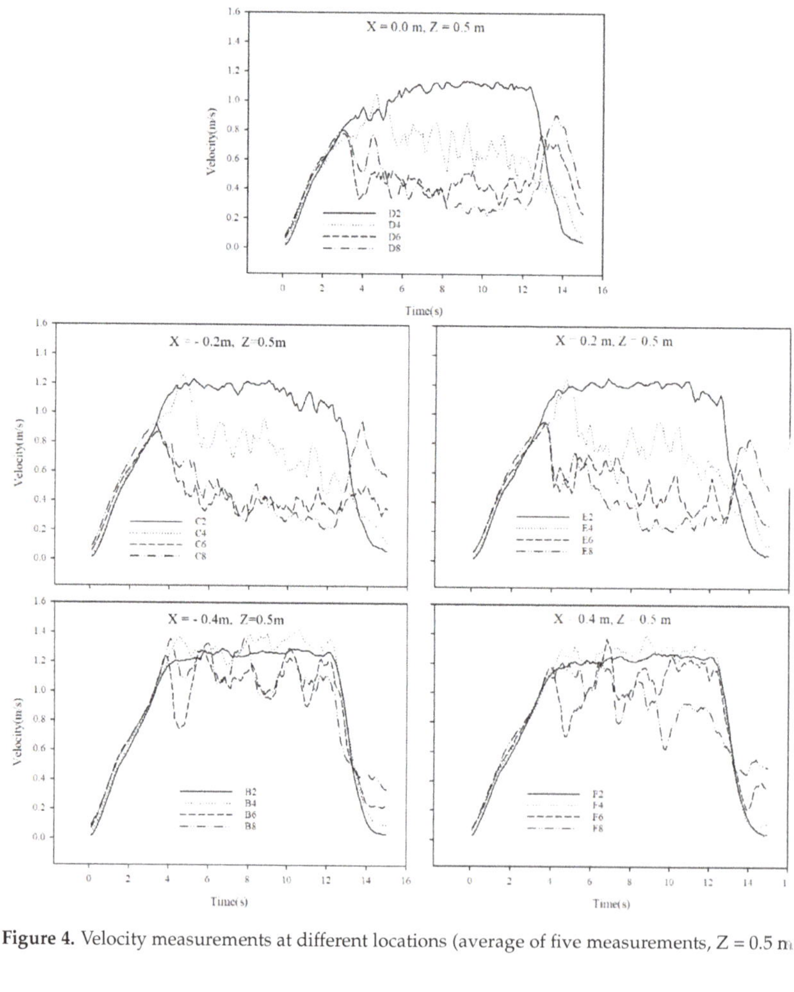

Figure 4. Velocity measurements at different locations (average of five measurements, Z = 0.5 m

3.2. Results of Cylinder Measurements and the Numerical Analysis

The average Reynolds number in the 5–6 s constant velocity section was calculated using the measurement results presented above. Figure 4 shows the variation in the dimensionless velocity ratio calculated by dividing the measured velocity u by the moving velocity U. Here, X/d is a dimensionless value calculated by dividing the width of the cylinder by the diameter, and Z/d is a dimensionless value calculated by dividing the distance between the cylinder and sensor support by the diameter of the cylinder.

Figure 5 shows that u/U approached 1 as the airflow increased with the increase in the distance from the rear of the cylinder. This was also confirmed by the measurements made in this study. The value of u/U at X/d = 0 increased toward 1 as Z/d increased, and the right and left sections of the graph at X/d = 0 were symmetrical at all heights. The values of u/U at X/d = −0.4, 0, or 0.4 were directly affected by the cylinder because sensor supports were positioned immediately behind the cylinder, and u/U increased toward 1 as Z/d increased.

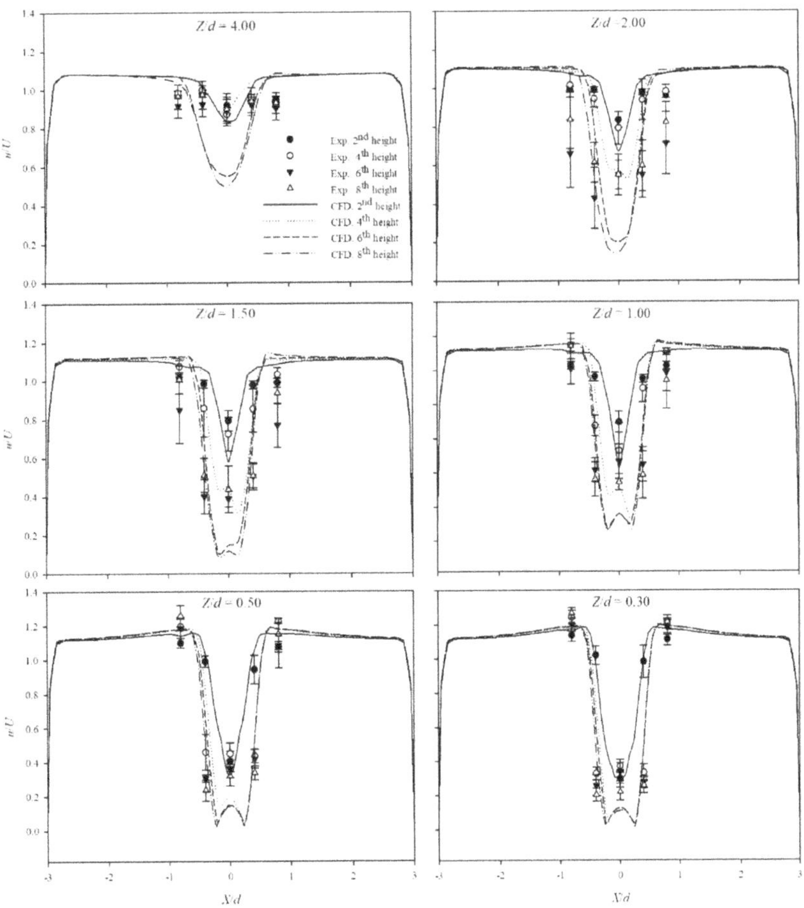

Figure 5. Profiles of normalized velocities at different Z/d locations.

The results of the numerical analysis and the u/U measurements are similar, with an approximate difference of only 0.023. This difference increased with Z/d, with the maximum difference (0.442) observed at the sixth and eighth height positions when $Z/d = 4$. However, the maximum difference at the second and fourth height positions was 0.089, which was not greater than that observed at the sixth and eighth height positions when $Z/d = 4$. This appeared to have been affected by the trailing vortex generated at the edge of the top of the cylinder [25].

Figure 6 shows the velocity profile according to Z/d when $X/d = 0$. The numerical analysis of U_X showed that the wind direction changed. The value of u_X/U_X was −0.130 in the opposite direction of the wind at all heights when Z = 0.15 m, whereas the value of u_X/U_X was −0.009 at the sixth and eighth height positions in the opposite direction of the wind for heights up to Z = 0.75 m. As shown in Figure 7, the value of u_X/U_X was negative because a vortex was generated when the cylinder moved, and the vortex increased as the height decreased. It was presumed that the point where the vortex was generated was the point where the direction of the measured value changed.

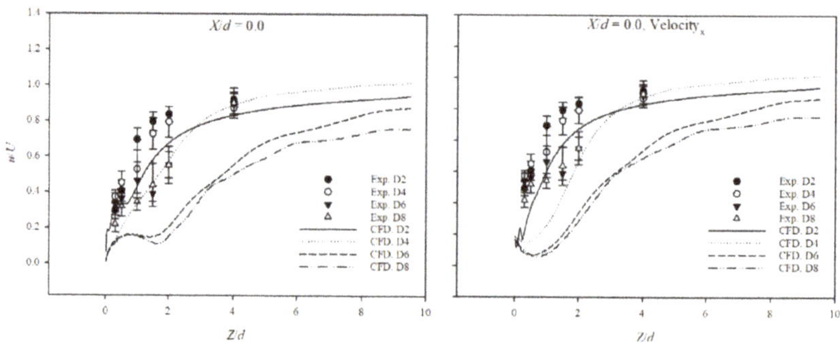

Figure 6. The normalized velocity profiles obtained by measurements and numerical analysis results.

Figure 7. Velocity vector profile of the cylinder in the y–z plane (x = 0 m).

Figure 8 shows the fluid flow at four heights. It also shows that the velocity increased rapidly to the left and right of the cylinder, and that a vortex was created behind it. The strength of the vortex increased toward the bottom.

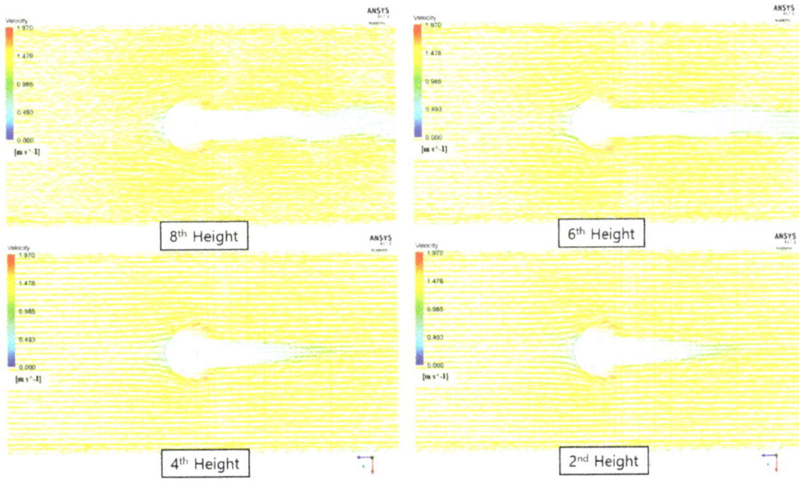

Figure 8. Time-averaged streamlines in different x–z planes.

Figure 9A shows the measurement results for the mannequin at the fourth height position (Y = 1.4 m). Figure 9B shows the measurement results according to various sensor heights taken at a distance of 0.5 m between the mannequin and sensor support. Patterns similar to those for Figure 9A,B of row D were observed. The average Reynolds number in the 5.6–8.0 s constant velocity section was calculated using the measurement results described above. Figure 10 shows the dimensionless velocity ratio calculated by dividing the measured velocity *U* by the moving velocity.

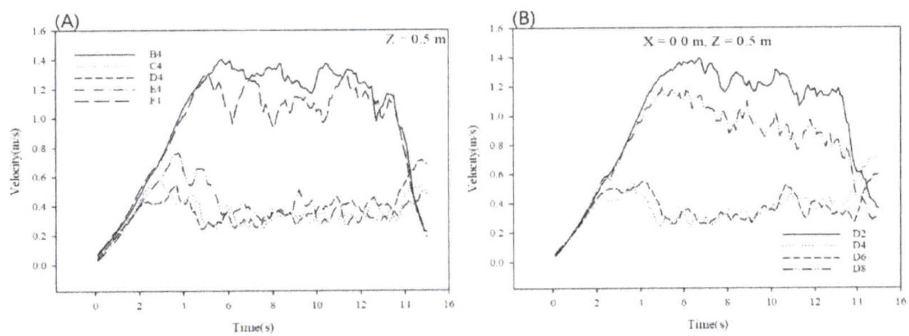

Figure 9. Results obtained at the 4th height position; (**A**) results for the mannequin at the fourth height position; (**B**) results according to various sensor heights taken at a distance of 0.5 m.

Figure 10 shows that as *u/U* approached 1, the air flow was more developed as the distance from the rear of the mannequin increased. This was also confirmed by the measurements in the study. The *u/U* at X (m) = 0 increased toward 1 as Z increased, and the right and left values at X (m) = 0 were symmetrical at all heights. The positions X (m) = −0.4, 0, or 0.4 were directly affected by the cylinder because they were positioned immediately behind the cylinder, and *u/U* increased toward 1 as *Z/d* increased.

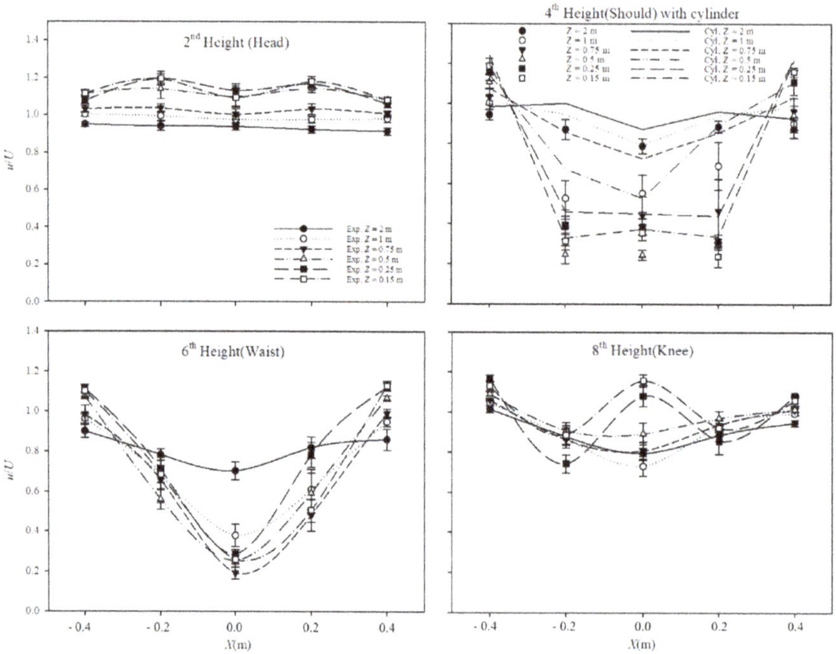

Figure 10. Results obtained for the cylinder and mannequin at the shoulder position (500 mm).

4. Conclusions and Discussion

In this study, a mobile measuring device was used to directly measure the slipstream generated when a cylinder of diameter 500 mm (the average shoulder width of an adult male) was moved at a velocity of 1.2 m/s (the average walking velocity of humans) to obtain the velocity profile of the rear side of a cylinder. The cylinder was then fixed, and a wind velocity of 1.2 m/s was created at the inlet to provide data for the numerical analysis; the results were compared with the measurements. The results of the measurements and numerical analysis of the area behind the cylinder are very similar, with a maximum u/U difference of 0.066 at Z/d = 0.3. The difference was 0.042 and was larger at the 2nd height position when X/d = 0.0 and Z/d = 4. The increase in the difference with increasing Z/d was attributed to the impact of the trailing vortex, and to the fact that the numerical analysis was performed with the cylinder in a fixed position. The direction of the measurement was estimated as per the position of the vortex obtained from the numerical analysis. The wake of the mannequin was measured in the same way as that of the cylinder. Similar measurement results were obtained at the shoulder height, which was the same diameter as the cylinder, and a velocity profile for the mannequin wake was obtained.

Previous experimental studies [20] on wakes were conducted in wind tunnels or as lab-scale experiments, whereas the present study used a mobile cylinder that can reveal the actual characteristic of wakes. In this manner, air flow characteristics were identified. This study presented a method based on a mobile measuring device to obtain the velocity profile of the slipstream of a moving object. If the moving velocity of the sensor support is accounted for, the mobile measuring device could be used to verify the results of simulations of the dispersion of airborne contaminants derived from moving objects.

Recently, the social and economic damage caused by viruses such as COVID-19 has increased. To prevent the spread of such airborne substances, a ventilation system can be used, along with restrictions on movement [26,27]. Droplet dispersion during coughing by people who are walking plays an important role in the transmission of COVID-19. A simulation showed that droplets in the air in a narrow space, such as a hallway, were transmitted below waist height (of the emitter) [28]. Wake measurements confirmed that the speed and distribution stabilized as the distance from the mobile slipstream at chest and waist height increased. The speed rapidly increased to the left and right of the mobile slipstream, and a vortex was created on the back side. The vortex formed as it moved to the bottom surface. Based on the results of this study, movement restrictions appear necessary to slow the spread of the virus, in accordance with the correlation between the wake velocity distribution and spread of the virus.

Numerical analysis results for a system comprising a moving object could not be compared with the measurement results. Therefore, in future studies, methods need to be devised that consider moving velocity when measuring wind velocity, and numerical analysis of a system including a moving object could be performed for comparison.

Author Contributions: D.P. planned the study and contributed the main ideas; M.K. was principally responsible for the writing of the manuscript; Y.L. revised the manuscript and methodology analysis. All authors have read and agreed to the published version of the manuscript.

Funding: This work was supported by a grant from the Subway Fine Dust Reduction Technology Development Project of the Ministry of Land Infrastructure and Transport (21QPPW-B152306-03).

Conflicts of Interest: The authors declare no conflict of interest.

References

1. Yu, I.T.S.; Li, Y.G.; Wong, T.W.; Tam, W.; Chan, A.T.; Lee, J.H.W.; Leung, D.Y.C.; Ho, T. Evidence of airborne trans-mission of the severe acute respiratory syndrome virus. *N. Engl. J. Med.* **2004**, *350*, 1731–1739. [CrossRef] [PubMed]
2. U.S. Department of Health & Human Services. *Centers for Disease Control and Prevention*; 2016. Available online: https://www.cdc.gov/coronavirus/mers/index.html (accessed on 20 July 2016).
3. Wei, J.; Li, Y. Airborne spread of infectious agents in the indoor environment. *Am. J. Infect. Control.* **2016**, *44*, S102–S108. [CrossRef] [PubMed]
4. Wang, J.; Chow, T.T. Numerical investigation of influence of human walking on dispersion and deposition of expiratory droplets in airborne infection isolation room. *Build. Environ.* **2011**, *46*, 1993–2002. [CrossRef]
5. Hang, J.; Li, Y.; Jin, R. The influence of human walking on the flow and airborne transmission in a six-bed isolation room: Tracer gas simulation. *Build. Environ.* **2014**, *77*, 119–134. [CrossRef] [PubMed]
6. Cheong Chang, H.; Seo, Y.M.; Lee, S.H.; Kang, J. Improvement of airborne infection prevention methods in emergency room by design case study. *J. Korean Soc. Living Environ. Syst.* **2016**, *23*, 433–442.
7. Min-Ki, S.; Shinsuke, K.; Jong-Hun, K. Airborne contaminant dispersion in the ward area of a hospital air-conditioned by multi zone VAV systems. *J. Korean Soc. Living Environ. Syst.* **2012**, *19*, 1–7.
8. Liu, Y.; Zhao, Y.; Liu, Z.; Luo, J. Numerical investigation of the unsteady flow characteristics of human body thermal plume. *Build. Simul.* **2016**, *9*, 677–687. [CrossRef]
9. Martinho, N.; Lopes, A.G.; da Silva, M.C.G. Evaluation of errors on the CFD computation of air flow and heat transfer around the human body. *Build. Environ.* **2012**, *58*, 58–69. [CrossRef]
10. Takada, S.; Sasaki, A.; Kimura, R. Fundamental study of ventilation in air layer in clothing considering real shape of the human body based on CFD analysis. *Build. Environ.* **2016**, *99*, 210–220. [CrossRef]
11. Ge, Q.; Li, X.; Inthavong, K.; Tu, J. Numerical study of the effects of human body heat on particle transport and inhalation in indoor environment. *Build. Environ.* **2013**, *59*, 1–9. [CrossRef]
12. Choi, J.-I.; Oberoi, R.C.; Edwards, J.R.; Rosati, J.A. An immersed boundary method for complex incompressible flows. *J. Comput. Phys.* **2007**, *224*, 757–784. [CrossRef]
13. Choi, J.-I.; Edwards, J.R. Large eddy simulation and zonal modeling of human-induced contaminant transport. *Indoor Air* **2008**, *18*, 233–249. [CrossRef] [PubMed]
14. Choi, J.-I.; Edwards, J.R.; Choi, J.-I.; Edwards, J.R. Large-eddy simulation of human-induced contaminant transport in room compartments. *Indoor Air* **2011**, *22*, 77–87. [CrossRef] [PubMed]
15. Choi, J.-I.; Edwards, J.R.; Rosati, J.A.; Eisner, A.D. Large Eddy Simulation of Particle Re-suspension During a Footstep. *Aerosol Sci. Technol.* **2012**, *46*, 767–780. [CrossRef]
16. Shih, Y.-C.; Chiu, C.-C.; Wang, O. Dynamic airflow simulation within an isolation room. *Build. Environ.* **2007**, *42*, 3194–3209. [CrossRef] [PubMed]
17. Zhang, Z.; Chen, X.; Mazumdar, S.; Zhang, T.; Chen, Q. Experimental and numerical investigation of airflow and contaminant transport in an airliner cabin mockup. *Build. Environ.* **2009**, *44*, 85–94. [CrossRef]
18. Poussou, S.B.; Mazumdar, S.; Plesniak, M.; Sojka, P.E.; Chen, Q. Flow and contaminant transport in an airliner cabin induced by a moving body: Model experiments and CFD predictions. *Atmos. Environ.* **2010**, *44*, 2830–2839. [CrossRef]

19. Mazumdar, S.; Poussou, S.B.; Lin, C.-H.; Isukapalli, S.S.; Plesniak, M.W.; Chen, Q. Impact of scaling and body movement on contaminant transport in airliner cabins. *Atmos. Environ.* **2011**, *45*, 6019–6028. [CrossRef]
20. Han, Z.Y.; Weng, W.G.; Huang, Q.Y.; Fu, M.; Yang, J.; Luo, N. Aerodynamic characteristics of human movement be-haviors in full-scale environment: Comparison of limbs pendulum and body motion. *Indoor Built Environ.* **2015**, *24*, 87–100. [CrossRef]
21. Milanowicz, M.; Kedzior, K. Active numerical model of human body for reconstruction of falls from height. *Forensic Sci. Int.* **2017**, *270*, 223–231. [CrossRef]
22. Liu, Y.; Liu, Z.; Luo, J. Numerical Investigation of the Unsteady Thermal Plume Around Human Body in Closed Space. *Procedia Eng.* **2015**, *121*, 1919–1926. [CrossRef]
23. Hemant, N.; Shaligram, T. Heat transfer and fluid flow characteristics from finite height circular cylinder mounted on horizontal plate. *Procedia Eng.* **2015**, *127*, 71–78.
24. Park, C.W.; Lee, S.J. Free end effects on the near wake flow structure behind a finite circular cylinder. *J. Wind. Eng. Ind. Aerodyn.* **2000**, *88*, 231–246. [CrossRef]
25. Kawamura, T.; Hiwada, M.; Hibino, T.; Mabuchi, I.; Kumada, M. Flow around a finite circular cylinder on a flat plate. *Bulletin of JSME.* **1984**, *27*, 2142–2151. [CrossRef]
26. Gola, M.; Caggiano, G.; De Giglio, O.; Napoli, C.; Diella, G.; Carlucci, M.; Carpagnano, L.F.; D'Alessandro, D.; Joppolo, C.M.; Capolongo, S.; et al. SARS-CoV-2 indoor contamination: Considerations on anti-COVID-19 management of ventilation systems, and finishing materials in healthcare facilities. *Ann. Ig.* **2021**, *33*, 381–392. [CrossRef] [PubMed]
27. Yang, Y.K.; Won, A.N.; Hwang, J.H.; Park, J.C. Simulation of splash diffusion analysis for prevention of infection in hospital. *KIEAE J.* **2018**, *18*, 121–127. [CrossRef]
28. Li, Z.; Wang, H.; Zhang, X.; Wu, T.; Yang, X. Effects of space sizes on the dispersion of cough-generated droplets from a walking person. *Phys. Fluids* **2020**, *32*, 121705. [CrossRef] [PubMed]

buildings

MDPI

Article

Window-Windcatcher for Enhanced Thermal Comfort, Natural Ventilation and Reduced COVID-19 Transmission

Odi Fawwaz Alrebei [1,*], Laith M. Obeidat [2], Shouib Nouh Ma'bdeh [2], Katerina Kaouri [3], Tamer Al-Radaideh [2] and Abdulkarem I. Amhamed [1,*]

1 Energy Department, Qatar Environment and Energy Research Institute (QEERI), Hamad Bin Khalifa University, Doha 34110, Qatar
2 Department of Architecture, Jordan University of Science and Technology, Irbid 3030, Jordan; lmobeidat@just.edu.jo (L.M.O.); snmabdeh@just.edu.jo (S.N.M.); t.radaideh@gmail.com (T.A.-R.)
3 School of Mathematics, Cardiff University, Cardiff CF24 4AG, UK; kaourik@cardiff.ac.uk
* Correspondence: oalrebei@hbku.edu.qa (O.F.A.); aamhamed@hbku.edu.qa (A.I.A.)

Abstract: We investigate and test the effectiveness of a novel window windcatcher device (WWC), as a means of improving natural ventilation in buildings. Using ANSYS CFX, the performance of the window-windcatcher is compared to a control case (no window-windcatcher), in three different geographic locations (Cardiff, Doha and Amman) which are representative of three different types of atmospheric conditions. The proposed window-windcatcher has been shown to improve both thermal comfort and indoor air quality by increasing the actual-to-required ventilation ratio by up to 9% compared to the control case as per the American Society of Heating, Refrigerating and Air-Conditioning Engineers (ASHRAE) standards. In addition, the locations with minimum velocities have been identified. Those locations correspond to the regions with a lower infection risk of spreading airborne viruses such as SARS-CoV-2, which is responsible for the COVID-19 pandemic.

Keywords: natural ventilation; thermal comfort; infection prevention; building cfd analysis; windcatcher

Citation: Fawwaz Alrebei, O.; Obeidat, L.M.; Ma'bdeh, S.N.; Kaouri, K.; Al-Radaideh, T.; Amhamed, A.I. Window-Windcatcher for Enhanced Thermal Comfort, Natural Ventilation and Reduced COVID-19 Transmission. *Buildings* **2022**, *12*, 791. https://doi.org/10.3390/buildings12060791

Academic Editors: Ashok Kumar, M Amirul I Khan, Alejandro Moreno Rangel and Michał Piasecki

Received: 11 April 2022
Accepted: 3 June 2022
Published: 9 June 2022

Publisher's Note: MDPI stays neutral with regard to jurisdictional claims in published maps and institutional affiliations.

1. Introduction

As one of the most significant threats to our lives, global warming needs to be tackled immediately and effectively. Global warming has been destroying the environment, thus affecting almost all aspects of our lives [1]. The construction industry is one of the main sectors contributing to global warming, through the emission of vast greenhouse gas (GHG), mainly CO_2 [2]. In addition, 40% of the CO_2 emissions is generated by buildings and around 40% of the global energy generated is consumed by buildings [3]. Energy consumption by buildings is expected to reach 64% of the total energy consumption by 2100, if no action is taken [4].

More than 60% of the energy consumption in buildings is used for heating, cooling, and ventilation [5]. This energy is obtained mainly from fossil resources [5]. In addition to the challenges of high energy consumption and CO_2 emissions, maintaining acceptable indoor air quality (IAQ) using mechanical HVAC systems can be challenging. On average, people spend up to 90% of their time working and living indoors. The risk of sick building syndrome (SBS), metabolic diseases and transmission of COVID-19 and other airborne viral diseases are increased in air-conditioned buildings compared to naturally ventilated buildings [6]. It is, thus, critical to ensure good IAQ to maintain health and productivity [5]. In this context, passive strategies implemented in the building's architecture, such as daylighting, natural ventilation, passive cooling and passive heating may provide significant benefits to users and to the environment as they lead to reduced energy consumption and CO_2 emissions, mitigating negative impacts on the environment and health. Implementing such passive strategies could also lead to significant cost savings [7].

Passive cooling techniques have been studied extensively [7]. Acceptable thermal comfort and IAQ using passive cooling can be achieved with only a small fraction of the energy consumed by mechanical ventilation systems [6]. Natural ventilation is one of the leading passive cooling strategies that effectively improve the indoor atmosphere by: (1) providing good IAQ and (2) improving thermal comfort, through affecting ventilation rates, air velocity, temperature and humidity [7]. Natural ventilation is air exchange between outdoor (fresh) air and indoor (used) air [1]. It occurs naturally, without mechanical assistance, by establishing a pressure difference or a temperature difference.

Indoor thermal comfort could be directly improved by increasing the cooling sensation through increased airflow or indirectly by night ventilation (night flushing) [7,8]. Night ventilation can be achieved through natural ventilation, especially in the context of adequate fluctuation in air temperature over the day and the night. For example, the temperature during the hot, sunny summer months in Amman, Jordan usually reaches 40 °C in the day and drops significantly, to around 20 °C in the night. (Average temperatures during the day and night are 36 °C and 22 °C, respectively [9].) Such a significant fluctuation in temperature provides great potential for night ventilation and improvement of the indoor thermal comfort [10] by providing a cool breeze during the night, which would flush out hot air and cool off the internal thermal masses to effectively delay the thermal gain during daytime [11].

Implementing effective natural ventilation solutions in multi-family residential buildings is challenging and sometimes not easily applicable. The internal spatial organization of the building [11], and to a great extent, its layout and limited shared exterior walls with the outdoor environment contribute to the difficulty. The limited shared exterior walls, especially in the generic architectural typology of the multi-story residential buildings, lead to little or even no condition of the opposite openings (inlet and outlet) necessary to achieve effective cross-ventilation [12]. In addition, even in the single-family detached house typology, cross-ventilation conditions can be difficult to achieve, especially for large houses where some rooms have only a single exterior wall with all window openings on the same wall. Various techniques and systems have been developed in order to exploit these natural phenomena and conditions to achieve adequate natural ventilation. These systems vary in performance, requirements, and settings: they include Trombe wall, double skin façade, solar chimney, solar walls, atrium, wind tower, windcatcher and fenestration (single-sided ventilation and cross ventilation) [7]. These systems can be intertwined and used for other passive design strategies.

A traditional and common natural ventilation system for buildings is the windcatcher [13] as it can provide good air quality and improve thermal comfort in an environmentally friendly manner, using, mainly, renewable wind energy [14]. Windcatchers have a long history with enhancing indoor environmental comfort in arid and semi-arid regions. They achieve harmony between built environments and the surrounding natural environments. A windcatcher or wind tower is generally defined as a tower-like architectural component designed to be mounted on the building roof "to 'catch' the wind at higher elevations and direct it into the inner environment of a building" [2].

Windcatchers operate mainly with wind-driven ventilation and stack (buoyancy) effects [2]. Moreover, windcatchers are low maintenance since they operate without moving parts [2]. However, windcatchers have limitations. A key limitation is their large size and centrality (i.e., located at the building's center). Since several windcatcher elements are generally required to achieve adequate natural ventilation, especially for large-scale buildings, restrictions are imposed on the building geometry. For example, windcatcher systems may limit future expansion and roof space use [3]. Many researchers have extensively studied their effectiveness and performance using different evaluation methods such as computational methods, experimental methods, analytical and empirical methods, or a combination. Each of these methods has its own advantages and limitations in terms of accuracy, cost, complexity of geometry, detail of the results and time to implement the method [15]. CFD is the most used computational method as it offers high accuracy and low financial cost (only the cost of the software package), and it is suitable for complex geometries, generating detailed results. Detailed information regarding the advantages of CFD compared to other methods can be found in [15].

According to [16,17], Environmental Controls (ECs) are based on methods for reducing concentrations of an infectious agent in the air and on surfaces in indoor environments. World Health Organization (WHO) guidelines recommend a combination of environmental control mechanisms to avoid the spread of viruses to health care workers (HCWs) and patients in health care settings [17]. The environmental regulations rely on the design of the healthcare environment and include (a) building materials, surfaces, and products used [17]; (b) indoor environmental factors (e.g., temperature, humidity, light, and airflow) [17]; and (c) indoor access to the outside. All of the above may influence the survival of infectious agents in the built environment.

Airflow and ventilation systems play a significant role in the airborne transmission of pathogens; improving ventilation decreases the risk of transmission. Identifying how the novel window-windcatcher improves ventilation is the focus of our work here [6,7]. The design of a ventilation system depends on the ability to contain, mitigate, and remove airborne pollutants through air change and inward indoor airflow [17].

Reducing the effect of overheating, and thus, improving thermal comfort in a building, is achieved mainly by two methods: building elements and ventilation [18]. The heat conductivity (k-value) of the building elements (such as walls, windows, etc.) can be reduced through selecting appropriate building elements. Ventilation is enhanced through increased air circulation, using, for example, window-windcatchers. The overheating is given by $H_{loss} = c_p \dot{m} \Delta T$, where c_p is the air specific capacity, $\dot{m}$ is the air mass flow rate and ΔT is the temperature difference between the internal and external domains. The window-windcatcher can increase H_{loss} by increasing $\dot{m}$.

Our work aims to investigate and test, using CFD, the design of a novel window- windcatcher device that can be mounted on exterior walls to capture the prevailing wind and redirect it into indoor spaces. We demonstrate that the ventilation rate in an indoor space increases when we use the novel window-windcatcher. According to the World Health Organization (WHO), viral diseases, such as COVID-19, can be more easily transmitted in poorly ventilated enclosed spaces which have low ventilation rates [19]. The proposed design could replace or complement traditional large-scale windcatchers by small-scale decentralized windcatchers which can be mounted on exterior walls as a window component. The design of the device is suitable for retrofitting existing buildings or for new buildings. We find that the device could enhance the effectiveness of natural ventilation (passive cooling) in buildings, significantly improving IAQ and thermal comfort by increasing the actual-to-required ventilation ratio, as per the ASHRAE standards, by up to 9% compared to the control case without a window-windcatcher.

This can be achieved by increasing the ventilation rate while ensuring minimal turbulence. Increasing the ventilation rate is primarily achieved by increasing air velocity; however, as the turbulence kinetic energy is dependent on the air velocity, improving the ventilation rate could potentially increase the turbulence kinetic energy. Therefore, it is crucial to ensure that the increase in the turbulence kinetic energy is kept sufficiently low as the velocity increases.

Portable air cleaners, also known as air purifiers or air sanitizers, are designed to filter the air in a single room or area [20]. Central furnace or HVAC filters are designed to filter air throughout a home. Portable air cleaners and HVAC filters can reduce indoor air pollutants, including viruses, that are airborne [20]. By themselves, portable air cleaners and HVAC filters are not enough to protect people from the virus that causes COVID-19 [20]. Air purifiers could be placed in regions of high turbulence kinetic energy. Hence, such regions shall be carefully identified in order to formulate recommendations on the use of air purifiers. Placing air purifiers in high turbulence kinetic energy regions will: (1) ensure that the highest air flow rate is entering the air purifier; and (2) prevent the building's residents to occupy those locations.

We outline the structure of the paper. The Introduction provides the rationale of the research, the benefits of implementing passive design techniques such as natural ventilation, the context of using the windcatcher natural ventilation system, our goals and objectives, and an overview of the used methodology. The Material and Methods section provides more detailed information about the proposed window windcatcher, building geometry, and the geographical locations of the three cities we study (Amman, Doha and Cardiff). In addition, this section provides information about the CFD method, software, sensitivity analysis, and inlet and outlet boundary conditions. The Results section consists of a qualitative and a quantitative part. The qualitative part presents visual comparisons of a case without or with a window windcatcher device, respectively. The comparison includes the turbulence kinetic energy, velocity, and velocity streamlines for the three selected cities, on selected planes of interest. The quantitative part shows the simulations with and without a window-windcatcher and the device's effect on the actual-to-required ventilation ratio. In the Discussion section, we present the effect of the windcatcher on the IAQ. In addition, potential locations for deploying air purifiers in indoor spaces are discussed. Lastly, the Conclusions section presents the key results; the window-windcatcher increases the actual-to-required ventilation ratio as per the ASHRAE standards by up to 9%.

2. Materials and Methods

2.1. Description of the Window-Windcatcher and of the Building

To examine the efficiency of the proposed window-windcatcher device, a simplified building model representing a typical single-family house is used—see Figure 1. This building model was used in several studies to investigate natural ventilation and passive cooling in Jordan [21]. For example, it was used to examine the efficiency of the Solar-Wall system (combination of Trombe wall and solar chimney) on enhancing indoor thermal comfort [21]. The selected room dimensions are 4 m × 3 m × 2.7 m (length × width × height), so the floor area is 12 $m^{2,}$ and the volume is 32.4 m^3. The external window of the room is 2 m in width, 1 m in length, and 1 m in sill height, with a total window-to-wall ratio of 18%. The window has an operable sliding glazing mechanism that allows up to 50% of its total area to be opened.

The proposed window-windcatcher aims to enhance natural ventilation in a particular room and in the whole residential unit—see Figure 1. The device is to be mounted on the envelope of existing or new buildings with minimal changes on the building shape or structure. Hence, the device could be used as a passive retrofitting technique. The design could be further developed to take into account requirements about privacy, daylighting, and aesthetic issues. Generally, as illustrated in Figure 2, the device consists of four vertical supporting elements (joists) that connect two horizontal planes, an upper and a lower plane. The distance between the upper and the lower plane is equal to the height of the window opening, in this case 1 m. The device consists of four fins (1 m height × 0.15 m width × 0.02 m thickness) tilted by 45 degrees located at the outside edge of the device and one curved element that spans from a point near the last fin in the group into the right internal corner of the two planes. The fins and the curved element are mounted between the two planes supported by the four supporting elements at the four corners of the horizontal planes. The aim is that the prevailing wind will be captured and pass through the device opening on the shorter side opposite the curved element and the areas between the tilted fins.

The vertical curved plane aims at enhancing the captured airflow toward the interior spaces. The tilting angle could be optimized by running the simulation for different angles; this is outside our research scope. Moreover, other issues could be investigated in future work, such as daylighting performance, privacy, and the finishing materials used for the various components of the proposed device.

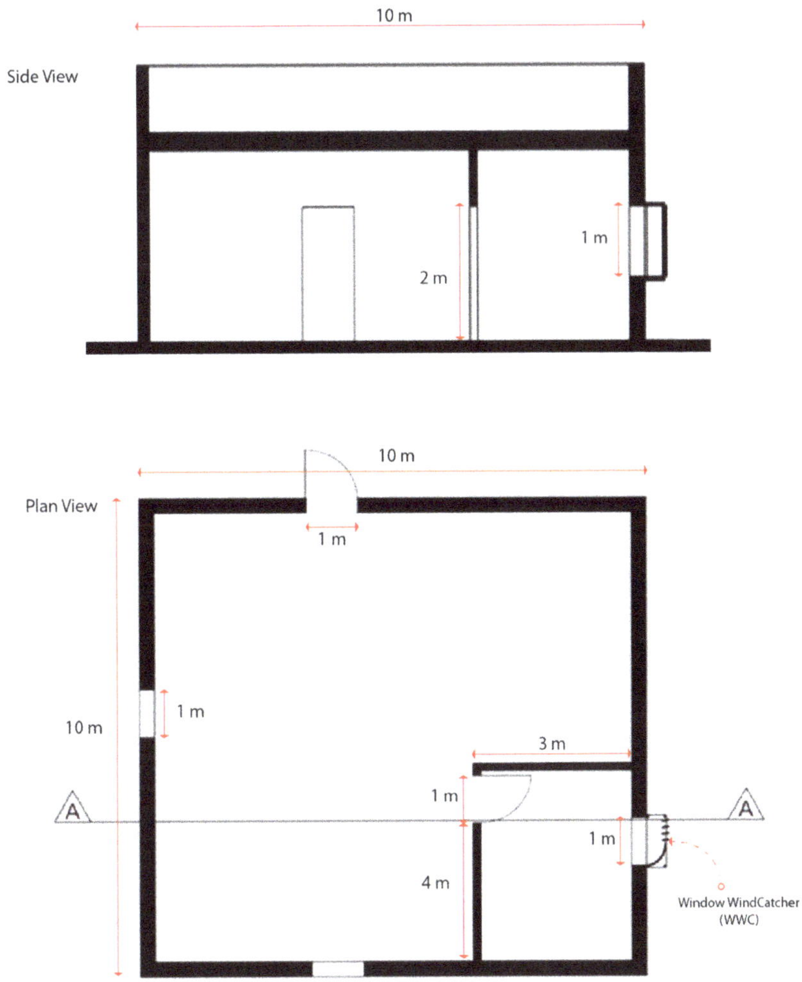

Figure 1. The dimensions of the building.

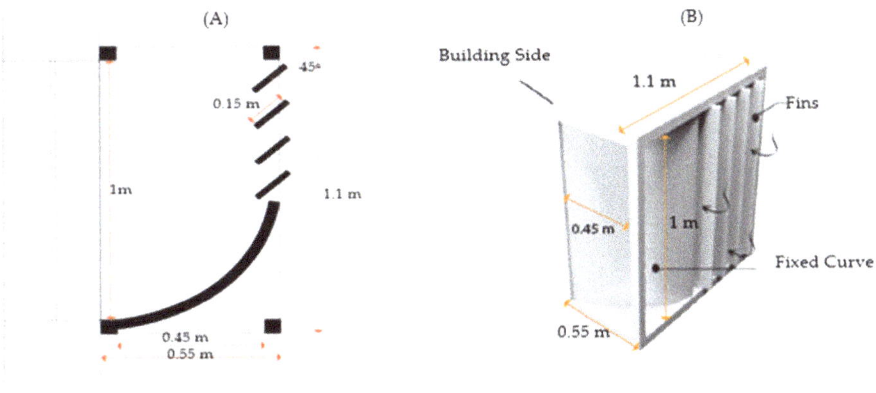

Figure 2. The design and dimensions of the proposed window-windcatcher. (**A**) 2D view (**B**) 3D View.

2.2. Case Studies

The proposed window-windcatcher's performance has been evaluated against a control case without a window-windcatcher, in three geographical locations: Cardiff, Doha and Amman—see Figure 3. The three cities are located within three different climatic zones: Amman in a hot-summer Mediterranean climate, Doha in a hot desert climate and Cardiff is in an Oceanic climate. The Total Wind Velocity (TWV) and temperature in each city have been obtained for 2021 [22]. The average temperature and TWV have been evaluated and plotted in Figure 4. We find, respectively, for Cardiff, Doha and Amman, these values to be [10.7 °C, 5.45 m/s], [27.8 °C, 4.2 m/s], and [22.3 °C, 3.6 m/s].

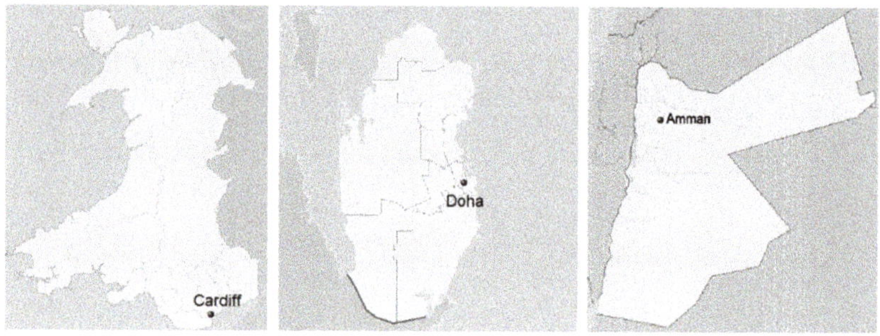

Figure 3. Geographical locations of the three cities we consider (Cardiff, Doha and Amman).

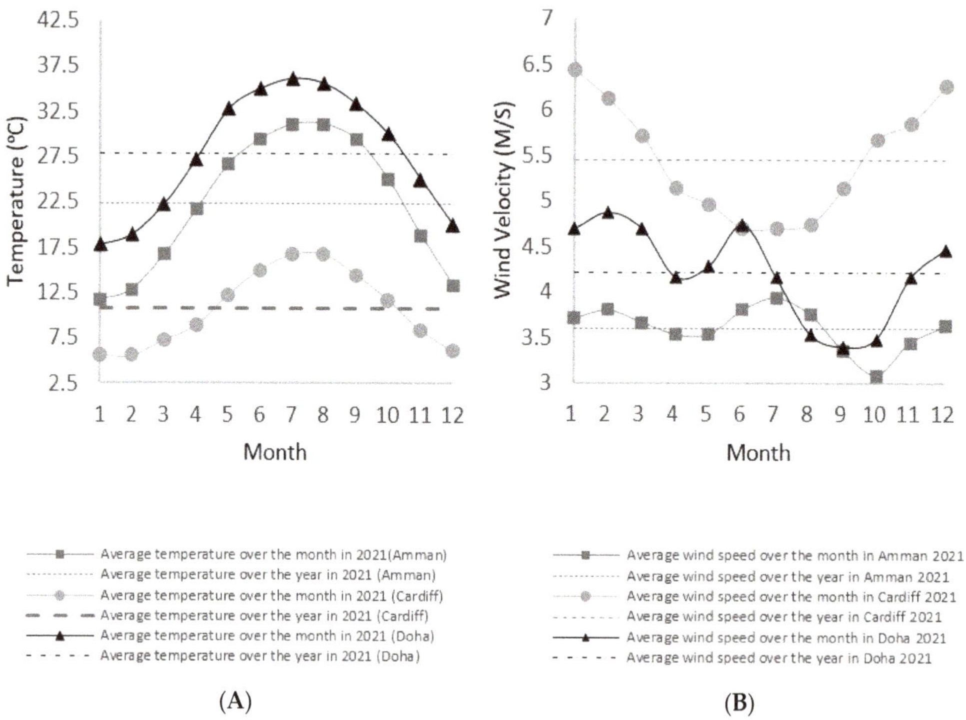

Figure 4. (**A**) Temperature and (**B**) Total Wind Velocity (TWV) in 2021 in Amman, Cardiff, and Doha.

As shown in Figure 5, the orientation of the building with respect to the direction of the average TWV is simulated for equal shear (SWV) and normal (NWV) wind velocity components (i.e., 3.85 m/s, 2.97 m/s and 2.55 m/s for Cardiff, Doha and Amman, respectively). The velocity components have been estimated, according to [23], as follows:

$$SWV^2 = NWV^2 = \frac{TWV^2}{2} \tag{1}$$

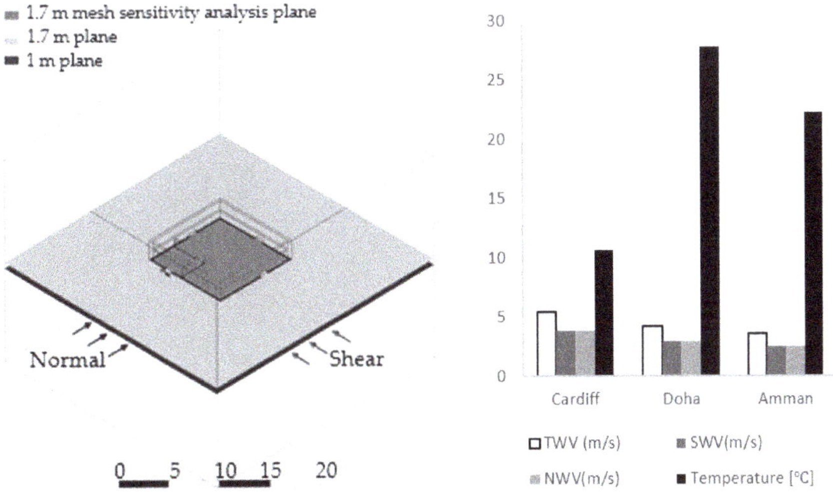

(**A**) (**B**)

Figure 5. (**A**) Internal and external computational domains—two planes at 1 m and two planes at 1.7 m; (**B**) computational setups of temperature and wind velocity.

2.3. CFD Simulations

CFD simulations of the airflow passing through the proposed window-windcatcher were performed with the ANSYS 2020 CFX package [24]. We used a virtual machine with computational capabilities of Processor Intel® Core™i7-7700 CPU @ 3.6 Hz, installed memory 32 GB and a 64-bit operating system. The computational time was approximately 12 h for each case study. The geometry of the building was modelled and loaded into ANSYS. The building model was created using the Boolean algorithm (i.e., the solid domain is subtracted from the internal and external fluid domain [25]—see Figure 5. Figure 6 shows the computational mesh for these domains, created with approximately 2.19×10^6 elements.

Performing experiments with the novel windcatcher is not currently possible as the device has not been manufactured. In fact, the focus of the work is generating CFD simulations that are as accurate as possible in order to assess this device before proceeding to manufacture it. We establish the accuracy of the simulations through performing mesh-sensitivity analysis for the building that ensures that the findings are independent of the mesh size. The WWC CAD model is created using AutoCAD. This approach has been adopted in our previous studies [26,27]. Figure 7 shows how the number of elements was determined following mesh sensitivity analysis. The mesh sensitivity study was done for the Amman case study using an average velocity across an interior plane with an offset of 1.7 m from the floor, which is around the average person's height [28]. At around 9.4×10^5 elements, the results do not change with the mesh size. Nevertheless, a much finer mesh with 2.19×10^6 elements was chosen for the simulation to give a high level of confidence and accuracy. In addition, the relative error to the selected mesh size has been estimated and shown to decrease when the mesh size decreases—see Figure 7. The velocity values converged with a relative error margin of 1%.

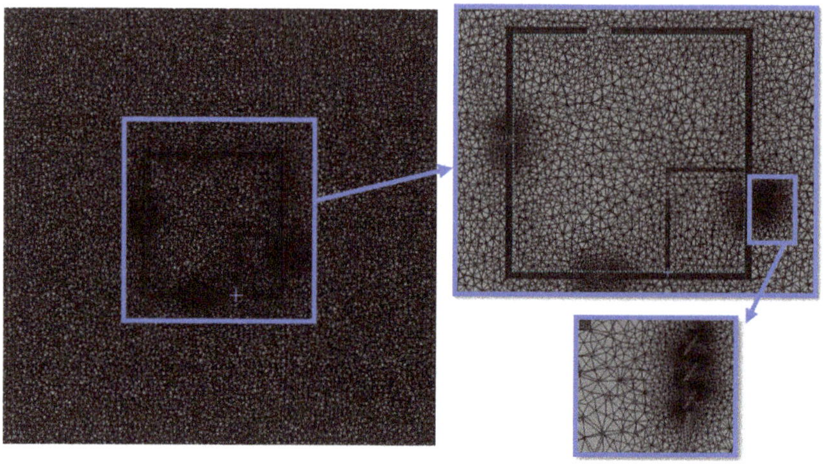

Figure 6. CFX mesh of the CAD model presented in Figures 2 and 3 (building and window-windcatcher).

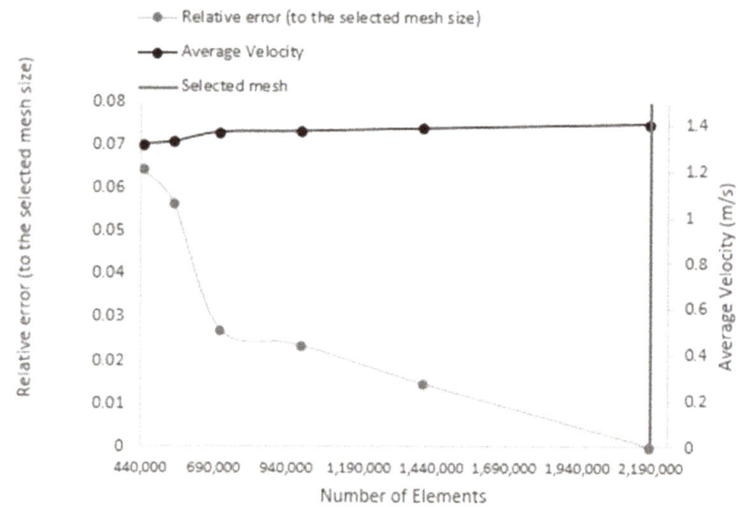

Figure 7. Mesh analysis—average velocity at 1.7 m offset (internal plane).

Furthermore, the mesh quality (Table 1) is consistent with previous studies [27–29]. The mesh is exported to CFX-PRE.

Using the k-ε turbulent flow model, we proceed with a steady-state analysis to determine the average velocities [27–29]. The fluid domain was chosen from the ANSYS library as air at 10.7 °C, 27.8 °C and 22.3 °C corresponding to the Cardiff, Doha and Amman case studies, respectively (as discussed in Section 2.2). The no-slip boundary conditions were implemented in ANSYS as 'No Slip Walls' [27–29].

The goal of this study is to demonstrate that the ventilation rate in an indoor space increases when we use the novel window-windcatcher. According to the World Health Organization (WHO), viral diseases, such as COVID-19, can be more easily transmitted in poorly ventilated enclosed spaces which have low ventilation rates [19].

Table 1. Mesh properties.

Property	Value
Elements maximum size (mm)	500
Number of elements	2.19×10^6
Growth rate	1.2
Defeature size (mm)	2.5
Curvature minimum size (mm)	5
Curvature normal angle (degree)	18
Skewness	0.21188
Orthogonal Quality	0.78694
Inflation transition ratio	0.75
Inflation number of layers	5

Finally, the inlet boundary conditions (as specified in Figure 5) were set to velocity inlets with a turbulence intensity of 5% (default setting in ANSYS).

The Turbulence Kinetic Energy (k) is a proxy for the flow mixing level [26,29]. TKE has been chosen as a quantity to study in this work since COVID-19 spread increases with mixing. Equations (2)–(5) [26,29] give TKE:

$$k = \frac{3}{2}(UI)^2 \tag{2}$$

$$\varepsilon = c_{\mu}^{\frac{3}{4}} k^{\frac{3}{2}} l^{-1} \tag{3}$$

$$I = 0.16Re^{-\frac{1}{8}} \tag{4}$$

$$l = 0.07L \tag{5}$$

We plot TKE in ANSYS CFX. In addition, the performance of the window-windcatcher in preventing the spread of COVID-19 by increasing the ventilation rate has been evaluated against the required ventilation rate (Q_{required}) as per the ASHRAE standards [30]. The acceptable ventilation rate in residential buildings, as defined by the ASHRAE standards, is given in Equation (6) [30]. The convergence of the results is shown in Figure 8.

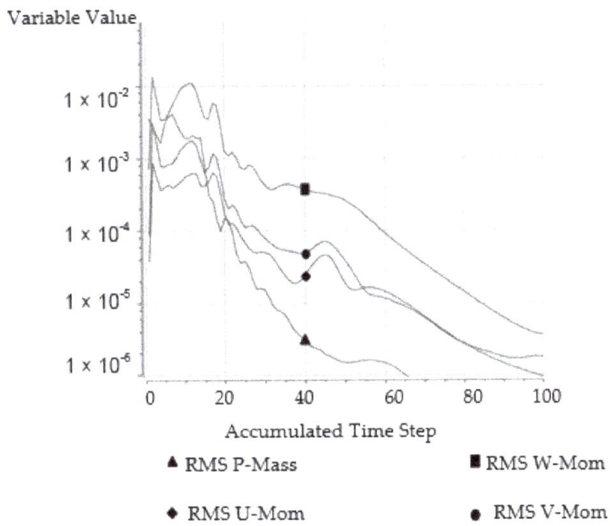

Figure 8. Convergence of results.

The actual ventilation rate (Q_{actual}) has been estimated computationally using ANSYS, and the ventilation performance has been benchmarked by the actual-to-required ventilation ratio (n_Q), Equation (7) [30]:

$$Q_{\text{required}} = 0.15A_{floor} + 3.5(N_{br} + 1) \tag{6}$$

$$n_Q = Q_{\text{actual}} / Q_{\text{required}} \tag{7}$$

The streamlines and contours of the velocity and TKE for the entire fluid domain are plotted in Figures 9–12. In addition, as shown in Figure 5, data have been displayed at two distinct heights (1.7 m and 1 m) for four planes (two planes for the internal domain and two for the external domain): the first height is 1.7 m above the floor (i.e., the breathing level of an average person [26]). The second is at the height of 1 m above the ground, which is about the same as the height of a sitting person.

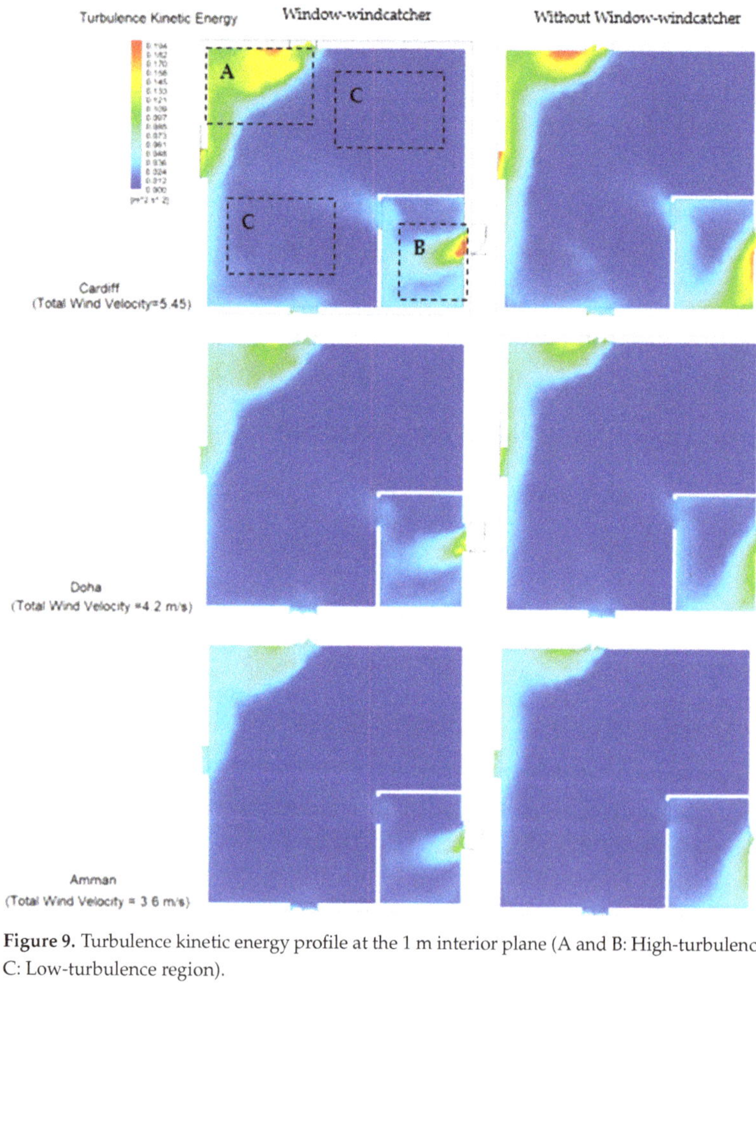

Figure 9. Turbulence kinetic energy profile at the 1 m interior plane (A and B: High-turbulence region, C: Low-turbulence region).

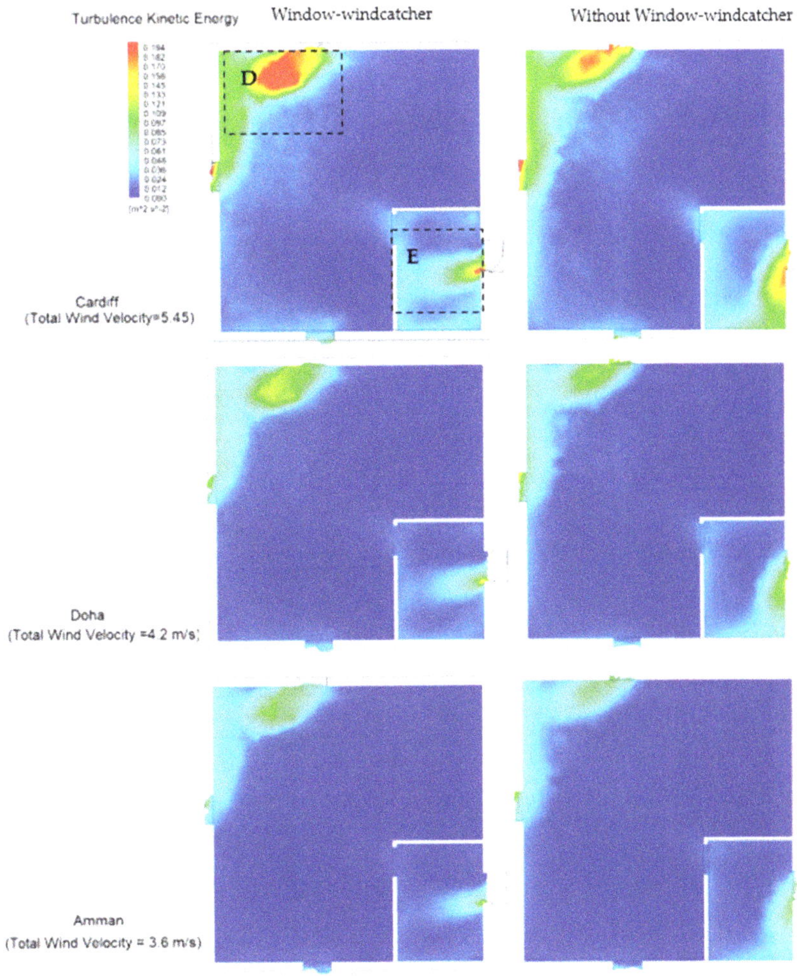

Figure 10. Turbulence kinetic energy profile at the 1.7 m interior plane (D: High-turbulence region, E: Low-turbulence region).

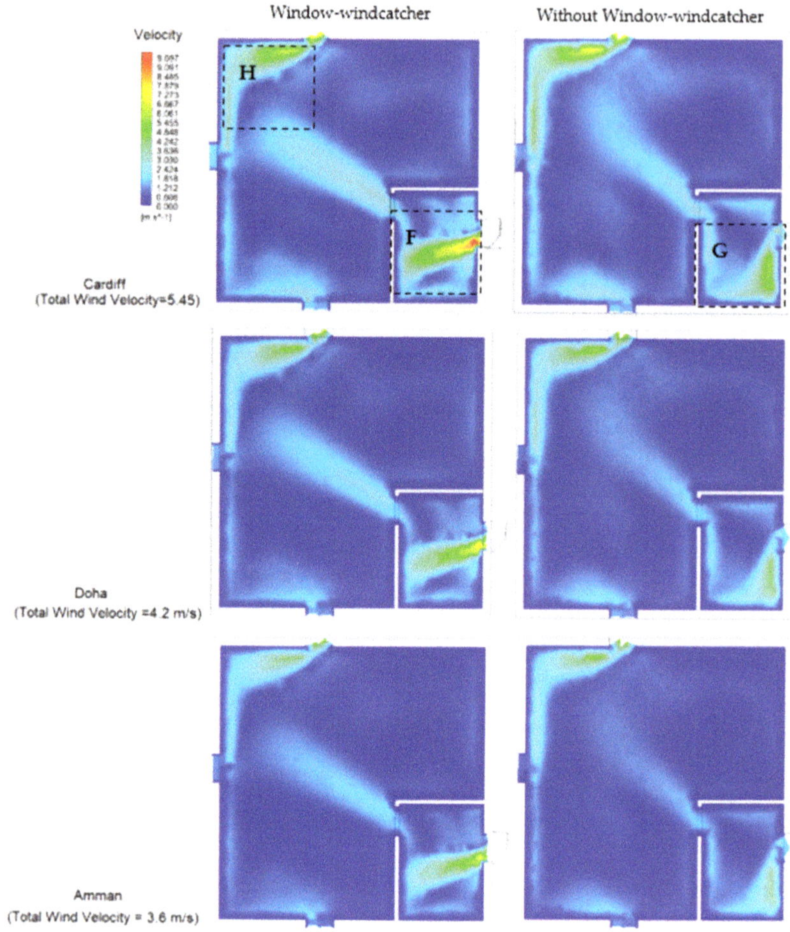

Figure 11. Velocity profile at the 1 m interior plane (H, F and G: High-velocity regions).

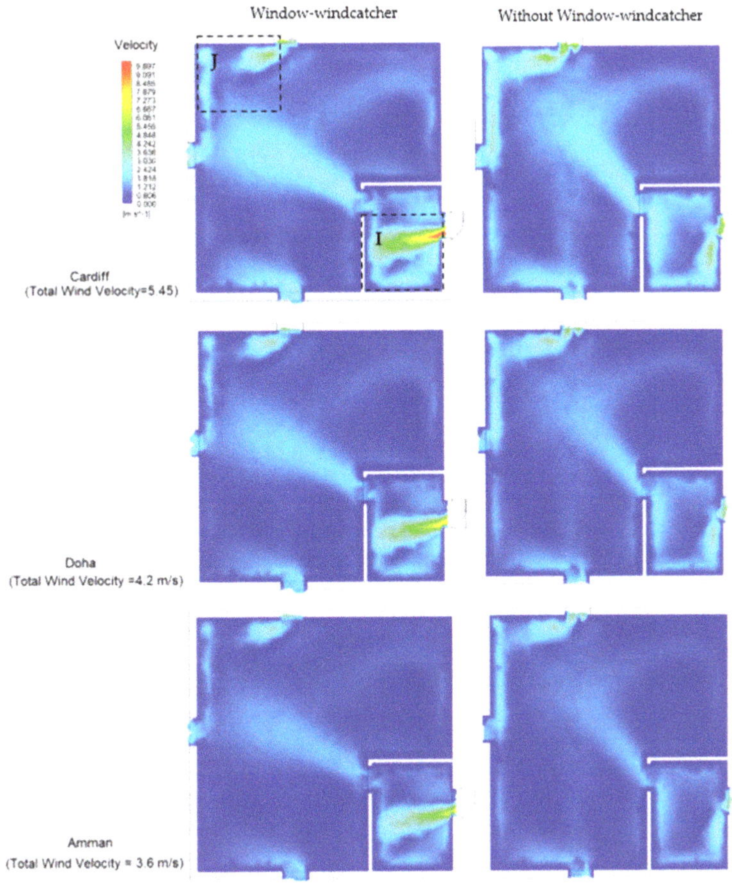

Figure 12. Velocity profile at the 1.7 m interior plane (I and J: High-velocity regions).

3. Results

3.1. *Qualitative Analysis*

As discussed in Section 2, we show how the novel window-windcatcher device we propose could increase the IAQ and hence mitigate the spread of COVID-19 indoors. This is essentially achieved by increasing the ventilation rate while ensuring minimal turbulence. Increasing the ventilation rate is primarily achieved by increasing air velocity; however, as the turbulence kinetic energy increases with the air velocity, increasing the ventilation rate would increase the turbulence kinetic energy.

Therefore, it is crucial to ensure that the increase in the turbulence kinetic energy is maintained at a low value. In addition, regions of high turbulence kinetic energy shall be carefully identified to inform other potential mitigations, for example placing air purifiers in relatively high turbulence regions. Therefore, the turbulence kinetic energy of the interior plane has been plotted for the 1 m (the average height for a seated person) and 1.7 m (the average height for a standing person) planes (Figures 9 and 10, respectively) for the three locations of interest (Cardiff, Doha and Amman).

As shown in Figure 10 for Cardiff, the window-windcatcher has slightly increased the TKE inside the building compared to the case without the window-windcatcher. On the other hand, this increase was less significant in Doha and Amman. This is attributed to the lower levels of wind velocity in Amman and Doha compared to Cardiff. Moreover, as shown in Figure 9, Regions A and B, the high-turbulence regions are located at the building corners while the central region (Region C) remains approximately unaffected.

By comparing the turbulence kinetic energy profiles at the 1 m plane (Figure 9) to those at the 1.7 m plane (Figures 9 and 10), it can be seen that the turbulence energy is higher at the 1.7 m plane (i.e., Region A in Figure 9 to Region D in Figure 10). Hence, Regions D and E could be good locations to place air purifiers.

The velocity profile of the interior plane has been plotted for the 1 m and 1.7 m planes (Figures 11 and 12, respectively) for Cardiff, Doha and Amman. As shown in Figure 11, the window-windcatcher has increased the air velocity inside the building compared to the case without the window-windcatcher (i.e., Region F in Figure 12 compared to Region G in Figure 11). In addition, by comparing Regions F and G, it can be noted that the window-windcatcher has directed the air velocity towards the centre compared to the case without the window-windcatcher, where air velocity tends to be more attached to the building's wall. This essentially indicates the window-windcatcher's capability in vectoring the shear wind towards the building's centre—thus increasing the ventilation rate.

Comparing the velocity profiles of the three case studies, the Cardiff case demonstrates higher velocity levels than Doha and Amman. This is directly related to the fact that the wind velocity in Cardiff is higher than in Doha and in Amman. By comparing the velocity profiles at the 1 m plane to those at the 1.7 m plane (Figures 11 and 12, respectively), while Region F in the 1 m plane (Figure 11) follows approximately the same profile as the velocity at the 1.7 m plane (Region I in Figure 12), Region H in the 1 m plane (Figure 11) differs from that in the 1.7 m plane (Region J in Figure 12). Region H has a more consistent velocity magnitude compared to Region I, where a drop in the magnitude of the velocity has been demonstrated.

The streamlines at the interior plane have been plotted for the 1 m and 1.7 m planes (Figures 13 and 14, respectively) for Cardiff, Doha and Amman. Streamlines are the fluid particle paths. Thus, they provide a visualization of the distribution of the air in the space. The locations with minimal velocities are also identified. These correspond to the regions with lower likelihood of spreading airborne viruses, such as SARS-CoV-2 [16,17]. Those locations correspond to the points where the velocity magnitude gradually decreases to approximately 0 m/s. Those locations are defined here as the near-zero-velocity regions. Correlating these regions to the potential of deploying air purifiers, it is recommended to avoid choosing those locations as those locations correspond to 'safe' regions. On the other hand, air purifiers could be deployed at locations with high velocity to maximise the airflow rate enters the air purifiers. As shown in Figures 13 and 14, the centre of safe near-zero-velocity regions (SNZVR) has been identified for the 1 m and 1.7 m planes, respectively.

In addition, a 70% household limit of the maximum velocity has been used to propose the locations to deploy air purifiers. Those locations have been defined as the air-purifier regions (APR). As shown in Figures 13 and 14, the streamline patterns at the 1 m follow closely the patterns in the 1.7 m plane. However, by comparing the case with the window-windcatcher to the case without the window-windcatcher, it is noted that the SNZVR in Region K without the window-windcatcher (Figure 12) is split into two smaller SNZVR when the window-windcatcher is deployed (Region L). This is attributed to the fact that the window-windcatcher directs the air velocity towards the center, thus splitting the SNZVR. The interaction of the interior and exterior plane streamlines has been plotted for the 1 m and 1.7 m planes (Figures 15 and 16, respectively) for Cardiff, Doha and Amman. This helps us understand the interaction with the interior plane. As shown in Region M of Figure 15, the window-windcatcher has redirected the shear wind towards the interior plane of the building. However, it can be seen that some high-velocity wind streamlines (Region N) are not directed towards the internal plane of the building. This essentially suggests that the WWC design could be further optimized to enhance its aerodynamic capabilities. The WWC design optimization could include the depth of the WWC, the angles of the slanted fins and the number and thickness of the fins.

By comparing the 1 m plane in Figure 15 to the 1.7 m plane in Figure 16, we see that the streamline patterns are quite similar. Nevertheless, comparing the Cardiff case to Amman and Doha, it is noted that the velocity in the building is higher. This is due to the fact that the average wind velocity in Cardiff is higher than the other two cases of study. Another crucial point to note is that, in Region O, where the window-windcatcher has not been deployed (compare to region M), most of the shear wind streamlines are not directed towards the interior plane of the building. This suggests that the ventilation rate could be further increased by installing more than one WWC in Region O. Optimizing the number and positions of WWCs for a given space could significantly enhance the ventilation rate; this is another direction for future work.

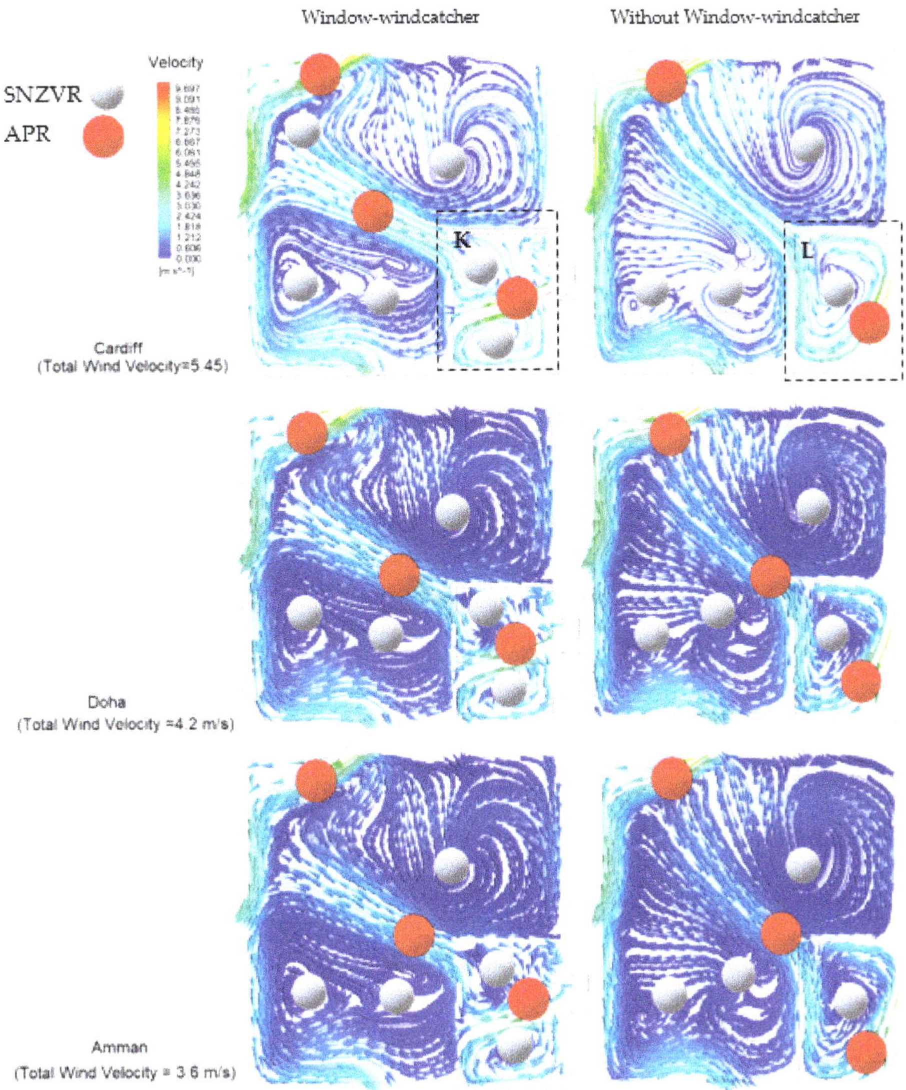

Figure 13. Streamlines at the 1 m interior plane (APR: Air purifiers region, SNZVR: safe near-zero-velocity regions).

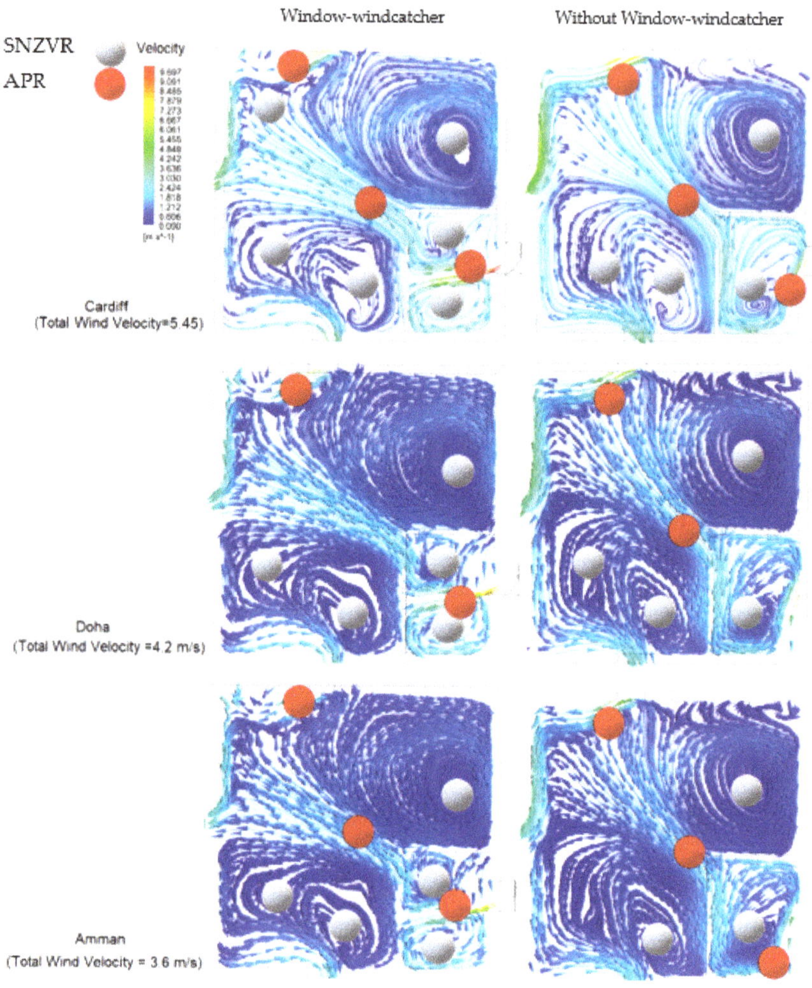

Figure 14. Streamlines at the 1.7 m interior plane (APR: Air purifiers region, SNZVR: safe near-zero-velocity regions).

3.2. Quantitative Analysis

Figure 16 displays the average turbulence kinetic energy of the two interior planes, 1 m and 1.7 m. It can be noted that the window-windcatcher has slightly increased the average turbulence kinetic energy at both planes, in all three cases of study. However, as discussed in Section 3.1, the turbulence kinetic energy increases in the regions that are less likely to be occupied by residents. The increase in the turbulence kinetic energy is directly caused by the increase in the velocity at those planes, as highlighted in Figure 17.

By correlating the average turbulence kinetic energy results in Figure 17 to the velocity results in Figure 18, in a case study with low average velocity (i.e., Amman), it can be noted that the window-windcatcher effect of increasing the turbulence energy is less significant than in the other two cases. This is due to the lower wind speed compared to the other two cases.

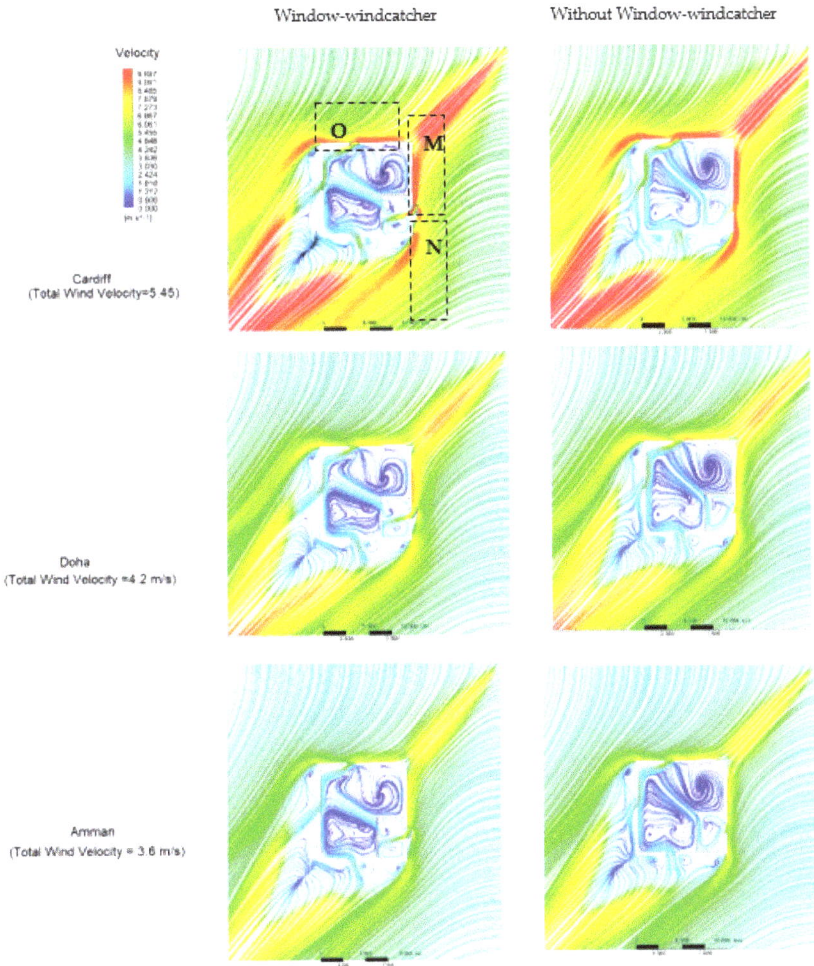

Figure 15. Streamlines at the 1 m plane (internal and external domain).

As shown in Figure 19, the ventilation rates using the window-windcatcher have increased for the three case studies compared to those without the window-windcatcher. In all three case studies, the ventilation rate using the window-windcatcher was increased by approximately 9% compared to the case without the window-windcatcher.

As discussed in Section 2, the ventilation rate has been evaluated against the required ventilation rate ($Q_{required}$) as per ASHRAE standards [30]. The acceptable ventilation rate in the studied residential building was estimated using Equation (6) [30] (i.e., approximately 168.5 L/s). The actual ventilation rate (Q_{actual}) has been estimated computationally using ANSYS, and the ventilation performance has been benchmarked by the actual-to-required ventilation ratio (n_Q) using Equation (7) [30]. As shown in Figure 19, the window-windcatcher for Cardiff has managed to increase the actual-to-required ventilation ratio by approximately 9% compared to the case without the window-windcatcher (n_Q increased from 96.7% to 106%). For Amman and Doha, n_Q has increased by approximately 6% (from 61.5% to 67.5%) and 7% (from 70% to 77.3%), respectively (Figure 20).

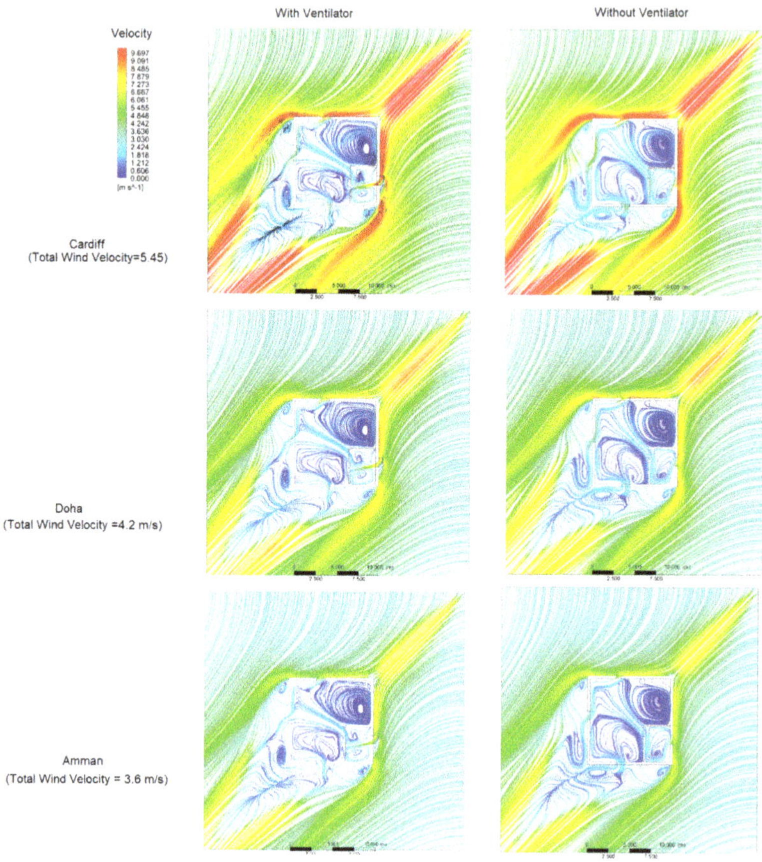

Figure 16. Streamlines at the 1.7 m full plane.

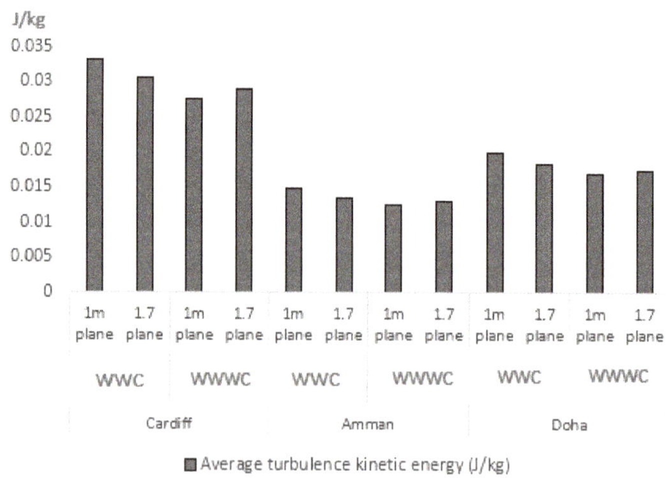

Figure 17. Average turbulence kinetic energy of the interior planes (1 m and 1.7 m) using a Window-WindCatcher (WWC) and Without Window-WindCatcher (WWWC).

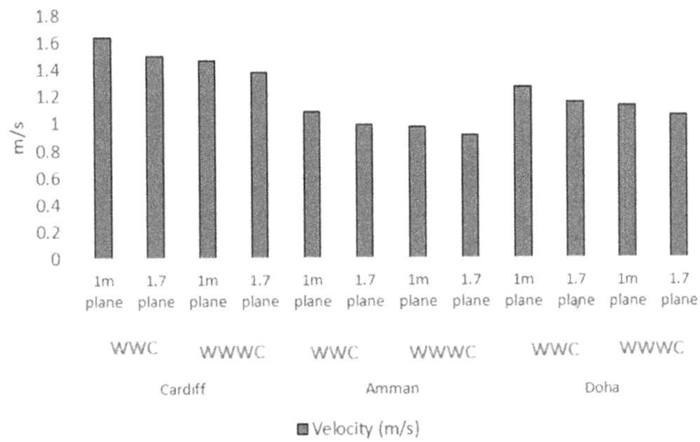

Figure 18. Average velocity of the interior planes (1 m and 1.7 m) using a Window-WindCatcher (WWC) and Without Window-WindCatcher (WWWC).

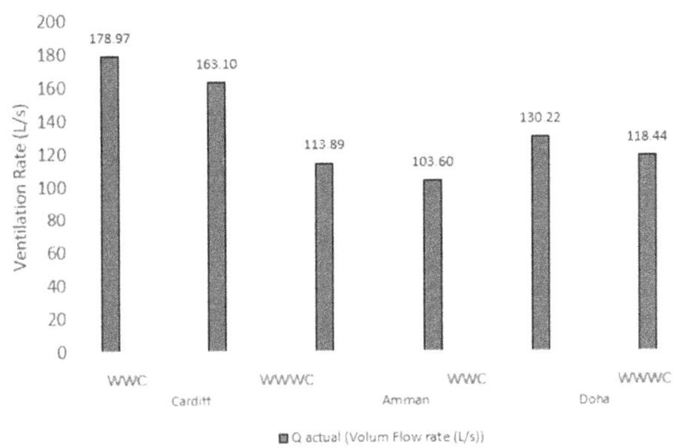

Figure 19. Actual ventilation rate using a Window-WindCatcher (WWC) and Without Window-WindCatcher (WWWC).

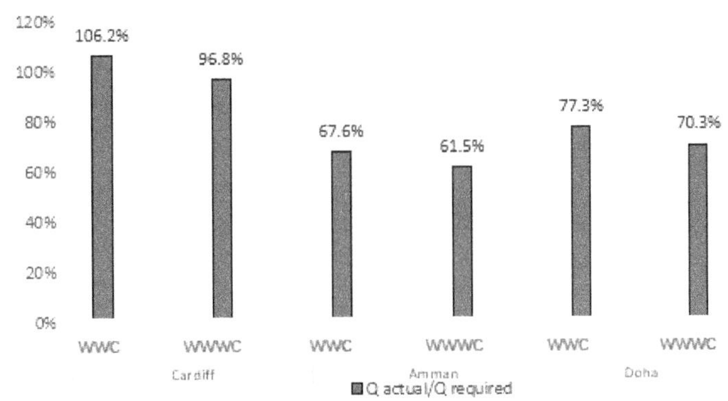

Figure 20. The actual-to-required ventilation ratio using Window-WindCatcher (WWC) and Without Window-WindCatcher (WWWC).

However, for Amman and Doha, although the actual-to-required ventilation ratio was increased using the window-windcatcher, the actual-to-required ventilation ratio is still less than 100%, that is, the actual ventilation rate is still lower than the required ventilation rate needed to fulfill the ASHRAE standards [30]. This suggests that deploying another window-windcatcher is necessary (possibly at Region O, as indicated in Figure 14). On the other hand, for Cardiff, the ASHRAE standards are fulfilled using only one window-windcatcher since the actual-to-required ventilation ratio is higher than 100% (i.e., n_Q = 106%).

To investigate how the performance of the window varies with boundary conditions, the actual ventilation rates of the three cities (which correspond to three different boundary conditions of wind velocities) are plotted against the total wind velocity in Figure 21. As the wind velocity increases, the window-windcatchers performance improves. In Figure 22, we plot the actual-to-required ventilation ratio of each city against the wind velocity (TWV), which also increases as the wind velocity increases.

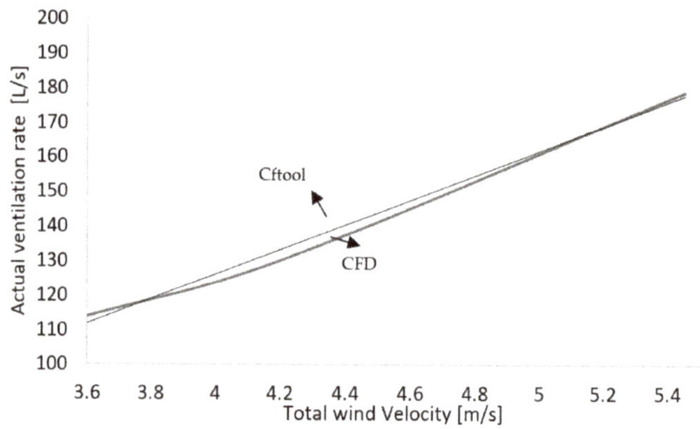

Figure 21. Actual ventilation rate with respect to the total wind velocity.

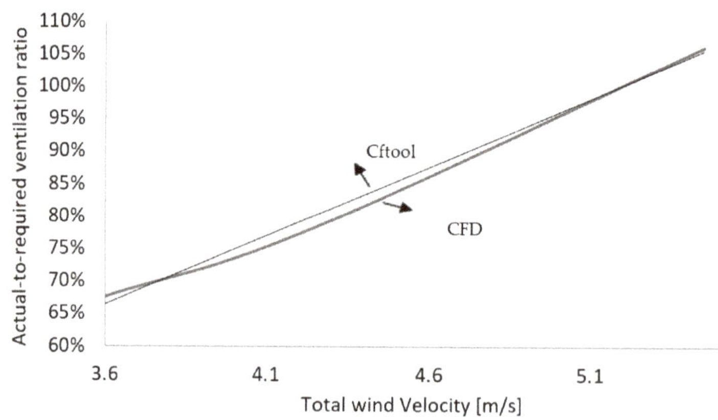

Figure 22. Actual-to-required ventilation with respect to the total wind velocity.

By utilizing the curve-fitting tool of Matlab "cftool", we determine the relationships (8) and (9) which describe, respectively, the actual ventilation rate and the actual-to-required ventilation ratio against the wind velocity:

$$Qact = 35.75\text{TWV} - 16.9 \quad (8)$$

$$n_Q = 0.212\text{TWV} - 0.009 \quad (9)$$

These relationships could then be applied to other geographical locations. In this study, we focus attention to specific regions and boundary conditions (in Amman, Doha and Cardiff); additional locations and hence boundary conditions could be investigated in future studies.

4. Discussion

The purpose of this study was to investigate, using CFD, the effectiveness of a novel window-windcatcher device that could be mounted on the exterior walls of new or existing buildings in order to capture and redirect prevailing wind into interior spaces. The proposed design could replace or supplement the typical large-scale windcatchers by utilising small-scale decentralised windcatchers on exterior walls as a window component. The suggested window-windcatcher is among the passive cooling approaches that have been shown in several studies to provide outstanding thermal comfort and indoor air quality while consuming only a fraction of the energy used by mechanical air conditioning systems [6]. Natural ventilation is one of the most popular passive cooling design strategies for improving indoor air quality and thermal comfort. The effectiveness of natural ventilation and passive cooling in buildings could be improved by using this new device, resulting in better indoor air quality and environmental comfort.

Furthermore, ensuring high indoor air quality is essential in mitigating the spread of COVID-19 and other viral diseases. Increasing air velocity is the most common way to increase ventilation rates; however, increasing ventilation rate increases turbulence kinetic energy. As a result, it is critical to keep the increase in turbulence kinetic energy as low as possible. In addition, high turbulence kinetic energy regions have been carefully identified to facilitate potential mitigation measures, such as the use of air purifiers in high turbulence/mixing areas (Figures 9 and 10).

By plotting the streamlines in Figures 15 and 16, the effect of the window-windcatcher on the airflow streamlines has also been evaluated. Streamlines trace fluid paths and, as a result, contribute to the understanding of the indoor air distribution. They also visualise the regions with the lowest velocities, and, therefore, with a lower risk of spreading airborne viruses like SARS-CoV-2 [16,17]. At those locations, the velocity magnitude gradually decreases to approximately 0 m/s; Figures 13 and 14 show the near-zero-velocity regions. By relating these regions to the possibility of deploying air purifiers, it is suggested that these locations should be avoided, as they correspond to 'safe' regions. Air purifiers, on the other hand, should be placed in areas with high velocity to maximise the airflow rate into the purifiers. In Figures 13 and 14, those locations have been labelled as air-purifier regions (APR).

Furthermore, we looked at the interaction of the interior and exterior planes' streamlines. Understanding the fluid interaction with the interior plane requires plotting the streamlines for the exterior planes. We also identified potential locations to place the window-windcatcher in order to increase the ventilation rate. The window-windcatcher redirects the shear wind towards the building's interior plane, as shown in region M of Figure 14. However, some high-velocity wind streamlines (Region N) are not directed towards the building's interior plane. This implies that the window-windcatcher design could be further improved in future work in order to enhance its aerodynamic capabilities.

Another important point is that, unlike Region M, where the window-windcatcher was not deployed, most of the shear wind streamlines are not directed towards the interior plane of the building in Region O (Figure 14). This means that, by deploying another window-windcatcher in Region O, the ventilation rate could be increased. According to the quantitative analysis (Section 3.2), the window-windcatcher has slightly increased the average turbulence kinetic energy at both planes in the three cases studied. The increase in turbulence kinetic energy, on the other hand, occurred in areas that are less likely to be occupied by people. However, the ventilation rate was compared to the required ventilation rate Q_{required}) as specified by the ASHRAE standards [30]. Compared to the case without the window-windcatcher (n_Q from 96.7 percent to 106 percent), the window-windcatcher managed to increase the actual-to-required ventilation ratio by approximately 9%. The actual-to-required ventilation ratio was increased by approximately 6% (from 61.5 percent to 67.5 percent) and 7% (from 70 percent to 77.3 percent) in the Amman and Doha cases, respectively.

5. Conclusions

This research aimed to investigate, using ANSYS CFX, the effectiveness of a design of a novel window-windcatcher device to be mounted on the exterior walls to capture the prevailing wind and redirect it into interior spaces. The performance of the proposed window-windcatcher has been evaluated in comparison to a control case (without a window-windcatcher) in three different geographical locations (Cardiff, Doha and Amman). The proposed window-windcatcher has proven to enhance thermal comfort and indoor air quality by increasing the actual-to-required ventilation ratio as per the ASHRAE standards by approximately 9% compared to the case without the window-windcatcher (n_Q from 96.7% to 106%). For Amman and Doha, the actual-to-required ventilation ratio was increased by approximately 6% (61.5% to 67.5%) and 7% (70% to 77.3%), respectively.

In addition, the location with minimal velocities has been identified by plotting the streamlines. Those locations correspond to the regions with a lower likelihood of spreading viral diseases such as COVID-19. Regarding the potential of deploying air purifiers, air-purifier regions (APR) with high velocity, where the airflow rate entering the air purifiers is increased, have been identified.

For future work, a prototype is recommended to be manufactured and tested in a wind tunnel to further examine the aerodynamic performance of the window-windcatcher.

Author Contributions: Conceptualization, O.F.A., L.M.O., S.N.M., K.K., T.A.-R. and A.I.A.; methodology, O.F.A., L.M.O., S.N.M., K.K., T.A.-R. and A.I.A.; software, O.F.A., L.M.O., S.N.M., K.K., T.A.-R. and A.I.A.; validation, O.F.A., L.M.O., S.N.M., K.K., T.A.-R. and A.I.A.; formal analysis, O.F.A., L.M.O., S.N.M., K.K., T.A.-R. and A.I.A.; investigation, O.F.A., L.M.O., S.N.M., K.K., T.A.-R. and A.I.A.; resources, O.F.A., L.M.O., S.N.M., K.K., T.A.-R. and A.I.A.; data curation, O.F.A., L.M.O., S.N.M., K.K., T.A.-R. and A.I.A.; writing—original draft preparation, O.F.A., L.M.O., S.N.M., K.K., T.A.-R. and A.I.A.; writing—review and editing, O.F.A., L.M.O., S.N.M., K.K., T.A.-R. and A.I.A.; visualization, O.F.A., L.M.O., S.N.M., K.K., T.A.-R. and A.I.A.; supervision, O.F.A., L.M.O., S.N.M., K.K., T.A.-R. and A.I.A.; project administration, O.F.A., L.M.O., S.N.M., K.K., T.A.-R. and A.I.A.; funding acquisition, O.F.A., L.M.O., S.N.M., K.K., T.A.-R. and A.I.A. All authors have read and agreed to the published version of the manuscript.

Funding: This publication was made possible by NPRP 13 Grant No. NPRP13S-0203-200243 from the Qatar National Research Fund (a member of the Qatar Foundation). The findings herein reflect the work and are solely the responsibility of the authors. Open Access funding is provided by the Qatar National Library.

Informed Consent Statement: Not applicable.

Data Availability Statement: Not applicable.

Acknowledgments: The authors gratefully acknowledge the support Oxford University through Ian Griffiths.

Conflicts of Interest: The authors declare no conflict of interest.

References

1. Wang, T.; Foliente, G.; Song, X.; Xue, J.; Fang, D. Implications and future direction of greenhouse gas emission mitigation policies in the building sector of China. *Renew. Sustain. Energy Rev.* **2014**, *31*, 520–530. [CrossRef]
2. Jomehzadeh, F.; Nejat, P.; Calautit, J.K.; Yusof, M.B.M.; Zaki, S.A.; Hughes, B.R.; Yazid, M.N.A.W.M. A review on windcatcher for passive cooling and natural ventilation in buildings, Part 1: Indoor air quality and thermal comfort assessment. *Renew. Sustain. Energy Rev.* **2017**, *70*, 736–756. [CrossRef]
3. Saadatian, O.; Haw, L.C.; Sopian, K.; Sulaiman, M. Review of windcatcher technologies. *Renew. Sustain. Energy Rev.* **2012**, *16*, 1477–1495. [CrossRef]
4. Santamouris, M. Cooling the buildings–past, present and future. *Energy Build.* **2016**, *128*, 617–638. [CrossRef]

5. Chenari, B.; Dias Carrilho, J.; Gameiro da Silva, M. Towards sustainable, energy-efficient and healthy ventilation strategies in buildings: A review. *Renew. Sustain. Energy Rev.* **2016**, *59*, 1426–1447. [CrossRef]
6. Ma'Bdeh, S.N.; Al-Zghoul, A.; Alradaideh, T.; Bataineh, A.; Ahmad, S. Simulation study for natural ventilation retrofitting techniques in educational classrooms—A case study. *Heliyon* **2020**, *6*, e05171. [CrossRef]
7. Zhang, H.; Yang, D.; Tam, V.W.; Tao, Y.; Zhang, G.; Setunge, S.; Shi, L. A critical review of combined natural ventilation techniques in sustainable buildings. *Renew. Sustain. Energy Rev.* **2021**, *141*, 110795. [CrossRef]
8. Faggianelli, G.A.; Brun, A.; Wurtz, E.; Muselli, M. Natural cross ventilation in buildings on Mediterranean coastal zones. *Energy Build.* **2014**, *77*, 206–218. [CrossRef]
9. Ababsa, M. Atlas of Jordan: History, Territories and Society. Presses de l'Ifpo. 2014. Available online: https://books.google.jo/books?id=RIcNCwAAQBAJ (accessed on 20 April 2021).
10. Geros, V.; Santamouris, M.; Tsangrasoulis, A.; Guarracino, G. Experimental evaluation of night ventilation phenomena. *Energy Build.* **1999**, *29*, 141–154. [CrossRef]
11. Al-Hemiddi, N.A.; Al-Saud, K.A.M. The effect of a ventilated interior courtyard on the thermal performance of a house in a hot–arid region. *Renew. Energy* **2001**, *24*, 581–595. [CrossRef]
12. Ahmed, T.; Kumar, P.; Mottet, L. Natural ventilation in warm climates: The challenges of thermal comfort, heatwave resilience and indoor air quality. *Renew. Sustain. Energy Rev.* **2021**, *138*, 110669. [CrossRef]
13. Reyes, V.; Moya, S.; Morales, J.; Sierra-Espinosa, F. A study of air flow and heat transfer in building-wind tower passive cooling systems applied to arid and semi-arid regions of Mexico. *Energy Build.* **2013**, *66*, 211–221. [CrossRef]
14. Esfeh, M.K.; Sohankar, A.; Shahsavari, A.; Rastan, M.; Ghodrat, M.; Nili, M. Experimental and numerical evaluation of wind-driven natural ventilation of a curved roof for various wind angles. *Build. Environ.* **2021**, *205*, 108275. [CrossRef]
15. Omrani, S.; Garcia-Hansen, V.; Capra, B.; Drogemuller, R. Natural ventilation in multi-storey buildings: Design process and review of evaluation tools. *Build. Environ.* **2017**, *116*, 182–194. [CrossRef]
16. Mabdeh, S.; Al Radaideh, T.; Hiyari, M. Enhancing Thermal Comfort of Residential Buildings through Dual Functional Passive System (Solar-Wall). *J. Green Build.* **2020**, *16*, 139–161. [CrossRef]
17. Weatherspark. Available online: https://weatherspark.com/ (accessed on 30 December 2021).
18. Toivanen, P.K.; Janhunen, P. Spin Plane Control and Thrust Vectoring of Electric Solar Wind Sail. *J. Propuls. Power* **2013**, *29*, 178–185. [CrossRef]
19. Alrebi, O.F.; Obeidat, B.; Abdallah, I.A.; Darwish, E.F.; Amhamed, A. Airflow dynamics in an emergency department: A CFD simulation study to analyse COVID-19 dispersion. *Alex. Eng. J.* **2021**, *61*, 3435–3445. [CrossRef]
20. Available online: https://www.epa.gov/coronavirus/air-cleaners-hvac-filters-and-coronavirus-covid-19 (accessed on 2 March 2022).
21. Obeidat, B.; Alrebei, O.F.; Abdallah, I.A.; Darwish, E.F.; Amhamed, A. CFD Analyses: The Effect of Pressure Suction and Airflow Velocity on Coronavirus Dispersal. *Appl. Sci.* **2021**, *11*, 7450. [CrossRef]
22. Ramponi, R.; Blocken, B. CFD simulation of cross-ventilation for a generic isolated building: Impact of computational parameters. *Build. Environ.* **2012**, *53*, 34–48. [CrossRef]
23. Yuan, F.-D.; You, S.-J. CFD simulation and optimisation of the ventilation for subway side-platform. *Tunn. Un-Derground Space Technol.* **2007**, *22*, 474–482. [CrossRef]
24. Average Height by Country 2021. Available online: https://worldpopulationreview.com/country-rankings/average-height-by-country2021 (accessed on 1 January 2022).
25. de Roode, S.R.; Jonker, H.J.; van de Wiel, B.J.; Vertregt, V.; Perrin, V. A diagnosis of excessive mixing in smagorinsky subfilter-scale turbulent kinetic energy models. *J. Atmos. Sci.* **2017**, *74*, 1495–1511. [CrossRef]
26. Paul Ninomura, P.; Richard Hermans, P. Ventilation standard for health care facilities. *ASHRAE J.* **2008**, *50*, 52–57.
27. ASHRAE Standards. Available online: https://www.ashrae.org/ (accessed on 30 December 2021).
28. Dimotakis, P.E. Turbulent mixing. *Annu. Rev. Fluid Mech.* **2005**, *37*, 329–356. [CrossRef]
29. Lee, S.C.; Harsha, P.T. Use of turbulent kinetic energy in free mixing studies. *AIAA J.* **1970**, *8*, 1026–1032. [CrossRef]
30. Learn | OpenEnergyMonitor. 2022. Available online: https://learn.openenergymonitor.org/sustainable-energy/building-energy-model/ventilation (accessed on 6 May 2022).

International Journal of
Environmental Research and Public Health

MDPI

Article

Experimental Methods of Investigating Airborne Indoor Virus-Transmissions Adapted to Several Ventilation Measures

Lukas Siebler *, Maurizio Calandri, Torben Rathje and Konstantinos Stergiaropoulos

Institute for Building Energetics, Thermotechnology and Energy Storage (IGTE), University of Stuttgart, Pfaffenwaldring 35, 70569 Stuttgart, Germany
* Correspondence: lukas.siebler@igte.uni-stuttgart.de; Tel.: +49-711-685-60785

Abstract: This study introduces a principle that unifies two experimental methods for evaluating airborne indoor virus-transmissions adapted to several ventilation measures. A first-time comparison of mechanical/natural ventilation and air purification with regard to infection risks is enabled. Effortful computational fluid dynamics demand detailed boundary conditions for accurate calculations of indoor airflows, which are often unknown. Hence, a suitable, simple and generalized experimental set up for identifying the spatial and temporal infection risk for different ventilation measures is more qualified even with unknown boundary conditions. A trace gas method is suitable for mechanical and natural ventilation with outdoor air exchange. For an accurate assessment of air purifiers based on filtration, a surrogate particle method is appropriate. The release of a controlled rate of either trace gas or particles simulates an infectious person releasing virus material. Surrounding substance concentration measurements identify the neighborhood exposure. One key aspect of the study is to prove that the requirement of concordant results of both methods is fulfilled. This is the only way to ensure that the comparison of different ventilation measures described above is reliable. Two examples (a two-person office and a classroom) show how practical both methods are and how the principle is applicable for different types and sizes of rooms.

Keywords: aerosol infection risk; SARS-CoV-2 transmission; measurement methods; surrogate particles; trace gas; ventilation measures

Citation: Siebler, L.; Calandri, M.; Rathje, T.; Stergiaropoulos, K. Experimental Methods of Investigating Airborne Indoor Virus-Transmissions Adapted to Several Ventilation Measures. *Int. J. Environ. Res. Public Health* **2022**, *19*, 11300. https://doi.org/10.3390/ijerph191811300

Academic Editors: Ashok Kumar, Michał Piasecki, M Amirul I Khan and Alejandro Moreno Rangel

Received: 15 August 2022
Accepted: 3 September 2022
Published: 8 September 2022

1. Introduction

The ongoing pandemic teaches us that the implementation of appropriate ventilation measures can significantly reduce indoor infection risks [1–4].

For fast and simple assessments, many calculation models regarding the infection risk of SARS-CoV-2 in indoor environments exist [5–10]. Often, these are based on idealised assumptions (e.g., ideal mixed ventilation). In reality, the condition of ideal mixed ventilation is impossible to achieve (finite velocity for distributing locally released substances), especially for larger rooms. Even for small to medium scales, the calculation models may not resolve aerosol dispersion appropriately.

In practice, different ventilation principles—natural ventilation and mechanical ventilation (mixing ventilation, displacement ventilation, downward ventilation)—are applied, depending on the type of use and the occupancy density of the room [11,12]. Depending on the meteorological boundary conditions such as wind velocity, natural ventilation can be classified between mixed ventilation and displacement ventilation [13]. These transient effects cannot be represented by a simple calculation model [14]. Furthermore, existing disturbance influences (leaks and opening of windows/doors, downdrafts, etc.) have to be considered for the respective ventilation type.

Displacement ventilation concepts, often applied in large halls, impede estimations of virus transmission to neighbors. In ideal theory, there would occur only unobjectionable vertical buoyancy flows. In reality, however, these are superimposed by disturbance effects [15–17], which might be critical regarding neighbor infection risks. If the relevant boundary conditions for these disturbing influences are unknown, the estimation is regarded to be even more critical.

For individual considerations and higher accuracies, experimental studies examine the effects of ventilation measures on airborne infections. Some of them deal with a real virus load of the indoor air with actually present infectious persons, without controlled boundary conditions [18]. In Li et al. [19], trace gas measurements and flow simulations for an actual infection scenario are conducted in order to reproduce transmission paths in detail. Transient and absolute considerations of virus loads are omitted in this context. Another research study examines the effects of ventilation measures, but does not take into account the transfer of substitutes to viruses and thus the actual infection risk [20]. As a result, only relative statements on the risk reduction are possible.

In general, ventilation measures can be divided into filtering recirculation methods (e.g., air purification) and ventilation principles with outside air exchange (e.g., natural/mechanical ventilation). However, there are no published studies on the comparative assessment of both measures with regard to the infection risk.

Previous experimental research is not yet suitable for a holistic individual assessment of the infection risk. Therefore, a comprehensive and standardized measurement procedure for any airborne transmitted disease is required. In this paper, two consistent measurement methods are presented, which allow for determining spatially and temporally resolved infection risks in rooms accurately. For the first time, the two consistent approaches can be used to evaluate both filtering recirculating air operations and ventilation principles with outdoor air exchange.

2. Theory of Airborne Virus Infections

In 1955, the first approach of assessing general infection risks was developed, which was improved and specified in 1978 on the disease measles [21,22]. The authors introduced the dose of inhaled quanta D_q as an indicator of whether an infection occurs. Taking into account the efficiency of masks, it can be calculated as:

$$D_\mathrm{q}(t) = \dot{V}_\mathrm{inh}\,(1-\eta_\mathrm{inh}) \int_0^t c_\mathrm{q}(t)\,\mathrm{d}t + D_{\mathrm{q}\,0} \tag{1}$$

with $\dot{V}_\mathrm{inh}$, η_inh, $c_\mathrm{q}(t)$, and $D_{\mathrm{q}\,0}$ as inhalation volume flow, mask filtration efficiency for inhaling, quanta concentration at time t and the initial value of D_q, respectively.

The approach of Wells et al. and Riley et al. allows the computation of the predicted infection risk via aerosols (PIRA), labeled as P_I [22]:

$$P_\mathrm{I} = 1 - \mathrm{e}^{-D_\mathrm{q}}. \tag{2}$$

As an alternative, the dose–response model follows a modified principle that is similarly referenced in science and should be roughly presented. Hereby, the number of pathogens that result in infections of a certain proportion of a group is usually determined on the basis of empirical animal experiments. Based on an analysis of how many pathogens a person exhales, the infection risk can be derived. The dose–response as well as a Wells–Riley model are accepted as valuable tools in epidemiological studies. When using these models, the respective advantages, disadvantages and uncertainties must be weighed [23].

In this paper, the Wells–Riley model is followed. However, the relevant equations can be easily modified to a dose–response model, due to substituting quanta emission rates (QER) with pathogen emission rates and an adaption of the risk assessment.

In general, infection risks can be reduced by either ventilation measures (mechanical and natural ventilation) or air purification concepts (without outside air exchange) can be used. For a non-spatially resolved estimate of the quanta concentration, the general differential Equation (3), which includes various ventilation concepts, has to be evaluated:

$$\frac{\mathrm{d}c_\mathrm{q}(t)}{\mathrm{d}t} = \underbrace{\frac{\dot{q}_\mathrm{out}\,(1-\eta_\mathrm{exh})}{V_\mathrm{r}}}_{\substack{\text{quanta release}\\ \text{of an infectious}\\ \text{person}}} - \underbrace{\frac{\dot{V}_\mathrm{dev/w}\,c_\mathrm{q}(t)\,\eta_\mathrm{dev}}{V_\mathrm{r}}}_{\substack{\text{quanta removal}\\ \text{of ventilation}}} - \underbrace{\dot{\Phi}\,c_\mathrm{q}(t)}_{\substack{\text{natural in-}\\ \text{activation/}\\ \text{deposition}}}\;,\; c_\mathrm{q}(0) = c_{\mathrm{q}\,0} \tag{3}$$

with $\dot{q}_\mathrm{out}$, η_exh, V_r, $\dot{V}_\mathrm{dev/w}$, η_dev, $\dot{\Phi}$ as quanta rate (output), mask filtration efficiency for exhaling, room volume, volume flow of device or window and device efficiency (filtration ratio for air purifiers, exhaust air to outdoor air exchange for ventilation systems, equals 0 for natural ventilation) and combined rate of natural inactivation and deposition of existing viruses, respectively. The last equation term can be described and modelled well in theory, but, in practice, it is challenging to include it in experimental settings. Integrating Equation (3) over time followed by using (1) and (2), the dose of inhaled quanta and finally PIRA can be calculated.

With these assumptions, it is possible to estimate infection risks using ventilation devices, air purifiers and natural ventilation under ideal mixed ventilation conditions. However, experimental methods of substance dispersion concerning the airborne transmission of virus infections enable accurate spatially and temporally resolved results for any ventilation principle even for unknown boundary conditions.

3. Experimental Methods

Airborne virus transmission is mostly dealing with particles below 10 µm of size [24,25]. These particles are meant to have negligible sink velocities and follow airflows almost exactly [26]. A common method investigating airflows quantitatively is releasing substances (which also follow the airflow) and measuring their concentrations. In order to evaluate the totality of the ventilation measures, suitable substances are trace gas and surrogate particles. For scenarios with outside air exchange, only trace gas is appropriate because of entering particles from the outside, which would falsify particle measurements. For recirculation devices based on filtration, however, trace gas is inapplicable since it is not filtered and therefore no particle removal can be measured. For this reason, two different methods are essential.

3.1. Trace Gas Method

The focus of previous indoor air investigations using trace gas, also conducted at the University of Stuttgart, has mostly been on evaluating the ventilation effectiveness rather than infection risks [27]. The method is based on the emission of trace gas, which is not present in the natural surrounding and whose concentration can be measured by infrared spectrometers (e.g., N_2O or SF_6). First, the room needs to be freed from trace gas from eventual previous measurements. By using a mass flow controller with gas-specific adapted properties, a constant and continuous mass flow of the trace gas is possible.

Along with the measured trace gas concentration, the quanta rate (output) and the respiratory rate following theoretical post processing lead to a calculation of the infection risk of a certain disease.

For trace gas, which is transported in a similar way to airborne particles and viruses (below 5 µm) [28], the following assumption without mask filtration efficiency is applied:

$$\frac{\dot{n}_\mathrm{in\,tg}(t)}{\dot{n}_\mathrm{out\,tg}} = \frac{\dot{q}_\mathrm{in}(t)}{\dot{q}_\mathrm{out}} \tag{4}$$

with $\dot{n}_\mathrm{in\,tg}$, $\dot{n}_\mathrm{out\,tg}$, $\dot{q}_\mathrm{in}$, $\dot{q}_\mathrm{out}$ as (fictitious) molar flow for trace gas (input), molar flow for trace gas (output), quanta rate (input) and quanta rate (output) respectively. Note that input and output represent a fictitious inhalation and exhalation.

From the (time dependent) quanta rate (input) $\dot{q}_{in}$, the dose of inhaled quanta D_q is determined by integration over time (assumption: $D_{q\,0} = 0$, $c_{q\,0} = 0$):

$$D_q = \int_0^t \dot{q}_{in}(t)\,dt = \frac{\dot{q}_{out}}{\dot{n}_{out\,tg}} \int_0^t \dot{n}_{in\,tg}(t)\,dt. \tag{5}$$

The molar flow for (fictitious) trace gas input is calculated by using $\dot{n} = \dot{m}/M$ and the assumption $c_{tg}(t) \ll 1\,mol_{tg}/mol_{air}$:

$$\dot{n}_{in\,tg}(t) = c_{tg}(t)\,\dot{n}_{inh} = c_{tg}(t)\,\frac{\rho_{air}\,\dot{V}_{inh}}{M_{air}} \tag{6}$$

with c_{tg}, $\dot{n}_{inh}$, ρ_{air}, and M_{air} as measured trace gas concentration, inhalation molar flow, density and molar mass of air, respectively.

The resulting equation for the dose of inhaled quanta D_q, considering mask filtration efficiency (see [29,30]), is:

$$\begin{aligned} D_q &= \int_0^t \dot{q}_{in}(t)\,dt \\ &= (1-\eta_{inh})\,(1-\eta_{exh})\,\frac{\dot{q}_{out}\,M_{tg}}{\dot{m}_{out\,tg}}\,\frac{\rho_{air}\,\dot{V}_{inh}}{M_{air}} \int_0^t c_{tg}(t)\,dt \end{aligned} \tag{7}$$

with M_{tg}, $\dot{m}_{out\,tg}$ as molar mass and mass flow of trace gas (output), respectively.

A numerical integration of the concentration of trace gas over time $c_{tg}(t)$ (e.g., via trapezoidal rule) allows the transfer of measurement data via Equation (2) into an infection risk for scenarios with outdoor air exchange. Furthermore, data for the quanta rate (output) are required, which can be obtained from literature or identified by a backward processing of this introduced approach, (see Section 6).

3.2. Surrogate Particles Method

To evaluate the function of an air purifier based on filtration, an alternative method is required because trace gas can not be filtered. Even though the approaches have analogous equations, they still involve different physical units and more elaborate conditioning, since the room needs to be initially particle-free. From then on, only particles that are actually released by particle generators are measured. In reality, it cannot be avoided that a certain number of particles is still present. Superimposing this concentration with high emissions is a reasonable measure. If the particle emission rate is set very high, particles coming from outside (e.g., via infiltrations) have no influence on the measurement results because their particle rate is several powers of ten lower. In this way, a simple and cost-efficient measuring technique is enabled, which can be widely applied.

A suitable substance for particles is Di-Ethylhexyl-Sebacat (DEHS). Besides the advantage that its particles keep the same size over time because of very low evaporation rates, the measured size distribution is similar to the exhaled particles of humans [25,31].

Any other possible particle sources (even persons) should be removed from the room of investigation or kept emitting as low as possible. Using several optical particle counters (OPC) or scanning mobility particle sizers (SMPS) on different positions allow a spatial and temporal measurement of the number concentration and size distribution of particles.

The measured surrogate particle concentration, the quanta rate (input) and the respiratory rate lead to the calculation of the infection risk for a room equipped with an air purifier. Furthermore, data for the quanta rate (output) are required, which can be obtained from literature.

Analogous to the trace gas method for surrogate particles, the following assumption without mask filtration efficiency is applied:

$$\frac{\dot{m}_{\text{in sp}}(t)}{\dot{m}_{\text{out sp}}} = \frac{\dot{q}_{\text{in}}(t)}{\dot{q}_{\text{out}}} \tag{8}$$

with $\dot{m}_{\text{in sp}}$, $\dot{m}_{\text{out sp}}$ as mass flow for surrogate particles input and output, respectively (fictitious inhalation and exhalation of particles).

Similar to the trace gas method, the dose of inhaled quanta D_{q} is (assumption: $D_{\text{q}0} = 0$, $c_{\text{q}0} = 0$):

$$D_{\text{q}} = \int_0^t \dot{q}_{\text{in}}(t)\,\text{d}t = \frac{\dot{q}_{\text{out}}}{\dot{m}_{\text{out sp}}} \int_0^t \dot{m}_{\text{in sp}}(t)\,\text{d}t. \tag{9}$$

Substituting the assumed constant mass flow (output) of surrogate particles ($\dot{m}_{\text{out sp}} = c_{\text{out sp}}\,\dot{V}_{\text{ag}}$) and a fictitious mass inhalation rate of surrogate particles ($\dot{m}_{\text{in sp}}(t) = c_{\text{in sp}}(t)\,\dot{V}_{\text{inh}}$) in (9) (considering mask filtration efficiency see [29,30]) results in:

$$D_{\text{q}} = \int_0^t \dot{q}_{\text{in}}(t)\,\text{d}t = (1-\eta_{\text{inh}})\,(1-\eta_{\text{exh}})\,\frac{\dot{q}_{\text{out}}}{c_{\text{out sp}}\,\dot{V}_{\text{ag}}}\,\dot{V}_{\text{inh}} \int_0^t c_{\text{in sp}}(t)\,\text{d}t \tag{10}$$

with $\dot{V}_{\text{ag}}$, $c_{\text{out sp}}$, $c_{\text{in sp}}(t)$ as volume flow of aerosol generator and mass concentration of surrogate particles (output and input), respectively.

With regard to suspected agglomeration effects, it seems appropriate to extend the detected bandwidth of the emission size distribution upwards compared to the emission bandwidth and to operate via mass-related units. If particles agglomerate, this has an influence on the particle number concentration but not on the particle mass concentration and the infectivity. Therefore, the mass concentration should be applied (in this case, up to an optical diameter of 10 µm, see also Section 6). This can be determined by cumulating mass concentrations of each size fraction by calculating their volumes and their weight with the density of the specific particle substance.

4. Comparison between the Two Methods

One key aspect of the study is to prove that both methods are concordant. Hence, a comparison between the two measuring methods for substance dispersion is essential. Bivolarova et al. [32] compare trace gases with different particle sizes on the basis of steady-state observations and decay curves of substance concentrations. A temporal resolution of these concentrations from the initial to the steady state—i.e., the dispersion of the substances—as well as a transfer to an infectious event is not focused here.

However, depending on the infectiousness of a disease and the exposure time, the transient dispersion is relevant to an infection process. In addition, the relation of substance release rates (emission) to emerging concentration profiles (emission) is not yet examined and thus a transfer to a fictitious unit such as quanta is not possible.

For these reasons, an experimental comparison is conducted by the authors with respect to transient quanta concentration courses in an airflow visualization laboratory with controlled boundary conditions.

In this laboratory, both a controlled supply and exhaust air volume flow is adjusted. At a specific position (see Figure 1), controlled flows of both a DEHS particle-laden aerosol (with known emission particle concentration) and a SF_6 trace gas are released simultaneously. Data of the aerosol generator for the particle release and the mass flow controller for trace gas are given in Table 1. OPCs and sampling tubes for the FTIR gas analyser are placed at six positions in the laboratory. This allows the concentrations of both the particles and the trace gas to be measured simultaneously. Since the authors have six OPCs but only one FTIR at their disposal, the suction of the six trace gas sampling points is changed automatically every minute. In order to take into account the time required for the gas to pass through these tubes to the FTIR, the measured values of each first 30 s are discarded. Switching the sampling points between six positions results in a 6-fold lower sampling rate compared to the OPCs (see Figure 2). In order to ensure that almost no outdoor particles enter the room, a HEPA 14 filter (corresponds with Minimum Efficiency Reporting Values (MERV) 19) was integrated into the duct of supply air. Otherwise, in addition to the released particles, those from the outside would also be measured and therefore corrupts the experimental data. A simultaneous release and measuring of particles and trace gas at the same position are expected to result in the same dispersion of both substances. In this case, the calculated course of the curves of quanta concentrations for both substances is supposed to be similar in all measuring positions.

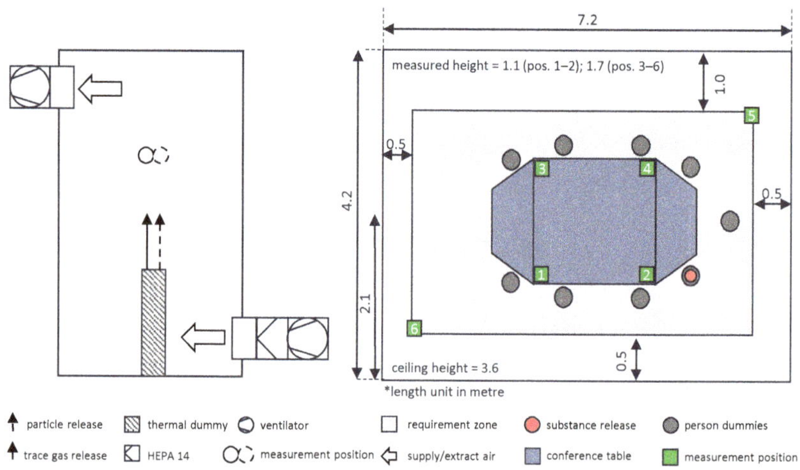

Figure 1. Set up to compare the two methods (**left**) and top view of the conference room (**right**).

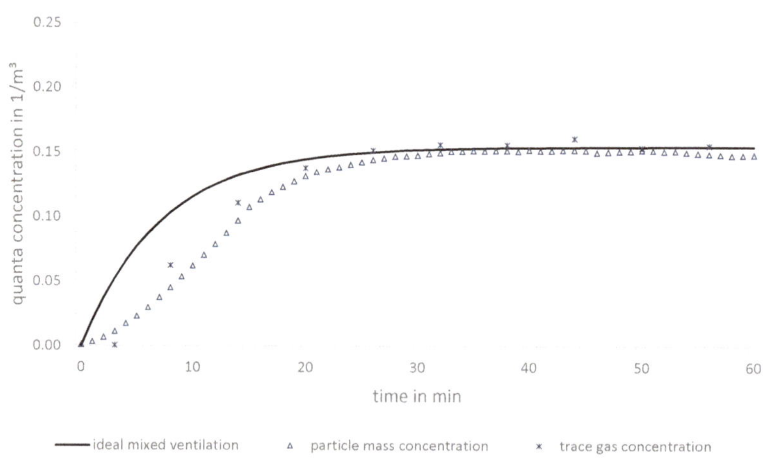

Figure 2. Comparison between particle and trace gas measurement as a function of quanta concentration over time exemplified in a conference room (position 3).

Table 1. Relevant parameters of the measurement devices.

Surrogate Particles		Trace Gas	
Quantity	**Value**	**Quantity**	**Value**
medium	DEHS	medium	SF_6
aerosol generator	Palas PAG 1000	MFC	Bronkhorst F-201CV
aerosol volume flow	168 L/h	trace gas volume flow	0.5 L/h
OPC	Palas AQ Guard	FTIR	Gasmet DX4015

In Table 1, the parameters of the measurement devices are shown.

The aerosol is generated with a particle number concentration of $1.5 \times 10^7\,\text{cm}^{-3}$, which are approximately logarithmic normal distributed (median optical diameter $\approx 0.3\,\mu\text{m}$). The OPCs are able to measure particle size distributions of 0.175...20 µm over 64 channels. Furthermore, data for the quanta rate (output) are required, which can be obtained from literature, see Peng et al. [33].

The experimental set up for the comparative measurement is presented in Figure 1. For the delta variant of SARS-CoV-2, a medium spreader is assumed by Peng et al. [33]. The corresponding boundary conditions are shown in Table 2.

Table 2. Relevant parameters of the comparative measurement.

Quantity	Value	Quantity	Value
room volume	$109\,\text{m}^3$	ventilation volume flow	$900\,\text{m}^3\,\text{h}^{-1}$
quanta rate (output)	$46.5\,\text{h}^{-1}$	exposition time	1 h
medium	SF_6/DEHS	number of persons	9

Deviating from usual recommendations of a certain air exchange rate, reference is given to the personal volume flow, see Kriegel et al. [2]. Depending on the viral load, exposition time, non-pharmaceutical measures, etc., this value may differ. However, this paper will focus on the comparison and concordance of the two measurement methods.

Over the entire measurement period, both quanta concentration courses are similar at all measurement positions. Therefore, it is expected that both methods are suitable and can be applied for different ventilation cases. In Figure 2, the exemplary result at a single measuring position (best fit) in the conference room is shown. In addition, it is worth emphasizing the small discrepancy between the two experimental curves compared to the theoretical one after a quasi-steady state has been reached. This is due to high air exchange rates and the possibility of accurate volume flow measurements (correlation to steady state concentration) in the laboratory. However, during the transient course, a discrepancy is generally observed, since substances in reality need time to disperse to a certain position.

Different measurement techniques can generally lead to different sampling rates. In this measurement, only one infrared spectrometer is used for the trace gas concentrations. By means of a measuring position switch, six positions are taken into account successively over one minute each. On the other hand, six OPCs simultaneously record the particle concentrations of a single measuring position every minute. Therefore, the sampling rate for trace gas is six times lower compared to particles.

5. Experimental Studies

In the following section, it is shown that both methods are practical. The measured scenarios go from small to medium scale and contain the two of three main ventilation types: a two-person office (air purifier) and a typical classroom (natural ventilation vs. air purifier). These investigated example scenarios are shown in detail.

Besides supply and extract air effects, indoor airflows are influenced by sub- and over-tempered surfaces (e.g., thermal sources). For an appropriate simulation of human heat outputs for a certain activity rate (low activity: 75 W) [34], thermal dummies with a surface area of an average human (1.8 m^2) [35] are recommended. Figure 3 shows a professional thermal person dummy and also a low cost variant (cartons with lightning bulbs inside) for substituting many persons in large rooms (e.g., Stuttgart Drama Theatre).

Figure 3. Professional thermal person dummy (**left**), low cost variants in Stuttgart Drama Theatre (**right**).

5.1. Spatially Resolved Measurements in a Laboratory

Under reproducible boundary conditions in an air visualisation laboratory, an air purifier has been investigated by the authors. The focus lies on the particle removal effectiveness of the device in a two-person office.

Thereby, one of both people is assumed to be infectious. Figure 4 shows a photo and the top view of the experimental set up; the relevant parameters of the experiments concerning the effectiveness of air purifiers are described in Table 3; for the corresponding parameters of the measurement devices, see Table 1.

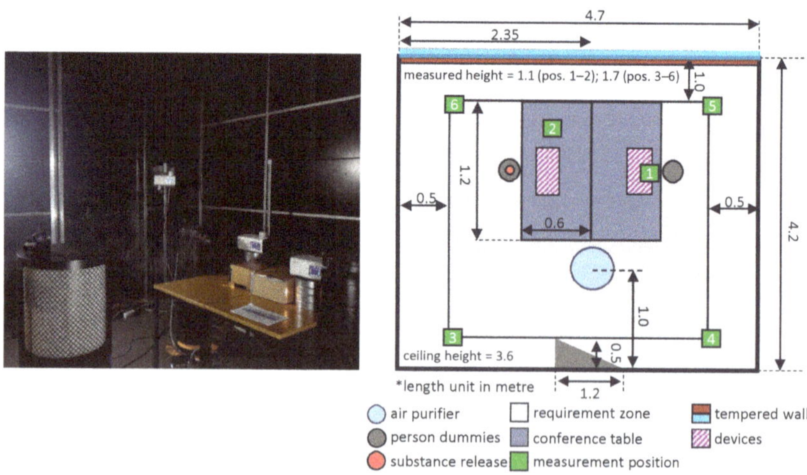

Figure 4. Photo (**left**) and the top view (**right**) of the experimental set up of a two-person office with air purifiers in an air visualisation laboratory. * length unit in metre.

Table 3. Relevant parameters of the experiments concerning the effectiveness of air purifiers.

Quantity	Value	Quantity	Value
room volume	$71\,m^3$	volume flow	$900\,m^3\,h^{-1}$
quanta rate (output)	$46.5\,h^{-1}$	exposition time	1 h
medium	DEHS	filtration class	HEPA 14
number of persons	2		

The particle measurement is analogous to the procedure described in Section 4. However, the filtered outdoor air is now replaced by recirculated air of a filtering air purifier. First, the room is freed from particles by the air purifier. Thereafter, the aerosol is subsequently emitted from the marked dummy (see Figure 4) with the properties of Table 1 over 60 min. The particle concentrations are determined by the OPCs at six different positions in the room in order to obtain spatial information about the substance removal.

The temporally-resolved data allow a computation of the infection risk (PIRA) at these positions using Equation (10). An exemplary measurement result is shown in Figure 5.

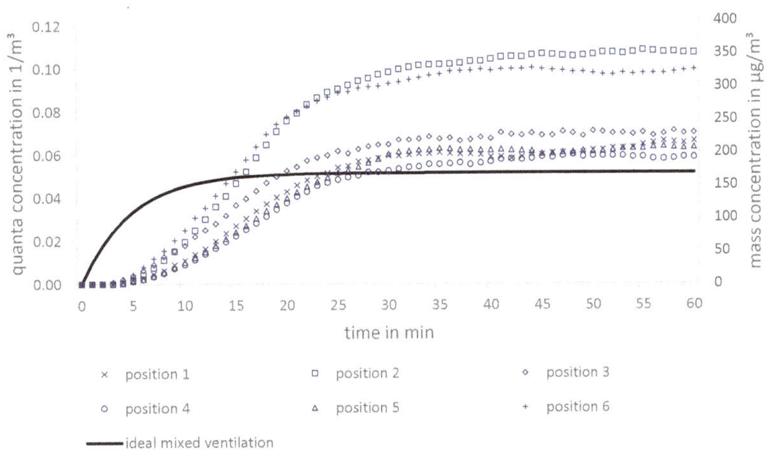

Figure 5. Theoretical (ideal mixed air) and measured quanta concentration (left axis) and their related mass concentration (right axis) of six positions in a two-person office.

Depending on the ventilation principles (mixing ventilation, displacement ventilation, downward ventilation), the spatial deviations from the assumption of ideal mixed ventilation (in relation to the entire room) may vary. The deviations of the individual positions among each other show a significant benefit of a spatial view. Moreover, quanta concentrations in Figure 5 do not only mismatch the ideal mixed ventilation in the transient range but also in the steady state. In this case for a duration of 1 h, the overall infection risk (PIRA) for a medium spreader (delta variant) by Peng et al. [33] using Equation (2) results in a range from 2.2% (position 4) to 4.0% (position 2).

5.2. Comparison of Ventilation Measures in Classrooms

Further investigations of ventilation measures in classrooms were conducted by the authors, in order to assess the effectiveness of periodic window ventilation, decentralised ventilation systems and air purifiers regarding infection risk and thermal comfort. For this study, it is required that both methods (trace gas and surrogate particles) perform similarly. The set up and the three ventilation measures are shown in Figure 6 exemplarily.

Figure 6. Experimental set up (**top**), exemplary window ventilation (**bottom left**), exemplary decentralised ventilation system (**bottom middle**), exemplary air purifier (**bottom right**).

Table 4 describes the relevant parameters of both experiments in an exemplary classroom, and Table 1 shows the corresponding parameters of the measurement devices. The weather data given are mean values of a meteorological station within the measurement period. The weather data are particularly important for window ventilation. They are irrelevant for the operation of the air purifier, since this experiment was carried out separately.

Table 4. Boundary conditions of the experiments in the classroom.

Quantity	Value	Quantity	Value
general parameters			
room volume	$210\,m^3$	number of persons	25
quanta rate (output)	$46.5\,h^{-1}$	exposition time	1.5 h
medium	SF_6/DEHS		
weather conditions [1]			
air temperature (outside)	14 °C	air temperature (inside)	22 °C
wind velocity	$1.5\,m\,s^{-1}$	wind direction	north north east
air purifier			
volume flow	$630\,m^3\,h^{-1}$	filter class	ePM1 85%/H13
west-facing windows (5×)		**south-facing windows (3×)**	
window type [2]	th (3×) | sh (2×)	window type [1]	th (3×)
window area [3](total)	$4.5\,m^2$ | $3.2\,m^2$	window area [3](total)	$4.5\,m^2$
tilt angle	17° | 90°	tilt angle	17°

[1] mean values. [2] th: top-hung, sh: side-hung. [3] clear opening.

Due to changing boundary conditions during this study (compared to reproducible conditions in the laboratory), only one exemplary classroom is considered for an air purifier and a periodic window ventilation (in this case, 20/5/20: 20 min closed, 5 min opened). For an assumed medium-spreader (SARS-CoV-2, delta variant) [33] and an exposition time of 1.5 h in both scenarios, there is the same position of the infectious person (substance release).

The investigation of air purification and natural ventilation is carried out successively. The experimental method for the air purifier is carried out in the same way as described in Section 5.1 using DEHS-particles. The reliable measurement of natural ventilation is conducted with trace gas. In this case, SF_6 is released in a controlled manner analogous to Section 4, and its concentration is measured at six different positions. The periodic window opening is carried out manually according to a stopwatch. The room geometry and dimensions as well as the detailed set-up of the experiment including the positions of the substance release, the measurement and the air purifier are shown in Figure 7.

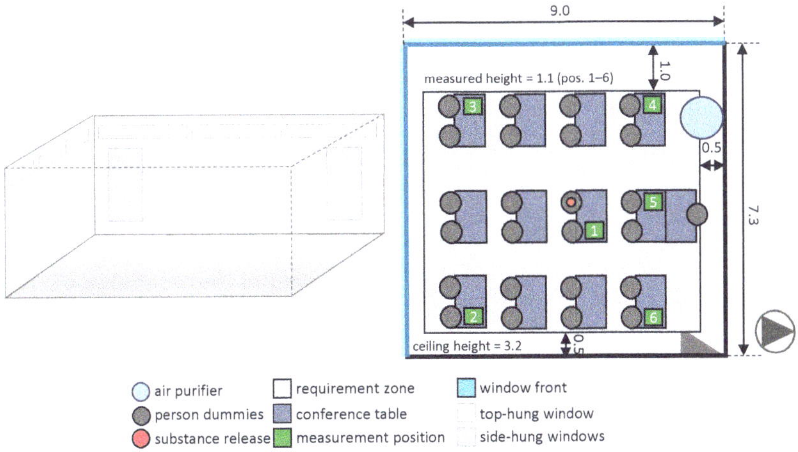

Figure 7. Draft (**left**) and the top view (**right**) of the experimental set up of a classroom with an air purifier.

At two different measurement positions (1 and 4), the quanta concentrations are illustrated in Figure 8. The varying curves show how valuable both spatial resolved methods are.

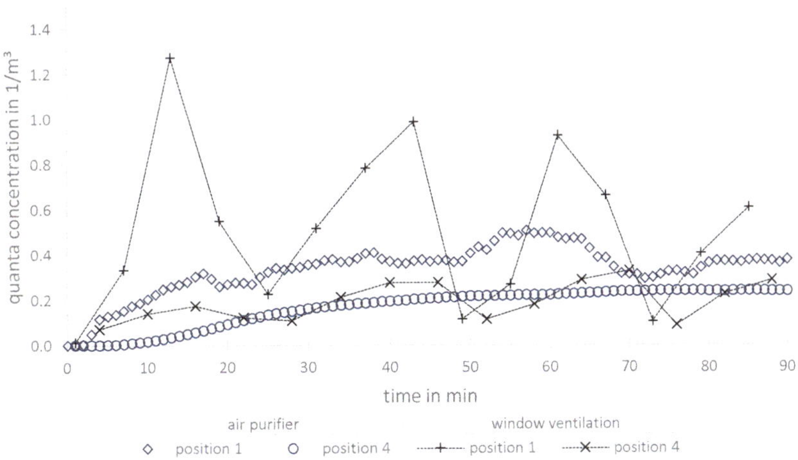

Figure 8. Comparison of quanta concentrations for a window ventilation and an air purification in a classroom.

Besides the position of an infectious person, the location of exposed persons and the air in-/outlets have a significant influence on the infection risks, especially for a non-continuous ventilation via windows. In this particular case, position 4 is proximate to the window front and therefore experiences higher local ventilation rates, which results in a lower quanta concentration course. Although this position is also close to the air purifier, in this situation, it experiences lower local ventilation rates than position 1 and thus a higher quanta concentration course. It is assumed that this anomaly is based on the occurring indoor airflow due to an upwards directed supply air. Besides the possibility of detailed local analysis, this plot emphasizes that the assumption of a theoretical ideal mixed ventilation is inappropriate in this example.

In scenarios with both principles (filtering device and ventilation with outdoor air exchange), like an air purifier combined with a window or mechanical ventilation, a new challenge arises. Outdoor air contains many particles of the same sizes as released by an aerosol generator, which means that an OPC cannot separate between surrogate and outdoor particles. One pre-study in this project shows that a simultaneous outdoor SMPS measurement of particle size distribution provides a solution. There are usually overlaps of the size distributions of outdoor particles and released ones. Consequently, if only particles outside this overlap are considered for both release and detection, the effect of both ventilation measures can be evaluated.

6. Discussion

There are two different models for estimating infection risks. Both Wells–Riley and dose–response models are accepted in the scientific community as valuable tools. Even though both experimental methods are easily adaptable, the formulas used in this paper are based on Wells–Riley. One of its criticisms is the uncertainty of quanta emission rate (QER) determination, using a backward calculation for the assumption of an ideal mixed ventilation [23]. Agreeing on that criticism, it should be suggested to use the two introduced experimental methods as well for an accurate determination of these values. With an experimental reconstruction of several infection scenarios, and a backward procedure to the one introduced in this paper, QER could be determined more reliably. By iteratively adjusting a still fictitious QER, infection risks could be derived for all exposed persons. Taking into account numerous scenarios and the persons actually infected, a mean resilient value could be identified using appropriate stochastic tools. This procedure enables a consideration of any kind of ventilation principle, instead of being limited to an ideal mixed ventilation.

A closer look at the experimental methods reveals that operating with surrogate particles (compared to trace gas) has higher uncertainties due to agglomeration, sedimentation and deposition effects. The intensity of agglomeration effects is discussed on the basis of measurements related to Figure 2, which is illustrated in a more detailed version (particle number concentration, particle mass concentrations PM1/PM2.5/PM10) in Figure 9.

The assessment on how well the quanta curves determined by surrogate particle method fit relatively to the ones by trace gas method is calculated as follows:

$$\Psi = \frac{\int_0^t |c_{\mathrm{q\,ref}}(t) - c_{\mathrm{q}}(t)|\,\mathrm{d}t}{\int_0^t c_{\mathrm{q\,ref}}(t)\,\mathrm{d}t} \tag{11}$$

with Ψ and $c_{\mathrm{q\,ref}}$ as curve agreement evaluation and reference quanta concentration (trace gas method), respectively. Table 5 shows the results of the evaluation on the curve agreement between the various approaches.

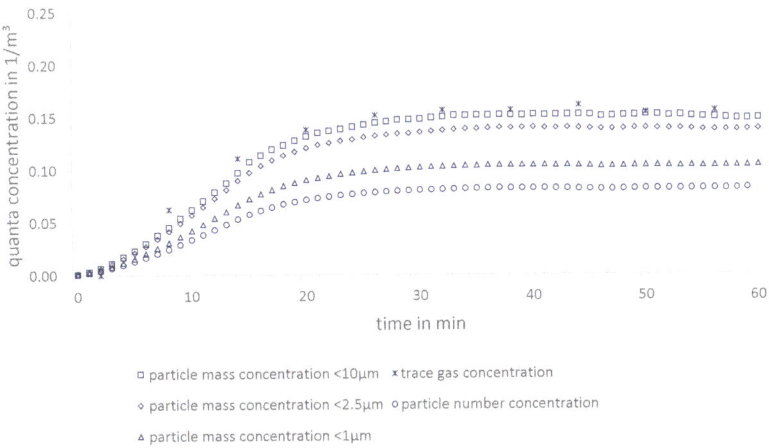

Figure 9. Comparison of quanta concentrations based on particle mass, particle number and trace gas concentrations in a conference room.

Table 5. Curve agreement evaluation of different approaches.

Approach	Curve Agreement Evaluation Ψ
trace gas (reference)	0%
particle number concentration	48.7%
particle mass concentration < 1 µm	35.0%
particle mass concentration < 2.5 µm	13.3%
particle mass concentration < 10 µm	5.6%

Since particle number concentration decreases due to agglomeration effects, this results in $\Psi = 48.7\%$. For mass concentrations considered below 1 µm, agglomeration might cause particles leaving the upper limit of the OPC's detection range, which results in lower calculated quanta concentrations compared to trace gas. For 2.5 µm, this effect becomes smaller because of a lower amount of large particles. It is even negligible for 10 µm, and its curve almost matches the trace gas course ($\Psi = 5.6\%$). To avoid underestimated infection risks, it is highly recommended to consider mass concentrations up to 10 µm even though the median size of particle release is below 1 µm. Several studies suggest that infectious particles, which remain suspended in the air, can be much larger [36] However, the release of particles with a median of less than 1 µm provides an overestimation of the infection risk. Apart from the lower filter removal efficiency for these particle sizes, they are also more likely to be airborne, resulting in fewer deposition effects. Even if in reality larger particles are emitted by humans, these two aspects ensure a conservative assessment of the infection processes.

Particle agglomeration further impacting both methods might be caused by wall effects, whereas trace gas should be reflected, and liquid particles are assumed to be trapped at walls. This might be one possible explanation for a lower curve of particle mass compared to trace gas concentration (Figure 9).

7. Conclusions

In order to estimate the infection risk of airborne indoor virus-transmissions, either calculation models or measurements can be carried out. The implemented simplifications of these calculation models (e.g., ideal mixed ventilation) might deliver fast but inaccurate results for certain scenarios. Previous experimental studies examine the effects of ventilation measures in more detail. However, instead of transient and absolute considerations of viral loads, they often regard relative statements of the infection risk.

Therefore, this study presents two experimental methods that are capable of determining a temporally and spatially resolved infection risk (absolute values) for different ventilation measures. Since particles entering from the outside would falsify the particle measurements, only the trace gas method is suitable for ventilation systems with air exchange and for natural ventilation. However, an accurate assessment of air purifiers based on filtration is only applicable by the surrogate particle method because trace gas is not filtered and therefore no device effect can be measured. For this reason, two different methods are essential.

Both methods are based on the theory that particles of relevant scales for infection procedures are airborne. The release of a controlled rate of either trace gas with a mass flow controller or particles with an aerosol generator allows a simulation of an infectious person releasing virus material. The measurement equipment includes an infrared spectrometer (trace gas method) or optical particle counters (surrogate particle method). For both approaches, the mathematical transfer of measured concentrations into infection risks is presented. In order to prove that the two methods are concordant, a comparison is essential. In an air visualisation laboratory with filtered outside air exchange, both methods are executed simultaneously. In fact, they provide similar results. This allows a first-time reliable experimental comparison of ventilation systems, natural ventilation and air purifiers.

Besides the detailed explanations and the comparison of both methods, several aspects that might influence the accuracy are discussed. Two exemplary scenarios show how practical both methods are and how scalable this principle is. Even if the ventilation concept deviates significantly from mixed ventilation, infection risks can be determined. Besides a two-person office, results of measurements performed in an exemplary classroom are presented. Both scenarios highlight the value of experimental investigations with temporal and spatial resolutions for determining infection risks. This allows, even for complex geometries, an assessment of the exposition time in rooms (e.g., workplace, events) and the identification of critical zones. On the one hand, the selection of a device and the related operating parameters such as volume flow can be determined. On the other hand, optimizations can be carried out (e.g., device positioning, orientation of supply air diffusers, permissible occupancy density). Furthermore, an evaluation of air purifiers beyond the quantity (Clean Air Delivery Rate, CADR) could be supplemented with information about locally resolved substance removal even under transient conditions.

Author Contributions: Conceptualization, L.S. and K.S.; methodology, L.S.; software, L.S., M.C. and T.R.; validation, L.S., M.C. and T.R.; formal analysis, L.S., M.C., T.R. and K.S.; investigation, L.S., M.C. and T.R.; resources, K.S.; data curation, L.S., M.C. and T.R.; writing—original draft preparation, L.S., M.C. and T.R.; writing—review and editing, K.S.; visualization, M.C. and T.R.; supervision, L.S. and K.S.; project administration, L.S. and K.S.; funding acquisition, K.S. All authors have read and agreed to the published version of the manuscript.

Funding: Investigations of Section 5.1 was funded by the Ministry of Science, Research and the Arts of Baden-Württemberg (MWK) as part of the project "Test aerosols and methods for efficacy testing of air purification technologies against Sars-CoV-2" with the grant number: 33-7533.-6-21/15/1.

Institutional Review Board Statement: Not applicable.

Informed Consent Statement: Not applicable.

Data Availability Statement: The datasets generated/analysed during the current study are available from the corresponding author on reasonable request.

Acknowledgments: We would like to thank the Ministry of Science, Research and the Arts of Baden-Württemberg (MWK) for funding the experiment of Section 5.1. Special thanks go to Michel Bauer for his scientific editing services.

Conflicts of Interest: The authors declare no conflict of interest.

Nomenclature

Quantity	Description	Unit
Roman Symbols		
c_q	quanta concentration	m^{-3}
c_sp	surrogate particle mass concentration	$\mathrm{kg\,m}^{-3}$
c_tg	trace gas concentration	$\mathrm{mol\,mol}^{-1}$
D_q	dose of inhaled quanta	–
M	molar mass	$\mathrm{kg\,mol}^{-1}$
$\dot{m}$	mass flow	$\mathrm{kg\,h}^{-1}$
$\dot{n}$	molar flow	$\mathrm{mol\,h}^{-1}$
P_I	predicted infection risk via aerosols	%
q	quanta rate	h^{-1}
t	exposition time	h
$\dot{V}$	volume flow	$\mathrm{m}^3\,\mathrm{h}^{-1}$
V_r	room volume	m^3
Greek Symbols		
η	device or mask filtration efficiency	–
ρ	density	$\mathrm{kg\,m}^{-3}$
Φ	combined rate of natural inactivation and deposition	h^{-1}
Ψ	curve agreement evaluation	%
Subscripts		
0	initial state	
ag	aerosol generator	
air	air	
dev	device	
exh	exhalation	
in	in	
inh	inhalation	
out	out	
q	quanta	
ref	reference	
sp	surrogate particles	
tg	trace gas	
w	window condition	

Abbreviations

The following abbreviations are used in this manuscript:

DEHS	di(2-ethylhexyl) sebacate
FFP2	filtering facepiece (class 2)
HEPA	high-efficiency particulate arrestance
MFC	mass flow controller
N_2O	nitrous oxide
OPC	optical particle counter
PIRA	predicted infection risk via aerosols
PM	particulate matter
SARS-CoV-2	Severe acute respiratory syndrome coronavirus 2
SF_6	sulfur hexafluoride
SMPS	scanning mobility particle sizer
MERV	minimum efficiency reporting values
QER	quanta emission rate, quanta rate (output)

References

1. de Oliveira, P.M.; Mesquita, L.C.C.; Gkantonas, S.; Giusti, A.; Mastorakos, E. Evolution of spray and aerosol from respiratory releases: Theoretical estimates for insight on viral transmission. *Proceedings. Math. Phys. Eng. Sci.* **2021**, *477*, 20200584. [CrossRef] [PubMed]
2. Kriegel, M.; Hartmann, A.; Buchholz, U.; Seifried, J.; Baumgarte, S.; Gastmeier, P. SARS-CoV-2 Aerosol Transmission Indoors: A Closer Look at Viral Load, Infectivity, the Effectiveness of Preventive Measures and a Simple Approach for Practical Recommendations. *Int. J. Environ. Res. Public Health* **2022**, *19*, 220. [CrossRef] [PubMed]
3. Blocken, B.; van Druenen, T.; Ricci, A.; Kang, L.; van Hooff, T.; Qin, P.; Xia, L.; Ruiz, C.A.; Arts, J.H.; Diepens, J.F.L.; et al. Ventilation and air cleaning to limit aerosol particle concentrations in a gym during the COVID-19 pandemic. *Build. Environ.* **2021**, *193*, 107659. [CrossRef] [PubMed]
4. Buonanno, G.; Morawska, L.; Stabile, L. Quantitative assessment of the risk of airborne transmission of SARS-CoV-2 infection: Prospective and retrospective applications. *Environ. Int.* **2020**, *145*, 106112. [CrossRef]
5. Lelieveld, J.; Helleis, F.; Borrmann, S.; Cheng, Y.; Drewnick, F.; Haug, G.; Klimach, T.; Sciare, J.; Su, H.; Pöschl, U. Model Calculations of Aerosol Transmission and Infection Risk of COVID-19 in Indoor Environments. *Int. J. Environ. Res. Public Health* **2020**, *17*, 8114. [CrossRef]
6. Hussein, T.; Löndahl, J.; Thuresson, S.; Alsved, M.; Al-Hunaiti, A.; Saksela, K.; Aqel, H.; Junninen, H.; Mahura, A.; Kulmala, M. Indoor Model Simulation for COVID-19 Transport and Exposure. *Int. J. Environ. Res. Public Health* **2021**, *18*, 2927. [CrossRef]
7. Xu, C.; Liu, W.; Luo, X.; Huang, X.; Nielsen, P.V. Prediction and control of aerosol transmission of SARS-CoV-2 in ventilated context: From source to receptor. *Sustain. Cities Soc.* **2022**, *76*, 103416. [CrossRef]
8. Kennedy, M.; Lee, S.J.; Epstein, M. Modeling aerosol transmission of SARS-CoV-2 in multi-room facility. *J. Loss Prev. Process Ind.* **2021**, *69*, 104336. [CrossRef]
9. Moreno, T.; Pintó, R.M.; Bosch, A.; Moreno, N.; Alastuey, A.; Minguillón, M.C.; Anfruns-Estrada, E.; Guix, S.; Fuentes, C.; Buonanno, G.; et al. Tracing surface and airborne SARS-CoV-2 RNA inside public buses and subway trains. *Environ. Int.* **2021**, *147*, 106326. [CrossRef]
10. Redder, C.; Fieberg, C. Sensitivity analysis of SARS-CoV-2 aerosol exposure. *GMS Hyg. Infect. Control* **2021**, *16*, Doc28. [CrossRef]
11. Santamouris, M.; Wouters, P. *Building Ventilation: The State of the Art*; Routledge: London, UK, 2006.
12. Cao, G.; Awbi, H.; Yao, R.; Fan, Y.; Sirén, K.; Kosonen, R.; Zhang, J. A review of the performance of different ventilation and airflow distribution systems in buildings. *Build. Environ.* **2014**, *73*, 171–186. [CrossRef]
13. Linden, P.F. The Fluid Mechanics of Natural Ventilation. *Annu. Rev. Fluid Mech.* **1999**, *31*, 201–238. [CrossRef]
14. Tan, G.; Glicksman, L.R. Application of integrating multi-zone model with CFD simulation to natural ventilation prediction. *Energy Build.* **2005**, *37*, 1049–1057. [CrossRef]
15. Nielsen, P.V. Displacement Ventilation. 1993. Available online: https://vbn.aau.dk/en/publications/displacement-ventilation (accessed on 10 August 2022).
16. Lin, Z.; Chow, T.T.; Tsang, C.F. Effect of door opening on the performance of displacement ventilation in a typical office building. *Build. Environ.* **2007**, *42*, 1335–1347. [CrossRef]
17. Tang, J.W.; Li, Y.; Eames, I.; Chan, P.K.S.; Ridgway, G.L. Factors involved in the aerosol transmission of infection and control of ventilation in healthcare premises. *J. Hosp. Infect.* **2006**, *64*, 100–114. [CrossRef]
18. Dinoi, A.; Feltracco, M.; Chirizzi, D.; Trabucco, S.; Conte, M.; Gregoris, E.; Barbaro, E.; La Bella, G.; Ciccarese, G.; Belosi, F.; et al. A review on measurements of SARS-CoV-2 genetic material in air in outdoor and indoor environments: Implication for airborne transmission. *Sci. Total Environ.* **2021**, *809*, 151137. [CrossRef]
19. Li, Y.; Qian, H.; Hang, J.; Chen, X.; Cheng, P.; Ling, H.; Wang, S.; Liang, P.; Li, J.; Xiao, S.; et al. Probable airborne transmission of SARS-CoV-2 in a poorly ventilated restaurant. *Build. Environ.* **2021**, *196*, 107788. [CrossRef] [PubMed]
20. Curtius, J.; Granzin, M.; Schrod, J. Testing mobile air purifiers in a school classroom: Reducing the airborne transmission risk for SARS-CoV-2. *Aerosol. Sci. Technol.* **2021**, *55*, 586–599. [CrossRef]
21. Keene, C.H. Airborne Contagion and Air Hygiene. William Firth Wells. *J. Sch. Health* **1955**, *25*, 249. [CrossRef]
22. Riley, E.C.; Murphy, G.; Riley, R.L. Airborne spread of measles in a suburban elementary school. *Am. J. Epidemiol.* **1978**, *107*, 421–432. [CrossRef] [PubMed]
23. Sze To, G.N.; Chao, C.Y.H. Review and comparison between the Wells–Riley and dose–response approaches to risk assessment of infectious respiratory diseases. *Indoor Air* **2010**, *20*, 2–16. [CrossRef] [PubMed]
24. Morawska, L.; Johnson, G.R.; Ristovski, Z.D.; Hargreaves, M.; Mengersen, K.; Corbett, S.; Chao, C.; Li, Y.; Katoshevski, D. Size distribution and sites of origin of droplets expelled from the human respiratory tract during expiratory activities. *J. Aerosol Sci.* **2009**, *40*, 256–269. [CrossRef]
25. Hartmann, A.; Lange, J.; Rotheudt, H.; Kriegel, M. Emissionsrate und Partikelgröße von Bioaerosolen beim Atmen, Sprechen und Husten. 2020, *Preprint*. [CrossRef]
26. Michaelides, E.E.; Crowe, C.T.; Schwarzkopf, J.D. (Eds.) *Multiphase Flow Handbook*, 2nd ed.; Mechanical and Aerospace Engineering; CRC Press Taylor & Francis Group: Boca Raton, FL, USA; London, UK; New York, NY, USA, 2017.
27. Adili, M.R.; Schmidt, M. Ventilation Effectiveness of Residential Ventilation Systems and Its Energy-Saving Potential. In *Sustainable Building for a Cleaner Environment: Selected Papers from the World Renewable Energy Network's Med Green Forum 2017*; Sayigh, A., Ed.; Springer International Publishing: Cham, Switzerland, 2019; pp. 451–462. [CrossRef]

28. Ai, Z.; Mak, C.M.; Gao, N.; Niu, J. Tracer gas is a suitable surrogate of exhaled droplet nuclei for studying airborne transmission in the built environment. *Build. Simul.* **2020**, *13*, 489–496. [CrossRef] [PubMed]
29. Asadi, S.; Cappa, C.D.; Barreda, S.; Wexler, A.S.; Bouvier, N.M.; Ristenpart, W.D. Efficacy of masks and face coverings in controlling outward aerosol particle emission from expiratory activities. *Sci. Rep.* **2020**, *10*, 15665. [CrossRef]
30. Hill, W.C.; Hull, M.S.; MacCuspie, R.I. Testing of Commercial Masks and Respirators and Cotton Mask Insert Materials using SARS-CoV-2 Virion-Sized Particulates: Comparison of Ideal Aerosol Filtration Efficiency versus Fitted Filtration Efficiency. *Nano Lett.* **2020**, *20*, 7642–7647. [CrossRef]
31. Palas GmbH. Datasheet DEHS. 2021. Available online https://palas.de/en/product/download/dehs/datasheet/pdf (accessed on 10 August 2022).
32. Bivolarova, M.; Ondráček, J.; Melikov, A.; Ždímal, V. A comparison between tracer gas and aerosol particles distribution indoors: The impact of ventilation rate, interaction of airflows, and presence of objects. *Indoor Air* **2017**, *27*, 1201–1212. [CrossRef]
33. Peng, Z.; Pineda Rojas, A.L.; Kropff, E.; Bahnfleth, W.; Buonanno, G.; Dancer, S.J.; Kurnitski, J.; Li, Y.; Loomans, M.; Marr, L.C.; et al. Practical Indicators for Risk of Airborne Transmission in Shared Indoor Environments and their Application to COVID-19 Outbreaks. *Environ. Sci. Technol.* **2022**, *56*, 1125–1137. [CrossRef]
34. DIN Deutsches Institut für Normung e.V. *DIN EN 16798-1 Energy Performance of Buildings—Ventilation for Buildings—Part 1: Indoor Environmental Input Parameters for Design and Assessment of Energy*; DIN Deutsches Institut für Normung e.V.: Berlin, Germany, 2021.
35. Haycock, G.B.; Schwartz, G.J.; Wisotsky, D.H. Geometric method for measuring body surface area: A height-weight formula validated in infants, children, and adults. *J. Pediatr.* **1978**, *93*, 62–66. [CrossRef]
36. Trivedi, S.; Gkantonas, S.; Mesquita, L.C.C.; Iavarone, S.; de Oliveira, P.M.; Mastorakos, E. Estimates of the stochasticity of droplet dispersion by a cough. *Phys. Fluids* **2021**, *33*, 115130. [CrossRef] [PubMed]

environments

MDPI

Review

Indoor Air Quality: A Review of Cleaning Technologies

Teresa M. Mata [1,*], António A. Martins [2,3], Cristina S. C. Calheiros [4], Florentina Villanueva [5], Nuria P. Alonso-Cuevilla [6], Marta Fonseca Gabriel [1,*] and Gabriela Ventura Silva [1,*]

1 LAETA-INEGI, Associated Laboratory for Energy and Aeronautics, Institute of Science and Innovation in Mechanical and Industrial Engineering, R. Dr. Roberto Frias 400, 4200-465 Porto, Portugal
2 LEPABE-FEUP, Laboratory for Process Engineering, Environment, Biotechnology and Energy, Faculty of Engineering, University of Porto, R. Dr. Roberto Frias s/n, 4200-465 Porto, Portugal
3 ALiCE—Associate Laboratory in Chemical Engineering, Faculty of Engineering, University of Porto, R. Dr. Roberto Frias, 4200-465 Porto, Portugal
4 Interdisciplinary Centre of Marine and Environmental Research (CIIMAR/CIMAR), University of Porto, Novo Edifício do Terminal de Cruzeiros do Porto de Leixões, Avenida General Norton de Matos s/n, 4450-208 Matosinhos, Portugal
5 Laboratorio de Contaminación Atmosférica, Instituto de Investigación en Combustión y Contaminación Atmosférica (ICCA), Universidad de Castilla-La Mancha, Camino de Moledores s/n, 13071 Ciudad Real, Spain
6 Atmosfree una Marca de Laberit Sistemas, Avenida Cataluña 9, 46020 Valencia, Spain
* Correspondence: tmata@inegi.up.pt (T.M.M.); mgabriel@inegi.up.pt (M.F.G.); gventura@inegi.up.pt (G.V.S.)

Citation: Mata, T.M.; Martins, A.A.; Calheiros, C.S.C.; Villanueva, F.; Alonso-Cuevilla, N.P.; Gabriel, M.F.; Silva, G.V. Indoor Air Quality: A Review of Cleaning Technologies. *Environments* **2022**, *9*, 118. https://doi.org/10.3390/environments9090118

Academic Editors: Alejandro Moreno Rangel, Ashok Kumar, M Amirul I Khan and Michał Piasecki

Received: 29 July 2022
Accepted: 20 August 2022
Published: 7 September 2022

Abstract: Aims: Indoor air quality (IAQ) has attracted increased attention with the emergence of COVID-19. Ventilation is perhaps the area in which the most changes have been proposed in response to the emergency caused by this virus. However, other strategies are possible, such as source control and the extraction of pollutants. The latter incorporates clean technologies, an emergent area with respect to IAQ. Method: Various air treatment technologies can be used to control contaminants, which are reviewed and discussed in this work, including physicochemical technologies (e.g., filtration, adsorption, UV-photocatalytic oxidation, ultraviolet disinfection and ionization) and biological technologies (e.g., plant purification methods and microalgae-based methods). Results and interpretation: This work reviews currently available solutions and technologies for "cleaning" indoor air, with a focus on their advantages and disadvantages. One of the most common problems in this area is the emission of pollutants that are sometimes more dangerous to human health than those that the technologies were developed to remove. Another aspect to consider is the limitation of each technology in relation to the type of pollutants that need to be removed. Each of the investigated technologies works well for a family of pollutants with similar characteristics, but it is not applicable to all pollutant types. Thus, the optimal solution may involve the use of a combination of technologies to extend the scope of application, in addition to the development of new materials, for example, through the use of nanotechnology.

Keywords: adsorption; activated carbon; filtration; indoor air quality; ionization; microalgae; nature-based solutions; photocatalytic oxidation; UV light disinfection; plants

1. Introduction

Increasing urbanization and modern lifestyles have contributed to humans spending an increasing amount of time inside buildings (e.g., at home, in offices, theaters, restaurants, stores, etc.), where they are exposed to indoor air pollutants [1]. Owing to the associated link between air quality and health, the WHO has recognized air pollution as one of the greatest environmental threats to human health [2]. To date, a considerable emphasis has been placed on reducing individual exposure to indoor air pollutants, making it necessary to analyze indoor sources and the possibility of reducing emissions from such sources. Thus, indoor air quality (IAQ), in all spaces where humans live and work, has become an issue of utmost importance and a significant determinant of human health and well-being. Several scientific studies have shown a direct relationship between improved air quality and positive impacts on human health [3–5]. The impact of indoor air pollutants on human health can be experienced in both the short and long term. Poor air quality results in unwanted health conditions and, in the worst-case scenarios, can lead to death [6].

Although the atmospheric composition, in terms of its main constituents (oxygen and nitrogen), is essentially the same indoors and outdoors, the types and amounts of indoor air pollutants differ from those found outdoors. Indoor air may contain a variety of contaminants, including particulate matter, tobacco smoke, radon, biological contaminants (e.g., mold, bacteria, fungi, dust mites, spores and pollen) and more than 400 organic and inorganic chemical compounds, with associated health effects [7,8]. Additionally, indoor air pollutants can reach concentrations of up to 10 times their levels in outdoor air, regardless of the building location [8]. Such pollutants are emitted by indoor activities (e.g., cooking and cleaning), products or materials (e.g., in furnishings and structures), to which other contaminants are added from outdoors that can penetrate indoors [9].

The concentration of pollutants in indoor air depends not only on indoor materials and activities but also on external factors [10]. Regardless of the insulation degree, even in naturally ventilated or mechanically conditioned and ventilated spaces, the internal atmosphere is an extension of the external atmosphere, i.e., the outdoor air quality directly influences the indoor air quality [11]. Non-reactive pollutants, such as carbon monoxide (CO), can penetrate the indoor environment and add to the indoor CO from unvented gas burners, defective cooking and heating devices, fireplaces, tobacco smoke and vehicle gases from attached garages [1,12]. On the other hand, reactive pollutants, such as sulfur dioxide (SO_2) and ozone (O_3), typically originating outdoors, quickly deplete after entering the indoor environment [11]. Carbon dioxide is considered an indicator of air quality in non-industrial indoor environments, such as homes, schools and offices and it is related to the presence of humans indoors and to human metabolism. It is also an indicator of the presence of other pollutants [13]. Although CO_2 at low concentrations has few or no toxicological effects on humans, at higher concentrations, it has direct health consequences. At concentrations higher than 5%, CO_2 causes the development of hypercapnia and respiratory acidosis, and at concentrations higher than 10%, it may cause convulsions, coma and death [14].

Humans are mostly exposed to air pollutants indoors via numerous sources, such as outgassing from furniture, floors, wall coverings, paints, glues, waxes, polishes, cleaning products, personal care products, tobacco smoke, heating appliances, cooking activities, etc. The indoor concentration of air pollutants can be affected by outdoor pollutant levels, as well as by other factors, such as door and window openings, air exchange rates, house age and size, and building renovations [15]. Cleaning agents and personal care products are common sources of volatile organic compounds (VOCs) and semi-volatile organic compounds (SVOCs), which are partially oxidized and condensed and therefore turn into fine particles. New furniture commonly emits formaldehyde [16]. Gas appliances such as stoves, boilers, smokers and cookers are important sources of indoor NO, NO_2, $PM_{2.5}$ and polycyclic aromatic hydrocarbons (PAHs) [17]. Ultrafine particles with a diameter between 5.6 and 560 nm are commonly detected in indoor air [18]. However, PM_{10} and $PM_{2.5}$ particles with a diameter of 10 and 2.5 μm or less, respectively, are more frequently detected indoors [18]. Laser printers emit ultra-fine particles, siloxanes and long-chained alkanes (C21–C45), and 3D printers are a source of nanoparticles [16]. The use of incense sticks and candles [19], toasting, frying, baking, open chimneys and older wood stoves are responsible for $PM_{2.5\text{-}10}$ emissions [16]. Biological pollutants are essentially composed of mites, hair, bacteria, molds, fungi, spores, endotoxins, mycotoxins and other types of living organisms with highly variable and complex characteristics [8,18].

Ventilation to dilute the indoor air contaminants is among the most important passive methods to improve indoor air quality in most buildings [12,20]. Natural ventilation can be achieved simply by opening windows. In modern and well-insulated buildings, it is also common to find mechanical ventilation systems, such as heat recovery ventilation (HRV) and energy recovery ventilation (ERV) systems. These systems continuously remove stale indoor air and replace it with fresh air from outdoors. However, if the outdoor air is more polluted or in certain situations where ventilation is not possible, other methods and/or air purification systems are required [21].

1.1. Scope and Objectives

Possible methods for air purification (Figure 1), which are reviewed and discussed in this work, include the physicochemical technologies (e.g., filtration, adsorption, ionization, UV-photocatalytic oxidation, ultraviolet disinfection) and the biological technologies (e.g., plant purification methods and microalgae-based methods).

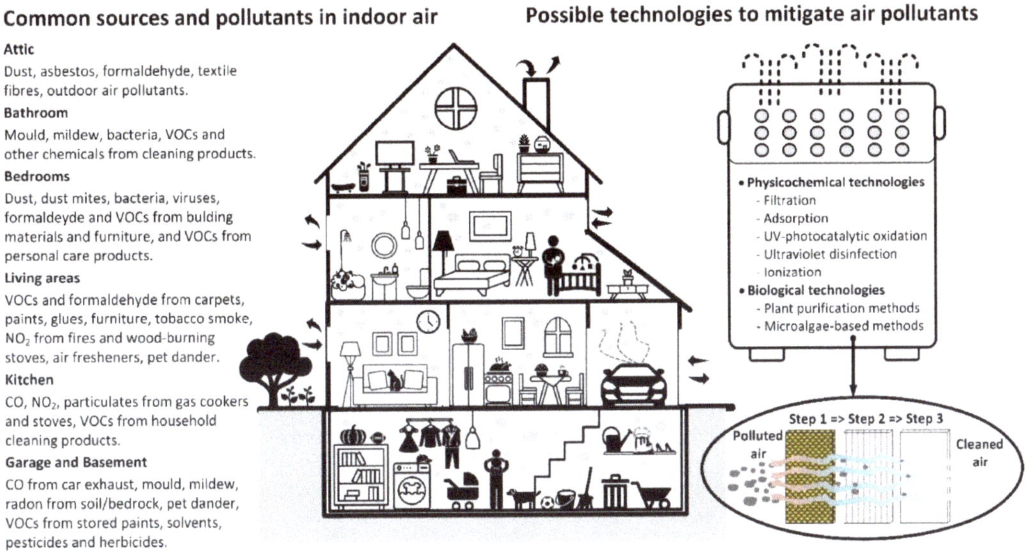

Figure 1. Common sources and pollutants in indoor air and some possible technologies to mitigate them (authors' own creation).

Generally, the conventional physicochemical technologies for capturing air pollutants, although effective in the short term, present some disadvantages in the longer term. Most of these methods cannot simultaneously remove all the major gaseous pollutants, some are unsafe due to the emission of ozone, all require regular and expensive maintenance, may have high energy consumption and generate secondary pollutants and waste, and have high installation costs. For example, filters and adsorbents are rapidly saturated and require regeneration or replacement to maintain the capture efficiency and prevent the growth of microorganisms in the organic matter retained in the filter material [10]. Air ionizers are limited due to low removal efficiency and production of harmful secondary products, such as O_3, NOx, and VOC oxidation intermediates [22]. After 3 to 6 months of use, adsorbents suffer from VOC saturation [23]. In addition to the saturation effects, some systems present ozone generation, reducing their practical application for air cleaning [24]. In addition, the high capital and operating costs of some of these technologies make them inaccessible to most consumers.

On the other hand, to maintain an acceptable IAQ, biotechnological solutions can offer a realistic alternative to engineering solutions. Indeed, in many situations, biological processes are the most cost-effective technology for treating VOCs and odors at low concentrations, below about 5 g m^{-3} [25]. This is based on the ability of microorganisms to convert VOCs into CO_2, water and biomass under ambient conditions of temperature and pressure. Biological methods typically generate fewer secondary pollutants and are less energy intensive, although some significant challenges remain. Thus, much of the scientific research developed recently is based on biological methods, highlighting nature-based solutions as promising alternatives [7,26]. These are based on existing solutions in nature to respond to human needs, following the principle of biomimetics [24], theorized in 1997 by Janine Benyus [27]. Numerous experimental studies have demonstrated the potential of the passive use of potted plants for a significant improvement in IAQ, with around 200 plant species tested so far for their VOC removal capacity, all with positive results. However, there has been little subsequent investigation to test the effectiveness of these potted plant passive systems in real environments and with extremely low airborne concentrations of VOCs [24].

A combination of different methods is also possible for better air purification efficiency. For example, promising results have been obtained with an air filtration system composed of plants and activated carbon [28]. Additionally, Salama and Zafar [29] determined the effectiveness of using nanotechnology, combined with plants, for the purification of ambient air, by using Saudi myrtle plants (*Myrtus communis*) treated with TiO_2 nanoparticles. The results showed a significant reduction in the air pollutants concentration (from 10% to 98%), including formaldehyde, NO_2, SO_2, CO and total volatile organic compounds (TVOCs).

The review organized by Szczotko et al. [30] focused on reducing microbial air contamination by using selected types of indoor air purifiers, showing that according to a wide range of articles on the topic, the actual effectiveness of the selected air purifiers is significantly lower, when applied to real conditions, than the values declared by manufacturers in their marketing materials and technical specifications. This is undoubtedly a major disadvantage of air purifiers offered to consumers.

Indoor air cleaning technologies can play an important role in improving indoor air quality. However, their effective application requires an adequate technical and environmental analysis of the real conditions for their use, as well as a characterization of the main pollutants existing in a given indoor environment. It may be necessary to use different air cleaning technologies simultaneously to more effectively maintain good indoor air quality. Hence, this work reviews the key indoor air treatment technologies, their target pollutants, main advantages and limitations.

1.2. Method

This review focuses on various air treatment technologies that can be used to control different types of contaminants, which can be physical (particulate matter), chemical (VOCs, NO_2, ammonia, etc.) or biological (bacteria, viruses, fungi, etc.). The technologies have been divided in two major groups: the physicochemical technologies and the biological technologies. Within the physicochemical technologies, this review covers filtration (mechanical and electronic), adsorption, UV photocatalytic oxidation, ultraviolet disinfection and ionization. In the case of biological technologies, plant purification methods and microalgae methods are covered.

This review presents some of the most relevant work in each technology, discussing the pros and cons of each one. Since it would not be possible to include all the studies published in recent years in this subject, a selection was made in order to give an overview of the diversity of research taking place around the world. Studies presenting a mix of technologies were also selected, as there is an increasing tendency to seek synergies between different methods in order to increase the range of pollutants covered. Studies with interesting technologies that can be applied in building materials, with the aim of degrading indoor air pollutants, were also reviewed and included in this article.

2. Physicochemical Technologies

2.1. Filtration

Two types of filtration technologies for air cleaning are commonly used to remove particles: mechanical filtration and electronic filtration; the latter also includes electronic air cleaners (e.g., ionizers and electrostatic precipitators).

2.1.1. Mechanical Filtration

Mechanical filtration is the most used air cleaning technology for particulate matter (PM) and it can be used even for removing respiratory droplets [31,32]. Mechanical filters use media with porous structures that contain fibers or stretched membrane material in a variety of fiber sizes, densities and media expansion configurations to remove particles from air streams. Some of the particles in the air that enter a filter bind to the medium and are removed from the air as it passes through the filter. Removal mainly occurs by impaction, interception and Brownian motion/diffusion, depending on the particle size. Some filters have a static electrical charge applied to the medium to increase particulate removal [33].

The main object of filtration is the removal of PM. There is a high variety of filter types, with a classification according to its efficiency to retain PM [34]. There are standards to classify filters, such as ISO 16890 [35], EN 1822 [36] in Europe and ANSI/ASHRAE 52.2 [37] in the USA. The ISO 16890 [35] classifies the filters used in general ventilation in four groups, based on the filter efficiency for a particle size: coarse, ePM_{10}, $ePM_{2.5}$ and ePM_1. To belong to each category, a filter must be capable of capturing at least 50% of the particles in that size range. The filters that capture less than 50% of PM_{10} (particles with diameters that are generally 10 μm and smaller) will belong to the coarse dust group. Both parameters, percentage of filtration and size, are equally relevant. For example, if the filters ePM_1 50% and $ePM_{2.5}$ 50% are compared, the first retains 50% of particles between 0.3 μm and 1 μm and the second 50% of particles between 0.3 μm and 10 μm. There are filters with high filtration efficiencies (EPA—Efficient Particulate Air, HEPA—High Efficient Particulate Air and ULPA—Ultra Low Penetration Air), which are used in environments that require a high degree of air asepsis, being classified by EN 1822 [36]. HEPA and ULPA filters can also be used for cleaning ultrafine or nanoparticles (<0.1 μm), such as bacteria and viruses that can even pass the membrane of our lung cells [38].

A very common particulate filter, mostly used in portable air cleaners, is the HEPA filter, which means that the single-pass efficiency of the filter media is ≥99.75% if the filter is classified as H13 and ≥99.97% for filters classified as H14. These filtration characteristics are set according to the efficiency of the 0.3 μm particles, which is the most penetrating particle size (MMPS).

These filters are normally part of a central heating and ventilation system, or part of air purification equipment, usually portable. In the first case, the filters act by filtering outdoor air, although they can filter indoor air if there is recirculation, and in the second case, the Portable Air Cleaners (PAC) exclusively purify indoor air, without air renovation. Real-time sensing has been applied to these devices to optimize their performance. These sensors monitor the ambient conditions online (temperature, humidity, concentrations of key pollutants) and activate the reduction units according to the needs of the occupants and their activities, with resulting energy savings [10]. However, PACs have different modes of operation in which the clean air flow provided is different (CADR—Clean Air Delivery Rate).

During the COVID-19 pandemic, PACs were recommended as a supplementary measure for ventilation or for those spaces in which natural or mechanical ventilation was not available, or was insufficient, in order to reduce the risk of transmission [39,40]. Experimental studies provided evidence for portable HEPA purifiers' potential to eliminate airborne SARS-CoV-2 [41]. Then, an air cleaner can be installed to remove particles potentially carrying viral particles from indoor air.

The air cleaner's effectiveness in reducing particles is defined by their CADR, typically expressed in m^3 per hour. Ventilation is defined parametrically as Air Change Rate (ACR) with its unit Air Changes per Hour (ACH, h^{-1}). The air change rate equivalent to the air cleaner's CADR is determined as follows:

During the pandemic it was recommended that 5–6 air changes per hour in classrooms should be achieved with ventilation and/or using PAC [42]. Therefore, the clean air flow required for a room, CADR, provided by a PAC (or several) can be calculated from Equation (1).

$$\text{ACR (cleaning)} = \text{CADR}/\text{Volume of air in the room} \quad (1)$$

Portable air cleaners have been widely used in different studies in order to assess the removal of aerosols in indoor air.

Cox et al. [43] performed a study in a total of 46 homes (43 of the homes completed the entire 3-month study, and an additional 3 homes completed a portion ($\leq$1-month)) to assess the effectiveness of a Portable Air Cleaner (PAC) with a HEPA filter in reducing indoor concentrations of traffic-related and other aerosols, including black carbon (BC), $PM_{2.5}$, ultraviolet absorbing particulate matter (UVPM) (a marker of tobacco smoke), and fungal spores. The PAC selected was a Whirlpool Whispure (Model AP51030K, Austin, TX) with a HEPA filter designed to capture 99.97% of 0.3 µm particles and with a CADR between 360 and 576 m^3/h (minimum to maximum speed). The CADR was selected according to the room size. The results showed that Portable Air Cleaners with HEPA filters could significantly reduce traffic-related and other aerosols in different residential environments, such as tobacco smoke, $PM_{2.5}$ and fungal spores.

Dubey et al. [44] have studied the effectiveness in reducing the concentration of different sized particulate matter (PM) and ions of two types of air purifiers equipped with HEPA filters in general indoor air and the presence of an external source (candles and incense). The first air purifier (API) comprised an anti-dust filter, activated carbon filter, active HEPA filter, electrostatic filter, vita ions, cold catalyst filter with programmable control panel, sleep mode, timer function, independent air ducts and a CADR of 120 m^3/h, while the second air purifier (APII) was equipped with six sense technology, a humidifier and a filter replacement indicator, along with filters viz. pre-dust filter, activated carbon filter, HEPA filter, nanocaptur filter; UV lamps, in addition to an ionizer function and a CADR of 150 m^3/h. The results showed that both devices reduced PM levels that varied from 12 to 53% for API and 37–68% for APII, depending on the scenario studied. In addition, both air purifiers reduced ions concentration significantly, while the concentration of some of the ions increased after the application of the air purifier. The increase in the mass concentration of ions after the application of the air purifier may be due to that air purifiers release ions continuously to purify the air. Overall, the study recommends the use of air purifiers with mechanical filters (HEPA) instead of those that release ions for air purification.

Blocken et al. [45] assessed aerosol levels in a gymnasium, and demonstrated that the existing mechanical ventilation systems alone are not efficient to decrease the levels. An air cleaning device (AC) alone with ACH = 1.39 h^{-1} had a similar effect as ventilation alone. Simplified mathematical models were engaged to provide further insight into ventilation, AC and deposition. It was shown that combining the above-mentioned ventilation and AC can reduce aerosol particle concentrations with 80 to 90%, depending on aerosol size. It should be stressed that it remains imperative that ventilation should be maintained at (at least) the minimum flow rates required by building codes, because many ACs do not remove gasses such as CO_2.

Lee et al. [46] assessed the effectiveness of aerosol filtration by portable air cleaning devices with HEPA filters used in addition to a standard building heating ventilation and air conditioning (HVAC) system. The test rooms, including a single-bed hospital room, were filled with test aerosols to simulate aerosol movement. Aerosol counts were measured over time with various portable air cleaning devices and room ventilation systems to quantify the overall aerosol clearance rate. It was found that PAC devices were very effective for the removal of aerosols. The aerosols were cleared five times faster in a small control room with PAC devices than in the room with HVAC alone. The single-bed hospital room (37 m^3) had an excellent ventilation rate (ACH = 14) provided by the HVAC system and cleared the aerosols in 20 min. However, with the addition of two air cleaning devices (CADR = 1458 m^3/h, ACH = 39 h^{-1}), the clearance time was three times faster.

Finally, Cheek et al. [47] carried out a systematic literature review to examine the impacts of portable air purification on indoor air quality ($PM_{2.5}$) and health, focusing on adults and children in indoor environments (homes, schools and offices). These authors [47] report positive long-term impacts with reduced $PM_{2.5}$ concentrations. The current evidence demonstrates that using a PAC results in short-term reductions in $PM_{2.5}$ in the indoor environment, which has the potential to offer health benefits.

It is consensual that filters can efficiently remove particles but are not effective for organic and inorganic chemical pollutants. A solution seems to be a combination of particulate filter and other air purification systems, or the development of filters with other properties, such as chemisorption. Regarding gas purification, the most effective and commonly used purification method is adsorption, with activated carbon filtration being the most prevalent approach due to their high surface area and high storage capacity, although other technologies are available [34,48].

Swamy [49] assessed the use of filters prepared with different percentages of NaOH doping on calcium silicate granules in order to reduce CO_2 concentration levels. The results showed an over 40% reduction in CO_2 concentrations with this purification system. Fresh air intake, to maintain the desired ventilation rates, has been reduced to over 50%, further reducing the heat load. Nanofibers can also be modified with adsorbent nanomaterials effective in the adsorption of VOCs [50]. Buyukada-Kesici et al. [51] have used cellulose nanocrystals and polyamide 6 to develop a porous electrospun material, which can adsorb around 50% of toluene in 45 min of trials, maintaining the same removal efficiency of conventional adsorbents in the form of powder or particles.

Protein-based nanofibers have also gained prominence in the air filtration field. The study performed by Kadam et al. [52] showed that Gelatin/β-CD composite nanofibers presented excellent adsorption of xylene (287 mg/g), benzene (242 mg/g) and formaldehyde (0.75 mg/g). The gelatin/β-CD biomaterial-based nanofibers filtered solid/liquid aerosols and gaseous pollutants simultaneously at a lower base weight with low air resistance.

Another interesting study was presented by Liu et al. [34], who developed a transparent polyacrylonitrile air filter to protect indoor air quality through natural passive ventilation windows. They obtained highly effective air filters, ~90% transparency, with a removal rate greater than 95% for $PM_{2.5}$, under extremely hazardous $PM_{2.5}$ concentrations (>250 $\mu g\ m^{-3}$). Its material is an excellent alternative for perspective windows, especially in large urban centers.

The studies presented are a small portion of all studies around new materials and new combinations involving filtration. With the advent of nanotechnology, there is enormous research potential in this area.

Concerning usual filtration, the traditional fibrous filters have numerous advantages, such as high removal efficiency, low initial cost and simple structure [34].

The main disadvantages are high pressure drop, high maintenance costs and filter colonization [34]. Another negative point is that filters are not effective for pollutants other than PM. The filtration efficiency of general fiber filters is directly proportional to the air pressure drop. High pressure drop means additional energy consumption and increased operating costs. Filter maintenance is often neglected during a system operating period. Filters must be replaced or cleaned regularly, otherwise they could become sources of pollution. The longer the filter operating time, the greater the possibility of potential pollution, by re-emission of VOCs or dissemination of fungi or bacteria by aerosols diffusion [53].

2.1.2. Electronic Filtration

There are two types of electronic filters for particles removal: electrostatic precipitators and ion generator or ionizers. Electronic filters include a wide variety of electrically connected air-cleaning devices that are designed to remove particles from airstreams. Removal, typically occurs by electrically charging particles, using corona wires or through the generation of ions (e.g., using pin ionizers), and by collecting the particles on oppositely charged deposition plates (precipitators), or by the particles' enhanced removal to a conventional media filter, or to room surfaces [33]. According to Bliss [54], the efficiency of electrostatic filters for a particle range of 0.3–6 μm is over 90%, while this value oscillates between 75 and 95% for ion generators. Some studies have found adverse health effects when using electrostatic precipitators such as the modification of cardiorespiratory function associated with the production of negative air ions, which may outweigh the potential benefits from PM reductions (e.g., Liu et al. [55]). In addition, the filters can become clogged over time, and so require regular cleaning. Generally speaking, electronic filters can generate hazardous charged particles [56] or new pollutants such as ozone, ultrafine particles and other compounds derived from VOCs ionization [57].

2.2. Adsorption

Adsorption consists of capturing air pollutants on the surface of an adsorbent material. It has been successfully applied for retaining both volatile organic compounds and inorganic pollutants on adsorbents, such as activated carbon, zeolites, silica gel, activated alumina, mineral clay and some polymers. The most commonly used are activated carbon and hydrophobic zeolites, due to their high surface area and adsorption capacity [18]. Activated carbon has high porosity and is a non-polar adsorbent. It can be produced from agricultural wastes such as sugarcane bagasse, apple pomace or coconut shell for more cost-effective pollutants removal [58]. Due to its microporous structure and large surface area, activated carbon is able to remove up to 100 mg m^{-3} of VOCs [59], although medium and high molecular weight volatiles are better adsorbed on activated carbon than low molecular weight volatiles.

Adsorbents can be easily incorporated into building materials and/or integrated into interior surfaces to remove air pollutants with no additional energy input and minimal byproduct formation; for this reason, they are classified as passive removal materials (PRMs). Passive removal materials enable ozone control, for example, in susceptible populations with health benefits, creating healthy indoor environments [60].

Hybrid technologies of adsorption combined with other methods have been proposed for pollutants removal from indoor air. For example, Jo and Yang [61] investigated the technical feasibility of an hybrid system composed of activated carbon and photocatalytic oxidation for controlling indoor air levels of BTEX (benzene, toluene, ethylbenzene, and xylenes) at low concentrations (of 0.1–1 ppmv). These authors [61] concluded that this hybrid system can enhance control efficiency of BTEX in indoor air levels with higher removal efficiencies (close to 100%) compared to using activated carbon alone (with removal efficiencies close to or higher than 90%), with a negligible addition to indoor CO levels from the photocatalytic oxidation process. However, some drawbacks of this technology include the decrease in removal efficiency with increasing relative humidity due to the capillary condensation of water vapor inside the activated carbon that blocks the adsorption sites. Additionally, the adsorption capacity of activated carbon decreases with increasing inlet concentrations. Furthermore, these authors [61] reported that a temperature of 300 °C is necessary to obtain significant desorption yields (75–95%) and the adsorbents need to be regularly replaced in order to avoid re-emission of already adsorbed compounds.

Ao and Lee [62] examined the effect of TiO_2 immobilized on activated carbon under different humidity levels for the removal of air pollutants from indoor air at parts-per-billion (ppb) levels. In this research [62], NO (200 ppb), BTEX (20 ppb) and SO_2 (200 ppb) were used as target pollutants. Different resident times and relative humidity levels were tested to investigate their mutual effect on TiO_2 and TiO_2 immobilized on activated carbon.

The results showed that the effect of TiO_2/AC is more significant with decreasing residence time and increasing levels of humidity. At a longer residence time, no significant pollutant removal difference is observed between TiO_2 and TiO_2 immobilized on activated carbon. At high humidity levels, the inhibition effect of water vapor is more significant compared to the presence of other pollutants, although it is still practically feasible to remove multiple pollutants under high humidity levels [62]. To further evaluate the performance for indoor air purification of a TiO_2 immobilized on activated carbon (TiO_2/AC) filter, Ao and Lee [63] examined it installed in a commercially available air cleaner. The authors tested it inside an environmental chamber, using NO and toluene as target pollutants. The original commercial air cleaner setting (AC + HEPA) showed no NO and little toluene removal. The TiO_2 filter removed 83.2% of NO but generated 12.9% of NO_2. Using TiO_2/AC, the NO removal efficiency increased to 97% and the generation of NO_2 decreased to 1.6%. The authors concluded that the TiO_2/AC filter not only increases the pollutants removal efficiency, but also reduces the release of intermediate compounds by the system.

Sidheswaran et al. [64] demonstrated the potential environmental and energy benefits of using activated carbon fiber filters for air cleaning in HVAC (heating, ventilation and air conditioning) systems. These filters are prepared from fabric precursors and have a very high specific BET surface area, typically higher than 1000 $m^2\ g^{-1}$ and low pressure drop, making them ideal for use in HVAC systems for VOC removal. In order to measure the removal efficiency of this activated carbon filter, the authors exposed it to a VOCs mixture of model pollutants, with concentrations in the range 20–30 ppbv (parts per billion by volume), composed of toluene, benzene, o-xylene, 1-butanol, limonene, undecane and formaldehyde at 29 °C and 30% relative humidity. The experiments showed the consistent removal (retaining) efficiencies of 70–80% for most VOCs [64].

Cheng et al. [65] evaluated the antibacterial and regenerated characteristics of a zeolite impregnated with metallic silver (Ag-Z) for removing bioaerosols (bacteria and fungi) in indoor environments, showing a 95% removal efficiency after 120 min of operation. These authors considered the 1 wt% Ag-Z to be more cost-effective, with an antibacterial efficiency near 90% in less than 60 min and an excellent repeated use performance up to nine times.

Adsorption materials can not only act as a sink for airborne pollutants, but also for excess moisture through adsorption. For example, a medium density fiberboard modified with walnut shell was investigated to regulate relative humidity, toluene, limonene, dodecane and formaldehyde [66]. A negative feature of the adsorption technology is the possibility of the deposition and development of airborne bacteria on the adsorbent surface due to the high biocompatibility of these materials [18]. Additionally, adsorption technology does not treat or destroy contaminants, but they are simply transferred from one phase to another, producing a hazardous solid waste that must be further treated and/or disposed of correctly.

2.3. UV-Photocatalytic Oxidation

UV-Photocatalytic Oxidation (PCO) is a very interesting air cleaning technology that has been the subject of much investigation in recent years. PCO is defined [33] as a light-mediated, redox reaction of gases and biological particles adsorbed on the surface of a solid pure or doped metal oxide semiconductor material or photocatalyst. The most common photocatalyst is TiO_2 (titanium dioxide), while zinc oxide (ZnO), tungsten trioxide (WO_3), zirconium dioxide (ZrO_2), cadmium sulfide (CdS), and iron (III) (Fe(III)-doped TiO_2), among others, are also used. To improve the efficiency of each elementary step, various strategies have been used to modify the physicochemical properties of nanomaterials. For example, element doping (metal or nonmetal) to induce impurity states in wide bandgap semiconductors has been used to extend the light absorption range, while plasmonic noble metal (Ag and Au) deposition is a popular way to enhance light absorption and inhibit photoinduced charge recombination. Several examples of these nanomaterials can be found in the review organized by Cao et al. [67]. The photocatalyst generates oxygen species (or reactive oxygen species) that remain surface-bound when exposed to light of particular wavelengths in the ultraviolet (UV) range. The oxygen species are highly reactive with adsorbed gases and biological particles. A variety of UV light sources can be used in PCO, including black lights (UV-A: long-wave; 400 to 315 nm), germicidal lamps (UV-C: short-wave; 280 to 200 nm), and lamps that generate ozone (vacuum UV [UV-V]: under 200 nm). Under reaction conditions allowing for deep oxidation (referred to as mineralization), carbon, hydrogen, and oxygen atoms in the reacting species will be converted completely via chemical reaction to water vapor and carbon dioxide. However, the oxidizing process can be incomplete, and origin reaction byproducts can be more toxic or harmful than the original constituents, as is the case for formaldehyde. Several studies [68–70] showed the generation of formaldehyde and acetaldehyde from the partial oxidation of ubiquitous VOCs such as alcohols. To minimize these problems, mixed technologies have emerged, which, for example, combine the use of PCO with filters. The combination of two techniques [71], or the development of filters with PCO properties, was found [72–74].

The research in this area is vast, and it would be impossible to list all the different nanomaterials developed to increase the PCO efficiency. Notably, in 2020, more than 9000 journal papers were published on the photocatalytic degradation of several pollutants [74]. Several review articles can be found [75] where an overview of the most recent studies for applications in indoor air cleaning is presented. In order to restrict the scope, this article presents some of the technologies ready (or near) to be used by consumers to clean indoor environments.

Kaushik and Dhau [71] presented a new air purifier (Molekule) that can trap pollutants and efficiently destroy harmful bio-active compounds using the photoelectrochemical oxidation (PECO) approach. The PECO technology is designed to drastically lower the atmospheric oxidation energy barrier using a specially designed catalyst coated on an air-cleaning filter. The Molekules technology is based on the synergy of nano-assisted efficient photoelectrochemical oxidation and filter membrane and have shown interesting performances. For example, for airborne viruses such as MS2 bacteriophage (a proxy virus for SARS-CoV-2, which travels in tiny droplets that can linger for hours before settling on surfaces) with 99.99% of removal in 30 min, and for formaldehyde with 81% of removal in 8 h.

Weon et al. [73] developed a new material: a TiO_2 Nanotubes Photocatalyst filter for Volatile Organic Compounds Removal. This filter was applied in a Commercial Indoor Air Cleaner, achieving an average VOCs removal efficiency of 72% (in 30 min of operation) in one 8 m^3 test chamber, showing promising results.

One of the most interesting applications is the incorporation of well-known and efficient photocatalytic materials into construction materials suitable for indoor applications to degrade priority air pollutants indoors and to inactivate various pathogens. Examples of such applications in confined spaces are TiO_2-based paints [76–78], roofing tiles [79], paper sheets [80], or textiles [81]. There is also the so-called indoor passive panel technology (IPPT), which includes as typical materials modified gypsum board, acoustic ceiling tiles, ceramic tiles, wallpaper and other coatings and pre-coated products relying on either sorptive or photocatalytic oxidation (PCO) processes [82]. Shayegan et al. [83] present a review focused on the application of passive removal materials to improve indoor air quality, which have recently gained interest due to their ability to remove pollutants without additional energy consumption and lower amounts of byproducts formation. Two types of materials are the object of this review: photocatalytic oxidation-based materials and sorptive-based materials. These authors [83] concluded that further scientific evaluation is necessary to assess the application of these passive materials in the indoor environment, and to better understand their impact on the IAQ.

Maggos et al. [77] developed an innovative paint material using a Mn-doped TiO_2 photocatalyst, which exhibits intense photocatalytic activity under direct and diffused visible light for the degradation of air pollutants, suitable for indoor use. A laboratory and a real scale study were performed using the above innovative photo-paint. The lab test was performed in a special design photo-reactor, while the real scale test was performed in a military's medical building. Nitrogen Oxide (NO) and Toluene concentration was monitored between "reference" rooms (without photo paint) and "green" rooms (with photo-paint) in order to estimate the photocatalytic efficiency of the photo-paint to degrade the above pollutants. The results of the study showed a decrease of up to 60% and 16% for NO and toluene, respectively, under lab scale tests, while an improvement in air quality of up to 19% and 5% under real world conditions was achieved.

In the study of Demeester et al. [79] through TiO_2 incorporation in roofing tiles, toluene was removed from air. At ambient conditions (T = 25 °C and RH = 47%) and toluene concentrations between 17 and 35 ppbv, toluene removal efficiencies between 23% and 63% were achieved. Other interesting data suggest that washing the TiO_2 containing building material with deionized water and simulating rainfall could partially (by a factor 1.3) regenerate photocatalyst activity.

Dong et al. [81] showed that the combination of TiO_2-loaded cotton fabrics, as wall cloth or curtains used in house rooms, produced using padding or coating methods with UV irradiation of 365 nm wavelengths can effectively eliminate gaseous ammonia in a photocatalytic reactor. The decomposition efficiency of ammonia was much affected by the dosage of TiO_2 aqueous dispersion, initial ammonia concentration, relative humidity and gas flow rate.

Zuraimi et al. [82] evaluated the performance of 3 photocatalytic oxidation (PCO)-based materials in controlled test chamber experiments with toluene, in order to determine removal rates, and ozone and carbonyl by-product formations. Toluene removal was found to be dependent on the type of light used. Only two PCO IPPTs are capable of performing under visible light. All PCO-based IPPTs generate ozone and carbonyls as byproducts, releasing up to 1.0 mg/h and 3.2 mg/h of ozone and formaldehyde, respectively. This is a concern, as exposures to ozone and formaldehyde are known to be associated with negative health outcomes.

From the exposed, it can be concluded that PCO is a promising cleaning technology, but studies show that there are aspects that need to be addressed before UV-photocatalytic oxidation can be used safely in buildings. The design of a photocatalytic air purification system is complex, and it is dependent on a wide variety of factors, including the intensity of the light falling on the catalyst, chemical makeup and pollutants concentration, the air flow rate through the device, moisture levels in the air, properties of the specific catalyst used, pollutant residence time, and how the device itself is configured [71].

However, the technology has several advantages:

(1) Use of solar light, a sustainable resource that is of major significance from the perspective of energy conservation and environmental remediation;
(2) Quick reaction rate and low energy consumption of heterogeneous photocatalytic oxidation;
(3) Relatively low pressure drop;
(4) Ability to treat a wide variety of compounds;
(5) Theoretically long-life cycle of reactive process (self-cleaning or regenerating feature of the photocatalyst).

The main disadvantage is the incomplete oxidation, which produces reaction byproducts that can be more toxic or harmful than the original constituents (e.g., formaldehyde). The catalysts can also be contaminated (poisoned) by airborne reagents and/or products of oxidation, which results in reduced or total efficiency failure of the process. In the cases where a lamp us utilized instead of solar light, the list of disadvantages includes the lamp energy consumption, lamp replacement costs, and the likelihood of ozone generation depending on the lamp source employed (e.g., UV-V lamps ~185 nm produces ozone) [33].

2.4. UV Light Technology-Based Disinfection Systems

As shown in Figure 2, there are four types of ultraviolet (UV) radiation, defined according to their wavelength range in nm: vacuum UV (100–200), UVC (200–280), UVB

(280–320) and UVA (320–400). Although all UV wavelengths are described to cause some photochemical effects, wavelengths within the UVC or UVGI range, specifically at 253.7 nm, are particularly harmful to cells, because it is absorbed by proteins, RNA and DNA. This process induces molecular breaks of the simple covalent bonds C, H, O and N of the nucleotide chain, resulting in irreversible molecular damage that leads to the inactivation of all types of microorganisms [84–86].

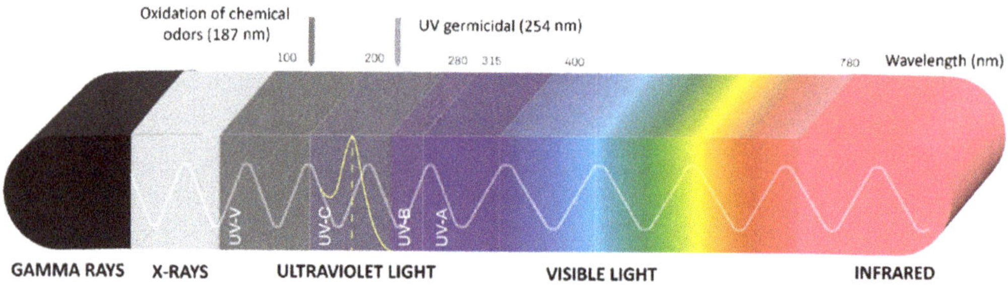

Figure 2. Electromagnetic spectrum including the types of UV radiation and the peak of UVGI higher effectiveness (254 nm). Adapted by Atmosfree with permission from Kowalski [84].

During the last century, several authors have studied the disinfection properties of ultraviolet (UVGI) light, at a first stage for water disinfection and, afterwards, for both air and surface disinfection purposes. In addition, throughout the years, efforts have been devoted to identify the configuration of an UVGI system that is most effective for each type of building ventilation system, as well as to disclose data on the effectiveness of UV in decreasing levels of microorganisms in indoor air and, consequently, the risk of developing health problems, such as respiratory infections and allergies [87–90]. The best-known application of UVGI disinfection in air is in buildings belonging to the healthcare sector [91–94]. However, a growing number of studies have provided robust evidence on the effectiveness of this air cleaning technology in several indoor environments, including offices, commercial areas, schools and universities [90,95,96]. For instance, although UVC systems have been used to disinfect hospital environments since 1936 [97], this approach was only formally recognized as being effective against airborne bio-pollutants by official authorities at the Center for Disease Control and Prevention (CDC) in 2003 [98]. Since then, UV light-based systems have been recommended by the CDC (2003) as an adjunct to routine chemical cleaning, as traditional cleaning and disinfection protocols can be insufficient for insuring proper disinfection in some contaminated areas [99]. Recently, ASHRAE and EPA recognized the importance of employing air cleaning solutions that include both filtration and UVC-based systems to prevent the spread of infectious diseases in indoor environments [100,101].

Air disinfection can be performed using UVC in several modalities, including irradiation in forced air or stand-alone systems, upper room, irradiation of an entire room (when the room is empty) and irradiation of the air circulating through a heating, ventilation, and air conditioning (HVAC) system, both in-duct and in the coils [100]. From the existing studies aiming at investigating the effectiveness of the use of UVGI for air treatment, it was particularly demonstrated that the use of in-duct in central ventilation systems, as well as upper-room and stand-alone systems, results in an effective reduction in the levels of microorganisms and endotoxins [90,101–107]. UVC systems in ducts are known to be cheaper and demand a lower energy consumption, as they are able to disinfect air and surfaces, while upper and stand-alone room devices only disinfect air [108].

Building ventilation systems are typically designed taking into consideration comfort needs. Even when ventilation systems are reconditioned to incorporate UV lamps there may be limitations related to air distribution and the removal of polluted air at the source [109].

Thus, based on the evidence, mainly for the indoor spaces with special needs of disinfection (e.g., hospitals) it is preferable to consider, in addition to filters, an UV disinfection technology, at an early stage of designing the ventilation system to serve the building. A very important criteria related to the choice/designing of the system to be installed is the type of lamp(s) to employ. Typically, low pressure (LP) mercury lamps, which radiate 95% of their energy at the wavelength 253.7 nm and are "monochromatic"; are described to have greater germicidal power than medium pressure (MP) polychromatic lamps, Xenon or UV LED [84]. The radiant energy flow of the systems should be determined, since systems, especially in ducts and stand-alone modalities, must be coated with material of high UV reflectance such as aluminum (not plastic) to reduce the number and size of lamps needed to be installed. Nevertheless, these conditions are difficult to standardize, given the geometry of the ducts and the eventual deterioration of reflectivity when internal surfaces are exposed to an airflow that carries can include variable levels of moisture and particles. This is why it is necessary to install lamps with a high UVC, preferably up to 30% of the rated power (e.g., Sanuvox technologies SL), as well as to correctly calculate and size each HVAC duct system, stand-alone, upper-room considering airflow, humidity, temperature, sizes, materials. In 1954, Harstad et al. [110] demonstrated that despite the installation of UV light in the air conditioner, there could still be airborne pollution from the growth of microorganisms in air conditioner components such as filters, cooling coils and duct surfaces [110]. In fact, one of the most widespread applications are UVC systems in cold batteries to destroy fungi, bacteria and endotoxins, avoiding their proliferation in the HVAC systems, achieving energy savings (average of 5–15%) and improving the efficiency of cooling transfer by reducing static pressure through the coil [90,108].

Each organism has a different sensitivity to UVGI light. Kowalski [84] and Malayeri [111] are some of the researchers who have collected data from several studies on the dose of UV needed to achieve the inactivation of bacteria, fungus, virus, protozoan and microalgae in vegetative forms and spores. Bedford [112] and Gates [113,114] were among the first to establish the UV doses needed for bacterial disinfection. Fulton and Coblentz [115] reported the UV doses for fungal inactivation, while data on the respective doses for viruses removal were first published by Rivers and Gates [116]. It is important to know the target pathogens to calculate the optimal UV dose based on their susceptibility constants, named K or z-value. This susceptibility, z-value, of each microorganism varies according to factors such as the pathogen biological structure, the conditions of environmental exposure and the distribution of the particles size, among others [84,105,117]. In fact, some environmental factors can influence the effectiveness of UV microbial inactivation. In this regard, there is evidence showing that airborne bacteria become more resistant to UV rays as relative humidity increases [84,105,117]. In addition, the use of an increased airflow rate passing through the UV system can result in a lower effectiveness of UV disinfection because microorganisms are exposed to UV rays for less time [84,105,106,118]. A low or a very high airflow temperature is also described to negatively affect the UV output, UV disinfection efficiency and susceptibility constants of microorganisms [84,105,106,117,118].

In addition to the selection of proper design, another aspect of utmost importance to consider is to ensure the proper sizing and operation of the systems. In fact, since the irradiance of the UV dose decreases with distance, to reach the same z-value, it can be necessary to operate the system with more time, in order to ensure effective disinfection [93]. Regarding the maintenance of the UV-based system, it is crucial to consider the nominal output potential of UVC lamps, which decreases over time. UVC lamps are classified into effective hours of UVC emission, and not at the end of the hours of electrical life. Many UVC lamps are designed to emit intensity levels at the end of their service life that are 50 to 85% or more than that measured in initial operation (after 100 h of burning time), although current models continue to emit blue visible light. Specification data from lamp manufacturers can verify depreciation over the useful life [119], the better the longer the lamp life, and the cost of spare parts and maintenance will be reduced (e.g., Sanuvox technologies SL lamps have a useful life of 17.000 h).

Importantly, in order to avoid any collateral health risks to the occupants, the potential release of toxic byproducts (such as ozone) by all kinds of UV systems should be carefully controlled. The devices must be tested by the manufacturer (and preferentially also by an independent third party laboratory) to ensure that the ozone concentration generated during operation respects the recommended maximum limits [100]. Another aspect to keep in mind is that there are limit values established for exposure to UVC light that cannot be exceeded. For systems that are closed (e.g., in ducts, cleaning of surface coils, autonomous systems), it is important to include a security system for opening doors that interrupts the operation of the lamps. In the case of upper room systems, these should be placed to an adequate distance from the ground that does not endanger people, because direct UVC light can induce damages to the eyes and skin [84,100,109].

2.5. Ionization

Bipolar ionization is generated when an alternating voltage (AC) source is applied to a special tube with two electrodes. This phenomenon can occur in nature, especially in mountain areas and waterfalls, where the production of positive and negative ions are reported to purify the air [120]. In the process of ionization, a neutral atom is given a positive/negative charge through the removal/addition of an electron, respectively. In bipolar ionization, positive (H^+) and negative (O^{2-}) ions are generated when water molecules are exposed to high-voltage electrodes. Although the mechanism associated with the biocidal effect of positive and negative ions have not been yet clearly established, the purposed mechanism involves the clustering of these ions around micro-organisms, resulting in the formation of OH radicals, which remove hydrogen, leading to the production of water vapor and to microbial inactivation [121]. Air ionization-based devices include those that generate only negative ions (i.e., unipolar ionizers) and those that generate positive and negative ions (i.e., bipolar ionizers). Bipolar ionization technologies, especially Corona Discharge and Needlepoint (NBPI), generally produce the same types of ions, which have the same theoretical mechanism of action when it comes to fighting pathogens, VOCs, and particles. However, a shared mechanism of action between the various air ionization technologies is not necessarily indicative of a shared method of ion creation [96]. Bipolar ionization technology has been around for decades, but the limited number of peer-reviewed studies in this topic makes it difficult to accurately support the effectiveness of this technology for air and surface disinfection purposes. Nevertheless, a growing body of recent evidence has presented the potential of using air ionization to decrease bacterial deposition on surfaces [122,123], inactivate airborne bacteria, viruses, and fungi [107,123–125] and to remove airborne particles and VOCs, being more effective when used in long-term applications [123,126].

Air ionization modules are often fitted directly into central air handling units to treat entire airflows. Modules can also be fitted into existing ductwork immediately downstream of central HVAC systems. Freestanding devices can also be placed into individual room spaces to meet immediate demands from internal sources. It is common to employ air ionization along with other technologies, such as air filtration [127], and some reports suggest that the efficiency of filtration increases when the ionizer is running [125]. Because the ions have a short service life of milliseconds, the distance from the ion generating equipment and the area to be treated must be estimated [127]. There are authors that recommend that the system should be installed vertically and deployed near both the inlet and return outlet for ensuring a better inactivation efficacy against airborne bacteria, especially in hospitals [128].

Since it has been seen that these systems can produce high levels of ozone and other organic compounds, similarly to UV-based systems, an aspect to consider is that the systems to be installed must have the certificate that accredits the non-generation of ozone [129]. In this regard, it has been described that when the energy potential produced through the ionization process is limited to 12 eV or less, ozone will not be produced because the oxygen has an ionization energy of 12.07 eV [120].

Some of the great advantages of NBPI systems are the elimination of VOCs, particles, odors and pathogens with reduced energy consumption and very low maintenance costs [123]. The main disadvantage is that while there is some evidence showing the efficacy of some of these approaches, the literature is still too scarce to draw robust conclusions-Thus, it is necessary to carry out more studies considering the implementation of air ionization-based technologies in real life situations and not only in controlled environments. Likewise, further work is needed to explore the potential capabilities that this technology has in combination with other systems to improve indoor air quality and reduce risks to human health.

3. Biological Technologies

3.1. Plant Purification Methods

Indoor greenery provides several benefits such as producing oxygen, generating humidity, pleasant aesthetical integration, passive acoustic insulation system [130], positive psychological effect on task performance, health, level of stress and comfort [131]. Besides that, the potential of plants for purifying and remediating the indoor atmospheric environment has long been identified (e.g., Wolverton [28]). Nevertheless, in the last twenty years, there has been a rising trend of more in-depth research on air purification mechanisms, technological solutions and methods [7,132,133]. Recently, in the context of the COVID-19 pandemic, the role of indoor plants in air purification and human health was looked at closely and considered as an alternative solution that could be used to reduce the viability of SARS-CoV-2 [134,135].

The purification methods mostly rely on phytoremediation, which is characterized by the use of plants to remove pollutants, or in this case from air, since it can be applied to water and soil, being based on a plant's ability to absorb, catabolize and degrade airborne pollutants, associated with their metabolic activities [130,132,133,136]. Regarding the plant microbiome, both the endobacteria and phyllobacteria may have an influence on the removal process to different extents, having in consideration the type of pollutant.

Interest associated with phytoremediation is high since it is considered an approach with low implementation cost and maintenance, compared with other technologies [137]. Moya et al. [130] provide a detailed description of the phytoremediation techniques. Additionally, Teiri et al. [138] revised different phytoremediation methods and the critical factors for the purification of indoor air, concluding that plants are able to efficiently remove different harmful contaminants from indoor air, including VOCs. This can be achieved through passive filtration using potted plants, or through active filtration using plant filters or green walls.

In general terms, active vegetation systems (in combination with mechanical systems) and passive vegetation systems (without additional energy requirements) can be considered for the present purpose [130,133]. Active systems increase the availability of polluting gases through the incorporation of mechanical ventilation devices; being associated with higher air-cleaning rates than passive systems. The passive ones are dependent on the diffusion of polluting gases, characterized by slower operation and lower concentrations [7].

Indoor plants are generally considered small shrubs and herbs that fit into the selected greenery system [132]. Plants used for indoor air phytoremediation are, in general, ornamental and limited to a small number of model species [133]. Following the recent review by Prigioniero et al. [133], the most widely considered species for this purpose is *Chlorophytum comosum* (Thunb.) Jacques, although other species are mentioned in the literature, often related with the type of pollutant to be removed [132,136,139]. An extensive list of indoor plants and their pollutant removal efficiency are mentioned in the literature [131,136]. Pollutant removal is plant specific and each part of the plant has different removal potential [131].

When using plant-based systems to promote indoor air quality, it is also important to consider the pollen load and allergenicity potential, such as flowering plants with strong fragrances [132]. Nevertheless, the main source of indoor pollen and fungi spores typically come from outdoors [140]. Plants also emit compounds, some of which are biologically active [141]. For example, plant volatile organic compounds (VOCs) are important in the ecosystem for chemical information transfer [132]. Gas exchange intensity and extent vary from night to day, and also depends on several factors such as temperature, humidity, light intensity, photosynthetic system, carbon dioxide concentration, and concentration of air pollutants [137,141].

The use of potted plants to promote air purification has been studied for a long time [28]. Although considered a passive approach, it has been investigated for the removal of harmful pollutants such NO_2, with promising results, for example with a combination of species *Spathip-hyllum wallisii* "Verdi", *Dracaena fragrans* "Golden Coast" and *Zamioculcas zamiifoli* [142]. Jung and Awad [143] demonstrated that indoor plants can improve the IAQ in University classrooms, showing that the increase in CO_2 concentration in classrooms with plant placement was lower (624 ppm) compared with the case without plant placement (about 1205 ppm). Later, Dela Cruz et al. [144] reviewed the use of potted plants to remove VOCs from indoor air, including the removal mechanisms and the relationship between plant, soil, and associated microorganisms. The literature mentions other pollutants, such formaldehyde and particulate matter, that are also affected by potted plants [132]. The extent of cleaning efficiency by plants can be increased by increasing the number of plants [145]. However, it is not possible to accurately estimate the number and size of plants needed to effectively purify indoor air. This is because different plant species have differences in photosynthesis, such as different optimal light intensity levels; some species grow slowly and others faster. Additionally, the type of plant and pollutant affects the phytoremediation efficiency. Moreover, the type of soil used for the plants to grow is another important factor, demonstrated in a study [138] using as a mixture of coco coir and activated carbon (for adsorption) as growing media. This significantly increased the VOCs removal efficiency (p-value > 0.05). Additionally, there is a lack of information concerning most contaminants in indoor air, thus it is very important to determine the concentration of indoor air pollutants.

Another challenge when using plants is the quantity needed to effectively improve the indoor air quality, which is not always practical in housing and/or offices with reduced areas. Thus, instead of using potted plants, several studies [146,147] suggested the use of "green walls" or "biowalls" with different plant species, which can simultaneously remove a mixture of different contaminants with less space requirement.

Biowalls are considered plant-based systems that mainly act to enhance the atmosphere and indoor environment and can be classified as living walls, vertical gardens or green facades, depending on their characteristics (type of plants and structural system) [148]. Figure 3 shows an example of a modular living wall system with planter boxes, implemented in an office building (Porto Office Park, Porto-Portugal). Figure 4 shows an example of a continuous system living wall with felt pockets, implemented in a Portuguese shopping center (Norteshopping, Matosinhos-Portugal).

Irga et al. [136] highlighted the importance of the technological advancements related to active botanical biofilters or functional green walls, which are becoming increasingly efficient and a rapidly growing field of research interest.

Several plant-based systems have emerged to support the improved indoor environment, such as the biofiltration system, where air is drawn through organic material (such as moss, soil and plants), resulting in the removal of organic gases and contaminants involving a mechanical system [130], and the nature-based air filtering system, which was installed at a students' residence, replacing an existing window with a mini-greenhouse, containing upwards of 30 plants connected to an air circuit to treat the indoor air [149]. The combination of systems can often boost and optimize the air purification effect, such as the combination of living wall systems with biofiltration. They are thus emerging technologies providing beneficial effects on the improvement of indoor comfort [130].

Figure 3. Modular system living wall with planter boxes in an office building (Porto Office Park, Porto-Portugal). Credits: Cristina Calheiros.

Figure 4. Continuous living wall system with felt pockets in a shopping center (Norteshopping, Matosinhos-Portugal). Credits: Cristina Calheiros.

The main recommendations associated with vegetation systems for indoor air quality promotion comprise a detailed selection of plant species, growth medium, irrigation systems, adequate light setting and abiotic conditions (e.g., temperature and humidity). The main research gaps center on the need for phytoremediation operational systems, which are important when considering a wider range of pollutants and plant organisms for indoor purposes [133]. Since the process performance depends on the interactions between pollutant, plant and microorganisms [130], it would be relevant to develop tools to support indoor air phytoremediation in order to further expand its use and allow a wider array of applications. For example, Thomas et al. [150] developed a mathematical model that takes into account the amount of plant material, building air volume, VOC concentrations and air exchange. More tools are needed to allow continuous and long-term monitoring of these systems performance.

3.2. Microalgae-Based Air Purification Systems

Microalgae are prokaryotic or eukaryotic microorganisms with a unicellular or simple multicellular structure. They are among the most efficient photosynthetic organisms on earth, with high biomass productivity and relatively low nutrient requirements, accumulating metabolites with several applications. They can live in harsh conditions, in seawater or freshwater, and multiply exponentially under favorable environments [151].

Microalgae for carbon capture via photosynthesis has gained increasing attention from the scientific community due to their ability to capture CO_2 and other pollutants, which they use to grow while producing O_2. In particular, microalgae are among the most efficient photosynthetic organisms, with high biomass productivity and relatively low nutrient requirements. They accumulate metabolites (e.g., pigments, fatty acids, etc.) with important biotechnological applications [152,153]. The biomass can be converted into chemicals and/or biofuels (e.g., biohydrogen, biodiesel, bioethanol, biobutanol, biomethanol and other biohydrocarbons), thus generating environmental and economic value [151,154] (Figure 5).

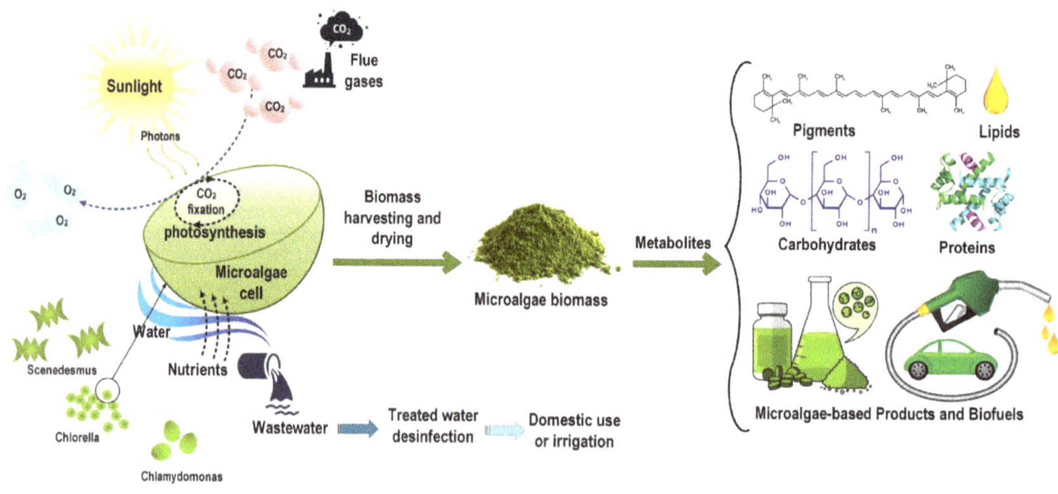

Figure 5. Microalgae as CO_2 biofixers, O_2 producers, and potential applications of microalgae biomass (adapted with permission from Mata et al. [7]).

The CO_2 bio-fixation by microalgae is a complex physicochemical process. Microalgae can tolerate up to a certain level of CO_2, after which it becomes detrimental to cell growth. This is due to the lowering of the medium pH, and to the environmental stress caused by higher CO_2 levels, reducing the cells' ability to fix more carbon. In an aqueous environment, inorganic carbon is available in different chemical forms, such as CO_2, H_2CO_3, CO_3^{2-} and HCO^{3-}. Depending on the species and on the physicochemical and hydrodynamic conditions, microalgae can biofix around 1.875 g of CO_2 per gram of biomass, [155]. Nonetheless, microalgae harvesting is still an energy intensive process due to the low cell density in the culture medium, typically in the range of 0.3–0.5 g/L, with exceptional cases reaching 5 g/L [156].

With the world's rapid urbanization and demand for renewable energy sources, a recent focus on the potential of microalgae is to contribute to the development of green cities and build a more sustainable future [157]. In particular, microalgae systems can be implemented as nature-based solutions to improve indoor air quality, along with other benefits [7], in alignment with the United Nations Sustainable development Goals (UN SDG) [158]. Moreover, their implementation will promote good health and well-being (Goal 3) and sustainable cities and communities (Goal 11), contributing to the European Commission's plans of Building a Green Infrastructure for Europe [159], allowing for thermal regulation and new architectural features [160]. Recommendations for sustainable urban planning include the implementation and, subsequently, the increase in urban greenery [148] as part of an urban renewal and rehabilitation strategy towards smarter and more sustainable development, and responding to global demands such as mitigation and adaptation to climate change [161].

With regard to the construction and architecture sectors, it is very common to find buildings with integrated photovoltaic energy. Despite the potential of microalgae biomass in the generation of renewable energy, its integration in buildings is still quite modest and at an early stage. In particular, microalgae have a great ability to biofix CO_2, produce O_2, treat wastewater, and produce biomass that can be used for bioenergy and bioproducts. The few examples of microalgae implementation in buildings and architectural design have demonstrated their significant contribution to energy efficiency, but they have never been tested for indoor air purification [7,162]. Recent studies have highlighted the potential of microalgae for indoor air purification, for example:

- Barati et al. [163] studied the influence of tobacco smoke on the cell growth, biodiesel characteristics and biochemical composition of two microalgae strains of *Chlamydomonas*. Upon exposure of this microalga to tobacco smoke, the specific growth rate (μmax) was unaffected in one of the strains, remaining around 0.500 days^{-1}, whereas in the other strain, the specific growth rate and the lipid content notably decreased from, respectively, 0.445 to 0.376 days^{-1} and from 15.55 to 13.37% DW (dry weight percentage) upon exposure to tobacco smoke. Therefore, the impact of smoke is strain dependent, thus making a prior selection of the candidate microalgae necessary.
- Yewale et al. [164] proposed a natural biological filter "Biosmotrap" to capture air pollutants made of a natural sponge gourd fiber support, impregnated with dry microalgae biomass. The results showed that the filter removed 60–80% of indoor pollutants from cigarette smoke and incense smoke.
- Lu et al. [165] studied the utilization of a microalgae-based air purifier for the removal of fine particles (PM2.5) in indoor air and oxygen production. The microalgae air purifier technology consists of a replaceable film (a cotton canvas) with a high density of microalgae attached (40.1 g m^{-2} of microalgae biomass dry weight), assessed during a 5-day usage. *Chlorella pyrenoidosa* is the microalgae species selected for this air purifier, isolated from a microbial consortium collected at a local lakeside (Nanchang, China). The innovative aspects of this microalgae air purifier are the high cell density microalgae film (instead of a large volume of liquid microalgae medium), reducing the energy consumption for maintaining the microalgae medium, easy film replacement by users, and the simultaneous removal of fine PM and O_2 production. The results showed that although the microalgae-based air purifier performed well for the intended purpose, the decrease in O_2 productivity (to less than 30 mg h^{-1}) and of the $PM_{2.5}$ removal efficiency (a 60% decrease) in a very short usage period (1 day)

is a technical barrier to its utilization. Thus, further development is required for the correct operation of this air purifier, in particular for better control of the moisture content and pH value.

- Thawechai et al. [166] studied the oleaginous microalgae *Nannochloropsis sp.* as a potential strain for CO_2 mitigation into lipids and pigments, analyzing the synergistic effects of light intensity and photoperiod. The authors obtained a 0.850 ± 0.16 g L^{-1} with a lipid content of $44.7 \pm 1.2\%$. The CO_2 fixation rate was 0.729 ± 0.04 g L^{-1} d^{-1}. The fatty acids were mainly C16–C18, indicating its potential use as biodiesel feedstock.

In buildings, microalgae can be cultivated in closed photobioreactors (PBRs) of different shapes (e.g., flat panels, multi-tubular, etc.) and dimensions that can act as dynamic shading devices (Figure 6). Depending on the density of microalgae biomass inside the PBRs, and the amount of sunlight absorbed by cells, various shading levels can be provided. On the other hand, the biomass density depends on the microalgae species, their growth cycle, the available carbon dioxide and sunlight, temperature of the culture medium, and frequency of biomass harvesting, among other factors. However, these conditions can be adjusted to the needs of the building's users. '

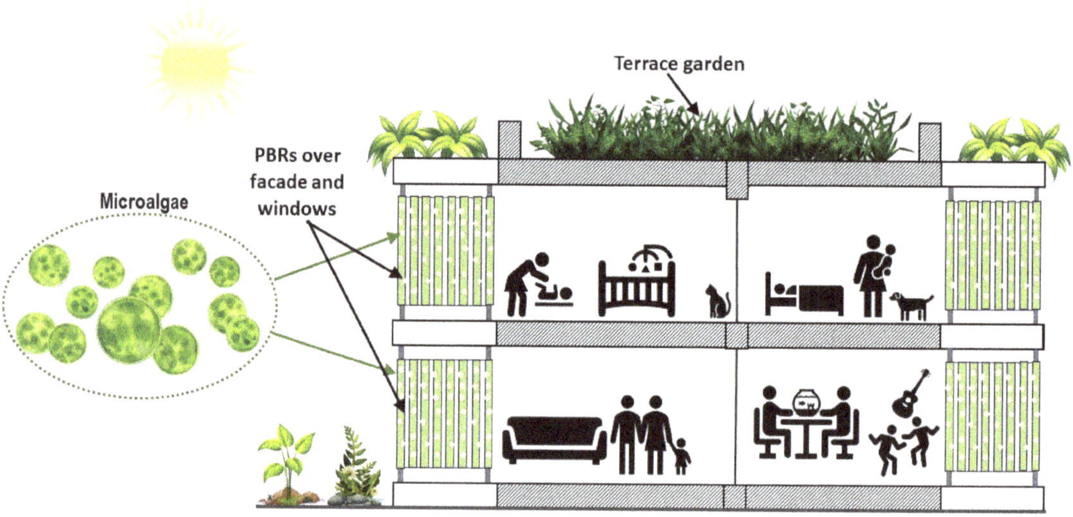

Figure 6. Example of integration of microalgae PBRs and plants in buildings (authors' own creation).

4. Conclusions and Future Trends

Indoor air quality has gained a new focus with the emergence of COVID-19. Ventilation is perhaps the most used strategy to decrease the concentration levels of indoor air pollutants. However, if outdoor air is more polluted, or in certain situations where ventilation is not possible, other strategies need to be applied, such as source control and pollutants extraction. The latter incorporates air cleaning technologies, one of the emergent areas on IAQ. Various air treatment technologies can be used to control contaminants, which are reviewed and discussed in this work and include physicochemical technologies (e.g., filtration, adsorption, UV-photocatalytic oxidation, ultraviolet disinfection and ionization) and biological technologies (e.g., plant purification methods and microalgae-based methods).

It is consensual that filters can efficiently remove particles but are not effective for organic and inorganic chemical pollutants. A solution seems to be a combination of particulate filter and other systems, or the development of filters with other properties, such as chemisorption. Nanofibers can be modified with nanomaterials to form effective adsorbent materials that can efficiently adsorb the different VOCs. With the advent of nanotechnology, there is enormous research potential in this area.

On the other hand, we have adsorption capable of capturing both volatile organic compounds and inorganic pollutants. Adsorbents can be easily incorporated into building materials and/or integrated into interior surfaces to remove air pollutants with no additional energy input and minimal byproduct formation; for this reason, they are classified as passive removal materials (PRMs). A negative aspect of the adsorption technology is the possibility of the development of airborne bacteria on the adsorbent surface due to the high biocompatibility of these materials. Additionally, adsorption technology produces a hazardous solid waste that must be further treated and/or disposed of correctly.

UV-Photocatalytic Oxidation (PCO) is a promising cleaning technology, ranging from organic to inorganic compounds, as well as microorganisms, but studies show that there are aspects that need to be addressed before UV-photocatalytic oxidation can be used safely in buildings. The design of a photocatalytic air purification system is complex and is dependent on a wide variety of factors, including intensity of the light falling on the catalyst, chemical makeup and concentration of pollutants, the air flow rate through the device, moisture levels in the air, properties of the specific catalyst used, pollutant residence time, and how the device itself is configured. The main disadvantage is the incomplete oxidation, which produces reaction byproducts that can be more toxic or harmful than the original constituents (e.g., formaldehyde).

Ultraviolet light is used mainly for disinfecting air in buildings belonging to the healthcare sector, focusing on microorganisms such as bacteria, virus, fungi, etc. However, a growing number of studies has provided robust evidence on the effectiveness of this air cleaning technology in several indoor environments, including offices, commercial areas, schools, and universities. Currently, ASHRAE and EPA also recognize the importance of employing air cleaning solutions that include both filtration and UVC-based systems to prevent the spread of infectious diseases in indoor environments. Importantly, in order to avoid any collateral risks to the health of occupant, the potential release of toxicant byproducts (as ozone) by all kinds of UV systems should be carefully controlled. Another aspect to keep in mind is that there are limited values established for exposure to UVC light that cannot be exceeded, and direct exposition should be avoided as direct UVC light can damage to the eyes and skin.

Air ionization-based technologies show potential, as there is some evidence showing their efficacy to improve IAQ, but the literature is still too scarce to draw robust conclusions. Nevertheless, a growing body of recent evidence has presented the potential of using air ionization to decrease bacterial deposition on surfaces, inactivate airborne bacteria, viruses, and fungi and to remove airborne particles and VOCs, being more effective when used in long-term applications. Similarly, to UV-based systems, these systems can produce high levels of ozone and other organic compounds, which requires surveillance.

Phytoremediation is characterized by the use of plants to remove pollutants, in this case from air. Interest associated with phytoremediation is high since it is considered an approach with low implementation cost and maintenance, compared with other technologies Different studies on the purification of indoor air have concluded that plants are able to efficiently remove different harmful contaminants from indoor air, including VOCs. This can be achieved through passive filtration using potted plants, or through active filtration using plant filters or green walls. When using plant-based systems to promote indoor air quality, it is also important to consider the pollen load and allergenicity potential, such as flowering plants with strong fragrances. Plants also emit compounds, some of which are biologically active. The main research gaps focus on the needs of phytoremediation operational systems, making it important to consider a wider range of pollutants and plant organisms for indoor purposes.

Microalgae have a great ability to biofix CO_2, produce O_2, treat wastewater, and produce biomass, which can be used for bioenergy and bioproducts. The few examples of microalgae implementation in buildings and architectural design have demonstrated their significant contribution to energy efficiency, but they have never been tested for indoor air purification in real situations. However, from the studies performed in lab, it seems to be a promising technology.

To conclude, all the technologies presented show advantages and limitations. One of the common problems is the emission of other pollutants, different and sometimes more dangerous to human health than those they were initially intended to remove. Another aspect is the limited type of pollutants removed. The solution seems be the use of combined technologies to extend the scope and of course the development of new materials, using nanotechnology. From this review, one conclusion can be taken: there is still a need for more research in order to consolidate the existing technologies and assure their safety for use in indoor spaces.

Furthermore, the current reality has shown the importance of good indoor air quality. Thus, these new technologies can contribute to its improvement, despite all their limitations. It is essential that people acknowledge the importance of clean air as equally as pure water. It will be necessary to define minimum parameters for the classification of good IAQ. Additionally, it would be important to see a generalization of IAQ audits, which would enhance source control and ventilation, the main vectors to ensure good IAQ.

Author Contributions: Conceptualization, T.M.M., M.F.G. and G.V.S.; methodology, validation, writing, review, and editing, T.M.M., A.A.M., C.S.C.C., F.V., N.P.A.-C., M.F.G. and G.V.S. All authors have read and agreed to the published version of the manuscript.

Funding: This work was financially supported by base funding of the following projects: LA/P/0045/2020 (ALiCE), UIDB/00511/2020 (LEPABE), and UIDB/50022/2020 (LAETA), funded by national funds through FCT/MCTES (PIDDAC). António Martins thanks the Portuguese National Funding Agency for Science, Research, and Technology (FCT) for funding through program DL 57/2016—Norma transitória. Teresa Mata gratefully acknowledge the funding of Project NORTE-06-3559-FSE-000107, co-financed by Programa Operacional Regional do Norte (NORTE2020), through Fundo Social Europeu (FSE). Calheiros C. is thankful to FCT—Fundação para Ciência e Tecnologia within the scope of UIDB/04423/2020 and UIDP/04423/2020.

Conflicts of Interest: The authors declare no conflict of interest. The funders had no role in the design of the study; in the collection, analyses, or interpretation of data; in the writing of the manuscript; or in the decision to publish the results.

References

1. Mannan, M.; Al-Ghamdi, S. Indoor Air Quality in Buildings: A Comprehensive Review on the Factors Influencing Air Pollution in Residential and Commercial Structure. *Int. J. Environ. Res. Public Health* **2021**, *18*, 3276. [CrossRef]
2. WHO. *Ambient Air Pollution: A Global Assessment of Exposure and Burden of Disease*; Department of Public Health, Environmental and Social Health Organization, World Health Organization: Geneve, Switzerland, 2016; pp. 1–121.
3. Sundell, J. On the history of indoor air quality and health. *Indoor Air* **2004**, *14*, 51–58. [CrossRef]
4. Coggins, M.A.; Semple, S.; Hurley, F.; Shafrir, A.; Galea, K.S.; Cowie, H.; Sanchez-Jimenez, A.; Garden, C.; Whelan, P.; Ayres, J.G. *Indoor Air Pollution and Health (IAPAH) (2008-EH-MS-8-S3)*; STRIVE Report Series No.104. EPA STRIVE Programme 2007–2013; EPA—Environmental Protection Agency: Wexford, Ireland, 2013; ISBN 9781840954852.
5. Jones, A.P. Indoor air quality and health. *Atmos. Environ.* **1999**, *33*, 4535–4564. [CrossRef]
6. Van Tran, V.; Park, D.; Lee, Y.-C. Indoor Air Pollution, Related Human Diseases, and Recent Trends in the Control and Improvement of Indoor Air Quality. *Int. J. Environ. Res. Public Health* **2020**, *17*, 2927. [CrossRef]
7. Mata, T.M.; Oliveira, G.M.; Monteiro, H.; Silva, G.V.; Caetano, N.S.; Martins, A.A. Indoor Air Quality Improvement Using Nature-Based Solutions: Design Proposals to Greener Cities. *Int. J. Environ. Res. Public Health* **2021**, *18*, 8472. [CrossRef]
8. Mata, T.M.; Felgueiras, F.; Martins, A.A.; Monteiro, H.; Ferraz, M.P.; Oliveira, G.M.; Gabriel, M.F.; Silva, G.V. Indoor Air Quality in Elderly Centers: Pollutants Emission and Health Effects. *Environments* **2022**, *9*, 86. [CrossRef]
9. Kelly, F.J.; Fussell, J.C. Improving indoor air quality, health and performance within environments where people live, travel, learn and work. *Atmos. Environ.* **2018**, *200*, 90–109. [CrossRef]
10. González-Martín, J.; Kraakman, N.J.R.; Pérez, C.; Lebrero, R.; Muñoz, R. A state–of–the–art review on indoor air pollution and strategies for indoor air pollution control. *Chemosphere* **2021**, *262*, 128376. [CrossRef]
11. Yocom, J.E. A Critical Review. *J. Air Pollut. Control. Assoc.* **1982**, *32*, 500–520. [CrossRef]
12. Borsboom, W.; De Gids, W.; Logue, J.; Berkeley, L.; Sherman, M.; Berkeley, L.; Wargocki, P. *Technical Note AIVC 68 Residential Ventilation and Health*; International Energy Agency, Energy in Buildings and Communities Programme: Lozenberg, Belgium, 2016.

13. Zhang, X.; Wargocki, P.; Lian, Z.; Thyregod, C. Effects of exposure to carbon dioxide and bioeffluents on perceived air quality, self-assessed acute health symptoms, and cognitive performance. *Indoor Air* **2016**, *27*, 47–64. [CrossRef]
14. Permentier, K.; Vercammen, S.; Soetaert, S.; Schellemans, C. Carbon dioxide poisoning: A literature review of an often forgotten cause of intoxication in the emergency department. *Int. J. Emerg. Med.* **2017**, *10*, 14. [CrossRef] [PubMed]
15. Chin, J.-Y.; Godwin, C.; Parker, E.; Robins, T.; Lewis, T.; Harbin, P.; Batterman, S. Levels and sources of volatile organic compounds in homes of children with asthma. *Indoor Air* **2013**, *24*, 403–415. [CrossRef] [PubMed]
16. Sokhi, R.S.; Moussiopoulos, N.; Baklanov, A.; Bartzis, J.; Coll, I.; Finardi, S.; Friedrich, R.; Geels, C.; Grönholm, T.; Halenka, T.; et al. Advances in air quality research–current and emerging challenges. *Atmos. Chem. Phys.* **2022**, *22*, 4615–4703. [CrossRef]
17. Hassanvand, M.S.; Naddafi, K.; Faridi, S.; Nabizadeh, R.; Sowlat, M.H.; Momeniha, F.; Gholampour, A.; Arhami, M.; Kashani, H.; Zare, A.; et al. Characterization of PAHs and metals in indoor/outdoor PM10/PM2.5/PM1 in a retirement home and a school dormitory. *Sci. Total Environ.* **2015**, *527–528*, 100–110. [CrossRef] [PubMed]
18. Luengas, A.; Barona, A.; Hort, C.; Gallastegui, G.; Platel, V.; Elias, A. A review of indoor air treatment technologies. *Rev. Environ. Sci. Bio. Technol.* **2015**, *14*, 499–522. [CrossRef]
19. Silva, G.V.; Martins, A.O.; Martins, S.D.S. Indoor Air Quality: Assessment of Dangerous Substances in Incense Products. *Int. J. Environ. Res. Public Health* **2021**, *18*, 8086. [CrossRef]
20. *EUR 14449 EN*; European Collaborative Action: Indoor Air Quality & Its Impact on Man. Environment and Quality of Life. Report No. 11—Guidelines for Ventilation Requirements in Buildings; Commission of the European Communities: Luxembourg, 1992; pp. 1–40.
21. *EN 16798-1*; Energy Performance of Buildings—Ventilation of Buildings—Part 1: Indoor Environmental Input Parameters for Design and Assessment of Energy Performance of Buildings Addressing Indoor Air Quality, Thermal Environment, Lighting and Acoustics. European Committee for Standardization: Brussels, Belgium, 2019.
22. Kim, K.-H.; Szulejko, J.; Kumar, P.; Kwon, E.E.; Adelodun, A.A.; Reddy, P.A.K. Air ionization as a control technology for off-gas emissions of volatile organic compounds. *Environ. Pollut.* **2017**, *225*, 729–743. [CrossRef]
23. Wang, Z.; Zhang, J.S. Characterization and performance evaluation of a full-scale activated carbon-based dynamic botanical air filtration system for improving indoor air quality. *Build. Environ.* **2011**, *46*, 758–768. [CrossRef]
24. Pacheco-Torgal, F.; Labrincha, J.A.; Diamanti, M.V.; Yu, C.P.; Lee, H.K. *Biotechnologies and Biomimetics for Civil Engineering*; Springer International Publishing Switzerland: New York, NY, USA, 2015.
25. Muñoz, R.; Daugulis, A.J.; Hernández, M.; Quijano, G. Recent advances in two-phase partitioning bioreactors for the treatment of volatile organic compounds. *Biotechnol. Adv.* **2012**, *30*, 1707–1720. [CrossRef]
26. European Commission. FUTURE BRIEF: The solution is in nature. European Union, Luxembourg. *Sci. Environ. Policy* **2021**, *24*, 83. [CrossRef]
27. Benyus, J.M. *Biomimicry: Innovation Inspired by Nature*; HarperCollins Publishers: New York, NY, USA, 2009.
28. Wolverton, B.C.; Johnson, A.; Bounds, K. *Interior Landscape Plants for Indoor Air Pollution Abatement*; NASA—National Aeronautics and Space Administration: Washington, DC, USA, 1989; p. 30.
29. Salama, K.F.; Zafar, M. Purification of Ambient Air by Novel Green Plant with Titanium Dioxide Nanoparticles. *Int. J. Prev. Med.* **2022**, *13*, 67. [CrossRef] [PubMed]
30. Szczotko, M.; Orych, I.; Mąka, L.; Solecka, J. A Review of Selected Types of Indoor Air Purifiers in Terms of Microbial Air Contamination Reduction. *Atmosphere* **2022**, *13*, 800. [CrossRef]
31. Miller, S.L.; Lohascio, C.; Nazaroff, W.; Macher, J. Effectiveness of In-Room Air Filtration and Dilution Ventilation for Tuberculosis Infection Control. *J. Air Waste Manag. Assoc.* **1996**, *46*, 869–882. [CrossRef] [PubMed]
32. Nazarenko, Y. Air Filtration and Severe Acute Respiratory Syndrome Coronavirus 2. *Epidemiol. Health* **2020**, *42*, e2020049. [CrossRef]
33. ASHRAE. *ASHRAE Position Document on Filtration and Air Cleaning*; ASHRAE: Atlanta, GA, USA, 2021.
34. Liu, G.; Xiao, M.; Zhang, X.; Gal, C.; Chen, X.; Liu, L.; Pan, S.; Wu, J.; Tang, L.; Clements-Croome, D. A review of air filtration technologies for sustainable and healthy building ventilation. *Sustain. Cities Soc.* **2017**, *32*, 375–396. [CrossRef]
35. *ISO 16890-1:2016*; Air Filters for General Ventilation—Part 1: Technical Specifications, Requirements and Classification System Based upon Particulate Matter Efficiency (ePM). International Organization for Standardization, Technical Committee: Geneva, Switzerland, 2016; pp. 1–27.
36. *EN 1822-1:2019*; High Efficiency Air Filters (EPA, HEPA and ULPA)—Part 1: Classification, Performance Testing, Marking. European Committee for Standardization: Brussels, Belgium, 2019.
37. *ANSI/ASHRAE Standard 52.2*; Method of Testing General Ventilation Air-Cleaning Devices for Removal Efficiency by Particle Size. American Society of Heating, Refrigerating and Air-Conditioning Engineers, Inc. (ASHRAE): Atlanta, GA, USA, 2017; pp. 1–55.
38. Bluyssen, P.M.; Ortiz, M.; Zhang, D. The effect of a mobile HEPA filter system on 'infectious' aerosols, sound and air velocity in the SenseLab. *Build. Environ.* **2020**, *188*, 107475. [CrossRef]
39. Villanueva, F.; Ródenas, M.; Ruus, A.; Saffell, J.; Gabriel, M.F. Sampling and analysis techniques for inorganic air pollutants in indoor air. *Appl. Spectrosc. Rev.* **2021**, *57*, 531–579. [CrossRef]
40. Zhao, B.; Liu, Y.; Chen, C. Air purifiers: A supplementary measure to remove airborne SARS-CoV-2. *Build. Environ.* **2020**, *177*, 106918. [CrossRef]

41. Liu, D.T.; Phillips, K.M.; Speth, M.M.; Besser, G.; Mueller, C.A.; Sedaghat, A.R. Portable HEPA Purifiers to Eliminate Airborne SARS-CoV-2: A Systematic Review. *Otolaryngol. Neck Surg.* **2021**, *166*, 615–622. [CrossRef]
42. Minguillón, M.C.; Querol, X.; Alastuey, A.; Riediker, M.; Felisi, J.M.; Garrido, T.; Bekö, G.; Nehr, S.; Wiesen, P.; Carslaw, N. Guide for Ventilation towards Healthy Classrooms. COST Action CA17136 Report. 2020. Available online: http://hdl.handle.net/10261/225519 (accessed on 2 July 2022).
43. Cox, J.; Isiugo, K.; Ryan, P.; Grinshpun, S.A.; Yermakov, M.; Desmond, C.; Jandarov, R.; Vesper, S.; Ross, J.; Dannemiller, D.K.; et al. Effectiveness of a portable air cleaner in removing aerosol particles in homes close to highways. *Indoor Air* **2018**, *28*, 818–827. [CrossRef]
44. Dubey, S.; Rohra, H.; Taneja, A. Assessing effectiveness of air purifiers (HEPA) for controlling indoor particulate pollution. *Heliyon* **2021**, *7*, e07976. [CrossRef] [PubMed]
45. Blocken, B.; van Druenen, T.; Ricci, A.; Kang, L.; van Hooff, T.; Qin, P.; Xia, L.; Ruiz, C.A.; Arts, J.; Diepens, J.; et al. Ventilation and air cleaning to limit aerosol particle concentrations in a gym during the COVID-19 pandemic. *Build. Environ.* **2021**, *193*, 107659. [CrossRef] [PubMed]
46. Lee, J.H.; Rounds, M.; McGain, F.; Schofield, R.; Skidmore, G.; Wadlow, I.; Kevin, K.; Stevens, A.; Marshall, C.; Irving, L.; et al. Effectiveness of portable air filtration on reducing indoor aerosol transmission: Preclinical observational trials. *J. Hosp. Infect.* **2021**, *119*, 163–169. [CrossRef] [PubMed]
47. Cheek, E.; Guercio, V.; Shrubsole, C.; Dimitroulopoulou, S. Portable air purification: Review of impacts on indoor air quality and health. *Sci. Total Environ.* **2020**, *766*, 142585. [CrossRef]
48. Bahri, M.; Haghighat, F. Plasma-Based Indoor Air Cleaning Technologies: The State of the Art-Review. *CLEAN Soil Air Water* **2013**, *42*, 1667–1680. [CrossRef]
49. Swamy, G. Development of an indoor air purification system to improve ventilation and air quality. *Heliyon* **2021**, *7*, e08153. [CrossRef]
50. De Almeida, D.S.; Martins, L.D.; Aguiar, M.L. Air pollution control for indoor environments using nanofiber filters: A brief review and post-pandemic perspectives. *Chem. Eng. J. Adv.* **2022**, *11*, 100330. [CrossRef]
51. Buyukada-Kesici, E.; Gezmis-Yavuz, E.; Aydin, D.; Cansoy, C.E.; Alp, K.; Koseoglu-Imer, D.Y. Design and fabrication of nano-engineered electrospun filter media with cellulose nanocrystal for toluene adsorption from indoor air. *Mater. Sci. Eng. B* **2020**, *264*, 114953. [CrossRef]
52. Kadam, V.; Truong, Y.B.; Schutz, J.; Kyratzis, I.L.; Padhye, R.; Wang, L. Gelatin/β–Cyclodextrin Bio–Nanofibers as respiratory filter media for filtration of aerosols and volatile organic compounds at low air resistance. *J. Hazard. Mater.* **2020**, *403*, 123841. [CrossRef]
53. Niu, M.; Shen, F.; Zhou, F.; Zhu, T.; Zheng, Y.; Yang, Y.; Sun, Y.; Li, X.; Wu, Y.; Fu, P.; et al. Indoor air filtration could lead to increased airborne endotoxin levels. *Environ. Int.* **2020**, *142*, 105878. [CrossRef]
54. Bliss, S. *Best Practices Guide to Residential Construction: Materials, Finishes, and Details*; Wiley: London, UK, 2005.
55. Liu, S.; Huang, Q.; Wu, Y.; Song, Y.; Dong, W.; Chu, M.; Yang, D.; Zhang, X.; Zhang, J.; Chen, C.; et al. Metabolic linkages between indoor negative air ions, particulate matter and cardiorespiratory function: A randomized, double-blind crossover study among children. *Environ. Int.* **2020**, *138*, 105663. [CrossRef] [PubMed]
56. Guieysse, B.; Hort, C.; Platel, V.; Munoz, R.; Ondarts, M.; Revah, S. Biological treatment of indoor air for VOC removal: Potential and challenges. *Biotechnol. Adv.* **2008**, *26*, 398–410. [CrossRef] [PubMed]
57. Waring, M.S.; Siegel, J.A. The effect of an ion generator on indoor air quality in a residential room. *Indoor Air* **2010**, *21*, 267–276. [CrossRef] [PubMed]
58. Anirudhan, T.; Sreekumari, S. Adsorptive removal of heavy metal ions from industrial effluents using activated carbon derived from waste coconut buttons. *J. Environ. Sci.* **2011**, *23*, 1989–1998. [CrossRef]
59. Xie, T. Indoor air pollution and control technology. *IOP Conf. Ser. Earth Environ. Sci.* **2018**, *170*, 032084. [CrossRef]
60. Gall, E.T.; Corsi, R.L.; Siegel, J.A. Barriers and opportunities for passive removal of indoor ozone. *Atmos. Environ.* **2011**, *45*, 3338–3341. [CrossRef]
61. Jo, W.-K.; Yang, C.-H. Granular-activated carbon adsorption followed by annular-type photocatalytic system for control of indoor aromatic compounds. *Sep. Purif. Technol.* **2009**, *66*, 438–442. [CrossRef]
62. Ao, C.; Lee, S. Combination effect of activated carbon with TiO2 for the photodegradation of binary pollutants at typical indoor air level. *J. Photochem. Photobiol. A Chem.* **2004**, *161*, 131–140. [CrossRef]
63. Ao, C.; Lee, S.-C. Indoor air purification by photocatalyst TiO2 immobilized on an activated carbon filter installed in an air cleaner. *Chem. Eng. Sci.* **2005**, *60*, 103–109. [CrossRef]
64. Sidheswaran, M.A.; Destaillats, H.; Sullivan, D.P.; Cohn, S.; Fisk, W.J. Energy efficient indoor VOC air cleaning with activated carbon fiber (ACF) filters. *Build. Environ.* **2012**, *47*, 357–367. [CrossRef]
65. Cheng, H.-H.; Hsieh, C.-C.; Tsai, C.-H. Antibacterial and Regenerated Characteristics of Ag-zeolite for Removing Bioaerosols in Indoor Environment. *Aerosol Air Qual. Res.* **2012**, *12*, 409–419. [CrossRef]
66. da Silva, C.; Stefanowski, B.; Maskell, D.; Ormondroyd, G.; Ansell, M.; Dengel, A.; Ball, R. Improvement of indoor air quality by MDF panels containing walnut shells. *Build. Environ.* **2017**, *123*, 427–436. [CrossRef]
67. Cao, J.-J.; Huang, Y.; Zhang, Q. Ambient Air Purification by Nanotechnologies: From Theory to Application. *Catalysts* **2021**, *11*, 1276. [CrossRef]

68. Hodgson, A.T.; Destaillats, H.; Sullivan, D.P.; Fisk, W.J. Performance of ultraviolet photocatalytic oxidation for indoor air cleaning applications. *Indoor Air* **2007**, *17*, 305–316. [CrossRef]
69. Geiss, O.; Cacho, C.; Barrero-Moreno, J.; Kotzias, D. Photocatalytic degradation of organic paint constituents-formation of carbonyls. *Build. Environ.* **2012**, *48*, 107–112. [CrossRef]
70. Farhanian, D.; Haghighat, F. Photocatalytic oxidation air cleaner: Identification and quantification of by-products. *Build. Environ.* **2014**, *72*, 34–43. [CrossRef]
71. Kaushik, A.K.; Dhau, J.S. Photoelectrochemical oxidation assisted air purifiers; perspective as potential tools to control indoor SARS-CoV-2 Exposure. *Appl. Surf. Sci. Adv.* **2022**, *9*, 100236. [CrossRef]
72. Aydin-Aytekin, D.; Gezmis-Yavuz, E.; Buyukada-Kesici, E.; Cansoy, C.E.; Alp, K.; Koseoglu-Imer, D.Y. Fabrication and characterization of multifunctional nanoclay and TiO2 embedded polyamide electrospun nanofibers and their applications at indoor air filtration. *Mater. Sci. Eng. B* **2022**, *279*, 115675. [CrossRef]
73. Weon, S.; Choi, E.; Kim, H.; Kim, J.Y.; Park, H.-J.; Kim, S.-M.; Kim, W.; Choi, W. Active {001} Facet Exposed TiO2 Nanotubes Photocatalyst Filter for Volatile Organic Compounds Removal: From Material Development to Commercial Indoor Air Cleaner Application. *Environ. Sci. Technol.* **2018**, *52*, 9330–9340. [CrossRef]
74. Wang, H.; Li, X.; Zhao, X.; Li, C.; Song, X.; Zhang, P.; Huo, P. A review on heterogeneous photocatalysis for environmental remediation: From semiconductors to modification strategies. *Chin. J. Catal.* **2022**, *43*, 178–214. [CrossRef]
75. Ren, H.; Koshy, P.; Chen, W.-F.; Qi, S.; Sorrell, C.C. Photocatalytic materials and technologies for air purification. *J. Hazard. Mater.* **2017**, *325*, 340–366. [CrossRef] [PubMed]
76. Monteiro, R.A.; Silva, A.M.; Ângelo, J.R.; Silva, G.V.; Mendes, A.M.; Boaventura, R.A.; Vilar, V.J. Photocatalytic oxidation of gaseous perchloroethylene over TiO 2 based paint. *J. Photochem. Photobiol. A Chem.* **2015**, *311*, 41–52. [CrossRef]
77. Maggos, T.; Binas, V.; Siaperas, V.; Terzopoulos, A.; Panagopoulos, P.; Kiriakidis, G. A Promising Technological Approach to Improve Indoor Air Quality. *Appl. Sci.* **2019**, *9*, 4837. [CrossRef]
78. Salvadores, F.; Alfano, O.; Ballari, M. Kinetic study of air treatment by photocatalytic paints under indoor radiation source: Influence of ambient conditions and photocatalyst content. *Appl. Catal. B Environ.* **2020**, *268*, 118694. [CrossRef]
79. Demeestere, K.; Dewulf, J.; De Witte, B.; Beeldens, A.; Van Langenhove, H. Heterogeneous photocatalytic removal of toluene from air on building materials enriched with TiO2. *Build. Environ.* **2008**, *43*, 406–414. [CrossRef]
80. Ichiura, H.; Kitaoka, T.; Tanaka, H. Removal of indoor pollutants under UV irradiation by a composite TiO2–zeolite sheet prepared using a papermaking technique. *Chemosphere* **2002**, *50*, 79–83. [CrossRef]
81. Dong, Y.; Bai, Z.; Liu, R.; Zhu, T. Decomposition of indoor ammonia with TiO2-loaded cotton woven fabrics prepared by different textile finishing methods. *Atmos. Environ.* **2006**, *41*, 3182–3192. [CrossRef]
82. Zuraimi, M.; Magee, R.; Won, D.; Nong, G.; Arsenault, C.; Yang, W.; So, S.; Nilsson, G.; Abebe, L.; Alliston, C. Performance of sorption- and photocatalytic oxidation-based indoor passive panel technologies. *Build. Environ.* **2018**, *135*, 85–93. [CrossRef]
83. Shayegan, Z.; Bahri, M.; Haghighat, F. A review on an emerging solution to improve indoor air quality: Application of passive removal materials. *Build. Environ.* **2022**, *219*, 109228. [CrossRef]
84. Kowalski, W. *Ultraviolet Germicidal Irradiation Handbook: UVGI for Air and Surface Disinfection*; Springer: Berlin/Heidelberg, Germany, 2009; ISBN 9788578110796.
85. Rauth, A.M. The Physical State of Viral Nucleic Acid and the Sensitivity of Viruses to Ultraviolet Light. *Biophys. J.* **1965**, *5*, 257–273. [CrossRef]
86. Bolton, J.R.; Cotton, C.A. *The Ultraviolet Disinfection Handbook*; American Water Works Association: Denver, CO, USA, 2008; ISBN1 1583215840. ISBN2 9781583215845.
87. Whyte, W. Bacteriological aspects of air-conditioning plants. *Epidemiol. Infect.* **1968**, *66*, 567–584. [CrossRef] [PubMed]
88. Cooley, J.D.; Wong, W.C.; Jumper, C.A.; Straus, D.C. Correlation between the prevalence of certain fungi and sick building syndrome. *Occup. Environ. Med.* **1998**, *55*, 579–584. [CrossRef] [PubMed]
89. Lee, L.D.; Delclos, G.; Berkheiser, M.L.; Barakat, M.T.; Jensen, P.A. Evaluation of multiple fixed in-room air cleaners with ultraviolet germicidal irradiation, in high-occupancy areas of selected commercial indoor environments. *J. Occup. Environ. Hyg.* **2021**, *19*, 67–77. [CrossRef]
90. Menzies, D.; Popa, J.; Hanley, J.A.; Rand, T.; Milton, D.K. Effect of ultraviolet germicidal lights installed in office ventilation systems on workers' health and wellbeing: Double-blind multiple crossover trial. *Lancet* **2003**, *362*, 1785–1791. [CrossRef]
91. Sánchez C, J.P.; Arias Echandi, M.; Armenta Prada, J.; Salas Segura, D. Germicidal ultraviolet light and environmental control of microorganisms in hospitals. *Rev. Costarric. Salud Pública* **2012**, *21*, 19–22.
92. Brais, N. Air disinfection for ART clinics using ultraviolet germicidal irradiation—Chapter 10. In *Clean Room Technology in ART Clinics*; Esteves, S., Varghese, A.C., Worrilow, K.C., Eds.; CRC Press, Taylor & Francis Group: Boca Raton, FL, USA, 2017; pp. 119–132.
93. De Souza, S.O.; Cardoso, A.A., Jr.; Sarmento, A.S.C.; D'Errico, F. Effectiveness of a UVC air disinfection system for the HVAC of an ICU. *Eur. Phys. J. Plus* **2021**, *137*, 37. [CrossRef]
94. MaHTAS. *Sterybox Air Disinfectant*; Evaluation Section (MaHTAS). Serial No. 008/08. 6; Health Technology Assessment Section, Medical Development Division, Ministry of Health: Putrajaya, Malaysia, 2008.
95. De Robles, D.; Kramer, S.W. Improving Indoor Air Quality through the Use of Ultraviolet Technology in Commercial Buildings. *Procedia Eng.* **2017**, *196*, 888–894. [CrossRef]

96. Krull, B.; Graham, D.; Lee, C. Bipolar Ionization: Understanding the Difference between Theory and Practice. Available online: https://synexis.com/wp-content/uploads/2021/02/BPI_TheoryAndPractice_WhitePaper.pdf (accessed on 2 July 2022).
97. Hart, D. *Sterilization of the Air in the Operating Room by Bactericidal Radiant Energy*; American Association for Thoracic Surgery: Beverly, MA, USA, 1937; Volume 1, ISBN 1213141516.
98. CDC. *Guidelines for Environmental Infection Control in Health-Care Facilities*; Healthcare Infection Control Practices Advisory Committee (HICPAC): Atlanta, GA, USA, 2003; p. 241.
99. Armellino, D.; Goldstein, K.; Thomas, L.; Walsh, T.J.; Petraitis, V. Comparative evaluation of operating room terminal cleaning by two methods: Focused multivector ultraviolet (FMUV) versus manual-chemical disinfection. *Am. J. Infect. Control.* **2019**, *48*, 147–152. [CrossRef]
100. ASHRAE. Ultraviolet air and surface treatment—Chapter 62. In *ASHRAE Handbook, HVAC Applications, SI Edition*; American Society of Heating, Refrigerating and Air-Conditioning Engineers (ASHRAE): Atlanta, GA, USA, 2019.
101. EPA. *Biological Inactivation Efficiency by HVAC In-Duct Ultraviolet Light Systems*; U.S. Environmental Protection Agency: Washington, DC, USA, 2006; pp. 1–23.
102. Levetin, E.; Shaughnessy, R.; Rogers, C.A.; Scheir, R. Effectiveness of Germicidal UV Radiation for Reducing Fungal Contamination within Air-Handling Units. *Appl. Environ. Microbiol.* **2001**, *67*, 3712–3715. [CrossRef]
103. Brickner, P.W.; Vincent, R.L.; First, M.; Nardell, E.; Murray, M.; Kaufman, W. The application of ultraviolet germicidal irradiation to control transmission of airborne disease: Bioterrorism countermeasure. *Public Health Rep.* **2003**, *118*, 99–114. [CrossRef]
104. Kujundzic, E.; Hernandez, M.; Miller, S.L. Ultraviolet germicidal irradiation inactivation of airborne fungal spores and bacteria in upper-room air and HVAC in-duct configurations. *J. Environ. Eng. Sci.* **2007**, *6*, 1–9. [CrossRef]
105. Zhang, H.; Jin, X.; Nunayon, S.S.; Lai, A.C.K. Disinfection by in-duct ultraviolet lamps under different environmental conditions in turbulent airflows. *Indoor Air* **2020**, *30*, 500–511. [CrossRef]
106. Yang, Y.; Zhang, H.; Nunayon, S.S.; Chan, V.; Lai, A.C.K. Disinfection efficacy of ultraviolet germicidal irradiation on airborne bacteria in ventilation ducts. *Indoor Air* **2018**, *28*, 806–817. [CrossRef] [PubMed]
107. Escombe, A.R.; Moore, D.A.J.; Gilman, R.H.; Ñavincopa, M.; Ticona, E.; Mitchell, B.; Noakes, C.; Martínez, C.; Sheen, P.; Ramirez, R.; et al. Upper-Room Ultraviolet Light and Negative Air Ionization to Prevent Tuberculosis Transmission. *PLoS Med.* **2009**, *6*, e1000043. [CrossRef]
108. Luongo, J.C.; Brownstein, J.; Miller, S.L. Ultraviolet germicidal coil cleaning: Impact on heat transfer effectiveness and static pressure drop. *Build. Environ.* **2017**, *112*, 159–165. [CrossRef]
109. Nardell, E.A. Air Disinfection for Airborne Infection Control with a Focus on COVID-19: Why Germicidal UV is Essential. *Photochem. Photobiol.* **2021**, *97*, 493–497. [CrossRef]
110. Harstad, J.B.; Decker, H.M.; Wedum, A.G. Use of Ultraviolet Irradiation in a Room Air Conditioner for Removal of Bacteria. *Appl. Microbiol.* **1954**, *2*, 148–151. [CrossRef]
111. Malayeri, A.H.; Mohseni, M.; Cairns, B.; Bolton, J.R.; Chevrefils, G.; Caron, E.; Barbeau, B.; Wright, H.; Linden, K.G. *Fluence (UV Dose) Required to Achieve Incremental Log Inactivation of Bacteria, Protozoa, Viruses and Algae*; IUVA Guidance Documents; IUVA—International Ultraviolet Association: Washington, DC, USA, 2006; pp. 1–41.
112. Bedford, T.H.B. The Nature of the Action of Ultra-Violet Light on Micro-Organisms. *Br. J. Exp. Pathol.* **1927**, *8*, 437–441.
113. Gates, F.L. A study of the bactericidal action of ultra violet light: I. The Reaction to Monochromatic Radiations. *J. Gen. Physiol.* **1929**, *13*, 231–248. [CrossRef]
114. Gates, F.L. A study of the bactericidal action of ultra violet light: III. The Absorption of Ultra Violet Light by Bacteria. *J. Gen. Physiol.* **1930**, *14*, 31–42. [CrossRef]
115. Fulton, H.R.; Coblentz, W.W. The fungicidal action of the ultraviolet. *J. Agric. Res.* **1929**, *38*, 159–168.
116. Rivers, T.M.; Gates, F.L. Ultra-violet light and vaccine virus. *J. Exp. Med.* **1928**, *47*, 45–49. [CrossRef] [PubMed]
117. Chang, C.W.; Li, S.Y.; Huang, S.H.; Huang, C.K.; Chen, Y.Y.; Chen, C.C. Effects of Ultraviolet Germicidal Irradiation and Swirling Motion on Airborne Staphylococcus aureus, Pseudomonas aeruginosa and Legionella pneumophila under Various Relative Humidities. *Indoor Air* **2012**, *23*, 74–84. [CrossRef] [PubMed]
118. Nguyen, T.T.; Johnson, G.R.; Bell, S.C.; Knibbs, L.D. A Systematic Literature Review of Indoor Air Disinfection Techniques for Airborne Bacterial Respiratory Pathogens. *Int. J. Environ. Res. Public Health* **2022**, *19*, 1197. [CrossRef]
119. ASHRAE. *Handbook, Heating, Ventilating, and Air-Conditioning Systems and Equipment*; American Society of Heating, Refrigerating and Air-Conditioning Engineers (ASHRAE): Atlanta, GA, USA, 2012; ISBN 978-1-936504-25-1.
120. Schurk, D.N. A Bipolar Ionization Primer for HVAC Professionals. *ASHRAE J.* **2021**, *63*, 40–46.
121. Tierno, P.M., Jr. Cleaning Indoor Air Using Bi-Polar Ionization Technology. 2017, pp. 1–12. Available online: https://ciright.com/wp-content/uploads/2020/06/Cleaning-Indoor-Air-Using-Bi-Polar-Ionization-Technology_Dr.-PhilTierno_NYU-SchoolMedicine_2017.pdf. (accessed on 2 July 2022).
122. Meschke, S.; Smith, B.; Yost, M.; Miksch, R.; Gefter, P.; Gehlke, S.; Halpin, H. The effect of surface charge, negative and bipolar ionization on the deposition of airborne bacteria. *J. Appl. Microbiol.* **2009**, *106*, 1133–1139. [CrossRef]
123. Sahay, R.; Mendez, J.; Wozniak, A.; Rivera, H. *Bipolar Ionization and Its Contribution to Smart and Safe Buildings*; A CABA White Paper; CABA—Continental Automated Buildings Association: Gloucester, ON, Canada, 2021; p. 45.
124. Kanesaka, I.; Katsuse, A.; Takahashi, H.; Kobayashi, I. Evaluation of a bipolar ionization device in inactivation of antimicrobial-resistant bacteria, yeast, Aspergillus spp. and human coronavirus. *J. Hosp. Infect.* **2022**, *126*, 16–20. [CrossRef]

125. Hyun, J.; Lee, S.-G.; Hwang, J. Application of corona discharge-generated air ions for filtration of aerosolized virus and inactivation of filtered virus. *J. Aerosol Sci.* **2017**, *107*, 31–40. [CrossRef]
126. Pushpawela, B.; Jayaratne, R.; Nguy, A.; Morawska, L. Efficiency of ionizers in removing airborne particles in indoor environments. *J. Electrost.* **2017**, *90*, 79–84. [CrossRef]
127. Daniels, S.L. Control of Volatile Organic Compounds and Particulate Matter in Indoor Environments of Airports by Bipolar Air Ionization. Available online: http://www.enginuity-llc.com/wp-content/uploads/2020/06/DrStacyDaniels-Report-to-FAA-on-BPI-Benefits-forAirports-2002-.pdf (accessed on 2 July 2022).
128. Zhou, P.; Yang, Y.; Lai, A.C.; Huang, G. Inactivation of airborne bacteria by cold plasma in air duct flow. *Build. Environ.* **2016**, *106*, 120–130. [CrossRef]
129. Zeng, Y.; Manwatkar, P.; Laguerre, A.; Beke, M.; Kang, I.; Ali, A.S.; Farmer, D.K.; Gall, E.T.; Heidarinejad, M.; Stephens, B. Evaluating a commercially available in-duct bipolar ionization device for pollutant removal and potential byproduct formation. *Build. Environ.* **2021**, *195*, 107750. [CrossRef]
130. Moya, T.A.; van den Dobbelsteen, A.; Ottelé, M.; Bluyssen, P.M. A review of green systems within the indoor environment. *Indoor Built Environ.* **2019**, *28*, 298–309. [CrossRef]
131. Deng, L.; Deng, Q. The basic roles of indoor plants in human health and comfort. *Environ. Sci. Pollut. Res.* **2018**, *25*, 36087–36101. [CrossRef] [PubMed]
132. Han, Y.; Lee, J.; Haiping, G.; Kim, K.-H.; Wanxi, P.; Bhardwaj, N.; Oh, J.-M.; Brown, R.J. Plant-based remediation of air pollution: A review. *J. Environ. Manag.* **2021**, *301*, 113860. [CrossRef]
133. Prigioniero, A.; Zuzolo, D.; Niinemets, U.; Guarino, C. Nature-based solutions as tools for air phytoremediation: A review of the current knowledge and gaps. *Environ. Pollut.* **2021**, *277*, 116817. [CrossRef]
134. El-Tanbouly, R.; Hassan, Z.; El-Messeiry, S. The Role of Indoor Plants in air Purification and Human Health in the Context of COVID-19 Pandemic: A Proposal for a Novel Line of Inquiry. *Front. Mol. Biosci.* **2021**, *8*, 709395. [CrossRef]
135. Megahed, N.A.; Ghoneim, E.M. Indoor Air Quality: Rethinking rules of building design strategies in post-pandemic architecture. *Environ. Res.* **2020**, *193*, 110471. [CrossRef]
136. Irga, P.J.; Pettit, T.J.; Torpy, F.R. The phytoremediation of indoor air pollution: A review on the technology development from the potted plant through to functional green wall biofilters. *Rev. Environ. Sci. Bio. Technol.* **2018**, *17*, 395–415. [CrossRef]
137. Gawronski, S.W.; Gawronska, H.; Lomnicki, S.; Sæbo, A.; Vangronsveld, J. Plants in Air Phytoremediation. *Adv. Bot. Res.* **2017**, *83*, 319–346. [CrossRef]
138. Teiri, H.; Hajizadeh, Y.; Azhdarpoor, A. A review of different phytoremediation methods and critical factors for purification of common indoor air pollutants: An approach with sensitive analysis. *Air Qual. Atmos. Health* **2021**, *15*, 373–391. [CrossRef]
139. Soreanu, G.; Dixon, M.; Darlington, A. Botanical Biofiltration of Indoor Gaseous Pollutants—A Mini-Review. *Chem. Eng. J.* **2013**, *229*, 585–594. [CrossRef]
140. Wang, Y.; Bakker, F.; de Groot, R.; Wörtche, H. Effect of ecosystem services provided by urban green infrastructure on indoor environment: A literature review. *Build. Environ.* **2014**, *77*, 88–100. [CrossRef]
141. Yang, D.S.; Son, K.-C.; Kays, S.J. Volatile Organic Compounds Emanating from Indoor Ornamental Plants. *HortScience* **2009**, *44*, 396–400. [CrossRef]
142. Gubb, C.; Blanusa, T.; Griffiths, A.; Pfrang, C. Potted plants can remove the pollutant nitrogen dioxide indoors. *Air Qual. Atmos. Health* **2022**, *15*, 479–490. [CrossRef]
143. Jung, C.; Awad, J. Improving the IAQ for Learning Efficiency with Indoor Plants in University Classrooms in Ajman, United Arab Emirates. *Buildings* **2021**, *11*, 289. [CrossRef]
144. Dela Cruz, M.; Christensen, J.H.; Thomsen, J.D.; Müller, R. Can ornamental potted plants remove volatile organic compounds from indoor air?—A review. *Environ. Sci. Pollut. Res.* **2014**, *21*, 13909–13928. [CrossRef] [PubMed]
145. Peng, Z.; Deng, W.; Hong, Y. Investigation of Indoor Air Quality and Identification of Plant's Capabilities in Removing Air Pollutants in Urban Residential Buildings. *IOP Conf. Ser. Earth Environ. Sci.* **2019**, *281*, 012018. [CrossRef]
146. Brown, E.; Enguillado, G.; McDermott, R.; Palumbo, N.; Smith, J.; Stanley, M.; Sulzbach, M.; Taylor, J. Bioremediation of Volatile Organic Compounds in Indoor Spaces Using a Novel Biowall Design: A Feasibility Study. Available online: https://drum.lib.umd.edu/handle/1903/20671 (accessed on 5 July 2022).
147. Auer, T.; Radi, M.; Brkovi, M. Green Facades and Living Walls—A Review Establishing the Classification of Construction Types and Mapping the Benefits. *Sustainability* **2019**, *11*, 4579. [CrossRef]
148. Francis, R.A.; Lorimer, J. Urban reconciliation ecology: The potential of living roofs and walls. *J. Environ. Manag.* **2011**, *92*, 1429–1437. [CrossRef]
149. Gattringer, H.; Efthymiou-Charalampopoulou, N.; Lines, E.; Kolokotroni, M. Nature based solution for indoor air quality treatment. *J. Phys. Conf. Ser.* **2021**, *2042*, 012133. [CrossRef]
150. Thomas, C.K.; Jin Kim, K.; Kays, S.J. Phytoremediation of Indoor Air. *HortScience* **2015**, *50*, 765–768. [CrossRef]
151. Mata, T.M.; Martins, A.A.; Caetano, N.S. Microalgae for biodiesel production and other applications: A review. *Renew. Sustain. Energy Rev.* **2010**, *14*, 217–232. [CrossRef]
152. Junior, W.G.M.; Gorgich, M.; Corrêa, P.S.; Martins, A.A.; Mata, T.M.; Caetano, N.S. Microalgae for biotechnological applications: Cultivation, harvesting and biomass processing. *Aquaculture* **2020**, *528*, 735562. [CrossRef]

153. Corrêa, P.S.; Júnior, W.G.M.; Martins, A.A.; Caetano, N.S.; Mata, T.M. Microalgae Biomolecules: Extraction, Separation and Purification Methods. *Processes* **2020**, *9*, 10. [CrossRef]
154. Branco-Vieira, M.; Martin, S.S.; Agurto, C.; dos Santos, M.A.; Freitas, M.A.V.; Mata, T.M.; Martins, A.A.; Caetano, N.S. Potential of Phaeodactylum tricornutum for Biodiesel Production under Natural Conditions in Chile. *Energies* **2017**, *11*, 54. [CrossRef]
155. Xing, Z. *Microalgae Removal of CO_2 from Flue Gas*; IEA Clean Coal Centre: London, UK, 2015; p. 95.
156. Klinthong, W.; Yang, Y.-H.; Huang, C.-H.; Tan, C.-S. A Review: Microalgae and Their Applications in CO2 Capture and Renewable Energy. *Aerosol Air Qual. Res.* **2015**, *15*, 712–742. [CrossRef]
157. Chew, K.W.; Khoo, K.S.; Foo, H.T.; Chia, S.R.; Walvekar, R.; Lim, S.S. Algae utilization and its role in the development of green cities. *Chemosphere* **2020**, *268*, 129322. [CrossRef]
158. UN SDG. United Nations Sustainable Development Goals. Available online: https://www.un.org/sustainabledevelopment/ (accessed on 22 June 2021).
159. European Commission. Directorate General for the Environment. Building a Green Infrastructure for Europe. Available online: https://data.europa.eu/doi/10.2779/54125 (accessed on 9 February 2021).
160. European Commission—DG Environment News. The Multifunctionality of Green Infrastructure. *Sci. Environ. Policy In-Depth Rep.* **2012**, *40*, 1–36. [CrossRef]
161. Pearlmutter, D.; Theochari, D.; Nehls, T.; Pinho, P.; Piro, P.; Korolova, A.; Papaefthimiou, S.; Mateo, M.C.G.; Calheiros, C.; Zluwa, I.; et al. Enhancing the circular economy with nature-based solutions in the built urban environment: Green building materials, systems and sites. *Blue Green Syst.* **2019**, *2*, 46–72. [CrossRef]
162. Elrayies, G.M. Microalgae: Prospects for greener future buildings. Renew. Sustain. *Energy Rev.* **2018**, *81*, 1175–1191. [CrossRef]
163. Barati, B.; Zafar, F.F.; Babadi, A.A.; Hao, C.; Qian, L.; Wang, S.; Abomohra, A.E.-F. Microalgae as a Natural CO2 Sequester: A Study on Effect of Tobacco Smoke on Two Microalgae Biochemical Responses. *Front. Energy Res.* **2022**, *10*, 881758. [CrossRef]
164. Yewale, P.; Wagle, N.; Lenka, S.; Bannigol, P.; Junnarkar, M.; Prakash, D.; Mandal, A.; Stigh, C.; Sahasrabudhe, T.; Vannalwar, T.; et al. Studies on Biosmotrap: A multipurpose biological air purifier to minimize indoor and outdoor air pollution. *J. Clean. Prod.* **2022**, *357*, 132001. [CrossRef]
165. Lu, Q.; Ji, C.; Yan, Y.; Xiao, Y.; Li, J.; Leng, L.; Zhou, W. Application of a novel microalgae-film based air purifier to improve air quality through oxygen production and fine particulates removal. *J. Chem. Technol. Biotechnol.* **2018**, *94*, 1057–1063. [CrossRef]
166. Thawechai, T.; Cheirsilp, B.; Louhasakul, Y.; Boonsawang, P.; Prasertsan, P. Mitigation of carbon dioxide by oleaginous microalgae for lipids and pigments production: Effect of light illumination and carbon dioxide feeding strategies. *Bioresour. Technol.* **2016**, *219*, 139–149. [CrossRef]

MDPI
St. Alban-Anlage 66
4052 Basel
Switzerland
Tel. +41 61 683 77 34
Fax +41 61 302 89 18
www.mdpi.com

MDPI Books Editorial Office
E-mail: books@mdpi.com
www.mdpi.com/books

www.ingramcontent.com/pod-product-compliance
Lightning Source LLC
Chambersburg PA
CBHW061557220926
51850CB00005B/359